PRAGUE & BUDAPEST

TOM DIRLIS

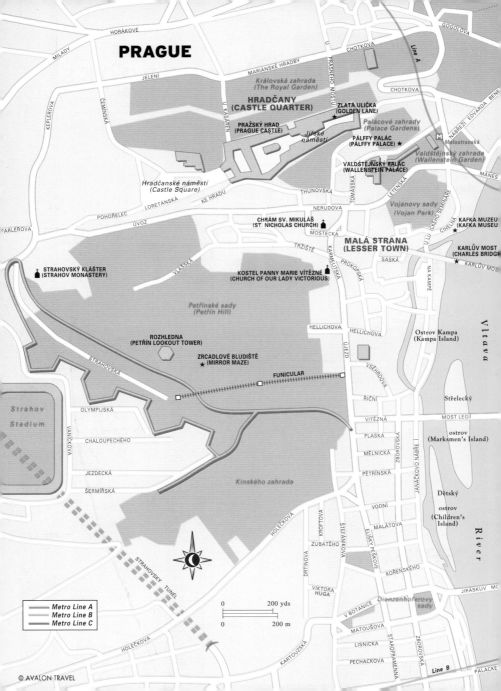

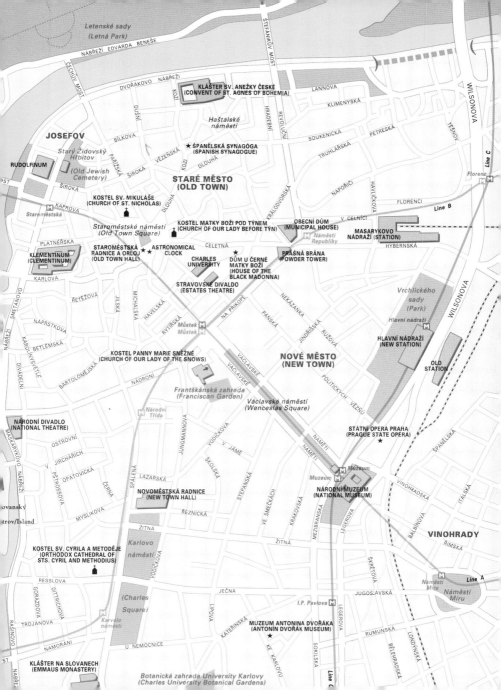

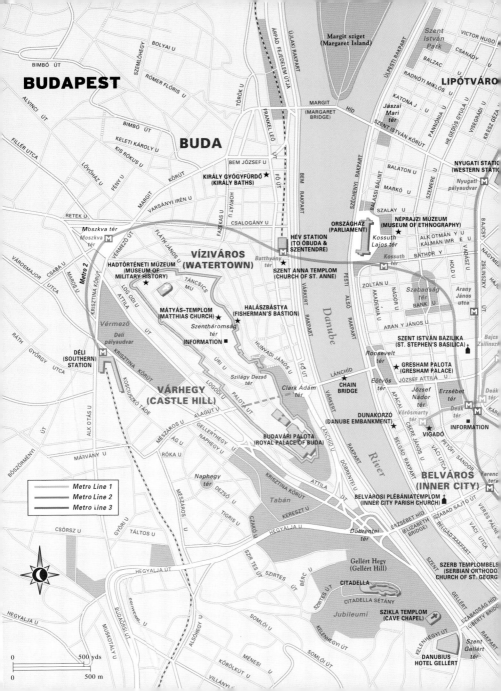

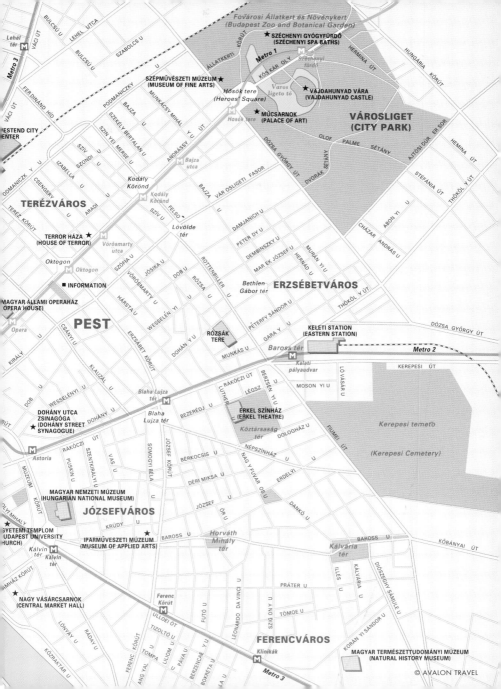

DISCOVER PRAGUE & BUDAPEST

Entering both the new millennium and the European Union, both Prague and Budapest have hit the ground running. No longer Communist children that could not be separated from Mother Russia, they are beacons of the future burning brightly for the entire world to see. No matter what time of year you choose to visit, it is guaranteed that you will leave affected, understanding that there is more to this life than Western concepts of materialism and wealth; there is also aesthetic beauty, the gravitas of history, and intangible mystery that we barely understand.

Prague, with its dark and illustrious history, along with breathtaking buildings that only the most insensitive would not stop to admire, is more reminiscent of a fairy tale than a Central

Old Town Square, Prague

European capital. From the top of Wenceslas Square to the hill that is home to Prague Castle, it is pound for pound just as beautiful as the fabled cities of Paris and Venice, though nowhere near as expensive and certainly more liberal-minded than either of its contemporaries. This is the capital of Bohemia, where beer is cheaper than bottled water and freedom of expression continued to rear its proud, socially conscious head, even during the darkest times when opening one's mouth could mean a sentence to prison or the afterworld.

Budapest, too, is a capital full of thrills and adventure, where warm, hospitable people still remember fighting the good fight, determined to lose their lives if need be for the simple, undeniable fact that living under unwanted rule simply wouldn't do. Faster,

Karlovy Vary, Bohemia

bigger, and rougher around the edges than Prague, its largesse never fails to inspire thoughts of what life must have been like when it was part of the Austro-Hungarian Empire. Whether it's the no-nonsense hustle of Pest or the nearly Dickensian back streets of Buda, the city abounds in beauty, harmony, and incontrovertible charm, while the people's passion for music, drink, and romance expresses itself brazenly at every conceivable corner.

During the summer months, both capitals are bombarded with tourists, all of whom have come to see what all the fuss is about. Streets are jammed, prices climb, and the shops, bars, hotels, and restaurants are filled to bursting. It's admittedly hard at times to fully appreciate each city's individual qualities when you're busy ducking out of photographs or trying to explain to hardened servants of the service industry that you're not the kind of tourist who uses their home as your own individual playground, but the kind who is sensitive to the history, land, and people; the kind who could even point out the countries on a map. The occasional bad

peacock in Vojan Park, Prague

apple and disgruntled local employee aside, however, the summer is a remarkable time. It is a season when everything is in full swing, from the fairs, festivals, and impromptu outdoor concerts to the unabashed and fleeting liaisons that bloom due to the irresistible, intoxicating atmosphere that pervades.

While the winter is, admittedly, a rather cold, dark, and harsh affair, it is an excellent time to come to Prague and Budapest. Shaking off the sweetness of summer, the cities fall back into their regular grooves, allowing travelers to get closer to the heart of what exactly makes these incomparable capitals tick. The streets are quiet, speaking volumes without having to say anything. Vast squares wait patiently for you to grace them with your presence, and you can have Charles Bridge and the Danube Promenade all to yourself. These are truly magical moments that anyone would be lucky to experience.

Ask anyone who has lived here long enough and they'll be able to list the myriad of changes both Prague and Budapest have gone

a view of Parliament from Várhegy, Budapest

through off the top of their head: Internet cafes, cell phones, the newest trends in all things fashion, entertainment, and ostentation. Things have changed and continue to do so at a surprisingly rapid rate. Their Communist hangovers nearly cured, Prague and Budapest push to join the ranks of more wealthy cities – not in pure emulation or out of adolescent idolatry, but, rather, in an effort to prove to the world that they can play this game we call consumerism, too, only with a balance of priorities and a decidedly distinct flavor. Come to Prague and Budapest and have your eyes opened and heart stirred with their effortless blending of the old with the new.

the Hungarian National Museum, Budapest

Výstaviště, Prague

Tihany, on Lake Balaton, Hungary

celebrating in Old Town, Prague

Contents

GERMANY

TEREZÍN

Elbe River

Karlovy Vary

☀ Prague

Kutná Hora

CZECH
REPUBLIC

Telč

Český
Krumlov

GERMANY

Danube   River

AUSTRIA

Drava

River

SLOVENIA   CROATIA

0   25 mi

0   25 km

MAP CONTENTS

POLAND

SLOVAKIA

UKRAINE

River

Tisza

Szentendre ○

Budapest ✦

HUNGARY

Danube River

Balatonfüred
Tihany
Siófok
Lake Balaton
eszthely

ROMANIA

SERBIA

© AVALON TRAVEL

The Lay of the Land

PRAGUE

Central and Eastern Europe's most successful post-Communist country also boasts one of the most beautiful capitals in the entire world. Magic Prague, the Golden City, is one of the hottest destinations in the region thanks to its well-preserved historic buildings, as well as its laid-back, anything-goes attitude, which continues to attract artists, foreigners, and just about anyone looking for a bit of the Bohemian in their lives. Whether it's the indisputable majesty of **Prague Castle,** the picturesque streets of **Malá Strana,** or the breathtaking beauty of **Charles Bridge** and **Old Town Square,** Prague is a city that touches everyone, leaving its indelible stamp on the entire world's imagination.

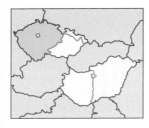

BOHEMIA

The greater of the Czech Republic's two regions is known primarily for being dotted with magical castles and quaint picturesque towns, many of which are in close proximity to the capital and therefore make for excellent day-trip options. **Karlštejn, Konopiště,** and **Křivoklát** all boast fascinating histories, not to mention remarkable castles unique in both their architecture and beauty. **Český Krumlov**'s castle, meanwhile, is the second-largest in the country, complementing in grandiose fashion the well-preserved medieval masterpiece of a town that it overlooks. Fans of the morbid and truly bizarre will be fascinated by the macabre bone church in **Kutná Hora,** while those looking to heal themselves amidst gorgeous natural surroundings need look no further than the curative springs of world-renowned spa town **Karlovy Vary.**

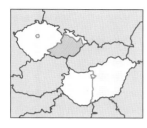

MORAVIA

Less visited by tourists but certainly no less interesting or exciting, Moravia is its own distinct region and serves as the Czech Republic's wine country. Steeped in tradition and home to a looser, friendlier breed of Czech, Moravians are proud of their land, as well as their capital **Brno,** Prague's natural rival and an excellent place to visit for a couple of days. Aside from its historic old town, it is the scene of countless cultural events and its being a university town only adds to the frenzy of social activity you're bound to run into on any night of the week. UNESCO-protected **Telč,** on the other hand, is known for having one of the prettiest squares in the country and its surrounding peaceful lakes and forests make it an excellent getaway destination. And let us not forget the enchanting town of **Mikulov,** which has been one of Moravia's leading wine centers for centuries. If you're looking to dive deep into the Czech Republic's heart of warmth and kindness, head for the Moravian border now.

BUDAPEST

The famed Danube River separates Buda's hilly west bank from Pest's bustling streets, offering travelers the best of both peaceful surroundings and the infectious energy that comes with a modern, cosmopolitan city. In Pest, visitors can enjoy any number of remarkable sights, from **St. Stephen's Basilica** to **Heroes' Square,** as well as enjoy romantic strolls along the **Danube Embankment** or shopping sprees down famed **Váci Street.** Then there's the nightlife, which rages well into the night, oftentimes letting up only when the sun decides to shine. In Buda, meanwhile, the ancient tranquility of centuries long gone persists in tiny neighborhood streets, the **Royal Palace of Buda,** and the otherworldly **Buda Hills.** Hungarians are a vibrant, fun-loving, and hospitable people who have tackled their accession to the EU with all the energy one could hope for, building countless new shops, hotels, and residences as they gear up for what is sure to be a memorable millennium.

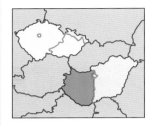

BEYOND BUDAPEST

While Budapest is clearly Hungary's most popular destination, it would be a shame if visitors didn't head out from the capital for at least a day or two. The pretty artist colony of **Szentendre,** for example—with its long promenade, Mediterranean-influenced restaurants, excellent museums, and numerous shops—continues to be one of the most popular day-trip excursions from the big city. **Esztergom,** the birthplace of St. Stephen, is a must for history fans, who will practically keel over at the sight of the magnificent Basilica, the largest church in the country. And then there's the legendary **Lake Balaton.** Central Europe's largest lake is also one of Hungary's most popular holiday destinations, attracting folks from around the world in search of non-stop parties in **Siófok** and wine-tasting in the more traditional villages up north. Easily accessible from Budapest by car, rail, or bus, there is little reason to miss these extraordinary experiences.

Planning Your Trip

Roughly 354 miles apart, Prague and Budapest can be easily combined to make for a memorable trip in Central Europe. Many "do" both capitals in a whirlwind week of activity, but if you'd like to truly get the most out of each cities' major attractions and possibly even squeeze in a day trip or two, then you're far better off planning for at least a 10-day trip.

Prague's major sights can be easily covered in three days as all of them are located in the zone designated "Prague 1," which spans Nové Město, Staré Město, and Malá Strana. This includes everything from Wenceslas Square, Josefov, and Charles Bridge to Kampa Island and, of course, Prague Castle. With an extra day or two, however, you'll also be able to take in Bohemian castles like **Karlštejn** or enjoy an overnight trip to either **Český Krumlov** or **Karlovy Vary,** both of which are spectacular. **Moravia,** too, would require at least a couple days, adding up to a full week or so should you want to experience a decent-sized chunk of the entire Czech Republic.

Budapest, on the other hand, requires three or four days of quick, on-the-move traveling in order to cover all of Pest, as well as Buda and its wonderful hills. While **Szentendre** and **Esztergom** make for very comfortable day trips, a journey out to **Lake Balaton** requires at least two or three days, depending on how much you'd like to see. Again, a week or so in Hungary would be ideal.

The capitals themselves are very easily explored on foot or via excellent public transport systems that take you right to the doorstep of each and every worthwhile sight. Prague in particular is not only easily accessible but compact as well, making walking a joy that is rarely experienced in North American capitals where driving is an absolute necessity.

Prague Castle

As a matter of fact, driving in both capitals is the worst (i.e., slowest) way to see things, thanks in large part to maddening one-way streets and growing traffic.

Due to a never-ending stream of trains and buses that take visitors between the countries and within them, traveling in the Czech Republic and Hungary is not only easy, but relatively inexpensive as well.

WHEN TO GO

Both Prague and Budapest have a rather night-and-day nature about them in respect to the atmosphere they exude throughout the year. From spring till fall, the streets, shops, sights, and bars are abuzz with activity and packed with tourists and locals soaking up the long, sunny days and warm, vibrant nights. In the winter, both capitals quiet down considerably as both temperatures and the number of visitors drop. There's never a bad or off time to visit but if you find yourself getting easily depressed by grey skies and wet, humid winters, you'll probably want to plan your visit for after Easter.

Badacsony, at the western end of Lake Balaton in Hungary

Spring is the season of rebirth and you can nearly taste it as both cities shake off winter's doldrums and prepare themselves for brighter times ahead. Flowers begin to blossom, the landscape returns to a healthy shade of green, and temperatures start to climb while crowds remain at reasonable levels. Fairs and festivals begin, too, with both Prague and Budapest hosting their own respective Spring Festivals. It is also the season when the gates to the Czech Republic's castles and gardens open again to the delight of tourists and history buffs the country over.

The **summer** season is, of course, the time when countless tourists descend. Prague in particular is overrun with tour buses pulling up to Prague Castle, as well as every conceivable monument and centrally located restaurant, while students and younger travelers fill the bars and clubs, turning an already energetic nightlife into one non-stop party.

In Budapest, meanwhile, finding a cov-eted table in any of its plentiful outdoor cafes becomes harder and harder as temperatures soar. Popular Danube Bend towns come alive once again and Lake Balaton becomes the best place in the country to let your hair down and meet likewise laid-back people from around the world.

Despite the crowds, it is a wonderful time to visit, with impromptu fairs, festivals, and outdoor concerts popping up everywhere, adding to the overall exuberance that envelops both cities.

Those not interested in sacrificing elbow room to the summer masses should consider visiting during the **autumn** months when cool breezes and lower prices turn Prague and Budapest into more affordable and comfortable destinations. It is a time when Prague's parks and the hills surrounding the castle, as well as Margaret Island and the Buda Hills, turn into red and golden paradises, providing picture-perfect backdrops to already breathtaking skylines. In the Czech Republic, it is the season for mushroom picking and long hikes in the woods, while wine lovers in Hungary head for the myriad of harvest festivals that take place throughout the country.

While admittedly cold and at times unnervingly dark, the **winter** is nevertheless a charming time to visit. Prague affects a Gothic, Kafkaesque aura whose mysterious beauty is compounded by historic, snow-capped buildings and a near-empty Charles Bridge. Budapest, in turn, is returned to Budapesters and once-bustling streets, squares, and avenues settle back down into the majestic, imperial beauty they've been renowned for throughout the centuries. Both cities boast popular Christmas markets and near legendary New Year's Eve festivities, while the ski resorts in Bohemia's modest mountains ring loudly with the hoots and hollers of snowboarders, skiers, and nighttime revelers. The main drawback to visiting at this time is that the Czech Republic's castles, gardens, and various historical attractions close down for the season, while Hungary's most important sites generally keep shorter visiting hours.

WHAT TO TAKE

Though certainly nowhere near the spirit-crushing cold of Russia or any of the Scandinavian countries, temperatures do dip in the winter and a properly packed suitcase will make all the difference between enjoying your stay and cursing yourself for not having thought

ahead. Bring a heavy coat, woolen cap, gloves, and boots with decent lining and treads as slush tends to build up, even if the snow doesn't. If you plan on doing extended trips throughout the region or simply love to walk, a pair of long underwear won't hurt either.

Frequent bouts of rain are not uncommon during the early spring or autumn so you may want to bring an umbrella with you, as well as an appropriately protective jacket. Sweaters, a fleece, and/or a relatively warm coat are good ideas as well due to evenings that tend to become rather chilly after relatively warm mornings and afternoons.

In the summertime, the general rule of thumb is to flaunt it if you got it. Short skirts, sandals, and halter tops generally dominate the female wardrobe while men tend to stick to shorts and t-shirts. Hats and sunglasses are also necessary accessories. A light, long-sleeved shirt or two won't hurt, nor will a sweater and light jacket if visiting near the beginning or end of the season. If camping, hiking, or spending time working on your tan, make sure to pack some bug spray and sun block to keep you comfortable and safe.

You'll find that both cities have an easy-going, laid-back, anything-goes atmosphere about them, but those planning on patronizing higher-end restaurants or clubs should consider bringing at least semi-formal attire with them. Suits and formal evening attire, on the other hand, are appropriate when visiting classical music concerts or the opera.

Explore Prague and Budapest

THE BEST OF PRAGUE AND BUDAPEST IN 10 DAYS

Ten days will be enough time to take in all the major sight both cities have to offer, but it does mean sticking to a tight schedule and forgoing a few museums. Be prepared to do a lot of walking and get your camera ready—you're about to experience a ton of Kodak moments.

Day 1

Fly into Prague's Ruzyně Airport and head for your hotel. Staying in Nové Město or the Old Town means being within spitting distance of a wide array of shops, restaurants, sights, bars, and all the action. Conversely, if a more peaceful, picturesque environment is what you prefer, Malá Strana is hard to beat.

Day 2

Start your first full day in beautiful Old Town Square, taking time to admire the gorgeous facades and wide array of beautiful buildings like the **Church of our Lady Before Týn** and **Church of St. Nicholas.** Drink in **Old Town Hall** and the **Astronomical Clock** and make sure to catch the wooden marionette show, "The Walk of the Apostles," performed at the top of every hour. From there, take a stroll down chic **Pařížská Street** with its trendy boutiques and designer cafes. Stop for coffee or lunch and then continue on to **Josefov,** Prague's famed Jewish quarter and home of the magnificent **Spanish Synagogue** and haunting **Old Jewish Cemetery.** Lose yourself amongst the winding, picturesque streets before settling in for an evening of traditional Czech food and a pint or two of the country's world-famous beers.

Day 3

Start your day bright and early by heading for **Prague Castle,** the city's most recognizable and visited landmark. Admire the view of

St. Vitus Cathedral, Prague

Prague down below before wandering through the courtyards and entering jaw-dropping **St. Vitus Cathedral.** Bask in the glory of its massive nave, stained glass windows, and ornate frescoes, then follow the crowds to tiny **Golden Lane,** one-time home to the incomparable Franz Kafka. Backtrack to the castle's front gates and ease on down Nerudova Street, peeking into its plethora of souvenir shops before arriving at **Malostranské náměstí,** Malá Strana's legendary square. Enjoy a traditional Czech lunch then burn those calories off with an enjoyable walk through Lesser Town's romantic, cobblestone streets. You'll find no shortage of art galleries, cafes, and glass shops but make sure to leave time for a visit to **Kampa Island.** Have a rest on one of its park benches and when you've

Municipal House, Prague

had enough of the remarkable view of Old Town and the lazy Vltava River, head for the **Charles Bridge** and see for yourself why it's widely considered one of Prague's most memorable structures. Take your pick from any one of the district's many fantastic restaurants and cap it off with a live show or drinks.

Day 4

Start at the top of Nové Město on the **National Museum**'s steps, where you can see the length of bustling **Wenceslas Square** stretch out before you. If natural history isn't your thing, forgo the museum and slowly make your way down the square. There are countless shopping possibilities on either side of the boulevard, as well as numerous cafes and restaurants that are perfect for people-watching. When you're ready to move on again, continue down to the bottom of the square, otherwise known as **Můstek.** On the right is Na Příkopě Street, which is filled with even more shops, cafes, and restaurants, as well as casinos and museums. Those interested in learning more about the Czech Republic's Communist past should definitely pay a visit to the highly informative **Museum of Communism.** Farther along Na Příkopě Street, you'll come upon the **Powder Tower** and Art

Nouveau masterpiece the **Municipal House.** Have dinner then consider taking in a classical concert or opera at either the Municipal House, National Theatre, or State Opera House for a memorable night of high culture.

Day 5

Today's a travel day so pack your bags and head for the nearest car rental office or main train station **Hlavní Nádraží.** Upon arriving in Budapest, settle into your hotel, freshen up, and hit the Belváros. **Vörösmarty Square** is the city's social hub and the site of the world-famous **Café Gerbeaud.** Don't miss the opportunity to grab a delicious cup of coffee and scrumptious dessert then on to **Váci utca,** the country's best-known pedestrian shopping district. All sorts of souvenir shops, boutiques, and restaurants line the street, offering visitors plenty of opportunities to spend some of their holiday cash. At the end of the street is the cavernous **Central Market Hall,** which, if still open by the time you reach it, will overwhelm you with countless stalls selling everything from paprika to traditional clothing and gifts. If you still have some energy left, take a romantic walk down Budapest's famed **Danube Embankment,** home to plenty of outdoor restaurants and cafes, not to mention beloved concert hall the **Vigadó** and gorgeous views of Buda Castle and Géllert Hill.

Day 6

Begin at the **Royal Palace of Buda** and if time or interest allows, spend a couple of hours admiring the artwork in the massive **Hungarian National Gallery.** A hop, skip, and a jump will take you to **Szentháromság Square** and monumental **Matthias Church,** as well as kitschy yet playful **Fisherman's Bastion.** Grab some lunch and when you're done admiring the maze of streets and royal views, head on back down the hill and over the striking **Chain Bridge.** Spend the afternoon exploring grand boulevard **Andrássy út,** whose numerous shops are bound to keep you occupied for some time. You'll soon come upon the grand **Opera House,** a tour of which is highly recommended for fans and non-fans of the music alike. A little farther on is **Nagymező utca,** Budapest's Broadway; it's the site of charming outdoor cafes, theaters, and the city's very own Moulin Rouge club. Just down from that is **Liszt Ferenc tér,** a bustling collection of outdoor restaurants, bars, and cafes, the perfect place to enjoy an excellent meal, fine wine, and a well-deserved evening of fun.

Day 7

Kick things off bright and early with gigantic **Heroes' Square.** It's flanked on either side by the **Palace of Art** and **Museum of Fine Arts,** both of which are perfect for fans of culture and high art. Nearby is eclectic **Vajdahunyad Castle** and its collection of Gothic, Renaissance, and Baroque buildings. If you have the time, soothe your aches and pains in one of Europe's largest spa complexes, the **Széchenyi Spa Baths.** If traveling with kids, visit family fave **Vidám Park,** full of old-world charm and home to a 100-year-old merry-go-round. Have some lunch on or around Andrássy út as you head back toward the center and over to **St.**

Stephen's Basilica, Hungary's largest church and resting place of the mummified right hand of St. Stephen himself. Enjoy a cup of coffee or light snack at one of the cafes bordering the square then continue on past peaceful **Szabadság Square** to **Kossuth Lajos Square** and the remarkable **Parliament** building, the largest in Europe. A tour of this remarkable building is highly recommended. As evening descends, treat yourself to a tasty Hungarian dinner and some excellent domestic wine.

Day 8

Spend a peaceful and relaxing morning on beautiful **Margaret Island,** where lazy strolls among its gardens and ruins will reward you with an amusing **Musical Fountain,** the historic **Dominican Convent,** and openair water complex **Palatinus Strand.** After lunch, head for the **Buda Hills.** Take a breathtaking ride up the hills via the Cog-Wheel Railway and Children's Railway, stopping to enjoy the serenity of Normafa before reaching **János-hegy** and Budapest's highest point. Make your way back down slowly, savoring the natural surroundings before returning to the realities of the big city. It's your last night in Budapest so a scrumptious meal and lots of last-minute fun are more than appropriate.

Day 9

Have a hearty breakfast (it is a travel day after all) and try to squeeze in the impressive **Dohány Street Synagogue,** the largest functioning of its kind on the continent. Then it's back to your car or Keleti train station for the trip back to Prague. If you get to Prague at a reasonable hour, take a final stroll around the city's magical streets and try to visit Charles Bridge one last time. You'll be happy you did.

Day 10

Head to Ruzyně Airport and start figuring out how soon you can conceivably come back.

WHEN IN PRAGUE . . .
FOUR DAYS OF LOCAL LIVING

Everybody knows what the main sights, bars, and restaurants are, but what if you'd like to live like a local and eat, drink, and stroll where they do? Well look no further because here are a few tips that should have you rubbing elbows with more than tourist-bus travelers in no time.

Day 1

Start your day with an affordable breakfast and bottomless cup of coffee at **Bohemia Bagel** by Charles Bridge. Pick up an extra bagel or two if you like because you'll be doing a lot of walking. Start with the streets of Malá Strana and work your way over to **Kampa Island.** Take the funicular or do as the brave do and slowly make your way up **Petřín Hill** on foot, resting and admiring the view below as often as you like. When you get to the top, stroll through the large grounds and, if you have the energy, climb up **Petřín Lookout Tower** for the excellent panoramic view. Continue on to the castle or stop for lunch at **Malý Buddha.** Head on over for more peaceful walking through both **Wallenstein and Vojan Parks** and say hello to the peacocks in the latter. Enjoy a delicious Balkan dinner at the unbeatable **Gitanes** and when you're ready to rock and roll with the local contingent, start drinking at **Klub Újezd,** where anything goes. If something a little more upscale but still friendly is to your liking, get on over to **Blue Light** for cocktails and impromptu conversations. Both bars stay open until very late so dig in and get ready to party like the Bohemians.

Day 2

Enjoy breakfast in charming **Cafe Louvre,** then make your way to **Stromovka Park,** one of Prague's more serene getaways, where you can breathe in the fresh air and clear your head amongst laughing children, playful dogs, and the fortunate locals who don't have a day job. Come out on the end where **Výstaviště** is located and take your pick from amusement rides, the **Lapidárium,** or **Sea World.** Have a light lunch at **La Creperie** or more hearty fare at **Na staré kovárně v Bráníku.** Walk it off with a romantic stroll through **Letná Park** and pull up a picnic bench at its popular

Kampa Island

a breathtaking view from Petřín Hill

beer garden for informal drinks and excellent views of the city below. Have dinner at nearby local favorite **La Bodega Flamenca** before moving a couple of doors down to **Fraktal,** where free-form conversation comes more naturally than you might think. Order a beer. Drink. Repeat.

Day 3

Take your pick from the countless restaurants along **Wenceslas Square** and have breakfast while watching the people go by. Next, it's shopping along **Na Příkopě Street,** whose boutiques, malls, and specialty shops will easily keep you busy till lunch. For a real local experience, break bread at **U Govindy Vegetarian Club.** Spend a few hours browsing the myriad of shops lining both **Celetná** and **Pařížská Street,** picking up gifts and mooning over outfits you can't afford. Have a cup of coffee with local artists and students at **Cafe Montmartre** then explore the back streets of **Old Town** while asking yourself if a downtown core can really be this beautiful. An exotic dinner at **Orange Moon** will provide the sturdy base you'll need for drinks at the always fun and rowdy **Harley's Bar.**

If cocktails and the in-crowd are more your speed, then a night at **M1** or **Tretter's** should do the trick.

Day 4

Have breakfast at **Kava Kava Kava** then wind your way over to the **Globe Bookstore & Coffeehouse** and pick up that book you've always been meaning to read, or catch up on your emails and tell everybody back home how much fun you're having. Lunch at **Dynamo** if you're in the mood for something traditional or **Lemon Leaf** if Thai food's what you've been missing. Walk along the Vltava and explore both **Střelecký** and **Dětský** islands. Head back to **Národní třída** and grab a snack before jumping on a tram and taking in a movie at **Kino Aero,** Žižkov's incomparable retro movie theater. Afterwards, discuss the movie's merits or lack thereof over a late dinner of exceptional Greek cuisine at **Olympos.** Since you're already in Žižkov, *the* neighborhood for Dionysian behavior, you might as well stay there. Descend into the legendary **Palac Akropolis** and if you still have energy left at the end of the night, stumble into **Blind Eye** then back out again when the sun comes up.

10 DAY TRIPS IN BOHEMIA AND MORAVIA

One advantage of living in a relatively small country such as the Czech Republic is the ability to see many of its sights through a series of day trips. These 10 possibilities can each be enjoyed within the course of a single day, using Prague as home base.

Day 1: Karlštejn

After breakfast, jump on a train or in the car, you're off to **Karlštejn Castle.** Enjoy the trip along the Berounka River and when you get to the castle, don't be put off by the busloads of tourists—there simply isn't a down time here. Settle on a tour of your liking and have fun roaming through the castle's various rooms and chapels. For lunch, try either **Koruna** or **U Janů** for tasty, traditional Czech fare. When you get back to Prague, continue on in historic fashion with a walk around **Old Town**'s winding cobblestone streets. Enjoy a modern Czech dinner menu at hugely popular **Kolkovna** and wash it down with their excellent dark Velkopopovický Kozel.

Day 2: Konopiště

Head to the Posázaví Region where you'll find **Konopiště Castle,** easily the area's most famous attraction. Choose a tour that reflects your particular interests and wander around the parlors and private apartments, not to mention the remarkable hunting collection of Archduke Ferdinand, which is simply mind-boggling. Have lunch at either **Stará Myslivna** or **Nova Myslivna,** or prepare a packed lunch before leaving Prague, and have a pleasant picnic in the castle's well-kept gardens. Stroll through the gardens at your leisure and return to Prague whenever the feeling hits. In the evening, take a walk around Malá Strana and follow the Archduke's lead by having a huge wild game dinner at the always fun **U Sedmi Švábů.**

Day 3: Terezín

A break from castles today as you learn more about the 20th century's darkest chapter at Terezín. Wander around the eerily silent grounds,

which include the **Magdeburg Barracks** and **Ghetto Museum,** imagining all the while how you'd fare under such trying conditions. Head back to Prague for a late lunch and spend the afternoon strolling through Prague's pretty **Jewish quarter,** admiring its synagogues and serene streets. Have a relaxing dinner at one of **Old Town**'s many restaurants, then spend the remainder of the evening walking around Prague's beautiful city center, taking extra care to appreciate everything you see, do, and have.

Day 4: Křivoklát

Křivoklát Castle, a far less touristy castle that's surrounded by tranquil woods and hills and boasts one of the country's finest interiors, is today's destination. From the **Royal Chapel** to the **Great Royal Hall** and dungeons of **Huderka Tower,** a walk through Křivoklát is an eye-opening, jaw-dropping experience. Grab a traditional, homemade lunch at **U Jelena** then spend the

Karlštejn Castle

Konopiště Castle

Český Krumlov Castle

better part of the afternoon walking around the castle's lush surroundings, a UNESCO biosphere preservation area. Upon your return to Prague, continue the theme of basking in gorgeous interiors by having dinner at **Restaurant Parnas,** whose white marble floors and chandeliers blend perfectly with the wonderful view of Prague Castle and Charles Bridge before you.

Day 5: Kutná Hora

Kutná Hora, part of UNESCO's World Cultural Heritage List, comprises today's activities and the masterfully Gothic **St. Barbara's Cathedral** is first on your list. Take your time admiring its remarkable interiors then set off for another memorable interior—the morbid yet fascinating **Sedlec Ossuary,** with its unbelievable collection of human bones. If you haven't lost your appetite, try **Pivnice Dačický** for a traditional Czech lunch or local fave **U Šneka Pohodáře** for yummy pizza pie. Depending on time or interest, check out the **Czech Silver Museum and Medieval Mine** or take a walk through town and soak up life in a slower, friendly Bohemia. When you get back to Prague, head to the castle after dinner for more Gothic goodies and feast on its massive grounds, which will be far less crowded and way more romantic.

Day 6: Český Krumlov

Leave Prague as early as possible because you'll want to maximize your time in the me-

dieval paradise that is Český Krumlov. Stroll through the town's historic center and stop for lunch at either **Tavern U dwau Maryí** or **Cikánská jizba,** then it's off to the castle, where tours through **Masquerade Hall** and **Mirror Hall** will simply astound. Don't forget to peer into the **Bear Moat** and if shopping's in the cards for you, then definitely stop by **Egon Schiele Art Centrum** for funky, creative souvenirs. Spend the rest of your time soaking up the town's abounding charm and tear yourself away long enough to get back to Prague. Have a late dinner or drink and take a walk along the Vltava and across the **Charles Bridge** before heading off to dreamland.

Day 7: Karlovy Vary

Up and at 'em nice and early again as today's journey takes you to the Czech Republic's largest and most famous spa, Karlovy Vary. Head straight for the **springs** and see whether you can actually stomach the metallic-tasting water. Enjoy walking around the town's five **colonnades,** stopping only for lunch, before wandering around the peaceful town some more. Visit historical sights like the **Russian Orthodox Church of St. Peter and Paul** or take a tour of the **Becherovka factory,** where one of the country's most popular liqueurs is made. Have an early dinner in town or a late one in Prague but get into bed early; Moravia's next.

Day 8: Brno

Have a hearty breakfast and hit the highway, it's time to visit the Moravian capital of Brno. Start with a lovely walk through historic **Old Town,** taking time to admire the buildings and appreciate the laid-back, distinctly Moravian vibe. Grab a bite to eat and head up to **Špilberk Castle,** check out the grisly casements then climb the castle tower and admire the view. If you're into the gruesome and grisly, pop into the **Capuchin Crypt** or climb up to the **Cathedral of St. Peter and Paul** for more great views of the town below. You'll find plenty of shops in the Old Town but if they're not enough try the 130 establishments that comprise **Galerie Vaňkovka.** If there's time for dinner before heading back, visit **Starobrno Pivovar** for authentic Czech cuisine and a pint of light, dark, or mixed Starobrno beer. Return to Prague and get plenty of rest as it's back to Moravia tomorrow.

Day 9: Telč

Hit the road early for a trip to the peaceful, picturesque, and UNESCO-protected town of Telč. The **town square,** one of the prettiest in the country, deserves a slow, appreciative stroll through it so take time to enjoy all the well-preserved examples of Renaissance and Baroque architecture. Have lunch on the charming summer terrace of **Šenk pod věží** then head up to remarkable **Telč Castle,** where a tour of its lavishly decorated halls will leave you breathless. If there's time, explore the countryside's numerous lakes and forests before heading back to Prague.

Day 10: Mikulov

The last day trip leads right into the heart of wine country and the town of Mikulov. Start with the remarkably well-preserved Renaissance buildings that characterize the **town square.** Pop your head into the **Church of St. Wenceslas** for a look at one of the country's most valuable church organs then settle in for lunch. Afterwards, up to **Mikulov Castle** you go where you can learn plenty about Moravia's wine history at the **Regional Museum of Mikulov,** as well as feast your eyes on Central Europe's second-largest wine barrel. Spend the rest of your time sampling the local wine at various wineries and wine cellars and make sure to buy a few bottles for friends and family back home. Now it's back to Prague and a well-deserved rest.

SPOILING YOURSELF ROTTEN IN BUDAPEST

Those who like to treat themselves to something extra special while on holiday will find no shortage of opportunities in Budapest to do so. From its famous baths to trendy cafes, upscale shops, and fine dining, this city has it all. Here are a few tips on how you can make your stay here an extra cozy one.

Day 1

Begin where everyone else does—on Váci Street. Ignore the plethora of souvenir shops with their knock-off t-shirts and cheap mugs. Head instead for the boutiques and name-brand outlets where you'll find everything from a new pair of shoes to that expensive but amazing item of clothing you wouldn't dare buy at home. Stop for a delicious lunch at famed **Café Gerbeaud** and make sure to leave for room for a scrumptious and sinful dessert. Shopping and eating can take a lot out of a person so get to the remarkable **Gellért Baths** and splash around in the lavish indoor pool or bask in the steam rooms and saunas. When you feel like moving again, opt for dinner and drinks on trendy **Ráday Street,** where you can take your pick from an amazing variety of top-notch restaurants and bars.

Day 2

Today's shopping experience begins at the one and only **WestEnd City Center,** Central Europe's largest shopping center. With over 400 shops at your disposal you'll not only find whatever it is you're looking for, but probably one or two things you weren't. For lunch, try **Kárpátia,** which has rich interiors that will make you feel like the king or queen you've always known you are. Burn a few calories by walking up to Buda's **House of Hungarian Wines.** Taste over 50 delicious domestic wines representing 22 of Hungary's wine-growing regions on your own or with the help of a friendly, informative guide. Since you're already on the Buda side, enjoy an upscale dinner at **Arany Kaviár,** where if you really feel like spoiling yourself, the "Gourmet Menu" is the only appropriate choice.

Day 3

The grand boulevard **Andrássy út** will definitely keep you busy for at least a couple of hours thanks to bountiful shops selling everything from high fashion to creative gift items. There are plenty of salons as well in case you feel like treating yourself to an aesthetic boost. Enjoy lunch on bustling **Liszt Ferenc tér** and watch the world go by. The **Széchenyi Spa Baths** are next, where you can relax in the gigantic outdoor swimming pool or head straight for the series of steam rooms, saunas, and Turkish baths. End the day with an impressive Hungarian dinner at **Gundel,** one of the country's most esteemed and respected restaurants.

Széchenyi Spa Baths

Day 4

Make a list and check it twice, you're off to the **Central Market Hall** to stock up on all picnic items your heart desires. Browse the countless stalls selling fresh fruits and vegetables, every kind of conceivable deli meat, tons of domestic wine, and a whole lot more. Now find your way over to heavenly **Margaret Island** and take a peaceful, romantic stroll through its spacious gardens until you find that perfect spot for some fun in the sun. When you're good and ready, enter immense open-air complex **Palatinus Strand.** With three thermal pools, a water slide, ping-pong tables, and trampolines, you may never want to leave. In the evening, continue on in the romantic vein by walking down Budapest's historic **Danube Embankment,** where you can choose from any number of restaurants offering excellent traditional fare and breathtaking views of Buda. It's the perfect nightcap to a perfect day.

BALATON, BABY!
A WEEK BY THE HUNGARIAN SEA

The lake attracts hundreds of thousands of visitors a year and for good reason. Whether you like to party till you drop, appreciate nature, or crave cultured evenings sipping the region's finest wines, Lake Balaton has something for everyone. A week is enough time to fully enjoy yourself and catch most of what the region has to offer, though many leave wishing they could've stayed longer.

Day 1

Get in the car or jump on one of the trains regularly leaving Keleti and Déli train stations and prepare yourself for **Siófok**—Lake Balaton's Dionysian capital. Upon arrival, find the hostel, guest house, or wellness center you've secured a room at, then waste no time heading for **Siófok Beach.** Work on that tan or stay in shape by joining a game of beach volleyball. When hunger strikes, grab a snack at any of the many kiosks or dive into a tasty traditional dish at the excellent **Csárdás Restaurant.** Spend some time walking down the tree-lined promenades and if you're looking for a different place to take an afternoon dip, check out either the **Gold Coast (Aranypart)** or **Silver Coast (Ezüstpart).** Freshen up and grab some dinner before beginning what is sure to be a long night. Head back to Siófok Beach for non-stop fun at the **Coca Cola Beach House** or hit the **Palace Dance Club** and/or **Bacardi Music Café** for dancing till dawn.

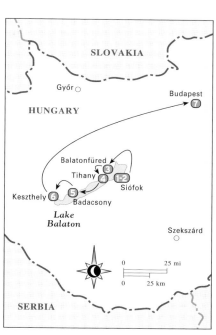

Day 2

Sleep in, shake off that hangover, and head back to whatever beach you fancy for more fun in the sun. Add some culture to your visit by checking out peaceful and romantic **Millennium Park**—the perfect antidote to the frenzy of activity that surrounds the rest of town. Head for the railway and have an unbelievable lunch at **Hintaló Vendéglő,** which is known to satisfy even the most finicky of diners. Drop by the unique **Evangelical Lutheran Church,** designed by Ybl prize–winning architect Imre Makovecz, then make your way through the shops and stalls of **Kálmán Promenade** and pick up a souvenir or two. After dinner, take a nice long walk, enjoy the sunset, and figure out whether you really want to knock off early in a town that was born ready to party.

Day 3

Head north to pretty **Balatonfüred,** where the old world meets the new. Check into your hotel then make your way to the center of town, where you'll find Lajos Kossuth Spring. Drink deeply from its curative springs and feel the debauchery of Siófok pleasantly fade away. Have lunch at the outdoor **Cimbora Grill Garden** and gorge on the wide array of grilled meat dishes, as well as the generous salad bar on offer. Walk around town admiring the tasteful villas and charming residential districts then spend some time at kitschy **Annagora Park**—a mock Greek village selling everything from souvenirs to souvlaki. Enjoy a fantastic meal on **Stefánia Vitorlás Restaurant**'s sunny terrace and make sure to save some room for one of the over 40 desserts available. If you feel rested enough and could do with another party, check out the spacious **Columbus Dance Club** or Mediterranean-themed **Club Santorini** for some serious after-hours fun.

Day 4

Take the boat over to **Tihany** and settle into a nice hotel or inn along the bay, amongst the vineyards or high atop **Felsőkopasz Hill** if you'd like some distance between yourself and the center of town. Give yourself a couple of hours to explore the peninsula's pretty interior, which includes the **Inner Lake** and **Outer Lake,** accessible via a trail from Tihany Village. Once you've built up an appetite, head for **Fogas Csárda,** Tihany's oldest traditional restaurant and a hit with both tourists and locals. Stroll along the cobblestone streets of charming Tihany village and have a look at all the handicrafts, wine, and embroidery for sale before moving on to impressive **Tihany Benedictine Abbey.** When you're done admiring the wood carvings and Baroque pulpit found inside, take the path to the left of the church leading up to **Echo Hill.** Enjoy gorgeous views of the lake and shout a few words when you get to the top to find out how the hill got its name.

Unwind with dinner at the superb **Ferenc Cellar Tavern** and finish the evening with a glass of wine or a pleasant walk.

Day 5

Take the train west to beautiful **Badacsony** and find yourself a nice hotel along the shore or guesthouse in the center of town. Take one of the many walking trails leading to the legendary **Basalt Hills** and lose yourself amongst the geological gems. For lunch, try the excellent pike-perch at the **Szent Orban Wine-House and Restaurant** and drink in the wonderful panoramic view from its summer terrace. Spend the rest of the day wine tasting, moving from wine cellar to wine cellar and enjoying the beautiful vistas along the way. If visiting during the end of July, make sure to stick around for at least one day and night of the **Badacsony Wine Festival.**

Day 6

Get up at a decent hour and head to **Keszthely,** located at the far western tip of the lake. Check into a pension along the shore or in the center of town and waste no time getting to **Festetics Palace,** Hungary's fourth-largest palace. Enjoy a tasty lunch at **La'Koma Restaurant** then spend a couple of hours at the highly informative **Balaton Museum** or enjoy an afternoon of walking around town checking out the shops, as well as **Keszthely's open-air market.** This is your last night at Lake Balaton so spoil yourself with a wonderful dinner and then cap off the night with drinks at **John's Pub** or the more alternative **512 Club.**

Day 7

Upon finishing breakfast, jump in the car or on the train and make your way back to the capital.

PRAGUE

Ever since the fall of Communism and the consequent flood of visitors to Central and Eastern Europe, Prague (Praha) has had to do little to establish itself firmly as one of the hottest destinations in the region, boasting numerous lush, wooded parks and beautiful buildings left untouched despite two World Wars. Visitors quickly come to feel they are walking through a fairy tale more so than an EU capital.

Who can remain unimpressed by the awe-inspiring Prague Castle and St. Vitus Cathedral, or the inherent beauty of Petřín Hill and Kampa Island? Is there anybody who has walked up and down Charles Bridge and not felt its palpable perfection deep in their heart? The simple truth is that Prague is a magical, melancholy city that mesmerizes all of its visitors without fail season after season. There are also thousands of expats who ended up making the capital their home, many of whom had initially arrived with the intention of staying for a month or two but couldn't resist, no matter how hard they tried, the city's famous "claws" Kafka once wrote of.

Not just a living, breathing museum of arresting architecture, Prague also boasts a legendary nightlife that has thousands of tourists shuttling in nearly every weekend to get a taste of the world's best beer and party with local Bohemians in the plethora of bars and clubs located throughout the city center and beyond. Others come to shop along trendy Pařížská and pricey Na Příkopě streets, while still others choose Prague as their honeymoon destination, strolling hand in hand down its cobblestone streets, sealing their lifelong pledge of love with a

© TOM DIRLIS

HIGHLIGHTS

◖ Václavské náměstí (Wenceslas Square): Commercial center by day, neon jungle by night, the hub of the city pulses with a lively mix of human traffic no matter what time it is (page 39).

◖ Obecní dům (Municipal House): Sit back and enjoy as the Prague Philharmonic Orchestra performs classical masterpieces in the city's finest example of Art Nouveau architecture (page 43).

◖ Národní divadlo (National Theatre): This icon of Czech culture is the perfect place to take in drama, opera, or the ballet. A tour of the magnificent playhouse is also available and recommended (page 45).

◖ Staroměstské náměstí (Old Town Square): Abuzz with shops, hotels, restaurants, and bars, this is *the* place to meet fellow travelers, take in some of the city's most jaw-dropping sights, and enjoy a vibrant nightlife (page 50).

◖ Karlův most (Charles Bridge): Take a long, romantic stroll past artists, musicians, and souvenir hawkers all vying for your attention (and money). One of the most beautiful sights Prague has to offer, with breathtaking views of the city (page 53).

◖ Rudolfinum: Focusing on contemporary Czech and international artists, this magnificent example of neo-Renaissance architecture also houses some of the city's most interesting and imaginative retrospectives (page 59).

◖ Petřínské sady (Petřín Hill): Take the funicular or walk all the way up Prague's highest and greenest hill. A perfect place to explore and have a picnic away from the maddening crowd (page 69).

◖ Pražský hrad (Prague Castle): Whether it's St. Vitus Cathedral, Golden Lane, or the Royal Garden that brings them in, this is the one place in town where *everybody* flocks to at some point during their stay. This is the epitome of Prague's national and international identity (page 70).

◖ Sbírka moderního a současného umění (National Gallery Collection of 19th-, 20th-, and 21st-Century Art): A little off the beaten track but worth the trip for anyone interested in 20th-century Bohemian art, including Cubism and Surrealism. Thought-provoking and often hair-raising Stalin-era works are also worth a look (page 81).

◖ Letenské sady (Letná Park): One of the finer outdoor places to people-watch and imbibe the world's best beer. Pull up a bench and drink in the city's mesmerizing skyline (page 81).

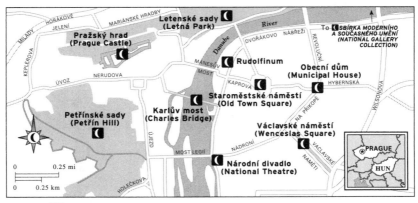

LOOK FOR ◖ TO FIND RECOMMENDED SIGHTS, ACTIVITIES, DINING, AND LODGING.

PRAGUE ADDRESSES AND DISTRICTS

Prague is separated into 10 postal districts, the numbers of which are generally included when giving an address. For example, the proper full address for the excellent Cafe Louvre would be written like this: Národní 20, Praha 1. Oftentimes, the address given will also state the specific neighborhood within the district, like so: Cafe Louvre, Národní 20, Praha 1, Nové Město. This, of course, makes it even easier to locate a particular address.

The most common districts and their corresponding neighborhoods are listed below.

Praha 1
The city's most central and by far most popular district, Prague 1 is home to the tourist-driven neighborhoods of Hradčany, Malá Strana, Staré Město, Josefov, and northern Nové Město. All the major sights are here, including Prague Castle, Charles Bridge, and Wenceslas Square, as well as the city's major shops, restaurants, hotels, and businesses.

Praha 2
Prague 2 is comprised of the tail-end of southern Nové Město, Vyšehrad, and western Vinohrady. A good deal of its charm lies in its quiet residential streets, cozy bars, intimate restaurants, and wooded parks.

Praha 3
Eastern Vinohrady and Žižkov make up the city's third district. Still close to the center, it's full of old, decrepit buildings, though it's currently experiencing a bit of a makeover. Žižkov, in particular, is known for its countless bars and rather bohemian expat residents.

Praha 5
Prague 5 is situated on the Vltava's left bank, just south of Malá Strana. Its main neighborhood, Smíchov, has undergone dramatic changes over the last five years, transforming itself from a dodgy area into a bustling commercial center full of cinemas, shopping centers, and administration offices.

Praha 6
Prague 6's main neighborhood is Dejvice. Home to Divoká Šárka, Břevnov Monastery, and Hvězda Summer Palace, it is mainly characterized by embassies, ambassadors' villas, university campuses, and residential areas.

Praha 7
Continuous reconstruction of Holešovice, Prague's former industrial zone, has made the seventh district one of the hotter locations to invest in real estate these days. This relatively central neighborhood is home to Stromovka, Letná Park, and Výstaviště.

TERMS
The Czech language is a notoriously difficult one, but learning a few of the terms below ought to help you navigate the city's streets with relative ease.

ulice (also abbreviated as *ul.*) – street
třída (also abbreviated as *tr.*) – avenue
náměstí (also abbreviated as *nám.*) – square
sady/zahrada – gardens
ostrov – island
nábřeží – quay
most – bridge
nádraží – train station
zastávka – bus, tram, subway stop

romantic, old-world kiss. Whether you come here to party, soak up the history, or simply check out what everybody's been buzzing about, it is absolutely guaranteed that Prague will stay under your skin long after you've reluctantly left.

PLANNING YOUR TIME
Many come to Prague for a quick whirlwind tour of the major sights and better-known bars

that rarely lasts longer than a weekend. While it's true that the city center and its surroundings can be easily covered in two or three days, four days offers you a better chance to truly get an authentic taste of all Prague has to offer, and five days is ideal should you want to get out of the center and investigate a few of the outlying neighborhoods and parks as well.

Prague is a breeze to get around, thanks to

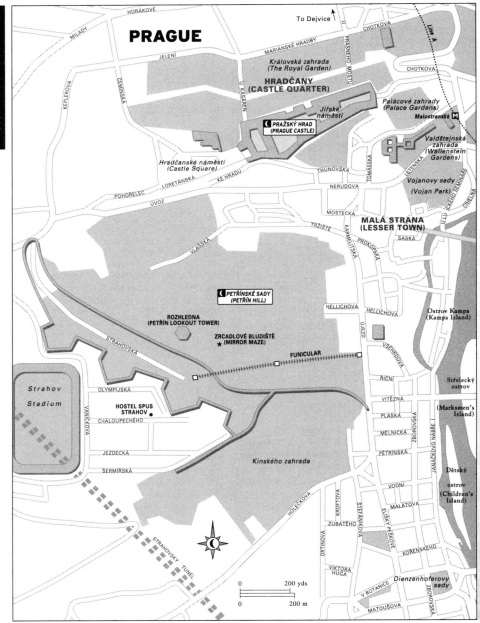

PRAGUE

HORÁKOVÉ

MILADY

JELENÍ

MARIÁNSKÉ HRADBY

To Dejvice

CHOTKOVA

Line A

KEPLEROVA

CEMINSKÁ

U KASÁREN

*Královská zahrada
(The Royal Garden)*

CHOTKOVA

**HRADČANY
(CASTLE QUARTER)**

*Jiřské
náměstí*

*Palácové zahrady
(Palace Gardens)*

Malostranská Ⓜ

🕯 **PRAŽSKÝ HRAD
(PRAGUE CASTLE)**

*Valdštejnská
zahrada
(Wallenstein
Gardens)*

LETENSKÁ

*Hradčanské náměstí
(Castle Square)*

POHOŘELEC

LORETÁNSKÁ

KE HRADU

ÚVOZ

THUNOVSKÁ

TOMÁŠSKÁ

NERUDOVA

*Vojanovy sady
(Vojan Park)*

MOSTECKÁ

ULU JÍČKÉHO SEMINÁŘE

CIHELNÁ

**MALÁ STRANA
(LESSER TOWN)**

TRŽIŠTĚ

VLAŠSKÁ

KARMELITSKÁ

PROKOPSKÁ

SASKÁ

🕯 **PETŘÍNSKÉ SADY
(PETŘÍN HILL)**

**ROZHLEDNA
(PETŘÍN LOOKOUT TOWER)**

HELLICHOVA

HELLICHOVA

*Ostrov Kampa
(Kampa Island)*

**ZRCADLOVÉ BLUDIŠTĚ
★ (MIRROR MAZE)**

ÚJEZD

VŠEHRDOVA

FUNICULAR

STRAHOVSKÁ

RIČNÍ

*Střelecký
ostrov*

*Strahov
Stadium*

OLYMPIJSKÁ

VITĚZNÁ

VANIČKOVA

**HOSTEL SPUS
STRAHOV** ●

PLASKÁ

*(Marksmen's
Island)*

CHALOUPECHÉHO

MELNICKÁ

ZBOROVSKÁ

JANÁČKOVO NÁBŘEŽÍ

JEZDECKÁ

PETŘÍNSKÁ

*Dětský
ostrov
(Children's
Island)*

ŠERMÍRSKÁ

Kinského zahrada

VODNÍ

MALÁTOVA

STRAHOVSKÝ TUNEL

HOLEČKOVA

KROFTOVA

ŠTĚFÁNIKOVA

ELIŠKY PEŠKOVÉ

KOŘENSKÉHO

DRTINOVA

ZUBATÉHO

VIKTORA
HUGA

*Dienzenhoferovy
sady*

V BOTANICE

ZBOROVSKÁ

VYSOKÁ

MATOUŠOVA

0   200 yds

0   200 m

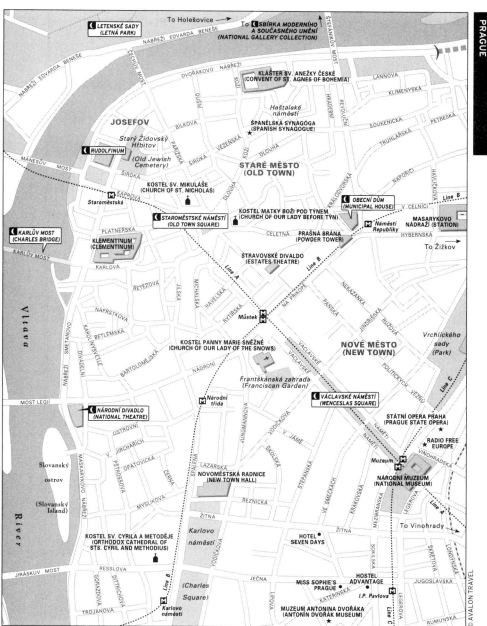

To Holešovice

To **⊆** SBÍRKA MODERNÍHO A SOUČASNÉHO UMĚNÍ (NATIONAL GALLERY COLLECTION)

⊆ LETENSKÉ SADY (LETNÁ PARK)

NÁBŘEŽÍ EDVARDA BENEŠE

ČECHŮV MOST

ŠTEFÁNIKŮV MOST

DVOŘÁKOVO NÁBŘEŽÍ

KLÁŠTER SV. ANEŽKY ČESKÉ (CONVENT OF ST. AGNES OF BOHEMIA)

LANNOVA

KLIMENTSKÁ

PETRSKÁ

NÁBŘEŽÍ EDVARDA BENEŠE

KOŽÍ

HRADEBNÍ

REVOLUČNÍ

SOUKENICKÁ

TRUHLÁŘSKÁ

JOSEFOV

Haštalské náměstí

BÍLKOVA

DUŠNÍ

ŠPANĚLSKÁ SYNAGÓGA (SPANISH SYNAGOGUE)

NAPORICI

Starý Židovský Hřbitov

⊆ RUDOLFINUM

(Old Jewish Cemetery)

PAŘÍŽSKÁ

ŠIROKÁ

VĚZEŇSKÁ

KOŽÍ

DLOUHÁ

STARÉ MĚSTO (OLD TOWN)

HAVLÍČKOVA

MÁNESŮV MOST

ŠIROKÁ

KAPROVA

KRÁLODVORSKÁ

Line B

M Staroměstská

KOSTEL SV. MIKULÁŠE (CHURCH OF ST. NICHOLAS)

DLOUHÁ

⊆ OBECNÍ DŮM (MUNICIPAL HOUSE)

V CELNÍCI

⊆ STAROMĚSTSKÉ NÁMĚSTÍ (OLD TOWN SQUARE)

KOSTEL MATKY BOŽÍ POD TÝNEM (CHURCH OF OUR LADY BEFORE TÝN)

M Náměstí Republiky

MASARYKOVO NÁDRAŽÍ (STATION)

⊆ KARLŮV MOST (CHARLES BRIDGE)

PLATNÉŘSKÁ

CELETNÁ

PRAŠNÁ BRÁNA (POWDER TOWER)

HYBERNSKÁ

KARLŮV MOST

KLEMENTINUM (CLEMENTINUM)

To Žižkov

KARLOVA

ŘETĚZOVÁ

STRAVOVSKÉ DIVADLO (ESTATES THEATRE)

Line B

NA PŘÍKOPĚ

NEKÁZANKA

Vltava

NÁPRSTKOVA

JILSKÁ

MICHALSKÁ

HAVELSKÁ

RYTÍŘSKÁ

Line A

PANSKÁ

JINDŘIŠSKÁ

RUŽOVÁ

BETLÉMSKÁ

KAROLÍNY SVĚTLÉ

SMETANOVO NÁBŘEŽÍ

DIVADELNÍ

M Můstek

Vrchlického sady (Park)

BARTOLOMĚJSKÁ

NÁDRAŽÍ

KOSTEL PANNY MARIE SNĚŽNÉ (CHURCH OF OUR LADY OF THE SNOWS)

VÁCLAVSKÉ

NOVÉ MĚSTO (NEW TOWN)

POLITICKÝCH VĚZŇŮ

Line C

MOST LEGIÍ

⊆ NÁRODNÍ DIVADLO (NATIONAL THEATRE)

OSTROVNÍ

Frantškánská zahrada (Franciscan Garden)

VÁCLAVSKÉ

⊆ VÁCLAVSKÉ NÁMĚSTÍ (WENCESLAS SQUARE)

Slovanský ostrov

V. JIRCHÁŘÍCH

OPATOVICKÁ

PŠTROSSOVA

ČERNÁ

M Národní třída

JUNGMANNOVA

VODIČKOVA

V. JÁMĚ

ŠKOLSKÁ

ŠTĚPÁNSKÁ

NÁMĚTÍ

STÁTNÍ OPERA PRAHA (PRAGUE STATE OPERA)

RADIO FREE EUROPE

VINOHRADSKÁ

MASARYKOVO NÁBŘEŽÍ

(Slovanský Island)

MYSLÍKOVA

LAZARSKÁ

SPÁLENÁ

NOVOMĚSTSKÁ RADNICE (NEW TOWN HALL)

M Muzeum M

NÁRODNÍ MUZEUM (NATIONAL MUSEUM)

Line A

ŽITNÁ

ŘEZNICKÁ

VE SMEČKÁCH

KRAKOVSKÁ

MEZIBRANSKÁ

LEGEROVA

To Vinohrady

River

KOSTEL SV. CYRILA A METODĚJE (ORTHODOX CATHEDRAL OF STS. CYRIL AND METHODIUS)

Karlovo náměstí

ŽITNÁ

VODIČKOVA

HOTEL SEVEN DAYS

SOKLSKÁ

SKŘETOVA

JUGOSLÁVSKÁ

LONDÝNSKÁ

JIRÁSKŮV MOST

RESSLOVA

JEČNÁ

MISS SOPHIE'S PRAGUE

KATEŘINSKÁ

HOSTEL ADVANTAGE

I.P. Pavlova

M I.P. Pavlova

LEGEROVA

Line C

GORAZDOVA

DITTRICHOVA

TROJANOVA

(Charles Square)

M Karlovo náměstí

VODIČKOVA

MUZEUM ANTONÍNA DVOŘÁKA (ANTONÍN DVOŘÁK MUSEUM)

LÍPOVÁ

RUMUNSKÁ

© AVALON TRAVEL

most of the important sights being situated in the zone designated Prague 1, starting from the top of Wenceslas Square in Nové Město, through to Old Town Square in Staré Město and over Charles Bridge into picturesque Malá Strana and Prague Castle that towers over it. While most prefer to stroll along the romantic cobblestone streets, others are more than satisfied with Prague's exceptional public transport system that covers the entire city, with subway stations near and around all sights and with numerous trams that lead you right to the doorstep of most significant monuments. Public transport is also the best and easiest way to reach outer neighborhoods like Dejvice, Holešovice, Vinohrady, and Žižkov. These particular districts will be of interest primarily to those who are looking to learn more about how the city really ticks. The deeper you delve into these areas, the more you'll shed the hordes of tourists that plague the center and the closer you'll come to understanding what exactly it is that makes Praguers so proud of their magical city.

ORIENTATION
Nové Město (New Town)
Located in Prague 1, Nové Město is one of the city's busiest districts and is characterized by Václavské náměstí (Wenceslas Square). Starting from its natural top at the National Museum, it stretches down towards Můstek, interrupted halfway by busy Vodičkova Street. Turning northeast at Můstek leads you down pedestrian Na Příkopě Street, which eventually ends at Náměstí Republiky; heading southwest from Můstek will take you to Národní třída and the Vltava River.

The major subway stops are Muzeum, Můstek, Náměstí Republiky, Karlovo náměstí, and Národní třída. The major tram lines are 3, 4, 5, 8, 9, 10, 14, 16, 18, 22, 23, 24, and 26.

Staré Město (Old Town)
The eastern tip of Celetná Street marks the border between Old Town and New Town. Heading west brings you to Staroměstské náměstí (Old Town Square). Walking past Old Town Hall takes you to jam-packed Karlova Street, which winds its way to the Old Town side of Charles Bridge. Behind the Jan Hus monument in Old Town Square is the start of fashionable Pařížská Street and the beginning of Josefov, Prague's Jewish quarter, which stretches all the way down to the Vltava River.

The major subway stop is Staroměstská. The major tram lines are 12, 17, and 18.

Malá Strana (Lesser Town)
Malostranské náměstí is the district's center and where all tourists make their way to at some point. This is where you'll find legendary Nerudova Street, lined with souvenir shops and restaurants as it stretches up to Prague Castle.

The major subway stop is Malostranská. The major tram lines are 12, 18, 20, 22, and 23.

Hradčany
Hradčany is defined by Prague Castle; the center of the castle complex is Jiřské Náměstí, which leads off to plenty of sights, including pretty Golden Lane. Opposite the castle's gates and entrance is gorgeous Hradčanské Náměstí, which is home to the Archbishop's Palace, Sternberg Palace, and Schwarzenberg Palace. Just west of the square is Loretánské náměstí, characterized by the magnificent Loreto.

The major subway stop is Hradčanská. The major tram lines are 1, 8, 15, 22, 23, and 25.

Dejvice
The center of the sixth district is the busy roundabout known as Vitězné náměstí. Evropská Street connects to this square and leads off to both Divoká Šárka and Ruzyně Airport.

The major subway stop is Dejvická. The major tram lines are 2, 8, 20, and 26.

Holešovice
Prague's seventh district is reached via Milady Horákove, which delves into the depths of Holešovice, passing Letná Park and busy commercial street Letenské náměstí, and stops at central Strossmayerovo náměstí. From there, it's just a few blocks to the National Gallery Collection of 19th-, 20th-, and 21st-Century

Art, Výstaviště's exhibition grounds, and Stromovka Park.

The major subway stops are Vltavská and Nádraží Holešovice. The major tram lines are 1, 5, 8, 12, 14, 15, 17, 25, and 26.

Žižkov

Žižkov is Prague's sprawling third district; its main square is Náměstí Jiřiho z Poděbrad. On the opposite side of the district is Žižkov Hill, as well as main road Seifertová, whose tram lines connect the area with the center of town.

The major subway stops are Florenc and Jiřiho z Poděbrad. The major tram lines are 5, 9, 10, 11, and 26.

Vinohrady

Vinohrady is located in the heart of Prague's second district and boasts two main squares: the heavily congested I.P. Pavlova, with its endless stream of trams, shoppers, and neighboring employees, and the grander, far more peaceful Náměstí Míru, whose comfortable benches and magnificent Church of St. Ludmilla provide the perfect antidote to I.P.'s bustle. The area's two main streets are Ječná, which leads to Karlovo náměstí, and Vinohradská, which starts/ends right behind the National Museum.

The major subway stops are Náměstí Míru and I.P. Pavlova. The major tram lines are 4, 6, 10, 16, 22, and 23.

Sights

NOVÉ MĚSTO (NEW TOWN)

Founded by Charles IV in 1348, Nové Město is a predominantly commercial district that is home to many of the city's finer shops, most of its financial institutions, as well as a plethora of restaurants, bars, and hotels. Bustling both day and night with all walks of life, it stretches north and east to Národní, Na Příkopě, and Revoluční where it borders Staré Město (Old Town).

Nové Město is constantly being redeveloped in an effort to keep the tourist dollars rolling in and the number of designer shops, boutique hotels, and department stores has grown dramatically in the last five years alone. There is one particular development that has drawn a lot of criticism, however: the steady increase of "night clubs" (i.e., brothels) that continue to attract hordes of rowdy British stag parties, giving Prague the unwanted reputation of being "that kind of town."

◖ Václavské náměstí (Wenceslas Square) and Vicinity

More a boulevard than a square, the 2,462-foot-long, 197-foot-wide Wenceslas Square is named after Saint Wenceslas; former duke and present patron saint of Bohemia who, legend has it, was murdered while on his way to church by mercenaries hired by his brother Boleslav.

The square operates as the unofficial hub of the city and was the site of nearly every major historical event the country underwent during the 20th century. On October 28, 1918, droves of Praguers filled the square to hear Czechoslovakia proclaimed an independent republic. During the Nazi occupation, the streets were the scene of mass demonstrations. The brief, hope-filled Prague Spring of 1968 came and went here and on January 19, 1969, university student Jan Palach set himself ablaze in protest of the Soviet invasion. It was here, too, on November 17, 1989, that the world tuned in to see hundreds of thousands of Czechs celebrating their first taste of democracy in over 40 years.

In the early morning, while locals head to work and tourists sleep off hangovers, the boulevard is relatively quiet, making it easy to drink in some of the historical buildings that line it. At #34 for example, you'll find the **Wiehl House,** a beautiful neo-Renaissance building designed in 1895–1896 that boasts colorful murals, gables, turrets, and a belfry. The **Melantrich Building** at #30 will stay in the hearts and minds of Czechs for a

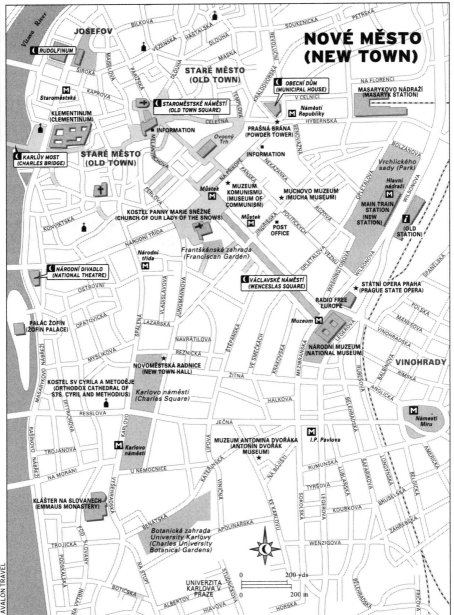

long time to come, as this is the spot where Václav Havel and Alexander Dubček stood on the second balcony and announced to a delirious crowd on November 24, 1989, that Communism was finally over. At #25 stands the infamous Art Nouveau **Grand Hotel Evropa,** which, despite its magnificent facade, has fallen way behind the times in the realm of hotel service and makes for a much better photograph than accommodation.

As the day unfolds, Wenceslas Square becomes a lively mix of hurried employees, shady money changers, reckless taxi drivers, and souvenir-laden visitors. It can all be slightly overwhelming but one way to avoid the crush of human traffic is to cross over to the island that runs down the middle of the boulevard. Lined with benches and well-manicured little gardens, the meridian is a far less crowded affair and makes for a perfect place to rest your feet, have a snack, or simply look around and admire the view. At night, Wenceslas Square sheds the day's overtly commercial slant and fills up with drunken revelers, prowling prostitutes, and a barrage of fun-seekers, giving the area a carnival-like atmosphere that extends well into the wee hours.

NÁRODNÍ MUZEUM (NATIONAL MUSEUM)

At the southern end of the square sits the National Museum (Václavské náměstí 68, tel. 224 497 111, www.nm.cz, May–Sept. 10 A.M.–6 P.M., Oct.–Apr. 9 A.M.–5 P.M., 120 Kč), a grand neo-Renaissance building that was built between 1885 and 1891 based on the designs of Josef Schulz. Weather-beaten and war-weary, it survived near-bankruptcy during the First World War and a German bomb circa 1945 during the second. Soviet soldiers senselessly opened fire on its facade in 1968 and underground blasting during the construction of the Museum metro station in 1978 caused further damage, as did the construction of what was then dubbed the "North–South Highway" (Wilsonova/Mezibranska Street), which runs past the front of the building.

Today, scores of tourists congregate at the top of the museum's steps to enjoy the view encompassing the length of the square before heading inside. Permanent exhibitions include the primeval history of Bohemia, Moravia, and Slovakia, as well as various zoological and mineral collections. The truth is that most of what's on display here is rather unimpressive, but the majestic lobby and opulent staircase are well worth a look. In front of the museum, you'll notice two small mounds embedded in the cobblestone street. They are there to commemorate Jan Palach, who set himself on fire in protest against the Soviets, as well as Jan Zajic, who followed suit a month later.

In front of the National Museum, on the other side of Wilsonova Street, is an imposing equestrian **statue of Saint Wenceslas** himself, designed by famed Czech sculptor Josef Myslbek. Affectionately dubbed "The Horse," it marks the beginning of the boulevard proper and is one of Prague's favorite meeting spots, not to mention the starting point of countless walking tours. Saint Wenceslas is kept company by fellow patron saints of Bohemia St. Agnes, Adelbert, Procopius, and Wenceslas' own grandmother, Ludmila. At the foot of the statue rests a **memorial to the victims of Communism,** depicting the images of Palach and Zajic, two protesters who sacrificed their lives for their beliefs.

RADIO FREE EUROPE

East of the National Museum is the former home of the Stock Exchange (1936–1938), which later on became the Federal Assembly Building in 1973 and stayed as such until Czechoslovakia was split into two republics in 1993. Today, the dull-looking building is the headquarters of Radio Free Europe (Vinohradská 1, tel. 221 122 114, www.rferl.org) and has been surrounded by concrete barriers and heavy security ever since a bomb threat was called in shortly after the tragic events of 9/11.

STÁTNÍ OPERA PRAHA (PRAGUE STATE OPERA)

East of Radio Free Europe is the pretty Prague State Opera (Wilsonova 4, tel. 224 227 266,

VELVET VÁCLAV

It is a very clear understanding that the only kind of politics that truly makes sense is one that is guided by conscience.

Václav Havel, 1999

Playwright, poet, political prisoner, and president, Václav Havel has been one of the foremost intellectual figures and moral forces in Eastern Europe, bringing the world's attention to the absurdity of regulated thought and speech under Communist rule and emphasizing the moral revival of the individual amidst changes of the social order. Born into an affluent family in Prague, Havel was denied entry to university due to his "bourgeois" background. He ended up studying at a technical college between 1955 and 1957 then served in the Czechoslovak army between 1957 and 1959 before joining the progressive "Theater on the Balustrade" in 1960. Starting as a stagehand, Havel eventually saw his first play, *The Garden Party*, performed on stage in 1963. It satirized modern bureaucracy and was a critical success both at home and abroad. In 1965, he picked up where he left off, writing *The Memorandum*, in which he introduced an artificial language constructed with the express purpose of creating greater precision in communication. The theme was further explored a few years later in 1968 with *The Increased Difficulty of Concentration*, which attacked fashionable sociological terminology, the era's own specific brand of political correctness. During this time, Havel was also a member of the editorial board of literary magazine *Tvár*, which quickly started to annoy the conservative Writer's Association. The magazine was ground to a halt in 1969, the same year Havel's passport was confiscated on the grounds that his writings were considered subversive and therefore dangerous to the state.

Communism's "normalization" period began in the 1970s, a period that saw tens of thousands of writers and artists arbitrarily threatened, expelled from the country, or simply locked away. Things began to look bleak and Havel saw his country becoming more and more apathetic and demoralized in the face of increased repression. In 1975, he sat down and wrote a letter to Gustav Husak, Czechoslovakia's then ruler, and lambasted him in systematic detail as to how totalitarianism was ruining the country: "So far, you and your government have chosen the easy way out for yourselves, and the most dangerous road for society: the path of inner decay for the sake of outward appearances; of deadening life for the sake of increasing uniformity; of deepening the spiritual and moral crisis of our society, and ceaselessly degrading human dignity, for the puny sake of protecting your own power." Broadcast over Radio Free Europe and illegally typed and distributed amongst numerous underground artistic and political circles, Havel's letter sent ripples of rebellion throughout the region, causing many to stop and realize that they too could stand up, ignore the potential consequences, and maybe put their oppressors on the defensive.

Havel continued to fight the good fight, sparking the Charter 77 movement that defended civil liberties, specifically rock music and its musicians who had recently been brought to the courts as dangers to society and the state. Imprisoned in 1979 for four and a half years for subversion of the republic, Havel was released in 1983 due to illness and instantly became the unofficial leader of the Czechoslovak human rights movement. He continued to write powerful plays and political essays, as well as deliver impassioned speeches and pleas that began gaining the attention and sympathy of neighboring western countries. In November 1989, Havel formed a political opposition group named the Civic Forum and was elected by direct popular vote as president of the Czech and Slovak Federal Republic when Communism finally fell. The so-called Velvet Revolution of 1989, named after Havel's favorite band The Velvet Underground, may very well have been a political inevitability, but it was Havel himself who stood up time and time again for the right of individuals to speak freely and, as he liked to put it, "live in truth."

www.sop.cz, box office Mon.–Fri. 10 A.M.–5:30 P.M., Sat.–Sun. 10 A.M.–noon, 1–5:30 P.M.), which opened on January 5, 1888, with a performance of Wagner's *The Mastersingers of Nürnberg*. Every season brings with it above-average artists hailing from all over Europe performing most of the classics, along with some lesser-known works peppered in to keep things interesting. Tickets are rather inexpensive compared to Western prices and the elegant neo-Rococo auditorium alone is worth the visit.

Northern Nové Město

The north side of Wenceslas Square is named Můstek, which in Czech means "little bridge." A bridge once connected Old and New Town here, the partial remains of which can still be seen down in the depths of the Můstek subway station. Today, Můstek is surrounded by a wide variety of shops, as well as food stands offering all kinds of greasy burgers, sausages, and hometown, late-night favorite *smažený sýr* (deep-fried cheese). Continuing straight past the square, with the National Museum at your back, you will eventually end up in Old Town Square. Turning southwest at Můstek will take you to southern Nové Město and eventually the Vltava River; heading northeast sends you down Na Příkopě, the world's 18th-most expensive street, filled with shops, restaurants, casinos, and cafes, not to mention museums, the Municipal House, and the Powder Tower.

MUZEUM KOMUNISMU (MUSEUM OF COMMUNISM)

Starting with the coup in February 1948 and spanning the years all the way to Communism's ultimate collapse in 1989, the thought-provoking Museum of Communism (Na Příkopě 10, tel. 224 212 966, www.muzeum komunismu.cz, daily 9 A.M.–9 P.M., 180 Kč) recreates a memorable account of the totalitarian regime that changed the face of the country and is still remembered by many today. The theme of the museum is "Communism—the Dream, the Reality, and the Nightmare" and visitors are invited to experience what life was like behind the Iron Curtain. An old school-room and interrogation room have been recreated, while news footage of the times in the museum's Television Time Machine both chill the heart and inspire it. This is a great introduction to the Communist era and a vivid reminder of what many Czechs lived through not all that long ago.

MUCHOVO MUZEUM (MUCHA MUSEUM)

Alphonse Mucha (1860–1939) is arguably the Czech Republic's most well-known visual artist. More than 100 exhibits featuring various paintings, photographs, and personal memorabilia of his can be found at the Mucha Museum (Kaunický palác, Panská 7, tel. 224 216 415, www.mucha.cz, daily 10 A.M.–6 P.M., 120 Kč). Most often remembered for the unconventional yet beautiful posters he designed for Sarah Bernhardt, he played a key role in influencing the French Art Nouveau at the turn of the 20th century. A half-hour video detailing Mucha's life and a recreation of his Parisian studio are also part of the exhibition on offer and visitors can purchase reprints of many of his colorful works from the museum's gift shop.

◖ OBECNÍ DŮM (MUNICIPAL HOUSE)

Prague's most prominent Art Nouveau building also happens to be one of its most beautiful. Situated on the site of the former Royal Court Palace, the Municipal House (Náměstí Republiky 5, tel. 222 002 101, www.obecnidum.cz, guided tours 150 Kč) was constructed between the years 1905 and 1911 and decorated with intricate stained-glass windows, gold trimmings, the finest in Czech crystal, and magnificent frescoes painted by the country's most talented 20th-century artists—including Alfons Mucha and Karel Spillar, who is also responsible for the mosaic above the building's main entrance, entitled "Homage to Prague." The Municipal House contains several upper-class restaurants, bars, conference rooms, and the like, but its essence can be found in Smetana Hall, which was named after the famous Czech composer and remains Prague's largest concert hall. Taking

© CORINE TACHTIRIS

the mighty and majestic Municipal House

in a classical concert here is an unforgettable experience and highly recommended to anyone who is a fan of the music.

PRAŠNÁ BRÁNA
(POWDER TOWER)

Next to the Municipal House is the 213-foot-tall Powder Tower (May–Oct. daily 10 A.M.–6 P.M., 50 Kč). This Gothic structure originally served as the gateway to the Royal Route that wound through Old Town, over the Charles Bridge, and up to the Castle. Built in 1475, it was one of Prague's original 13 city gates and was originally named Mountain Tower. The change came in the 17th century when the structure was used to store gunpowder. Renovated in the 1990s, visitors can now climb the 186 steps up to the top for excellent views of the city, as well as a permanent exhibition dealing with the history of Prague and its towers.

MUZEUM HLAVNÍHO MĚSTA PRAHY
(PRAGUE CITY MUSEUM)

Tracing Prague's development from the earliest settlement of the Prague Basin all the way to the late 18th century, the Prague City Museum (Na Poříčí 52, tel. 224 816 773, www.muzeum prahy.cz, Tues.–Sun. 9 A.M.–6 P.M., 80 Kč) is an interesting and educational way to spend an hour or two. Full of historical artifacts, weapons, maps, and signs, its most prized possession is a huge, remarkable cardboard model of the city designed 1826–1837 by Antonín Lanweil. Masterfully crafted, this model accurately depicts the city as it was before large areas of the center were cleared during the 19th and 20th centuries.

Southern Nové Město
FRANTIŠKÁNSKÁ ZAHRADA
(FRANCISCAN GARDENS)

Located behind Světozor Cinema off Vodičkova Street are the Franciscan Gardens, formerly a monastic garden built by—you guessed it—the Franciscans. The small park is a peaceful oasis amidst the rush and rumble of Nové Město and is often inhabited by office workers on their lunch break, students playing hooky, or just about anybody else looking to rest on one of the many comfortable benches. This is a relatively well-kept secret and a perfect place to take a break from the hordes.

PALÁC ADRIA
(ADRIA PALACE)

Located southwest of Můstek is Jungmannovo náměstí and it is at #28 where the Adria Palace rests. Built in 1925, it is arguably the city's finest example of Rondocubist architecture. It's now home to modern offices, apartments, and shops but still makes for an excellent photograph.

KOSTEL PANNY MARIE SNĚŽNÉ
(CHURCH OF OUR LADY OF THE SNOWS)

Founded in 1347 by Charles IV, the Church of Our Lady of the Snows (Jungmannovo náměstí 18, tel. 222 246 243, pms.ofm.cz, daily 6:30 A.M.–7:30 P.M.) was intended to be Prague's most exalted place of worship. The Hussite Wars put an end to that dream, however, and only a third of the church was ever completed. Visitors will nevertheless be impressed by the church's vaulted ceilings and altarpiece, as well as the 95-foot-tall main altar that was designed in the mid-17th century and still stands as Prague's tallest.

◖ NÁRODNÍ DIVADLO
(NATIONAL THEATRE)

The National Theatre (Ostrovní 1, tel. 224 901 448, www.narodni-divadlo.cz, box office daily 10 A.M.–6 P.M.) is one of the country's strongest symbols of a Czech people who wanted to unify their nation and culture. Funded fully with money donated from people of all social strata, the ceremonious foundation stone was laid on May 16, 1868, with the theater opening officially on June 11, 1881, in honor of Crown Prince Rudolph's visit. Tragedy struck scarcely two months later, however, when a fire broke out while further work was being done on the building, destroying the copper dome, stage, and auditorium. Once again the Czech people got together and amassed an incredible one million florins in just 47 days. Finally, on November 18, 1883, the theater opened officially with a performance of Smetana's opera *Libuše*.

THE ROYAL ROUTE: WALKING IN THE FOOTSTEPS OF KINGS

One of the most enjoyable ways to see the best of what Prague has to offer is to follow the Royal Route – the historical path that was the site of coronation processions of Bohemian monarchs on their way to being crowned at Prague Castle's St. Vitus Cathedral. The route starts at the Powder Tower located next to the magnificent Municipal House. It continues down colorful Celetná Street, home to countless souvenir shops, as well as beautiful murals, facades, and important pieces of architecture including the House of the Black Madonna. Following Celetná will lead you to Old Town Square and all of the beauty that comes with it: the astronomical clock, Týn Church, and St. Nicholas Church, among others. Continue on down Karlova Street and its wide array of shops and restaurants until you hit Charles Bridge, one of Prague's most celebrated attractions. Here you can enjoy the wonderful view of Prague Castle, the lovely Vltava River, buskers, artisans, and 30 remarkable statues that cause everybody to stop, stare, and admire. Coming off the bridge, take adjoining Mostecká Street up to Malostranské náměstí and pause for a moment to enjoy its collection of historical buildings, which include the awe-inspiring St. Nicholas Church. From there, it's on to steep Nerudova Street and its never-ending shops, restaurants, and cafes filled with tourists and locals, all enjoying the grandeur of times long gone but not forgotten. At the top of Nerudova, follow the curve to the right and you'll come upon Matthias Gate and the Prague Castle, which served as the official end of the coronation procession. The path itself is very easy to navigate but if you find yourself confused or feel that you've lost your way, look down – there are silver arrows in the ground labeled "Silver Line" outlining the entire path.

Today, the theater continues to be a beacon of culture and entertainment, offering sold-out audiences filled with schools, couples, families, and society's elite the very best ballet, opera, and drama the country has to offer.

The neo-Renaissance building is beautiful, with its golden dome and balustrade lined with wild, kicking horses. Tours of the National Theatre are scheduled three times a month. The cost is 50 Kč per person and the tour lasts about 25 minutes. For information on specific dates, email tourinfo@pis.cz.

PALÁC ŽOFÍN
(ŽOFÍN PALACE)

This gorgeous neo-Renaissance mansion located on Slovanský Island (Slovanský ostrov 226, tel. 224 924 112, www.zofin.cz) was built during 1885–1887 in honor of the Archduchess Sophie, mother of Emperor Franz Josef I. Offering tremendous views of the city, as well as Prague Castle, it has seen some of the world's finest composers perform here, including Smetana, Dvořák, Berlioz, Liszt, and Wagner. Its huge halls were ideal for concerts and balls, both of which continue to this day, along with congresses, gala receptions, and major business events.

MÁNES GALLERY

Designed by Otakar Novotný and completed in 1934, the functionalist-looking Mánes Gallery (Masarykovo nábřeží 250, tel. 224 930 794, www.galeriemanes.cz, Tues.–Sun. 10 A.M.–6 P.M., admission varies) is home to three spacious floors of regularly scheduled international art shows as well as popular exhibits of contemporary Czech artists. If you have time afterward, make sure to check out the gallery's restaurant terraces and unwind with a cup of coffee and a wonderful panoramic view of the city.

Karlovo náměstí
(Charles Square) and Vicinity

Charles IV took it upon himself to create a square large enough to rival the one found in Old Town. He certainly accomplished what he set out to do; originally a cattle market, Charles Square remains the largest square in the capital.

Choked by busy roads and an endless stream of trams, the park in the middle of the square is nevertheless an enjoyable place to walk the dog, read a book, or soak your tired feet in the fountain. Plenty of shops, restaurants, and offices are to be found in the area, as are interesting historical sights including New Town Hall, the Baroque Cathedral of St. Ignatius, Emause Monastery, and the Faust House. Though an excellent place to take a stroll and soak up some rays, the park is known to become a rather popular place for drug users and petty criminals at night; use extreme caution should you insist on walking through the square after dusk.

NOVOMĚSTSKÁ RADNICE
(NEW TOWN HALL)

Operating as the home of New Town authorities from 1377–1784, New Town Hall (Karlovo náměstí 23, tel. 224 948 229, www.novomestskaradnice.cz, May–Sept. Tues.–Sun. 10 A.M.–6 P.M., free admission) was also the site of Prague's First Defenestration. On July 30, 1419, an angry mob led by Jan Želivský demanded the release of Hussite prisoners that were being held in the building. When the Catholic councilors refused, the outraged crowd stormed the building and went about throwing all present councilors out the window. Those who somehow managed to survive the fall were beaten to death. It was here then, that Prague's first protest and the beginning of the Hussite Revolution took place. Today, the building's three lovely halls are used for much more enjoyable purposes, including various cultural and social events, as well as weddings.

KOSTEL SV. IGNÁCE
(CHURCH OF ST. IGNATIUS)

The full-on gilding and flamboyant stucco work found on the Church of St. Ignatius (Karlovo náměstí, corner of Ječná and Resslova) is quite typical of the kind of Baroque churches the Jesuits were apt to build in order to leave an indelible impression and convince others of the power of their faith. It was built by Carlo Lurago in 1665 and finished off in 1687 by Paul Ignatz Bayer, who added the church's tower.

Both architects were also responsible for the adjoining Jesuit College, which was converted into a military hospital in 1773 and now serves Charles University as a teaching hospital.

FAUSTŮV DŮM
(FAUST HOUSE)

Although closed to the public, the Faust House (Karlovo náměstí 40-41) is associated with so much bizarre history that it's well worth a look. Built in the 14th century, it was first owned by alchemist Prince Václav of Opava, then by famous alchemist Edward Kelley in the 16th century, and Count Ferdinand Mladota in the 18th century. (The count's experiments would oftentimes go awry, resulting in minor explosions and consequent holes in the roof.) Under Rudolf II, an astrologer named Jakub Krucinek lived here with his two sons, the younger of which killed the other in the name of large amounts of treasure that were purportedly hidden in the house. In the 19th century, Karl Jaenig moved in and proceeded to cover the walls with scribbled funereal texts. He fashioned a working gallows in his home and slept in a wooden coffin. His final wish was to be buried facing the bottom of said coffin. With all the crazy things that have gone down within these walls, perhaps the authorities know what they're doing by not letting the public in. Visit at your own risk.

KOSTEL SV. CYRILA A METODĚJE
(ORTHODOX CATHEDRAL OF
STS. CYRIL AND METHODIUS)

Built in the 1730s by Kilián Ignáz Dientzenhofer, the Baroque Orthodox Cathedral of Sts. Cyril and Methodius (Resslova 9a, tel. 224 920 686, pravoslavnacirkev.cz, Mar.–Sept. Tues.–Sun. 10 A.M.–5 P.M., Oct.–Feb. Tues.–Sun. 10 A.M.–4 P.M., 50 Kč) is known primarily for being the scene where Czech nationalists took their last stand after the successful assassination of Reinhard Heydrich, the Nazi SS Obergruppenfuhrer and General of Police, on May 27, 1942. Hiding in the cathedral's crypt and betrayed before they could escape, they found themselves on June 18 surrounded by hundreds of Gestapo soldiers whose orders were to capture the "criminals" alive. Fighting valiantly, three Czech soldiers died while defending the nave; the remaining four soldiers fought until they were down to their last four bullets, which they then used on themselves.

KLÁŠTER NA SLOVANECH
(EMMAUS MONASTERY)

Consecrated on Easter Monday in 1372 in the presence of King Charles IV, the Emmaus Monastery (Vyšehradská 49, tel. 221 979 211, www.emauzy.cz, Mon.–Fri. 9 A.M.–4 P.M., 40 Kč) has been through a lot, to say the least. It was first ravaged during the Hussite Wars and then again during the brief French occupation of Prague in the 18th century. By the late 19th century the church was in such dire condition that it was in danger of being torn down. The worst came during the 1940s and '50s, however, when both the Nazis and Soviets took turns taking over the premises and brutally killing most of the monks who made their home here. The monastery was finally returned to the Benedictine order after the fall of Communism and massive efforts to painstakingly restore this wonderful piece of history continue to this day.

BOTANICKÁ ZAHRADA
UNIVERSITY KARLOVY
(CHARLES UNIVERSITY
BOTANICAL GARDEN)

If you're looking to do something a little different during your stay, try the oft-overlooked Charles University Botanical Garden (Benátská 2, tel. 224 918 970, www.natur.cuni.cz, Dec.–Feb. daily 10 A.M.–5 P.M., Mar.–Nov. daily 10 A.M.–6 P.M., 15 Kč). Inaugurated in 1898, it serves as a public garden as well as an educational paradise for students of the university. Outside, there is a fine collection of central European flora, including the valuable *Ginko biloba cv. Praga*—the only specimen of its kind in the world. There are also incredible greenhouses on the premises housing the oldest *Cycas* in the country, along with a collection of cacti, papayas, huge primeval plants, orchids, and a whole lot more.

CZECH CUBISM

Inspired by the work of Braque and Picasso, four remarkably talented and avant-garde artists – Pavel Janák, Josef Gočár, Josef Chochol, and Vlastislav Hofman – took French Cubist principles and adapted them to furniture, decorative objects, and buildings, ignoring the arguments of their predecessors and pushing Cubism further than anyone else dared to. Characterized by sharp points, slicing panes, and crystalline shapes, the Czech Cubists believed that the only way an object's internal energy could be properly freed was by smashing the vertical and horizontal surfaces that restrained it. Using the pyramid as the zenith of architectural design and the crystal as the quintessential natural form, they introduced angled planes to everyday objects, giving them a dynamism that transformed them into works of art. The Cubist movement was vastly supported by Bohemia's cultural elite, who enjoyed the daring new designs that found their way into their desks, chairs, villas, and offices. Art historian Miroslav Lamac explained the phenomenon thusly: "Prague became the city of Cubism with Cubist apartment blocks full of Cubist flats furnished with Cubist furniture. The inhabitants could drink coffee from Cubist cups, put flowers in Cubist vases, keep the time on Cubist clocks, light their rooms with Cubist lamps and read books in Cubist type." Some of the finer surviving examples of Cubist architecture about town are the House of the Black Madonna (Ovocný trh 19 in Staré Město), the apartment building at Elišky Krásnohorské 10-14 in Josefov, and Adria Palace (Jungmannovo náměstí 28 in Nové Město). Those interested in learning more about this fascinating movement are strongly urged to visit the Museum of Czech Cubism housed in the aforementioned House of the Black Madonna.

STARÉ MĚSTO (OLD TOWN)

Since its founding in 1231, Staré Město has been the heart and soul of the capital and remains as such today, attracting visitors from all over the world who stand open-mouthed at the staggering beauty accumulated over a millennium's worth of architecture. In Old Town Square alone one can see Romanesque, Gothic, Rococo, and Art Nouveau buildings blending in nicely with the upsurge of tourist-dependent businesses that have cropped up throughout the district. Trendy restaurants and cocktail bars have replaced old-school eateries and pubs, and the once-quiet cobblestone streets are now filled with throngs of tourists desperate to experience the magic and Bohemian lifestyle that have been immortalized in countless books, plays, and films. Despite the increase in overpriced cafes and upscale shops, however, Staré Město remains as elegant, romantic, and intoxicating as ever—a feat that is as impressive as it is admirable.

Celetná ulice (Celetná Street)

Stretching between the Powder Tower (in Nové Město) and Old Town Square is the lively pedestrian lane Celetná, named as such due to the plaited bread rolls (called *calty*) that were baked here in the 13th century. It is one of the city's oldest streets and was part of the royal coronation route of Czech kings that ran all the way to Prague Castle. Lined with picturesque houses, as well as numerous shops, cafes, and restaurants, it bustles with activity during the day and reverts to one of Prague's most romantic streets at night. Many of the houses here are of historical significance, including the Pachta Palace (#36), which began as a mint in the Middle Ages and became a court building in 1849 that employed a young Franz Kafka. The House at the Golden Angel (#29) used to operate as an inn and extended its hospitality to revered guests such as Mozart. And let us not forget the House at the Three Kings (#3),

PRAGUE

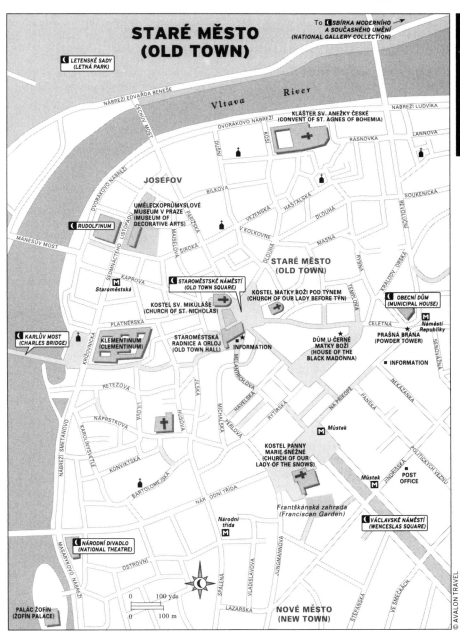

STARÉ MĚSTO (OLD TOWN)

To **☾** SBÍRKA MODERNÍHO A SOUČASNÉHO UMĚNÍ (NATIONAL GALLERY COLLECTION)

☾ LETENSKÉ SADY (LETNÁ PARK)

NÁBŘEŽÍ EDVARDA BENEŠE

ČECHŮV MOST

Vltava River

DVOŘÁKOVO NÁBŘEŽÍ

NÁBŘEŽÍ LUDVÍKA

KLÁŠTER SV. ANEŽKY ČESKÉ (CONVENT OF ST. AGNES OF BOHEMIA)

RÁSNOVKA

LANNOVA

DUŠNÍ

KOSÍ

DVOŘÁKOVO NÁBŘEŽÍ

JOSEFOV

BÍLKOVA

HAŠTALSKÁ

VEZEŇSKÁ

SOUKENICKÁ

UMĚLECKOPRŮMYSLOVÉ MUSEUM V PRAZE (MUSEUM OF DECORATIVE ARTS)

DLOUHÁ

REVOLUČNÍ

☾ RUDOLFINUM

PAŘÍŽSKÁ

V KOLKOVNE

MASNÁ

MÁNESŮV MOST

MAISELOVA

SIROKÁ

DLOUHÁ

RYBNÁ

STARÉ MĚSTO (OLD TOWN)

KRÁLODV. OPSKÁ

SEDMNÁCTEHO LISTOPADU

KAPROVA

M Staroměstská

☾ STAROMĚSTSKÉ NÁMĚSTÍ (OLD TOWN SQUARE)

TEMPLOVÁ

☾ OBECNÍ DŮM (MUNICIPAL HOUSE)

M Náměstí Republiky

KOSTEL MATKY BOŽÍ POD TÝNEM (CHURCH OF OUR LADY BEFORE TÝN)

KOSTEL SV. MIKULÁŠE (CHURCH OF ST. NICHOLAS)

PLATNÉŘSKÁ

CELETNÁ

PRAŠNÁ BRÁNA (POWDER TOWER)

SENOVÁŽNÁ

☾ KARLŮV MOST (CHARLES BRIDGE)

KŘIŽOVNICKÁ

KLEMENTINUM (CLEMENTINUM)

STAROMĚSTSKÁ RADNICE A ORLOJ (OLD TOWN HALL)

MELANTRICHOVA

■ INFORMATION

DŮM U ČERNÉ MATKY BOŽÍ (HOUSE OF THE BLACK MADONNA)

NEKÁZANKA

■ INFORMATION

RETĚZOVÁ

LILIOVÁ

JILSKÁ

MICHALSKÁ

PERLOVÁ

HAVELSKÁ

RYTÍŘSKÁ

NA PŘÍKOPĚ

PANSKÁ

NÁPRSTKOVA

HUSOVA

Můstek

POLITICKÝCH VEZŇŮ

KAROLÍNY SVĚTLÉ

KONVIKTSKÁ

KOSTEL PANNY MARIE SNĚŽNÉ (CHURCH OF OUR LADY OF THE SNOWS)

NÁBŘEŽÍ SMETANOVO

BARTOLOMĚJSKÁ

NÁR. ODNI TŘÍDA

Můstek **M**

JINDŘIŠSKÁ

■ POST OFFICE

Frantškánská zahrada (Franciscan Garden)

☾ VÁCLAVSKÉ NÁMĚSTÍ (WENCESLAS SQUARE)

Národní třída **M**

☾ NÁRODNÍ DIVADLO (NATIONAL THEATRE)

MASARYKOVO NÁBŘEŽÍ

OSTROVNÍ

SPÁLENÁ

VLADISLAVOVA

JUNGMANNOVA

ŠTĚPÁNSKÁ

VE SMEČKÁCH

0   100 yds

0   100 m

LAZARSKÁ

NOVÉ MĚSTO (NEW TOWN)

PALÁC ŽOFÍN (ŽOFÍN PALACE)

© AVALON TRAVEL

where Kafka lived between 1896 and 1907. No matter how long you stay in Prague, this is one street that deserves your attention.

DŮM U ČERNÉ MATKY BOŽÍ (HOUSE OF THE BLACK MADONNA)

On the corner of Celetná Street and Ovocný Trh you'll find one of the world's most striking examples of Cubist architecture. The House of the Black Madonna (Ovocný trh 19, tel. 224 211 746, www.ngprague.cz, Tues.– Sun. 10 A.M.–6 P.M., 100 Kč) came to be after wholesale merchant František Josef Herbst commissioned respected Czech architect Josef Gočár to design a department store. Built between 1911 and 1912, the building was a sensitive addition to a historic city center and remains one of Prague's most aesthetically pleasing buildings. It now houses the Museum of Czech Cubism, which is run by the National Gallery and offers a comprehensive collection of paintings, prints, and sculptures that reflect the period of 1910–1919, which were the style's most significant years.

◖ Staroměstské náměstí (Old Town Square)

For most people, entering Old Town Square for the first time is like walking into a movie set in the 18th century, when colorful facades and architectural styles ranging from the Gothic to the Baroque were par for the course. Not only is it the country's most beautiful square, it is undoubtedly one of the entire continent's as well. It has been Prague's economic and political center since the 10th century, acting as marketplace, execution site, and location of nation-changing announcements—including the beginning of the Communist takeover. Its first houses were built in the 12th and 13th centuries, and the square is home to some of the city's most spectacular buildings, including Old Town Hall with its famous Astronomical Clock, St. Nicholas Church, and the Church of Our Lady Before Týn.

The ever-growing number of tourists who flock to the city has changed the face of the square, fueling an overt commercialism that includes a line of stalls on the west side selling kitsch to the swarms of tour groups that descend on the square daily. Despite the hordes, however, it is still one of the most wondrous places in town—a space often filled with smiling faces, people posing for photographs, swing jazz bands, and lovers enjoying the romance in the air which is as old as it is palpable. Cafes, bars, and restaurants have gotten in on the act, too, setting out tables and chairs that offer the finest views available. Throughout the summer, the square is often the site of world music concerts, art exhibits, and a wide variety of traditional cultural events. In the winter, it is the setting of Prague's biggest Christmas market, a jolly, outdoor affair augmented by a gigantic, brilliantly lit tree.

The center of the square is characterized by the Jan Hus monument, dedicated to the Protestant reformer who was labeled a heretic and burnt at the stake on July 6, 1415. It was designed by Ladislav Šaloun and presented to the public in 1915 on the 500th anniversary of Hus's death. The base of its steps used to be a popular meeting point, as well as a perfect place for locals and visitors alike to take a breather and drink in the square's charm. Unfortunately, countless overzealous (and drunken) tourists repeatedly tried climbing the monument, prompting authorities to install a ring of flowerbeds and benches around it.

Near the monument lies a brass strip in the ground that marks the site of the former Marian Column of 1650. When the column's shadow fell on the meridian at noon, a senior timekeeper in the observation tower of the Klementinum would wave a flag, prompting all of Prague's timekeepers to synchronize their clocks.

STAROMĚSTSKÁ RADNICE A ORLOJ (OLD TOWN HALL AND ASTRONOMICAL CLOCK)

One of the most striking and popular buildings of Old Town Square is the Old Town Hall and Astronomical Clock (Staroměstské náměstí, Apr.–Oct. Mon. 11 A.M.–6 P.M., Tues.–Sun. 9 A.M.–6 P.M., Nov.–Mar. Mon. 11 A.M.–5 P.M., Tues.–Sun. 9 A.M.–5 P.M., 50 Kč). The Town

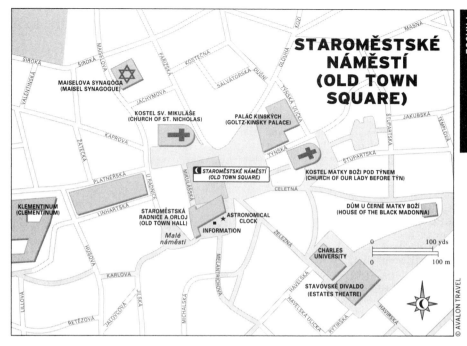

STAROMĚSTSKÉ NÁMĚSTÍ (OLD TOWN SQUARE)

Hall was established in 1338 and is actually an amalgamation of neighboring buildings that were joined together over the years, resulting in a mixture of Renaissance and Gothic architectures. There is a nearly 200-foot-tall viewing tower inside the building, which is well worth the time and money as it affords remarkable views of the square and Old Town in general.

The most intriguing feature of Town Hall is, of course, the Astronomical Clock that was incorporated into the structure in 1490. Legend has it that Master Hanuš, the clock's maker, was blinded by the town's council in order to prevent him from recreating his marvelous achievement elsewhere in Europe. Seeking revenge, Hanuš is purported to have stuck his hands in the machinery, thereby ending his life and damaging the clock (for the time being at least). The clock itself is an intricate piece of machinery and consists of three main components: an astronomical dial showing the position of the sun and moon in relation to the zodiac, a calendar dial with medallions representing the months of the year, and the crowd favorite, "The Walk of the Apostles"—an hourly (8 A.M.–8 P.M.) show where wooden statuettes appear from mini trap doors and move from left to right while a skeletal figure signifying Death pulls a rope to the rhythm of the chimes. In actual fact, the "puppet show" is a rather anti-climactic affair but worth a look should you happen to be in the square at the top of the hour.

KOSTEL MATKY BOŽI POD TÝNEM (CHURCH OF OUR LADY BEFORE TÝN)

The Church of our Lady Before Týn (Staroměstské náměstí 604, tel. 222 322 801, services Wed.–Fri. 6 P.M., Sat. 8 A.M., Sun. 9:30 A.M. and 9 P.M., free admission) is the grand Gothic building dominating one side of Old Town Square and easily recognizable thanks to its twin towers capped by four small spires. Impressive by day, it adds to the overall fairy-tale feel of "Magic Prague" when lit up at night, causing many visitors to stop in mid-step and simply admire it in silence. It was founded in 1385 during the reign of Charles IV and possesses one of the most remarkable Baroque interiors to be found in the city. Brightly stained glass, a Rococo altar on the northern wall, and a black and gold organ are just some of its features, with the most interesting being the tomb of famed astronomer Tycho Brache, who served as Rudolf II's personal "consultant."

KOSTEL SV. MIKULÁŠE (CHURCH OF ST. NICHOLAS)
Designed by Kilian Ignaz Dientzenhofer, the Church of St. Nicholas (Staroměstské náměstí, Mon. noon–4 P.M., Tues.–Sun. 10 A.M.–4 P.M., free admission), not to be confused with the one in Malá Strana, is a gorgeous Baroque building on the corner of Old Town Square. It was completed in 1735 and is a favorite with tour groups and visitors in general as it hosts a number of classical music concerts (typically 500 Kč) on any given day of the week. Tickets can be bought in front of the church, which is also the site of the occasional busker or two, including a crowd-pleasing, well-dressed elderly man who plays jazz standards on the saxophone.

PALÁC KINSKÝCH (GOLTZ-KINSKY PALACE)
Standing on a site that was previously occupied by two medieval dwellings, Goltz-Kinsky Palace (Staroměstské náměstí 12, tel. 224 810 758, Tues.–Sun. 10 A.M.–6 P.M., 100 Kč) is a late Baroque building with a gorgeous pink and white Rococo facade that does much to add to the square's overall beauty. It was built between 1755 and 1765 by Anselmo Lurago according to the designs of Kilian Ignaz Dientzenhofer. The palace operated as a German grammar school and had a quiet student named Franz Kafka enrolled here from 1893–1901. His father Hermann was

the Church of St. Nicholas in Old Town Square

around as well, running a haberdashery on the main floor. A far more chilling historical event occurred on the palace's balcony on February 25, 1948, when then Communist leader Klement Gottwald informed the crowds below that the Communist era had officially begun. Today, the palace hosts various collections of the National Gallery, including one permanent exhibit detailing Czech landscapes from the Baroque to the present day.

DŮM U KAMENNÉHO ZVONU (HOUSE AT THE STONE BELL)
Dating back to the second half of the 13th century and recognized as Prague's oldest Gothic building, the House at the Stone Bell (Staroměstské náměstí 13, tel. 224 827 526, www.citygalleryprague.cz, Tues.–Sun. 10 A.M.–6 P.M., 90 Kč) was painstakingly restored in the late 1980s and now boasts an enchanting Baroque courtyard along with three floors of exhibitions run by the City Gallery of Prague. It is the site of occasional concerts and various artistic events as well.

On the Way to Charles Bridge

The easiest and by far most popular way to reach Charles Bridge is via the twisting, cobblestone street known to all as Karlova. Numerous Baroque and Renaissance facades line the way, including the former residence of famed astronomer Johannes Kepler, who lived at #4. Countless shops on either side of the narrow street offer the usual tourist grab bag of t-shirts, marionettes, and glass, making for a jam-packed route that can become rather frustrating at times. To fully appreciate Karlova, try taking a stroll during the early hours of the morning or late at night when the street is near empty and at its most enchanting.

Malé náměstí (Little Square) marks the beginning of Karlova just past Old Town Hall. At its center is a Renaissance fountain protected by a pretty wrought-iron grill from the 16th century. The small square is surrounded by expensive shops like the colorful Rott Building, as well as hotels, taxis, and antique cars offering hour-long tours of the area at typically inflated prices.

KLEMENTINUM (CLEMENTINUM)

The Clementinum (Mariánské náměstí 4/ Klementinum 190, tel. 221 663 111, www .klementinum.cz, tours daily 10 A.M.–6 P.M. every hour, 190 Kč) is a massive Baroque complex located right by the Charles Bridge that can be accessed from Mariánské náměstí and/ or Karlova Street. It is now home to the National Library of the Czech Republic and holds over six million volumes, including the surviving remnants of Tycho de Brahe's library, as well as collections from Count Kinsky and the Lobkowicz family.

On the premises is a pretty Mirror Chapel that was built around 1720. It boasts slick marbled walls and floors, gorgeous ceiling frescoes, and murals depicting the life of the Virgin Mary. Mozart used to play here occasionally and the chapel continues to host classical music concerts daily. There is also a breathtaking Baroque Library Hall, finished in 1722; it has a tremendous trompe l'oeil ceiling symbolizing antique wisdom with a Dome of Wisdom acting as its centerpiece. The hall has remained virtually untouched over the years and is as good an example of an authentic Baroque library as you're going to get. Finally, the Astronomical Tower, which was built around the same time as both the chapel and library hall, served as an astronomical observatory that was fitted out with the latest devices the era could offer by Jesuit Jan Klein. It was from here that the Prague Meridian was determined and a signal, followed by a cannon shot, was fired every noon to let the entire city know that the middle of the day had arrived. Tours of all three sights are offered daily.

◖ Karlův most (Charles Bridge)

Apart from the Prague Castle, Charles Bridge is easily the city's most popular attraction and is synonymous with Prague's world-renowned beauty and mystique. Thousands of visitors cross the bridge daily, stopping to get their portrait painted, posing for one-of-a-kind photographs, and taking slow, romantic strolls hand in hand. Adding to the historic atmosphere are buskers, artists, and vendors selling everything from panoramic pictures of the bridge to handcrafted souvenirs and jewelry. Though packed in the summertime (so much so that it makes it almost impossible to enjoy the bridge's beauty), the crowds do thin out come evening time. The most magical moments to enjoy the glorious view are at night when the castle and near mystical surroundings are brilliantly lit. The truly lucky may even get the entire bridge to themselves, though it'll have to be very late at night or early in the morning before the professional photographers appear, hoping for the day's best and brightest light.

It is interesting to note that the Charles Bridge was not the first bridge to stand in its present location. It was the Judith Bridge, built in 1172, that served the capital until its unfortunate collapse in 1342 due to heavy flooding. Holy Roman Emperor Charles IV himself laid the foundation stone of the Charles Bridge on July 9, 1357, at exactly 5:31 A.M. The date and time are of numerological significance as several odd numbers were aligned. Starting with the year then taking the date, month, and time, the numbers read 1-3-5-7-9-7-5-3-1. Head of the bridge's construction was architect extraordinaire Petr Parléř, who was also responsible for the majestic St. Vitus Cathedral at Prague Castle. The story goes that he mixed egg yolks into the mortar in an effort to strengthen the bridge's construction.

The bridge itself is 1,692 feet long, 31 feet wide, has 16 spans with radiuses ranging 54.5–77 feet, and is situated 43 feet above the river's surface. Although now strictly a pedestrian zone, horse-drawn buggies ran across it from 1883; they were then replaced by trams in 1905, along with buses and cars that drove across the bridge all the way up to 1965.

One of the most beautiful aspects of the bridge is its gorgeous Baroque statues, which total 30 in all (plus one just beyond the railing). Most are replicas, though many of the originals can be viewed at the Lapidarium. One thing to look for is the Archbishop's five-star brass cross, located on the bridge's balustrade near the statue of St. John the Baptist. Superstition dictates that those who put their hands on the cross so that each of their fingers touches one of the stars will be rewarded with their most secret desire coming true.

STAROMĚSTSKÁ MOSTECKÁ VĚŽ (OLD TOWN BRIDGE TOWER)

At the eastern end of the Charles Bridge on the Staroměstská side is the blackened but beautiful Old Town Bridge Tower (Křížovnické náměstí/Charles Bridge, tel. 224 220 569, Mar. daily 10 A.M.–6 P.M., Apr.–May and Oct. daily 10 A.M.–7 P.M., June–Sept. daily 10 A.M.–10 P.M., Nov.–Feb. daily 10 A.M.–5 P.M., 50 Kč). It was designed by Petr Parléř in the Gothic style and completed in 1380, serving as both watchtower and part of Prague's defense system. There is a relatively boring exhibition on the tower's history but don't miss the opportunity to climb all the way up for a fantastic view of the city center.

On the other end of the bridge is the Lesser Town Bridge Tower, in Malá Strana.

STATUES

The following is a list of statues found on the Charles Bridge. In parentheses, the statue's sculptor and date it appeared on the bridge are given. We start on the Old Town side with statue #1 being the first statue on your left; statue #2 is the first on your right-hand side, statue #3 is the second on your left, etc.

1. St. Ivo (M. B. Braun, 1711). Notable 11th-century bishop of Chartres, France. Counselor to King Philip, he fought against the greed of his contemporaries and was imprisoned for a time for opposing King Philip's plans to leave his wife Bertha and marry Bertrade of Anjou.

2. St. Bernard (M. V. Jackel, 1709). Founding abbot of Clairvaux Abbey in Burgundy, he was one of the most important Church leaders of the first half of the 12th century, as well as a powerful propagator of Cistercian reform.

3. SS Barbara, Margaret, and Elizabeth (J. Brokoff, 1707). St. Barbara was the extremely beautiful daughter of wealthy Dioscorus, who, fearing his daughter would be demanded in marriage, shut her in a tower to protect her from the outside world. She gradually came to accept the Christian faith, which outraged her father. The prefect of the province sentenced her to death by beheading, a task Dioscorus happily volunteered for. On his way home to do the dirty deed, he was struck by lightning, which is the reason that Barbara is today considered to be the patron saint in times of danger, thunderstorms, fires, and sudden death.

While watching the flocks of her mistress, St. Margaret was approached by Roman prefect Olybrius, who was determined to make her his concubine or wife. When she resisted and it became clear she wouldn't back down, Olybrius had her brought before him in a public trial. Threatened with death unless she renounced her Christian faith, Margaret stuck to her guns. Set on fire, the flames that were meant to burn her fizzled out. Bound hand and foot and then thrown into a cauldron of boiling water, her bonds broke and she stood up unharmed. Having had enough, the prefect did the only thing he could think of: Off with her head, he ordered. Nobody knows why exactly, but this eternal virgin is widely considered to be the patron saint of pregnant women.

Born in Hungary in 1207, St. Elizabeth married into royalty but led a simple, pious life, devoting her time to works of charity. After her husband's death, Elizabeth left the royal court for good, denounced the world and devoted herself to the care of sick children until her death. She is the patron saint of bakers, children, widows, young brides, the homeless, and the falsely accused.

4. The Madonna with St. Dominic and Thomas Aquinas (M. V. Jackel, 1708). Founder of the Order of Preachers (Dominicans), St. Dominic traveled all over Italy, Spain, and France preaching the good word and attracting numerous followers due to his harmonization of intellectual life with the needs of the people. He is the patron saint of astronomers.

A member of the Dominican order, Thomas Aquinas is perhaps best known for his synthesis of Christianity with Aristotelian philosophy, which became the Roman Catholic Church's official doctrine in 1879.

5. The Lamenting of Christ (E. Max, 1859). Depicts Jesus lying in the Virgin Mary's lap, with St. John in the center and Mary Magdalene on the right.

6. Crucifixion (W. E. Brohn, J. J. Heermann, E. Max, 1696/1861). The Hebrew inscription in gold reads, "Holy, Holy, Holy, Lord God Almighty"; it was paid for by a local Jew as punishment for allegedly blaspheming in front of the statue in 1696.

7. St. Joseph (1854, E. Max). Well-known husband of Mary and father of Jesus of Nazareth.

8. St. Anne (M. V. Jackel, 1707). Mother of Mary and grandmother to Jesus himself.

9. St. Francis Xavier (F. M. Brokoff, 1711). Pioneering missionary who co-founded the Jesuit Order, St. Francis Xavier is the patron saint of Navarre, Spain and missionaries. He is considered by the Catholic Church to have converted more people than anyone save for St. Paul.

10. SS Cyril and Methodius (Karel Dvořák,

1928). The two saints who were responsible for bringing Christianity to the Slavs in the 9th century.

11. St. Christopher (E. Max, 1857). One of the 14 Holy Helpers, St. Christopher wandered the world and one day came upon a hermit who served others by guiding them to places that were safe to cross. Christopher took over for the hermit but instead of doling out advice, would carry travelers safely across the stream he lived by. One day, he carried a child across who was so heavy, the weight nearly crushed him. It turned out to be Jesus, who bore the weight of the world upon himself. Christopher is the patron saint of travel and travelers.

12. St. John the Baptist (J. Max, 1857). Widely considered the forerunner of Jesus Christ, St. John the Baptist was a preacher and ascetic who is regarded as a prophet by Christianity, Islam, Mandaeanism, and the Bahá'í faith.

13. St. Francis Borgia (F. M. Brokoff, 1710). A duke at the relatively young age of 33, St. Francis Borgia lived happily with his wife and eight children. Upon his wife's death, he gave it all up and became a Jesuit priest, humbling himself continuously and without argument to his superiors. He was eventually made Superior General of the Jesuits and was an instrumental force in the spread of the Jesuit faith.

14. St. Norbert (J. Max, 1853). Dionysian in nature while growing up, St. Norbert faced certain death one day when he was caught in a horrendous thunderstorm. He managed to utter the question, "Lord, what do You want me to do?" The answer that came back from above was "Turn from evil and do good. Seek peace and pursue it." That is exactly what he did, fighting the prejudices of those who didn't believe his sudden change of heart and eventually climbing the ecclesiastical ladder all the way up to archbishop.

15. St. Ludmila (M. B. Braun, 1784). Grandmother of St. Wenceslas and patroness of Bohemia.

16. St. John of Nepomuk (M. Rauchmiller, J. Brokoff, W. H. Herold, 1683). The oldest and most popular statue on the bridge depicts the patron saint of Czechs who, legend has it, was thrown off the bridge after refusing to reveal the secrets of the Queen's confession. More likely is that he simply got caught up in one of King Wenceslas IV's rages against the church. A bronze relief below the statue details his unfortunate story and the belief is that if you rub it, you'll not only receive good luck, but come back to Prague again one day as well.

17. St. Francis of Assisi (E. Max, 1855). Founder of the Franciscan order and famed patron saint of ecology and animals, many of which he preached the word of God to.

18. St. Anthony of Padua (J. O. Mayer, 1707). Made a Doctor of the Church by Pope Pius XII in 1946, St. Anthony was known for his dedication and ability to teach the word of God to even the most uneducated and inexperienced. Much beloved, he was canonized a mere year after his death, which came at the tender age of 36.

19. SS Vincent Ferrer and Procopius (F. M. Brokoff, 1712). Patron saint of builders, St. Vincent Ferrer became as such due to his uncanny ability to strengthen the church through his inexhaustible preaching, teaching, and missionary work.

Born in Jerusalem, St. Procopius was a reader in Scythopolis when he was arrested by the Roman authorities and martyred when he became the first victim of the persecution of the Church in Palestine by Emperor Diocletian.

20. Bruncvik (L. Simek, 1884). Located beyond the railing, he is the hero of the 11th-century epic poem *Song of Roland*.

21. St. Jude Thaddeus (J. B. Kohl, 1708). A disciple of Jesus, St. Jude Thaddeus is "The Miraculous Saint" and patron saint of lost causes. He is the one to call when all hope is lost and there's no one else to turn to.

22. St. Augustine (J. B. Kohl, 1708). St. Augustine is the patron saint of brewers due to his conversion from a life full of old-world sex, drugs, and worldly ambitions to bishop and revered saint. He continues to inspire those who struggle to remain on the wagon.

23. St. Nicholas of Tolentino (J. B. Kohl, 1708). A 13th-century pastor who ministered to the poor and criminal, he gained a reputation as a wonder worker after curing the sick with bread that was blessed by Mary herself, who thoughtfully answered his prayers.

24. St. Luthgard (M. B. Braun, 1710). A highly esteemed mystic of the Middle Ages, St. Luthgard was a Cistercian nun who envisioned Christ, levitated, and had the sign of stigmata before going blind near the end of her life.

25. St. Cajetan (F. M. Brokoff, 1709). Fighting the good fight against corruption and licentiousness, St. Cajetan established the Theatine order and remains the saint people pray to when the Church troubles them and causes doubt.

26. St. Adalbert (F. M. Brokoff, 1709). Became the bishop of Prague in 982. Disliked by the nobility and facing mounting unpopularity, he left for Rome and became a Benedictine monk. Pope John XV sent him back to Prague where he founded Břevnov Monastery.

27. St. Philip Benitius (M. B. Mandel, 1717). General of the Servite order, the papal tiara lying at his feet symbolizes his refusal of the papacy in 1268.

28. SS John of Matha, Felix of Valois, and Ivo (F. M. Brokoff, 1714). Both John of Matha and Felix of Valois lived in a hermitage at Cerfroid before founding the Order of the Most Holy Trinity (the Trinitarians) upon receiving the blessing of Pope Innocent III. (See above for St. Ivo.)

29. St. Vitus (M. Brokoff, 1714). One of the 14 Holy Helpers, St. Vitus is the patron saint of epileptics, dancers, and actors, as well as being a protector against storms. The remarkable cathedral at Prague Castle is named after him as well.

30. St. Wenceslas (J. Fuhrich, J. K. Bohm, 1858). The one and only martyr, prince of Bohemia, and patron saint of the Czech Republic.

31. SS Cosmas and Damian (J. O. Mayer, 1709). Saints Cosmas and Damien were twin brothers who excelled in the practice of medicine in the 4th century, always preaching the word of Jesus to their patients and never accepting a dime for their services.

Josefov

Situated between Old Town Square and the Vltava River, Josefov's main street is Pařížská—a chic, pricey avenue full of designer boutiques, swanky restaurants, and trendy cocktail bars. Packed with tourists and the city's fashion-conscious, it is a far cry from the Jewish quarter of the 13th century, when Jews were ordered to vacate their homes and move into their new (and walled) neighborhood. It wasn't until 1781 that the Toleration Edict was issued by Emperor Joseph II of the Austrian Empire, granting Prague's Jews their civil rights. The former ghetto was named Josefstadt and was incorporated into the city in 1850. A vast redevelopment of the area was undertaken during 1893–1913, giving it the look that remains to this day. Six synagogues survived, as did the Jewish Town Hall and Old Jewish Cemetery. Most historical sights fall under the jurisdiction of the Jewish Museum and a single ticket will

get you into everything except for the Old-New Synagogue, which has its own admission fee.

STARONOVÁ SYNAGÓGA (OLD-NEW SYNAGOGUE)

The heart of the Jewish community is without a doubt the Old-New Synagogue (Červená 2, tel. 222 317 191, Sun.–Thurs. 9:30 A.M.–5 P.M., Fri. 9 A.M.–4 P.M., 200 Kč). Built around the year 1270, this remarkable Gothic building is Europe's oldest active synagogue and therefore one of its most valuable. Over 700 years of continuous prayer has occurred here, with the only exception being during the Nazi occupation of 1941–1945. This was the synagogue Franz Kafka attended and the setting of his bar mitzvah. The legend of the Prague Golem is also connected to the synagogue. According to the story, Rabbi Lowe created a monster made of clay that would help the Jews in times of trouble. Unfortunately, the Golem got a little too big for his britches, becoming aggressive and violent until it became necessary to put him down. It is said that pieces of the Golem

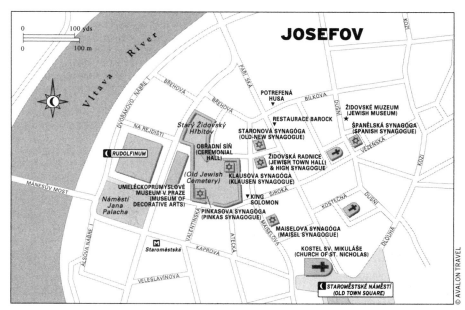

© AVALON TRAVEL

are still kept in the synagogue today and that he can be "awakened" again should the need ever arise.

ŽIDOVSKÁ RADNICE
(JEWISH TOWN HALL)

Located next to the Old-New Synagogue, the Jewish Town Hall (Maiselova 18) was built by Pankras Roder in the 1560s and financed by the district's Mayor Mordecai Maisel, a man of incredible wealth. Its pretty-in-pink Rococo facade was added in the 18th century, but the building's most famous characteristic is the Hebraic clock up on the roof, which is decorated in Hebrew and has hands that turn counterclockwise.

Attached to the Town Hall is the High Synagogue, which got its name due to having its prayer room located on the second floor—a bit of a novelty back in the 16th century when it was built. Also partly financed by Mayor Maisel, the synagogue continues to provide services to non-Orthodox Jews but is closed to tourists and the general public. There is, however, a Jewish Museum shop (tel. 221 711 511, Nov.–Mar. Sun.–Fri. 9 A.M.–4:30 P.M., Apr.–Oct. Sun.–Fri. 9 A.M.–6 P.M., closed Sat. and Jewish holidays) on the main floor.

ŽIDOVSKÉ MUZEUM
(JEWISH MUSEUM)

The original mission of the Jewish Museum (U Staré Školy 1, tel. 221 711 511, www.jewish museum.cz, Nov.–Mar. Sun.–Fri. 9 A.M.–4:30 P.M., Apr.–Oct. Sun.–Fri. 9 A.M.–6 P.M., closed Sat. and Jewish holidays) was to preserve artifacts from the synagogues that were demolished during the district's great renovation that occurred during the turn of the 20th century. The museum's exhibitions are located in six different historical sights: Maisel Synagogue, Spanish Synagogue, Pinkas Synagogue, Old Jewish Cemetery, Klausen Synagogue, and Ceremonial Hall. Tickets cost a reasonable 300 Kč.

Maiselova synagóga (Maisel Synagogue): Like most of the district at the time, Maisel Synagogue (Maiselova 10) was built by the mayor of the same name. Established in 1592, it is said to have been the finest of all synagogues in the area until a terrible fire in 1689 destroyed it, along with over 300 houses and a further 10 synagogues. A neo-Gothic synagogue was built between 1893 and 1905 during a massive reconstruction of the entire district. Today it houses an interesting collection of Jewish books, textiles, and silver.

Klausova synagóga (Klausen Synagogue): The fire of 1689 destroyed the original Klausen Synagogue (U Starého hřbitova 3A, tel. 222 310 302) but it was rebuilt in 1694 by the same craftsmen responsible for many of Prague's Baroque churches. Built by the omnipresent Maisel in honor of a visit paid to the ghetto by Emperor Maximilian II in 1573, it takes its name from the German word "Klausen," meaning "small buildings," as it used to be comprised of three, well, small buildings. Currently, the synagogue houses a thorough and rather interesting exhibition outlining many Jewish traditions and customs including bar mitzvahs, weddings, and the everyday Jewish household.

Španělská synagóga (Spanish Synagogue): Considered by many to be Prague's most beautiful synagogue, the Spanish Synagogue (Vězeňská 1, tel. 224 819 464) was built in 1868 on the former site of the oldest Prague Jewish house of prayer—"the Old Shul." Designed in the Moorish style by Vojtěch Ignátz Ullmann, its large dome and incredibly colorful interior includes stained-glass windows, stylized Islamic motifs and gorgeous floral designs in red, gold, and green. Closed for over 20 years, it reopened again on its 130th anniversary and currently houses a permanent exhibition outlining the history of the Jews in Bohemia and Moravia entitled "From Emancipation to the Present."

Pinkasova synagóga (Pinkas Synagogue): Founded by Rabbi Pinkas in 1479, the Pinkas Synagogue (Široká 3) was turned into a memorial after World War II commemorating the Jews in Bohemia and Moravia who were killed in the Holocaust. Over 80,000 names are inscribed on its walls, along with the victims' personal data and name of the community they belonged to. There is also a remarkably moving exhibition of drawings done by children who were held at Terezín before being shipped off to the death camps of the east.

Starý Židovský Hřbitov (Old Jewish Cemetery): Established in the first half of the 15th century, the Old Jewish Cemetery (Široká 3) is a haunting, solemn reminder of what was once a thriving and vibrant community. The cemetery contains roughly 12,000 tombstones, but it is estimated that over 100,000 people are actually buried here. The inconsistency arises due to the fact that Jews were not allowed to expand the grounds when the cemetery was full. They were consequently forced to bury their dead one on top of the other, resulting in some areas having graves layered 12 deep. The oldest grave on the premises dates back to 1439 and belongs to poet and scholar Avigdor Karo. By far the most well-known person buried here is Rabbi Lowe, who is famously associated with the story of Golem. Mordecai Maisel, Joesfov's former influential mayor is also buried here, about 30 feet southwest of the Rabbi's grave. For those who may be wondering, Franz Kafka is not buried here as the last burial took place in 1787, long before the great writer passed on.

At the cemetery's exit you'll find the **Obřadní síň,** or Ceremonial Hall (U Starého hřbitova 3A, tel. 222 317 191). Built between 1911 and 1912 in a pseudo-Romanesque style by J. Gerstl, it was initially used by the Prague Burial society but was soon after converted into an exhibition venue. Today, one can enjoy displays and presentations outlining a number of Jewish customs and traditions.

Northern Staré Město

As you walk past the Church of St. Nicholas with Old Town Square at your back, you'll come upon Kaprova Street, which leads towards the river. There, along the banks of the Vltava, is Náměstí Jana Palacha (Jan Palach Square), named after the student who lit himself on fire in protest of the Soviet invasion. Crossing the bridge (Mánesův Most) will take you to Malostranská, but it's the grandiose neoclassical Rudolfinum in the middle of the square that everyone stops to gawk at.

◖ RUDOLFINUM
Built between 1876 and 1884, Rudolfinum (Alšovo nábřeží 12, tel. 227 059 270, www .rudolfinum.cz, gallery Tues.–Sun. 10 A.M.–6 P.M., box office Mon.–Fri. 10 A.M.–6 P.M., closed mid-July–mid-Aug., 100 Kč) now serves as home stage to the Czech Philharmonic Orchestra in what has to be one of the most stunning concert halls on the continent. Decorated with statues of the world's most famous composers, it was the one of Jewish composer Felix Mendelssohn that was particularly bothersome to the Nazis during their occupation of the city. Having ordered the removal of the statue for obvious reasons, the job was given to a couple of Czech laborers who unfortunately had no idea what Mendelssohn looked like. Remembering their lessons in "racial science," they decided to get rid of the statue that had the biggest nose. It was only after they had finished the job that they realized the statue they had pulled down was Richard Wagner's.

KLÁŠTER SV. ANEŽKY ČESKÉ (CONVENT OF ST. AGNES OF BOHEMIA)
The Convent of St. Agnes of Bohemia (U Milosrdných 17, tel. 224 810 628, www .ngprague.cz, Tues.–Sun. 10 A.M.–6 P.M., 100 Kč) was founded in 1231 by Přemyslid Princess Anežka (Agnes), the sister of King Václav I. It was Prague's first Gothic building and operated as a convent, as well as the Přemyslid burial grounds. It was renovated in 1963 in order to serve the National Gallery and now holds an excellent exhibition of Bohemian and Central European Medieval and early Renaissance art.

UMĚLECKOPRŮMYSLOVÉ MUSEUM V PRAZE (MUSEUM OF DECORATIVE ARTS)
Designed by Josef Schulz and built between 1897 and 1899, the neo-Renaissance Museum of Decorative Arts (17. listopadu 2, tel. 251 093 111, www.upm.cz, Tues. 10 A.M.–7 P.M., Wed.–Sun. 10 A.M.–6 P.M., permanent and temporary exhibitions 120 Kč, permanent exhibitions 80 Kč, free entry Tues. 5–7 P.M.) is a veritable feast for the eyes. The facades alone

are worth a few moments. Above the first-floor windows are various reliefs depicting a number of crafts and trades including weaving, jewelry-making, wood-carving, and stone masonry. Above the second-floor windows you'll find the emblems of various Czech towns like home team Staré Město, Hradec Králové, Kutná Hora, and Plzeň. The interiors are just as lavish, with stained glass windows reflecting allegories of the decorative arts and trade, ornately decorated halls and a second-floor balustrade made from exquisite Carrara and Slivenec marble. The actual exhibitions are fascinating, spanning four halls and detailing 16th–19th century artifacts, including tapestries, pottery, clothing, ceramics, and glass. Anyone with even the slightest of interest in this field should put this at the top of their to-do list.

MALÁ STRANA (LESSER TOWN)

Located at the foot of Prague Castle, Malá Strana has long been the home of Bohemia's poets and drunkards, as well as the country's politicians and foreign ambassadors, striking a seemingly impossible balance between the Dionysian and diplomatic. Characterized by quiet, cobblestone streets filled with old-world buildings and charming art galleries and cafes, it is arguably Prague's prettiest district and one of its busiest as well, attracting busloads of tourists throughout the year. Despite its growing number of overpriced souvenir, crystal, and jewelry shops, it has somehow managed to maintain an intimate neighborhood feel about it, thanks to its rustic restaurants, lively nightlife, and well-preserved churches and historical buildings.

Malostranská mostecká věž (Lesser Town Bridge Tower)

On the Malá Strana side of Charles Bridge, two towers (late Mar.–early Nov. daily 10 A.M.–6 P.M., 60 Kč) stand that used to fortify the bridge's predecessor, the Judith Bridge. The southern tower (on the left as seen from the bridge) was reconstructed in the Renaissance style in 1591, while the tower next to it reflects the Gothic style and was built in the late 15th

century. The gateway located between the two towers dates back to the 15th century as well.

Mostecká ulice (Mostecká Street)

Leading up to Malostranské náměstí from Charles Bridge is Mostecká Street, a short, bustling strip filled primarily with souvenir shops, restaurants, and currency exchange outlets. In the summer, you're bound to sidestep visitors munching on snacks, pointing at buildings, or simply crashed out on the sidewalk in need of a break from the day's sightseeing.

The first street on the right is Josefská and at the end of it, on the right-hand side, is the small and intimate **Church of St. Joseph** (Josefská 8, Mon. 10 A.M.–noon, 5–7 P.M., Tues. 10 A.M.–noon, 7:30–8:30 P.M., Wed.–Fri. 10 A.M.–noon, free admission). Built in 1686–1692, it possesses a Dutch Baroque exterior while the interior is comparatively plain, apart from a series of Baroque altars. Mass is performed here in Czech on Thursdays at 7 P.M. and in French on Sundays at 11 A.M.

Across the street, on the other side of the tram tracks, is the decidedly more impressive **Church of St. Thomas** (corner of Letenska and Josefska, tel. 257 532 675, www.augustiniani.cz, Mon.–Sat. 11 A.M.–1 P.M., Sun. 9 A.M.–noon, 4:30–5:30 P.M., free admission), still a very active church performing worship services on Sundays in English, Spanish, and Czech. Originally a Gothic church founded for the Order of Augustinian Hermits in 1285 and completed in 1379, it was accompanied by an Augustinian Monastery and St. Thomas' Brewery. Inside are copies of two Rubens' paintings (the originals of which can be found in the National Gallery's Collection of European Art in Šternberg Palace) as well as the skeletal remains of St. Boniface and St. Just, which are dressed in costumes of the period and kept in glass-fronted coffins.

Back on Mostecká, at the top of the street, is McDonald's, which, despite sticking out like a sore thumb, is usually packed with those in dire need of a fast-food fix or timid souls not yet ready to try out the local cuisine. Opposite

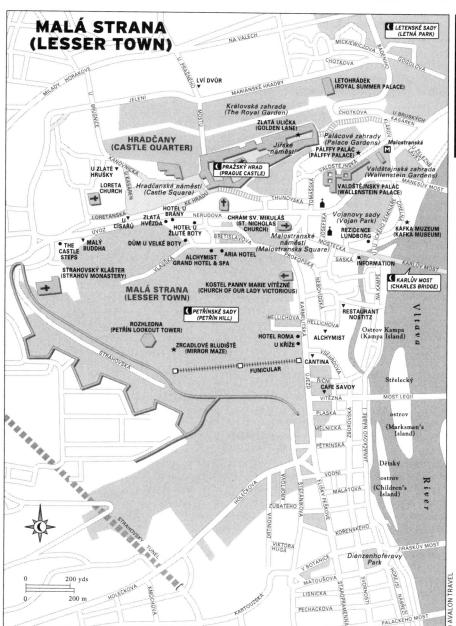

MALÁ STRANA (LESSER TOWN)

LETENSKÉ SADY (LETNÁ PARK)

NA VALECH

MICKIEWICZOVA

CHOTKOVA

GOGOLOVA

BADENIHO

MILADY HORÁKOVÉ

U PRAŠNÉHO

LVÍ DVŮR

MARIÁNSKÉ HRADBY

LETOHRÁDEK (ROYAL SUMMER PALACE)

JELENÍ

U BRUSNICE

MOSTU

CHOTKOVA

U BRUSKÝCH KASÁREN

Královská zahrada (The Royal Garden)

ZLATÁ ULIČKA (GOLDEN LANE)

KLÁROV

ŽELEZNÁ LÁVKA

HRADČANY (CASTLE QUARTER)

Jiřské náměstí

Palácové zahrady (Palace Gardens)

PÁLFFY PALÁC (PÁLFFY PALACE)

Malostranská

VALDŠTEJNSKÁ

KANOVNICKÁ

U KASÁREN

Hradčanské náměstí (Castle Square)

PRAŽSKÝ HRAD (PRAGUE CASTLE)

Valdštejnská zahrada (Wallenstein Gardens)

MÁNESŮV MOST

U ZLATÉ HRUŠKY

VALDŠTĚJNSKÝ PALÁC (WALLENSTEIN PALACE)

TOMÁŠSKÁ

LORETA CHURCH

KE HRADU

THUNOVSKÁ

LORETÁNSKÁ

HOTEL U BRÁNY

NERUDOVA

CHRÁM SV. MIKULÁŠ (ST. NICHOLAS CHURCH)

JOSEFSKÁ

Vojanovy sady (Vojan Park)

U LUŽICKÉHO SEMINÁŘE

CIHELNÁ

U ZLATÁ CÍSAŘŮ HVĚZDA

HOTEL U ŽLUTÉ BOTY

BŘETISLAVOVA

REZIDENCE LUNDBORG

KAFKA MUZEUM (KAFKA MUSEUM)

ÚVOZ

MALÝ BUDDHA

DŮM U VELKÉ BOTY

Malostranské náměstí (Malostranska Square)

MOSTECKÁ

THE CASTLE STEPS

VLAŠSKÁ

ALCHYMIST GRAND HOTEL & SPA

ARIA HOTEL

PROKOPSKÁ

SASKÁ

NA KAMPĚ

INFORMATION

KARLŮV MOST

STRAHOVSKÝ KLÁŠTER (STRAHOV MONASTERY)

MALÁ STRANA (LESSER TOWN)

KOSTEL PANNY MARIE VÍTĚZNÉ (CHURCH OF OUR LADY VICTORIOUS)

NEBOVIDSKÁ

KARLŮV MOST (CHARLES BRIDGE)

Vltava

PETŘÍNSKÉ SADY (PETŘÍN HILL)

HELLICHOVA

HELLICHOVA

RESTAURANT NOSTITZ

Ostrov Kampa (Kampa Island)

STRAHOVSKÁ

ROZHLEDNA (PETŘÍN LOOKOUT TOWER)

ZRCADLOVÉ BLUDIŠTĚ (MIRROR MAZE)

KARMELITSKÁ

HOTEL ROMA

U KŘÍŽE

ALCHYMIST

VŠEHRDOVA

Střelecký

FUNICULAR

ÚJEZD

CANTINA

ŘÍČNÍ

CAFE SAVOY

MOST LEGII

STRAHOVSKÁ

VÍTĚZNÁ

ostrov

PLASKÁ

ZBOROVSKÁ

(Marksmen's Island)

MĚLNICKÁ

JANÁČKOVO NÁBŘEŽÍ

PETŘÍNSKÁ

Dětský

VODNÍ

ostrov

HOLEČKOVA

KROFTOVA

ŠTEFÁNIKOVA

ELIŠKY PEŠKOVÉ

MALÁTOVA

(Children's Island)

River

ZUBATÉHO

STRAHOVSKÝ TUNEL

DRTINOVA

KOŘENSKÉHO

V BOTANICE

VIKTORA HUGA

JIRÁSKŮV MOST

Dienzenhoferovy Park

MATOUŠOVA

STAROPRAMENNA

SVORNOSTI

HOŘEJŠÍ NÁBŘEŽÍ

LISNICKÁ

HOLEČKOVA

KMOCHOVA

KARTOUZSKÁ

PECHÁČKOVA

PALACKÉHO MOST

0   200 yds

0   200 m

© AVALON TRAVEL

on the way to Malostranské náměstí

the Golden Arches is majestic Malostranska Square (Malostranské náměstí), the lifeblood of all things Malá Strana.

Malostranské náměstí (Malostranska Square) and Vicinity

Founded in 1257, Malá Strana's main hub of activity from day one has been Malostranské náměstí, which began life as a large marketplace on the outskirts of Prague Castle. Brimming with shops, restaurants, pubs and palaces, it's easy to see that little has changed over the centuries, with many of the Renaissance and Baroque buildings left virtually untouched.

CHRÁM SV. MIKULÁŠ (ST. NICHOLAS CHURCH)

Dominating Malostranska Square and splitting it in two is the remarkable St. Nicholas Church (Malostranské náměstí 556/29, tel. 251 512 516, www.psalterium.cz, Mar.–Oct. daily 9 A.M.–5 P.M., Nov.–Feb. daily 9 A.M.–4 P.M., 50 Kč), considered by many to

be the finest example of high Baroque architecture in Prague—if not the country. Completed in 1752, it was the masterpiece of father-son architect team Christoph and Kilian Ignaz Dientzenhofer, the latter being responsible for the immense dome and bell tower that is now an integral part of Prague's left bank skyline. Sadly, neither stayed alive long enough to see their work completed.

Inside, the myriad of statues, frescoes, and paintings continue on in flamboyant style, representing the astounding work of the epoch's finest craftsmen and artists. It's the Main Nave, however, whose vault is covered by an awe-inspiring fresco depicting the life of St. Nicholas himself that commands most people's attention. An art gallery can be found on the second level of the church and those not afraid of heights can climb the bell tower for a small fee. Concerts are held here on occasion as well, celebrating, no doubt, the time when Mozart played the church's 2,500-pipe organ in 1787.

LICHTENŠTEJNSKÝ PALÁC (LICHTENSTEIN PALACE)

Opposite St. Nicholas Church is Lichtenstein Palace (Malostranské náměstí 13), designed by Domenico Egidio Ross for Karel von Lichtenstein, better known as "Bloody Lichtenstein." He was the one who, in the name of Emperor Ferdinand II, sentenced and executed 27 Protestant leaders that dared revolt after their loss on Bílá Hora (White Mountain) in 1621. The 27 cast-iron heads on stone pillars now found at the front of the palace commemorate the event. Visitors don't have to worry about "losing their heads" these days, however, as the palace is now used by the peace-loving music faculty of the Academy of Performing Arts.

OTHER BUILDINGS OF NOTE

Other noteworthy buildings around the square include **Old Town Hall** (Malostranské náměstí 21), which is now the rock and blues joint Malostranská beseda; **Smiřický Palace** (Malostranské náměstí 18), with its unmistakable turrets and hexagonal towers, housing the Parliament of the Czech Republic; and

© TOM DIRLIS

PRAGUE

Kaiserstein Palace (Malostranské náměstí 23), which used to be the former home of late great Czech soprano Emmy Destinn. Today it hosts numerous banquets and conferences with the occasional classical concert being performed in Emmy Destinn Hall on the second floor.

SOUTH OF THE SQUARE
Following the tram lines south of Malostranska Square is the world-famous **Kostel Panny Marie Vítězné** (Church of Our Lady Victorious; Karmelitská 9, tel. 257 533 646, daily 8:30 A.M.–7 P.M., museum and gift shop Mon.–Sat. 9:30 A.M.–5:30 P.M., Sun. 1–6 P.M., free admission). Built in 1613 by Giovanni Maria Filippi for the German Lutherans and originally named the Holy Trinity, the Church of our Lady Victorious not only houses one of the most revered images in Catholicism, it also represents Prague's first Baroque building. Enshrined in a glass case on the right side of the church is the Holy Infant of Prague or *Il Bambino di Praga,* a wax effigy of the Infant Jesus that is believed to possess miraculous healing powers. Brought from Spain and donated to the church by Princess Polyxena of Lobkowitz in 1628, it continues to attract visitors from around the world—so much so that the church has not been able to hold a regular service there in years. A tiny museum adjacent to the church traces the wunderkind's history while a gift shop full of baby replicas, books, and handiwork addresses all your holy needs.

Northern Malá Strana
Adjacent to Malostranska Square is picturesque Nerudova Street, which stretches all the way up to the Castle grounds. At the foot of Nerudova is Zámecká Street, which ends on Thunovská. A quick left on Thunovská will bring you in front of the **New Castle Steps** (Nové zámecké schody)—a peaceful route up to the Castle proper that is a little less trying than taking Nerudova Street. If you take Thunovská the opposite way, you'll come across the British Embassy and U Hrocha, one of the few local bars that has managed to maintain a sense of true Czech drinking culture.

VALDŠTĚJNSKÝ PALÁC (WALLENSTEIN PALACE)
While one end of Thunovská Street brings you to the New Castle Steps, the opposite end leads to Sněmovní Street, a left onto which will bring you head to head with Czech parliamentary buildings as well as the Venezuelan Embassy. Following Sněmovní down and to the right will bring you out to Valdštejnské naměstí where, at #4, you'll find Wallenstein Palace (Sat.–Sun. 10 A.M.–4 P.M., free admission), which is also the seat of the Czech Senate. Built by Andrea Spezza in 1624–1630 for General Albrecht of Wallenstein, Commander of the Catholic forces during the Thirty Years War, the palace's sheer size is enough to make your jaw drop. The main hall alone measures roughly two stories in height, the ceiling of which is adorned with a fresco of Wallenstein himself portrayed as Mars, Roman God of War.

PÁLFFY PALÁC (PÁLFFY PALACE)
Pálffy Palace (Valdštejnská 14) is one of the more significant contributors to Prague's Baroque architecture. More or less identical to how it looked after its restoration in 1853, the palace has a rather unconventional design with its first floor acting as mezzanine and the second floor boasting a richly gilded stucco mirror hall, highbrow restaurant, private room, and terrace.

PALÁCOVÉ ZAHRADY POD PRAŽSKÝM HRADEM (PALACE GARDENS BELOW THE PRAGUE CASTLE)
Located on the southern slope of Prague Castle hill are the Palace Gardens Below the Prague Castle (Valdštejnská 12, tel. 257 010 401, www.palacovezahrady.cz, Apr.–Oct. daily 10 A.M.–6 P.M., 90 Kč), a stunning, intertwining collection of five gardens: Ledebourk Garden, Small Palffy Garden, Great Palffy Garden, Kolowrat Garden, and Small Fürstenberg Garden. Decorated with Baroque statues, fountains, water jets, and small pavilions, no visitor should miss the opportunity

NERUDOVA STREET

Bearing the name of Jan Neruda, Malá Strana's most famous poet and journalist, Nerudova Street is a breathtaking (literally – it's steep) cobblestone street leading up to Prague Castle as the final leg of the Royal Route. Jam-packed with souvenir shops, art galleries, cafes, and restaurants, it does what it can to coax those hard-earned dollars of yours out of your pocket and into the local economy.

Word to the wise: While dodging traffic and ducking out of countless photographs you may be tempted to dine in one of the many establishments advertising "traditional" Czech cuisine like goulash (which is Hungarian, by the way). Sadly but truly, these restaurants are infamous for serving up sub-par food at inflated prices, preying on tourists who walk through their doors with the hope of experiencing something authentic. For a true Czech dining experience, you're far better off trusting one of the Czech restaurants listed in this guide than any of the many who stand outside of these "genuine" restaurants and try to lure you in.

Of course, one would be remiss if they didn't mention the magnificent architecture that abounds. A fine example is the beautiful Church of Our Lady of Unceasing Succour & St. Kajetan on Nerudova 22, which now recreates Mozart's illustrious time in Prague by putting on professional performances of his work with musicians dressed in original costumes from the 18th century. Nearby are two stunning examples of Baroque architecture: Thun-Hohenstein Palace (1714) on Nerudova 20, which houses the Italian Embassy, and Morzin Palace (1721) on Nerudova 5, which is home to the Romanian Embassy.

Another unique feature on Nerudova is the way many of its buildings are marked with interesting symbols. Up until the introduction of numbers for addresses in 1770, all the houses were distinguished by signs. As you make your way up or down the street, keep an eye out for some of the more interesting ones including At the Red Eagle (U červeného orla) at Nerudova 6 and At the Two Suns (U dvou slunců), Jan Neruda's previous residence, up near the top at Nerudova 47.

Below is a full list of all the signs:

5/256   At the Black Stag (U mouřenínů)
6/207   At the Red Eagle (U červeného orla)
11/253   At the Red Ram (U červeného beránka)
12/210   At the Three Fiddles (U tří housliček)
15/249   At the Golden Crown (U zlaté koruny)
16/212   At the Golden Cup (U zlaté číše)
18/213   Of St. John of Nepomuk (U sv. Jana Nepomuckého)
23/245   At the White Pigeon (U bílé holubice) – in disrepair at time of writing; hopefully the beloved little bird will fly back one day
27/243   At the Golden Key (U zlatého klíče)
28/217   At the Golden Wheel (U zlatého kola)
34/220   At the Golden Horseshoe (U zlaté podkovy)
35/239   Of the White Angel (U bílého anděla)
39/237   At the White Beet (U bílé řepy)
40/223   At the Prison of St. John (U žaláře sv. Jana)
41/236   At the Red Lion (U červeného lva)
42/224   At the Three Steps (U tří stupňů)
43/236   At the Green Lobster (U zeleného raka)
47/233   At the Two Suns (U dvou slunců)
49/232   At the White Swan (U bílé labutě)
51/231 At the Green Stag (U zeleného jelínka)

to enjoy the nearly 30 garden terraces open to the public, each of them offering their own unique layout and view.

Farther on down the road you'll find the double-winged late Baroque **Kolovratský palác** (Kolowrat Palace, Valdštejnská 10), the Czech Senate's second home, which is closed to the public. Farther still, you'll come across the delightful **Fürstenbersk Gardens,** which, sadly, were closed for repairs at the time of this writing; the gardens are expected to reopen in 2008.

VALDŠTEJNSKÁ JÍZDÁRNA (WALLENSTEIN RIDING SCHOOL)

At the end of Valdštejnská Street is the Malostranska metro station. It is here where you'll find the entrance to Wallenstein Riding School (tel. 257 073 136, www.ngprague .cz, Tues.–Sun. 10 A.M.–6 P.M., 100 Kč), which served as Prague's largest riding school until the end of the 17th century. Nowadays, its space is used to display various short-term art exhibits, which, truth be told, are rather hit and miss.

VALDŠTEJNSKÁ ZAHRADA (WALLENSTEIN GARDENS)

Facing the Malostranská metro station entrance, you'll find the entrance to Wallenstein Gardens (Apr.–Oct. daily 10 A.M.–6 P.M., free admission) on the left. Built in the Baroque style at the same time as Wallenstein Palace, the gardens are arguably the best kept in the city and are often full of locals enjoying their lunch, reading a book, or simply basking in the refuge from Malá Strana's merry madness. Many of the statues and fountains are copies of Dutch artist Adrian de Vries' works, a necessity seeing as the originals were plundered by the Swedes in 1648. At the far end of the grounds is the pretty Sala Terrena, which figured prominently in the film *Amadeus* and occasionally holds classical concerts of its own. Close by you'll find a wall built from artificial stalactites, as well as an aviary for exotic birds.

MALOSTRANSKÁ METRO STATION AND VICINITY

The courtyard of the Malostranska metro station is a favorite meeting place of tour groups, students, and folks who simply need to take a load off. Outside the station, head for the street lights. To the left is Mánesův Bridge, which leads to Old Town Square. To the right is Letenská Street, which winds it way back to Malostranské náměstí. (It also offers a secondary entrance to Wallenstein Gardens.) Straight ahead, however, is U Lužického semináře Street. Crossing the lights and coming on to the street proper, you will soon come to a fork in the road. On the left is the relatively new Glamour Café. Those not interested in paying tourist prices for a cup of coffee or the day's sweets can do as the locals do and pull up a seat on the handful of benches located in front of the cafe. With Charles Bridge on the right, Rudolfinum on the left, this is a wonderful place to relax, drink in the view, and, if you're lucky, hang out with some of the neighborhood's swans. This entire area was submerged under water during the flood of 2002 but was rebuilt quickly to the delight and relief of both residents and tourists alike.

KAFKA MUZEUM (KAFKA MUSEUM)

Where U Lužického semináře turns into Cihelná, you'll find the Kafka Museum (Cihelná 2b, tel. 257 535 507, www.kafka museum.cz, Jan.–Feb. daily 11 A.M.–5 P.M., Mar.–Dec. daily 10 A.M.–6 P.M., 120 Kč). On display are many first editions of Kafka's works, as are his diaries, manuscripts, photographs, and letters. For those who want to take a little piece of the famed writer home with them, the gift shop offers all of his works, as well as postcards, calendars, mugs, mouse pads, and a whole lot more. The pretty courtyard in front of the shop is decorated with a quirky statue of two naked men, complete with shifting torsos, urinating into a fountain. Many take a moment to photograph the amusing piece but don't realize that nearby are some stairs that, if you follow them down, will bring you to a small clearing with a couple of secluded park benches. This is a great, somewhat secret place to rest your feet and enjoy another wondrous view of Charles Bridge.

VOJANOVY SADY (VOJAN PARK)

A tranquil oasis in the heart of the city, Vojanovy sady (U Lužického semináře 17, winter daily 8 A.M.–5 P.M., summer daily 8 A.M.–7 P.M.) is one of Prague's oldest parks, dating back to around 1300. In the 17th century it belonged to the Convent of Barefoot Carmelites but today it functions as a perfect spot for a picnic, game of Frisbee, or leisurely stroll. Two chapels can be found here—the

FRANZ KAFKA

Perhaps no other writer managed to capture the debilitating atmosphere of 20th-century alienation better than Franz Kafka (1883-1924). His nightmarish worlds of dehumanization, totalitarianism, and bureaucratic catch-22s captured the imagination of millions of readers and remain as relevant today as when they were first published. Born in Prague on July 3, 1883, he was the son of domineering Hermann Kafka and delicate mother Julie (Löwy). Kafka also had three sisters, all of whom went on to die in Nazi concentration camps. It was Kafka's father in particular who was the impetus for a large part of his writings, as he explained once in a letter to him: "My writing was all about you; all I did there, after all, was to bemoan what I could not bemoan upon your breast. It was an intentionally long-drawn-out leave-taking from you."

Educated at both the German National and Civic Elementary School and German National Humanistic Gymnasium, he entered Ferdinand-Karls University in 1901 and received a doctorate in law in 1906. It was during this time that Kafka began keeping company with a small circle of Prague intellectuals that included Franz Werfel, Oskar Baum, and close friend Max Brod, who encouraged him to write as much as possible.

Kafka's best-known works include the bizarre *Metamorphosis* (1915), where he famously turns into a despicable bug, as well as his novels *The Trial* (1925) and *The Castle* (1926), both of which were published posthumously and deal with the darker side of the law where crimes are doled out freely and anonymously. His unfinished novel *Amerika* (1927) was also published after his death and portrayed a young Karl Rossmann, who enters New York Harbor and sees the Statue of Liberty brandishing a sword instead of her famous lamp. A mere six chapters were all that Kafka managed to complete before dying of tuberculosis on June 3, 1924. Despite Kafka's wishes to have all of his work destroyed upon his death, long-time friend Max Brod ignored the request and made public all of Kafka's unpublished work, a gift that all lovers of literature continue to be most thankful for.

Chapel of Elijah and another dedicated to St. Theresa. In the depths of the park is a staircase leading up to a tiny parkette where, on a good day, you just might come across a couple of peacocks out for a pleasant walk of their own.

Upon exiting Vojanovy sady, you can either turn left and head back to Malostranská metro or head right and continue on towards Charles Bridge and the beginning of Kampa Square. Before you reach it, however, turn right on a tiny street named **Mišenská**. Here you'll find one of the film industry's favorite streets to shoot on; it has been well preserved and can easily be made to look like any European city from a few centuries before. (Indeed, this entire area is oftentimes filled with movie types.) A few intimate cafes are located here, including local haunt Veronský Dům, which serves delicious wine and dessert to neighborhood artists. When done, follow the street to its end and voila! You're back at Mostecká.

MALTÉZKÉ NÁMĚSTÍ (MALTESE SQUARE)

To the south of Malostranska Square is tiny and peaceful Maltese Square (Maltézké náměstí), which took its name from the Priory of the Knights of Malta who used to occupy this part of Malá Strana. It's characterized by a statue of St. John the Baptist—part of a fountain that was built in 1715 to mark the end of the plague epidemic. Opposite the square rests the striking Church of our Lady Beneath the Chain, complemented by two large towers that remind passersby of its previous function as a fortified priory. Founded in the 12th century, it remains Malá Strana's oldest church and was originally used to guard the approach to the old Judith Bridge, precursor to the Charles Bridge. The Hussite Wars led to the abandonment of further construction, which is why an ivy-covered courtyard exists today in place of a nave. For those who may be wondering, the church's odd name refers to the chain used during the Middle Ages to close the monastery's gatehouse. Classical concerts are held regularly, affording one the opportunity to enjoy the well-preserved interior that is otherwise closed to the public.

Nearby, at Maltézké náměstí 1, is the beautiful Baroque Nostický palác (Nostitz Palace), which was built in 1658–1660 and now houses both the Ministry of Culture and the Dutch Embassy. Concerts are often held here in the summertime and tend to be rather popular affairs. A few steps past the palace marks the beginning of Nosticova Street, which leads to an unassuming little park frequented mostly by dog walkers, young lovers, and the occasional homeless person. Most don't stay long however, preferring to walk right through it, entering from the side, as it were, a much bigger, much more impressive piece of property: Kampa Island.

Ostrov Kampa (Kampa Island) and Vicinity

Roughly two-thirds of the way down Charles Bridge (en route to Malá Strana), you'll notice a divided stairway on the left. It is at the bottom of these stairs where **Na Kampě,** otherwise known as Kampa Square, officially begins. Lined with restaurants, inns, park benches, and acacia trees, it is one of the more picturesque parts of the city and often holds fairs and outdoor exhibits during the summer months.

Kampa Island lies directly ahead but before entering, take the tiny street on the right named Hroznová and follow it as it curves left. It will lead you to a small opening where, on your right, you'll spot a little bridge that carries pedestrians over **Čertovka** (Devil's Stream), a burbling offshoot of the Vltava River. You'll also see the Grand Prior's Millwheel, which continues to turn despite the termination of the mill in 1936.

Over the little footbridge and out you come onto Velkopřevorské náměstí. On the right is the colorful and historically poignant **John Lennon Peace Wall.** On the left is **Buquoy Palace** (Velkopřevorské náměstí 2), yet another beautiful Baroque building, which has operated as the French Embassy for many

pretty and peaceful Kampa Island

JOHN LENNON PEACE WALL

On December 8, 1980, Mark David Chapman walked calmly up to John Lennon and shot him dead in front of his then wife Yoko Ono. The murder of the former Beatle sent shock waves around the world, including here in Prague, where simply singing his songs in public could land one in jail on the grounds of perpetrating "subversive activities against the state." Risking capture and severe punishment, an anonymous group of youths stole away in the still of the night and set up a mock grave to honor their underground hero. This simple yet dangerous act of defiance caught the attention of the Communist secret police and captured the imagination of the population at large.

Despite repeated warnings from the state, fans of Lennon's music, as well as believers of his message of peace, would slip into the square unnoticed to write down their own "rebellious" thoughts on the subject. The wall was whitewashed over and over again but paintings of the icon, along with his lyrics of love and hope, continued to appear. Within a short period of time, the wall became an informal political forum for those daring enough to voice their grievances against the Communist regime.

Shortly after the Velvet Revolution in 1989, the wall was returned to its original owners, the Knights of Malta, as part of a generous restitution package. Proving to be no more understanding than their predecessors, the Knights were on the verge of whitewashing the wall yet again when an unlikely savior in the form of the French Ambassador, whose office looked directly onto the graffiti covered wall, called up the municipal authorities and asked them to leave it as it is. The event sparked a minor diplomatic incident but the wall remained.

New messages continued to appear in the 1990s but most were in the form of lightweight (and at times crude) thoughts scrawled down by tourists who knew little, if anything, of the wall's original significance. In 1998, the Prague-based "John Lennon Peace Club" joined forces with the Knights of Malta and began reconstructing the crumbling facade. The wall's original plaster had been ravaged by tourists who wanted to take a "piece of peace" home with them and was consequently replaced by a solid white surface. The two groups then threw a "happening" wherein local hipsters, backpackers, and anyone else who wanted to join in were invited to add their opinions on all things John. Not surprisingly, none of the new messages packed the punch of the old. Anti-Communist/pro-freedom slogans were replaced with flowers, butterflies, and tiresome cliches – all of which were put down for posterity with brushes and paint provided by the church.

The Knights of Malta have, at times, painted over slogans they deemed to be either too large or not in line with their own beliefs. This has caused concern amongst some who feel the wall has lost its value as a venue for free speech. If you look hard enough, however, you can still find the occasional heartfelt message from somebody somewhere who continues to imagine all the people living life in peace.

years. Continuing on straight ahead will take you to Maltézské náměstí, but if you head back to Hroznová and continue to the right, you'll end up directly in front of the entrance to Kampa Island.

Back in the day (think Middle Ages), Kampa Island was composed primarily of gardens and was mainly used for washing clothes or bleaching linens. These days, Kampa has little to do with laundry and everything to do with fun and relaxation. Pull up a seat on one of the benches overlooking the Vltava and let the river lull you into a state of happiness and relaxation. This is a perfect place to read a book, whisper sweet nothings into your lover's ear, or daydream about quitting your job and staying here for good. Filled in the summertime with neighborhood dogs, students strumming guitars, tourists, picnickers, and sunbathers, Kampa Island is the kind of place you want to stroll through slowly, paying close attention to its quiet simplicity. Do that and the chirping of the birds, the laughter of young and old, and the hushed flow of the mighty Vltava will stay with you forever.

Kampa Island is also the setting of renovated **Kampa Museum** (U Sovových Mlýnů 2, tel. 257 286 147, www.museumkampa.cz, daily 10 A.M.–6 P.M., 80 Kč), which houses international contemporary art and a private collection of important Czech modernist works. Highlights include selections of seminal Czech abstractionist Frantisek Kupka's work as well as 18 bronze sculptures by Czech artist Otto Gutfreund, one of Eastern Europe's first Cubists.

Walking through the museum grounds or past them and turning left brings you up close and personal with the Vltava. A few benches are scattered around for your convenience, providing an even quieter place to reflect upon all things Bohemian. Further along, near the southern end of the island is the 13th-century **Chapel to St. John of the Laundry** (Kaple sv. Jana Na Pradlé)—a testament to the area's previous function.

Střelecký ostrov (Marksmen's Island)

Located in the middle of the Vltava River opposite Kampa near the National Theatre, the island is accessible from Legií Bridge via a large stone stairway. It is the perfect place to take a romantic stroll and have a pleasant dinner or drink at the Střelecký Ostrov Restaurant and Terrace. Concerts are held here during the warmer months and there's even an outdoor cinema screening movies once a week June– September. This shaded oasis is an excellent way to escape the bustle of the center or enjoy a variety of cultural events.

Dětský ostrov (Children's Island)

Those of you traveling with children will not want to miss out on this pretty little island dedicated to your little darlings. Sitting opposite Střelecký Ostrov next to the big lock full of boats traveling up and down the river, it is easily accessible from the left bank of the Vltava via a small bridge. A large playground offers plenty of things for the kids to do here, including sandpits, swings, and ramps. The play area is fenced in and there's a supervisor present to make sure everyone is playing nicely. This is a wonderful way to subdue the kids after they inevitably grow tired of sightseeing.

◖ Petřínské sady (Petřín Hill)

Located west of Malá Strana and stretching up to a height of 1,043 feet is Petřín Hill, a loose network of eight different parks offering visitors a haven from the hectic goings-on down below, as well as a jaw-dropping panoramic view of the entire city. In the 12th century the area was covered with vineyards that were later on transformed into gardens and orchards. It is also interesting to note that much of the stone used to build various sites around Prague came from the quarry that originally operated here. Extremely popular in the spring when the fruit trees begin to bloom, the hill attracts scores of young lovers, some of whom come to lay flowers on the monument dedicated to Karel Hynek Mácha, the Czech Republic's most famous Romantic poet.

A leisurely walk up the hill is a particularly rewarding experience but most prefer to save their energy and take the **funicular** (Nov.–Mar. daily 9 A.M.–11:20 P.M., Apr.–Oct. daily 9 A.M.– 11:30 P.M., 18 Kč), reached via Újezd Street. Halfway up the hill, the funicular stops close to Restaurant Nebozízek (Petřínské sady 411, tel. 257 315 329, www.nebozizek.cz), a rather touristy establishment that nonetheless offers its patrons a magnificent view of the city, not to mention an eye-level view of Prague Castle.

Traversing the southern edge of the hill is the **Hunger Wall** (Hladová Zed'), built during 1360–1362 by order of Charles IV, whose purpose, it is argued, was not strategic, as was once believed, but rather to feed the city's poor by offering them a way to make some muchneeded money.

ROZHLEDNA (PETŘÍN LOOKOUT TOWER)

Built out of recycled railway tracks in 31

days for the 1891 Jubilee Exhibition, Petřín Lookout Tower (tel. 257 320 112, Jan.–Mar. Sat.–Sun. 10 A.M.–5 P.M., Apr. daily 10 A.M.–7 P.M., May–Sept. daily 10 A.M.–10 P.M., Oct. daily 10 A.M.–6 P.M., Nov.–Dec. Sat.–Sun. 10 A.M.–5 P.M., 50 Kč) has managed to survive all these years despite an order issued by Adolf Hitler to have it removed, as well as the Communist regime's utter lack of interest in it during their 40-year run. Modeled after the Eiffel Tower, it was renovated after the Velvet Revolution and now serves as a symbol of Czech independence. The tower itself is only 197 feet in height but factor in its location on top of Petřín Hill and you start to understand why, on a clear day, you can see as far as Sněžka Mountain, the Czech Republic's highest peak located roughly 93 miles away.

ZRCADLOVÉ BLUDIŠTĚ (MIRROR MAZE)

Next to Petřín Lookout Tower stands a mock medieval castle that is home to the Mirror Maze (tel. 257 315 212, Jan.–Mar. Sat.–Sun. 10 A.M.–5 P.M., Apr. daily 10 A.M.–7 P.M., May–Aug. daily 10 A.M.–10 P.M., Sept. daily 10 A.M.–7 P.M., Oct. daily 10 A.M.–6 P.M., Nov.–Dec. daily 10 A.M.–5 P.M., 50 Kč), another leftover of the 1891 Jubilee Exhibition. Although small, the maze still manages to delight children and their accompanying adults after all these years. There is also a marvelous diorama depicting one of the Czech Republic's proudest moments in history: their defending of the Charles Bridge during the Swedish invasion of 1648.

HVĚZDÁRNA (STEFANIK OBSERVATORY)

Stefanik Observatory (tel. 257 320 540, www .observatory.cz, 40 Kč) dates back to 1928 and was completely reconstructed in the 1970s, giving it the appearance it maintains today. Mostly used as an incentive to get people hooked on astronomy, the observatory allows visitors to catch glimpses of sunspots and solar flares by day and the moon, stars, and planets by night. The observatory is open January–February Tuesday–Friday 6–8 P.M., Saturday–Sunday 10 A.M.–noon, 2–8 P.M.; March and October Tuesday–Friday 7–9 P.M., Saturday–Sunday 10 A.M.–noon, 2–6 P.M., 7–9 P.M.; April–August Tuesday–Friday 2–7 P.M., 9–11 P.M.; Saturday–Sunday 10 A.M.–noon, 2–7 P.M., 9–11 P.M.; September Tuesday–Friday 2–6 P.M., 8–10 P.M. Saturday–Sunday 10 A.M.–noon, 2–6 P.M., 8–10 P.M.; November–December Tuesday–Friday 6–8 P.M., Saturday–Sunday 10 A.M.–noon, 2–8 P.M.

HRADČANY

Founded in the year 1320 during the reign of John of Luxembourg, Hradčany is a picturesque, mostly residential area that stretches north across the hilltop and west to Strahov Monastery. It is, of course, home to the Prague Castle, easily the most famous of Prague's sights, as well as its most visited. While a tour of the castle grounds is mandatory for any visitor, the district's surrounding streets are also worth a look for they are tiny, twisting pockets of the past: a blend of Gothic, Renaissance, and the Baroque that stirs the heart and captures the imagination.

◖ Pražský hrad (Prague Castle)

High atop a hill on the left bank of the Vltava River sits the Prague Castle—the most recognizable structure in the entire Czech Republic. It is not only a grandiose fixture on an already bewitching skyline, but a great source of national unity and pride as well. Constructed by Prince Bořivoj in the second half of the 9th century, it began as a wooden fortress and underwent four major reconstructions before reaching the form we recognize today. Its biggest development came during the 14th century when Charles IV made the grounds his residence and ordered the building of the awe-inspiring St. Vitus Cathedral. Each ruler who sat here made changes to suit his own personal tastes and the result is a marvelous mixture of architectural styles ranging from the Romanesque to the Baroque. It is the largest ancient castle in the world, measuring 1,870 feet long and an average of 420 feet wide, with a

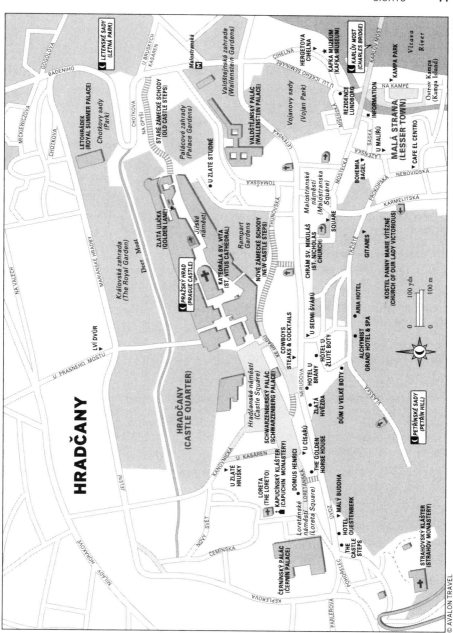

HRADČANY (CASTLE QUARTER)

LETENSKÉ SADY (LETNÁ PARK)

LETOHRÁDEK (ROYAL SUMMER PALACE)

Chotkovy sady (Park)

STARÉ ZÁMECKÉ SCHODY (OLD CASTLE STEPS)

Paláncové zahrady (Palace Gardens)

Valdštejnská zahrada (Wallenstein Gardens)

VALDŠTEJNSKÝ PALÁC (WALLENSTEIN PALACE)

Vojanovy sady (Vojan Park)

● U ZLATÉ STUDNĚ

KAFKA MUZEUM (KAFKA MUSEUM)

KARLŮV MOST (CHARLES BRIDGE)

KAMPA PARK

Vltava River

Ostrov Kampa (Kampa Island)

HERGETOVA CIHELNA

REZIDENCE LUNDBORG

INFORMATION

NA KAMPĚ

● U MALÍŘŮ

MALÁ STRANA (LESSER TOWN)

▼ CAFE EL CENTRO

BOHEMIA BAGEL ▼

Malostranské náměstí (Malostranska Square)

CHRÁM SV. MIKULÁŠ (ST. NICHOLAS CHURCH)

GITANES ▼

Královská zahrada (The Royal Garden)

Deer Moat

ZLATÁ ULIČKA (GOLDEN LANE)

Jiřské náměstí

PRAŽSKÝ HRAD (PRAGUE CASTLE)

KATEDRÁLA SV. VÍTA (ST. VITUS CATHEDRAL)

Rampart Gardens

NOVÉ ZÁMECKÉ SCHODY (NEW CASTLE STEPS)

COWBOYS STEAKS & COCKTAILS

● U SEDMI ŠVÁBŮ

HOTEL U ŽLUTÉ BOTY

● ARIA HOTEL

ALCHYMIST GRAND HOTEL & SPA

KOSTEL PANNY MARIE VÍTĚZNÉ (CHURCH OF OUR LADY VICTORIOUS)

HOTEL U BRÁNY

ZLATÁ HVĚZDA

DŮM U VELKÉ BOTY

● U ZLATÉ HRUŠKY

LORETA (THE LORETO)

KAPUCÍNSKÝ KLÁŠTER (CAPUCHIN MONASTERY)

DOMUS HENRICI

Loretánské náměstí (Loreta Square)

● MALÝ BUDDHA

THE GOLDEN HORSE HOUSE

● U CÍSAŘŮ

SCHWARZENBERSKÝ PALÁC (SCHWARZENBERG PALACE)

Hradčanské náměstí (Castle Square)

HRADČANY (CASTLE QUARTER)

LVÍ DVŮR ▼

ČERNÍNSKÝ PALÁC (ČERNIN PALACE)

HOTEL QUESTENBERK

THE CASTLE STEPS

STRAHOVSKÝ KLÁŠTER (STRAHOV MONASTERY)

PETŘÍNSKÉ SADY (PETŘÍN HILL)

0   100 yds
0   100 m

© AVALON TRAVEL

total area of roughly 18 acres. It has operated as the official seat of Czech presidents since 1918 and is by far the most visited site in the county. A tour of the grounds requires a half a day (not including museum visits) and you can expect things to get pretty crowded during the summer season. If you'd like a little more elbow room, try coming early in the morning or late in the afternoon, or, if entering the actual sights doesn't particularly interest you, do as the natives do and come late at night, when the grounds are near empty and the air electric with magic and romance.

Admission to the castle grounds is free but you will need a ticket for many of the main sights. These can be bought at the Tourist Information Center (Second Courtyard tel. 224 372 423, Third Courtyard tel. 224 373 368, tourist.info@hrad.cz, summer daily 9 A.M.–6 P.M., winter daily 9 A.M.–4 P.M.), which can also arrange guided and audio tours. A regular "long tour" ticket costs 350 Kč and allows access to the Old Royal Palace, the permanent exhibition "The Story of Prague Castle," St. George's Basilica, the Convent of St. George and its National Gallery exhibit, Golden Lane with Daliborka Tower, and the Prague Castle Picture Gallery. A "short tour" ticket costs 250 Kč and gets you into the Old Royal Palace, St. George's Basilica, and Golden Lane with Daliborka Tower.

During the high season (Apr.–Oct.), the castle complex is open from 5 A.M. to midnight, while those sights requiring a ticket are generally open from 9 A.M. to 6 P.M. The castle's gardens and Stag Moat are open April and October daily 10 A.M.–6 P.M., May and September daily 9 A.M.–7 P.M., June–July daily 9 A.M.–9 P.M., August daily 9 A.M.–8 P.M. In the winter (Nov.–Mar.), sights requiring tickets are open daily from 9 A.M.–4 P.M., while the castle gardens and Stag Moat are closed.

FIRST COURTYARD

The official and most impressive entrance to the castle grounds is the main gate on Hradčanské náměstí, characterized by Ignatz Platzer's enormous, 18th-century, Baroque **statues of**

one of Hradčany's many quiet, picturesque streets

© TOM DIRLUS

battling Titans. The two statues tower over the castle guards standing beneath them and are a favorite of professional and amateur photographers alike. There is a **changing of the guard** every hour on the hour 5 A.M.–10 P.M., the most impressive of which occurs at noon when the change is accompanied by a brass band playing from Plečníkova síň (Plečnik Hall) overlooking the First Courtyard. The Second Courtyard is reached via Matyášova brána (Matthias Gate), Bohemia's earliest Baroque work dating all the way back to 1614.

SECOND COURTYARD

Passing through Matthias Gate, you can't help but notice the Second Courtyard's centerpiece—a beautiful 17th-century Baroque **fountain.** You'll often find visitors taking a break here or dousing themselves with water on a particularly hot day. To the right is **Kaple svatého Kříže** (Chapel of the Holy Cross), which was built in 1736. Formerly the treasury of St. Vitus Cathedral, it now operates as a gift shop and the castle's box office.

In the northern wing of the courtyard stands the great gold and white **Španělský sál** (Spanish Hall), named as such after Rudolf II's popular Spanish horses, which were kept in the stables below the hall. Decorated lavishly with large mirrors and golden chandeliers, as well as sculptures by Adrien de Vries representing allegories of the Arts, Science, Commerce, and Industry, it is now used primarily for state receptions and rare concerts. It is open to the public only twice a year: May 8, which marks the Czech's liberation from Germany at the end of World War II, and October 28, which was the date an independent Czechoslovak state was established.

THIRD COURTYARD

A passage on the Second Courtyard's eastern side leads you to the castle's third and most important courtyard. At its center is the monumental St. Vitus Cathedral, which never fails to leave an indelible impression.

Katedrála sv. Víta (St. Vitus Cathedral): St. Vitus Cathedral is without a doubt the religious heart and soul of the country. Not only is it one of the Czech Republic's finest examples of Gothic architecture, it's also the lifeblood of the nation's spirit, where coronations of kings were held and the land's patron saints buried. In 1344, Charles IV secured an archbishopric for his beloved Prague and construction on the cathedral began under the watchful eye of French architect Matthew of Arras. Petr Parléř took over the reins in 1352 upon Matthew's death but despite the tremendous efforts of sovereigns to continue construction, the masterwork remained unfinished for centuries. It wasn't until the late 19th century when the unimaginatively named Union for the Completion of the Building of St. Vitus Cathedral took control and finally realized Parler's original plans. The cathedral was finally consecrated in 1929.

St. Vitus' exterior is characterized by the prominent **Great Tower**, topped with a Baroque dome and home to Sigismund, Bohemia's largest bell, which was made in the mid-16th century and weighs well over 33,000 pounds. To the right of the tower you'll find the cathedral's **southern doorway,** which formerly operated as the main entrance. Known as the Golden Gate, it is unmistakable due to the large, multi-colored Venetian-glassed mosaic depicting the Last Judgment.

The **western door** of the cathedral, found opposite the passageway connecting the Second and Third Courtyards, now serves as the main entrance and is decorated with reliefs depicting various stories and legends of St. Wenceslas and St. Adalbert. This entire section of St. Vitus is in fact its newest addition, dating back to the late 19th and early 20th centuries.

Inside, the massive **nave** is almost overwhelming at first and the beautiful stained glass windows on the left add an ethereal quality to an already otherworldly atmosphere. Looking closely, the third window stands out in both color and style. No wonder, as it was done by Alfons Mucha, one of the country's most famous artists.

On the far right of the cathedral is the awe-inspiring **Chapel of St. Wenceslas.** It is located directly on the site where Wenceslas was buried and was built in 1345 by Charles IV in honor of the saint. Although closed to the public, visitors can still crane their necks at the chapel's entrance and admire the ornate frescoes covering an area of nearly 2,500 square feet portraying scenes from both the Bible and St. Wenceslas' life. The chapel is also decorated with over 1,300 priceless gems and contains the decorated tomb of the saint himself in the middle of the chapel, along with some of his belongings, including his armor and helmet. It is interesting to note that every coronation in Czech history took place here, with kings often coming to pray as well. Today, mass is held every year on September 28—St. Wenceslas Day. In the southwestern corner of the chapel stands a door leading to a chamber containing the heavily protected crown jewels. The door is locked with the help of seven keys that are kept separately by seven different state and church officials.

A further note of interest is the **tombstone of St. John of Nepomuk,** whose pedestal and statue contain a mind-boggling two tons of silver. Nearby, in front of the high altar, is the entrance to the cathedral's **underground mausoleum and royal crypt,** which contains the graves of various Czech sovereigns and patron saints including Rudolf II and Charles IV himself.

Starý Královský palác (Old Royal Palace): In the courtyard's eastern end is the Old Royal Palace, which was founded in the late 9th century as nothing more than a wooden building with a stone foundation wall. It was rebuilt into a Romanesque palace made of stone by Prince Sobeslav in the early 12th century. A number of kings used it as their residence during the course of the next 600 years, each one of them converting the premises to fit their own tastes and style of the respective period.

The jewel of the palace is beyond a doubt the impressive **Vladislav Hall,** which was designed by Benedict Reid at the turn of the 16th century. It boasted the largest secular space in the city at the time and was arguably the grandest late Gothic hall in all of central Europe. Back then, the hall was used primarily for coronations, balls and markets, as well as indoor jousting tournaments, which explains the presence of the Jezdecké schody or Rider's Steps that allowed knights to enter the area while remaining on horseback. Note the difference in architectural styles when comparing its fantastic vaulted ceiling representing Gothic's last gasp, with the large square windows exemplifying the beginning of the Renaissance. Today, the hall is where the National Assembly elects its new president and was the setting for the swearing in of Vaclav Havel in 1990—the country's first president after over 40 years of Communist rule.

At the eastern end of the hall is a balcony that overlooks **All Saints' Church,** which was built by Petr Parléř during the second half of the 14th century. It was destroyed by fire in 1541, leaving only its peripheral walls intact and was redone in the Renaissance style near the end of the 16th century. The church is open to the public only during religious services and for the occasional concert.

Above the hall is the **Bohemian Chancellery,** site of a major turning point in Czech history,

for it was here in 1618 where Protestant nobles rebelled against the Habsburg emperor and promptly threw two governors and their secretary out the window. This bold move sparked what was to become the Thirty Years' War.

The **Diet Chamber,** which can be accessed via a stairway to the right of the Rider's Steps, is also worth a look. It, too, possesses a wonderfully vaulted ceiling, along with crests from all of Bohemia's most important families and volumes from the court library.

JIŘSKÉ NÁMĚSTÍ (GEORGE SQUARE) AND SURROUNDINGS

Just east of St. Vitus Cathedral is Jiřské náměstí, the center of the castle complex. Its main street, Jiřská, stretches from St. George's Basilica to the castle's eastern gate.

Bazilika sv. Jiří (St. George's Basilica): Founded by Prince Vratislav in 921, St. George's Basilica is Prague's second oldest church. Its eye-catching, red and cream Baroque facade marks a stark contrast from its austere Romanesque interior, which houses the tombs of some of the Přemyslid dynasty of princes in its main nave. The church now serves as a classical music concert hall with excellent acoustics. Left of the basilica is the sober-looking Convent of St. George, which was established in 973 by Boleslav II. Today it acts as a branch of the National Gallery and offers an interesting exhibit of Renaissance and Baroque works.

Zlatá Ulička (Golden Lane): Down the hill from St. George's is Golden Lane: a tiny, colorful street comprised of 11 historic homes that came to be after the northern wall of Prague Castle was constructed. Dating back to the 16th century, it was originally the residence of castle servants (likely goldsmiths and castle marksmen), with most homes remaining occupied until World War II. Its most-famous resident by far was the one and only Franz Kafka, who stayed at #22 with his sister Ottla, although, judging by the minute size of the home, one has to wonder how. These picturesque, pint-sized houses are charming to say the least. However, when seen by day, one hardly has a chance to appreciate them as the narrow street is choked with tourists craning their necks to get a better look. What's more, the interiors of the homes have all gone the way of souvenir shops, causing even more beleaguering bustle. A ticket is required to enter the street but if you go after hours, admission is free. For those who would truly like to enjoy the atmosphere of this marvelous little street, pay a visit during the evening when the castle grounds are nearly empty. The result is an atmospheric, romantic experience you won't soon forget.

At the eastern end of the lane are stairs which lead you under the last house to **Daliborka** (Dalibor Tower). A former prison, it took its name after the knight Dalibor of Kozojedy, who was held here as punishment for providing shelter to peasants who were part of a local uprising. Legend has it that he passed his time while awaiting execution by playing the violin. The music was apparently so beautiful that it enchanted all who heard it. Well-known classical composer Bedřich Smetana's 1868 opera *Dalibor* pays tribute to the man and his story.

Muzeum Hraček (Toy Museum): Covering two floors and seven rooms of exhibits, the Toy Museum (Jiřská 6, tel. 224 372 294, daily 9:30 A.M.–5:30 P.M., 60 Kč) is the second-largest of its kind in the world. Showcasing toys from ancient Greece to modern-day Barbie, kids will find themselves either loving this place or hating it as most toys are kept well out of reach.

Královská zahrada (The Royal Garden)

Founded in 1534 by Ferdinand I, the Royal Garden was originally designed in the Renaissance style and intended as a gift for his wife Queen Anne. Sadly, the queen never had a chance to enjoy the lovely grounds as she died while giving birth to her 15th child. Over the years, the garden gained an enviable reputation across the continent due to its collection of rare and exotic plants, which then included orange, lemon, and fig trees. It went through a couple of transformations including being designed in the Baroque style during the first half of the 18th century, then later taking on the form of

an English-style park, which it continues to resemble today. There are still plenty of Baroque and Renaissance reminders, however, including a lovely giardenetto. Closed to the public for centuries, the garden is now open to the public (except during winter) and can be accessed via U Prašného mostu, as well as through the castle's second courtyard.

LETOHRÁDEK (ROYAL SUMMER PALACE)

At the eastern end of the garden is the beautiful Belvedere, or Royal Summer Palace. It is Prague's finest example of Italian Renaissance architecture and sports a green copper roof, Ionic columns, and arcades. Designed by Paolo della Stella, it was built between 1538 and 1564. In front of the building is the Singing Fountain, which was built between 1562 and 1568 by Master Jaroš. Made of bronze and bell metal, its jets produce a "musical" sound when the water hits the fountain's resonating bronze plate.

MÍČOVNA (BALL GAME COURT)

On the garden's southern side, overlooking the Stag Moat, is the elegant Míčovnaor Ball Game Court, easily recognized by its black and white sgraffito. Built by Bonifac Wohlmut between 1567 and 1569, it was used by the emperor's courtiers for various sports activities and competitions and also served as a riding school and stable. Today it is mainly used for a variety of art exhibitions, concerts, and state social events.

JELENÍ PŘÍKOP (STAG MOAT)

Below the ramparts of the castle is the wonderful and peaceful getaway known as the Stag Moat. Rudolf II kept a choice selection of animals here including deer, lions, and tigers, though there hasn't been a stag sighting here since the 17th century. Closed for years and reopened by Havel while serving as President, this shady and secluded natural path stretches all the way to Malá Strana and is perfect for those looking to avoid the castle's inevitable crowds.

Hradčanské náměstí (Hradčany Square)

Opposite the entrance to the Prague Castle grounds is Hradčanské náměstí, arguably the city's prettiest square, characterized by grand buildings and offering the finest views of Prague proper. Originally kept separate from the castle grounds by a system of fortifications and moats, the area's houses were burned to the ground during the great fire of 1541 and later rebuilt into magnificent palaces by church dignitaries and the town's elite. Little has changed since then, allowing visitors the opportunity to marvel at various architectural styles that have come and gone including Renaissance, Baroque, and Rococo.

On the north side of the square is the **Arcibiskupský palác** (Archbishop's Palace; Hradčanské náměstí 16), a wonderful example of Rococo that came into the hands of Archbishop Anton Brus in 1562 and has served as the seat of Prague's archbishop and the archdiocese ever since. It consists of four wings and just as many courtyards but is unfortunately closed to the public.

ŠTERNBERSKÝ PALÁC (STERNBERG PALACE)

Built between 1697 and 1707 for Count Vaclav Vojtech of Sternberg, Sternberg Palace (Hradčanské náměstí 15, tel. 233 090 570, www.ngprague.cz, Tues.–Sun. 10 A.M.–6 P.M., 150 Kč) is located next to the Archbishop's Palace and is a fine example of Baroque architecture that is currently owned by the National Gallery. There is a permanent exhibition here entitled *European Art from the Classical Era to the Close of the Baroque* that particularly emphasizes the 14th–18th centuries. Noteworthy works from great artists that include El Greco, Goya, and Rubens—along with the very well-known *The Feast of the Rosary* by Albrecht Dürer—make this a memorable visit for any fan of art.

SCHWARZENBERSKÝ PALÁC (SCHWARZENBERG PALACE)

Opposite Prague Castle and Sternberg Palace is Schwarzenberg Palace (Hradčanské náměstí 2), one of the city's most beautiful Renaissance buildings—easily recognizable by its decorative sgraffiti. It was built between 1545 and 1563 by Agostino de Galli and up until recently housed the Military Museum. The palace was acquired by the National Gallery in 2002, however, and a massive 260-million-crown renovation of the premises was completed in early 2007. In 2008 the Gallery opened a new permanent exhibition featuring roughly 160 sculptures and 280 examples of late Renaissance and Baroque art made between the late 16th and late 18th centuries in the kingdom of Bohemia. Some of the key figures whose work is highlighted are Vaclav Vavrinec Reiner, Anton Kern, and Norbert Grund.

Loretánské náměstí (Loreta Square)

A short walk west from Hradčanské náměstí will lead you to Loreta Square. Created in the 18th century while construction of Černín Palace was underway, the builders at the site were shocked to uncover a strange pagan cemetery full of headless skeletons. The bones were never identified and the earth that was dug up remained untouched until it was eventually used to form the embankment that divides the square into two levels today. The square's main attractions are Černín Palace and the Loreto, but make sure to stroll through Nový Svět (New World) as well. Located behind the square, it is a charming little neighborhood full of some of the most romantic homes and streets Prague has to offer.

ČERNÍNSKÝ PALÁC (ČERNÍN PALACE)

Located between Prague Castle and Strahov Monastery, Černín Palace (Černínská 5) is yet another example of early Baroque architecture. Built between 1669 and 1682, it was designed by Francesco Caratti for Count Humprecht Jan Černín of Chudenice, one of then Bohemia's richest and most powerful men. It is Prague's third largest palace and boasts an impressive 492-foot-long facade punctuated by 30 continuous semi-columns. Gestapo interrogations were held here during the Nazi occupation, but the palace is better known for being the site of Jan Masaryk's death in March of 1948. The son of the first Czech president, he died mysteriously two weeks after the Communists gained power. Originally thought to be a suicide, police finally confirmed in 2004 that it had indeed been murder that ended his life. Today, the palace serves as the Ministry of Foreign Affairs and is sometimes opened to the public during the summer.

LORETA
(THE LORETO)

The Loreto (Loretánské náměstí 7, tel. 220 516 740, www.loreta.cz, Tues.–Sun. 9 A.M.–12:15 P.M., 1–4:30 P.M., 90 Kč) is a remarkable Baroque pilgrimage site containing beautiful chapels and chambers dating back to 1626. Its central point is the Santa Casa that is modeled after the original building that stood in the town of Nazareth—purportedly the site of the famed Incarnation where archangel Gabriel announced to the Virgin Mary that she would give birth to the son of God. Legend has it that this Santa Casa was miraculously transported by angels to the small town of Loreto in Italy, spawning a rash of knock-offs of the building across Europe. This particular version was built on the orders of Kateřina of Lobkowicz as part of the Catholic campaign after the Czech Protestants were defeated at the Battle of White Mountain. Other buildings of note are the Church of the Nativity, which holds the fully clothed, skeletal remains of two Spanish saints, St. Felicissimus and St. Marcia, as well as the Chapel of Our Lady of Sorrows. This latter building is home to a painting of a bearded woman (St. Starosta) hanging from a cross. Apparently she had taken a vow of virginity, which was threatened by her father's announcement of her marriage to the king of Sicily. God took pity on the woman and helped her grow a beard in an effort to make her undesirable. Horrified, her father had her crucified and she now has the dubious honor of being the saint of unhappily married women. Also worth a visit is the treasury where you'll be dazzled by the amazing Prazske slunce (Prague Sun), a

diamond monstrance made of solid silver and gold that's studded with 6,222 stones.

KAPUCÍNSKÝ KLÁŠTER
(CAPUCHIN MONASTERY)

At the northern end of Loretánské náměstí stands the Capuchin Monastery (Loretánské náměstí 6, tel. 220 516 738, www.kapucini .cz). Built in 1600, it is the oldest monastery of its kind in the country. Unfortunately, it is closed to visitors save for exceptional occasions and even then certain areas are still off-limits. There is, however, a pretty life-size nativity scene erected every Christmas that adds to its rather mystical charm.

STRAHOVSKÝ KLÁŠTER
(STRAHOV MONASTERY)

The Premonstratensians are a Roman Catholic order founded in 1120 by St. Norbert; they have been at Strahov Monastery (Strahovské nádvorí 1, tel. 220 517 278, www.strahovmonastery .cz, daily 9 A.M.–noon, 1–5 P.M., 80 Kč) ever since it was founded in 1143, making it one of the oldest monasteries of the Premonstratensian Order in the world. All the monastery buildings have something interesting to offer visitors, starting with the Strahov Church, otherwise known as The Basilica of Our Lady. Dedicated to St. Norbert, it is beautifully adorned with frescoes by Neunhertz depicting the Virgin Mary and life of the order's founder. The church's organ is of particular significance as it was played by Mozart during his visit here in 1787. There is also Strahov's famous library, a collection of roughly 200,000 books that is located in both the Theological and Philosophical Halls and includes works from famous printers like influential Renaissance humanist Christoffel Plantin from Antwerp. The Cabinet of Curiosities, meanwhile, houses a fascinating natural science collection whose prize possession is the remains of the now-extinct dodo bird. Finally, the ancient printing presses located downstairs are also worth visiting, as are the remains of St. Norbert himself, which were brought here in 1627 upon his becoming an official patron saint of Bohemia.

MUZEUM MINIATUR (MUSEUM OF MINIATURES)

Generally unknown and rarely advertised, the Museum of Miniatures (Strahovske Nádvoři 11, tel. 233 352 371, daily 9 A.M.–5 P.M., 50 Kč) is tucked away in the courtyard of Strahov Monastery and houses the remarkable work of Siberian-born Anatolij Koněnko. Using the provided magnifying glasses and lenses, visitors are stunned to see the portrait of Anton Chekhov designed on half a poppy seed, the Lord's Prayer written on a human hair and a three-dimensional miniature replica of the Eiffel Tower in the eye of a needle. You'll also find mini copies of famous paintings by masters such as Dali, Matisse, and da Vinci, as well as the world's smallest book—a 30-page re-creation of "Chameleon" by Chekhov.

DEJVICE

To the north of Hradčany lies Dejvice, a sprawling neighborhood characterized by embassies, ambassadors' villas, university campuses, and residential areas for the middle-class and upwardly mobile. This was an area that radiated plenty of prestige in the first half of the 20th century and still carries some of that tradition today with current president Václav Klaus, as well as his famous predecessor Václav Havel, both making their homes here. While admittedly registering low on the sights-to-see scale, a walk through Dejvice can be a very relaxing and pleasant experience, not to mention one that's well away from the throngs of tourists found elsewhere. The easiest way to reach the area is by taking the A (green) subway line and alighting at Dejvice station.

Divoká Šárka

Just off Evropská Street, on the way to Ruzyně Airport, is the wild and wonderful Divoká Šárka, Prague's best known and (arguably) favorite park. The easiest way to get there is to take tram #20 or #26 to the Divoká Šárka tram stop (hard to miss thanks to the large McDonald's looming over it). Named after the legendary warrior Šárka, said to have thrown herself off the cliffs in despair, this vast valley offers everything from hiking and bike trails, climbing, golfing, and, of course, swimming. Hordes of people young and old make their way to Džbán Reservoir in the west end of the park to cool off with a refreshing swim before sprawling out against the rocks to sunbathe. There is also a public pool open on hot days which is stream-fed, so be prepared for the water to be cold! Although you won't be able to get any swimming in, Divoká Šárka is also a great place to visit in the wintertime. Blanketed by snow and quiet to the point of eeriness, it's a perfect place to clear your head, get in touch with nature, or do a bit of cross-country skiing before entering the real world again.

Břevnovský klášter (Břevnov Monastery)

Břevnov Monastery (Markétská 28/1, tel. 220 406 111, www.brevnov.cz, tours Apr.–Oct. Sat.–Sun. 10 A.M., 2 P.M., 4 P.M., Nov.–Mar. Sat.–Sun. 10 A.M., 2 P.M., 50 Kč) was founded by Bishop Vojtech and King Boleslav II in 993 and bears the honor of being Bohemia's very first monastery. Its current Baroque form is owed to prolific father-son architect team Christoph and Kilian Ignaz Dientzenhofer and dates back to the early 18th century. Its altarpieces, sculptures, woodcarvings, and ceiling frescoes represent the delightful handicraft of the period, while the crypt located in the choir of the church dates back to its original Romanesque beginnings. Comprised of the Church of St. Margaret, the convent and prelature, outbuildings, entrance gate, and garden, the monastery is now home to 13 Benedictine monks who go about their business peacefully—something that wasn't possible during the Communist years of 1948–1989 when some of the grounds were used by the secret police.

Letohrádek Hvězda (Hvezda Summer Palace)

Designed by and built for Archduke Ferdinand of Tyrol in the 1550s, Hvezda Summer Palace (Obora Hvězda—Bílá Hora; tel. 235 357 938; Apr. and Oct. Tues.–Sun. 10 A.M.–5 P.M.,

May–Sept. Tues.–Sun. 10 A.M.–6 P.M., 30 Kč) is a three-storied Renaissance summer palace in the shape of a six-pointed star—a design which apparently reflected the Archduke's beliefs on the construction of the universe. If that sounds confusing, don't worry. Nobody to this day has been able to figure out what he was thinking, either. Now functioning as the rather modest Museum of Czech Literature, one can also visit a permanent exhibition outlining the history of this interesting building, see a model of the historic Battle of White Mountain that was fought here, and, of course, stroll through the lovely wooded park.

Crowne Plaza Hotel

Officially declared a national monument, the Crowne Plaza Hotel (Koulova 15, tel. 296 537 111, www.crowneplaza.cz) is a triumphant example of Marxist-Leninist decor and an imposing reminder of the not too distant past. Built in the 1950s, it was originally called the Hotel International and was inspired by the design of Moscow University's Tower. Today, the facade above the entrance depicting Russian war heroes being greeted by Czech peasants seems rather absurd, considering the droves of businessmen and nouveau riche who now occupy the hotel's bars.

Baba Settlement

On the hill above the Crowne Plaza Hotel is an interesting collection of private residences known as the Baba Settlement, built in the 1930s. Designer and prominent Czech architect Pavel Janák invited three generations of fellow architects to help him present various aspects of modernism. Predominantly functionalist, the settlement includes houses suitable for newlywed couples and all the way up to large families. Soon after its construction, the settlement was recognized as a stellar example of Czech modernism and remains a proud part of Czech cultural history to this day.

HOLEŠOVICE

In the past, Holešovice was primarily known as a bustling industrial zone that was also home to Prague's main harbor and docklands. Over the years, however, the area experienced a decline that saw the closing of numerous factories and a once lively port turn to a sleepy backwater. The flood of 2002 didn't help matters much either as Holešovice was one of the districts that was hardest hit.

Things have begun to change. An ambitious new building development aims to revitalize the area by creating a massive new 1,506,960-square-foot embankment that will include large sections of residential housing, state-of-the-art office buildings, and modern retail outlets. There are also tentative plans to build a new harbor that will make room for yachts and pleasure boats. Add the fact that Praguers have been steadily buying up property here over the last few years and one quickly begins to see that this former blue-collar neighborhood may soon become the city's hottest "new" district.

Výstaviště

Built to house the Jubilee Exhibition of 1891, Výstaviště (U Výstaviště 1, tel. 220 103 111/484, www.incheba.cz, Tues.–Fri. 2–9 P.M., Sat.–Sun. 10 A.M.–9 P.M., free admission Tues.–Fri., 20 Kč Sat.–Sun.), in all its wrought-iron glory, is a 3,444,480-square-foot multifunctional area that nowadays plays host to trade fairs ranging from the literary to the downright pornographic. On its grounds you'll also find Křižíková Fontána, the Lapidárium, Lunapark, and Sea World (Mořský svět).

KŘIŽÍKOVÁ FONTÁNA (KRIZIK'S FOUNTAIN)

If you're still at the exhibition grounds by the time dusk settles in, stick around and watch the water and light show at Křižíková Fontána (U Výstaviště 1, tel. 220 103 280, www.krizikovafontana.cz, Mar. hourly 7–9 P.M., Apr.–Oct. hourly 8–10 P.M.). Spinning, spraying, gurgling, and gushing to classical works such as *Swan Lake* and *Rusalka,* as well as more contemporary music including Queen and numerous film scores, the Fountain entertains die-hard fans and curious onlookers

Výstaviště, Prague's exhibition grounds

daily. Tip: If possible, stay for the late show when it's properly dark and the lights can do their thing to the fullest.

LAPIDÁRIUM

If you manage to make it to the exhibition grounds for a visit, do not miss the opportunity to check out the Lapidárium (U Výstaviště 1, tel. 233 375 636, www.nm.cz, Tues.–Fri. noon–6 P.M., Sat.–Sun. and holidays 10 A.M.–6 P.M., free admission). Housing over 400 stone sculptures dating from the 11th–19th century, this wonderful museum is a crash course in monuments long gone (but not forgotten). Included in this fascinating exhibition are 10 of Charles Bridge's original statues, the Lions of Kouřim (Bohemia's oldest surviving stone sculpture), parts of the Renaissance Krocín Fountain that once stood proudly in Old Town Square, as well as equestrian statues of past Austrian Emperors, just to name a few.

LUNAPARK

Popular with kids of all ages is Prague's version of Lunapark (U Výstaviště 1, tel. 220 103 111/484, www.incheba.cz, Tues.–Fri. 2–9 P.M., Sat.–Sun. 10 A.M.–9 P.M., free admission; pay for rides separately). Rides include a Ferris wheel, rollercoaster, haunted house, and any number of vomit-inducing attractions for all those brave enough to hop aboard. St. Matthew's Fair is held here every year as well, which brings in an additional 130 rides for fun-lovers and thrill-seekers.

MOŘSKÝ SVĚT (SEA WORLD)

Sea World (U Výstaviště 1, tel. 220 103 275, www.morsky-svet.cz, daily 10 A.M.–7 P.M., 240 Kč) is the Czech Republic's largest aquarium and has been a hit with locals and tourists ever since it opened in the summer of 2002. Sporting an exhibition space of over 10,764 square feet, Sea World's state-of-the-art aquariums simulate the sea's natural environment, including high and low tide, natural sunlight, and the moon's phases when night falls. Some of the aquarium's well-taken-care-of inhabitants include a sand tiger shark, barracudas, whitefish, zebra fish, lobsters, crabs, and numerous colorful corals and coral fish that can be observed in an 82-foot-long submarine cave. Lots of fun for all and pretty darn educational, too.

Stromovka

Next to Výstaviště is sprawling Stromovka Park, whose origins begin in 1268 when Czech King Přemysl Otakar II developed it into his royal hunting grounds. It has managed to survive numerous disasters over the years, the last of which was the flood of 2002 when over 600 trees were lost. It was renovated and opened once again in April 2003 and remains as popular as ever. You'll find plenty of people here in-line skating, walking the dog, strolling hand in hand, and spending quality time with the kids by the pond, and it's one of the best places in the city to do so.

PLANETÁRIUM PRAHA (PRAGUE PLANETARIUM)

Tucked inside Stromovka Park, just west of Výstaviště, is Planetárium Praha (Královská obora 233, tel. 220 999 001-3, www.planetarium .cz, Mon.–Thurs. 8:30 A.M.–noon, 1–8 P.M., Sat.–Sun. 9:30 A.M.–noon, 1–8 P.M., 120 Kč). Its main room, Cosmorama Hall, accommodates up to 210 people and boasts the country's largest projection screen at 9,074 square feet. Most programs are in Czech only but there are two that can be heard in English. The first is "Astrology & Alchemy in the Court of Rudolph II," which takes audiences back to 1600 and delves into all things alchemic. The second is "The Night Sky," a journey through stars, constellations, and celestial highlights that comes complete with laser effects.

◖ Sbírka moderního a současného umění (National Gallery Collection of 19th-, 20th-, and 21st-Century Art)

Veletržní palác (Trade Fair Palace) was built in 1929 and housed countless trade fairs before becoming home to the National Gallery Collection of 19th-, 20th-, and 21st-Century Art (Veletržní palác, Dukelských hrdinů 47, tel. 224 301 024, www.ngprague.cz, Tues.–Sun. 10 A.M.–6 P.M., 160 Kč) in 1996 following a heavy facelift. The first floor is where you'll find various temporary exhibitions, along with foreign artists like Klimt, Ernst, and Picasso. The second floor is dedicated to Czech art from 1930–2000, including a very interesting screening room showing short, silent films made between the two world wars and showcasing the beginning of Czechoslovakia's experimental movement. Some of the films are of particular interest as they depict a Prague now long gone, including images of old trams that used to cross over the Charles Bridge. The third floor is where some of the country's biggest names, such as František Kupka and Josef Čapek, are to be found. There is also a very interesting wing exhibiting French art that displays works by Rodin, Monet, Degas, and Renoir, to name but a few. The fourth floor is where the 19th-century art is kept, along with a healthy collection of famed Czech sculptor Josef Václav Myslbek's grander works including his most famous piece "Hudba" (Music). A couple of other paintings to look for here are Gabriel Max's "A Prevorst Prophetess in Ecstasy" and E. K. Liška's "Cain." If you plan on visiting, make sure to set aside at least two hours of comfortable gawking.

◖ Letenské sady (Letná Park)

The weekend of the Velvet Revolution was a cold, wintry affair, but that didn't stop roughly one million people from gathering at Letná Park to celebrate national sovereignty and the return of democracy. Situated on a plateau high above the city proper, the park today is a hotspot for in-line skaters, kite flyers, skateboarders, and just about anybody else wishing to enjoy a sunny afternoon or warm summer evening. In the center of the park is Letenský zámeček (Letenské sady 341, daily 11 A.M.–11 P.M.), an excellent outdoor beer garden where you'll find Czechs and foreigners chilling under the chestnut trees and enjoying the picture-perfect view of Prague below with an ice cold beer. A leisurely stroll down any of the park's wide walkways will inevitably lead you to a marble plateau, which is now the stomping grounds of skateboarders and their groupies. From 1955 to 1962, however, it was the spot where Stalin's Monument used to stand—a monstrous 51-foot-high, 72-foot-long statue dedicated to the Soviet dictator that overlooked the city until it was removed. A giant metronome was installed in its place in 1991 to symbolize the passage of time.

Národní technické muzeum (National Technology Museum)

Although its name might not inspire immediate interest, the National Technology Museum (Kostelní 42, tel. 220 399 111, www.ntm.cz, Tues.–Fri. 9 A.M.–5 P.M., Sat.–Sun. 10 A.M.–6 P.M., 70 Kč) is a fascinating look at the role science and technology played in Czechoslovakia throughout the years. Filled to the brim with steam trains, antique motorcycles, gleaming old planes, bicycles, and cars, this collection reminds visitors how advanced Czechoslovakian society was in the early 20th century before Communism put a big red stop to it. A realistically reconstructed coal mine offers tours in English and the chance to see just how claustrophobic you may or may not be. Rounding out the collection is an impressive photography and cinematography section, a mock TV studio, rare astronomical instruments, and timekeeping technology. Told you it was interesting.

ŽIŽKOV

Named after one-eyed Hussite hero Jan Žižka, working-class Žižkov has always been one of Prague's more notorious districts, characterized by lively 24-hour bars and neighborhood bordellos. While some of its buildings close to the center are getting much-needed makeovers, a significant portion of the district remains old and rundown, abandoned buildings and spotty streets serving as reminders that not all of Prague is as picture perfect as may seem. Nevertheless, it is a part of town where one can get a true feeling of Prague's rarely publicized underbelly, a place where the city's

PANELÁKY

Though Prague is known throughout the world for its breathtaking architecture that somehow survived the continent-wide devastation of the Second World War, there is another form of architecture that rarely gets any attention. The *panelák* or *paneláky* (plural) are what we would call "tenements" in American English or a "block of flats" in British English. Essentially, *paneláky* are a series of high-rise apartment blocks made from prefabricated, reinforced concrete panels. Each apartment block contains hundreds of identical apartments and each estate is comprised of a handful to a dozen identical apartment buildings. The result is a veritable concrete jungle: dull grey-looking suburban communities with zero aesthetic appeal. The apartments themselves are nothing to write home about either. Boxy, poorly laid-out, and separated by flimsy partition walls, they are a claustrophobic's nightmare and an eavesdropper's dream come true.

Built during the Communist period to champion uniformity and raise a disparaging eye towards individualism, *paneláky* remained a cheap housing option for many years after the Velvet Revolution. Today, however, many of these unimaginative apartments are getting makeovers, with owners rebuilding walls, laying down proper floors, and replacing bathrooms and kitchens with modern designs in mind. The result is a far more comfortable living arrangement that has begun to attract a wide array of tenants ranging from students to doctors, all of whom find the still reasonable rent and contemporary design very much to their liking.

You'll find *paneláky* all over the outer parts of town but the biggest collection of them is in Jižní Město, located at the southeastern edge of the city. To get there, take the subway to Háje, Opatov, or Chodov (all located on the red line) and head for the huge grey buildings dotting the skyline.

upscale stores and Western European influences are replaced with mom-and-pop eateries, neighborhood shops, and local watering holes that care little, if at all, about catering to the tourist trade.

Kostel Nejsvětějšího Srdce Páně (The Church of the Most Sacred Heart of our Lord)

Proudly sporting Prague's largest clock, The Church of the Most Sacred Heart of our Lord (Náměstí Jiřiho z Poděbrad 19, services Mon.– Sat. 8 A.M. and 6 P.M., Sun. 7 A.M., 9 A.M., 11 A.M., and 6 P.M.) is also one of the more interesting and inspiring pieces of 20th-century architecture to be found in the city. Built between 1928 and 1932 by Slovenian architect Jozef Plečnik (who was also responsible for some of the additions to Prague Castle), the Church still triggers debates amongst the locals, half of whom find it to be an eyesore while the other half couldn't imagine the neighborhood, let alone the square, without it.

© CORINE TACHTIRIS

Žižkov's TV Tower – Praguers either love it or hate it.

Žižkovská televizní věž (Žižkov TV Tower)

Arguably the most dominant structure in Prague's third district and, according to your taste, either the most striking or ugly building in the district, is the Žižkov TV Tower (Mahlerovy sady 1, tel. 242 418 778, www .tower.cz, daily 10 A.M.–11 P.M., 60 Kč). Standing proudly as the Czech Republic's highest structure (709 feet), its completion in 1992 was met with immediate criticism, among which were concerns of it giving children cancer. The tower stuck it out however and is now considered to be the area's defining landmark. Visitors should head to the observation tower, which, on a clear day, affords a view that stretches as far as 62 miles in any direction. There is also a fully functional restaurant that serves up dishes to amused tourists at a height of 216 feet. And for those who are unsure whether their eyes are playing tricks on them or not, yes, those *are* babies climbing up the side of the tower. They're the work of resident rebel artist David Černý.

Národní památník na Vítkově (National Memorial)

The National Memorial (U památniku 1900, www.pamatnik-vitkov.cz, Mon.–Fri. 8:30 A.M.–3 P.M. though times may vary; advanced booking required through Prague Info Service) on Vítkov Hill in Žižkov is hard to miss. It is a somber building devoid of windows and accompanied by a massive equestrian statue featuring Czech military commander Jan Žižka astride his horse. Designed in the late 1920s by Jan Zázvorka, its original purpose was to honor the remains of Czech legionnaires who battled against the Austro-Hungarian Empire during World War I. When the Communists took over, it became the resting place of state and party leaders. There was speculation after the revolution in 1989 as to what the grounds should function as but nobody could come up with a viable answer. In the year 2000, however, management duties fell to the National Museum, which has vowed to revamp the grounds as a strong symbol of Czech sovereignty by the end of the decade.

Olšanské Hřbitovy (Olšany Cemetery)

Built in an effort to solve the escalating number of plague victims who began dying en masse in 1680, Olšany Cemetery (Vinohradská 153, tel. 272 739 364, Nov.–Feb. daily 9 A.M.–4 P.M., Mar.–Apr. and Oct. daily 8 A.M.–6 P.M., May–Sept. daily 8 A.M.–7 P.M.) is Prague's largest burial ground. When the plague reared its diseased head once again in 1787, Emperor Joseph II banned the burial of bodies within the city's limits and declared Olšany the city's central graveyard for hygienic purposes. Two very famous faces from Communism lay buried here. The first is Jan Palach, the country's most famous anti-Communist martyr who set himself ablaze on Wenceslas Square in 1969 in protest of the Soviet invasion. The second is first Communist president Klement Gottwald, who, ironically, died shortly after catching a cold at Stalin's funeral in March 1953.

Nového Židovského Hřbitova (New Jewish Cemetery)

Not to be confused with the Old Jewish Cemetery in Old Town Square, the New Jewish Cemetery (Izraelská 1, Oct.–Mar. Mon.–Fri. 9 A.M.–2 P.M., Sun. 9 A.M.–4 P.M., Apr.–Sept. Mon.–Fri. 9 A.M.–2 P.M., Sun. 9 A.M.–5 P.M., closed Sat. and Jewish holidays) is located opposite the Želivského metro station at the tail end of the green subway line. At the top of the escalator, follow the exit straight ahead marked "Židovské Hřbitovy." When you emerge from the station, the cemetery will be on your immediate right. Franz Kafka is buried here and you'll find his grave by taking the first path on the right and following it four entrance gates down to lot 21. His rather unassuming tombstone is decorated with the occasional bouquet of flowers and some have left coins on the rocks directly in front of his grave with what seem to be messages hidden underneath. Many make the pilgrimage to this very spot every June 3—the day the great writer died.

© CORINE TACHTIRIS

Náměstí Míru's centerpiece, the Church of St. Ludmilla

VINOHRADY

Literally meaning "vineyards" because its entire area was once covered with such, Vinohrady today is a popular residential area that has also seen an increase in small-to-medium independent (and oftentimes artistically oriented) businesses. Beautiful Art Nouveau buildings complement tree-lined neighborhoods, including prominent Náměstí Míru and Riegrovy sady, one of Prague's premier outdoor drinking spots. Located a few minutes from the center and home to a myriad of excellent restaurants, bars, and shopping facilities, Vinohrady remains one of Prague's most attractive and desirable districts.

Kostel sv. Ludmily (Church of St. Ludmilla)

The centerpiece of Náměstí Míru (Liberty Square) and Vinohrady proper, the Church of St. Ludmila is an impressive, neo-Gothic, two-spire basilica beauty that was built between 1888 and 1893 based on the designs of Josef Mocker. Above the main entrance is a relief of Jesus Christ with St. Wenceslas and St. Ludmilla on

VYŠEHRAD

South of Nové Město, you'll find historic Vyšehrad, whose slightly mysterious-looking outline of spires is an indelible part of Prague's skyline. Steeped in legend, it is the site of Princess Libuše's foretelling of Prague's future glory, a vivid vision that prompted her to send her horse out to find Přemysl the Ploughman, the man she would eventually take as husband and king before founding the capital and Přemysl dynasty. What actually happened was that a fortified castle was built here in the middle of the 10th century and enjoyed a brief period as the seat of ultimate political power under King Vratislav II before the Přemyslid rulers decided to pack up and head to Prague Castle.

To see all that Vyšehrad has to offer, take the subway (red line) to Vyšehrad station. Walk past the rather ugly-looking Congress Center and through the Baroque gateway into the park proper. As you enjoy your leisurely stroll through the peaceful surroundings, you'll come upon the Rotunda of St. Martin. This is Prague's oldest surviving Romanesque building and though it dates back all the way to the 11th century, it still holds evening Mass to this very day. Continuing on, the next sight of interest is the neo-Gothic Church of SS Peter and Paul. Built during the beginning of the 20th century, it was based on the designs of Joseph Mocker and boasts an exquisite Art Nouveau-influenced interior. Next door is Slavin, Vyšehrad's famous cemetery, which is home to some of the country's most important cultural and political figures. Amongst the arcades and pretty memorials rest such giants as Antonín Dvořák, Bedřich Smetana, Karel Čapek, Jan Neruda, and Josef Václav Myslbek.

If you happen to have some time on your hands and don't really feel like seeing Prague Castle or Charles Bridge yet again, do yourself a favor and head for Vyšehrad. Its beauty, tranquility, and historical context are enough to rival any of the city's better-known sights.

---

either side of Him. Open only for services, the church now acts mostly as a popular meeting place for the many in town who prefer to soak up the scene on the neighboring benches, rather than engage in any ecclesiastical activities.

Divadlo na Vinohradech (Vinohrady Theatre)

Opposite Náměstí Míru is the gorgeous Art Nouveau building better known as the Vinohrady Theatre (Náměstí Míru 7, tel. 224 257 601, www.dnv-praha.cz, box office Mon.–Fri. 11 A.M.–7 P.M., Sat. 1–7 P.M.). Opened in 1907, it stands as one of Prague's oldest theaters and has managed to remain one of its premiere venues for Czech theater and the ballet.

Muzeum Antonina Dvořáka (Antonín Dvořák Museum)

Classical composer Antonín Dvořák (1841–1904) is arguably the Czech Republic's most widely known personality abroad and is a national hero at home. An exhibition of his memorabilia is on display at the Antonín Dvořák Museum (Villa Amerika, Ke Karlovu 20, tel. 224 923 363, Apr.–Sept. Tues.–Sun. 10 A.M.–5:30 P.M., Oct.–Mar. Tues.–Sun. 9:30 A.M.–5 P.M., 50 Kč), which is tucked behind the wrought-iron gates of Villa Amerika—a pretty 18th-century palace that has also served as a cattle market and restaurant in the past. Concerts are held regularly here and tend to fill up quickly.

Riegrovy sady (Riegrovy Park)

Located behind the National Museum off Italská Street, Riegrovy sady is a fantastic outdoor beer garden populated by locals and expats happily quenching their thirst. Completed in 1908, there are pretty gardens leading up to the drinking area, lined by benches often filled with couples who prefer a little privacy. The beer garden itself consists of a few hundred people seated at long tables with benches pounding back beers and catching up with old friends. A large screen occasionally projects various sports events and a kiosk offers up sausages, chips, and peanuts should all that drinking make you hungry. This is a great place to experience Prague at its most relaxed and authentic.

Entertainment and Events

Prague has been a respected capital of culture for centuries, something that doesn't seem likely to change any time soon. No matter what the time of day, night, or year, there is always something going on in the Golden City to keep its visitors and residents occupied. There are the local pubs and trendy cocktail bars, as well as the swanky yet welcoming clubs teeming with revelers and rabble-rousers. Those looking for a more cultivated level of entertainment will certainly find no shortage of ballets, orchestral concerts, and operas to keep them occupied, while theater and film fans have an inexhaustible selection to choose from thanks to the plethora of homegrown and imported talent gracing the city's stages and filling its silver screens.

BARS

Prague's nightlife is legendary, satisfying the entire spectrum of nocturnal taste ranging from smoky cellar bars to upscale lounges. No matter what your poison or pleasure, you can rest assured you'll find it here.

Nové Město

Tiny and extremely cozy, **Al Capone's Cocktail Bar** (Bartolomějská 3, tel. 224 212 192, www .alcapone.cz, Mon.–Thurs. 5 P.M.–2 A.M., Fri.–Sat. 6 P.M.–3 A.M., Sun. 6 P.M.–midnight) is a great place to unwind with friends or spend an evening of serious cocktail experimentation. The old wooden furniture and friendly staff will add to your comfort and the bar's darkened corners will make you feel like the criminal mastermind you've always wanted to be.

Centrally located and open 24 hours a day, *everybody* has ended their night of debauchery at **Batalion Hard Rock Café** (28. října 3,

tel. 220 108 147, www. batalion.cz, open 24 hours) at one point or another. Popular with off-the-clock bar staff, not-ready-to-pack-it-in-yet tourists, and natives going the extra mile, this bare-bones, two-floor, rowdy yet friendly bar will happily ply you with beer until you either pay up or pass out. A true rite of passage.

Rocky o'Reillys (Štěpánská 32, tel. 222 231 060, www.rockyoreillys.cz, daily 10 A.M.–1 A.M.) is Prague's biggest Irish pub, boasting mouth-watering Irish pub food in authentic Irish surroundings. Whether you grab a Guinness at the bar or sip on a glass of wine by the log fire, this is a great place to unwind and get away from the bustle of Wenceslas Square. Unfortunately, Rocky's also attracts large groups of British soccer fans and is occasionally overrun by "the lads" who have had a little too much to drink. Ye takes your chances.

Despite the constant complaints regarding overly aggressive bouncers and waitstaff who happily ignore you or over-charge you, **Solidní nejistota** (Pštrossova 29, tel. 224 933 086, www.solidninejistota.cz, daily 6 P.M.–6 A.M.) is a brightly painted, medium-sized meat market that continues to thrive. Packed to the gills every weekend with eager-to-score tourists, in-the-know natives, and the occasional local celebrity, this is the kind of place you'll either love or hate.

Sleek, stylish, and spacious, **Ultramarin** (Ostrovní 32, tel. 224 932 249, www.ultramarin.cz, daily 11 A.M.–4 A.M.) offers the late, *late* crowd the finest chilled-out option available in Nové Město. Many argue over the quality of the international menu, which tends to be a hit-or-miss affair, but nobody complains about the drinks or ambience and effort in making those wee

DO I REALLY WANT TO TRY ABSINTHE?

In the mid-to-late 19th century, there was hardly an artist anywhere who didn't cite absinthe as his drink of choice. Picasso, Van Gogh, Wilde, Toulouse-Lautrec, Baudelaire, Poe, and Hemingway were but a few of the Bohemian bourgeoisie who enjoyed a glass or two of "The Green Muse." Their extravagant descriptions of the drink's mind-altering effects went a long way in shaping its popularity and mystique, though closer inspection and study has shown that those claims were largely exaggerated and based on little more than a tipsy imagination.

The mythic drink's origins can be traced back to the end of the 18th century when French doctor Pierre Ordinaire began using wormwood (*Artemisia absinthium*) together with anise, fennel, hyssop, and numerous other herbs distilled in an alcoholic base as an herbal remedy for his patients. The curious concoction eventually ended up in the hands of Henri-Louis Pernod who, upon opening his first distillery in 1805, went on to produce "Extrait d'absinthe," sparking the Pernod dynasty as well as a national phenomenon. Numerous reports regarding the drink's harmful effects began to emerge, though most, if not all, were alarmist and/or reflected the opinions of the rich and powerful who were either for the banning of alcohol or wanted to eliminate the competition absinthe had brought to France's wine industry. "The Green Fairy," as it was known in some circles, was banned in France in 1914 due to mounting reports of its dangerous side effects, which we now know were the result of cheap, knock-off brands who were looking to make a quick franc. Nevertheless, it was the end of an era and Pernod's plant, which was home to 110 years of profitable production, served as a field hospital during World War I before being sold on December 31, 1917, to Nestlé.

Today, absinthe is still banned in most countries but you'll find it readily available in plenty of Prague bars who play up the drink's magical history. If you decide to give it a whirl, it will be served to you in a small glass, along with a teaspoon and packet of sugar. Pour some sugar onto the spoon then soak the spoonful with absinthe and light it in order to caramelize the sugar. When the flame goes out, stir the sugar into your drink, buck up, and drink down. You'll soon realize why all bars have a two-absinthe maximum.

---

hours enjoyable ones. A must for those looking to end the night with laid-back style.

Velryba (Opatovická 24, tel. 224 931 444, daily 11 A.M.–midnight) is a simply furnished, spartanly decorated local hangout that has long been a favorite with students and artists thanks to its cheap beer and very affordable pub grub. Not too many tourists find their way in here despite its central location, so if you really want to rub shoulders with the locals, here's one place to do so. If you have the time, make sure to check out the small art gallery they have in the back showcasing some of the more interesting homegrown talent.

Staré Město

If you're looking to bump and grind alongside an international, fun-loving crowd,

Bombay Cocktail Bar (Dlouha 13, tel. 721 882 557, Sun.–Wed. 4 P.M.–4 A.M., Thurs.–Sat. 4 P.M.–5 A.M.) is the place to be. The bar itself stretches all the way down one side of the room, which makes getting served a relatively painless affair, no matter how packed the place gets. So order up a margarita or one of the many exotic beers on offer and dance the night away in one of the more loose atmospheres the city has to offer.

Bugsy's (Pařižská 10, tel. 224 810 943, www.bugsysbar.cz, daily 7 P.M.–2 A.M.) used to be the only place in town that knew how to make a proper cocktail and still boasts an impressive drinks list. Thanks to its swank Pařížská location, wanna-be New York decor, and exorbitant prices, the place attracts an older crowd—representing the city's suits,

FERNET

Fernet is another herbal liquor that is hugely popular with Czechs and anyone else who likes the strong stuff. There are two variants to the drink: Fernet Stock (bitter) and Fernet Citrus (lemon flavored). Although the recipe is heavily guarded, we do know that some of Fernet's 14 ingredients include gentian root, quinine, orange peels, and Roman chamomile. First produced in 1927 by Italian businessman Lionello Stock in his liquor factory in Plzen, it quickly became one of the country's most sought after drinks and consistently places in the world's Top 100 best-selling international liquor brands today. Best served cold or with ice, it also makes for a potent shooter.

hustlers, and nouveau-riche—that fills the place nightly.

If you're from the UK and feeling a little homesick, **Caffrey's** (Staroměstské náměstí 10, tel. 224 828 031, www.caffreys.cz, Sun.–Thurs. 9 A.M.–1:30 A.M., Fri.–Sat. 9 A.M.–2 A.M.), with its English pub atmosphere, predominantly British expat/tourist clientele, and sky-high prices, will make you feel like you never left. It does boast one of the finest views of Old Town Square, however, and a relaxing drink on their spacious patio is definitely worth your while.

If you're in the mood to rub elbows with Prague's seedier side or young Americans who finally figured out which guy to buy weed from, then the blood red **Chateau Rouge** (Jakubská 2, tel. 222 316 328, www.chateaurouge.cz, Mon.–Thurs. noon–4 A.M., Fri. noon–6 A.M., Sat. 4 P.M.–4 A.M., Sun. 4 P.M.–2 A.M.) is most definitely for you. This place has been wild, grungy, and one of the most popular and happening hangouts since the day it opened. Something is *always* going on here.

Located a stone's throw from Charles Bridge and yet somehow devoid of tourists, **Duende** (Karoliny Světlé 30, tel. 604 269 731, www .duende.cz, Mon.–Fri. 1 P.M.–1 A.M., Sat.

3 P.M.–1 A.M., Sun. 4 P.M.–1 A.M.) may just be Prague's best-kept secret. Uniquely decorated (e.g., life savers and wooden tigers), this Latin-themed cafe-bar fills up nightly with a free spirited, artistic crowd looking for a laid-back place to sip a glass of wine or two. Make sure to try the walnut liqueur *Ořechovka.*

If you're aching for a dose of Americana, Southern-rock style, head to **Harley's Bar** (Dlouhá 18, tel. 227 195 195, www.harleys .cz, Sun.–Thurs. 6 P.M.–4 A.M., Fri.–Sat. 6 P.M.–5 A.M.) and join resident mascot Jack (Daniels) for one bourbon, one scotch, and one beer. A fun, loose atmosphere and pleasant bar staff keep this stylish biker bar packed with locals and tourists well into the night.

Right in the heart of Old Town, **Kozička** (Kozí 1, tel. 224 818 308, www.kozicka.cz, Mon.–Fri. noon–4 A.M., Sat. 6 P.M.–4 A.M., Sun. 6 P.M.–3 A.M.) is a spacious basement bar that fills up with locals and tourists on a nightly basis. Popular and unpretentious, this homey hangout is a breath of fresh air in what's become an increasingly commercialized area.

Celebrating South and Central American culture on the outskirts of Old Town Square, **La Casa Blu** (Kozí 15, tel. 224 818 270, www .lacasablu.cz, Sun.–Thurs. 11 A.M.–midnight, Fri.–Sat. 11 A.M.–2 A.M.) is a brightly lit bar with battered yet comfy furniture that's a big hit with students, tourists, and just about anybody else who winds up here. Tasty burritos, cool mojitos, and a lively atmosphere are just a few of the reasons why this place should not be missed.

M1 Secret Lounge (Masná 1, tel. 227 195 235, www.m1lounge.com, Sun.–Thurs. 6 P.M.–3 A.M., Fri.–Sat. 6 P.M.–4 A.M.) established itself early on as one of the trendiest places to be seen in Prague and things haven't changed much. Amid the soft lights and long red couches, expats mix with models who mix with film people who mix with fat cats on the rise. Jam-packed on weekends, M1 is also a great place to visit midweek as it's one of the few places in Old Town that serve up cocktails and ambience until the wee hours.

Molly Malone's (U Obecního dvora 4, tel.

224 818 851, www.mollymalones.cz, Sun.–Thurs. 11 A.M.–1 A.M., Fri.–Sat. 11 A.M.–2 A.M.) was Prague's first Irish bar and if you ask its regulars, it's still the best. Mismatched chairs complement tables put together out of old beds and sewing machines while the Pogues and U2 play nonstop on the stereo. Filled with mostly backpackers and easy-going British locals, Molly's is a warm, atmospheric place where anybody can feel at home. If you're in town in the wintertime, the roaring log fire will be one more reason you won't want to leave.

With up to 200 concoctions available on the menu, **Tretter's** (V kolkovně 3, tel. 224 811 165, www.tretters.cz, daily 7 P.M.–3 A.M.) is truly a cocktail lover's dream. Sporting an elegant, old New York–style interior complete with red upholstery, classy tables, and a long dark-wood counter, this gin joint is a hit with fashion, film, and business types and was Owen Wilson's drinking hole of choice while on location here.

Soaked in both beer and tradition, **U Zlatého tygra** (Husova 17, tel. 222 221 111, www.uzlatehotygra.cz, daily 3 P.M.–11 P.M.) is a must for those interested in seeing where some of the country's greatest writers, like the late great Bohumil Hrabal, used to get inebriated. Vaclav Havel and Bill Clinton have also raised their glasses here and you just never know who else might come on in. The two medium-sized rooms start filling up as soon as the doors open, so get here early and stay awhile.

Malá Strana

Unpretentious and reasonably priced, **Bar Bar** (Všehrdova 17, tel. 257 312 246, www.bar-bar.cz, Sun.–Thurs. noon–midnight, Fri.–Sat. noon–2 A.M.) is a breath of fresh air in heavily commercialized Malá Strana. The menu is packed with hearty and delicious continental fare and the bar staff is one of the friendliest you'll find in town. Both of their bright and spacious rooms are perfect for an early dinner or a laid-back evening over cocktails with friends.

Tucked away a little farther up from the U.S. Embassy, **Baráčnická rychta** (Tržiště 23, tel. 257 532 461, www.baracnickarychta.cz, Mon.–

Sat. 11 A.M.–11 P.M., Sun. 11 A.M.–9 P.M., varying cover charge) is a refreshing, authentic change from the throngs of tourists and the shops that cater to them. A small beer hall filled with students and laborers is what you'll usually find on the ground floor, but those who venture downstairs will find a large, Communist-era music hall that stages local rockers and swing bands on any given night. This is the place to come to when you've had your fill of sightseeing and shopping and want a taste of what things used to be like in Malá Strana.

Located on an unassuming street just past Charles Bridge on the Malá Strana side, **Blue Light** (Josefská 1, tel. 257 533 126, www.bluelightbar.cz, daily 7 P.M.–4 A.M.) is a small bar that's a big hit with just about anybody who passes through its doors. Ice-cold cocktails are served up by a friendly staff to an attractive clientele that's ready to party till the sun comes up. Get here early if you want one of the few tables available or sidle up to the bar and make some new friends; it's that kind of place.

Just down the street from the U.S. Embassy, **J.J. Murphy's** (Tržiště 4, tel. 257 535 575, www.jjmurphys.cz, daily 9 A.M.–1 A.M.) is a spacious, friendly Irish pub where locals and tourists regularly settle in for a delicious pint of Guinness. Perfect for lunch, dinner, or a drink or two with friends, J.J.'s also offers sports fans an upstairs lounge that showcases the day's main matches.

Loud, smoky and devoid of attitude, **Pod Petřínem** (Hellichova 5, tel. 257 007 327, daily 11 A.M.–midnight) is Malá Strana's old-school jewel. Not only does it serve the cheapest drinks in the neighborhood, the waiters will continue plopping down beers in front of you until you beg them to stop. Heavy smoke, long wooden benches, and daily binge drinking makes this about as traditional as a Czech bar gets and is not for the faint-hearted. A must for those in search of no-frills, genuine Prague experiences.

Located in a beautiful UNESCO-listed building dating back to 1554, the **St. Nicholas Café** (Trziště 10, tel. 257 530 204, Sun.–Thurs. noon–2 A.M., Fri.–Sat. noon–3 A.M.) offers much-needed respite from the tourist bustle of Malostranské náměstí. Housed in a dark vaulted basement decorated in quasi-Moroccan fashion, one feels transported to a bygone era upon entering. Great for an evening of drinks and warm and snuggly in the wintertime, St. Nick's is an excellent place to unwind with friends or spend time with that special someone.

Part cafe, part bar, and part art gallery, **Tato Kojkej** (Kampa Park, tel. 257 323 102, www.tatokojkej.cz, daily 10 A.M.–midnight) has slowly carved out a rather chic name for itself. Maybe it's because of the eclectic furniture, or maybe it's due to the overpriced art for sale. Either way, this laid-back place tucked away in lovely Kampa Park is perfect for taking a load off during the day or hanging out with close friends at night.

Back in the day, dreadlocks, dogs, and dime bags were all necessary accessories if one was to enjoy a night at **Klub Újezd** (Újezd 18, tel. 257 316 537, daily 2 P.M.–4 A.M.) properly. Things have calmed down a little since then but if you want a true Prague experience, put this on your "to-drink" list. Don't let its rough, wooden, unrefined appearance sway your opinion. It may not look like much, but Újezd has been a hit with both locals and tourists for many a moon.

"Little Glen's" or **U Malého Glena** (Karmelitská 23, tel. 257 531 717, www.malyglen.cz, daily 10 A.M.–2 A.M., 100–150 Kč cover charge) is a smallish, typical-looking pub that has long been on the scene, serving up tasty soups, sandwiches, and Tex-Mex to both expats and Czechs alike. Friendly and easy-going, this is a place worth visiting when in need of a break from the Malá Strana madness. If you visit in the evening, make sure to check out the tiny jazz cellar located downstairs, which regularly features some of Prague's hottest talent.

U Hrocha (Thunovská 10, daily noon–11:30 P.M.) is a small, smoky traditional pub in the heart of Malá Strana that time seems to have forgotten. Frequented mostly by government employees working nearby, as well as a motley crew of laborers, locals, and students, it's managed to maintain a distinct authentic

flavor throughout the years while the rest of the neighborhood continues to redevelop itself. An excellent choice for those craving a taste of local color.

Holešovice

Popular from the get-go, **Fraktal** (Šmeralova 1, tel. 777 794 094, www.fraktalbar.cz, daily 11 A.M.–1 A.M.) is a cozy, cheerful bar full of expats and Czechs who are serious about having a good time. Few tourists make it out here but if you find yourself weary of the downtown core, make the trip out to Holešovice and join in the fun. Also known as one of the few places in town where one can get a proper hamburger.

Tasty tapas and smooth sangrias are what you're in for at **La Bodega Flamenca** (Šmeralova 5, tel. 233 374 075, www.labodega.cz, Sun.–Thurs. 4 P.M.–1 A.M., Fri.–Sat. 4 P.M.–3 A.M.). The walls are lined with bench-style seats and they fill up fast so if you feel like sitting, get there early. Otherwise, do as the Spanish do and show up no earlier than midnight. Things usually don't start to heat up until then anyway.

If a small lounge/club with a DJ is what you crave, **Wakata** (Malířská 14, tel. 233 370 518, www.wakata.cz, Mon.–Thurs. 5 P.M.–3 A.M., Fri.–Sat. 5 P.M.–5 A.M., Sun. 6 P.M.–3 A.M.) is sure to satisfy. Catering to a younger crowd of late teens and twentysomethings draped coolly from welded bar stools, DJs from all over the world come here to spin anything from jungle, hip-hop, Latin, and ska. This place tends to stay open later than their advertised hours if something fun's going on, which is usually the case.

Žižkov

A long-time favorite with backpackers and Czechs, **Blind Eye** (Vlkova 26, www.blind eye.cz, daily 11 A.M.–5 A.M.) is a chilled-out, extremely dark bar that plays house to Prague's grungier set. The walls are fashionably vandalized, the booths are sufficiently grubby, and the music is liable to range from Madonna to Motorhead in a matter of minutes. This is definitely one place to drop in on if you happen to be in the neighborhood.

Long a neighborhood staple, **U Sadu** (Škroupovo náměstí 5, tel. 222 727 072, www .usadu.cz, Mon.–Fri. 8 A.M.–4 A.M., Sat.– Sun. 9 A.M.–4 A.M.) is an absolute must and well worth going out of your way for a visit. Decorated with Socialist-era relics, including meat grinders and gas masks, this institution has "traditional" written all over it. Whether it's copious amounts of beer you're looking to consume or the stinky yet delicious *nakladany hermelin* (pickled cheese) you've come to relish, U Sadu will convince you to stay longer than you had originally intended.

One of the more unique bars in Žižkov, **U vystřeleného oka** (U božích bojovníků 3, tel. 222 540 465, Mon.–Sat. 4:30 P.M.–1 A.M.), meaning "At the Shot-Out Eye," sits beneath the famous statue of General Jan Žižka. When it's warm, most opt for the three-level outdoor beer garden where they can sip their suds and watch the local trains rumble past. Inside, drinkers of all walks of life wax drunkenly amidst the grotesque artwork of Martin Velíšek. A must if you're in the neighborhood and well worth the trip if you're not.

CLUBS

The club scene in Prague is a vibrant and varied one that ranges from the down-and-dirty vibe of Palac Akropolis to swank and trendy institutions like Mecca and Radost FX. Club attire is just as diverse as it's common to see anything from the completely casual to the bluntly provocative, often in the same group of friends. Clubs tend to get busy around midnight and stay that way till the wee hours, with most clubbers heading home as others begin their day. Most offer different musical programs depending on the night of the week so check local listings to make sure you find the right fit for you.

Karlovy Lázně (Novotneho Lavka 5, Staré Město, tel. 222 220 502, www.karlovylazne.cz, daily 9 P.M.–5 A.M., 100 Kč) is Central Europe's largest dance club. Boasting four floors and five clubs for the price of one, this is the place where most serious clubbers eventually end up. Very touristy and rather pricy, the club nevertheless packs them in most nights and you'd be wise to get there early (around 10 P.M.) if you want to avoid the long, inevitable line.

Next to Karlovy Lázně is **Klub Lávka** (Novotného lávka 1, Staré Město, tel. 221 082 299, www.lavka.cz, open 24 hours, 100 Kč), a place where scores of young, good-looking tourists and locals go to shake their money-makers on the cramped dance floor downstairs or enjoy one of the grandest views of Prague on the club's outdoor patio. If you happen to be on the Charles Bridge at night, the loud music and even louder roars of merriment may just twist your arm enough to double back and join in the debauchery.

One of Prague's better-known meat markets, **La Fabrique** (Uhelný trh 2, Staré Město, tel. 224 233 137, www.lafabrique.cz, Sun.–Thurs. 5 P.M.–3 A.M., Fri.–Sat. 5 P.M.–4 A.M., no cover charge) actually offers up some tasty international dishes, but nobody comes here to eat. It's all about the boogie here, so order up a drink, smile flirtatiously, and head for the cramped dance floor downstairs. Everybody else does.

Long heralded as one of the better techno clubs in Prague, **Mecca** (U Průhonu 3, Holešovice, tel. 283 870 522, www.mecca.cz, varying cover charge) often attracts huge numbers of the young, beautiful, and aspiring. Soft white couches adorn an industrial lounge that leads to a large dance space that's filled most nights. For those who tire easily of body-rocking beats, there's a large chill-out space in the basement that allows you to collect your thoughts. Not as central as other clubs in town but worth the visit if you don't mind springing for a cab.

A veritable institution and still the most-popular bar in the district, **Palac Akropolis** (Kubelíkova 27, Žižkov, tel. 296 330 911, www .palacakropolis.cz, daily 11:30 A.M.–3 A.M., no cover charge) is a bar, club, and concert venue all rolled into one. Beer flows freely upstairs but it's downstairs where all the action happens. Rub elbows with travelers and arty types over battered tables and blazing beats. This is the place to be if a night of true-blue Bohemian behavior is what you're after.

Radost FX (Belehradská 120, Vinohrady, tel. 224 254 776, www.radostfx.cz, daily 11 A.M.–5 A.M., 150 Kč) is where Prague's in-crowd parties most nights of the week. The space itself is an appealing mix of nightclub, cocktail bar, art gallery, and vegetarian cafe, all of which are top-notch. Lush decor, sexy clientele, and stylish bar staff have helped make Radost one of Prague's premiere nightspots for years now and things don't seem like they're going to change anytime soon.

Plagued for years by rumors that it would be shut down due to angry neighbors complaining about the constant noise, the **Roxy** (Dlouhá 33, Staré Město, tel. 224 826 296, www.roxy .cz, daily 7 P.M.–5 A.M., varying cover charge) has nevertheless managed to stay open and remains as popular as ever. Some of the world's top DJs and live acts have performed here and the slightly dilapidated interior, along with a relaxed and tolerant vibe, makes this a big hit with locals, expats, tourists, and just about anybody else who likes their drum 'n' bass, jungle, and techno. This is arguably Prague's most famous nightspot and is a must for any serious clubber.

LIVE MUSIC

Considering the sheer volume of bars and clubs in the capital, it should come as no surprise that the live music scene is a thriving one. Whether it's international acts playing smaller, more intimate venues or established local bands rocking the Kasbah, there is always something going on, no matter what the day of the week. The handful of jazz clubs in town host shows by the finest musicians in the country for a relative pittance, while other music clubs hold a wide variety of concerts ranging from funk and reggae, to straight-out rock, punk, and thrash. There are also a whole host of cover bands (called "revivals") that add an element of amusement to an already-enjoyable show. Cover charges are low, crowds are laidback, and the air is always thick with smoke and sweat. Make sure to keep an eye out for the weekly music schedules posted all over town to see who'll be performing during your stay.

One of the better mid-sized venues in town

is **Lucerna Music Bar** (Vodičkova 36, Nové Město, tel. 224 217 108, www.musicbar.cz, daily 8 P.M.–3 A.M., varying cover charge), which boasts a long list of famous and eclectic artists who've graced its stage. Weekends give way to tremendously popular '80s DJ nights where locals who are way too young to remember the decade do The Safety Dance.

Smack dab in the center of town is **Rock Café** (Národní 20, Nové Město, tel. 224 933 947, www.rockcafe.cz, Mon.–Fri. 10 A.M.–3 A.M., Sat. 5 P.M.–3 A.M., Sun. 5 P.M.–1 A.M., varying cover charge), proud bringer of lesser-known alternative and punk bands to Prague. Albeit lacking in ambience and service, it does offer weekly movie screenings and more cover bands than you can shake a stick at. Your best bet is to check out the music program in advance and take it from there.

Housed in the same building as Rock Café is **Reduta Jazz Club** (Národní 20, Nové Město, tel. 224 933 487, www.redutajazzclub.cz, daily 9 P.M.–12:30 A.M., 150 Kč). More or less unchanged in decades, it affects an old-school atmosphere what with the cramped seating and coat-check guy running after you in hopes of a tip. Most don't appreciate the lack of air circulation and over-priced drinks but it's a well-known fact that some of the continent's best jazz musicians come through here.

Across the street from Rock Café is **Vagon** (Národní 25, Nové Město, tel. 221 085 599, www.vagon.cz, Mon.–Sat. 6 P.M.–5 P.M., Sun. 6 P.M.–1 A.M.), a spacious, smoky cellar serving up cheap beer, unsigned rock and reggae bands, and free-for-all jam nights. This is a great place to chill out with the locals until well past your bedtime. A cover is sometimes charged, generally ranging 80–150 Kč.

Located conveniently close to Old Town Square is **Agharta Jazz Centrum** (Železná 16, Staré Město, tel. 222 211 275, www .agharta.cz, daily 6 P.M.–12:30 A.M., 150 Kč), one of the better venues in town to enjoy home-grown jazz. Featuring well-known live acts in a warm, cozy environment, Agharta fills up early so you may want to book seats in advance. Don't forget to check out their record store either, where you'll find plenty of local (and affordable) recordings.

One of the finer places to catch modern, contemporary, and Latin jazz is **U Staré Paní Jazz Club** (Michalská 9, Staré Město, tel. 603 551 680, www.jazzlounge.cz, daily 7 P.M.–2 A.M., 150 Kč), where most of the hottest players in town come to swing. Jams will last all night if the mood's right and if you get the munchies in between sets this is the only jazz club in town that'll be able to come to your rescue.

Founded in 2000, **Ungelt Jazz & Blues Club** (Týn 2, Staré Město, tel. 224 895 748, www.jazzblues.cz, daily 8 P.M.–12:30 A.M., 150 Kč) is located mere steps from Old Town Square and is home to some of the finest jazz, blues, and funk you're liable to hear around these parts. Situated in cellar rooms dating back to the 15th century, the club attracts many tourists who come to enjoy the nation's top musicians. This is the most expensive jazz club in Prague but still relatively reasonable by Western standards.

THE ARTS

The arts scene in Prague strikes a balance between the time-honored and cutting-edge, accommodating and nurturing both to the delight of theater, music, and film fans everywhere. From standards like *Pygmalion* and *La Traviata* to groundbreaking domestic dance troupes and avant-garde filmmakers, artistic expression is alive and well in the bosom of Bohemia. What else could one expect from a country whose former president was a dissident playwright?

Theater

Sitting majestically alongside the banks of the Vltava River is **Národní Divadlo** (National Theatre; Ostrovní 1, Nové Město, tel. 224 901 448, www.narodni-divadlo.cz, box office daily 10 A.M.–6 P.M.), one of Prague's most important cultural landmarks. Built between 1868 and 1881, this neo-Renaissance building with the gleaming golden roof plays host to some of the city's finest ballet and opera performances. If *Carmen* or *Swan Lake* isn't your thing, a tour of this magnificent building (held daily) is still worth the time.

At the forefront of contemporary theater, dance, and music is the critically acclaimed **Divadlo Archa** (Archa Theatre; Na Poříčí 26, Nové Město, tel. 221 716 333, www.archatheatre.cz, box office Mon.–Fri. 10 A.M.–6 P.M.). Its versatile space attracts rather avant-garde productions and has hosted such well-known artists as David Byrne, Allen Ginsberg, The Royal Shakespeare Company, and The White Stripes.

Housed in the odd-looking glass addition to the National Theatre is **Laterna Magika** (Magic Lantern; Národní 4, Nové Město, tel. 224 931 482, www.laterna.cz, box office Mon.–Sat. 10 A.M.–8 P.M.), a black light theater that has been delighting audiences for decades. Not knowing the Czech language doesn't affect one's enjoyment of the performance as there are no words spoken. Rather, the performances rely on a combination of film projection, dance, sound, lights, and pantomime.

Popular with tourists and children alike is the **Národní divadlo marionet** (National Marionette Theatre; Žatecká 1, Staré Město, tel. 224 819 322, www.mozart.cz, box office daily 10 A.M.–8 P.M.), which has been entertaining audiences with its unique portrayal of Mozart's *Don Giovanni* since 1991. No humans on stage here, just classically carved marionettes. While relying more on cuteness than anything else, these performances are nevertheless skillful adaptations of the original masterpiece by some of the country's top puppeteers.

Located on trendy Pařížská Street is yet another black light endeavor—the **Divadlo Image** (Image Theatre; Pařížská 4, Staré Město, tel. 222 314 448, www.imagetheatre.cz, box office daily 9 A.M.–8 P.M.). Focusing mainly on contemporary dance and music, the theater puts on three or four productions a month as well as a medley of their more successful bits in a production entitled "Best of Image."

In December 2002, **Švandovo Divadlo** (Švanda Theatre; Štefánikova 57, Smíchov, tel. 234 651 111, www.svandovodivadlo.cz, box office daily 2–7 P.M.) opened its door to the public again after a lengthy period of reconstruction and hasn't looked back since. Theater lovers will find much diversity here ranging from Chekhov to Shakespeare to Havel to McDonagh. Most performances offer English subtitles—a relief to non-Czech-speaking foreigners who have few opportunities here to enjoy a night at the theater. The suburb of Smíchov is located just south of Malá Strana and can be easily reached by taking the subway's yellow line to Anděl station. A number of trams serve the area as well, the most popular of which are the 4, 7, 9, 10, 12, and 20.

Classical Music and Dance

Next door to Radio Free Europe is the midsized yet elegant **Státní Opera Praha** (State Opera; Wilsonova 4, Nové Město, tel. 224 227 266, www.sop.cz, box office Mon.–Fri. 10 A.M.–5:30 P.M., Sat.–Sun. 10 A.M.–noon, 1–5:30 P.M.), where classics are performed daily by artists hailing from all around the world. Overshadowed a little by the magnificence of the National Theatre, the State Opera is nevertheless an excellent venue to watch top-notch performances of all the master works.

The **Municipal House** (Náměstí Republiky 5, tel. 222 002 101, www.obecnidum.cz, box office daily 10 A.M.–7 P.M.) is home to the Prague Symphony, as well as the main venue of the very popular Prague Spring International Music Festival. A stunning example of Art Nouveau, it is the center of cultural life in Prague thanks to the numerous conferences, balls, and concerts that are held in its elaborately decorated rooms.

Standing proudly at the edge of Staré Město is the neoclassical style **Rudolfinum** (Alšovo nábřeží 12, Staré Město, tel. 227 059 352, www.rudolfinum.cz, box office Mon.–Fri. 10 A.M.–6 P.M.), arguably one of the most beautiful concert halls in Europe. Home stage to the Czech Philharmonic Orchestra as well as to world-class musicians from all four corners of the globe, this magnificent building is well worth visiting for its sublime interior alone.

Built in 1783, the **Stavovské Divadlo** (Estates Theatre; Ovocný trh 1, Staré Město, tel. 224 901 448, www.stavovskedivadlo.cz, box office daily 10 A.M.–6 P.M.) is not only a breath-taking example of late-Baroque architecture, but Prague's oldest theater as well. The Czech national anthem was first performed here as part of the comic opera *Fidlovacka,* as was *Don Giovanni,* conducted by Mr. Mozart himself in 1787. Today, both opera and theater are performed here to a packed house of (mostly) tourists eager to get a sense of how things must have been like in a time long gone.

Cinemas

Offering up a mix of new releases and offbeat independent films, **Světozor** (Vodičkova 39, Nové Město, tel. 224 946 824, www.kino svetozor.cz) attracts a wide range of people from the popcorn-munching filmgoer to the all-out cinephile. It also hosts a variety of film festivals throughout the year so make sure to check out the cinema's schedule should you be interested in taking in a film while here.

Situated opposite the Světozor is the Art Nouveau **Lucerna** (Vodičkova 36, Nové Město, tel. 224 216 972, www.lucerna.cz), a pretty, old-fashioned European cinema complete with coat check and balcony. Hollywood films have been slowly giving way to foreign works from around the globe, with the occasional Czech film accompanied by English subtitles being shown as well. This is a great place to see a movie if you'd like a change from the usual mind-numbing multiplex experience.

Straddling the border between Old Town and New, **Palace Cinemas Slovanský Dům** (Na Příkopě 22, Nové Město, tel. 257 181 212, www.palacecinemas.cz) boasts 10 screens showing the latest films from Hollywood and around the world. Its slick, modern interior and excellent sound system make for an enjoyable film-going experience and you can even reserve tickets in advance either online or in person.

True film aficionados will want to have a look at what **Kino Aero** (Biskupcova, Žižkov, tel. 271 771 349, www.kinoaero.cz) is offering during their stay. A retro theater with rough-around-the-edges old-school charm, it manages to secure showings of films no other theater in town seems to even consider, let alone pursue. There is also a popular and extremely comfortable cafe/bar to add to your evening's enjoyment.

FESTIVALS AND EVENTS

Unlike other cities whose festival season tends to center around the summer months, Prague's calendar is full of culture and fun all year-round. Whether it's classical music or contemporary dance, Shakespeare or the latest in European cinema, fans of all artistic mediums and disciplines are sure to find something that will both entertain and enlighten.

Spring

Originally scheduled in January, **Febiofest** (Růžová 13, tel. 221 101 111, www.febiofest .cz) now runs during late March and features roughly 300 films from over 60 countries every year. Some of contemporary cinema's most important films are screened at various venues around the city, as are debut and sophomore efforts of Europe's up-and-coming filmmakers. A favorite of the festival is its retrospective series, which in the past has featured such high-profile names as Pasolini and Antonioni.

Continuing a tradition that dates way back to 1595 is **Matejská pout'** or St. Matthew's Fair (U Výstaviště, tel. 220 103 204, late Feb.–mid-Apr. Tues.–Fri. 2–9 P.M., Sat.–Sun. 10 A.M.–9 P.M.), held annually at Prague's Exhibition Grounds in Holešovice. Kids of all ages are invited to take part in the over 120 attractions on hand. Admittedly, the rides are pretty cheesy but it's the laid-back heralding of warmer weather that most people seem to enjoy.

Marking the death of winter and the birth of spring is **Pálení čarodějnic,** better known as Witches' Night (April 30). In an effort to purge the land of winter spirits, faithful citizens light bonfires around the country and burn an effigy of a hag (or witch). Some of the more daring participants will even try to jump over the flames. This is always a fun night in the Czech Republic that comes complete with loud music, good food, and, you guessed it—beer. This tradition is alive

celebrating Masopust in Old Town

and well in most Czech villages. In Prague, you can usually hear a witch's death screams coming from Petřín Hill or near the student dorms in Strahov.

One of the more romantic days in Prague occurs on May 1, loosely referred to as **May Day**. Lovers of all walks of life make the trek to Petřín Hill, locating the statue of 19th-century Romantic poet Karel Hynek Mácha and kissing under the cherry blossom tree next to it. A kiss under the tree ensures a year full of love and judging by all the smooching going on this day, there'll be plenty of love to last decades. A recent development worth noting is the expat chicken party—an all-day affair where anyone is welcome to bring their own chicken dish and partake in all the other tasty poultry delights that have been prepared by fellow foreigners. Very informal, lots of fun, and a great way to meet people in the expat community; just look for the large group on the hill devouring chicken wings.

Growing steadily in numbers every year is the **Prague International Marathon** (various routes throughout the city, tel. 224 919 209, www.pim.cz, mid-May), which takes runners through a mostly flat course that includes some of the city's most beautiful buildings. There's also a six-mile race whose route is no less picturesque. A massive street party is held afterwards where runners, organizers, and beer lovers in general refresh themselves with Bohemia's finest brews.

Literature lovers are treated to readings and Q&A sessions with some of the world's best-known writers during the **Prague Writer's Festival** (various venues, tel. 224 241 312, www.pwf.cz, mid-May–early June). Past guests include Martin Amis, Harold Pinter, Margaret Atwood, and Salman Rushdie.

One of Prague's more unique festivals is **Mezi ploty** (Ústavní 91, tel. 272 730 623, www.meziploty.cz, last weekend in May), a two-day festival showcasing professional, amateur, and mentally/physically disabled artists, dancers, and musicians. Very popular and loads of fun, the weekend's events are held on the grounds of Bohnice Psychiatric Hospital.

Lovers of classical music would be wise to attend Prague's most popular music festival—**Prague Spring** (various venues, tel. 257 312 547, www.festival.cz, mid-May–early June). The festivities kick off on the anniversary of the death of Czech composer Bedřich Smetana with a rousing performance of his tone poem *Má Vlast* (My Country). Showcasing some of the world's most outstanding performing artists, symphony orchestras, and chamber music ensembles, Prague Spring is not to be missed. Booking in advance is essential.

Summer

Fans of traditional Gypsy music, as well as those interested in learning more about Roma culture, would be wise to check out **Khamoro** (various venues, tel. 222 518 554, last week in May, www.khamoro.cz). This is a lively festival that holds concerts at various venues around the city and offers numerous informative and entertaining workshops and seminars.

Growing in prestige and popularity year by year is the modern dance festival **Tanec Praha** (various venues, tel. 224 817 886, www.tanecpha.cz, throughout June). Offering a 400,000 Kč ($20,000) development prize for Dance Discovery of the Year, Tanec Praha is an exciting event and a wonderful opportunity to see the world's finest performers in some of the city's better theaters.

The quiet Vltava riverfront turns into a non-stop concert during the **United Islands of Prague** (various venues, www.unitedislands.cz, throughout June), a high-energy festival that offers fans the opportunity to enjoy a multitude of musical genres such as world, ethno, folk, jazz, blues, and rock. Some of the festival's past artists include Fishbone, Placebo, and Martin, Medeski & Wood.

Even though all the performances are in Czech, lovers of Shakespeare will most definitely want to attend Prague's annual **Summer Shakespeare Festival** (Burgrave Palace, Prague Castle, tel. 226 200 830, www.shakespeare.cz, late June–early Sept.). Originally initiated by former President and playwright Václav Havel, a handful of The Bard's works are put on every year to the delight of all. Language barriers aside, it truly is a memorable experience watching a masterpiece under a warm, summer sky with the Prague Castle as backdrop.

Autumn

Since its inception, the **Prague Autumn Festival** (various venues, tel. 222 540 484, www.pragueautumn.cz, mid-Sept.–early Oct.) has focused on major classical works dating from the 18th century to the present. Russian, German, and Czech orchestras and choirs perform regularly in some of Prague's most beautiful venues. Recent years have added surprises such as Chinese opera and the Xalapa Guitar Orchestra from Mexico. This event has been growing in popularity over the years, making the advance booking of tickets essential.

Despite the fact that the country no longer exists, the **Anniversary of the Birth of Czechoslovakia** (Oct. 28) continues to be observed. Fireworks displays and the consumption of large amounts of beer are usually on the menu. If near a weekend, the city empties as most Czechs and many locals head for cottage country.

Celebrating the fall of Communism and the ushering in of a new era, the **Anniversary of the Velvet Revolution** (Nov. 17) is a surprisingly subdued affair. Flowers are laid and candles are lit at both the top of Wenceslas Square and Národní třída, but one gets the feeling that most people are busy enjoying their TVs and Western products more than remembering the way things used to be.

Winter

Smaller than most jazz festivals but certainly no less respectable is the **Prague Jazz Festival** (various venues, tel. 224 235 340, www.jazz festivalpraha.cz, second half of Oct.), which has been host to some of the biggest names in the business, including Herbie Hancock, Wynton Marsalis, Buddy Rich, and Count Basie. Sponsored by the AghaRTA Jazz Club, most performances are held at Lucerna Music Bar with a few other jazz venues occasionally thrown in for good measure.

One of the more charming and colorful traditions in Prague is **Mikuláš** (Dec. 5, all over town—particularly Old Town Square), a sort of judgment day for kids. Typically, a group of three characters: St. Nicholas, an Angel, and a Devil roam the streets and stop kids randomly, asking them whether they've been naughty or nice. Most kids admit to having been good and sing a song or recite a short poem to prove it. They are then rewarded with a piece of candy by the Angel. The "bad" kids are supposed to get a sack of coal or potatoes instead of sweets but you'll be hard-pressed to find that happening these days.

When people hear of Carnivals or Masquerades, most think of New Orleans or Rio de Janeiro. **Masopust** (various venues in Žižkov, www.praha3.cz, mid-Feb.), while nowhere near in scope or international attention, is a whole lotta fun nonetheless. Faces are painted, meat is grilled, and merry-making rings loudly throughout the city. Events, parades, and nighttime activities revolve around the borough of Žižkov, which happily brings this colorful tradition to life year after year.

Shopping

The beginning of Prague's burgeoning tourist industry brought with it an increased exposure to Western styles and habits, which, when coupled with a slow but steady increase in wages, helped shape the average Czech's approach to shopping and created a consumer savvy unseen in these parts before. The inevitable result was a tremendous and seemingly overnight growth of designer boutiques, multinational brands, and sprawling shopping malls. Although they may be wont to admit it, today's Czech is just as liable to spend a weekend out shopping as they are relaxing at the cottage—something that was unthinkable a scant 10 years ago. Increased consumer awareness has led to increased spending, resulting in Prague reaching a level of sophistication that now rivals the same Western markets that were once on the wrong side of the curtain.

SHOPPING DISTRICTS

The first of the city's central shopping districts is the mighty **Wenceslas Square,** starting at the top of Muzeum and stretching all the way down to the bottom of Můstek. Along the way are bookshops, clothing stores, jewelry dealers, department stores, and arcades brimming with well-known brands and typically hefty price tags. There are a handful of souvenir shops kicking around as well, hawking the same cheaply manufactured kitsch one can easily find in Old Town Square or Malá Strana. At the bottom of the square on the right is the beginning of **Na příkopě Street.** Home to all things multinational and fashionable, it was recently ranked 18th in a survey called "Main Streets of the World," behind Manhattan's Fifth Avenue, London's Oxford Street, and the like. Any international brand worth a dime has a shop here.

Two streets dominate the shopping scene in Old Town Square: **Pařížská** and **Celetná.** The first is home to trendy, expensive, and well-known designer boutiques including Louis Vuitton, Boss, and Dior. The second is full of crystal, Bohemian glass, and souvenir shops that range from the elegant and expensive to the crappy and overpriced. The rest of the common pedestrian areas are dominated by shops selling tacky souvenirs including annoying "Czech me out!" t-shirts and cheaply made beer mugs. There are, however, a small number of tiny shops selling antiques, old books, and prints that are tucked away down side streets and require a bit of hunting around to track down.

Crossing the Charles Bridge and into Lesser Town will bring you face to face with two main shopping drags. The first is **Mostecká,** which runs from the end of the bridge to Malostranské náměstí and is packed with jewelry, crystal, glass, and souvenir shops. The second is **Nerudova,** which offers more of the same. Prices are typically higher on this side of the river but a bit of legwork and comparison shopping should help you find a few reasonably priced items.

NOVÉ MĚSTO
Antiques

If you're looking for an authentic slice of the past, try **Hamparadi Antik Bazar** (Pštrossova 22, tel. 224 931 162, daily 10:30 A.M.–6 P.M.). There are plenty of unique and interesting items to be found here, from knick-knacks to ceramics to glass, most of which is affordably priced. Feel free to ask the staff for help if you haven't found what you're looking for. If they don't have it, they'll know someone who will.

Books and Music

Long an expat haven and institution, **The Globe Bookstore & Coffeehouse** (Pštrossova 6, tel. 224 934 203, www.globebookstore.cz, daily 9:30 A.M.–midnight) has been serving up used books and fine food since its original location in Holešovice. Operating out of New Town for the last few years now, it remains one of the best places in Prague to pick up new releases, meet fellow foreigners, grab a bite, or

© TOM DIRLIS

a small sample of antiques

simply catch up on email. Under new management recently, its live music, book launches, and a whole host of other events continue to keep the Globe as lively and supportive of the artistic community as it ever was.

One of the wider selections of books in English can be found at **Palác knih Luxor** (Václavské náměstí 41, tel. 221 111 364, www .neoluxor.cz, Mon.–Fri. 8 A.M.–8 P.M., Sat. 9 A.M.–7 P.M., Sun. 10 A.M.–7 P.M.) on Wenceslas Square. New arrivals can be found on the main floor, along with a healthy variety of popular magazines like *National Geographic* and *Rolling Stone*. Literature ranging from classics to crime to contemporary best sellers is located downstairs in a spacious setting that may take up a bit more of your time than originally expected.

Although microscopic compared to North American and Western European megamusic stores, **Bontonland Megastore** (Václavské náměstí 1, tel. 224 473 080, www .bontonland.cz, Mon.–Sat. 9 A.M.–8 P.M., Sun. 10 A.M.–7 P.M.) is Prague's largest and carries a decent selection of music, movies, and video games. CD prices are rather high in this country and can easily reach 600 Kč ($29). You may find something obscure here, however, making it well worth it to spend a bit of time browsing through some of the more interesting European releases.

Department Stores

Kotva (Náměstí Republiky 8, tel. 224 801 111, www.od-kotva.cz, Mon.–Fri. 9 A.M.–8 P.M., Sat. 10 A.M.–7 P.M., Sun. 10 A.M.–6 P.M.) has been serving the public for over 30 years now and it's starting to show. There's nothing too cutting-edge to be found here, although the prices are relatively cheap. Jewelry, perfume, and snacks are some of the goodies you'll find on the first floor, while men's and women's clothing, sporting goods, furniture, and a whole lot more await you on higher floors. There's also a supermarket where you can stock up on rations before hitting the sightseeing trail again.

Twelve million people pass through **Tesco** (Národní třída 26, tel. 222 003 111, www.tesco -shop.cz, department store Mon.–Fri. 8 A.M.–9 P.M.,

Sat. 9 A.M.–8 P.M., Sun. 10 A.M.–7 P.M., supermarket Mon.–Fri. 7 A.M.–10 P.M., Sat. 8 A.M.–8 P.M., Sun. 9 A.M.–8 P.M.) every year, which explains why it oftentimes resembles a zoo. There's a decent-sized supermarket downstairs while the department store offers four floors of affordably priced wares ranging from cosmetics to fashion to electronic goods.

Popular British department store **Debenhams** (Václavské náměstí 21, tel. 221 015 028, www.debenhams.cz, Mon.–Sat. 9 A.M.–8 P.M., Sun. 10 A.M.–8 P.M.) is one of Wenceslas Square's newer additions, giving tourists (mostly) a chance to see what the fuss is all about. There's a supermarket in the basement, cosmetics, footwear and leather on the main floor, and women's and men's fashions above that. Most Czechs walk by unimpressed, however, preferring something that sounds Italian, or at the very least French.

Fashion

Pour Pour (Voršilská 6, tel. 777 830 078, www.pourpour.com, Mon.–Fri. 11 A.M.–7 P.M., Sat. noon–6 P.M.) is a small shop specializing in trendy, original clothing designed by young, up-and-coming Czech artists. Started up in 2004, it quickly became one of the must-visit places for those who like to be on top of all things current and chic. Very funky and very affordable.

Pietro Filipi (Národní 31, tel. 224 231 120, www.pietro-filipi.com, Mon.–Fri. 10 A.M.–7 P.M., Sat.–Sun. 11 A.M.–6 P.M.) produces popular lines of clothing for both men and women at reasonable prices. Focusing primarily on Italian fashion, design, and culture, the clothing strikes a balance between elegance and simplicity, as well as invention and convention.

Senior Bazar (Senovážné náměstí 18, tel. 224 235 068, Mon.–Fri. 9 A.M.–5 P.M.) is one of the better-known second-hand clothing shops in town and arguably the best. Budget shoppers will be delighted to find it filled to the brim with all sorts of odds and ends, all of which are of standard quality or higher. A must if you're looking to pick up a top or two on the cheap.

Galleries

At the forefront of showcasing independent art is **Gallery Art Factory** (Václavské náměstí 15, tel. 224 217 585, www.galleryartfactory.cz, Mon.–Fri. 10 A.M.–6 P.M.). Its 5,382-square-foot exhibition space serves both internationally respected artists as well as the hungrier ones who are just coming up. The gallery's biggest triumph is its annual event, "Sculpture Grande," where large, thought-provoking sculptures are exhibited publicly all up and down Wenceslas Square.

The finest painters and sculptors in the country are regularly exhibited at **Galerie Gambit** (Mikulandská 6, tel. 224 910 508, www.gambit.cz, Tues.–Fri. noon–6 P.M.). Anything goes here, from more traditional works inspired by the streets of Prague to airy, metallic installations that bend perspectives and meaning. A must for any art aficionado.

The **Jiří Švestka Gallery** (Biskupský dvůr 6, tel. 222 311 092, www.jirisvestka.com, Tues.–Fri. noon–6 P.M., Sat. 11 A.M.–6 P.M.) is the Czech Republic's first and foremost private gallery, showcasing internationally known Czech artists like Krištof Kintera and Jiří Černický, as well as young artists looking to carve their niche in the global art scene. Modern, contemporary art is the gallery's focus, with a particular taste for the unapologetically innovative.

Gifts

As their website says, **Hard-de-core** (Senovážné náměstí 10, tel. 777 094 421, www.harddecore.cz, Mon.–Fri. 11 A.M.–7 P.M., Sat. 11 A.M.–5 P.M.) is an art workshop, design studio, and boutique all in one. You'll find plenty of original clothing here, as well as accessories, ceramics, jewelry, books, and a whole lot more. Art classes are also held on the premises, where aspiring artists or mere hobbyists can take a variety of classes, including pottery, painting, and interior design.

A veritable institution, **Jan Pazdera** (Vodičkova 28, tel. 224 216 197, Mon.–Sat. 10 A.M.–6 P.M.) is the first shop all photographers visit when they need to replace a piece of equipment without breaking the bank. You'll find all sorts of used cameras here sitting alongside lenses, binoculars, microscopes, and various hard-to-find Russian cameras like Smenas and Zenits, as well as Leicas. If you're interested in photography or know somebody who is, this shop is a must.

Body Basics (Myslbek Center, Na příkopě 19-21, tel. 224 236 800, Mon.–Sat. 9 A.M.–8 P.M., Sun. 10 A.M.–7 P.M.) is a bath-taker's dream. Wall-to-wall lotions, scrubs, soaps, shower gels, and bath salts are the shop's signature, with plenty of helpful gift-basket options for men who can't help but feel a little overwhelmed.

Glass

One of the few interesting shops in Černa růže shopping center is **Moser Praha** (Na Příkopě 12, tel. 224 211 293, www.moser-glass .com, Mon.–Fri. 10 A.M.–8 P.M., Sat.–Sun. 10 A.M.–7 P.M.). Established by Ludwig Moser in Karlovy Vary in 1857, Moser went on to become one of the most respected glassmakers in the world. Known for its elegant beauty and extravagant designs, Moser Glass always makes for a unique, if slightly expensive, gift.

Slovimex Praha (Betlémské náměstí 2, tel. 222 220 521, www.slovimex-crystal.cz, daily 10 A.M.–6 P.M.) is one of the finest shops in Prague specializing in handcrafted products made from glass and crystal. Using production methods dating back to the 14th century, all items are manufactured by masters in their field who have been involved with this work for a number of generations. From candle-sticks to decanters, vases to carafes, lovers of glass are sure to find something that strikes their fancy.

Jewelry

BeldaFactory (Mikulandská 10, tel. 224 933 052, www.belda.cz, Mon.–Thurs. 10 A.M.–6 P.M., Fri. 10 A.M.–5 P.M.) is a unique Czech jewelry company founded in 1915. Known for their classy, contemporary and original designs, their name has become synonymous with quality and style. If you're interested

in buying the special woman in your life a special gift, this is the place to start looking.

Jablonex (Dům módy, Václavské náměstí 58, tel. 234 101 114, www.jablonexgroup.com, daily 10 A.M.–7 P.M.) is a world-renowned Czech costume jewelry manufacturer representing the traditions of glass and jewelry production that are unique to north Bohemia. Their two new luxury brands, Amorike and Fried Freres, have met with great success, with the latter making a splash in Parisian fashion circles. At their Wenceslas Square branch you'll find classic Czech glass design along with trendy fashion pieces at reasonable prices.

Markets

Market at the Fountain (Spálena 30, daily 7:30 A.M.–7 P.M.) is a congregation of kiosks located right behind Tesco. Out-of-town farmers come in to peddle their fruit and vegetables, most of which are both cheaper and a fair taste better than what you'll find at, well, Tesco, for example. Various snacks, knick-knacks, and weather-appropriate clothing are also sold here at a reasonable price.

Shopping Centers

The **Palladium** (Náměstí Republiky 1, tel. 225 770 250, www.palladiumpraha.cz, daily 7 A.M.–3 A.M.) opened in October 2007, reviving the commercial area surrounding Náměstí Republiky. Designed with a sense of both the traditional and modern in mind, its natural lighting, fountains, and shopping pavilions have been a big hit so far with shoppers, who have roughly 160 stores and 30 restaurants and bars to choose from. With popular shops like Sony, Body Shop, Puma, and Marks & Spencer, as well as restaurants representing the most popular cuisines from around the world, odds are the Palladium will be a strong commercial contender for a long time to come.

Rather uninspired despite a couple of name brands like Adidas and Pierre Cardin, **Černa růže** (Na Příkopě 12, www .cernaruze.cz, Mon.–Fri. 9 A.M.–8 P.M., Sat. 10 A.M.–7 P.M., Sun. 11 A.M.–7 P.M.) leaves most of its visitors feeling like spending their money elsewhere. Worth taking a peek on the off-chance you'll find a bargain, but don't say you weren't warned.

Myslbek Center (Na Příkopě 19-21, tel. 224 239 550, www.myslbek.com, Mon.–Sat. 8:30 A.M.–8:30 P.M., Sun. 9:30 A.M.–8:30 P.M.) bustles from the opening bell, with tourists and locals darting in and out of name-brand stores looking for the day's best deal. Pizza Coloseum and Sushi Point are located on the ground floor and first floor respectively, giving shoppers and non-shoppers at least two excellent reasons to come here.

Slim, over-priced pickings in the fashion department does not a successful mall make, which is why a visit to **Slovanský Dům** (Na Příkopě 22, tel. 221 451 400, www.slovansky dum.cz, daily 10 A.M.–8 P.M.) only makes sense if you are visiting the excellent Kogo Ristorante or Ambiente Brasileiro. There is a Palace Cinemas Multiplex, too, which makes for an entertaining and air-conditioned option should you need a break from the crowds or summer heat. Matinee, anyone?

STARÉ MĚSTO
Antiques
If you're looking for accessories that date back to the 1920s or '30s, **Art Deco** (Michalská 21, tel. 224 223 076, Mon.–Fri. 2–7 P.M.) is your best bet. This fun, swingin' store has tons of interesting clothing and bric-a-brac from Prague's golden age and the friendly staff will help you sift through all the stuff until you find that treasure you've been looking for all these years.

Bric a Brac (Týnská 7, tel. 222 326 484, daily 11 A.M.–7 P.M.) is a small shop that is crammed floor to ceiling with countless pieces ranging from the antique to the truly bizarre. Antique vases, typewriters, musical instruments, cigarette cases, and Communist-era signs and uniforms are but a few of the interesting items available here. Although slightly pricy, a bit of hunting around should uncover a few bargains. This should be one of your first stops if you're stuck for souvenir or gift ideas.

Lovers of Art Deco design will do themselves a great service by paying a visit to **Kubista** (Ovocný trh 19, tel. 224 236 378, Tues.–Sun. 10 A.M.–6 P.M.). Located on the ground floor of Dům U Černé Matky Boží (House of the Black Madonna), visitors have the opportunity to buy exclusive reproductions of original designs by Czech Art Deco masters like Pavel Janák and Josef Gočár. Original furniture from the period, as well posters, postcards, and books are also available.

Books and Music
Anagram Bookshop (Týn 4, tel. 224 895 737, www.anagram.cz, Mon.–Sat. 10 A.M.–8 P.M., Sun. 10 A.M.–7 P.M.) can be accessed either through its lovely courtyard on Týn or via Štupartská Street. An excellent selection of all the newest releases can be had here, as well as interesting volumes covering art, design, history, and science to name but a few. Their new location at Ruzyně Airport mercifully ensures travelers they'll have more to choose from than usual suspects John Grisham and Danielle Steel.

Conveniently located between Náměstí Republiky and Old Town Square is **BigBen Bookshop** (Malá Štupartská 5, tel. 224 826 565, www.bigbenbookshop.com, Mon.–Fri. 9 A.M.–6:30 P.M., Sat. 10 A.M.–5 P.M., Sun. noon–5 P.M.), where you'll find an excellent selection of new titles, classics, travel guides, children's books, and non-fiction. The shop's friendly staff is always ready to lend a helping hand and will happily order whatever book you're desperately trying to track down. A must for all book lovers.

Disko Duck (Karlova 12, tel. 222 221 696, www.diskoduck.cz, daily noon–7 P.M.) is situated a stone's throw from the Charles Bridge and offers pretty much everything today's hip DJ needs. New 12" vinyl and CDs from around the world are imported regularly, adding to their already 5,000-strong record collection ranging from house, hip-hop, techno, and jungle. DJ equipment like turntables, mixers, needles, and headphones is also available. Who said vinyl was dead?

Fashion

Timoure et Group–TEG (V Kolkovně 6, tel. 222 327 358, www.timoure.cz, Mon.–Fri. 10 A.M.–7 P.M., Sat. 11 A.M.–5 P.M.) is a well-known Czech fashion design duo that is popular with local celebrities. Creating minimalist ready-to-wear collections in their own distinct, downplayed style, you'll find their sophisticated line of clothing and accessories are perfect for any occasion.

Klara Nademlynska (Dlouhá 3, tel. 224 818 769, www.klaranademlynska.com, Mon.–Fri. 10 A.M.–7 P.M., Sat. 11 A.M.–6 P.M.) is one of the most respected fashion designers in the country. Known for her originality, imaginative combinations, and seductive, classy clothing, her boutique is full of her unique Bohemian chic.

Parazit (Karlova 25, www.parazit.cz, Mon.–Sat. 11 A.M.–8 P.M.) is an alternative fashion dream come true with non-conformist and independent Czech designers showcasing their original clothing and accessories. A wide range of tastes is represented, from extravagant to casual to haute couture. This is where hip, in-the-know-locals come to do their shopping.

Boheme (Dušní 8, tel. 224 813 840, www.boheme.cz, Mon.–Fri. 11 A.M.–7 P.M., Sat. 11 A.M.–5 P.M.) is the brainchild of Hana and Jan Stocklassa and has been producing top-quality clothing since 1991. Their bread and butter is knitwear that includes sweaters, turtlenecks, cardigans, and skirts, but they also have some fantastic leather and suede, along with the appropriate accessories. A favorite of local celebrities, Boheme manages to strike a balance between classy yet comfortable clothing.

Galleries

Galerie Jakubská (Jakubská 4, tel. 224 827 926, www.galeriejakubska.cz, daily 11 A.M.–7 P.M.) revolves around the bold work of Ukrainian-born impressionist painter Alexandr Onishenko. Exhibited all over the world, his vibrant paintings depict lush landscapes, life-like animals, and a haunted, Gothic view of Prague many attempt to capture but fail. Many of the paintings available here stay with you long after you've left.

Galerie Art Praha (Staroměstské náměstí 20, tel. 224 211 087, www.galerieartpraha.cz, Mon.–Sat. 10:30 A.M.–7 P.M.) has an extensive collection of paintings from some of the more daring and innovative Czech and Slovak artists of the 20th century. The staff here is extremely helpful and knowledgeable and will be more than happy to help you find exactly what it is you're looking for, even if you're unable to properly express what exactly that is.

The Prague branch of the **Dorotheum** (Ovocný trh 580, tel. 224 222 001, www.dorotheum.cz, Mon.–Fri. 10 A.M.–7 P.M., Sat. 10 A.M.–5 P.M.) was founded in 1992 and it began to hold auctions regularly in 1995. Today, it ranks as the country's largest auction house, hosting four of them a year at the Renaissance Hotel. Its modern gallery shop boasts an excellent range of artwork that includes paintings, antiques, jewelry, glass, silver, and porcelain, making it not only one of the more comprehensive galleries in town, but one of the best as well.

Gifts

Just off Na Příkopě is **Dům Hraček Sparkys** (Havířská 2, tel. 224 239 309, www.sparkys.cz, Mon.–Sat. 10 A.M.–7 P.M., Sun. 10 A.M.–6 P.M.). Three colorful floors are filled with toys ranging from stuffed animals to board games and action figures. Affordable and centrally located, this is the place to come to when it's time to get something for the kids.

Growing all the necessary ingredients on their organic Gardens Complex in the tiny village of Ostrá, **Dr. Stuart's Botanicus Shops** (Týn 3, tel. 234 767 446, www.botanicus.cz, daily 10 A.M.–6:30 P.M.) offer health and beauty products with a natural touch. Whether it's cosmetics, soaps, teas, spices, or candles you're looking for, you'll be able to buy it here and feel good about not hurting dear Mother Earth in the process.

Herrero (Karlova 23, tel. 224 221 232, www.herrero.cz, daily 10 A.M.–9 P.M.) proudly carries the time-honored tradition of blacksmithing into the new millennium. Specializing in household furniture and furnishings, they combine centuries-old techniques with modern stylistic trends to produce unique items for the home such as beds, tables, chairs, and candlestick holders. This is an excellent opportunity to pick up something with authentic Czech history attached to it that will last longer than most trinkets found on this street.

Glass

One of the more creative consumer combinations in Old Town is **Arzenal** (Valentinská 11, tel. 224 814 099, www.arzenal.cz, daily 10 A.M.–midnight), which showcases original work by world-renowned artist Borek Šípek and houses an excellent gourmet Thai restaurant as well. Šípek was commissioned to build the Kyoto Opera in Japan, along with fashion designer Karl Lagerfeld's shop in Paris, and was responsible for architectural changes made to Prague Castle in the early 1990s. Admired all around the world, this beautiful shop never fails to impress with his wide range of colorful, expressive designs. The restaurant downstairs is well worth sampling, too.

Cristallino (Celetná 12, tel. 224 225 173, www.cristallino.cz, Jan.–Mar. daily 9 A.M.–7 P.M., Apr.–Dec. daily 9 A.M.–8 P.M.) is a huge shop near Old Town Square offering one of Prague's largest selections of both traditional and modern glassware from the country's foremost designers. Bohemian crystal, porcelain, and jewelry can be found here, too, not to mention gorgeous chandeliers and unique folk art that make for memorable gifts. The friendly and knowledgeable service you get here is a breath of fresh air from other, stuffier establishments.

Located in a beautifully restored, neo-Renaissance building between Old Town Square and Charles Bridge, **Rott Regena Crystal** (Malé náměstí 3, tel. 224 229 529, www.czech crystal.com, daily 10 A.M.–9 P.M.) is home to four floors of gorgeous glassware, ceramics, and jewelry, as well as fine Bohemian and imported crystal that would look great in any home. Easily one of the prettiest shops in Prague, it is also one of its priciest.

Jewelry

Blue Rabbit (Karlova 12, tel. 222 220 121, daily 10 A.M.–7 P.M.) is a brightly colored jewelry store specializing in handmade accessories that go perfectly with all things fun. Filled with earrings, necklaces, brooches, and more, you're bound to find something here for either you or your best friend. Affordable and innovative, this shop is a welcome relief from all the neighboring, mass-produced schlock passing for souvenirs.

Markets

Melantrichova Street picks up where Wenceslas Square leaves off, connecting it with Old Town Square. Halfway to the Old Town, you'll come upon open-air **Havelský Market** (Havelská Street, Mon.–Fri. 7:30 A.M.–6 P.M., Sat.–Sun. 8:30 A.M.–6 P.M.). This is still an excellent place to get fresh fruit and vegetables, although many of the stalls have given themselves over to the tourist trade, hawking anything from paintings to wooden knick-knacks. Careful browsing should land you a decent deal or two.

Specialty Shops

Qubus (Rámová 3, tel. 222 313 151-2, www .qubus.cz, Mon.–Fri. 10 A.M.–6 P.M.) is undoubtedly one of Prague's coolest home decor boutiques. Selling conceptual pieces by Czech designer Maxim Velčovský, as well as a diverse selection of European furnishings, the shop is full of sleek and modern furniture, cute utensils, and accessories and popular gift items like flower vases shaped like a pair of white porcelain boots.

de.co by de.fakto (Perlová 6, tel. 224 218 326, www.defakto.cz, daily 10 A.M.–8 P.M.) is a funky boutique specializing in decorations for the home and designer kitchenware. Loads of interesting gift ideas here from subtly silver clocks to brightly colored cutlery, glasses, and bowls.

Smokers may be a dying breed, but don't tell **Baker Street** (Celetná 38, tel. 224 231 117, www.baker-street.cz, Mon.–Fri. 10 A.M.–7 P.M., Sat. 10 A.M.–6 P.M., Sun. 1–5 P.M.). A full-on smoke shop dedicated to a habit that's still going strong in Europe, this is where one can find high quality pipes, cigars, chewing tobacco, lighters, humidors, and a decent selection of top-notch cognacs and whiskeys. You won't find the healthiest of gifts in this shop but if you or someone you know smokes, you'll definitely find an appropriate gift here.

MALÁ STRANA
Antiques
Ahasver (Prokopská 3, tel. 257 531 404, www.ahasver.com, Tues.–Sun. 11 A.M.–6 P.M.) is a pretty little shop in the prettiest part of town dealing primarily with antique and folk clothing. A wide range of gowns and accessories are available, including purses, brooches, jewelry, and lace. A step back in time if there ever was one.

Vetešnictvi (Vítězná 16, tel. 257 530 624, daily 10 A.M.–4 P.M.) is a veritable grab bag of antiques, historically significant items, and good old-fashioned junk. Dig around and you'll find just about anything here, including furniture, tools, medals, postcards, beer mugs, and god knows what else. A lot of this stuff is from the Communist era, which might explain the bust of Lenin overseeing the shop.

Books and Music
Shakespeare & Sons (U Lužického semináře 10, tel. 257 531 894, www.shakes.cz, daily 11 A.M.–7 P.M.) does little to curb the exorbitant prices locals are forced to pay in order to remain literate but you will find an excellent selection of books ranging from cookbooks to gender studies to psychology and sci-fi. Lots of Czech authors and high lit as well, which make for a pleasant afternoon of reading in nearby Kampa Park.

Fashion
A new addition to the Malá Strana scene is vintage tattoo-wear king **Ed Hardy** (Karmelitská 22, tel. 774 100 699, www.edhardy.cz, daily 10 A.M.–8 P.M.), whose colorful clothing has made a splash with celebrities and the street-conscious alike. This is the biggest shop of its kind in Europe and second only to HQ in Los Angeles. Clothes and accessories include fashionable jackets, pants, hats, and bags.

Another fashionable shop for the younger, urban set is **Represent** (Saská 6, tel. 257 535 321, www.represent.cz, daily 10 A.M.–8 P.M.). Located on a tiny side street just behind Charles Bridge, its shelves and walls are full of casual, trendy clothing and accessories for the skateboarder, snowboarder, and/or hip-hop star in all of us.

Galleries
If you'd like a painting of Prague that isn't a cheap knock-off bought from Charles Bridge, have a look at what's on offer at **Gallery Left Bank** (Mišenská 10, tel. 257 534 940, www.gallery-leftbank.com, daily 10 A.M.–6 P.M.). Co-owned by Jiři Štastný, whose work is also on display, the gallery is home to lively, colorful paintings depicting the lighter side of the capital in all its Bohemian glory. There are also plenty of abstract and representational works by various Eastern European artists portraying all aspects of life ranging from the sublime to the macabre. This is one of the more imaginative galleries in a neighborhood choked with them.

Galerie Kodl (Vítězná 11, tel. 251 512 728, www.galeriekodl.cz, Mon.–Fri. 10 A.M.–1 P.M., 2–6 P.M.) is a family tradition that dates back over 100 years. Both an auction house and gallery, the paintings, drawings, graphics, and sculptures on display represent some of the finest talent working in the country today. Known throughout the continent for their professionalism and expertise, this is a must stop for art lovers looking to expand their collections.

The work of internationally acclaimed Ukrainian artist Roman Zuzuk is on display at the **Zuzuk Gallery** (U Lužického semináře 20, tel. 257 533 403, www.zuzuk.cz, daily 9 A.M.–7 P.M.), just around the corner from Charles Bridge. Inspired by nature and the folklore of his native land, his pictures are bright with an occasional twist of the humorous or grotesque. Run by his happy-go-lucky brother Miro, the gallery also plays host to up-and-coming Ukrainian artists looking to make a name for themselves in the art world.

Gifts

Just a few steps past Charles Bridge, in a building that was once known as U bílé růže (At the White Rose), sits the highly successful **Manufaktura** (Mostecká 17, www.manufaktura.biz, daily 10 A.M.–7 P.M.). Describing themselves as "inspired by nature," their products are 100 percent Czech made and include wooden toys, Czech crafts, and natural cosmetics. A refreshing alternative to the usual fare found on this street.

A gift from Prague that never fails to make an impression is a hand-crafted marionette, which is exactly what you'll find under Charles Bridge at **ObchodPod Lampou** (U Lužického semináře 5, tel. 606 924 392, www.marionety.com, daily 10 A.M.–8 P.M.). A far cry from the mass-produced, miniature examples one can find on any tourist-lined street, this shop takes special care in order to preserve the unique quality any fine doll should have. Sure it's a little pricey, but it'll remind you of magical Prague for the rest of your long life.

If you take your first left coming off Charles Bridge, you'll find the **Czech Beer Shop** (Lázeňská 15, tel. 257 532 687, www.czechbeershop.com, daily 10 A.M.–6 P.M.) selling bottles and cases and kegs, oh my! Just about any Czech beer worth its salt is available here and you'll be wise to inform yourself of whatever customs laws apply to you before making a large, impulsive purchase. Then again, you could always take your haul to Kampa Park and imbibe it there.

From teddy bears to bedroom sets, **L'Architecte de l'Enfant** (Karmelitská 18, tel. 257 530 421, www.vibel.com, Tues.–Fri. 10 A.M.–6:30 P.M., Sat. 9 A.M.–3 P.M.) has got everything your adorable young son or daughter might need. Vibrant colors and imaginative themes such as Space, Fish, and Cat create a warm, affectionate environment any parent would envy. Buying the heavy furniture on display certainly isn't practical but you're bound to find some very pretty accessories that might not be available back home.

Sports and Recreation

Keeping active and fit is a national pastime in the Czech Republic, which explains why the problem of obesity that has plagued North America hasn't reared its ugly head here. Traditional activities like hiking and swimming are de rigueur on the weekends, as Czechs head for their cottages and spend countless hours in their beloved forests and rivers. Cycling and in-line skating are very popular, too, with countless couples and groups of friends suiting up and hitting the trails. The upwardly mobile and business-oriented have gotten in on the act as well, generating an interest in golf and squash that was practically non-existent a mere five years ago. Interest in sport has continued to grow, bringing with it an increase and improvement in facilities that have made it easier than ever for visitors to maintain a healthy lifestyle during their stay.

CLIMBING

Rock climbing has been growing in popularity in the Czech Republic for some years now and the spacious **Sport Centrum Evropská** (José Martího 31, Dejvice, tel. 220 172 309, www.sportcentrumevropska.cz, daily 7 A.M.–11 P.M.) offers enthusiasts one of the better indoor walls to practice on. The multi-purpose sports center also offers squash, bowling, table tennis, and aerobics. Reservations are a very good idea, if not essential.

CYCLING

One fun way to travel around Prague is by bicycle and **City Bike** (Králodvorská 5, Staré

Město, tel. 776 180 284, www.pragueonline .cz/citybike, Apr.–Oct. daily 9 A.M.–7 P.M., 3 bike tours 10 A.M., 2 P.M., and sunset) is the place to seek out should you feel the same way. Their rental rates are affordable, and they also offer free group rides three times a day, led by locals who know the city well.

FITNESS CENTERS

Delroy's Gym (Zborovská 4, Smíchov, tel. 257 327 042, www.delroys-gym.cz, Mon.– Fri. 7 A.M.–10 P.M., Sat. 9 A.M.–9 P.M., Sun. 9 A.M.–10 P.M.) has been the martial arts center of choice for Czechs, foreigners, politicians, visiting celebrities, and the like since Delroy Scarlett established it in 1993. Friendly, affordable, and relatively near the center, this is a great place to go if you need to take out some frustration on a punching bag or simply hit the weights in a friendly environment.

Housed in the relatively new Marks & Spencer Building is the **Oasis City Relaxation Center** (Václavské náměstí 36, Nové Město, tel. 224 210 146, www.oasiscity.cz, Mon.–Sat. 8 A.M.–9 P.M., Sun. 8 A.M.–10 P.M.), a state-of-the-art fitness center whose sole purpose is to relieve you of the day's troubles. Aside from an excellent aerobics room, the center also boasts its own Aqua Spa—a wonderfully relaxing facility that comes complete with sauna, steam room, and whirlpool. In a continuing effort to pamper their clientele, Oasis City also offers manicures, pedicures, massage, and hairdressing services. Children are welcome, too, as friendly, qualified staff are more than happy to keep them occupied on Robinson Crusoe's Island—home to clowns, theater, painting, and a whole lot more.

If all that heavy Czech food is starting to make you feel a little sluggish, head for **Sportcentrum YMCA** (Na Poříčí 12, Nové Město, tel. 224 875 811, www.scymca.cz, Mon.–Fri. 6:30 A.M.–10 P.M., Sat.–Sun. 10 A.M.–9 P.M.). You'll find the same services that people have come to expect from the YMCA, including a weight room, swimming pool, sauna, and massage. Less busy than most gyms and more affordable to boot, the Y is a

reasonable alternative when you're looking for a simple workout without the frills.

Certainly the most central and arguably the most fashionable, **World Class Fitness Center Prague** (Václavské náměstí 22, Nové Město, tel. 234 699 100, www.worldclassfitness.net, Mon.–Fri. 6 A.M.–11 P.M., Sat. 7 A.M.–10 P.M., Sun. 10 A.M.–10 P.M.) is an enormous, multi-level health club spanning over 19,000 square feet and offering everything any health nut could want. Whether it's aerobics, weights, saunas, tanning beds or a wide range of cardio machines you're looking for, look no further. Popular with the young and affluent set, you can avoid the crowds by coming here in the middle of the day.

GOLF

Golf has started to catch on in the Czech Republic and the **Erpet GolfCentrum** (Strakonická 2860/4, Smíchov, tel. 257 321 177, www .erpet.cz, daily 8 A.M.–11 P.M.) has established itself firmly as *the* indoor golf center in town. The center comes complete with a two-story driving range, four golf simulators offering players more than 30 world-renowned courses to choose from, as well as the Astar Learning system, which helps users perfect their swing. Popular with the emerging business class, reservations are recommended should you feel like hitting the links.

Golf Club Praha (Plzeňská 401/2, Smíchov, tel. 257 216 584, www.gcp.cz, daily 7 A.M.–sunset) is Prague's only outdoor course, a nine-hole affair that also includes a training area, clubhouse, and restaurant. Falling short of most golf enthusiasts' expectations, the course may cure your immediate itch to get a game in, but won't satisfy it completely.

ICE SKATING

Attached to the Hotel Hasa is the **USK Praha Hotel Hasa** (Sámova 1, Vršovice, tel. 271 747 128, www.hotelhasa.cz, Mon., Tues., Thurs., Fri. 9 A.M.–11 A.M., Wed. 9 A.M.–11 A.M., 4–5:30 P.M., Sat.–Sun. 10 A.M.–noon), a large ice rink that is open to the public when not being used by the USK Praha figure skating team. The hours listed are tentative so make sure you call ahead to confirm that the rink isn't booked by the country's future Olympians.

Zimní stadion Štvanice (Ostrov Štvanice 1125, Holešovice, tel. 602 623 449, www.stvanice .cz) is the oldest indoor ice rink in the Czech Republic and it shows. Rickety and more than a little rather rough around the edges, it's open to the public when not hosting tournaments or house league games. Worth a stop if you happen to find yourself in the Holešovice area. Its hours are: Monday 10 A.M.–noon, 2:30–4:15 P.M., Tuesday 10:30 A.M.–noon, 3–6 P.M., Wednesday 10 A.M.–noon, 3–5 P.M., 6:45–8:15 P.M., Thursday 10 A.M.–noon, 3–6 P.M.; Friday 10:30 A.M.–noon, 3–6 P.M., 6:30–9:30 P.M., Saturday 9 A.M.–noon, 2–5 P.M., 8–10 P.M., Sunday 9 A.M.–noon, 2–5 P.M.

IN-LINE SKATING

Arguably the best place for in-line skating in Prague, **Ladronka In-line Park** (Ladronka Park—Ke Kotlářce and Plzeňska Streets, Dejvice, tel. 775 082 858, www.ladronka.cz, daily noon–9 P.M.) provides a flat, perfectly refurbished, 2.4-mile-long surface completely devoid of pedestrians, dogs, or baby carriages (they have their own path). Admittedly, Ladronka's a little off the beaten path but many flock to it, having tired of the incessant crowds at both Letná and Stromovka Parks.

SQUASH

You can imagine how quickly a mere three courts fill up when located right on Wenceslas Square. **ASB Squash Centrum Praha** (Václavské náměstí 13-15, Nové Město, tel. 224 232 752, www.asbsquash.cz, Mon.–Fri. 7 A.M.–11 P.M., Sat.–Sun. 8 A.M.–11 P.M.) is usually booked solid by the white-collar contingent, which leaves you no other choice but to reserve early and hope the economy's having a busy day.

A big hit with the business crowd, **Squash Centrum Haštal** (Haštalská 20, Staré Město, tel. 224 828 561, www.squashe.cz, daily 7 A.M.–11 P.M.) serves up top-of-the-line squash courts in a soothing, temperature-controlled environment. Typically full before normal

working hours begin (7–9 A.M.) as well as after they end (5–7 P.M.), your best bet is to try your hand—or racket—during the middle of the day. Reservations are recommended, however, as the place does steady business thanks to its central location.

SWIMMING

Prague's outdoor pools tend to fill up quickly during the summer but if crowds aren't what you're looking for, try the indoor pool at **Hotel Axa** (Na Poříčí 40, Nové Město, tel. 227 072 150, www.hotelaxa.com, Mon.–Fri. 7 A.M.–11 P.M., Sat.–Sun. 9 A.M.–9 P.M.). Rarely occupied and open all year long to both guests and the public, this 82-foot-long pool is a great place to get in a good swim either at the beginning or the end of your day.

A veritable landmark in the field of sports facilities, **Plavecký Stadion Podoli** (Podolská 74, Podoli, tel. 241 433 952, www.pspodoli .cz, pool daily 6 A.M.–9:45 P.M., sauna Mon.–Fri. 10 A.M.–9:30 P.M., Sat.–Sun. 9 A.M.–7:30 P.M.) hasn't changed much over the decades but remains as popular as ever. The large outdoor pool is jam-packed during the warmer months with people of all ages while the Olympic-sized indoor pool attracts a far more dedicated and athletic group. You'll also find a weights room, sauna, and fitness shop on the premises, as well as a huge lawn for soaking up rays during the summer.

Located in the middle of **Divoká Šárka** in Dejvice is an excellent outdoor swimming pool that is open daily 10 A.M.–6 P.M. in June and 9 A.M.–7 P.M. in July and August (may be open in September if weather permits). Admission is 50 Kč for those over the age of 10, 20 Kč for kids 5–10, free for kids under 5, and 40 Kč for senior citizens.

TENNIS

Founded in 1893, **ČLTK** (Štvanice 38, Holešovice, tel. 222 316 317, www.cltk.cz, daily 7 A.M.–midnight) is easily the Czech Republic's oldest and most prestigious tennis club. Located on Štvanice Island in Holešovice, the complex offers 14 outdoor clay courts as well as 6 indoor courts. Their central court hosts up to 8,000 people and is the annual scene of various ATP and WTA tournaments. Reservations here are absolutely necessary.

Neighboring the Letná Beer Garden is **Tenisový Klub Slavia Praha** (Letenské sady 32, Holešovice, tel. 233 374 033, www.volny.cz/tkslavia, indoor Nov.–Mar. daily 7 A.M.–11 P.M., outdoor Apr. 15–Oct. 15 daily 7 A.M.–9 P.M.). Equipped with eight outdoor clay courts along with a tennis bubble for the colder months, this well-respected tennis club also offers tennis lessons and hosts year-round tournaments.

YOGA

Located right off Old Town Square is **Centrum Lotus** (Dlouhá 2, Staré Město, tel. 224 814 734, www.centrumlotus.cz, various times), a very friendly Buddhist center that is also one of Prague's better-known spots for yoga. Some classes are offered in English but if you find they're all full, try a Czech one. The classes are relatively simple and the instructor will occasionally offer a few words in English to help you follow. Tai-chi classes are also on offer here, as are a variety of interesting lectures and seminars for fellow Buddhists.

Laid-back, friendly, compassionate, and refreshingly down-to-earth are just some of the adjectives used to describe Monica Angelucci of **Prague Yoga with Monica Angelucci** (Plavecká 12, Nové Město, tel. 777 028 371, www.pragueyoga.cz, various times). A big hit with foreigners, Monica tailors her classes specifically to whatever exercises the group feels like pursuing on any given day, adjusting the level of difficulty accordingly. Always available to her students, she is well known for her unwavering patience with beginners and also offers classes especially designed for pregnant women and those with special injuries.

SPECTATOR SPORTS

If you ask a Czech what the national sport is, odds are they'll shrug their shoulders and tell you it's a toss-up between hockey and soccer. When it comes to the former, the Czech Republic has plenty to boast about. Not only have they consistently placed near the top of every important international tournament, including winning the gold medal at the 1998 winter Olympics, they also have a remarkable amount of superstars dominating the NHL, including Jaromir Jagr and Dominik Hašek. And while their soccer team isn't quite as impressive, world-famous players like Pavel Nedvěd have kept World Cup hopes alive and fans riveted to their TV sets. Most players who demonstrate excellence in either sport tend to head for larger markets and bigger paychecks, but that doesn't stop Czechs from following both sports religiously, filling up hockey rinks and soccer stadiums every time playoff season arrives. Tickets are very affordable and the possibility of seeing tomorrow's stars play their hearts out today adds an element of excitement to the games that is often lacking in more established leagues.

Ice Hockey

Having settled in nicely at Sazka Arena, **HC Slavia Praha** (Sazka Arena, Ocelářská ulici, Vysočany, www.hc-slavia.cz) finally won its first championship in 2003. The team's die-hard fans make going to any game a unique experience but if you really want to see them go rabid with emotion, make sure to get a ticket when they play long time rivals HC Sparta Praha.

HC Sparta Praha (T-Mobile Arena, Za elektárnou 419, Holešovice, tel. 266 727 443, www.hcsparta.cz) is Prague's most popular hockey team. Well-financed and well-managed, they dominate during the regular season and are consistently a force to be reckoned with during the playoffs. Tickets are always available for home games, though you might want to think about reserving in advance when it comes to post-season play.

Soccer

AC Sparta Praha (Toyota Arena, Milady Horákové 98, Holešovice, tel. 220 570 323, www.sparta.cz) is without a doubt the most successful soccer team in the country. They won their 34th Czech championship in 2007 and continue to be a thorn in the side of larger, better-known teams during international tournaments. Known for their rowdy and faithful fans, a trip to one of their matches is a must for any serious fan of the game.

Playing in a modestly sized stadium to fans who for the most part look like they cashed their pension checks on the way to the game, **FK Viktoria Žižkov** (Stadion FK Viktoria Žižkov, Seifertova 130, Žižkov, tel. 222 722 045, www.fkviktoriazizkov.cz) is the city's underdog, to say the least. Nobody expects much from this team, especially since they were relegated in 2003 and nailed for match-fixing in 2004. Back in the first division, nobody considers them to be a challenge for the league title but that doesn't stop their loyal fans from coming out and enjoying the day, if not the game.

Despite its devoted fans and ability to occasionally overcome unbeatable odds, **SK Slavia Praha** (Stadion Evžena Rožického, Strahov, tel. 233 081 751, www.slavia.cz) continues to place second in the division standings behind cross-town rivals Sparta Praha. Currently, the team plays in Rožicky stadium, which has suffered plenty of criticism due to its location atop a steep hill and atmosphere-crushing running track that encircles the playing field.

Horse Racing
Running April–October, **Chuchle** (Radotínská 69, Radotin, tel. 257 941 431, www.velka-chuchle.cz) offers flat racing every Sunday starting at 2 P.M. The Czech Derby is held here in June, giving fans one last opportunity to enjoy a day at the track before closing up shop till the end of August. Those interested in betting on the ponies should take note that bookmakers are not allowed at the track. Rather, a tote betting system is in place that pools all bets and shares the total among the winning tickets. There is also a very unpopular 5 percent betting tax added to all bets.

Accommodations

Prices keep going up as Prague continues to establish itself as one of Europe's hottest travel destinations. Great deals can still be found online, however, with many hotels offering package deals and holiday specials. Booking in advance will save you some cash, as will having your meals and drinks away from the hotel's premises, where prices are considerably cheaper.

NOVÉ MĚSTO
New Town is the hub of all things commercial and tourist-oriented, which means staying here guarantees you a wide selection of hotels, restaurants, and shops. It also means you'll be right in the thick of things, part of the mass that moves up and down Wenceslas Square and the surrounding area. Many like the energetic feel of the district, while others tire quickly of the bustle and late-night antics of drunken revelers. Its proximity to Old Town, as well as Vinohrady and Žižkov, make staying here a strategically wise choice if you plan on doing some exploring outside of the downtown core.

1,000-2,000 Kč
What **AZ Hostel** (Jindřišská 5, tel. 224 241 664, www.hostel-az.com, 1,200 Kč d) may lack in character, it more than makes up for in location. Being within spitting distance of Wenceslas Square is about as central as it gets and it guarantees you will see all of what downtown has to offer without ever having to step foot on a subway or tram. The 1–6-bed rooms plus dormitory are clean and spacious, and the staff is on call 24 hours a day should you need assistance. It may not have the charm of some of the more colorful hostels in town but you'll get maximum value in terms of price and convenience.

Opinions vary wildly as to the quality of the **Golden Sickle Hostel** (Vodičkova 10, tel. 222

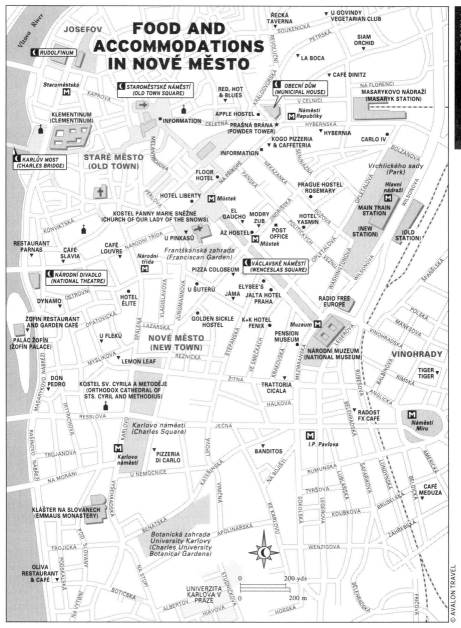

FOOD AND ACCOMMODATIONS IN NOVÉ MĚSTO

230 773, www.goldensickle.com, 1,400 Kč d) but nobody can argue with its location a mere stone's throw away from Wenceslas Square. Average-sized with relatively clean rooms and free Internet, the major complaints seem to be the lack of security (insist on a locker!) and the fact that people tend to stumble in drunk at the end of night, crossing through your room to get to theirs. Very laid back and an excellent place to meet fellow travelers, this hostel will do just fine if you're only planning on staying a handful of days.

Another affordable option just minutes from both Wenceslas and Old Town Square is **Prague Hostel Rosemary** (Růžová 5, tel. 222 211 124, www.praguecityhostel.cz, 1,400 Kč d). On offer are 1–6-bed rooms with private bathroom and kitchen, less-expensive 2–6-bed private rooms that share a bathroom, and a dormitory. Clean and friendly, there are two computers that offer free Internet and a common room where you can meet other like-minded travelers. Pretty basic fare but the price is right and the location is top-notch.

Considering its close proximity to Wenceslas Square, Old Town Square, and Charles Bridge, **Apple Hostel** (Náměstí Republiky 7, entrance Králodvorská 16, tel. 224 231 050, www.applehostel.cz, 1,700 Kč d) is ridiculously cheap. Then again, no one has ever accused it of being super-clean or comfortable. Very bare bones and a magnet for the hungover and restless, it may not be for everybody—especially non-smokers. Good for a couple of days if you can handle roughing it a little and need to save your cash.

2,000-3,000 Kč

Pension Museum (Mezibranská 15, tel. 296 325 186, www.pension-museum.cz, 2,920 Kč d) is located literally steps from the National Museum and the top of Wenceslas Square. Most rooms are relatively clean and of a decent size, although it's in your best interest to request one facing away from the street as tourists and cars galore travel up and down it all day and night. Nothing too fancy here and the staff is rather hit and miss. But if not wanting to deal with taxis

or needing somewhere to lay all those shopping bags down before going out to dinner is important to you, then this is one affordable place you should definitely consider.

3,000-4,000 Kč

Reasonably priced and located a mere 330 feet from Wenceslas Square, **U Šuterů** (Palackého 4, tel. 224 948 235, www.usuteru.cz, 3,100 Kč d) is an excellent choice for those looking to spend moderately without sacrificing comfort and convenience. The loft at the top of the hotel's spiral staircase is lovely, as are the rest of the rooms, which are decorated with traditional period furniture. Their restaurant is also known throughout the city for its excellent goulash and is frequented by local politicians and celebrities.

Floor Hotel (Na Příkopě 13, tel. 234 076 300, www.floorhotel.cz, 4,000 Kč d) finds itself right on Na Příkopě, Prague's busy pedestrian shopping area, which just happens to be conveniently close to Old Town and Wenceslas Square. Focusing on classical luxury balanced out with a healthy dose of modernism, the Floor Hotel should appeal to most travelers who like being smack dab in the middle of a city's ebb and flow. Those preferring a quiet, secluded type environment should definitely seek elsewhere. All the expected amenities are to be found here and more than one guest has mentioned enjoying staying in room 101.

4,000-5,000 Kč

Opened in the spring of 2006, **Hotel Yasmin** (Politických vězňů 12, tel. 234 100 100, www.hotel-yasmin.cz, 4,700 Kč d) has been the accommodation of choice for those who like their hotels modern yet warm. Pale green walls, big hairy sculptures, floating trees, and ornaments are just some of the decorative curiosities you'll be surrounded in. All rooms and suites are immaculately kept and come equipped with minibar, air conditioning, LCD-screen TVs, and Internet. There's a nice gym and sauna as well, and their Restaurant Café Bar "Noodles" offers tasty cuisine hailing from all four corners of the earth. Although situated on a relatively quiet side street, take the extra precaution if you're a light sleeper and request a room on one of the higher floors or facing away from traffic.

Like all K+K Hotels, the **K+K Hotel Fenix** (Ve Smečkách 30, tel. 225 012 000, www .kkhotels.com, 4,950 Kč d) offers its guests spacious and tidy communal areas, clean and comfortable rooms, and excellent facilities that include sauna, fitness center, and massage. The breakfast served is one of the better to be found around town and comes complete with champagne. Its location near a couple of cabaret clubs may be a little off-putting to some but is in no way threatening. Plenty of shops, restaurants, theaters, and sights are within a few minutes' reach and the reception desk will happily suggest and set up any type of program you please.

5,000-6,000 Kč

Many are initially surprised to find the entrance to **Elysee** (Václavské náměstí 43, tel. 221 455 111, www.hotelelysee.cz, 5,400 Kč d) located inside a shopping arcade just off Wenceslas Square. Despite its close proximity to the unceasing bustle of the boulevard, most of the 70 rooms here are very quiet, although some are enclosed and therefore don't offer a view. Modern furnishings, tight security, and an overall clean environment make this hotel a smart option in the center of town.

Housed in a 14th-century building on a quiet side street located minutes from Wenceslas Square, Old Town, New Town, Malá Strana and more, the **Hotel Élite** (Ostrovni 32, tel. 224 932 250, www.hotelelite.cz, 5,950 Kč d) is what you'd expect from a typical, quaint European hotel. The rooms are on the small side but clean and the staff is helpful and friendly. Try to get a room overlooking the courtyard or splurge for the junior suite if romance is why you're in town.

Over 6,000 Kč

Hotel Liberty (28. října 11, tel. 224 239 598, www.hotelliberty.cz, 6,200 Kč d) offers 32 colorful and luxurious rooms and suites that come complete with antiques, chandeliers, and all the modern amenities one looks for in a boutique

hotel. Some rooms offer a balcony or terrace, affording guests pretty views of Prague Castle. Their motto, loosely translated, is "Our rooms don't only have numbers, they have souls as well," and one does sense that their stylish, spacious rooms are indeed living things, as opposed to the often stark, characterless accommodations of the bigger chains.

You'll find 94 clean, modern, and functional rooms smack dab in the center of tourist town at **Jalta Hotel Praha** (Václavské náměstí 45, tel. 222 822 111, www.jalta.cz, 6,750 Kč d). Some of the rooms overlook Wenceslas Square offering wonderful views in both directions and the courteous staff is more than happy to arrange anything you might need. The trendy and reputable HOT restaurant is located on the ground floor as well, which is definitely worth a meal or two should you have the time or inclination.

Opulent, elegant, and unforgettable are just some of the words visitors use to describe **C Carlo IV** (Senovážné náměstí 13, tel. 224 593 111, www.boscolohotels.com, 9,000 Kč d), located in a neoclassical building just a short walk away from the Powder Tower. From its grand reception hall to its very comfortable (although sometimes small) rooms, one is immediately and completely immersed in old-world charm and style. The fantastic spa and pool area boasts subdued lighting, as well as fruit and drinks, making it the perfect spot for some much needed rest and relaxation.

STARÉ MĚSTO

From humble hostels to old-world luxury and charm, Old Town's got it all. Unlike Nové Město's commercial vibe, the streets here radiate history, the architecture makes you feel like you're on the set of a fairy tale, and the nightlife is arguably the finest the city has to offer. Most of your time will probably be spent in and around Old Town anyway so why not set up camp here as well?

1,000-2,000 Kč

If you're planning on staying in one of the dorms, you can forget about getting any sleep at **Travellers' Hostel** (Dlouhá 33, tel. 224 826 662, www.travellers.cz, 1,300 Kč d). People come and go at all hours and the aftermath of any given night looks like a frat party gone wrong. Opt instead for one of the rooftop apartments, which are simple but clean, comfortable, and spacious. Being a block away from Old Town Square has its obvious advantages, as does staying next to the Roxy—one of Prague's biggest and best clubs. Keep in mind that there tends to be a very long waiting list here so make sure you book well in advance, particularly during the high season.

Relatively new on the scene, **Old Prague Hostel** (Benediktská 2, tel. 224 829 058, www.oldpraguehostel.com, 1,320 Kč d) is one minute's walking distance from Old Town Square and all the restaurants, bars, and sights that come with it. Free breakfast, linen, lockers, and Internet are definite pluses here, as is the availability of non-smoking rooms—always hard to find in Prague. There are rooms ranging from 2–8 beds, along with a suite that accommodates five. The staff hasn't been accused of being the friendliest, but that's a common enough complaint. One tip is to make sure you don't get a room that's attached to the common room. Not if you want to get any sleep, that is.

2,000-3,000 Kč

Simple yet tasteful rooms is what you get at **Pension Corto** (Havelská 15, tel. 224 215 313, www.corto.cz, 2,950 Kč d), a very affordable and very centrally located boutique-style bed-and-breakfast. First-floor rooms look out onto outdoor market Havelská Tržnice, while guests staying on the top floor (the fifth) should be aware that there is no elevator, due to the buildings historic, and therefore heritage-protected, status. As a result, the newly reconstructed attic rooms up top come at a slightly cheaper price. All rooms come with satellite TV, WiFi, and kettle. Excellent value is what you can expect here.

3,000-4,000 Kč

If it's an unconventional holiday you're after, try staying at the **Botel Albatros** (Nábřeží Ludvíka Svobody, tel. 224 810 547, www.botelalbatros.cz, 3,080 Kč d). This boat-hotel on the tranquil Vltava River offers 82 rooms and four apartments; while the boat's quarters may not be the most spacious and luxurious you've ever seen, its summer terrace and bar offer outstanding views of Hradčany and Prague Castle more than makes up for it. Located away from the hustle and bustle, though only a 5–10-minute walk away from it, this is a great option for those who seek something a tad adventurous while keeping the costs down.

Haštal Hotel (Haštalská 16, tel. 222 314 335, www.hastal.cz, 3,500 Kč d) is situated on quiet Haštal Square opposite St.Haštal Church. Nothing fancy here: just simple, spacious, and secure rooms with comfortable bathrooms and a summer courtyard/cafe out back. If you can, request room #22, which comes with a pretty wrought-iron balcony overlooking the church and square. Two doors down is Chez Marcel, an excellent French bistro that is perfect for either dinner or drinks. Note that the hotel offers a 20 percent discount if you reserve online.

U Zlaté studny (Karlova 3, tel. 222 220 262, www.uzlatestudny.cz, 3,500 Kč d) is located in a beautiful UNESCO-protected building whose history can be traced back to the 16th century. Lots of charm here with wooden beams, antique furniture, and the occasional hand-painted ceiling providing guests with a sense of history and culture that eludes the international chains. Its location in the heart of Old Town's busy pedestrian area will either have you lauding its proximity to everything or cursing the human traffic. Choose wisely.

◖ **U Zlatého jelena** (Štupartská 6/Celetná 11, tel. 222 317 237, www.hotel-u-zlateho-jelena.cz, 3,600 Kč d) is a charming little hotel whose lack of pretension gives guests that "home away from home" feel that's getting harder and harder to find these days. The staff is pleasant, the rooms are large and decorated with antique furnishings, the bathrooms are luxurious, and the breakfast is generous. Being located about 100 paces from Old Town Square doesn't hurt either. This is where you

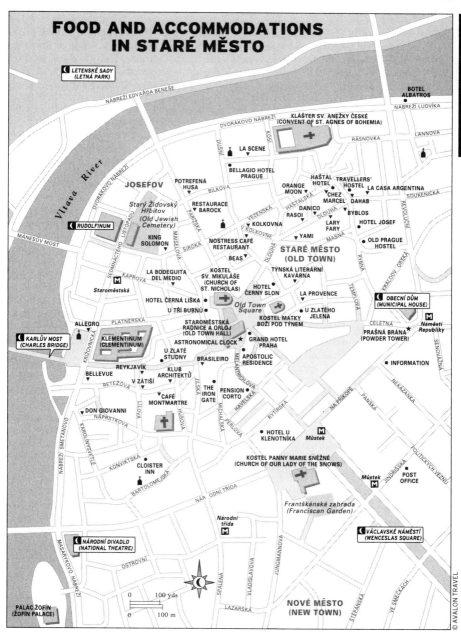

FOOD AND ACCOMMODATIONS IN STARÉ MĚSTO

want to be if you favor the down-home and authentic over the slick, plastic, and contrived.

Built in the 15th century and located a little over 300 feet from Old Town Square is **U Tří Bubnů** (U radnice 8 & 10, tel. 224 214 855, www.utribubnu.cz, 3,700 Kč d). There is a very strong sense of the traditional and unspoiled here, with large, tastefully decorated rooms providing a much warmer atmosphere than most of the slick, new hotels springing up these days. Part of its traditional atmosphere includes the lack of an elevator, however, so those not interested in climbing the original stone staircase every day should arrange for a room on one of the lower floors.

Hotel U Klenotníka (Rytířská 3, tel. 224 211 699, www.uklenotnika.cz, 3,800 Kč d) is a small, three-star, family-run operation located a few steps away from Wenceslas Square and a couple of minutes from Old Town Square. There are 11 tastefully furnished, air-conditioned rooms available and the friendly staff is always willing to advise on nearby restaurants or help you plan a daily trip out of the city. Those not insisting on or looking for the luxury that comes with five-star hotels will be more than happy here. One note: There is no elevator and climbing a healthy number of steps every day can be a rather trying experience for some. Mercifully, a dumbwaiter deals with the luggage.

4,000–5,000 Kč

Hotel Černý slon (Týnská 1, tel. 222 321 521, www.hotelcernyslon.cz, 4,900 Kč d) is a Gothic building that was built during 1330–1340 and is UNESCO-listed and protected. Sixteen big rooms with wooden floors are available, some of which look out onto charming Old Town Square streets where one can lose hours watching the people pass by. Quaint, cozy, and competitively priced, it fills up fast so make sure to reserve well in advance. There is no elevator so book accordingly.

5,000–6,000 Kč

Built in the second half of the 14th century, the building now housing **Hotel Černá Liška**

(Mikulášská 2, tel. 224 232 250, www.cernaliska .cz, 5,100 Kč d) has survived through some hairy times, including a fire in 1945 during the Prague uprising. Today it offers 12 lovely rooms, most of which overlook Old Town Square all the way across to Týn Church. The rooms are comfortable and spacious, blending modern touches with old-world design like wooden beams and beautiful painted ceilings. Some may not like the fact that staying here means you're right in the thick of things tourist-wise, while others will find it a godsend.

Arguably the hippest boutique hotel in Old Town, the ◖ **Hotel Josef** (Rybná 20, tel. 221 700 111, www.hoteljosef.com, 5,400 Kč d) offers 109 stylish, sound-proofed rooms: many of which are non-smoking and overlook a pretty and rather large courtyard. Bathrobe, slippers, Aveda bath products, and complimentary daily mineral water are just a few of the perks that come with staying here, and their famous glass-walled bathrooms (found in the Superior rooms) are something you won't forget any time soon. Rooms 704 and 801 are especially luxurious and come with impressive views of Prague Castle and the countless spires of Old Town Square.

While certainly not a luxurious hotel, the **Cloister Inn** (Konviktská 14, tel. 224 211 020, www.cloister-inn.com, 5,700 Kč d) offers excellent value for the money. A very helpful and efficient staff keeps the large, spacious rooms here clean as a whistle and is more than willing to advise you on the large number of restaurants, bars, and shops in the vicinity. Minutes away from Old Town Square, Wenceslas Square, and the Vltava makes it a very practical and convenient choice.

Over 6,000 Kč

Directly opposite the Astronomical Clock is the fantastic **Apostolic Residence** (Staroměstské náměstí 26, tel. 221 632 206, www.prague -residence.cz, 6,300 Kč d). The large and immaculate rooms are furnished with antiques and sport luxurious bathrooms that are very well appointed. Those with a bit of money to burn should opt for the impressive attic apartment, which consists of two bedrooms, linked by a spiral staircase, with en-suite baths. It also boasts soaring ceilings, huge beams, and oak floors, not to mention an incredible view of the Astronomical Clock and the people that gather on an hourly basis to watch its mini puppet show. The noise of drunkards spilling out onto the square at the end of the night might bother some, so make sure your room has double glazing or bring some earplugs. If you're a particularly light sleeper and don't mind sacrificing the tremendous view, ask for room 205, which overlooks a quiet courtyard.

Owned by the same folks who run Apostolic Residence, the neighboring **(C Grand Hotel Praha** (Staroměstské náměstí 22, tel. 221 632 556, www.grandhotelpraha.cz, 6,300 Kč d) is another luxurious hotel offering jaw-dropping views of the Astronomical Clock and Týn Church. Elegant yet understated, the hotel offers all modern amenities, including wireless in the rooms and an office area, along with a wonderful sauna and outdoor/indoor cafe—which at times results in the hotel smelling a lot like a warm, fuzzy pastry. Lots of gleaming woods, green marble, and brass fittings, a delicious buffet-style breakfast, and large, comfortable rooms (#211 and #213 are excellent examples) make this a sure shot. Make sure to book a room with a view, however. There really is no point to pay this much otherwise.

Originally a residential building, the **Bellagio Hotel Prague** (U Milosrdných 2, tel. 221 778 999, www.bellagiohotel.cz, 6,500 Kč d) was completely rebuilt during 2002–2003 and is now a four-star hotel offering 46 luxurious rooms in the heart of Josefov. Designed in a warm Italian style, the hotel goes out of its way to make you feel at home with some of the most helpful and pleasant staff you'll find anywhere. Another plus is that its location is not in the middle of all the nonstop activity of Old Town and Wenceslas Square. However, those sights, as well as a plethora of restaurants, museums, shops, bars, etc. are only a few minutes' walk away. Large enough to warrant its four-star rating yet small enough for it be personal

and relaxed, the Bellagio continues to make its guests' stay a memorable one.

The Iron Gate (Michalská 19, tel. 225 999 902, www.irongate.cz, 9,400 Kč d) is located on a quiet side street just off Old Town Square, away from the throngs of tourists. Decorated with remarkable wooden painted ceilings and frescoes dating back to the 14th century, it provides guests with that old European charm many pay top dollar to experience. Rooms range in size from the Deluxe Room (410 square feet) to the stunning Tower Suite (764 square feet) which spans three floors and has a heart-shaped bedroom. An excellent and omnipresent staff does everything they can to make your stay as comfortable as possible, including leaving chocolates on pillows and Evian on the table. Pricey but memorable.

MALÁ STRANA

The hotels are a little pricier in Lesser Town but considering Charles Bridge, Kampa Park, Petřín Hill, and Prague Castle are all close by, that little extra goes a long way. Smaller in size than either Nové or Staré Město, its small, winding side streets provide intimacy and comparative quiet when night comes, as stag parties and pleasure seekers migrate back over to the other side of the Vltava.

2,000–3,000 Kč

Spanning three buildings on Nerudova and two a little higher up on Úvoz, **The Castle Steps** (Úvoz 3 & 26, Nerudova 4, 10 & 33, tel. 257 216 337, www.castlesteps.com, 2,000 Kč d) is perfect for the frugal-class traveler. Visitors have a choice of choosing from rooms and apartments, with most rooms being decently sized and, although rather Spartan, very clean. The drawback for some guests might be that they must share a bathroom with another room. The apartments are bigger, boast private bathrooms, fridges, kettles, and some even have their own kitchen. Considering its proximity to the Castle and Malá Strana, there really is no better value around these parts than this. Two things to keep in mind, however: The steps are numerous (as the hotel's name implies) so if you're not that mobile, don't bother staying here. Secondly, the breakfast that comes with the price is vegan, which may or may not interest you. Should you decide to go with this place make sure to book early as all five buildings fill up rather quickly.

3,000–4,000 Kč

For excellent value at the foot of Petřín Hill, try **U Kříže** (Újezd 20, tel. 257 313 272, www .ukrize.com, 3,650 Kč d). Reliable, friendly service and a peaceful atmosphere is what you can expect here, with Kampa Park, Charles Bridge, and the National Theatre only minutes away. The 16 rooms and suites are furnished simply and kept extremely clean. Some overlook Petřín, which makes for a pleasant view but light sleepers might be kept up at night due to the trams that run past. If that's the case, just ask for a room overlooking the atrium.

Another great deal to be found in Malá Strana is **Hotel U žluté boty** (Jánský vršek 11, tel. 257 532 269, www.zlutabota.cz, 3,700 Kč), on a quiet side street near the foot of Prague Castle. Its seven double rooms and one studio make this a small, intimate hotel/B&B, which is reflected in the friendly, helpful attitude of the staff. Very clean, super comfortable, and enveloped in warmth, you'll get excellent value here. One slight drawback to consider is that the walls are paper thin, so fingers crossed for a quiet neighbor!

If you like family-run hotels that offer professional service and care, then **Dům U velké boty** (Vlašská 30, tel. 257 532 088, www .dumuvelkeboty.cz, 3,760 Kč d) is for you. This 12-room bed-and-breakfast is operated by the very hospitable Rippl family and is one of the best-kept secrets (until now) Malá Strana has to offer. Large, clean rooms furnished with comfortable beds and lovely antiques await you. While there is no TV in any of the rooms, you'll hardly miss it. Minutes away from Charles Bridge and Petřín Hill makes the location hard to beat and the hotel's peaceful surroundings will help you enjoy the kind of sleep you look forward to when going on vacation. If a friendly personal touch, coupled with

simple yet elegant surroundings, is what you're looking for, then look no further.

Situated at the foot of lovely Petřín Hill stands the **Hotel Roma** (Újezd 24, tel. 222 500 222, www.hotel-roma-prague.com, 3,500 Kč d), a relatively new, modern-looking hotel featuring 25 gorgeous suites and 62 spacious double rooms. The hotel's lovely reception area houses a bar, offers free Internet, and is home to a terrific aquarium that includes an impressive-looking and mostly friendly shark. Close to many sights including Charles Bridge, Kampa Park, and the National Theatre, the hotel is also near to many excellent restaurants, including Le Bastille, Cantina, and Bohemia Bagel. A tip for those who appreciate a good balcony: Make sure to ask for room #310.

Located on a quiet side street a mere stone's throw from Malostranské náměstí is the **Hotel U Tří Čápů** (Tomášská 20, tel. 257 210 779, www.utricapu.com, 3,900 Kč d). Boasting 10 deluxe double rooms, eight standard double rooms, and two single rooms, the hotel is the neighborhood's newest addition in luxury accommodations. All rooms are equipped with air-conditioning, minibar, safe, telephone, LCD TV, and DVD player with a wide array of films available. Spacious, clean, and modern, and sporting one of the friendliest hotel staff in town, the Hotel U Tří Čápů is an excellent choice for those wanting to spoil themselves in the middle of picturesque Malá Strana.

5,000–6,000 Kč

Halfway up Nerudova on the way to Prague Castle, **Hotel U Brány** (Nerudova 21, tel. 257 534 050, www.ubrany.cz, 5,700 Kč d) offers 10 large apartments in a 15th-century, modestly decorated building. As there are relatively few rooms, the atmosphere is a very homey one and owner Vanda Topinková works effortlessly to keep that vibe alive. All rooms come with private bathroom, satellite TV, minibar, and safe and the huge attic apartment offers a pretty, panoramic view of Prague Castle. The semi-steep climb to get to the hotel may not be for everyone, but it's well worth it considering its very central location and proximity to all major sights.

Over 6,000 Kč

At the top of Nerudova Street you'll find **Zlatá hvězda** (Nerudova 48, tel. 257 532 867, www .hotelgoldenstar.com, 6,300 Kč d), whose building dates back to 1372 when it functioned as the Mayor of Hradcany's residence. Located a convenient two-minute walk away from Prague Castle and St. Vitus Cathedral, its rooms are bright, high-ceilinged, and well furnished. Do yourself a favor and request (in advance) a room on the fourth floor, where the views are simply mesmerizing. Friendly and helpful staff top off this excellent choice.

Rezidence Lundborg (U Lužického semináře 3, tel. 257 011 911, www.lundborg .se, 6,500 Kč d) is a luxurious Baroque hotel housed in a 700-year-old building offering 13 apartments and suites (no rooms) that are located literally at the end of Charles Bridge. All suites come fully equipped with TV, free Internet, whirlpool tub, kitchen, sound system, original wooden Renaissance ceilings, and magnificent views overlooking the bridge. Suites range from the Junior Suite (323 square feet) to the Imperial Suite (1507 square feet), and all are bathed in quality and comfort, making this one of the better places in town to rest your weary head.

If you're a lover of music, start saving your money now for a stay at the incomparable **◖ Aria Hotel** (Tržiště 9, tel. 225 334 111, www.ariahotel.net, 8,500 Kč d). Each of its four floors is dedicated to a particular genre of music, with every stylishly decorated room honoring an artist in said genre. From Vivaldi to the Beatles, all rooms are stocked with original artwork, books, and music that pay tribute to the artist in question. Apart from the beautiful decor peppered with fresh, exotic flowers throughout, this boutique hotel also boasts an executive conference room, private screening room for up to 40, music salon, winter garden, fitness center, and much, much more. All rooms also have a computer and DVD hook-up with an extensive library of movies and music available at your fingertips. Exceptional staff and extras like complimentary fruit bowls, dressing gowns, slippers,

and Molton Brown toiletries only add to the unique experience and may be enough to keep you from wondering what might be going on in the Bob Marley room.

Depending on your point of view, being located next to the heavily guarded American Embassy makes the **◖ Alchymist Grand Hotel & Spa** (Tržiště 19, tel. 257 286 011, www.alchymisthotel.com, 9,400 Kč d) either the safest or most dangerous place in Prague. This remarkable boutique hotel showcases Italian opulence at its finest with an abundance of Rococo, Art Deco, and gold mirrors decorating its premises. An incredible spa and steam room are available, as is a gorgeous swimming pool that comes complete with overhanging chandelier. For those who like to mingle, there's a gathering every evening at 5:30 P.M. with complimentary wine and cheese. A few of the amenities to be found in the Deluxe Rooms (which are smallest) are plasma TV, DVD/CD player, safe, Internet, and gorgeous marble-floored bathrooms. The suites, meanwhile, are in a class of their own. Although one of the more expensive hotels in town, the Alchymist is also one of the finest you'll find in Europe.

HRADČANY

Accommodation in the castle district is going to cost you, but most would argue that a stay in this peaceful, historic, and incredibly romantic part of town is absolutely priceless. Slightly removed from the action yet close enough to all the main sights and districts, Hradčany is an excellent choice for families or couples looking for a quieter type of getaway.

1,000–2,000 Kč

The Golden Horse House (Úvoz 8, tel. 603 841 790, www.goldenhorse.cz, 1,650 Kč d) is the perfect choice for the unpretentious traveler on a budget. Two simple, self-contained apartments are offered, each with their own bathroom, TV, and Internet connection. Clean, Spartanly furnished and two minutes from the Castle, this is easily the best deal in the district. Book well in advance.

4,000-5,000 Kč

Domus Henrici (Loretánská 11, tel. 220 511 369, www.domus-henrici.cz, 4,800 Kč d) is hidden down a quiet street in the middle of Prague Castle, Strahov Monastery, and the Loreto, offering its guests a warm, neighborhood-type feel away from the hordes of tourists that dominate the city's center. Redesigned in 2006, it boasts four double rooms, three deluxe doubles, and a suite, all of which come equipped with HDTV, Dolby surround stereo, and corner baths. Room #6 has a magnificent view of the city and a leisurely stroll downhill will take you into Malá Strana and beyond. Those who shudder at the thought of walking back uphill, fear not. Prague's excellent public transport system will whisk you right up and deposit you just up the road from the hotel. Excellent value for the money means you should book well ahead.

5,000-6,000 Kč

Situated a few steps away from Prague Castle between Strahov Monastery and Loreta Square is **Hotel Questenberk** (Úvoz 15, tel. 222 407 600, www.questenberk.cz, 5,300 Kč d), a beautiful Baroque building that underwent complete reconstruction in 2002. Looking more like a church than an upscale hotel, it sports 26 double rooms with four king suites that are tastefully furnished. The hotel's finest room is #406, which is set in the attic with original wooden beams, has two windows offering panoramic views of Golden Prague and boasts a superb en-suite bathroom. Book well in advance.

The **C Romantik Hotel U Raka** (Černínská 10, tel. 220 511 100, www.romantikhotel-uraka.cz, 5,600 Kč d) is a charming, unique, and above-all comfortable hotel within walking distance of the Palace Gardens. Run and designed by photographer Alexandr Paul and his daughter Aneta, guests are made to feel welcome immediately upon arrival—so much so that they come to feel they are staying at a five-star hotel rather than an intimate rustic inn with a combined total of six rooms. Once settled in, take a stroll through picturesque Nový Svět, a street well known for its ability to spark romance and conveniently located just 10 minutes away from Prague Castle. After the day's sightseeing is over, return to the hotel and relax in its peaceful garden with a glass of champagne and wonder why anyone would want to stay anywhere else. This is a perfect place for romantic couples—not so much for families or party animals. Book early.

Over 6,000 Kč

Originally the residence of Roman Emperor and Bohemian King Rudolf II, as well as famous astronomer Tycho de Brahe, **U Zlaté studně** (U Zlaté studně 166, tel. 257 011 213, www.goldenwellhotel.com, 6,900 Kč d) is drenched in history. Renovated in 2000, it has all the modern amenities one looks for in a hotel without sacrificing any of its old-world charm. Four floors house 18 rooms and two suites, all designed with beautiful reproductions of antique pieces from the 17th, 18th, and 19th centuries. The service is courteous and professional, starting with a champagne reception upon each guest's arrival. Make sure to check out their pillow menu—one more detail to help make your stay as comfy as possible. And consider this fair warning: The view of Prague stretching out before you while having breakfast or coffee on their terrace will make you think twice about getting to the airport on time.

Charming, old fashioned, and swanky enough for the likes of Madeleine Albright, Sean Connery, and the Red Hot Chili Peppers, **Hotel Savoy** (Keplerova 6, tel. 224 302 430, www.hotel-savoy.cz, 10,200 Kč d) is a five-star hotel with a price tag to match. Large comfortable rooms with luxurious baths and excellent views (particularly on the eighth floor) are topped off with complimentary robes, slippers, and minibar. Top-of-the-line facilities include a whirlpool tub, fitness center, sauna, and a more-than-competent masseuse who can always be found in the hotel's "Relax Center." Located in Prague's diplomatic quarter, the Savoy makes for a quiet, elegant, and rather extravagant choice.

DEJVICE

Primarily a residential district, Dejvice is also home to gorgeous Divoká Šárka and a large number of beautiful ambassador's villas. The airport and city center are a mere 20 minutes away by both bus and metro, making this area a favorite with those who prefer some distance between where they play and where they stay.

Under 1,000 Kč

They certainly aren't much, but the rooms offered at Strahov college student dorm **Hostel SPUS Strahov** (Chaloupeckeho ul. Block 4, tel. 220 513 419, open July 1–Sept. 20, 540 Kč d) are easily the best deal around. Spartan as they come, each room has two simple beds, while shower and toilet facilities are located on each floor and shared. There are a couple of bars on a campus, as well as a small shop, and Prague Castle is only a 10–15-minute walk away. This is an ideal choice for the backpacker on a tight budget who just needs a basic yet clean place to crash and isn't worried about any frills.

5,000-6,000 Kč

Deep in Dejvice lies **Hotel Villa Schwaiger** (Schwaigerova 59/3, tel. 233 320 271, www .villaschwaiger.cz, 5,400 Kč d), a pretty villa offering 22 luxurious rooms amongst ambassadors' residences and sprawling, soothing Stromovka Park. The specialty rooms like the Zen-like "Chinese Room" or the "Provencal Room," with its southern flavor and flair, are interesting additions to this very well-kept and professional hotel. One drawback to this otherwise lovely place is its distance from public transport, forcing guests to either learn the bus/metro system quickly or shell out for a cab. On the other hand, the excellent restaurant-pub Na Slamníku is located directly across the street. It may not look like much from the outside, but venture in and enjoy an authentic Czech experience, including excellent Czech cuisine and beer at local (i.e., cheap) prices.

Over 6,000 Kč

The **Diplomat Hotel Prague** (Evropská 15, tel. 296 559 111, www.diplomatpraha.cz,

6,500 Kč d) is the last stop on the airport bus's route and is located next to the Dejvicka subway station. This may explain why vast numbers of tour groups regularly fill its 398 rooms and suites. The decor is dated and the service, while good, may not live up to some peoples' Western standards, but the rooms are spacious, clean, and more than adequate. Depending on your taste, you'll find its being away from the city center either a plus or minus. However, Malá Strana is two subway stops away, Old Town Square is three, and Wenceslas Square is four. All can be reached within minutes, as can lovely Divoká Šárka, one of Prague's finest (and largest) parks.

HOLEŠOVICE

Slightly off the beaten path, Holešovice is nevertheless a good choice for those who want to throw themselves into an authentic Prague environment. Small, locally owned businesses are what you'll find here, along with a healthy mixture of hip locals and expats who populate the area's bars and restaurants. Letná and Stromovka parks are nearby, too, enabling one to enjoy pleasant afternoon walks and hours of beer garden goodness.

1,000-2,000 Kč

Completely renovated in 2005, **A&O Hostel** (U Výstaviště 1, tel. 220 870 252, www.aohostels .com, 1,250 Kč d) is a clean, comfortable option located directly opposite Prague's Exhibition Grounds and sprawling Stromovka Park. All rooms come with their own private facilities and single and double rooms have cable TV as well. The famous "Underground Bar" is located in a spacious, well-lit wine cellar that is home to spontaneous parties and the infamous A Bombs (absinthe and Red Bull) that are served at midnight. A metro station, three trams, and a night tram make everything you want to see around town easily accessible.

❰ Sir Toby's Hostel (Dělnická 24, tel. 283 870 635, www.sirtobys.com, 1,450 Kč d) is hands down one of the finest hostels in town. The rooms are quiet, clean, bright, and spacious, complete with rolling lockers found under the bed and loads of hot water. The staff is friendly and helpful and there's free Wi-Fi and coffee and tea to boot. The 90 Kč all-you-can-eat breakfast is tasty but pricey; those who hunt around will easily find better deals. Its location away from the center may not appeal to some but it's a simple 10-minute tram ride away and most people come to appreciate the distance from the maddening crowds. This is a perfect place for those on a budget and not interested in the typical drink-till-you-drop hostel atmosphere.

3,000-4,000 Kč

Well it ain't fancy, but the **Hotel Belvedere** (Milady Horákové 19, tel. 220 106 111, www .hotelbelvedere.cz, 3,600 Kč d) gets the job done at a relatively reasonable price. The rooms are basic but clean and come with all the essentials: comfortable bed, safe, writing desk, coffeemaker, and decent-sized bathroom. Although a little far from the center, Stross-mayerovo náměstí is just down the street and all sorts of trams and buses can get you over the river and into Old Town in roughly 10 minutes. There are also a few good restaurants in the area, including Italian eatery Capua, which serves tasty and affordable fare. You won't see any monuments or tourist-filled squares here, but you'll be close and spend a fraction of the cost. Ideal for the frugal traveler who likes staying local and doesn't mind a lack of frills.

ŽIŽKOV AND VINOHRADY

Both districts are known for their numerous restaurants, pubs, and wine bars, as well as loyal residents who wouldn't change their location for the world. Close to the center yet far away enough to not be overwhelmed by it, both areas are perfect for those seeking vibrant surroundings and local character.

1,000-2,000 Kč

Its central location just a block and a half away from busy I.P. Pavlova and its corresponding metro station make **Hostel Advantage** (Sokol-ská 11, tel. 224 914 062, www.advantagehostel .cz, 1,350 Kč d) a very convenient and strate-gic choice. Rather large, it offers clean, spacious rooms with single beds (as opposed to bunks), as well as cheap beer and free Internet access (although you'll have to fight for computer time). There is also a *jídelna* across the street with cheap, tasty food—perfect for a backpacker's budget. On the downside, the bathroom and shower facilities lack privacy and smoking is allowed in the bedrooms.

The trek up the hill to get to **Clown & Bard** (Bořivojova 102, tel. 222 716 453, www .clownandbard.com, 1,400 Kč d) is not an en-viable one, especially if your backpack is on the heavy side, or if you're stumbling home after having had a little too much to drink. Never-theless, its relaxed, open, and extremely friendly atmosphere continues to attract travelers of all walks of life. The 32-bed dorm up top is as noisy as you'd expect it to be, but the smaller suites are considerably quieter. Cheap Internet, 24-hour reception, and a large breakfast are a few pluses, as is its location a mere 15 minutes from the center. Some are turned off by the rough-around-the-edges, dive-type feel that permeates throughout. While it's admittedly not for the squeamish, those who enjoy a little adventure in their hostelling will like it just fine.

Located on the edge of Žižkov, a breezy 15-minute walk from the center, is **Hostel Elf** (Husitská 11, tel. 222 540 963, www.hostelelf .com, 1,440 Kč d), a friendly, colorful environ-ment that seems to attract some of the better guests that come through town. Free Internet, breakfast, coffee, and tea are available and the 24-hour staff is usually very happy to help you find whatever it is you might need. There is also a common area that includes comfy couches and outdoor benches, which are often occupied by easy-going people you can talk to or have a drink with. The bathrooms could be a little bit cleaner and it can get noisy at night, but those staying for a relatively short while will hardly notice or care.

If a hostel exists out there that can be de-scribed as upscale, Ⓒ **Miss Sophie's Prague** (Melounova 3, tel. 296 303 530, www.miss -sophies.com, 1,790 Kč d) is it. Modern art and furniture evoke a cool, trendy setting where you can casually put up your feet and relax in style and comfort. The beds are soft, the pillows fluffy, the rooms spotless, and the staff polite to a fault (almost). Truth be told, Miss Sophie's is better than some of the higher-priced, over-rated hotels in the center trying to pass themselves off as comfortable lodgings. A tad more expensive than other hostels, but you'll notice where that little extra went immediately.

3,000-4,000 Kč

The **Hotel Seven Days** (Žitná 46/572, tel. 222 923 111, www.hotelsevendays.com, 3,300 Kč d) is housed in a building that dates back to 1888 and is now protected by the UNESCO Heritage List. Its 50 air-conditioned, tastefully furnished rooms come complete with cable/pay TV and Internet access, along with sufficiently spacious, clean bathrooms. Located within a couple minutes' walking distance from the National Museum and Wenceslas Square, you'll save a bundle on taxis and drop a few pounds in the process. Don't let the presence of a couple of sex shops across the street influence your opinion on the neighborhood. This is Bohemia, after all.

Over 6,000 Kč

Although it advertises itself as a four-star hotel, the **Ametyst** (Jana Masaryka 11, tel. 222 921 921, www.hotelametyst.cz, 6,300 Kč d) may fall short of some guests' Westernized expectations of that rating. Nevertheless, its 84 rooms are clean and comfortable and come with all the amenities one looks for while on holiday. Located in the heart of Vinohrady, it's a little farther away from the city's sights than other hotels, but the nearest metro stop is a five-minute walk away and Wenceslas Square a mere 15 minutes away. Vinohrady is an excellent residential district to explore and one can find many restaurants and wine bars full of Czechs and expats alike. One excellent example is nearby Hlučná Samota, a well-known restaurant/bar with affordable meals and delicious beer.

There are not enough superlatives to describe the experience at ❰ **Le Palais** (U Zvonařky 1, tel. 234 634 111, www.palais hotel.cz, 9,500 Kč d). A boutique hotel with 60 gorgeous rooms and 12 deluxe suites, it's the small touches that set this fantastic hotel apart. From the warm welcoming and hotel tour upon arrival, to the free minibar, turn-down service, chocolate on the pillow, and surprise rose petals and candles lining your bathtub, Le Palais goes out of its way to make you feel like royalty. The staff's kindness and attention to detail is unparalleled—so much so that you'll wish you had booked a longer stay. Highly recommended.

Food

Over the course of the last 10 years, Prague's restaurant scene has gone from dreary to diverse, resulting in a wide variety of cuisines and gourmet dining options. Apart from traditional Czech establishments serving classic mains like goulash, *svíčková* (beef in cream sauce), and pork, dumplings, and cabbage, diners can now gorge on any number of international dishes hailing from Afghanistan all the way to Zagreb. Service continues to improve as well, though it still has a way to go before reaching the friendly and prompt attention Western-ers are used to. Nevertheless, what was once a barren wasteland of unimaginative meat-heavy dishes and bland sauces has flourished into a tantalizing terrain of culinary sophistication even the most finicky palates can enjoy.

NOVÉ MĚSTO
American

Jáma (V Jámě 7, tel. 224 222 383, www.jama pub.cz, daily 11 A.M.–1 A.M., mains 125–355 Kč) is a friendly, American-run pub that has been a staple of the expat community since

1994. Serving up hearty hamburgers and tasty Tex-Mex with a smile, this is a good place to visit if you want to meet local foreigners or simply need a healthy dose of home.

Located opposite Kotva department store, **Red, Hot & Blues** (Jakubská 12, tel. 222 314 639, www.czrb.cz, daily 8 A.M.–midnight, mains 139–399 Kč) is another American-run establishment that set up shop shortly after the Velvet Revolution and has remained popular with the expat crowd after all these years. The menu centers on Tex-Mex and Cajun cuisine but also offers more traditional American fare like burgers and buffalo wings. Local bands provide live entertainment on a regular basis and there's even an adjoining video store stocked with all the latest titles.

Asian

Lemon Leaf (Myslíkova 14, tel. 224 919 056, www.lemon.cz, Mon.–Thurs. 11 A.M.–11 P.M., Fri. 11 A.M.–12:30 A.M., Sat. 12:30 P.M.–12:30 A.M., Sun. 12:30–11 P.M., mains 127–355 Kč) has won over some pretty loyal customers over the last couple of years—and with good reason. The menu includes standard steak and pasta dishes but it's the Thai food people come for. Crisp spring rolls and spicy chicken meatballs make for unbeatable appetizers, while the Panang curry pork with coconut milk, chili, lemon leaves, and rice seems to put a few smiles on faces as well. Elegant without being stuffy, this is a popular expat hangout and is the perfect place for a dinner date. A very affordable 99 Kč lunch special is offered during weekdays and includes a main course, soup, and/or rice.

Wenceslas Square is a bit of a culinary wasteland but one bright spot has opened up recently with new kid on the block **Modrý zub** (Jindřišská 5, tel. 222 212 622, www.modryzub .com, Mon.–Fri. 10 A.M.–midnight, Sat. 11 A.M.–midnight, Sun. 11 A.M.–11 P.M., mains 145–175 Kč) serving inexpensive, respectable Thai food to downtown's hipsters and food fans. The front area is reminiscent of a cafe and offers attentive and friendly service at the tables. Most of the action happens in the back, however,

where the take-out stand is. The menu ranges from Thai to Japanese to Indian and many swear by the *lab mu* or one of the various curries. The pad thai is a hit-and-miss affair, but Modrý zub is definitely worth the risk should you need a fast-food fix and can't bear the thought of another Big Mac or KFC combo.

Siam Orchid (Na Poříčí 21, tel. 222 319 410, www.siamorchid.cz, daily 10 A.M.–10 P.M., mains 160–280 Kč) is a no-frills, family-run establishment that offers tasty Thai food at very low prices. Located next to Bílá Labuť and hidden on the first floor of a building that also houses the Thai Fit massage salon, this colorful and friendly restaurant is a great place to stock up on chicken satay, fried tofu, and any number of spicy dishes before hitting the streets again and carrying on with your busy day.

Cafes

The first thing that strikes you about **Café Dinitz** (Na poříčí 12, tel. 222 314 071, www .dinitz.cz, daily 9 A.M.–3 A.M., mains 135–380 Kč) is its pretty Art Deco interior. It's enough to simply sip your coffee and admire the high ceilings, massive black tables, and leather-bound chairs until you're ready to leave. There's an upper floor as well that operates as a whiskey bar and when night falls, live music (either jazz or salsa) kicks in, prompting some merrymakers to jump out of their seats and groove along. The menu includes meat dishes, pastas, sandwiches, and burgers, and there's a business lunch menu offered during weekdays that's usually a steal.

Café Louvre (Národní 22, tel. 224 930 949, www.cafelouvre.cz, Mon.–Fri. 8 A.M.– 11:30 P.M., Sat.–Sun. 9 A.M.–11:30 P.M., mains 109–299 Kč) is a spacious, Parisian-style cafe right in the heart of downtown. Founded in 1902, it has seen the likes of Kafka and Einstein pass through its doors and is now regularly filled with tourists, local artists, and the business class. This is a perfect place to take a break from the bustling streets and unwind with a cup of coffee in elegant surroundings. The food is hit and miss, however, as are the desserts, so be warned. Non-smokers will be happy to know that a room has been provided for them and there are five pool tables that can be rented by the hour as well, should you care to get a game in before hitting the streets.

Opposite the National Theatre sits **Café Slavia** (Smetanovo nábřeží 1012/2, tel. 224 218 493, www.cafeslavia.cz, daily 8 A.M.–11 P.M., mains 139–339 Kč), a pleasant, Art Deco cafe that used to be the unofficial meeting place of the city's artists and intellectuals, including former President Václav Havel who was a regular during his dissident years. These days it's usually frequented by tourists during the day and the after-theater crowd at night. Try securing one of the window tables that offer gorgeous views of either the National Theatre or Prague Castle.

Continental

Lime green, local, and lively are just some of the things that spring to mind when visiting **Dynamo** (Pštrossova 29, tel. 224 932 020, daily 10 A.M.–midnight, mains 100–300 Kč). This is where the local hip crowd noshes on traditionally heavy Czech dishes, delectable salads, and vegetarian offerings like their popular grilled eggplant. Very reasonably priced and a whole lotta fun, Dynamo is an excellent choice this side of Národní. Their extensive collection of single-malt scotch is nothing to sneeze at either.

Offering generous portions of Czech and international dishes at modest prices has earned **Hybernia** (Hybernská 7, tel. 224 226 004, www.hybernia.cz, Mon.–Fri. 8 A.M.–11:30 P.M., Sat.–Sun. 10:30 A.M.–11:30 P.M., mains 129–490 Kč) a very loyal customer base, particularly at lunch time. Businesspeople, locals, and heads of state all drop in regularly, filling up its three rooms and (during the warmer months) quiet outdoor courtyard. Popular dishes include the ginger-marinated duck breast and chicken skewer with smoked salmon, bacon, and vinegar herb sauce.

Czech

A relatively high-priced Czech menu is what

Restaurant Parnas (Smetanovo nábřeží 1012/2, tel. 224 239 604, www.restaurant parnas.cz, daily noon–11 P.M., mains 290–590 Kč) is known for, along with having one of the most exquisite Art Deco interiors in the city, complete with white marble floors and chandeliers. The various grilled meat dishes are most popular here, which go down nicely while admiring the excellent view of Prague Castle and Charles Bridge that stretch out before you.

Housed in a building that dates all the way back to 1499, **U Fleků** (Křemencova 11, tel. 224 934 805, www.ufleku.cz, daily 9 A.M.–11 P.M., mains 185–365 Kč) is a pub, restaurant, and micro-brewery that is as traditional as they come. A large complex of rooms designed in true beer hall fashion is packed to the gills daily with tour groups and visitors looking for a taste of the authentic. The menu favors meat and wild game dishes that can (and should) be washed down with a glass of their home-brewed dark beer. The waiters here can leave a lot to be desired as some of them can seem grumpy or as though they have a chip on their shoulders. Feel free to ignore them and turn your attention to the lively accordion shows performed intermittently throughout the day and night.

Beer aficionados will be wise to mark down ◖ **U Pinkasů** (Jungmannovo náměstí 16, tel. 221 111 150, www.upinkasu.cz, restaurant daily 11 A.M.–11 P.M., cellar pub daily 4 P.M.–4 A.M., mains 129–309 Kč) on their must-see list. Legend has it that in 1843, this very same establishment was the first to serve Pilsner Urquell to its happy customers and the suds have been flowing ever since. It is one of the few places in Prague that serve the brew unpasteurized; you'll notice the difference in taste immediately. The menu is chock-full of traditional Czech dishes and wild game delicacies that include duck, hare, and boar—all of which come in very generous portions. Centrally located yet remarkably cheap, this place is highly recommended for those looking for a taste of the unpolished and authentic.

The beautiful neo-Renaissance Žofin Palace is located on tiny Slovanský Island situated opposite the National Theatre. Inside is **Žofin Restaurant and Garden Café** (Slovanský ostrov 226, tel. 224 934 548, www.gastrozofin .cz, daily 11 A.M.–midnight, 260–890 Kč), a mainstay with the Czech elite, as well as a favored site for galas, government functions, and celebrity bashes. Its large banquet rooms and pretty garden offer diners a level of luxury and European charm that's hard to beat, making the nouveau Czech cuisine and Moravian vintages offered even more enjoyable than they already are.

Latin American

Located inside the Hotel Salvator is the warm and inviting **La Boca** (Truhlářská 10, tel. 222 312 073, www.salvator.cz, daily 8:30 A.M.–11 P.M., mains 165–345 Kč). The internal terrace garden is the focal point here, with a few booths and even a children's play area rounding out the rest of the space. The tomato soup and Caesar salad are excellent starters while just about any of the pastas, tapas, or salads (most of which are too large too finish) will leave you more than satisfied. To top it all off, the waitstaff is one of the friendliest in town.

Sizeable portions and thick cuts of rib-eyes, top sirloin, tenderloins, and T-bones make **El Gaucho** (Václavské náměstí 11, tel. 221 629 410, www.el-gaucho.cz, daily 11:30 A.M.–midnight, mains 220–1,140 Kč) a must for steak aficionados. Food is prepared on a *parilla* (authentic Argentinean grill), and the chefs attribute the unbeatable taste to a top-secret combination of organic tenderizing and carefully calculated cooking over a charcoal fire. Grilled chicken and fish dishes are also available, but it's the steaks people come here for. If you're with a fellow meat lover, try the mix grill for two, or if unsure, simply ask the pleasant waitstaff decked out in traditional gaucho attire what they recommend.

Mediterranean

Located just off Wenceslas Square, **Pizza**

Coloseum (Vodičkova 32, tel. 224 214 914, www.pizzacoloseum.cz, Mon.–Sat. 11:30 A.M.–11:30 P.M., Sun. noon–11:30 P.M., mains 120–300 Kč) is a cozy, subterranean pizzeria with large brick ovens and comfortable tables. Aside from traditional pizza and pasta dishes, Coloseum also serves delicious salads and a few fish and seafood entrees. This is a great choice if you want to have some above-average food but need to keep the costs down. There is also a second central location at Palác Myslbek, Ovocný Trh 8 (tel. 224 238 355).

Inside Slovanský Dům, **Kogo Pizzeria & Caffeteria** (Na Příkopě 22, tel. 221 451 259, www.kogo.cz, daily 11 A.M.–11 P.M., mains 220–950 Kč) fills up regularly with families, businesspeople, and couples who can't wait to sink their teeth into the excellent and consistent Italian and Mediterranean menu. The risotto con roba di mare is particularly popular, as is the linguine with lobster, shrimp, and zucchini. Brightly lit, full of energy, and very affordable considering the portions and location, Kogo is one of the surer bets in town.

Yes, olives are the running motif at **Oliva Restaurant & Café** (Plavecká 4, tel. 222 520 288, www.olivarestaurant.cz, Mon.–Sat. 11:30 A.M.–3 P.M., 6 P.M.–midnight, mains 265–395 Kč), beginning with the three olive oils and homemade bread that form your complimentary starter. The menu focuses on simplicity with dishes like the grilled duck breast and tuna steak, two excellent examples of well-prepared fare without all the unnecessary bells and whistles. The warm chocolate gateau with pistachio cream is one of the restaurant's most commonly ordered desserts and one taste of it will make you a believer, too. Cozy, pleasant, and worth every penny, Oliva is an excellent choice for either lunch or dinner.

Laying it on a little thick what with the mural of Mykonos and the incessant bouzouki music, **Řecká Taverna** (Revoluční 16, tel. 222 317 762, www.gyros-gr.com, daily 11 A.M.–midnight, mains 140–400 Kč) is nevertheless a fine choice should you find yourself at Náměstí Republiky and desire a taste of the Mediterranean. The gyros, spanakopita, and dolmades are typically top-notch and the staff is usually attentive and prompt, demonstrating the warmth Greeks are well known for. Traditional Greek wines, along with ouzo and retsina, are also available to complete the authentic experience, although breaking plates and yelling "Opa!" was still frowned upon last time I checked.

Vegetarian
Cheap, simple, and extremely popular, **U Govindy Vegetarian Club** (Soukenická 27, tel. 224 816 631, daily 11 A.M.–5 P.M., main of the day 85 Kč) is a self-service vegetarian restaurant owned and operated by Prague's Hare Krishna community. Diners share tables and floor cushions, although more conventional seating is available upstairs. All of the food served is grown on their organic farm outside the city, making it one of the healthier options in town.

STARÉ MĚSTO
Asian
Not just another Thai restaurant, **◖ Orange Moon** (Rámová 5, tel. 222 325 119, www.orange moon.cz, daily 11:30 A.M.–11:30 P.M., mains 165–365 Kč) also offers mouth-watering Burmese, Indian, and Indonesian cuisine that has won over almost everybody lucky enough to walk through their doors. Delicious starters like their classic veggie spring rolls or *tom yum kai,* along with mains such as their *phad kra pao,* have made believers out of the staunchest food critics, which is probably why both floors are usually packed with tourists, Czechs, and expats no matter what the hour. Reservations recommended.

YAMI (Masná 3, tel. 222 312 756, www .sushi-yami.cz, daily noon–midnight, sushi sets: 350–480 Kč) is a relative newcomer to Old Town Square and the sushi scene in general, offering over 70 different sushi specialties in an authentic environment. There's a Korean menu available, too, with what has to be the spiciest kimchi in the country. The Tolsot bibimbap, served in a stone pot that includes rice, sliced cucumbers, carrots, and grilled beef

topped with a sunny-side-up egg, is worth the visit alone.

Cafes
Despite its proximity to the Charles Bridge, **Café Montmartre** (Řetězová 7, tel. 222 221 244, Mon.–Fri. 8 A.M.–11 P.M., Sat.–Sun. noon–11 P.M., mains 48–110 Kč) has somehow managed to stay relatively tourist-free. Around since the first Republic and once a favorite watering hole of the town's literati, you'll now find students, artists, and office workers kicking back with a drink or enjoying a sandwich or dessert. A true survivor and well worth a visit.

Tucked away on tiny Týnská Street, **Týnská literární kavárna** (Týnská 6, tel. 224 827 807, www.knihytynska.cz, Mon.–Fri. 9 A.M.–11 P.M., Sat.–Sun. 10 A.M.–11 P.M., mains 55–95 Kč) is where you'll find local writers and students sipping on wine or devouring pub food like fried cheese or pickled fish. A large patio is open during the summer months while the winter offers a more intimate setting inside the cafe's series of arched rooms. Somehow managing to stay tourist-free despite it being located mere meters from Old Town Square, Týnská literární kavárna is a wonderful place to put a few drinks away before rejoining the masses.

Continental
Located in a 12th-century cellar with a decor that is arguably more interesting than the menu, **Klub Architektů** (Betlémské náměstí 5a, tel. 224 401 214, daily 11:30 P.M.–midnight, mains 120–250 Kč) captures the imagination with its open kitchen, exposed air ducts, and overall dungeon feel. A variety of vegetarian meals, along with standard Czech dishes and house specialties that include beef strips with apples in cream sauce and chicken with ham and pineapple, make this one of the more unique options in town. Some of the meals on offer can seem a little too experimental for certain tastes but if you'll be fine if you stick to the simpler fare. Don't forget to check out the bookstore and architecture exhibition before you leave.

Competing for the finest dining experience in Prague is ◖ **Bellevue** (Smetanovo nábřeží 18, tel. 222 221 443, www.zatisigroup .cz, daily noon–3 P.M., 5:30–11 P.M., mains 490–790 Kč), whose window seats provide a picture-perfect view of Charles Bridge and Prague Castle. Live piano music in the evenings provide a romantic backdrop as diners dig in to all kinds of beef, fish, pasta, and duck dishes, washing it all down with a bottle chosen from the elegant and comprehensive wine list. Many opt for the "Best of Bohemia Menu" and some of the braver souls spoil themselves with the extraordinary fillet of fallow deer. Sunday brunch has live jazz and all the Bohemia Sekt you can drink. Highly recommended, as are reservations.

Split over two levels, **La Provence** (Štupartská 9, tel. 296 826 155, www.kampa group.com, daily noon–11 P.M., mains 285–695 Kč) offers guests a quasi-formal Parisian Brasserie setting at the entrance level and a more romantic Provençal village dining space downstairs that has candles on the tables and live piano music during the evenings. The menu is filled with delicious mains ranging from lamb to traditional casseroles, but it's the fresh fish and seafood platters that include oysters, salmon, escargots, and foie gras that command one's attention. A little on the pricey side, La Provence is nevertheless worth a visit if budgeting isn't an issue.

The **Nostress Café Restaurant** (Dušní 10, tel. 222 317 007, www.nostress.cz, daily 10 A.M.–midnight, mains 230–580 Kč) is a category-defying space that operates as an art gallery, lifestyle shop, and fusion restaurant all at once. Simple tables rest amidst antiques and towering works of art while business folk, shoppers on a lunch break, and high-end tourists from the ritzier hotels dive into delicious helpings of chicken curry panang and salmon steak. A great place to have a relaxing lunch in one of Prague's busiest restaurant districts, you may even find yourself picking up some wrought-iron furniture on your way out.

V Zátiší (Liliová 1, tel. 222 221 155, www .vzatisi.cz, daily noon–3 P.M., 5:30–11 P.M.,

mains 495–795 Kč) was one of the first restaurants in town to open its doors after the Velvet Revolution of 1989. It won the Best Restaurant in Central & Eastern Europe award in 1996 and the Best Restaurant in Prague award in 2001, solidifying its reputation as one of the finer establishments about town. Intimate and elegant, its four rooms are decorated in unique style, including artists' easels placed randomly about the premises and paintings from the country's finest artists gracing the walls. The service can be spotty (always a problem in Prague) and the menu changes often but typically includes creative examples of French, Asian, and Czech cuisines. A big hit with celebrities, foodies, and the town's elite, this is a place no diner will forget any time soon.

Cuban

Modeled after Papa Hemingway's old stomping grounds in Havana, **La Bodeguita del Medio** (Kaprova 5, tel. 224 813 922, www .bodeguita.cz, daily 10 A.M.–2 A.M., mains 345–695 Kč) is a little slice of salsa just off Old Town Square proper. Begin the evening with one of the mouthwatering Cuban dishes on offer like the two-person Hemingway seafood platter or the unforgettable mixed grill special "Che Guevara." And what better way to wash it down than with a nice cool mojito? (The bar claims they serve over 300 on any given day.) Live music courtesy of Cuban troupe Clave Mixta is complemented by scantily-clad salsa dancers who always manage to drive diners out of their seats and onto their tables or the bar, turning La Bodeguita into a writhing free-for-all before the night's done. Fun is the key word here.

Czech

Kolkovna (V Kolkovně 8, tel. 224 819 701, www.kolkovna.cz, daily 11 A.M.–midnight, mains 165–429 Kč) is a very popular restaurant that combines traditional Czech cuisine with modern gastronomy, all under the banner of mighty Pilsner Urquell. Located a hop, skip, and a jump from Pařížská Street and Old Town

Square, this pub/restaurant is typically packed to the gills with visitors sampling the local food and beer, two standouts of which are the ribs and the dark Velkopopovický Kozel. Though incredibly popular, there have been numerous reports lately of terrible service and a decline in the quality of food. Not everyone agrees but if the waitstaff starts off by giving you attitude, it may be worth your while to simply get up and leave rather than stick it out.

Continuing on in the tradition of chain restaurants, **Potrefená Husa** (Bílkova 5, tel. 222 326 626, www.pivovarystaropramen .cz, daily 11 A.M.–midnight, mains 145–359 Kč) is owned by the Staropramen brewery and this location in Old Town Square is just one of 19 found throughout the country. Czech standards such as *guláš* (goulash) and *svíčková* (beef sirloin in cream sauce) can be found here, as well as a handful of more international dishes including various pastas and steaks. Very popular with the young and upwardly mobile business crowd, there are nevertheless many who believe the service has spiraled downward the last couple of years and that the prices (although reasonable by US standards) are not worth the dining experience. Reservations recommended.

French

A long-time favorite with the French expat crowd, **Chez Marcel** (Haštalská 12, tel. 222 315 676, www.chezmarcel.cz, Mon.–Sat. 8 A.M.–1 A.M., Sun. 9 A.M.–1 A.M., mains 150–350 Kč) is an excellent cafe/bar whose quiche and authentic bistro dishes like rabbit in mustard sauce keep them coming back for more. By day, the place affects a lazy kind of charm; it's a perfect spot to unwind with a cup of coffee and the day's *Le Monde*. At night, hipsters and couples start filing in, ordering up carafes of wine and adding to the overall joie de vivre.

La Scene (U Milosrdných 6, tel. 222 312 677, www.lascene.cz, Mon.–Fri. noon–2 P.M., 7 P.M.–midnight, Sat.–Sun. 7 P.M.–midnight, mains 280–580 Kč) is the type of place you spend hours in, drinking up the minimalist design, soft lighting, and background music. Study the menu with an aperitif at the lounge bar before heading to the restaurant proper to enjoy any number of classic French creations. Foie gras, scallops, lamb, duck, and swordfish await you, and when you're all done, head off to the Champagne Club downstairs to enjoy live swing, jazz, or Latin music with an after-dinner drink. Reservations recommended.

Indian

Located next to the popular Bombay Café is the **Rasoi** (Dlouhá 13, tel. 222 324 040, www.rasoi.cz, daily noon–11 P.M., mains 280–480 Kč), which many argue is the finest Indian restaurant in town. Spiced according to the guest's demands, traditional dishes like palak paneer, lamb biryani, and chicken lababdar become art forms even those with the most sensitive of palates can enjoy. The entire dining experience is distinctly Indian, as gracious waiters dressed in traditional garb escort you to your table before leaving you to admire the wonderful interiors decorated tastefully with paintings of rural India. Slightly pricey but a must if you're a fan of the cuisine.

If you're in Old Town Square and don't feel like spending 250 Kč and upwards for something to eat, try **Beas** (Týnská 19, tel. 608 035 727, www.beas-dhaba.cz, Mon.–Sat. 10 A.M.–8 P.M., Sun. 10 A.M.–6 P.M., mains 78–128 Kč), arguably the best Indian food in town at such a low price. Specializing in vegetarian cuisine, they offer a handful of daily specials and a couple of sides, all of which are cooked fresh and richly spiced. There isn't much to the decor or atmosphere of the place, but if you're looking for something quick and tasty, you won't find a better deal nearby.

International

Pařížská is one of the trendier streets in Prague and **Restaurace Barock** (Pařížská 24, tel. 222 329 221, www.barockrestaurant.cz, daily 10 A.M.–1 A.M., mains 395–615 Kč) does its best to fit in. Large, stylish, and sleek, it attracts the ultra-cool and ultra-wannabe set, complete with pouty looks and Versace sunglasses. Owned by

Tommy Sjoo and Nils Jebens, who also operate the flawless Kampa Park restaurant, the international menu does have its moments, particularly the sushi, as well as other, more imaginative Asian fusion dishes. In the end, some will like the high-end attitude that overflows here, while others will be turned off completely, preferring a sandwich on the fly.

Walking into **Lary Fary** (Dlouhá 30, tel. 222 320 154, www.laryfary.cz, daily 11 A.M.–midnight, mains 295–590 Kč) you might wonder what the decorator was smoking before settling on a decor that can only be described as "eclectic," or Morocco meets Polynesia meets the supernatural. The food is just as diverse, ranging from Brazilian to Asian to Czech, with their signature trademark being a 1.5-foot-long skewer that needs to be fastened to your table and swings above you like the sword of Damocles. There's sushi, too, which is so good that the Japanese embassy has chosen Lary Fary to cater their events. A little on the pricey side but well worth spoiling yourself at least once.

Jewish/Kosher

Across the street from Pinkas Synagogue sits **King Solomon** (Široká 8, tel. 224 818 752, www.kosher.cz, Sun.–Thurs. noon–11 P.M., Fri. dinner and Sat. lunch reservations only, mains 250–900 Kč), Prague's oldest and most well-known kosher restaurant. Specialties include Wiener schnitzel, holishkes, roasted duck, and gefilte fish, all of which are served during dining hours that adhere to the Sabbath. There is a long and rather impressive list of Israeli, American, and Moravian kosher wines available as well. Keep in mind that while the food here is generally very good, the prices are geared towards well-to-do tourists and are therefore quite high.

Latin American

La Casa Argentina (Dlouhá 35/730, tel. 222 311 512, www.lacasaargentina.cz, daily 10 A.M.–2 A.M., mains 150–720 Kč) is a theme restaurant complete with fedoras, Maradona jerseys, and sexy tango dancers. The main dining room has been made to resemble a typical Argentine street scene. Another room has water running down its walls and a caged lizard. There's also a bar in the back decked out in nautical theme. Many will find this to be a little too kitschy for their taste. Still others will wonder whether the waitstaff could be any more useless. Why then do people insist on coming here? In a word: steak. Imported from Argentina, the steak served here will help you quickly come to understand why the country eats more red meat than any other. Be warned: Everything about this place, including the menu, is a hit-and-miss affair. But the steak . . . it's so good you'll forgive just about anything for one more bite.

Owned by the highly reputable Ambiente group, **⟨ Brasileiro** (U Radnice 8, tel. 224 234 474, www.ambi.cz, daily 11 A.M.–midnight, 465 Kč all you can eat) is an all-you-can-eat Brazilian bonanza that can do no wrong. Meat is grilled in the churrasco style and served by churasqueros, who are both your waiters and cooks. Winding their way amongst the tables, they happily offer diners various meats off their skewers, explaining the differences in taste and preparation of each. This is primarily a carnivore's paradise but vegetarians can pay half-price and gorge themselves on the salad bar, which includes sushi, stuffed mushrooms, fresh greens, and marinated peppers, just to name a few. You'll be hard-pressed to find another restaurant in town that offers as much bang for your buck.

Mediterranean

Allegro (Veleslavínova 2a, tel. 221 427 000, www.fourseasons.com, daily 6:30 A.M.–11:30 P.M., mains 650–1,800 Kč) is the main dining room of the Four Seasons Hotel, which immediately explains the exorbitant prices. Its chef, however, is famed Vito Mollica, and he has without question turned Allegro into one of the finest restaurants in town, performing miracles with various Italian, Mediterranean, and classic Continental dishes. The diner is left overwhelmed and consequently quite aware of why Mr. Mollica has won raves all around the world. There is a downside, though. The ambience, truth be told, isn't exactly the most alluring. It is the Four Seasons, after all, and its formulaic decor seems somewhat distasteful and not at all related to anything remotely Prague.

Lovers of Italian food will not want to hesitate visiting **Don Giovanni** (Karolíny Svetlé 34, tel. 222 222 062, www.dongiovanni .cz, daily 11 A.M.–midnight, mains 260–980 Kč). Affording remarkable views of Charles Bridge and Prague Castle, its neoclassical surroundings affect a formal but comfortable atmosphere wherein one can sample true-blue Mediterranean delights such as Parma ham or pappardelle with cream sauce before digging into melt-in-your-mouth mains like *scaloppina di vitello al limone o vino marsala*. Mama mia!

An affordable *and* worthwhile Italian restaurant in Old Town Square? Doesn't sound possible but **dANico** (Dlouhá 21, tel. 222 311 807, www.danico.cz, daily 11 A.M.–1 A.M., mains 110–360 Kč) pulls it off with flying colors. Classy yet relaxed, this intimate space offers a menu that includes popular mains like lamb and swordfish carpaccio, as well as a top-notch vegetarian lasagna that might convince you to give up meat altogether. For dessert try their tasty tiramisu and wash it all down with one (or two) of the over 300 wines available. A definite treat.

Middle Eastern
Located inside Burzovni Palac in a small passage behind Kotva department store is the incomparable **Byblos** (Rybná 14, tel. 221 842 121, www.biblos.cz, Mon.–Fri. 9 A.M.–midnight, Sat.–Sun. 11 A.M.–11 P.M., mains 150–350 Kč). Many find the hanging-gardens-of-Babylon-type setting to be a little on the kitschy side, but nobody argues about the menu, which boasts over 30 mezze dishes like baba ghanouj, tabbouleh, hummus, and spiced lamb sausages. Without a doubt, the best thing on offer is the unbelievable "Byblos Mezze Menu for Two," which can easily satisfy two ravenous adults. You'll wonder whether the

plates will ever stop coming. Pizza and pasta dishes can be had here as well, but what's the point? Tip: Avoid the Lebanese wines as they're overpriced and truly disappointing.

Entering **Dahab** (Dlouhá 33, tel. 224 827 375, www.dahab.cz, daily noon–1 A.M., mains 225–800 Kč) feels like walking into a Middle Eastern oasis—a veritable world away from the traffic and hustle of Dlouhá Street. Delectable delights like hummus, tahini, couscous, and a wide range of sweets are on offer, as is a variety of teas and Turkish coffee. Should you feel like unwinding with a good smoke, table-top hookahs are available, along with a number of fruit and non-tobacco products. Service can be spotty at times but if you're lucky, you'll have a pleasantly exotic experience before re-entering reality.

Seafood
Located on Karlova Street right in the heart of tourist central is **Reykjavík** (Karlova 20, tel. 222 221 218, www.reykjavik.cz, daily 11 A.M.–midnight, mains 200–530 Kč), a self-described "Icelandic seafood saga." Seafood is flown in daily from the motherland and served up in decent portions, particularly the lobster and salmon steak, which tends to win raves. The decor relies heavily on wood adorned with curiosities collected from all over the world, giving it more of a pub-like feel than anything elegant or overtly formal. Rather pricey and occasionally underwhelming, it nevertheless continues to be a tourist favorite.

MALÁ STRANA
American
Walking around Malá Strana can really work one's appetite into a frenzy but help is available in the form of **Cowboys Steaks & Cocktails** (Nerudova 40, tel. 296 826 107, www.cowboys restaurant.cz, daily noon–11 P.M., mains 245–985 Kč), a steakhouse with all the fixin's. Billing itself as having the biggest, best, and sexiest steaks in town, the focus here is on quality and fun. Friendly waitstaff bedecked in Stetsons and leather vests serve generous portions of steaks, seafood, poultry, and vegetarian

dishes to your cowhide-covered booth, or, if the weather's right, to your table on the heated rooftop terrace that offers an exceptional panoramic view of the city. Very popular and very satisfying, just make sure to leave room for dessert in the form of good old-fashioned American cheesecake or chocolate brownies.

Hearty soups and sandwiches, along with free coffee and soda refills (still a very foreign concept here) are just some of the reasons why **Bohemia Bagel** (Lázeňská 19, tel. 257 310 694, www.bohemiabagel.cz, Mon.–Fri. 7 A.M.–midnight, Sat.–Sun. 8 A.M.–midnight, mains 70–169 Kč) continues to do big business with tourists and locals alike. This is the only place in town where you'll find fresh bagels and cream cheese and their "Wake and Bake" breakfast specials are a good reason to get out of bed and make it to one of their two central locations by 11 A.M. Friendly, informal, and a great place to meet expats. (There's a second location: Másna 2, tel. 224 812 560.)

Balkan

As you approach the American embassy on Tržiště Street, tantalizing smells waft through the air, accompanied by the percussive, rhythmic sounds of Gypsy music. Follow your nose a little further and you'll come to 🄲 **Gitanes** (Tržiště 7, tel. 257 530 163, www.gitanes.cz, daily noon–midnight, mains 150–450 Kč), a jewel of Balkan cuisine in the middle of Malá Strana. Decorated with colorful icons, paintings, and photographs of the former Yugoslavia, its two rooms emanate a warmth and hospitality that's hard to find in Prague. The menu relies heavily on Yugoslavian cuisine but mixes in a few Italian specialties as well. The roasted peppers stuffed with cheese make for a wonderful appetizer and the chef's specialty Pasta alla Trieste—an Italian-Yugoslavian combo of fettuccine with lamb on onion and vegetables that will be enough to convince you to come back again before your trip is over.

Cafes

The **Glamour Café** (U Lužického semináře 42, tel. 257 531 799, www.glamourcafe.cz, daily

11 A.M.–midnight, mains 185–465 Kč) joined the Malá Strana scene in the summer of 2006, offering all hungry passersby excellent seafood dishes such as tiger prawns, halibut, and Canadian lobster. Its swanky Spartan interior is complemented by a large terrace that looks out over the Vltava and onto Charles Bridge, making it a popular choice with both tourists and locals alike.

Tucked away down a quiet cobblestone street not far from Charles Bridge, **Veronský Dům** (Mišenská 8, tel. 603 745 414, daily 7 A.M.–11 A.M., 1 P.M.–1 A.M.) is a charming little cafe and wine bar, home to thirsty tourists during the day and local artists and residents at night. Its intimate, tastefully decorated space is often the site of lively parties, particularly as the night wears on.

Continental

Although occasionally plagued by stories of poor or rude management, **Pálffy palác** (Valdštejnská 14, tel. 257 530 522, www.palffy .cz, daily 11 A.M.–11 P.M., mains 430–765 Kč) continues to remain at the top of most peoples' lists as one of the best and most romantic dining spots in Prague. Housed in the elegant Baroque palace of the same name, tourists, young professionals, and the occasional politician take their time poring over the menu, which offers such delicacies as oysters, swordfish, and salmon steak stuffed with lemon sole fillets and Dublin Bay prawns. This is one lunch or dinner you won't soon forget.

Quiet Maltézské náměstí is the home of **U Malířů** (Maltézské náměstí 11, tel. 257 530 000, www.umaliru.cz, daily 11:30 A.M.– 11:30 P.M., mains 490–1,480 Kč), a highly reputable and very popular vaulted and frescoed tavern that excels at every level. Everything on the menu is good here, be it the duck, game, beef, lamb, or fresh seafood flown in daily. Many consider this the finest dining Prague has to offer and is a must for those whose budgets will allow it.

U Maltézských rytířů (Prokopská 10, tel. 257 533 666, www.umaltezskychrytiru .cz, daily 1–11 P.M., mains 400–1,250 Kč) is an exceptional restaurant whose specialty is wild game dishes, particularly the roast saddle of boar on briar sauce and the fillet of pork with leeks and bacon baked on lard. The main floor is a vaulted Renaissance affair offering three cozy tables but it's downstairs where you'll find the jewel of the place: two romantic Gothic vaults offering intimate lounges that have been the site of many a celebrity party and marriage proposal. Low lighting and jazzy piano music complete the scene. Reservations a must.

Previously a decadent coffeehouse at the turn of the 20th century, the **Cafe Savoy** (Vítězná 5, tel. 257 311 562, www.ambi.cz, Mon.–Fri. 8 A.M.–10:30 P.M., Sat.–Sun. 9 A.M.–10:30 P.M., mains 178–385 Kč) is now an excellent choice for settling in with a drink or light meal and soaking up the ambience. The restored ceiling alone—a triumphant trompe l'oeil that interweaves leaves, apples, grapes, and ribbons—is worth a visit and the dining area on the upper level provides an excellent view of the three enormous crystal chandeliers that light up the main room. The menu consists of decent roast meats including the Wiener schnitzel and grilled chicken breast, which are quite popular, as is the delicious weekend brunch special.

Czech

Often overlooked by visitors is the consistently excellent **Restaurant Nostitz** (Nosticova 2a, tel. 257 007 681, www.nostitz.cz, daily 11 A.M.–midnight, mains 129–649 Kč), a large, upmarket yet inexpensive place whose summer terrace overlooks lovely Kampa Park. The cuisine is a mix of traditional Czech recipes (including wild game) along with pasta, fish, and meat dishes, all of which are delicious. The mix grill for two is very popular here, as are the finger-licking-good chicken wings.

Roughly halfway up Nerudova Street on your way to the castle, a flight of stairs leading downwards appears on your left. Take it and you'll find **U Sedmi Švábů** (Jánský vršek 14, tel. 257 531 455, www.svabove.cz, daily 11 A.M.–11 P.M., mains 155–690 Kč), one of Prague's more interesting and enjoyable restaurants. Admittedly, it looks like a tourist trap from the outside but open the heavy door and step right into 1493: a year that comes complete with dark lighting, large oak tables, tightly bodiced maidens, gypsy dancers, fire eaters, and even an executioner or two! All in good fun, the menu offers tons of traditional Czech dishes, including some that date back to the Middle Ages. Not to be missed is the wild boar goulash and roasted pork knuckle with horseradish and mustard, which most find impossible to finish. Feel free to chat up your neighbors as the emphasis here is on fun and entertainment, something that is accentuated by the numerous shows that are performed, much to the delight of all.

International

There are many words one can use to describe the interiors at **Alchymist** (Hellichova 4, tel. 257 312 518, www.alchymist.cz, Tues.–Sun. noon–midnight, mains 445–635 Kč) and "opulent" is certainly one of the better ones. Relying on a mix of European, Moorish, and Baroque styles, you come to feel like you're dining in the 18th century more so than modern-day Malá Strana. The sea bass and tuna are two surefire hits here, as is the homemade crème brulée, all of which is brought to you by an extremely professional and polite waitstaff. The pinot grigio is also one of the finest you'll find in any restaurant around town.

Opposite the Kafka Museum sits an 18th-century building that originally served as a brick factory or *cihelna*. Today, it's the home of **Hergetova Cihelna** (Cihelná 102/2, tel. 257 535 534, www.cihelna.com, daily 11:30 A.M.–1 A.M., mains 225–695 Kč), a chic restaurant, cocktail bar, cafe, and music lounge all rolled into one. The delicious and well-presented international menu ranges from Asian to Continental to American, offering something for those with even the most finicky tastes. There's also a large summer terrace overlooking the river, providing an unforgettable, picture-perfect view of the Charles Bridge.

Střelecký Ostrov Restaurant and Terrace (Střelecký Ostrov 336, tel. 224 934 026, www.streleckyostrov.cz, daily noon–1 A.M., mains 160–480 Kč) is a particularly popular choice for tourists, who can't seem to get enough of the restaurant's excellent patio, which offers grand views of both the Vltava and National Theatre. Serving up a handful of seafood and vegetarian dishes, along with traditional Czech specialties like venison goulash and roasted duck, this is an affordable choice and a consistently pleasant dining experience.

Mediterranean

Authentic Spanish cuisine served by refreshingly cheerful waitstaff is what you'll find at **Cafe El Centro** (Maltézské náměstí 9, tel. 257 533 343, www.elcentro.czrb.cz, daily noon–midnight, mains 140–349 Kč). Its arched doors, vaulted ceilings, and suspended smoked hams provide an ambience that is half Czech pub, half Spanish bodega, and all culinary comfort. Just about everything on the extensive menu is good and the portions are very generous, particularly two-person dishes like the paella, rabbit montanesa, and the fish plate featuring salmon, redfish, trout, and swordfish.

Smack dab in the middle of Malostranské náměstí is **Square** (Malostranské náměstí, tel. 257 532 109, www.squarerestaurant.cz, daily 8 A.M.–1 A.M., mains 185–595 Kč), a conveniently located people-watcher's paradise. Formerly known as Malostranská kavárna, it was patronized often by the likes of Jan Neruda and Franz Kafka. Nowadays, tourists and locals alike gorge on a diverse range of Italian and Mediterranean dishes, as well as scrumptious Spanish tapas. Aside from the modish central dining area, there is also a cozy cellar complete with fireplace, along with a heated outdoor terrace that faces the square.

Mexican

Opposite Petřín Hill is **Cantina** (Újezd 38, tel. 257 317 173, daily noon–midnight, mains 149–329 Kč), a veteran of the Mexican restaurant scene that still has patrons waiting at the bar in the off-chance that somebody's reservations fall through. Pseudo-rustic and slightly kitschy what with the burlap-covered ceiling and vintage tequila posters, the menu nonetheless impresses time and time again. The gorditas are as just as good as any you'll find back home and the fajitas are usually a sure bet as well. Slightly overshadowed now by newer, bigger Mexican restaurants that have recently arrived on the scene, Cantina still manages to hold its own this side of the river. Reservations a must.

Seafood

Consistently ranking as one of Prague's finest dining establishments, **(Kampa Park** (Na Kampě 8b, tel. 296 826 102, www.kampa group.com, daily 11:30 A.M.–1 A.M., mains 435–895 Kč) is an experience you won't soon forget. The selection of fresh seafood, wild game, and contemporary meat dishes is second to none, as is the extensive range of wines on offer (numbering more than 150). Excellent service, unbeatable quality, and the most magnificent riverside views of Charles Bridge and beyond are just some of the reasons why locals, tourists, and visiting dignitaries continue to flock here—including Hillary Clinton, who was quoted as saying, "I wanted our last night at Kampa Park to go on forever."

HRADČANY

Asian

Advertising itself as an "Oriental tearoom and restaurant," the extremely popular **(Malý Buddha** (Úvoz 46, tel. 220 513 894, www .malybuddha.cz, Tues.–Sun. noon–10:30 P.M., mains 100–220 Kč) offers diners a serene alternative to the chaos of Prague Castle. Comprised of a series of vaulted spaces that culminate in a shrine dedicated to a large orange Buddha, this unique establishment is also one of the few in Prague that is completely non-smoking. The menu boasts over 50 types of tea, as well as enticing entrees like shark with garlic and chili.

Some offerings even promise curing powers, such as, "Our snake wine increases virility." This is a very affordable, highly recommendable alternative to the usual fare found in the immediate area.

Czech

Having played host to a number of dignitaries including George and Barbara Bush, Margaret Thatcher, and Mikhail Gorbachev, it would be accurate to say that **U Císařů** (Loretánská 175/5, tel. 220 518 484, www.ucisaru.cz, daily 9 A.M.–1 A.M., mains 200–490 Kč) is a pretty safe bet. The interiors are reminiscent of a small castle, complete with original antiques, arched doorways with wrought-iron gates, and paintings of former Czech rulers gracing each table. Attentive waiters are more than happy to explain the traditional Czech dishes on offer and a pianist tickles the ivories to ensure that a relaxed and pleasurable time is had by all.

Set in the Royal Gardens, **Lví dvůr** (U Prašného mostu 6/51, tel. 224 372 361, www .lvidvur.cz, daily 11 A.M.–midnight, mains 220–990 Kč) manages to combine original period pieces with contemporary touches to create an unforgettable dining experience. Traditional Czech food is on offer with roast pig on a spit, accompanied by kettle chips, salad, and appropriate sauces being the house specialty, although the Castle Skewer (a mixed meat kebab) with roast potatoes, vegetables, and sauces is also well worth trying. The service here is typically excellent and during the summer months an ample terrace is opened to the public, allowing awe-inspired diners romantic views of St. Vitus Cathedral and the Castle Towers.

Plenty of local game and fish is what you'll find at **U Zlaté hrušky** (Nový svět 3, tel. 220 514 778, www.uzlatehrusky.cz, daily 11:30 A.M.–3 P.M., 6:30 P.M.–midnight, mains 390–1,580 Kč), set in a charming 17th-century cottage. Diners have the choice of sitting in the cozy, wood-paneled dining room, or, weather permitting, in the delightful outdoor garden that seats up to 150. Food is rather pricey, so the majority of the clientele tends to be tourists or visiting celebrities, with the occasional high-powered Czech sprinkled in. If you decide to throw caution to the wind and loosen the purse strings a bit, go for the venison in pear sauce or let one of the friendly waiters make a suggestion. Reservations recommended.

DEJVICE
Czech

A favorite with locals and packed to the rafters when soccer's on, **Bruska** (Dejvická 20, tel. 224 322 946, www.restaurace-bruska .com, Mon.–Sat. 11 A.M.–11:30 P.M., Sun. 11:30 A.M.–10 P.M., mains 150–300 Kč) is a laid-back neighborhood restaurant featuring tasty traditional Czech dishes and some of the finest beer in the district. Well worth a trip if you're interested in trying the local cuisine, and if you happen to be there on a weekend, go for the ribs; you won't be disappointed.

French

Relocated in 2005 to the swanky Villa Schwaiger, **Le Bistrot de Marlene** (Schwaigerova 59/3, tel. 224 921 853, www .bistrotdemarlene.cz, Mon.–Fri. 11 A.M.–2 P.M., 7–10:30 P.M., Sat. 7–10:30 P.M., mains 410–810 Kč) has been a hit with the local French community and other expats for many years now. The veal and lamb are divine here, as are the various desserts and the numerous wines on offer. Authentic French cuisine does come with a price, however, and the bill at the end of a meal usually rivals Western standards. Reservations are a must.

Indian

Located a stone's throw from Hradčanská metro station, **Haveli** (Dejvická 6, tel. 233 344 800, www.haveli.cz, daily 11 A.M.–midnight, mains 195–495 Kč) serves mouth-watering Indian dishes to delightfully surprised tourists and in-the-know locals who keep coming back for more. The service is excellent here and the menu boasts one of the broader vegetarian selections in town. Arguably the best Indian restaurant in Prague and a must if you're anywhere near the vicinity.

Mexican

Expanded in 2007, **Fiesta** (Václavkova 2, tel. 224 324 448, Mon.–Thurs. 8 A.M.–11 P.M., Fri. 8 A.M.–11:30 P.M., Sat. 10 A.M.–11:30 P.M., Sun. noon–11 P.M., mains 150–300 Kč) serves up generous portions of some of the finest Mexican food this side of the river. The Azteca soup is delicious, as are the steaks and fajitas, and if you're really hungry, the Tacos Mexicanos are for you. An outdoor patio is erected in the summer and it fills up fast, so get there early and find out why the locals keep coming back for yet another Fiesta fix.

Middle Eastern

A veteran of the Middle Eastern restaurant scene, **U Cedru** (Národní obrany 27, tel. 233 342 974, daily 11 A.M.–11 P.M., mains 225–295 Kč) continues to draw them in thanks in large part to their homey atmosphere and delicious appetizers (mezze). The grilled dishes are excellent, particularly the chicken shaworma, and the baba ghanouj is wonderful as well. It may not be as fancy as some of the newer Middle Eastern establishments that have popped up recently, but U Cedru is still a solid choice if you happen to be in the area.

HOLEŠOVICE

Czech

Owned by Lou Fanánek Hagen, lead singer of legendary Czech rock band Tři Sestry, **Na staré kovárně v Bráníku** (Kamenická 17, tel. 233 371 099, Mon.–Sat. 11:30 A.M.–1 A.M., Sun. 11:30 A.M.–11:30 P.M., mains 135–260 Kč) is a cross between an old-school, table-sharing Czech pub and a modern restaurant with an emphasis on fun. Ignore the motorcycle dangling from the ceiling and flip through the extensive menu, which offers some colorful Czech dishes like "Xena—Is She a Woman" and "Alcoholic's Treat." Keep in mind that the full menu is only available after 2:30 P.M. so plan your time accordingly or get there early and down some of the tastier

beer this side of Holešovice with all the other local long-hairs.

French

La Creperie (Janovského 4, tel. 220 878 040, www.lacreperie.cz, daily 9 A.M.–11 P.M., mains 55–120 Kč), known for its savory galettes—thin crepes served open-faced—is a tiny piece of Paris in otherwise very local, very Czech Holešovice. The soft, dreamy *chansons* coming from the speakers, coupled with the snippets of French you can't help but overhear from neighboring tables, is enough to make you forget where you are and order up another coffee or *cidre*. This is a wonderful place to start your day and a great choice for a lazy Sunday brunch.

ŽIŽKOV AND VINOHRADY

American

Part of the highly successful Ambiente chain, **Ambiente Manesova** (Mánesova 59, tel. 222 727 851, www.ambi.cz, Mon.–Fri. 11 A.M.–midnight, Sat.–Sun. noon–midnight, mains 149–595 Kč) continues on in the same vein, offering delicious food in friendly surroundings at affordable prices. Most of the menu focuses on American staples including mouth-watering wings and all you can eat ribs. There are a few Creole dishes available, as well as some Tex-Mex; the fajitas are very well known amongst the expat community. This is one of the few sure bets in town—a place where you know the food will be excellent, reasonably priced, and served to you with a smile.

Frequented by expat regulars and friendly foreigners staying in hotels nearby, **Banditos** (Melounova 2, tel. 224 941 096, daily 9 A.M.–1 A.M., mains 150–240 Kč) offers standard Tex-Mex fare in very generous portions. The burritos and quesadillas are a hit, as are the daily specials and all-day breakfasts. Some have complained about the less-than-hospitable service, but if a waitress's smile isn't the most important factor in your dining experience, give it a try.

Asian

Some of Prague's finest Korean food and

sushi can be had at **Hanil** (Slavíkova 24, tel. 222 715 867, Mon.–Sat. 11 A.M.–2:30 P.M., 5:30–11 P.M., Sun. 5:30–11 P.M., mains 240–450 Kč). Informal and reasonably priced, the place fills up regularly with friends and businessmen gorging on sushi/sashimi/maki sets, as well as house specialties like bibimbap and bulgogi. Reservations are recommended.

Located slightly off the tourist trail, **Tiger Tiger** (Anny Letenské 5, tel. 222 512 084, www.tigertiger.cz, Mon.–Fri. 11:30 A.M.–11 P.M., Sat.–Sun. 5–11 P.M., mains 145–325 Kč) is a popular choice for foreigners who need their Thai food fix. Depending on whom you ask, this is either one of the better places for said cuisine, or one of the worst. The red curry chicken (Kaeng Ped Gai) is usually a good bet but the pad thai tends to be hit or miss. A little more expensive than other, more consistent establishments, but worth taking a chance on if in the vicinity.

Cafes

Café Meduza (Belgická 17, tel. 222 515 107, www.meduza.cz, Mon.–Fri. 10 A.M.–1 A.M., Sat.–Sun. noon–1 A.M., snacks 50–100 Kč) is a very local, very cozy hangout for university students and aspiring artists still looking for that big break. Most come for the coffee or the mulled wine but there are a number of tasty treats to be had here including a wide array of sweetened pancakes, open-faced sandwiches, and a handful of vegetarian delights—all at prices that are more than reasonable.

International

Considered by many resident foreigners to be one of the more romantic dining spots in town, **⟨** **Mozaika** (Nitranská 13, tel. 224 253 011, www.restaurantmozaika.cz, Mon.–Fri. 11:30 A.M.–midnight, Sat. 2 P.M.–midnight, Sun. 4 P.M.–midnight, mains 174–368 Kč) is also known for its wildly changing international menu. The goat cheese au gratin is a popular starter and the duck breast is a solid main, as is the burger, which many argue is the best in town. This is a lovely local restaurant

whose ambience, service, and cuisine are well worth the effort of leaving the center and joining the locals.

Latin American

There's an ongoing debate around town as to which restaurant serves the best steaks but most say you'll find them at **Don Pedro** (Masarykovo Nábřeží 2, tel. 224 923 505, www.donpedro.cz, daily 11:30 A.M.–11 P.M., mains 180–350 Kč), a festively decorated Colombian restaurant that is at the top of many local diners' lists. The Caldo de Costilla is a highly recommended starter and apparently a sure-fire hangover cure as well. Also delicious is the churrasco, a 10.6-ounce grilled steak that will leave you yearning for warmer climes. Be forewarned, however: The food takes its time getting to your table so make sure you're not in a hurry when you order.

Mediterranean

"Simplicity, tradition, passion" is the motto at **Aromi** (Mánesova 78, tel. 222 713 222, www.aromi.cz, Mon.–Sat. noon–11 P.M., Sun. noon–10 P.M., mains 195–595 Kč) and they deliver on all three counts. A simply prepared menu dominated by seafood and pasta is what people keep flocking to here, especially the sea bass baked in sea salt and the ravioli with calamari and red sauce. For dessert, try the grand marnier chocolate fondant, or, if you just can't decide on what to order, ask any of the very attentive waitstaff who'll be happy to help. Highly recommended, as are reservations.

Partly hidden down a side street on Karlovo náměstí is **⟨** **Pizzeria di Carlo** (Karlovo náměstí 30, tel. 222 231 374, www.dicarlo.cz, daily 11 A.M.–10:30 P.M., mains 115–295 Kč), a hometown favorite that bustles with brisk business from the moment it opens its doors. Casual, friendly, and boasting a menu of seemingly countless Italian dishes, their generously portioned pastas and brick-fired pizzas win over their diners time and time again. In a city where quality is rarely a given, Pizzeria di Carlo is one you can bet on.

Located across the street from St. Ludmilla's Church, **Pizzeria Grosseto** (Francouzská 2, tel. 224 252 778, www.grosseto.cz, daily 11:30 A.M.–11 P.M., mains 120–390 Kč) is a friendly, brightly lit pizzeria that's been a staple in the expat community for years. Specializing in tasty and affordable pizzas and pastas, this is a great place to bring friends, family, or that special someone you've been meaning to impress. Many tend to linger over a glass of wine after dinner, preferring to soak up some more of the ambience before paying, so you're better off avoiding the usual wait by booking a table in advance.

Considered by many to be the best Greek restaurant in town, **Olympos** (Kubelíkova 9, tel. 222 722 239, www.taverna-olympos.eu, Mon.–Sat. 11:30 A.M.–midnight, Sun. 11:30 A.M.–11 P.M., mains 180–500 Kč) sits high atop Žižkov hill, offering diners traditional Greek delights like souvlaki and gyros, along with mouth-watering veal and lamb dishes. Using original ingredients that have been shipped all the way from the mother country, Olympos does a solid job recreating an authentic Greek dining experience. This is especially true during the warmer months

when the sunny outdoor patio is open for business.

Regularly patronized by Prague's Italian community, **Trattoria Cicala** (Žitná 43, tel. 222 210 375, trattoria.cicala.cz, Mon.–Sat. 11:30 A.M.–10:30 P.M., mains 120–590 Kč) is a charming cellar restaurant that is a must for fans of Italian cuisine. Pretty much everything on offer here is delicious but if you can't decide on anything, feel free to ask the staff for suggestions or simply allow friendly owner Aldo to cook something spontaneous up for you.

Vegetarian

Adjoined to one of the hippest clubs in town, the **Radost FX Café** (Bělehradská 120, tel. 224 254 776, www.radostfx.cz, daily 11:30 A.M.–3 A.M., mains 140–285 Kč) is usually full of hipsters who can't seem to get enough of the delicious vegetarian menu. Ranging from Greek, Indian, Thai, and Mexican, this is one of the few places in Prague that serves mouth-watering meals well into the wee hours. Weekends offer a highly popular brunch menu and Sunday nights focus on a wide range of Italian specialties. Highly recommended.

Information and Services

TOURIST INFORMATION OFFICES

The Prague Information Service (tel. 221 714 444, www.pis.cz, Mon.–Fri. 8 A.M.–7 P.M.) is the first and foremost tourist authority on all things Praha. Whether it's basic information regarding the country, culture, transportation, accommodation, cultural events, day trips, or organized tours, you'll find everything you need right here. Plenty of maps and brochures can be picked up at their four branches: Rytířská 31, Apr.–Oct. daily 9 A.M.–7 P.M., Nov.–Mar. daily 9 A.M.–6 P.M.; Staroměstské náměstí 1, Apr.–Oct. Mon.–Fri. 9 A.M.–7 P.M., Sat.–Sun. 9 A.M.–6 P.M., Nov.–Mar. Mon.–Fri. 9 A.M.–6 P.M., Sat.–Sun. 9 A.M.–5 P.M.; Wil-

sonova 8, Apr.–Oct. Mon.–Fri. 9 A.M.–7 P.M., Sat.–Sun. 9 A.M.–6 P.M., Nov.–Mar. Mon.–Fri. 9 A.M.–6 P.M., Sat.–Sun. 9 A.M.–5 P.M.; Lesser Town Bridge Tower, Malá Strana, Apr.–Oct. daily 10 A.M.–6 P.M.

EMERGENCY SERVICES

Should you need the assistance of the police, the main station is located a short walk from Wenceslas Square at Jungmannovo náměstí 9 and is open 24 hours a day. Sadly, however, the police in Prague have got a less than stellar reputation and are usually not very helpful at all. Odds are that whatever you have lost will most likely stay that way. If you somehow lose possession of your passport, report it to your embassy immediately. Keep in mind that knowing your passport number or having it written down somewhere will significantly speed up the process of getting it replaced.

In case of emergency, the numbers to call are:

• Ambulance: 155

• Police: 158

• Fire: 150

• General emergency: 112

MEDICAL SERVICES

There are a number of hospitals in Prague but the two that can provide 24-hour emergency care in English are Motol Hospital (V Úvalu 84, tel. 224 431 111, emergency tel. 224 433 682, pediatrics tel. 224 433 690) and Na Homolce Hospital (Roentgenova 2, tel. 257 272 146, emergency tel. 257 272 191, pediatrics tel. 257 272 043), which is home to the city's best-equipped facilities. Both are located in Prague 5.

The Canadian Medical Center in Prague 6 (Veleslavínská 30, tel. 235 360 133, www.cmc.praha.cz, Mon.–Fri. 8 A.M.–6 P.M.) is one of the longest-running international clinics in town and consistently voted one of the best by resident foreigners. Opposite the National Theatre, the PolyClinic at Národní (Národní 9, tel. 222 075 120, emergency tel. 720 427 634, www.poliklinika.narodni.cz, Mon.–Fri. 8:30 A.M.–5 P.M.) is run by US Board Certified Physicians and has a variety of specialists available, as well as a lab and physical therapy. Also in Prague 6, the Unicare Medical Center (Na Dlouhém Lánu 11, tel. 235 356 553, 24-hour emergency service tel. 608 103 050 or 602 201 040, www.unicare.cz, Mon.–Fri. 8 A.M.–8 P.M., Sat. 9 A.M.–4 P.M.) is highly reputable and can be contacted 24 hours a day.

For expert dental care, contact centrally located Erpet Medical Centrum (Pštrossova 10, tel. 221 595 000, emergency tel. 724 511 547, www.erpet.cz, Mon.–Thurs. 7 A.M.–5 P.M., 5–9 P.M. with appointment only, Fri. 7 A.M.–5 P.M., 5–7 P.M. with appointment only)

or the European Dental Center (Václavské náměstí 33, 2nd floor, tel. 224 228 984, 224 228 993-4, www.edcdental.cz, Mon.–Fri. 8 A.M.–11 P.M., Sat. 9 A.M.–6 P.M.).

The Czech word for pharmacy is *lékárna*. Only over-the-counter medicine is available at these pharmacies with their general operating hours being 7:30 A.M.–6 P.M. on weekdays. All pharmacies in Prague are required to post contact information for the city's 24-hour pharmacies. A few of the more handy ones are Lékárna Palackého (Palackého 5, tel. 224 946 982) in Prague 1 and Lékárna U Svaté Ludmily (Belgická 37, tel. 224 237 207) in Prague 2. If it's late and the door is locked, simply ring the buzzer and wait. Keep in mind that a small additional fee will be added for the after hour service.

BANKS AND CURRENCY EXCHANGE

Banks in Prague generally offer the best rates of exchange but are only open 8 A.M.–5 P.M. Most of the big players are found in the center, a few of which are: CitiBank (Rytířská 24, tel. 233 062 355, www.citibank.cz), Komerční Banka (Na příkopě 33, tel. 800 111 055, www.kb.cz), Ebanka (Na příkope 19, tel. 841 841 841, www.ebanka.cz), and Živnostenská Banka (Na příkopě 20, tel. 800 122 412, www.zivnostenska.cz). Most banks tend to offer the same rates and the best deal can easily be found thanks to their close proximity to one another.

There are plenty of currency exchange outlets around town, but those in the thick of the tourist trade generally offer terrible rates, oftentimes covered up by their advertising "no commission" on the exchange. Don't be fooled. The most reputable exchange office about town these days is AktivChange (Národní 24, tel. 224 934 761, www.aktivchange.cz, daily 8:30 A.M.–8 P.M.).

POSTAL SERVICES

Post offices are scattered throughout the city but confusingly have varying business hours and levels of competent service. If you just need a stamp, you're better off asking at kiosks, newsstands, or anywhere you see postcards being sold. The main post office, Hlavní Pošta (Jindřišská 14, tel. 221 131 111, daily 2 A.M.–midnight), is your best bet for further services and has a pretty interior you can gaze at while waiting for your number to come up.

INTERNET

Prague is overrun by Internet cafes now, whereas you could hardly find any a scant eight years ago. Prices and comfort vary enormously from cafe to cafe; you can be sure that those located in Malá Strana and Old Town Square will be considerably more expensive than all other areas. Feel free to compare prices but if time is of the essence, you can't really go wrong with the following: Grial Internet Café (Belgická 31, tel. 222 516 033, www.grial.cz, Mon.–Fri. 9 A.M.–11 P.M., Sat.–Sun. 11 A.M.–11 P.M., 40 Kč/hour), Bohemia Bagel (Masná 2, tel.

224 812 603, www.bohemiabagel.cz, Mon.–Fri. 7 A.M.–midnight, Sat.–Sun. 8 A.M.–midnight, 120 Kč/hour), and Internet Café Spika (Dlážděná 4, tel. 224 211 521, www.netcafe.spika.cz, daily 8 A.M.–midnight, 80 Kč/hour). Free Wi-Fi is sometimes available, while other establishments might charge a nominal fee before giving you the necessary password.

LAUNDRY

There are a handful of launderettes in Prague; the two most-popular are Prague Andy's Laundromat (Korunní 14, tel. 222 510 180, www.volny.cz/laundromat, daily 8 A.M.–8 P.M.), near the Náměstí Míru subway station, and Laundry Kings (Dejvická 16, tel. 233 343 743, www.laundry.czweb.org, daily 8 A.M.–10 P.M.), near the Hradčanská stop. Both offer DIY or full service, Internet, English-language magazines and newspapers, as well as plenty of opportunities to meet locals and like-minded travelers killing time between spin cycles.

Getting There

BY AIR

Ruzyně Airport (tel. 220 113 314, www.csl.cz) is located in Dejvice, roughly 12.5 miles northwest of the downtown core. The airport is comparatively small and easy to navigate as the Arrivals Hall and Departures Hall are next to each other.

The taxi situation in Prague is pretty abominable all around, but most cabs set a fixed fee for service from the airport to anywhere in town. These days, the going rate is 700 Kč. A far cheaper alternative is the Čedaz (tel. 220 114 296, www.cedaz.cz) shuttle bus that leaves the airport every half-hour 6 A.M.–9 P.M. and drops passengers off at Dejvická subway station (90 Kč) or downtown near Náměstí Republiky (120 Kč). You can also take the friendly Prague Airport Shuttle (www.prague-airport-shuttle.com), which will take up to four passengers anywhere in town for a fixed price of 600 Kč.

BY TRAIN

All international trains make their final stop at either Nádraží Holešovice (Holešovice Station; Vrbenského 1, Holešovice, tel. 220 806 790) or Hlavní nádraží (Main Station; Wilsonova 2, Nové Město, tel. 972 241 883). Both train stations are on the subway's red line, making them easy to reach and traveling in and around the city a piece of cake.

The Main Station is located right downtown, a couple minutes' walk away from Wenceslas Square. There is an information desk at the station, as well as kiosks and shops where you can grab a sandwich or drink. Be wary of anyone who approaches you offering accommodations or bar tips. The station is a haven for drug addicts and the homeless and, while relatively safe, there is no reason to stick around the station any longer than you have to.

Stations serving domestic routes include Masarykovo nádraží and Smíchovské nádraží. Masarykovo nádraží (Masaryk Station; Hybernská, Nové Město, tel. 224 611 111), situated in Prague 1 between Náměstí Republiky and Florenc subway/bus station, serves a large number of cities and towns located in northern and eastern Bohemia. Smíchovské nádraží (Smíchov Station; Nádražní, Smíchov, tel. 221 111 122), in Prague 5, serves all major towns and cities located in the south and west of the Czech Republic.

Trains from Budapest to Prague leave 5–6 times a day, and the trip takes 7–9 hours.

Visit www.idos.cz for schedules and fares of all trains, buses, and planes both leaving and crisscrossing the country.

BY BUS

Florenc bus station (Křižíkova 4, Žižkov, tel. 900 144 444, www.csad.cz) is where all domestic and international coaches come and go. As with the train station, spending any more time here than absolutely necessary is not recommended. Pickpockets, drunks, and various odds and ends lurk about so take care of business and keep on moving. Luckily, the station is served by two subway lines that will quickly take you pretty much anywhere you need to go. On the premises is a Eurolines office (Křižíkova 6, tel. 224 218 680, www .eurolines.cz, daily 5:45 A.M.–10:15 P.M.), which can help you reserve a seat on any one of their numerous buses connecting Prague with the rest of the continent.

Buses leave Budapest for Prague three times a week. The trip lasts 7.5 hours, and a round-trip ticket costs 15,900 Ft.

BY CAR

A valid UK, U.S., or Canadian license is required for you to lawfully drive in the Czech Republic. The country's highways are continually being upgraded, which means that traffic jams and various delays are not out of the ordinary. For travel on the highways, a sticker needs to be bought at a border crossing, gas station, or post office and affixed to your windshield. The validity of coupons is as follows: "R" is valid for one year, "M" for one month, and "D" for one week.

If you're approaching Prague from the east, you'll cross through Zilina, Slovakia; those from the south will pass through Linz, Austria. If coming from the west, Waldhaus/Rozvadov will serve as your border and Reitzenhain/Pohranicí will greet those coming from the northwest.

While Prague boasts highway connections from five major directions, the country's highway network leaves plenty to be desired, as it is incomplete and suffers from poor upkeep. Nevertheless, two major highways lead to the Czech border: the D5 (or international E50) stretches southwest past Plzeň and on to Germany, while the D1 (or international E65) heads to Brno and continues on to Slovakia.

With regard to distances, Budapest is 347 miles, Vienna is 194 miles, Warsaw is 320 miles, and Berlin is 220 miles.

Getting Around

Prague's excellent public transportation system makes it a snap to get around town, connecting all the city's major hubs and hotspots by either tram or subway. Taxi rides are a little risky as plenty of drivers are looking for the next great sucker but it usually beats driving around town, which is usually a remarkably frustrating experience. When all is said and done, by far the best way to get around this beautiful capital is the old-fashioned way—walking.

BY PUBLIC TRANSPORT

Early birds and night owls will both be happy to know that Prague's public transportation system runs 24 hours a day. Regular service typically starts around 5 A.M. and stops 10 or so minutes after midnight. Night trams and buses (all numbered in the 50s) continue on throughout the wee hours, whisking the tired and the drunk to their final destinations. Many stand confused at bus and tram stops trying to decipher the timetables. It's quite easy, really. The stop you are currently waiting at will be highlighted. Look for the stop you are headed to. If it's located below the one you are currently at, then you're going the right way. If it's located above your current position, cross the street and take the bus/tram heading in the opposite direction.

Prague's subway system consists of three lines that cover pretty much the entire city and easily get you to any and all of the major sights and squares. They run every two minutes during peak times and roughly every seven or eight minutes in the evening. Trams are also an excellent way to get around the city, particularly the #22, which leads up to the castle. They run every 5–8 minutes during peak hours and every 10–20 minutes as the day unfolds. Buses are rarely used by visitors as they tend to serve the outer districts and everything worth seeing can be reached by either subway or tram. Nevertheless, they run approximately every 5–15 minutes during the busier hours and every 20–30 when things start to slow down.

Dopravní podnik hl. m. Prahy (Prague Public Transit Company) runs Prague's public transport system. For more information regarding all things public transport, check out www.dpp.cz.

Tickets

Tickets are pre-bought at kiosks, newsstands, and machines at various stops and all subway stations. There is a wide variety of tickets available, including day and week passes, but most need only concern themselves with two types. The first is the 18 Kč ticket, which is good for a 20-minute ride on any form of transport or up to five stops on the subway. The second is a 24 Kč ticket that lasts 75 minutes and allows unlimited travel within

the city, including transfer between subway, bus, and tram.

If you are planning on sticking to the center of Prague, a pass of any kind will not be necessary as most sights are easily reached on foot. For longer trips to the Castle or outlying neighborhoods, odds are you'll save money by simply purchasing individual tickets. Should you, however, plan on doing a lot of traveling in and around the city, or are not able or interested in doing much walking, then a pass will definitely come in handy. The current rates for passes are 100 Kč for a 24-hour pass, 330 Kč for a three-day pass, and 500 Kč for a seven-day pass.

All tickets must be validated when you board a bus or tram or upon entering the "ticket holders only" area of the subway. Stamp your ticket (face up) in the yellow ticket machines found on buses and trams, as well as at the entrances of all subway stations. There are plenty of ticket inspectors patrolling all forms of transport and there is no hiding the fact that they prey on tourists, heading immediately towards large groups speaking foreign languages that may or may not have bothered to pay their way.

BY TAXI

Prague's reputation of having some of the most corrupt cab drivers on the planet remains true and you'll be wise to follow a few simple steps in order to avoid any unfortunate incidents. First of all, never approach taxis that are waiting in line at any of the city center's sights. They will charge you exorbitant fees and may not even be all that friendly while doing so. Secondly, don't flag down a cab unless absolutely necessary. They aren't all out to get your money, but many are and those sitting on the fence won't think twice once they realize you're a tourist. The best thing to do is simply call ahead and request a cab from any of the following cab companies: AAA (tel. 222 333 222, www.aaataxi. cz), City Taxi (tel. 257 257 257), or Profi Taxi (tel. 261 314 151). Doing this will dramatically cut down on the possibility of you being

© TOM DIRLIS

Parking in Prague requires patience.

ripped off and having to deal with what can quickly escalate into an ugly situation.

Rates in Prague tend to change often. Currently, a basic charge of 34 Kč is applied upon entering the taxi. If you hail a cab, the maximum charge is 25 Kč per kilometer, while arranging a cab over the phone will reward you with a lesser charge of 20 Kč per kilometer traveled.

BY CAR

Driving is by far the worst way to get around the city as the central areas that typically attract visitors are either pedestrian zones or clogged with endless traffic. Roads leading out of the city on Fridays and Saturdays are equally terrible, as are the roads leading back into the city on Sundays.

Parking

Parking in Prague can be a nightmare, thanks to a limited amount of spaces and a relatively high rate of auto theft. Remain patient while searching for a spot and, if possible, never leave anything of value in the car.

Tickets, which should be displayed face-up on your dashboard and made plainly visible through the windshield, can be purchased from coin-operated parking meters located on the respective street or lot.

The streets in Prague's center break down into three distinct types of parking zones: blue, orange, and green. The blue zones are reserved for local residents and companies. (This law is strictly enforced so avoid these spots no matter how tempting they may look.) The orange zones accommodate parking for a maximum of two hours. Rates vary from 10 Kč for 15 minutes to 40 Kč for an hour. Green zones are for those looking to park for up to six hours and charge 15 Kč for half an hour, 30 Kč for an hour, and 120 Kč for the full six hours.

Car Rental

The car rental scene in Prague can be both an expensive and frustrating one, with rates climbing year after year and service—particularly in regards to choice of car and management of reservations—still leaving something to be desired. Nevertheless, the overall situation is improving and the companies below tend to be hits more than misses.

Avis (Klimentská 46, tel. 221 851 225, www.avis.cz, Mon.–Fri. 8 A.M.–4:30 P.M., Sat. 8 A.M.–2 P.M., Sun. 10 A.M.–2 P.M., from 3,000 Kč/day) is expensive but reliable. Alimex (Tusarova 39, tel. 233 350 001, www .alimex.eu, daily 8 A.M.–6 P.M., from 750 Kč/day) gives you the best bang for your buck, though reservations ahead of time are essential. Budget (Cistovická 100, tel. 235 325 713, www.budget.cz, Mon.–Fri. 8 A.M.–4:30 P.M., from 2,100 Kč/day) and Hertz (Karlovo náměstí 15, tel. 225 345 041, www.hertz.cz, daily 8 A.M.–8 P.M., from 1,500 Kč/day) also sport decent reputations about town. These companies (with the exception of Alimex) have offices at Ruzyně Airport.

Try to arrange your car rental a few days ahead of time for best possible results and remember to bring your international driving license, passport, and credit card along with you.

BOHEMIA

Easily the more popular of the country's two regions, Bohemia is characterized by its majestic castles, well-preserved towns, rolling hills, and lush river valleys. Located in what can only be described as the heart of Europe, it attracts visitors from all over the continent who are stunned time and time again by the multitude of sights and scenery on offer, as well as by the difference in attitude and traditions of Czechs not interested in living in their country's famed capital. The proximity of marvelous and majestic castles like Karlštejn, Konopiště, and Křivoklát make for leisurely and enchanting day trips back in time and away from the hordes that regularly swarm Prague's center. Those interested in the darker side of things can't miss the opportunity to visit Kutná Hora's macabre Os-

suary, and history buffs will learn plenty from Terezín's memorial to one of the 20th century's darkest chapters. To the west lies Karlovy Vary, site of the country's renowned international film festival and the mother of all spa towns, whose wide array of hotels, restaurants, and curative services blend peacefully with its graceful hilly surroundings. To the south, one finds the unbelievably romantic Český Krumlov, home to the country's second-largest castle and a perfectly preserved medieval town center. Beer and Becherovka are the region's poisons of choice, and you'll find no shortage of either in the endless number of pubs that happily offer the world's best brews to anyone who walks through their doors. With all major destinations being easily reached by either bus or train, it is now easier than

© CORINE TACHTIRIS

HIGHLIGHTS

🌙 **Hrad Karlštejn (Karlštejn Castle):** Located in the pretty Český kras region, the castle is one of the country's most popular destinations thanks to its picture perfect exterior and close proximity to Prague (page 148).

🌙 **Hrad Křivoklát (Křivoklát Castle):** Boasting Central Europe's second-largest late-Gothic hall, this castle is a local favorite; its location in the pretty Berounka Valley offers the perfect backdrop for a romantic drive or walk (page 152).

🌙 **Kostnice Sedlec (Sedlec Ossuary):** Built from the bones of over 40,000 peo-

ple, this macabre chapel's interior gives new meaning to the phrase, "waste not, want not" (page 158).

🌙 **Zámecké divadlo (Castle Theatre):** Whether you're a fan of the period or not, Český Krumlov's Baroque theater is one of the best preserved in the world and comes complete with gorgeous costumes and still-functional machinery (page 163).

🌙 **Vřídla (Karlovy Vary's Springs):** The peaceful, picturesque surroundings and curative waters of the Czech Republic's largest spa have helped everyone from Casanova to Kafka. Why not you too? (page 168)

LOOK FOR 🌙 TO FIND RECOMMENDED SIGHTS, ACTIVITIES, DINING, AND LODGING.

ever for visitors to escape Prague's maddening crowds and enjoy a truly authentic Bohemian experience.

PLANNING YOUR TIME

Due to the close proximity of most locations to Prague, many visitors opt for day trips to a respective town or sight and then return to the capital for dinner and a nightcap. This is definitely the easiest way to take in as much as possible, but should you want to leave the

magic city behind and travel the Bohemian countryside at a leisurely pace, then a week's time ought to be enough to cover everything. Distances between the respective sights are short by North American standards, which means less time in the car and more time to explore the region's history and beauty.

Karlštejn, Konopiště, Křivoklát, and Terezín can each be done in a morning or afternoon as there is little else to see other than the particular sights they are known for. It would

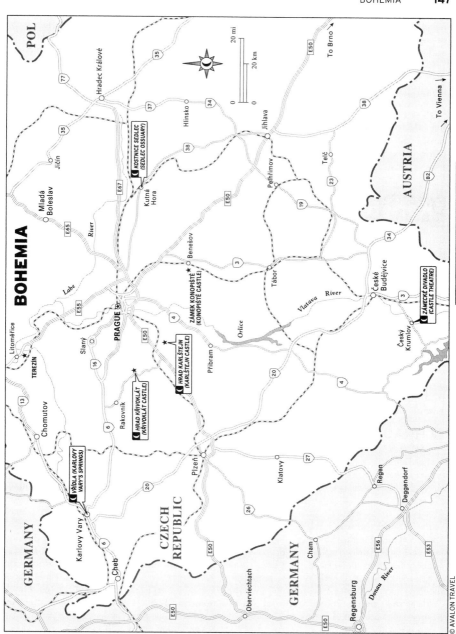

BOHEMIA

© AVALON TRAVEL

be relatively easy, in other words, to double up on sights and visit Karlštejn in the morning and Křivoklát, for example, in the afternoon. This, however, would require some advance planning and sticking to a tight schedule, which may or may not jibe with your idea of a vacation.

Kutná Hora can also be covered in a day but offers a charming selection of bars, restaurants, and shops that can, according to your tastes, twist your arm into staying overnight. If time permits, both Český Krumlov and Kar-

lovy Vary definitely deserve overnight stays. While they can each be done in a day, their charm and overall atmosphere are infectious, and many who leave the same day they arrived do so wishing they had planned for an extra day's visit. Do yourself a favor and grant yourself enough time to properly absorb and appreciate the grandeur of Český Krumlov's castle and magical town square as well as the spas of Karlovy Vary, which will have you feeling good as new after a peaceful and relaxing couple of days.

Karlštejn

Karlštejn village is situated along the banks of the Berounka River in the picturesque region of Český kras. It is located roughly 18 miles southwest of Prague and is home to the country's second-most popular tourist destination—Karlštejn Castle. Open longer throughout the year than any other sight in the country, the castle is typically overrun by busloads of tourists from all around the world, bringing with it an onslaught of souvenir stalls, ice-cream vendors, and inflated prices. Despite the crowds, a visit to this beautiful castle makes for an excellent day trip and is close enough to Prague that you can be back for dinner.

◖ HRAD KARLŠTEJN (KARLŠTEJN CASTLE)

Constructed by Charles IV in order to keep safe the royal treasures—particularly his collection of holy relics and coronation jewels of the Roman Empire—Karlštejn Castle (tel. 274 008 154-5-6, www.hradkarlstejn.cz) took nine years to build and was ultimately finished in 1365. Situated on a rocky outcrop surrounded by forests, vineyards, and hills, it is not only a stronghold against potential danger, but a thing of remarkable beauty as well. As a matter of fact, the King and son Wenceslas oftentimes used the castle as their summer home and royal palace. Besieged on a number of occasions, the worst of it coming at the hands of the Hussites in 1422,

the castle nevertheless survived one way or another throughout the years. A major renovation took place in the 19th century, giving us the extraordinary exterior we so admire today.

In order to see the interior of the castle, which, by the way, has been sadly neglected for no clearly understandable reason, visitors can choose from two tours. The first runs for 50 minutes and takes you through the Courtier's Hall, Royal Bedroom, Audience and Banquet Halls, Hall of Ancestors, Treasury and Jewels Hall, and former castle prison. Admission is 220 Kč. The second tour lasts 70 minutes and visits the Church of Our Lady, Chapel of St. Catharine, former Sacristy, wooden bridge, lapidary museum, picture gallery, and the Holy Rood Chapel, famous for the more than 2,000 precious and semiprecious inlaid gems adorning its walls. Please note that the second tour requires booking in advance and costs 300 Kč. There is an additional 20 Kč reservation fee for the first tour (reservation optional) and 30 Kč fee for the second.

The castle is open Tuesday–Sunday and has the following hours of operation: May, June, and September 9 A.M.–noon and 12:30–5 P.M.; July and August 9 A.M.–noon and 12:30–6 P.M.; April and October 9 A.M.–noon and 1–4 P.M.; November, December, and March 9 A.M.–noon and 1–3 P.M.; January 1–6 9 A.M.–noon and 12:30–3 P.M.

ENTERTAINMENT AND EVENTS
Karlštejn Vintage

For two whole days in late September, both the village and castle grounds of Karlštejn are transformed into one large medieval experience. Performances abound, including a number of traditional music concerts along with those by royal trumpeters and jesters. There is so much to see one doesn't know whether to begin with the grand royal joust, the fencing performances, the Gothic and Renaissance fashion show, or the fire-eating and magic demonstrations. A huge medieval fair in the village offers delicious, meat-heavy culinary delights from the period and there is plenty of local wine to be imbibed as well. For those who would like to live in a completely different dimension of time for a day or two, make sure to circle this event as it's one that always attracts a large, fun-seeking crowd. Admission is 100 Kč on Saturday, which allows you access to both days, and 50 Kč on Sunday. Children 15 and under get in for free. For more information, check out www.hradkarlstejn.cz.

ACCOMMODATIONS

The **Romantic Hotel Mlýn Karlštejn** (Karlštejn 329, tel. 311 744 411, mlyn@ europehotels.cz, 3,100 Kč d) sits on the Berounka River next to the castle. Its 21 tastefully furnished rooms have all the modern necessities a traveler could want, including TV and Internet, and its warm, down-home friendly restaurant makes for an excellent place to enjoy a tasty, traditional meal. Plenty of sporting opportunities are available as well, including a fitness center on the premises and a professional golf course a mere five minutes away.

Situated quite close to the castle is the **Hotel Koruna Karlštejn** (Karlštejn 13, tel. 311 681 465, www.korunakarlstejn.cz, 1,000 Kč d). Sporting 14 rooms with the basic amenities, it is a comfortable and affordable choice should you want to spend the night and explore the region. The staff is helpful and the hotel's restaurant, lounges, and summer terrace are wonderful spots to enjoy a meal, morning coffee, or after-dinner cocktail.

FOOD

Its appeal not limited to just its guests, the **Koruna Restaurant** (Karlštejn 13, tel. 311 681 465, www.korunakarlstejn.cz, daily 10 A.M.–10 P.M., mains 170–400 Kč) is a part of the hotel with the same name, serving up traditional meals in newly reconstructed surroundings, including a lovely summer terrace seating 120. For those who like wild game, their venison dishes tend to be top of the line.

U Janů (Karlštejn 90, tel. 311 681 210, www.ujanu.cz, daily 11 A.M.–10 P.M., mains 150–250 Kč) is another restaurant in the vicinity that serves up authentic Czech fish and turkey dishes, not to mention a mouth-watering mix-grill plate. The setting is traditional, the service friendly, and the prices affordable.

SHOPPING

The tiny souvenir shops and stalls located all around the castle and village sell typical fare that can be found just about anywhere in the country. Products range from Czech garnet, Bohemian crystal, handicrafts, and tacky t-shirts. If considering some of the more valuable items as gifts, a good idea is to have an idea of what the prices are in Prague and compare. You may be surprised to find that some products are actually cheaper in the capital. This is due to the massive influx of tourists that arrives daily and is eager to buy. Another tip is to bring snacks or water from Prague, as the shops at the base of the village tend to sell these things at heavily inflated prices.

SPORTS AND RECREATION

Although still very much a new and growing sport in the Czech Republic, golf has begun to catch on and **Golf Resort Karlštejn** (Běleč 272, Liteň, tel. 311 604 999, www.karlstejn-golf .cz, May–Aug. daily 7 A.M.–9 P.M., Sept. daily 8 A.M.–7 P.M., Apr. and Oct. daily 8 A.M.–6 P.M.) is one of the finer courses around. Opened in 1993 and designed by Canadians Les Furber and Jim Eremko, the course's hilly landscape, gorges, lakes, and multiple sand traps combine to make these 18 holes an "easy bogey but difficult birdie" kind of place. Albeit not on par (pun intended)

BOHEMIA

with some of the more famous courses in the world, there is something to be said about enjoying an afternoon of golf with majestic Karlštejn Castle in the background. Greens fees are 2,000 Kč Monday–Friday (1,000 Kč Mon.–Wed. till 11 A.M.), 3,000 Kč Saturday–Sunday.

INFORMATION AND SERVICES

There is no official tourist center, but any and all information regarding Karlštejn can be found either online at the castle's website or from any information center in Prague. Any additional information you may want can be had by joining one or both of the tours of the castle.

GETTING THERE
By Train

Most people prefer to travel to the castle by train. They leave from either Prague's Hlavní nádraží or Smíchovské nádraží roughly every hour, with the trip itself lasting a pleasant 40–45 minutes along the Berounka River. A second-class ticket with return costs 50 Kč. The village and castle are about a 15-minute walk from the station.

By Car

Karlštejn is 19 miles from Prague. If you have a car and would like to drive through the Czech countryside, there are two ways to get to the castle. The first and more scenic route is to leave Prague in a southwesterly direction along Highway 4 in the direction of Strakonice. Take the Karlštejn cutoff and follow the signs. The second route follows Route 5 out of Prague towards Plzeň. You'll find the Karlštejn cutoff about 20 minutes into your trip. Both routes take about a half an hour.

Konopiště

The Posázaví Region is a peaceful, picturesque area that has been a favorite with Praguers desperately looking to escape from the rigors of the big city. It seems like there are woods, castles, churches, and charming little towns everywhere you turn and a drive or train ride through these parts remind one of the curative powers of both travel and nature. There is no question that Konopiště Castle near Benešov is the region's most famous attraction, second only to Karlštejn in popularity. Located a mere 30 miles from Prague, a visit to the castle makes for an easily managed and enjoyable day trip—a remarkable step back in time that you won't forget in the near future.

ZÁMEK KONOPIŠTĚ (KONOPIŠTĚ CASTLE)

Konopiště Castle (tel. 317 721 366, www .zamek-konopiste.cz) was originally founded as a Gothic fortress in 1300 in the Sázava River valley. It went through a handful of architectural changes before undergoing extensive reconstruction in the 19th century. In 1887, the castle came under the ownership of Archduke Franz Ferdinand, whose eventual death in 1914 triggered the First World War. In the 1890s, St. George renovated the castle adding such modern touches as flush toilets, electricity, and an elevator. There is no doubt that the Archduke lived luxuriously here with his Czech wife Sophie, entertaining nobility and constantly feeding his one great obsession—hunting.

According to his records, the Archduke shot roughly 300,000 creatures in his lifetime, including foxes, deer, tigers, bears, wild boar, and birds. To put that in perspective, that means he shot 20 animals every day for roughly 41 years. More than 100,000 of these animals decorate the walls at Konopiště, making a tour through the trophy and antler rooms a rather overwhelming and spooky experience.

There are three guided tours available, all of which need a separate ticket. Tour 1 (50 min-

© CORINE TACHTIRIS

Konopiště Castle

utes, 190 Kč) takes you through Ferdinand's remarkable hunting collection on display, which, despite only representing roughly 1 percent of his entire collection, still ranks as one of Europe's largest. Visitors are also treated to the castle's parlors, which have been meticulously restored. Tour 2 (55 minutes, 190 Kč) deals with the Great Armory, which boasts one of the largest and most impressive collections of weapons, along with the chapel and "Gentlemen's Club," which was out of bounds to women at the time. Tour 3 (60–70 minutes, 300 Kč) is considerably more expensive but allows guests to visit the private apartments used by the Archduke and his family, which have been left virtually untouched since the state took possession of the castle in 1921. The castle is open April and October Tuesday–Friday 9 A.M.–3 P.M., Saturday–Sunday 9 A.M.–4 P.M.; May–August Tuesday–Sunday 9 A.M.–5 P.M.; September Tuesday–Friday 9 A.M.–4 P.M., Saturday–Sunday 9 A.M.–5 P.M.; closed November–March.

Before leaving, make sure to allow yourself enough time to stroll through the well-kept gardens, still home to a number of quails, pheasants, and peacocks. There are several open areas that make perfect spots for a romantic picnic as well. Should you feel like picnicking, however, make sure to do your shopping beforehand as there are no grocery stores anywhere near the castle.

ACCOMMODATIONS

The **Hotel Benica** (Ke Stadionu 2045, Benešov, tel. 317 725 611-12, www.benica.cz, 1,700 Kč d) is located about a half a mile from Konopiště Castle in tranquil countryside surroundings. There are 67 rooms and 3 suites in all and a pretty, well-maintained outdoor swimming pool as well. Comfortable and close to any and all sights and shops, the hotel also boasts an excellent trattoria known for cooking up Czech favorites, Italian specialties, and fantastic pizza.

Situated right by the Konopiste Chateau, the **Hotel Nová Myslivna** (Konopiště 22, tel. 317 722 496, www.e-stranka.cz/novamyslivna, 700 Kč d) offers its guests modern facilities in warm, friendly surroundings as well as excellent traditional meals at a quarter of the price you'd pay in Prague. If you plan on staying in town overnight, this place is hard to beat.

FOOD

Restaurace Stará Myslivna (Konopiště 2, tel. 317 721 148, www.staramyslivnakonopiste .cz, daily 11 A.M.–11 P.M., mains 120–280 Kč) means "Old Gamekeeper's Lodge"—a fitting name for this homey, rustic restaurant. Traditional, meat-heavy meals that include venison specialties are on offer and go very well with a glass of ice-cold Pilsner Urquell beer.

Located just under the castle, **Restaurace Nova Myslivna** (Konopiště 22, tel. 317 722 496, www.e-stranka.cz/novamyslivna, daily 11 A.M.–11 P.M., mains 120–280 Kč), or "New Gamekeeper's Lodge," offers excellent traditional Czech food in elegant surroundings. Known for its social events, it oftentimes is the setting to huge parties that include barbecues on the terrace, sword-fighting shows, and nights filled with folk and dance music. Make

BOHEMIA

sure to check out the website for listings or simply pay a visit and enjoy the fantastic fare.

SHOPPING

There aren't too many shopping opportunities available, except at the castle courtyard and terrace. There you'll find a small array of souvenirs, postcards, books, and classical music CDs.

SPORTS AND RECREATION

If you're staying overnight and love golf, you cannot miss the opportunity to tee-off at **Golf Resort Konopiště** (Tvoršovice 27, Benesov, tel. 317 784 044, www.gcko.cz, Mar.–Oct. daily 8 A.M.–dusk). Two 18-hole master courses await, as do a driving range, various short-game areas, and a 9-hole public course for beginners. There's even an indoor facility should you visit during the winter. Their renovated chateau—complete with clubroom, pro shop, restaurant, and hotel—have thus far gotten raves. Greens fees for 18 holes are 1,600 Kč Monday–Thursday, 2,000 Kč Friday–Sunday.

INFORMATION AND SERVICES

There is no official information center per se. Any questions you might have can be answered at the castle ticket window or online at the castle's official website.

GETTING THERE
By Bus

Buses leave Prague's Florenc station roughly every 45 minutes, with the trip lasting about an hour. A round-trip ticket costs 51 Kč.

By Train

Trains leave hourly from Prague's main train station, Hlavní nádraží, with tickets costing 64 Kč. There is no train station in Konopiště however, so you'll have to get off at Benešov station and then either catch one of the infrequent local buses headed for the castle or walk 1.25 miles. If walking, turn left as you leave the station then left across the bridge over the railway and follow Konopištská Street west.

By Car

Konopiště is 22 miles from Prague. Take the D1 expressway heading south and exit near Benešov, following the signs for Konopiště. The trip lasts about 45 minutes. The parking lot by the castle costs 50 Kč and is your best (and pretty much only) bet.

Křivoklát

Křivoklát is located roughly 28 miles west of Prague in the lush and peaceful Berounka River Valley. Apart from the castle's wooded, hilly surroundings being a thing of remarkable natural beauty, they are also a UNESCO biosphere preservation area, making Křivoklát an exceptional place to go for a walk or hike. The castle itself dates back to the 12th century and was a favorite of King Wenceslas IV, who preferred it to his father's Karlštejn lodgings. During the course of its history, it served as both a fortress and prison that once held English alchemist Edward Kelly, who was kept here after Rudolf II grew tired of waiting for him to turn base metals into gold.

Less crowded and nowhere near the tourist attraction its upstream neighbor Karlštejn is, Křivoklát is a wonderful reason to escape the modernity and bustle of the city and enjoy one of the oldest and most well-known castles in the country.

◖ HRAD KŘIVOKLÁT (KŘIVOKLÁT CASTLE)

Largely unknown to tourists, Křivoklát Castle (Křivoklát 47, tel. 313 558 440, www.krivoklat .cz, 150 Kč) nevertheless boasts one of the finest interiors to be found in the country. A tour of the grounds includes the late Gothic **Royal Chapel,** affectionately dubbed the "pearl" of the castle, which was originally open only to royalty and nobility. It is characterized by a 15th-century altar of the Virgin Mary, which looks to the right in the direction of where the king sat with his family. The intricate carvings decorating the pews are both beautiful and slightly unnerving as they are of angels holding medieval torture instruments. If the chapel is the pearl of the castle, then the magnificent **Great Royal Hall** is its heart. Measuring an impressive 79 feet long, it is Central Europe's second-largest late-Gothic hall and features remarkable Gothic ribbing, as well as a replicated throne and collection of statues that gives the feeling of somehow transported back in time to an audience with the King. The **Knight's Hall** is equally magical with its fantastic collection of late Gothic art and the **Furstenberg Picture Gallery** has the distinct honor of being one of the Czech Republic's largest castle libraries, with a collection numbering well over 50,000 volumes. Finally, there are the **castle's dungeons,** as well as those of **Huderka Tower,** which have preserved various torture devices, including a rack and Iron Maiden. A walk through here chills the blood and serves as a reminder of the period's shocking cruelty, offering a very different picture from the majesty distinguishing the rest of the grounds.

Tours of the castle are offered April and September Tuesday–Sunday 9 A.M.–noon, 1–4 P.M.; May–August Tuesday–Sunday 9 A.M.–noon, 1–5 P.M.; October Tuesday–Sunday 9 A.M.–noon, 1–3 P.M.; November–December Saturday–Sunday 9 A.M.–noon, 1–3 P.M.; January–March for booked groups of 10 people minimum only.

ENTERTAINMENT AND EVENTS

The annual Křivoklání Festival (mid-Oct.) is a step back in time and then some. Held at the castle, the festival focuses on all things medieval, including fencing tournaments, medieval music concerts, jugglers, and a harrowing presentation of what is politely called "The Executioner's Art." The festival is also accompanied by a fun-filled fair where visitors can try their hand at archery or taste the Czech specialty known as *medovina* (hot mead).

ACCOMMODATIONS

Although it certainly doesn't look like much from the outside, the **Hotel Sýkora** (Náměstí Svatopluka Čecha 85, tel. 313 558 114, www .hotel-sykora.krivoklatsko.com, 400 Kč d) is just fine for travelers who are comfortable with the bare essentials. Comfortable, rustic, and sporting a generally friendly staff, guests will find themselves comfortable here should they want to spend a night in town.

Perfect for the budget traveler, the **Hotel Roztoky** (Roztoky u Křivoklátu 14, tel. 607 854 425, www.hotelroztoky.cz, 250–470 Kč d) offers clean and comfortable dorm-type single, double, and triple rooms. The attached restaurant serves traditional Czech cuisine at very affordable prices (mains 80–150 Kč) and the location a mere half-mile away from the castle is not too shabby, either.

FOOD

Seating 60 and serving up traditional Czech dishes just like grandma used to make is **Penzion a Restaurace U Jelena** (Hradní 53, tel. 313 558 529, www.u-jelena.cz, Mon.–Thurs. and Sun. 10 A.M.–10 P.M., Fri.–Sat. 10 A.M.–midnight, mains 120–350 Kč). A common location for banquets, wedding receptions and the like, it has earned a decent reputation for its venison, fish and poultry dishes.

INFORMATION AND SERVICES

There is no official information center per se. Any questions you might have can be answered at the castle ticket window or online at the castle's official website.

GETTING THERE
By Train

Trains heading directly to Křivoklát are rare. The best thing to do is to catch one of the regularly departing trains for Beroun from either Prague's Smíchovské nádraží or Hlavní nádraží. Then change trains at Beroun for Křivoklát. The whole trip lasts a little over an hour and a half and costs approximately 100 Kč.

By Car

Křivoklát is 28 miles from Prague. Follow the E50-D5 in the direction of Beroun. Turn off at junction 14 and take the Berounka Valley west in the direction of Rakovník.

Terezín

Knowing his empire was under threat of attack by Prussian forces, Emperor Joseph II had a fortress town built here in 1780. Roughly 160 years later, Nazi forces took command of the area, establishing a terrifying transit camp that held approximately 140,000 people in total, over half of whom were shipped off to Auschwitz and Treblinka. Terezín is also remembered as the site where the Nazis fooled the world. On June 23, 1944, foreign visitors, including two from the Red Cross, came to inspect the grounds in order to ascertain whether the rumors of atrocities committed against the Jews were true. What they found instead was children studying at schools, shops stocked with goods, and a thriving cultural life that even included a jazz band. Completely fooled by the carefully choreographed stunt, the visitors left satisfied that everything was aboveboard. By the time Russian forces liberated Terezín on May 10, 1945, over 35,000 Jews had died due to disease, starvation, or suicide.

TEREZÍN MEMORIAL
Hlavní Pevnost
(Main Fortress)

Upon entering the Main Fortress, an eerie silence hangs heavily in the air, enveloping the town's gloomy, grid-pattern streets. The **Ghetto Museum,** the main sight here, lies just off the main square. Opened in 1991 in the town's former school, it chronicles the rise of Nazism in Czechoslovakia, as well as daily life in the ghetto. The exhibitions have been arranged with the help of those who survived the ghetto, adding an element of authenticity that hits visitors that much harder.

The **Magdeburg Barracks** is the Ghetto Museum's second branch. Opened in 1997, it features a reconstructed prison dormitory from the period, as well as exhibits detailing the remarkable music, art, literature, and theater that somehow managed to develop here under such terrible conditions.

Malá Pevnost
(Small Fortress)

During 1940–1945, the Small Fortress served as the Prague Gestapo's prison. In front of the fortress is the Národní hřbitov (National Cemetery), where the bodies of 10,000 victims are buried and overseen by a gigantic wooden cross. Above the fortress gate hangs a chilling sign that reads Arbeit Nacht Frei ("Work Sets One Free"). A free map, obtainable from the ticket office, helps guide you through the workshops, isolation cells, prison barracks, and execution grounds, each one becoming harder and harder to absorb.

Practicalities

The Ghetto Museum and Magdeburg Barracks are open November–March daily 9 A.M.–5:30 P.M., April–October daily 9 A.M.–6 P.M. The Small Fortress is open November–March daily 8 A.M.–4:30 P.M., April–October daily 8 A.M.–6 P.M. Tickets for the Ghetto Museum and Magdeburg Barracks or the Small Fortress are 160 Kč, while a combined entrance ticket costs 200 Kč.

Further information about the memorial (tel. 416 782 225) can be found at www.pamatnik-terezin.cz. There's an onsite information center (Ghetto Museum, tel. 416 782 616) open during the memorial's hours.

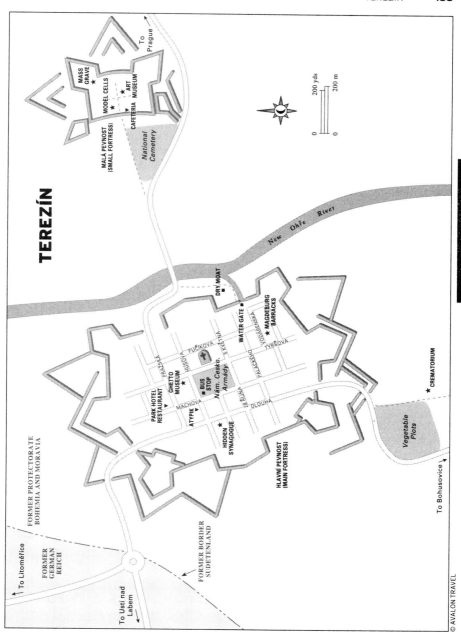

TEREZÍN

MALÁ PEVNOST (SMALL FORTRESS)

MASS GRAVE ★

MODEL CELLS ★

ART MUSEUM ★

CAFETERIA ▼

National Cemetery

To Prague

0 — 200 yds
0 — 200 m

New Ohře River

DRY MOAT ■

WATER GATE ■

MAGDEBURG BARRACKS ★

FUČÍKOVA

5 KVĚTNA

VODÁRENSKÁ

TYRSOVA

HUSOVA

PRAŽSKÁ

Nám. Česko. Armády

PALACKÉHO

BUS STOP ■

GHETTO MUSEUM ▼

PARK HOTEL RESTAURANT ▼

MACHOVA

28 ŘÍJNA

DLOUHA

ATYPIK ▶

HIDDEN SYNAGOGUE ★

HLAVNÍ PEVNOST (MAIN FORTRESS)

CREMATORIUM ★

Vegetable Plots

To Bohusovice

FORMER PROTECTORATE BOHEMIA AND MORAVIA

FORMER GERMAN REICH

FORMER BORDER SUDETENLAND

To Litoměřice

To Ústí nad Labem

© AVALON TRAVEL

ENTERTAINMENT AND EVENTS

There are no set cultural events that happen annually or on a regular basis at Terezín. However, there are competitions, concerts, and plays performed on occasion. The Attic Theatre in the Magdeburg Barracks has been known to put on both musical and dramatic performances from children's theaters here in the Czech Republic and abroad. Well-known Jewish classical musicians visit and perform here on occasion as well. Check Terezín's official website for current details.

FOOD

Terezín isn't exactly a town known for its restaurant scene, as most visitors prefer to leave soon after they've done the rounds. However, if you're feeling a tad peckish, try the goulash or other Czech standards at **Atypik** (Máchova 91, tel. 416 782 780, Mon.–Fri. 9:30 A.M.–9 P.M., Sat. 11 A.M.–9 P.M., Sun. 11 A.M.–6 P.M., mains 100–150 Kč). It's a standard cafe on the main square and as good a place as any to have a coffee or bite to eat while absorbing what you've just seen.

INFORMATION AND SERVICES

Find everything you need to know about Terezín and its history at the Tourist Information Center (Náměstí Čs armády 179, tel. 416 782 616, Mon.–Thurs. 8 A.M.–5 P.M., Fri. 8 A.M.–1:30 P.M., Sun. 9 A.M.–3 P.M.). You can also find useful information online at www .pamatnik-terezin.cz.

GETTING THERE
By Bus

Buses leave Prague's Florenc station hourly, with the journey lasting roughly an hour. Tickets cost approximately 60 Kč.

By Car

Terezín is located 31 miles northwest of Prague. At Holešovice, join Route 8 or the E55 via Veltrusy and follow it all the way to Terezín.

Kutná Hora

The discovery of rich silver ore deposits in the second half of the 13th century sparked an economic boom in Kutná Hora that turned this sleepy miner's settlement into the second-most important town in Bohemia, rivaling Prague in terms of economic, political, and cultural importance. King Wenceslas II declared it a royal town in 1307 and the Royal Mint, established in Kutná Hora a year later, went on to produce roughly one-third of Europe's total production of silver. As the town's wealth grew, so did the number of grandiose palaces and churches, forming one of the continent's most beautiful city centers. Things started taking a turn for the worse at the beginning of the 16th century, however, when Germany's dramatic increase of silver production, coupled with huge amounts of silver being now imported from America, began weakening Kutná Hora's power signifi-

cantly. The gradual depletion of ore deposits and the destruction caused by the Thirty Years' War were the industry's final death blows, leading to the closing of the Royal Mint in 1727 and the official end of a remarkable era.

Today, Kutná Hora remains one of Bohemia's most popular day-trip destinations thanks in large part to its charming historical center, which joined UNESCO's World Cultural Heritage List in December 1995. Further sites of interest are the chilling Sedlec Ossuary, the Czech Silver Museum and Medieval Mine, and the town's most spectacular achievement, St. Barbara's Cathedral.

CHRÁM SV. BARBORY (ST. BARBARA'S CATHEDRAL)

Named after the patron saint of miners, St. Barbara's Cathedral (Barborská Street, tel. 327

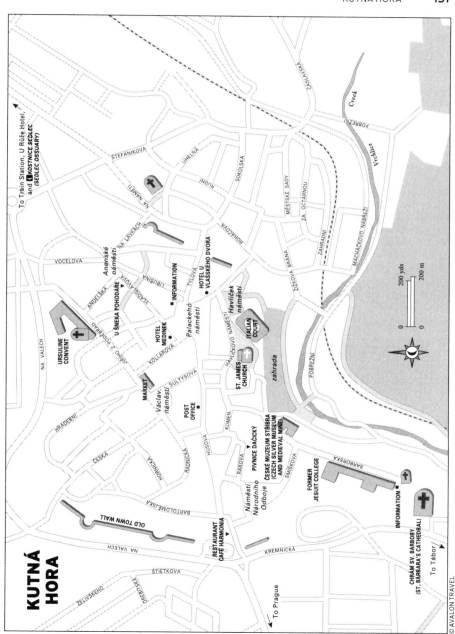

BOHEMIA

KUTNÁ HORA

To Train Station, U Růže Hotel, and KOSTNICE SEDLEC (SEDLEC OSSUARY)

STEFANIKOVA

UHELNÁ

Creek

Vrchlice

POBŘEŽNÍ

SOKOLSKÁ

RUDNÍ

MĚSTSKÉ SADY

ZA OCTARNOU

MACHÁČKOVO NÁBŘEŽÍ

NA NÁMĚTI

NA LÁVKÁCH

VOCELOVA

Anenské náměstí

VLADISLAVOVA

LIBUŠINA

INFORMATION

TYLOVA

HOTEL U VLAŠSKÉHO DVORA

ROHÁČKOVA

ZAHRADNÍ

ŽIŽKOVA BRÁNA

200 yds

200 m

ANDĚLSKÁ

U ŠNEKA POHODÁŘE

JIŘÍHO Z PODĚBRAD

Palackého náměstí

Havlíčkovo náměstí

HOTEL MEDINEK

KOLLÁROVA

HAVLÍČKOVO NÁMĚSTÍ

ITALIAN COURT

NA VALECH

URSULINE CONVENT

MARKET

Václav. náměstí

ŠULTYSOVA

ST. JAMES CHURCH

zahrada

POBŘEŽNÍ

HRADEBNÍ

POST OFFICE

KOMEN.

HUSOVA

ČESKÁ

RADNICKÁ

HORNICKÁ

RÁKOVA

PIVNICE DAČICKÝ

ČESKÉ MUZEUM STŘÍBRA (CZECH SILVER MUSEUM AND MEDIEVAL MINE)

SMÍŠKOVA

FORMER JESUIT COLLEGE

BARBORSKÁ

Náměstí Národního Odboje

OLD TOWN WALL

BARTOLOMĚJSKÁ

RESTAURANT CAFÉ HARMONIA

NA VALECH

KREMNICKÁ

INFORMATION

CHRÁM SV. BARBORY (ST. BARBARA'S CATHEDRAL)

ŠTIETKOVA

ŽELIVSKÉHO

OŘEBITSKÁ

To Prague

To Tábor

© AVALON TRAVEL

512 115, Oct.–Apr. Tues.–Sun. 10 A.M.–4 P.M., May–Sept. Tues.–Sun. 9 A.M.–6 P.M., 30 Kč) is quite simply one of the world's most remarkable examples of Gothic architecture. Based on the initial designs of Petr Parléř (who was also responsible for Prague's St. Vitus Cathedral), construction began in 1388 but was interrupted for an extended period of time due to the Hussite Wars. Work on the building ended in 1558 when the mines and money began to run out, but sporadic renovations and additions continued until the end of the 19th century. The cathedral's soaring arches and countless spires set the stage for a stunning interior dominated by the main altar and decorated with gorgeous frescoes depicting religious motifs and scenes inspired by its rich mining past. Overhead, four wooden statues symbolizing Justice, Bravery, Caution, and Temperance hang from a mind-boggling height, but perhaps the cathedral's most inspired achievement is its enormous glass windows, designed specifically to allow in as much brilliant white light as possible.

KOSTNICE SEDLEC (SEDLEC OSSUARY)

Roughly a mile south from Kutná Hora train station is Sedlec, home to Sedlec Ossuary (Zámecká 127, Sedlec, tel. 327 561 143, www.kostnice.cz, Nov.–Feb. daily 9 A.M.–noon, 1–4 P.M., Apr.–Sept. daily 8 A.M.–6 P.M., Oct. and Mar. daily 9 A.M.–noon, 1–5 P.M., 40 Kč), a macabre chapel decorated with the bones of approximately 40,000 people. The story began in 1278 when King Otakar II sent Henry, the abbot of Sedlec, on a diplomatic mission to Jerusalem. Henry returned with a small amount of earth taken from Golgotha and sprinkled it over the cemetery of Sedlec Monastery. The grounds were declared holy and the cemetery grew in fame throughout Central Europe, becoming the most sought-after burial site of the powerful and wealthy. The bodies began piling up during the plague epidemics of the 14th century and the Hussite Wars in the 15th, prompting the building of an underground chapel that was to be the final destination of the ever-increasing number of remains. When the Schwarzenberg family bought the monastery in the late 1800s, they hired local woodcarver František Rint, who hit upon a creative solution to the massive buildup of centuries-old bones. The result is the Ossuary as we know it today: a remarkable collection of bones arranged into crosses, columns, chalices, and monstrances, as well as giant bells in each of the chapel's corners and an enormous chandelier in the center of the nave containing every bone in the human body. There is even an impressive coat of arms of the Schwarzenberg family. Slightly surreal and bordering on the grotesque, this is one experience you will never forget.

ČESKÉ MUZEUM STŘIBRA (CZECH SILVER MUSEUM AND MEDIEVAL MINE)

Hrádek is a pretty 15th-century castle housing the Czech Silver Museum and Medieval Mine (Barborská 28, tel. 327 512 159, www.cms-kh .cz, Apr. and Oct. Tues.–Sun. 9 A.M.–5 P.M., May, June, and Sept. Tues.–Sun. 9 A.M.–6 P.M., July–Aug. Tues.–Sun. 10 A.M.–6 P.M., Nov. Tues.–Fri. only by prior arrangement, Sat.–Sun. 10 A.M.–4 P.M., Tour I 60 Kč, Tour II 110 Kč, combined ticket 130 Kč), offering visitors two tours that detail Kutná Hora's illustrious past. The first tour is entitled "The Town of Silver" and outlines the history of Hrádek, as well as the town's geological and architectural development. It's the second tour, however, "The Way of Silver," that most people opt for. A short explanation of the process of developing silver ore into coins is given before guests are equipped with lamps, helmets, and protective suits and led down into the medieval mines. Reservations are strongly recommended for this tour, as it is more popular by far.

ENTERTAINMENT AND EVENTS
Kutná Hora Music Festival

This classical music festival (mid-Sept.) is held in many of the town's most impressive historical landmarks, including the spectacular St.

Barbara's Cathedral. Leading Czech musicians are joined by prominent artists from around the world in performing immensely popular compositions from the 13th–20th centuries. Taking in a performance in any one of the town's breathtaking Gothic buildings makes for a truly memorable evening.

Královské stříbření Kutné Hory (Silver Mining Festival)

The Silver Mining Festival (second half of June) is a colorful Gothic festival that takes place every year and celebrates Kutná Hora's glory days in the 15th century. The festivities begin with the "arrival" of King Wenceslas IV, which is full of playful pomp and circumstance. Locals join actors by dressing up in costumes of the period and indulge in the non-stop concerts, dances, jousts, and competitions that animate the town for an entire weekend.

ACCOMMODATIONS

The **❰ Hotel U Vlašského dvora** (28. října 511, tel. 327 514 618, www.vlasskydvur.cz, 1,550 Kč d) is located in the historical center of town, offering guests beautiful views of the area's steeples, churches, and weather-beaten rooftops. Stylish and trendy, the hotel's clean, spacious rooms should satisfy even the finickiest of travelers and the friendly staff will be more than happy to do whatever they can to make your stay a pleasant one.

The **U Růže Hotel** (Zámecká 52, tel. 327 524 115, www.ruzehotel.cz, 1,300–1,600 Kč d) is one of the more charming places to rest your head in town. It's decorated with antique furniture and old collectibles; you'll find yourself feeling at peace the moment you walk in. The rooms are clean and spacious, the staff friendly and helpful, and the hotel restaurant offers tasty Czech and international cuisine. Within walking distance of the Ossuary, the only thing that may turn some off is the lack of an elevator.

The **Hotel Medinek** (Palackého náměstí 1, tel. 226 201 910-13, www.pragueholiday.cz/medinek-hotel-kutna-hora, 1,600 Kč d) is an affordable option that is situated opposite the tourist information center in the town's central square. Fifty clean double rooms and apartments, helpful staff happy to organize tours and events, fitness center, sauna, and an excellent restaurant serving Czech and international fare should be enough to convince anyone to stay here. If you do, make sure to book a room overlooking the square for the best possible views.

FOOD

❰ Pivnice Dačický (Rakova 8, tel. 327 512 248, www.dacicky.com, Mon.–Fri. 11 A.M.–11 P.M., Sat.–Sun. 11 A.M.–midnight, mains 149–299 Kč) is a veritable institution in town and has been operating for over 400 years. Serving up traditional Czech delicacies, international specialties, and extremely interesting "alchemical dishes," this is a warm, inviting, and reputable restaurant that should not be missed.

U Šneka Pohodáře (Vladislavová 333, tel. 327 515 987, Sun.–Thurs. 11 A.M.–10 P.M., Fri.–Sat. 11 A.M.–midnight, mains 95–180 Kč) is an excellent pizzeria and a local favorite. The chicken and broccoli pizza is particularly good, though there are plenty of combinations to choose from. The service is very friendly, the decor is warm and inviting, and you get great value for the money. An excellent choice should you feel like Italian during your stay.

Restaurant Cafe Harmonia (Husova 105, tel. 327 512 105, daily 10 A.M.–11 P.M., mains 70–180 Kč) is a popular stop that's located to the rear of the St. James Church. Excellent soups, salads, and lighter fare are served up to both locals and visitors enjoying the sun on one of the nicer terraces in town.

SHOPPING

Puppets/marionettes and glass are two of the biggest-selling souvenirs in Kutná Hora. There are numerous shops throughout town selling them and your best bet is to do a little comparison-shopping. Typically, the shops along the main tourist routes will be slightly more expensive than the ones hidden around corners or down side streets. Either way, all prices here are generally 25–50 percent cheaper than in Prague.

Antikvariát Felix Jenewein (Barborská 23, tel. 327 514 304, www.antikvariat-kutna -hora.cz, Mon.–Sat. 9 A.M.–noon, 1–5 P.M., Sun. 10 A.M.–noon, 1–4 P.M.) is a used bookstore that has been kicking around since 1991. Filled with old maps, books, paintings, postcards, and antiques, this is a place to check out should you be looking for a piece of Kutná Hora's history to take home with you.

INFORMATION AND SERVICES

Whatever information you need can be provided to you at the Information Center (Sankturinovský dům, Palackého náměstí 377, tel. 327 512 378, www.kutnahora.cz, Apr.–Sept. daily 9 A.M.–6 P.M., Oct.–Mar. Mon.–Fri. 9 A.M.–5 P.M., Sat.–Sun. 10 A.M.–4 P.M.). There are plenty of materials here to get you started and the staff is always on top of all the special events and interesting things to do about town. There are also very useful signs posted everywhere for the benefit of tourists, which make navigating the town a snap.

GETTING THERE

By Bus

Buses leave 2–3 times hourly from Prague's Florenc station, with the trip lasting roughly 90 minutes. Tickets cost 59–71 Kč.

By Train

Trains leave hourly from Prague's Hlavní nádraží, Holešovice, and Masarykovo nádraží. The journey lasts approximately one hour, with the exception of trains leaving from Masarykovo nádraží, which take two hours. The main Kutná Hora station is actually located in Sedlec, requiring transfer onto a local train that will take you into Kutná Hora proper. Round-trip tickets are 98–110 Kč.

By Car

Kutná Hora is 44 miles from Prague. Take Vinohradská Street, which runs east behind the National Theatre, all the way to Kutná Hora. Once out of Prague, note that the road turns into Highway 333. The whole trip shouldn't take longer than 50 minutes or so.

Český Krumlov

Legend has it that the name "Krumlov" comes from the German "Krumme Aue" which, loosely translated, means "crooked meadow." The name is appropriate, as the Vltava snakes its way through town, adding its own layer of unique beauty to what has become one of the Czech Republic's most popular weekend destinations. With its winding cobblestone streets, lazy riverside cafes, and refusal to allow any modern development in its historic town center, Český Krumlov resembles a preserved medieval paradise where time has happily stood still—a feeling that is accentuated by its magnificent castle, which overlooks the picturesque countryside and is second only to Prague's in size and stature. Added to UNESCO's World Heritage List in 1992, Český Krumlov is widely considered to be the prettiest town in south Bohemia and the perfect romantic getaway no matter what the time of year.

STÁTNÍ HRAD A ZÁMEK ČESKÝ KRUMLOV (ČESKÝ KRUMLOV CASTLE)

Consisting of 40 buildings and palaces, as well as five castle courts and a park spread out over an area of over 17 acres, Český Krumlov Castle (Zámek 59, tel. 380 704 710, www.castle .ckrumlov.cz) dominates the landscape. It was bought in 1602 by Emperor Rudolf II and changed hands a number of times before becoming the property of the Czechoslovak State in 1950. Two major tours are available to the public, taking them through the castle complex's well-preserved interiors that date back to the 16th century. Tours of the Castle Tower and Baroque Castle Theatre are also available and highly recommended.

Tour I (100 Kč) is the most extensive and includes **St. George's Chapel; Renaissance**

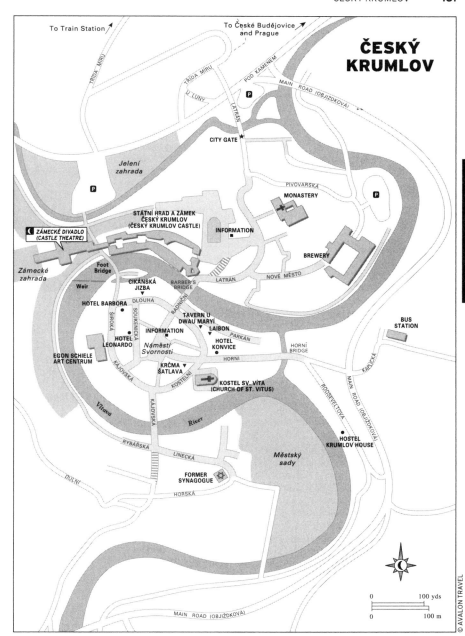

BOHEMIA

ČESKÝ KRUMLOV

To Train Station

To České Budějovice and Prague

TŘÍDA MIRU

TŘÍDA MIRU

U LUNY

POD KAMENEM

MAIN ROAD (OBJIZDKOVÁ)

LATRÁN

CITY GATE

Jelení zahrada

PIVOVARSKÁ

MONASTERY

STÁTNÍ HRAD A ZÁMEK ČESKÝ KRUMLOV (ČESKÝ KRUMLOV CASTLE)

INFORMATION

ZÁMECKÉ DIVADLO (CASTLE THEATRE)

BREWERY

Zámecké zahrada

Foot Bridge

Weir

LATRÁN

NOVÉ MĚSTO

CIKÁNSKÁ JIZBA

BARBER'S BRIDGE

HOTEL BARBORA

DLOUHÁ

RADNIČNÍ

BUS STATION

TAVERN U DWAU MARYÍ

LAIBON

PARKÁN

SIROKÁ

SOUKENICKÁ

INFORMATION

HOTEL LEONARDO

Náměstí Svornosti

HOTEL KONVICE

HORNÍ BRIDGE

HORNÍ

KÁJOVSKÁ

RODESEVELTOVA

MAIN ROAD (OBJIZDKOVÁ)

EGON SCHIELE ART CENTRUM

KRČMA ŠATLAVA

KOSTELNÍ

KOSTEL SV. VÍTA (CHURCH OF ST. VITUS)

Vltava

River

HOSTEL KRUMLOV HOUSE

KÁPLICKÁ

RYBÁŘSKÁ

LINECKÁ

Městský sady

PIVNÍ

FORMER SYNAGOGUE

HORSKÁ

0   100 yds

0   100 m

MAIN ROAD (OBJIZDKOVÁ)

© AVALON TRAVEL

Český Krumlov Castle

Hall, with its four lavish rooms decorated with original paintings, panel ceilings, and tapestries from the early 16th century; and the **Schwarzenberg Baroque Suite,** which takes up the entire first floor of the castle and is home to the **Golden Carriage,** a gilded masterpiece built in 1638 in honor of Pope Urban VIII's visit. The highlight of the tour is undoubtedly **Masquerade Hall,** a masterpiece of the Rococo decorated with wall-to-wall paintings of aristocrats enjoying themselves at a masquerade ball. It served as a sort of waiting room where the town's elite would gather before a performance in the Castle Theatre and its sheer size and meticulous attention to detail is simply breathtaking. It is home to a number of classical concerts in the summer that are hugely popular with tourists and locals alike. Adjacent to it is the equally stunning **Mirror Hall,** which was originally designated a palace and was also the scene of many a social gathering. Its magnificent stonework and gorgeous paintings bearing a musical motif is worth the price of admission alone.

Tour II (80 Kč) focuses completely on the Schwarzenberg family, who inherited the castle in the first half of the 18th century. The tour includes the **Schwarzenberg Portrait Gallery** and their **19th-century suite,** as well as that of **Duchess Marie Eleonora zu Schwarzenberg,** which includes a reception room, dining room, dressing room, and bedroom, all painstakingly renovated to reflect an authentic look back at the period. Although not as varied as the first tour, it nevertheless provides a fascinating look at just how luxuriously the other half lived.

Tours run April, May, September, and October Tuesday–Sunday 9 A.M.–5 P.M.; June–August Tuesday–Sunday 9 A.M.–6 P.M.

Zámecká věž (Castle Tower)

Situated on a rocky promontory, the Castle Tower (Apr., May, Sept., and Oct. Tues.–Sun. 9 A.M.–4:30 P.M., June–Aug. Tues.–Sun. 9 A.M.–5:30 P.M., 35 Kč) is located between the castle's first and second court-

© CORINE TACHTIRIS

the Bear Moat at Český Krumlov Castle

yards and surrounded by the residential palace of the Little Castle. It is a rounded, six-story Gothic and Renaissance beauty that rises 179 feet in the air and serves as the town's official symbol, immortalized by many a Czech artist, including the renowned Karel Čapek. A tour of the tower is a rewarding experience as visitors are afforded remarkable views of the town and its surroundings from the tower's gallery.

◖ Zámecké divadlo (Castle Theatre)

Dating back to the late 17th century, the Castle Theatre (May–Oct. Tues.–Sun. 10 A.M.–4 P.M., 110 Kč) is one of the most well-preserved Baroque theaters in the world. Remarkable as it sounds, the theater's original equipment—machinery, decorations, costumes, and lighting—continues to work, including various acoustic tools that re-create sounds of the elements (wind, rain, and thunder). The castle's archive contains over 2,400 librettos, operas, and ballets, as well as nearly

authentic 600 costumes from the time. Perhaps the most striking of the theater's features is how it reproduces the effect of candlelight, down to its color and flickering quality, via an electrical system that creates the illusion of a natural flame perfectly. This is an absolute must for fans of the Baroque period.

Medvědí příkop (Bear Moat)

Situated between the castle's first and second courtyards is the very popular bear moat, which has been delighting children of all ages for years. Bears have been kept in the moat since 1707; there are four of them being held there today. They are old-timers Kateřina and Vok, along with their son Hubert and his gal Marie Terezie. The bears are beloved local celebrities and there is even a Bear Festival that is held in their honor every Christmas Eve. The castle's official bear keeper starts off the day at 6 A.M. by placing a number of spruces decorated with various sweets, biscuits, and fruit in the moat and invites the public to come in and leave their Christmas offerings. It is the only time of the year where the public is allowed into the moat (the bears are kept in a separate room). Folks bring numerous gifts, including sweets and honey, all of which are inspected by the bear keeper to ensure nothing harmful is given to the bears. At around 10 A.M., the bears are let back into the moat and the public has a ball as they watch their furry friends go at their gifts with a gusto befitting the holiday season.

KOSTEL SV. VÍTA (CHURCH OF ST. VITUS)

Opposite the castle complex on the other side of the Vltava is Český Krumlov's second dominant structure, the Church of St. Vitus (Horní 156, tel. 380 711 336, summer Mass Mon. and Wed.–Sat. 6 P.M., Tues. 7:30 A.M., Sun. 9:30 A.M., winter Mass Mon. and Wed.–Sat. 5 P.M., Tues. 7:30 A.M., Sun. 9:30 A.M., free admission). Construction of the church began in 1340 but it wasn't until after the Hussite Wars that it was finally completed. It sports three naves with a five-sided presbytery, along with multiple-storied sacristies, the Chapel of Resurrection, and the Chapel of St. John of Nepomuk. Other notes of interest are the Statue of Piety from 1350, two organs, and the tombs of the local aristocracy, including Vilem of Rozmberk, who at the time was a diplomat, politician, and one of the highest-ranking noblemen in the Czech Kingdom.

ENTERTAINMENT AND EVENTS
Nightlife

Horor Bar (Másna 11, daily 3 P.M.–2 A.M.) is located downstairs in a dungeon-type space filled with whips, chains, skeletons, bats, and even a coffin in the back room. Prices are reasonable, the atmosphere is great, and absinthe is served here, as is *skoumavky*—little test tubes filled with blood red liquor. Who knew ghouls had so much fun?

Zapa Bar (Latrán 15, tel. 380 712 559, www.zapabar.cz, daily 6 P.M.–1 A.M.) is an excellent choice for those who prefer cocktails to beer. There is a huge whisky selection as well

and the Mexican-themed decor is something of a novelty in town. This place is popular with both foreigners and locals, all of whom agree that the mojitos here are some of the best they've ever tasted.

Festivals and Events

The **International Music Festival Český Krumlov** (July–Aug.) has already enjoyed 16 successful seasons of concert music that touches all musical genres. During the five-week festival, performers from around the world dazzle audiences with their unique brands of homegrown music, including classical, jazz, and rock. Culinary delights are also on offer during various themed nights, which have included French and Irish nights in the past.

ACCOMMODATIONS

Located a mere 40 feet off the main square, the **Hotel Leonardo** (Soukenická 33, tel. 380 725 911, www.hotel-leonardo.cz, 2,400 Kč d) is a comfortable, historic hotel that has managed to retain a lot of its original Renaissance charm. Rooms are spacious and elegantly furnished and the service is top-notch, as is the buffet breakfast. One potential drawback is the hotel's proximity to all the nighttime action, which occasionally results in being within earshot of drunken revelers returning home.

The **Hotel Konvice** (Horní Ulice 144, tel. 380 711 611, www.boehmerwaldhotels.de, 1,500–1,800 Kč d) is known for its friendly owners and excellent views of the old town and castle. Rooms are a bit on the smallish side but nevertheless clean, comfortable, and reasonably priced. The stylish period furniture suits this building, which dates back to 1539, and guests feel like they're experiencing the charm of old Europe without roughing it or overpaying.

The **Hotel Barbora** (Široká č. 89, tel. 380 712 791, www.hotelbarbora.cz, 2,700–3,300 Kč d) consists of two buildings built in the 16th century. Small and full of character, some of the 16 comfortable rooms have original wooden ceilings hand-crafted in the 16th century, while others overlook the river and castle. Located very near the central square, its restaurant was reconstructed in 2006 and has been getting raves ever since, as has its helpful staff, who will go out of their way to make your trip as enjoyable as possible. An excellent choice for those who appreciate a personal touch.

The ◖ **Hostel Krumlov House** (68 Rooseveltova, tel. 380 711 935, www.krumlov house.com, 600–900 Kč d) is a clean, friendly, and completely smoke-free hostel that earns positive reviews. The helpful staff is happy to help you find the best bars and restaurants around town, as well as organize various activities, including biking, hiking, and horseback riding. If that sounds too strenuous, just chill out in the lounge, filled with games, musical instruments, and DVDs, or cook up some comfort food in the clean and well-equipped kitchen. If there's a relaxed and rustic hostel out there that feels a little bit like home, this is it.

FOOD

For excellent food in a medieval environment, try **Krčma Šatlava** (Horní 157, tel. 380 713 344, www.satlava.cz, daily 11 A.M.–midnight, mains 180–220 Kč). This cellar restaurant uses candles as its only light source and serves up classic meat dishes cooked on an open fire. Wild boar, baked duck, and mixed grill plates are just some of what's on offer, and the period music, costumes, and sword fighting somehow manage to escape the trappings of kitsch. This is a very popular place so reserving a table ahead of time is recommended.

The historic **Tavern U dwau Maryí** (Parkán 104, tel. 380 717 228, daily 11 A.M.–midnight, mains 130–270 Kč) is located in a medieval house that dates back to the mid-16th century. Restored wooden ceilings and intricate iron work set the scene where diners sink their teeth into traditional Bohemian fare, including chicken, smoked ham, and the immensely popular "Old Time Bohemian Feast," consisting of several meat specialties. This is a great and affordable place to enjoy traditional cuisine but it's only open April–December.

Being vegetarian is not easy in the Czech Republic but thank God for **Laibon** (Parkán 105, tel. 728 676 654, www.laibon.cz, daily

11 A.M.–9 P.M., mains 92–149 Kč), Český Krumlov's only veggie restaurant. Laid back, friendly, and atmospheric, Laibon's menu is filled with delicious vegetarian options like spicy dahl and unbelievable soya steaks. There is also a peaceful tearoom and terrace where you can enjoy your meals right along the riverside. A must for those who need a break from the heavy fare found just about everywhere else.

◖ **Cikánská jizba** (Dlouhá 31, tel. 380 717 585, Mon.–Thurs. 11 A.M.–2 P.M., 3–11 P.M., Fri.–Sat. 11 A.M.–2 P.M., 3 P.M.–midnight, mains 90–130 Kč) is an extremely popular Gypsy restaurant that cooks up some of the finest Czech food you'll ever taste. Their goulash is astounding, as is the Gypsy pasta with meat and their house specialty of fruit dumplings. Located in a wine cellar that served as the local jail once upon a time, this tiny (seven tables), atmospheric restaurant is a can't-miss choice. If you visit on the weekend, you may get a chance to see live Gypsy music, too.

SHOPPING

You'll find pretty much the same souvenirs in Český Krumlov as in Prague. There is certainly no shortage of wooden toys, amber, crystal, puppets, ceramics, and gingerbread, so your best bet is to take your time strolling through the center and doing some good old-fashioned comparison shopping. Most of the trinkets offered are kitschy or overpriced but you may find a bargain or two if you're lucky.

One store that stands out, however, is the **Egon Schiele Art Centrum** (Široká 71, tel. 380 704 011, www.schieleartcentrum.cz, daily 10 A.M.–6 P.M.), a wonderful museum and shop specializing in prints by Schiele, along with plenty of other international artists. There are plenty of books available, as well as graphics, posters, postcards, and various souvenirs, including coffee mugs and funky t-shirts. If you're stuck for gift ideas, try this place.

SPORTS AND RECREATION

One thing that's really worth your while is to rent a boat and travel along the water, which is where **Maleček půjčovna lodí** (Rooseveltova 28, tel. 380 712 508, www.malecek.cz) comes in. The outfitter allows you to choose your route and boat and enjoy a trip through town along the river the way past generations used to. Inflatable rafts for 2–6 people are available, as well as two-person canoes and kayaks. Paddles, life jackets, canoe bags, and maps are provided; prices vary depending on routes taken and time spent. This is an excellent way to see the city, and, if you're feeling particularly athletic, its surroundings as well.

Cestovní agentura Vltava (Kajovska 62, tel. 380 711 988, www.ckvltava.cz) also offers rafting possibilities but does not stop there. Bikes are available for rent here, too, and you can even arrange to go yachting and horseback riding. If you're the kind of person who likes to stay active and isn't afraid to break a sweat while on holiday, make sure to check this place out.

INFORMATION AND SERVICES

Located in the pedestrian zone in the old town center, the Tourist Information Center (Náměstí Svornosti 2, tel. 380 704 622, www.ckrumlov .cz/info, Nov.–Mar. daily 9 A.M.–5 P.M., Apr.–May and Oct. daily 9 A.M.–6 P.M., June and Sept. daily 9 A.M.–7 P.M., July–Aug. daily 9 A.M.–8 P.M.) should be the first stop for any-one new to town. Besides offering the most up-to-date information regarding sights and events, the helpful people here can also help you find accommodations, arrange trips, or even exchange money.

GETTING THERE
By Bus
Far more comfortable than the train, the bus for Český Krumlov leaves six times a day from Prague's Florenc bus station. The trip takes roughly two hours, 50 minutes, and costs about 160 Kč. Reserving your ticket at least a day before is a good idea as this is a very popular route.

By Train
This is by far the most inconvenient way to go. Trains leave Prague's Hlavní nádraží a few times a day but require a stop and transfer in České Budějovice. Furthermore, the train station in Český Krumlov is located an inconvenient 20 minutes away from the center of town. The trip can last anywhere from 3.5–5.5 hours depending on route taken and costs approximately 160 Kč.

By Car
Český Krumlov is about 112 miles from Prague. Leave Prague taking Route 4 south towards Strakonice and make your way via Písek.

Karlovy Vary

Approximately 80 miles west of Prague at the confluence of the Teplá and Ohře Rivers, lies Karlovy Vary—the Czech Republic's largest and most famous spa. Also known by its German name, Karlsbad, the town is surrounded by a romantic hilly countryside, which, when coupled with its pedestrian promenades, turn-of-the-20th-century Art Nouveau buildings, and sleepy, dreamlike pace, offers visitors an elegance and serenity unrivalled in the entire country. Founded in 1350 by King Charles IV, the town's character and curative waters have attracted many illustrious guests over the years, including Casanova, Beethoven, Mozart, Kafka, Paganini, and Chopin to name but a few. Today, the town hosts the highly respected Karlovy Vary International Film Festival and produces a number of highly popular products like Moser glass, Thun porcelain, Mattoni mineral water, and Becherovka, the nation's beloved herbal liqueur. Aside from the spas and springs, its most renowned landmarks include the Colonnades, Municipal Theatre and Russian Orthodox Church of St. Peter and Paul.

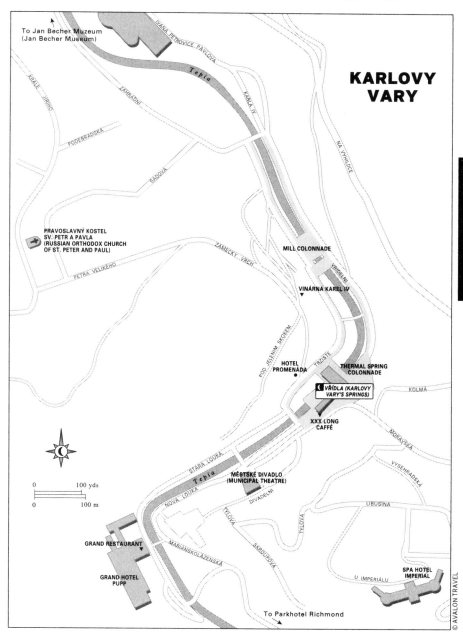

KARLOVY VARY

BOHEMIA

© AVALON TRAVEL

◖ VŘÍDLA (THE SPRINGS)

Karlovy Vary's famous healing springs annually attract hundreds of thousands of visitors from around the world who are looking to cure various metabolic, digestive, arthritic, and gynecological ailments. The springs share many similarities in their basic compositions, with the main differences (resulting in their varying effects) lying in their temperature and amounts of carbon dioxide they possess. Colder springs tend to have a slight detoxifying effect, while warmer waters slow down the forming of bile and gastric stomach juices. The springs range 102–163°F and are all clearly marked with a plaque detailing their mineral elements and temperature. The springs themselves are: **Hot Spring** (Hot Spring Colonnade, daily 6 A.M.–6:30 P.M.), **Charles IV Spring** (Market Colonnade, open 24 hours), **Lower Castle Spring** (Castle Colonnade, open 24 hours), **Upper Castle Spring** (Castle Colonnade, open 24 hours), **Market Spring** (Market Colonnade, open 24 hours), **Mill Spring** (Mill Colonnade, open 24 hours), **Nymph Spring** (Mill Colonnade, open 24 hours), **Prince Vaclav Spring** (Mill Colonnade, open 24 hours), **Libuše Spring** (Mill Colonnade, open 24 hours), **Rock Spring** (near Mill Colonnade, open 24 hours), **Freedom Spring** (near Spa III, open 24 hours), **Park Spring** (Military Spa Sanatorium, open 24 hours), **Snake's Spring** (Park Colonnade, open 24 hours), **Štěpánka Spring** (Spa IV, open 24 hours). The springs are free to the public.

KOLONÁDY (THE COLONNADES)

Built during the 19th and 20th centuries, Karlovy Vary's five colonnades are generally busy with people from around the world looking to restore their powers by drinking the town's curative waters. The **Park Colonnade** (daily 6 A.M.–6:30 P.M.) in Dvořák Park was designed by Viennese architects Ferdinand Fellner and Herman Helmer and completed in 1881. It was part of a concert hall and restaurant called the Blanenský Pavilion and originally served as a promenade connecting the concert hall with the Park Spring. The **Mill Colonnade** (open 24 hours) is the town's

THE TEN COMMANDMENTS OF KARLOVY VARY'S DRINKING CURE

1. The thermal mineral waters of Karlovy Vary should only be imbibed after having consulted a qualified spa physician.
2. Water should be consumed at the springs in order for the drinker to feel its full medicinal effects.
3. Use only the widely available, traditionally shaped porcelain or glass cups.
4. Do not smoke or drink alcohol. Secondhand smoke is considered to be just as harmful.
5. Combine the drinking cure with light physical exercise such as walking.
6. Try to remain in a relaxed, peaceful state of mind as much as possible.
7. Repeat the drinking cure as recommended by your physician.
8. Do not disturb other patients, regardless of how kind and friendly your motives might be.
9. Do not use the mineral water to water nearby plants and take special care to not spill it on the floor in the colonnades.
10. Do not touch the spring stand or pipes while taking water from the fountain.

largest, measuring 433 feet long and 43 feet wide. Designed by Josef Zítek between 1871 and 1881, it is easily recognizable thanks to its 124 Corinthian columns supporting a roof that covers five different springs, each labeled with its unique mineral composition and temperature. Drawing its inspiration from the Swiss architectural style, the wooden **Market Colonnade** (daily 6 A.M.–6:30 P.M.) was built in 1883 by Ferdinand Fellner and Herman Helmer and was meant to cover the Market and Charles IV springs for a short while only. Time flew by apparently and after nearly 100 years, local authorities thought it would be a shame to tear it down and thankfully ordered an overall reconstruction instead. Located above the

Market Colonnade is the **Chateau Colonnade** (daily 6 A.M.–7 P.M.), which was designed by Friedrich Ohmann and built between 1911 and 1913. It is comprised of the Horní pramen (Upper Spring Colonnade) and the Dolní pramen (Lower Spring Colonnade), the latter of which is decorated with a pretty brownstone Spring Spirit relief, added in the 1930s. Closed down for numerous years, it was finally reopened in 2001 following lengthy reconstruction. The **Thermal Spring Colonnade** (daily 6 A.M.–7 P.M.) was originally a cast-iron work by Ferdinand Fellner and Herman Helmer that was taken down near the beginning of World War II. A temporary wooden colonnade was put in its place, and it stayed until its present glass incarnation was finished in 1974. It is Karlovy Vary's most popular colonnade as it houses the town's main spring, Vřídlo, which shoots water some 50 feet high.

MĚSTSKÉ DIVADLO (MUNICIPAL THEATRE)

The first incarnation of this theater (box office tel. 353 224 302, daily 2–5:30 P.M. and up to one hour prior to performance) was built in 1717 and stood on a tree-lined avenue behind the Grand Hotel Pupp. Made of wood, it eventually burned down in 1787 and was reconstructed nearly 100 years later (1884–1886), based on the designs of prominent Viennese architects Ferdinand Fellner and Herman Helmer. In 1993, the theater underwent a general reconstruction that lasted six years and cost over 250 million Kč. Its interiors are filled with elegant touches, including Rococo lamps on the stairway and a chandelier cast in bronze, but it's the theater's curtain that attracts everyone's attention. Entitled "An Apotheosis of Poetic Art," it was designed by young (and then still relatively unknown) Art Nouveau artists Franz Matsche, Ernst Klimt, and Gustav Klimt. The theme is theatrical art and its relation to the muses and depicts a poet surrounded by three muses who encourage him to gain inspiration from a group of lovers seen on the horizon. Notice as well the two groups in the lower corners. On the right are self-portraits of the artists: Matsche and his violin, Ernst Klimt with

BECHEROVKA

Becherovka is one of the country's most popular drinks and is available in pretty much every bar in the Czech Republic. A product of Karlovy Vary, it is devoid of any chemical conservatives, artificial coloring, or emulsifiers, making it a 100 percent natural alcoholic drink whose recipe hasn't changed in over 200 years. Becherovka's maturation process unfolds in dark oak barrels, some of which date back to the beginning of the 19th century. The sweet herbal liquid spends a few weeks mellowing, turning darker and sharpening its taste before it is filtered and bottled. Although hugely popular amongst Czechs, it is an acquired taste; give it a try but don't be embarrassed if it's not to your liking. Here are a few of the more popular cocktails that use Becherovka as a base:

Beton
4 centiliters (1.4 oz.) Becherovka
1 centiliter (0.3 oz.) lemon juice
20 centiliters (6.8 oz.) tonic water

Red Moon
4 centiliters (1.4 oz.) Becherovka
15 centiliters (5 oz.) black currant juice
5 centiliters (1.7 oz.) soda water

Magic Sunset
4 centiliters (1.4 oz.) Becherovka
15 centiliters (5 oz.) orange juice
1 centiliter (0.3 oz.) grenadine

BOHEMIA

a mandolin, and Gustav Klimt with a flute. On the left are Gustav Klimt's sisters, who apparently acted as models for three of the muses.

PRAVOSLAVNÝ KOSTEL SV. PETRA A PAVLA (RUSSIAN ORTHODOX CHURCH OF ST. PETER AND PAUL)

This gorgeous five-domed church (třída Krále Jiřího, free admission) was designed by Gustav

© TOM DIRLIS

Jan Becher Museum

Wiedemann and completed in 1898. Reflecting a classic Byzantine style, it was modeled after a church in Ostankino near Moscow and has survived in large part thanks to healthy donations from wealthy Russian guests whom the church has been serving for over 110 years. Its interior is decorated with gorgeous paintings and icons (some of which were also gifts) that can keep one occupied for a very long time, and its relief of Russian czar Peter the Great continues to strike pride in the hearts of all Russians who come for a visit.

JAN BECHER MUZEUM (JAN BECHER MUSEUM)

Becherovka is one of the nation's most-consumed domestic drinks and one of Karlovy Vary's better-known exports. At the Jan Becher Museum (T.G. Masaryka 57, tel. 359 578 156, www.becherovka.cz, daily 9 A.M.–5 P.M., 100 Kč), visitors are taken on a tour of the production plant and learn the basic history, manufacturing, and storage of the liqueur. Aside from the instructional film, exhibitions, and

trip through some of the plant's original cellars, guests are also invited to imbibe the country's pride and joy in the museum bar.

ENTERTAINMENT AND EVENTS
Nightlife

Becher's Bar (Mírové náměstí 2, tel. 353 109 483, www.pupp.cz, daily 7 P.M.–4 A.M.) is an upscale cocktail bar in the Grand Hotel Pupp and pretty much the only one in town. Fashioned after a typical post–World War I London pub, the bar has a drinks menu of over 100 cocktails that should keep you busy, and there are plenty of gourmet specialties available as well. Open far later than any other establishment in town, this is a reasonably priced choice for nighthawks and the nightly live jazz will satisfy any fan of the genre.

Festivals and Events

The **Karlovy Vary International Film Festival** (first half of July, www.kviff.com) is the most important of its kind in Central and Eastern Europe and ranks fourth in importance on the continent—behind Cannes, Berlin, and Venice, respectively. The festival ran for the first time in 1946 and suffered under the Communist regime before having life breathed back into it in 1994 by new organizers Jiří Bartoška and Eva Zaoralová. Today, it remains one of the most important cultural events on the country's calendar, attracting thousands of visitors, not to mention actors and directors from all over the world looking to promote their projects. Any fan of the medium will want to visit during the festival's eight-day run and drink up the transformation of this sleepy spa town into one of glamour and excitement. Should you be seriously considering a visit during this time, make sure to book a room well in advance as all accommodations are spoken for months before opening night.

ACCOMMODATIONS

Hotel Promenáda (Tržiště 31, tel. 353 225 648, www.hotel-promenada.cz, 1,590–1,890 Kč d) is a charming, intimate hotel located in the heart of the city's spa center. The service is warm and welcoming, the rooms are immaculate and the restaurant is one of the better ones in town. If you're looking for a first-rate, reasonably priced hotel in a city known for being overly expensive, book a room here now.

The **Parkhotel Richmond** (Slovenská 567/3, tel. 353 177 111, www.richmond.cz, 1,300–2,800 Kč d) is a spa hotel situated slightly away from the action of the city center. It is surrounded by a beautiful park with an original Japanese meditation garden, adding to the overall comfort of guests looking for a bit of R&R. Its 116 rooms are tastefully furnished, as are the excellent restaurant, cafe, piano bar, and billiards lounge. The spa treatments run from the traditional kind to more specialized programs, including anti-stress and weight loss. This is an excellent choice for those who don't want to stay right in the center of town.

Up on a hill overlooking the city is the beautiful and grand **◖ Spa Hotel Imperial** (Libušina 18, tel. 353 203 111, www.imperial .kv.cz, 2,300–3,000 Kč d). Spacious and stylish rooms with marble bathrooms await, as does the Imperial sports center with tennis courts, fitness center, and aerobics, not to mention indoor golf with two full-swing simulators of six world-famous courses. There is also a beauty salon, indoor pool, and concert hall and the friendly staff will happily help you plan any trips or events you might want to enjoy should you actually feel like leaving the premises.

FOOD

Located in the center of town at the Colonnades is **XXX LONG caffé** (Vřídelní 23, tel. 353 224 232, www.xxxlong.com, daily 11 A.M.–11 P.M., mains 120–350 Kč). Their extensive menu is full of Italian and international dishes, focusing primarily on seafood, pastas, and a wide array of pizzas. Stylish, welcoming, and reasonably priced, this is a good bet any day of the week.

Formerly the hunting lodge of Karel IV, the **◖ Vinárna Karel IV** (Zámecký vrch 2, tel. 353 227 255, daily noon–11 P.M., mains 120–380 Kč) is a wonderfully romantic restaurant dating back to the early 17th century. The extensive menu showcases traditional Czech and Continental cuisine that also includes fish and vegetarian options. If visiting in the summer, make sure to take advantage of the terrace—the perfect place to unwind in the evening after a long day's sightseeing. Reservations in advance are highly recommended.

Seeing as it's located in the magnificent Grand Hotel Pupp, it's no surprise that the **Grand Restaurant** (Mírové náměstí 2, Grandhotel Pupp, tel. 353 109 646, www .pupp.cz, daily noon–3 P.M., 6–10 P.M., mains 280–590 Kč) offers some of the finest dining in town. Luxurious, neoclassical surroundings set the stage for the excellent Czech and international fare on the extensive menu. Generous portions are professionally prepared by some of the country's finest chefs and served to you by a friendly and efficient waitstaff. Slightly on the expensive side but well worth the extravagance, the Grand Restaurant is an elegant dining experience you won't soon forget.

SHOPPING

There are plenty of shopping opportunities in Karlovy Vary but be forewarned: Prices are not what you'd expect them to be outside of the capital. Most goods are expensive since the spa resort attracts a certain affluence, but with the right kind of perseverance you'll find what you're looking for and not have to pay an arm and a leg to get it.

Becherovka, the sweet yet spicy domestic drink that can be found in every Czech bar in the country, is produced here and is available in most shops for a decent price. Gold and fur are two more rather common goods around here and can be easily found at numerous shops throughout the city. The most popular items bought in Karlovy Vary, however, are crystal and porcelain, both of which can be found at **Moser** (Tržiště 7, tel. 353 235 303, www .moser.cz, Mon.–Fri. 10 A.M.–7 P.M., Sat.–Sun. 10 A.M.–6 P.M.), the country's most respected name in glassware.

INFORMATION AND SERVICES

The Information Center of Karlovy Vary (Lázeňská 1, tel. 353 224 097, www .karlovyvary.cz, Apr. 1–Nov. 15 Mon.–Fri. 9 A.M.–7 P.M., Sat.–Sun. 10 A.M.–6 P.M., Nov. 16–Mar. 31 Mon.–Fri. 9 A.M.–5 P.M., Sat.– Sun. 10 A.M.–5 P.M.) is your first stop should you have any questions concerning the city's sights and/or cultural events. The friendly, multilingual staff will be happy to arrange tickets for you as well as any activities around town you might be interested in. Make sure to ask for a copy of *Promenáda* magazine, a helpful publication with a concise list of events around town, as well as a map of the down-town core.

Čedok (Dr Davida Bechera 21-23, tel. 353 222 994, Mon.–Fri. 9 A.M.–6 P.M., Sat. 9 A.M.– noon) is an alternative to the town's information center where visitors can obtain information and tickets for various events and concerts around town (excluding the film festival).

GETTING THERE
By Bus

Buses leave every 15–30 minutes from Prague's Florenc station. The trip lasts about 2 hours, 15 minutes, with tickets costing approximately 140 Kč.

By Train

Trains leave Prague's Hlavní nádraží at least three times a day. Tickets cost 192 Kč, with the journey lasting roughly 3.5 hours. The train takes an indirect route and is one hour longer than the bus. For maximum comfort, use the train as a last resort only.

By Car

Karlovy Vary is 81 miles from Prague. Take Highway E48 west from Prague all the way to Karlovy Vary. The roads are generally busy so make sure to use caution. The drive shouldn't take longer than two hours.

MORAVIA

Stretching out to the south and east, Moravia is the Czech Republic's famed and beloved wine country—a region characterized not only by its vineyards, lowlands, and wooded hillsides, but also by the loose love of life that inevitably comes with the grown grape. Those who venture into Brno and beyond are struck by the less hurried pace, the warm and friendly demeanor of the typical Moravian, and the maintenance of the culture's customs. Colorful folk costumes, infectious traditional music, and vibrant village festivals highlight the region's cultural calendar, while its countless biking and hiking trails afford nature enthusiasts an unforgettably sensuous and serene experience no matter what the time of year. Whereas pubs are Bohemia's natural gathering point, it is the neighborhood *vinárna* (wine bar) here that prevails, attracting locals and those from nearby towns curious as to what has been growing in the neighboring ground. The strong, sharp taste of *slivovice* (plum brandy) is the liqueur of choice. When it is homemade, it is as much as matter of painstaking preparation as it is pride, and it oftentimes sparks the beginning of a lively and late night. Moravians' food also differs from that of their Bohemian brothers, involving far spicier ingredients more akin to Slovakian and Hungarian palates. Whether it's the animated nightlife and historic Old Town of burgeoning Brno, or the sleepy, timeless beauty of Mikulov and Telč, visitors to the region will undoubtedly experience a lust for leisure and life rarely duplicated in other parts of the Czech Republic.

HIGHLIGHTS

◖ Staré Město (Brno's Old Town): Spend an afternoon taking in all of the Moravian capital's historic sights, then come back in the evening and let your hair down alongside natives who insist (and prove) that Brno can be a whole lot more fun than Prague (page 176).

◖ Kapucínská krypta (Capuchin Crypt): Grotesque maybe, morbid sure, but Brno's Capuchin Crypt nevertheless continues to pack them in. Past monks and society's big shots are all here in open coffins, decaying clothes and all (page 180).

◖ Náměstí Zachariáše z Hradce (Telč's Town Square): Spend some time admiring one of the country's most ex-quisite town squares. Perfectly preserved Renaissance and Baroque houses capped off with St. Jacob's Church's 200-foot-tall tower and its inspiring views make for the perfect romantic morning or afternoon (page 182).

◖ Státní zámek (Telč Castle): You will be hard-pressed to find more exquisite examples of Renaissance architecture complete with lavishly decorated interiors guaranteed to make your jaw drop (page 183).

◖ Pálava Vintage Wine Festival: The most important cultural event in Mikulov is also its most fun, attracting thrill seekers, wine lovers, and anyone else committed to having a great time (page 188).

LOOK FOR ◖ TO FIND RECOMMENDED SIGHTS, ACTIVITIES, DINING, AND LODGING.

PLANNING YOUR TIME

Moravia's sights are significantly further away than those of Bohemia, but they can be done in a relatively short time if need be. Three days are enough to do a quick tour through the countryside, grab a bottle of home-grown wine, and beat it back to Prague before your flight leaves. For a deeper understanding of this palpably different part of the country, however, four to five days are ideal.

The obvious choice is to begin with the Moravian capital of Brno. Spend all the time you want strolling through its historic center or climbing up to Špilberk Castle and Cathedral of St. Peter and Paul for a taste of history and fantastic panoramic views of the city below. Always bustling with activity, Brno will guarantee you an experience you won't soon forget, whether it's an evening at the theater, dinner at a traditional restaurant,

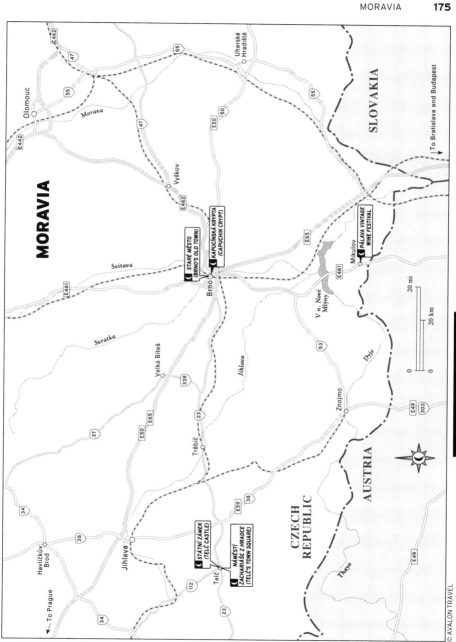

© AVALON TRAVEL

or a night out at any of its numerous bars, cafes, or clubs.

From there, either Mikulov or Telč makes sense, though leaving Mikulov for last will mean having to go through Brno again on your way back to Prague—something you may or may not want to do. Either way, Mikulov, with its castle, nature trails, and countless wineries and private wine cellars is easily an overnight trip for anybody interested in the great outdoors or the finer side of grapes. Telč, meanwhile, can be enjoyed in a single day, so leaving it for last may make the most sense, as you can fully enjoy its gorgeous town square and castle, and also pick up a number of souvenirs, before heading back to Prague in the late afternoon or evening.

Brno

Roughly 140 miles southeast of Prague lies the Moravian capital of Brno; its population of over 370,000 makes it the Czech Republic's second-largest city. Established over 800 years ago, it prospered quickly due to its proximity to Prague, Vienna, Bratislava, and Budapest—a geographical luxury it continues to profit from today. While certainly not as pretty as Prague, it would be wrong to focus solely on Brno's plethora of concrete functionalist buildings and write it off as just another industrial city. Its historic city center, for example, is full of architectural gems ranging from the Gothic to Art Nouveau and its two most famous attractions, Špilberk Castle and Cathedral of St. Peter and Paul, rise above the city majestically, adding elegance and historical context to its unique skyline.

Being home to a number of universities, theaters, clubs, and cafes, it's only natural that Brno would have a dynamic nightlife—one that is known to rival that of their cousins in the capital. Whether it's a stroll through the streets, a visit to the castle, or an all-nighter that includes lots of tasty Moravian wine, Brno's easy-going, fun-loving lifestyle is sure to please anyone who gives it a chance.

◖ STARÉ MĚSTO (OLD TOWN)

Though Brno is fairly large and spread out, visitors tend to stay in the compact Old Town, where most of the historical buildings and all of the action is. Somewhat oval in shape, Old Town stretches a little over half a mile north to south and about half that from east to west.

Náměstí Svobody (Freedom Square)

This is Brno's main square and heart of the city. "Square" isn't exactly the right word for it, as it's actually triangular in shape, forming a large reversed "A." It is always busy with visitors and locals out for a stroll or simply going about their business, and is also the site of numerous concerts, exhibitions, and various other cultural events throughout the year. At the center of the square is the **Marianne Column,** an attractive and ornate late 17th-century plague column, which, aside from being a noteworthy piece of sculpture, also serves as one of the city's more popular meeting points. The southern end of the square leads off to **Masarykova Street.** Lined primarily with shops, it is Brno's busiest and most commercialized street. Make sure to keep looking up, as many of the buildings have fantastic Art Nouveau facades that make for plenty of photo ops and a very pleasant stroll.

Stará radnice (Old Town Hall)

Old Town Hall (Radnická 8) is Brno's oldest secular building, dating all the way back to the 13th century. A quick look will reveal that it has gone through a number of renovations; characteristics of the Gothic, Renaissance, and Baroque periods are all evident. The building's

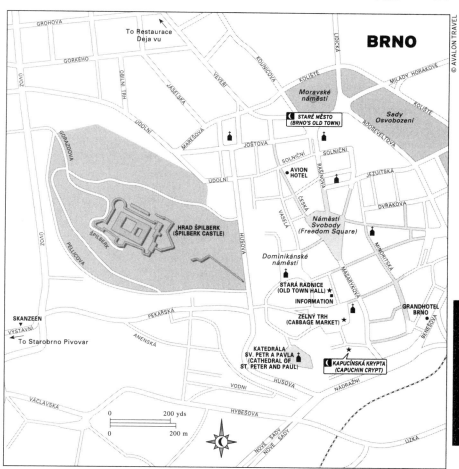

door and Gothic portal are of particular historical significance. Designed by Anton Pilgram in 1510, it is said that town officials flatly refused the architect's appeal for an advance on the sum they had agreed upon. Enraged and deeply offended, Pilgram exacted his revenge by ordering his workers to bend the portal's highest turret out of shape.

Suspended in the Hall's gateway are two of Brno's most famous attractions. The first is the **Brno Dragon,** which is actually a large al-

ligator whose history is as varied as it is uncertain. The second is the **Wagon Wheel,** which is believed to have come from Jiří Birek, a carpenter from Lednice. The story goes that he bet locals he could cut down a tree, make a wheel out of it, and roll it the 25 miles back to Brno all in a single day. "You're on," said the townspeople, who nearly fainted when he pulled it off. Convinced he was in cahoots with the Devil, the people of Brno never did business with him again.

THE BRNO DRAGON

The Brno Dragon is one of the town's most recognizable symbols yet nobody seems to really know what the truth is regarding its origin. One explanation is that it was killed by Sir Albrecht Trut's servants while the town was being established. Some believe it was brought back by crusaders who were returning home from one of their many adventures, while others maintain it was a gift for the members of Town Hall by a visiting sultan from Turkey.

The most popular story, however, is that the dragon lived in a cave along the Svratka River, devouring everything within sight and terrorizing the local population. A reward of 100 gold coins was offered to whoever was brave enough to rid the town of the beast, but nobody rose to the challenge. One day, a butcher who roamed the continent looking for work entered the Blue Lion Inn and overheard the natives jabbering excitedly about the scaly beast. Listening intently and interest piqued upon mention of the reward, he stood up and exclaimed, "I shall rid you of that dragon. Just fetch me a large ox pelt and a sack of lime." The townsfolk didn't know what to make of the stranger but they nevertheless provided him with what he asked for and watched him carefully as he sewed the lime into the ox pelt, loaded it into his wagon, and left. When the butcher located the dragon's lair, he laid his pelt on the ground and waited. It wasn't long before the dragon emerged from hiding, gobbled up the pelt and washed it down with the Svratka River's finest. That's when the lime that had been sewn into the ox pelt started to work its magic, beginning to boil and expanding until the fearsome dragon blew up into tiny bits. The butcher returned triumphant, pocketed the reward and left the natives of Brno dancing in the streets. Life has been relatively quiet in the Moravian capital ever since.

Zelný trh (Cabbage Market)

South of Old Town Hall is busy Cabbage Market, which has functioned as a farmers market since the 13th century. Here, next to **Parnas Fountain**—the town's main water source when it was built in 1699—are plenty of opportunities to buy fresh fruit and vegetables, as well as a wonderful array of colorful flowers.

HRAD ŠPILBERK (ŠPILBERK CASTLE)

Špilberk Castle has been an inseparable part of Brno's skyline for over seven centuries and is one of its most defining features. Built somewhere around the mid-13th century by King Přemysl Otakar II, the castle's looks and relevance changed vastly over the years, beginning as a royal castle and official seat of Moravian margraves, adapting with the times to become a significant Baroque fortress, changing into a widely feared prison during the Austro-Hungarian Empire, and finally finishing off as a barracks. It was declared a national heritage monument in 1962 and today houses Brno's leading cultural center, the Brno City Museum. Visitors to Špilberk can also see the castle's casements, a lapidary, a carillon, Baroque pharmacy, and castle tower that offers pretty views of the city's landscape.

Muzeum města Brna (Brno City Museum)

The Brno City Museum (Špilberk 1, tel. 542 123 611, www.spilberk.cz, May–Sept. Tues.– Sun. 9 A.M.–6 P.M., Oct. and Apr. Tues.– Sun. 9 A.M.–5 P.M., Nov.–Mar. Tues.–Sun. 10 A.M.–5 P.M., 120 Kč) is one of the city's more important cultural centers. It hosts plenty of concerts and happenings throughout the year and is the place to go to learn everything there is to know about the region and city's colorful past. There are always new temporary exhibitions being held, while some of the more popular permanent ones include "Špilberk—From Castle to Fortress," which outlines the castle's development in great detail; "Brno at Špilberk," which presents some of the most important chapters in Brno's history; and

MILAN KUNDERA

Born in Brno in 1929, Milan Kundera is one of the 20th century's most notable writers, blending philosophy, essayistic elements, and narrative to create a unique writing style that has produced critically acclaimed novels described as "a feast of many courses." Educated at Charles University and the Film Faculty of the Academy of Music and Dramatic Arts in Prague, Kundera worked as a manual laborer and jazz musician before becoming a professor of literature at the Institute for Advanced Cinematographic Studies. He joined the Communist party in 1948 and was expelled not once, but twice, for his unorthodox opinions. At the age of 38, Kundera published his first novel *The Joke* (1967), a darkly funny, illuminating work revealing how reality under Communist rule takes its revenge on those who play with it. Not surprisingly, Kundera was one of the authors who were banned from libraries and publication after the Russians invaded Czechoslovakia in 1968 and was fired from his teaching post less than a year later. In 1975, Kundera moved with his wife Vera Hrabánková to France, where he worked as a professor of comparative literature at the University of Rennes. In 1980, he was appointed professor at École des Hautes Études in Paris. His breakthrough novel, *The Unbearable Lightness of Being*, was published in 1984 and solidified his position as one of Central Europe's, if not the world's, most important and influential writers.

"From Renaissance to Modernism," an exhibition of significant pieces from some of Brno's most distinguished artists from 1570 to 1945.

Kasematy (Casemates)

The castle's casemates (May, June, and Sept. Tues.–Sun. 9 A.M.–6 P.M., July–Aug. daily 9 A.M.–6 P.M., Oct.–Apr. Tues.–Sun. 9 A.M.–5 P.M., 70 Kč) are one of Brno's most-visited tourist sites despite their grisly history. In 1783, Emperor Joseph II decided to use the dark, windowless rooms as a prison for the land's hardest and most dangerous criminals. The following year, he had wooden cells built; prisoners serving life sentences were hanged from the walls. Špilberk prison quickly gained the reputation of being the most brutal of all such facilities within the Austrian monarchy and remained as such until 1855, when Emperor Francis Joseph I put an end to the cruel and unusual punishment.

KATEDRÁLA SV. PETR A PAVLA (CATHEDRAL OF ST. PETER AND PAUL)

Perched atop Petrov Hill overlooking the old town is the Cathedral of St. Peter and Paul (Petrov 9, tel. 543 235 031, church daily 8 A.M.–6 P.M., tower daily 10 A.M.–6 P.M., crypt Mon.–Sat. 11 A.M.–5 P.M., Sun. 11:45 A.M.–5 P.M., tower 30 Kč, crypt 30 Kč), one of the city's most recognizable landmarks. Built as a Gothic cathedral on the presumed site of former Brno castle, it was converted into the Baroque style in the 18th century and attained its current neo-Gothic form at the turn of the 20th. Its interior is unspectacular, with a sculpture of the Virgin Mary being of minor interest. There is an original crypt from the 12th century now open to visitors but it is the cathedral's tower that is worth the effort, as it offers excellent views of the old town and beyond. One thing you might notice while here is that the cathedral's bells strike noon at 11 A.M. This can be traced back to a quick-thinking monk who somehow learned during the Thirty Years' War that the Swedes were planning to take the town by noon. If unsuccessful by then, they would move on. Not wanting to take any chances against the powerful Swedish army he rang the bells at 11 A.M., prompting the Swedes to pack up and leave and thus saving his beloved Brno.

◧ KAPUCÍNSKÁ KRYPTA (CAPUCHIN CRYPT)

Below Petrov Cathedral and adjacent to Zelný trh is the Capuchin Monastery, whose biggest attraction is the rather morbid yet intriguing Capuchin Crypt (Kapucínské náměstí 5, tel. 542 213 232, 20 Kč). Founded in the middle of the 17th century, it was the final resting spot for many of society's deceased until 1787, when Josef II prohibited burials within town limits. Today, the remains of various monks and Brno's more distinguished citizens of the day are on display in open coffins, their clothing and skin clearly decaying. Although a popular and somewhat fascinating sight, the crypt should be avoided by young children and the faint-hearted. The crypt's hours are February–April Tuesday–Saturday 9 A.M.–noon, 2–4:30 P.M., Sunday 11 A.M.–11:45 A.M., 2–4:30 P.M.; May–September Monday–Saturday 9 A.M.–noon, 2–4:30 P.M., Sunday 11 A.M.–11:45 A.M., 2–4:30 P.M.; October–December Tuesday–Saturday 9 A.M.–noon, 2–4:30 P.M., Sunday 11 A.M.–11:45 A.M., 2–4:30 P.M.

ENTERTAINMENT AND EVENTS
Nightlife

Charlie's Hat (Kobližná 12, tel. 542 214 459, Mon.–Thurs. 11 A.M.–4 A.M., Fri. 11 A.M.–5 A.M., Sat. noon–5 A.M., Sun. 3 P.M.–4 A.M.) is a fun party place located right in the old town. Head on down to the no-frills, rustic-looking cellar and rub shoulders with students, foreigners, and local party people. Rock and pop music fills the air till the wee hours every night, much to everybody's delight. Be forewarned—its location in a cellar makes it very easy to lose track of time. Don't be surprised if you walk out and the sun has already come up.

Absolut Cocktail Bar (Jánská 21, tel. 542 214 155, www.absolutbar.cz, Mon.–Fri. 4 P.M.–2 A.M., Sat.–Sun. 6 P.M.–2 A.M.) is a laid-back cocktail bar that is a load of fun on the right night. The comfortable booths and long bar are almost always filled with merrymakers. Excellent cocktails, expert service, and

smiles all around make this one of the more enjoyable places to have a drink with friends and let your hair down.

Krokodýl Fashion Club (Kounicova 1, tel. 732 307 766, www.krokodylclub.cz, Mon.–Thurs. 8 P.M.–2 A.M., Fri.–Sat. 8 P.M.–6 A.M.) spins funk, hip-hop, and reggae beats, along with the top dance hits of the day, whipping the crowd into a frenzy that doesn't end till the final bell. The huge dance floor in the center of this fun club is always packed with the tanned and well-dressed, so make sure to look your best and be prepared to stay a while.

Festivals and Events

Moravian Autumn (www.mhf-brno.cz, late Sept.–early Oct.) is a highly enjoyable two-week run of classical music concerts performed around the city to the delight of thousands of fans. Symphony orchestras, vocal ensembles, soloists, quartets, and dance troupes all find their way to the stage in some of Brno's finest venues, including the Brno Philharmonic Concert Hall, Janáček Theatre, and Brno City Theatre. This is a wonderful opportunity to hear superb artists from the Czech Republic and elsewhere in Europe perform music that still strikes a chord after all these years.

ACCOMMODATIONS

The **Grandhotel Brno** (Benešova 18-20, tel. 542 518 111, www.grandhotelbrno.cz, 3,200 Kč d) is a huge four-star hotel located directly opposite the train station on the edge of the historic old town. Rooms range from small and plain to huge and opulent; get one facing away from the train station or else getting some sleep may be a more of a challenge than you care for. The staff is courteous and the hotel's recent reconstruction has made it comparable to Western European standards. Slightly pricey but worth it if money is not an issue.

The **Hotel Myslivna** (Nad Pisárkami 1, tel. 547 107 111, www.hotelmyslivna.cz, 1,550 Kč d) is a quiet hotel located in a wooded area overlooking Brno's Exhibition Center, a short 10-minute drive away from the center of town. The staff is quite friendly and the rooms are simple, comfortable, and cheerful. There's a sauna, fitness center, and billiards table on the premises and the hotel's restaurant serves fantastic Czech and wild game dishes. This hotel offers excellent value for the money and is perfect for those who prefer some distance between them and the hubbub of the city.

The **◖ Avion Hotel** (Česká 20, tel. 542 215 280, www.avion-hotel.cz, 2,020 Kč d) dates back to 1928 and is the work of famous Czech architect Bohuslav Fuchs. Located in the center of town in a pedestrian-only zone, the hotel offers its guests clean, simply furnished rooms at an affordable price. There aren't too many bells and whistles to be found here but if you don't need the newest technology in your room or the highest standard of hotel living in order to enjoy your holiday, then this may be the right hotel for you.

FOOD

Restaurace Deja vu (Srbská 4, tel. 541 233 018, www.dejavu-restaurace.cz, Mon.–Fri. 11 A.M.–midnight, Sat. noon–midnight, Sun. noon–10 P.M., mains 109–259 Kč) is a very rare thing indeed. It's not often that pretty much anything on a restaurant's menu is superb, but Deja vu pulls it off. Sporting a sleek, spacious, and classy Mediterranean interior, it attracts all walks of life. Diners come to sink their teeth into any number of chicken, salmon, calamari, trout, pasta, lamb, and Argentinean steak dishes that are remarkably affordable. The fine folks here are so sure of their cooking prowess that they even have three different meals prepared for your pet dog should he suddenly get the munchies. Though somewhat outside the city center, it is very much worth the trip should you have the time. Reservations recommended.

Starobrno Pivovar (Hlinky 160, tel. 543 516 111, www.starobrno.cz, daily 11 A.M.–midnight, mains 115–255 Kč) is not only where Starobrno beer is brewed, it's also the setting of one of the city's finest dining experiences. If you're looking for authentic Czech cuisine like _gulaš_ or pork and dumplings, look no further. The indoor seating area is huge and is decorated like any other traditional Czech restaurant, while the outdoor summer terrace buzzes with activity during the warmer months. If you're really hungry, go for the very filling spare ribs and make sure to wash it all down with a freshly tapped light, dark, or mixed Starobrno beer.

◖ Skanzeen (Pekařská 80, tel. 543 244 962, www.skanzeen.cz, daily 11 A.M.–midnight, mains 119–289 Kč) is a centrally located restaurant that has been getting rave reviews from both the press and diners for its fantastic food. The menu focuses primarily on Slovakian dishes, which are meat-heavy like Czech meals but prepared with slightly different spices. Set in a rustic setting with traditional live music performed regularly, Skanzeen is an excellent choice for those who'd like to try something a little different from the usual local fare.

SHOPPING

Prices are generally cheaper in Brno than in Prague so odds are you'll find a few deals. For crystal, jewelry, or any number of gift items, check out the pedestrian shopping zone stretching from Náměstí Svobody to the train station.

Galerie Vaňkovka (Ve Vaňkovce 1, tel. 533 110 110, www.galerie-vankovka.cz, Mon.–Sat. 9 A.M.–9 P.M., Sun. 10 A.M.–8 P.M.) is a large shopping center located on the edge of the historical city center between the main train and coach stations. Consisting of 130 shops spread out over two floors, the center offers a wide range of internationally known shops like Levis, Nike, and Quicksilver, as well as Interspar (daily 7 A.M.–10 P.M.), a reputable and popular grocery store in the Czech Republic.

INFORMATION AND SERVICES

The new and improved Turistické Informacní Centrum (Radnická 8, tel. 542 211 090, www .ticbrno.cz) provides visitors with pretty much any and all information they'll need in order to take full advantage of their time in Brno. From hooking up accommodations to swinging tickets for the hottest shows in town, the fine folks here will be happy to serve you.

Hours are October–March Monday–Friday 9 A.M.–6 P.M., Saturday 9 A.M.–5:30 P.M., Sunday 9 A.M.–3 P.M.; April–September Monday–Friday 8:30 A.M.–6 P.M., Saturday–Sunday 9 A.M.–5:30 P.M.

There is also a second office across from the train station (Nádrazní 8, tel. 542 214 450, Oct.–Mar. Mon.–Fri. 9 A.M.–6 P.M., Apr.–Sept. Mon.–Fri. 8:30 A.M.–6 P.M.).

GETTING THERE
By Bus
Buses leave Prague's Florenc station for Brno every hour. The trip takes 2.5–3 hours and tickets cost roughly 170 Kč. Please note that tickets should be bought in advance if you're planning on traveling during peak hours or weekends.

By Train
Trains leave hourly for Brno from Prague's Hlavní nádraží, with the trip lasting 3–3.5 hours. Tickets cost 206 Kč.

By Car
Brno is 139 miles from Prague. Driving to Brno is a straightforward, if at times boring, drive. Simply take the E50 (a.k.a. D1) from Prague all the way to Brno. The trip should take approximately two hours.

GETTING AROUND
There are a number of car rental agencies in Brno, including Avis (Best Western Hotel, Husova 16, tel. 542 122 670, www.avis .com, Mon.–Fri. 8 A.M.–4:30 P.M., starting at 1,900 Kč/day), Budget (Brno Turany Airport, tel. 545 521 144, www.budget.com, Mon.–Fri. 9 A.M.–6 P.M., starting at 1,300 Kč/day), and Hertz (Millenium Center, Hybesova 42, tel. 225 345 071, www.hertz. cz, Mon.–Fri. 8 A.M.–7 P.M., starting at 3,150 Kč/day). Booking through the company's website may very well land you a far better deal than renting in person. Check online for more details.

Telč

Anyone interested in peace, quiet, and the picturesque should definitely consider a trip to Telč, widely considered one of the most beautiful holiday spots in this part of Europe. Dating back to 1099, this gorgeous little town located on the cusp of Bohemia and Moravia is surrounded by lakes, forests, and a countryside dotted with enough castles and ruins to keep any history buff busy. Its pretty, Renaissance-influenced square and castle are popular destinations for visitors hailing from all around the world and the perfect spots to lose yourself in the fairy-tale atmosphere that blankets the entire town. Small wonder that it was added to UNESCO's World Heritage List.

◖ NÁMĚSTÍ ZACHARIÁŠE Z HRADCE (TOWN SQUARE)
You'll be hard-pressed to find a more enchanting square in the country, lined as it is with arcades and meticulously preserved Renaissance houses complemented by picture-perfect facades. Many of these houses were originally built in the Gothic style during the second half of the 15th century and now boast individually built fronts and gables sporting Baroque features. Some of the buildings worthy of attention are **Town Hall** (#10), whose appearance dates back to 1574; the house at **#48,** which was rebuilt in the Baroque style in the 18th century; the Renaissance house with a Baroque front at **#57;** and the sgraffito-covered building at **#61** with Old Testament motifs. And let us not forget 17th-century **St. Jacob's Church** (May and Sept. Sat.–Sun. 1–5 P.M., June–Aug. Mon.–Sat. 10 A.M.–noon, 1–6 P.M., Sun. 1–6 P.M., 20 Kč), whose nearly 200-foot-tall tower affords breathtaking views of Telč, its surrounding lakes, and beyond.

© TOM DIRLIS

the pretty Renaissance houses of Telč's town square

◖ STÁTNÍ ZÁMEK (TELČ CASTLE)

Telč Castle (tel. 567 243 943, www.zamek-telc
.cz, Apr. and Oct. Tues.–Sun. 9 A.M.–noon,
1–4 P.M., May–Sept. Tues.–Sun. 9 A.M.–noon,
1–5 P.M., Tour A 80 Kč, Tour B 70 Kč) is easily one of the most remarkable examples of Renaissance architecture in the Czech Republic,
boasting carefully preserved original interiors
that prove the overwhelming influence Italian
art had in Central Europe. It was built in the
second half of the 14th century in the Gothic
style but was changed into what we see today
by Baldassare Maggi in 1550. Visitors have the
opportunity to choose from two tours of these
magnificent grounds. The first tour takes you
through enormous, lavishly decorated halls
with coffered ceilings and astonishing trompe
l'oeil works, as well as the Knight's Hall, filled
with numerous suits of armor, and the African
Hall, complete with the stuffed heads of exotic
animals hanging from the walls. The second
tour takes visitors through the castle's residential quarters, including the library, dining
room, salon, and bedroom—all painstakingly
recreated according to original designs of the
period. While it doesn't overwhelm the senses
like the first tour, it is nevertheless a fascinating look at what daily life was like for Moravian nobility.

ENTERTAINMENT AND EVENTS

Hot-Air Balloons above Telč (late July) has
been operating since 1997, offering contestants
the opportunity to compete in two categories:
sport ballooning and romantic ballooning.
The number of participants seems to grow
every year, with over 20 balloons flying high
over Telč last year. If you're anywhere near the
area, stop in for a visit and admire the skies
as you've never seen them before. There's also
a raffle during the course of the proceedings.
First prize? A ride in a balloon, of course. For
more information, check out the city's official
website at www.telc-etc.cz/telc.

Take a couple of steps back in time during the colorful and animated **Zacharias's**

Historic Celebrations (mid-August), a day dedicated to Telč's most important historical figure. Zacharias z Hradce (Zacharias of Hradec) was a wealthy nobleman who gained control of the town in the 16th century. Since he was a great admirer of the Italian Renaissance, he invited Italian architects to Telč and they proceeded to transform the town's once Gothic style into the Renaissance paradise it remains today. There are plenty of things to see on Zacharias's day, including sword fights, dance and theater performances, music concerts, and a full-on medieval fair complete with food, handicrafts, and drink of the period. This is a lot of fun for the whole family and a taste of what things were like many moons ago. Further information can be found at the tourist information office.

ACCOMMODATIONS

The **Hotel Celerin** (Náměstí Zachariáše z Hradce 43, tel. 567 243 477, www.hotelcelerin

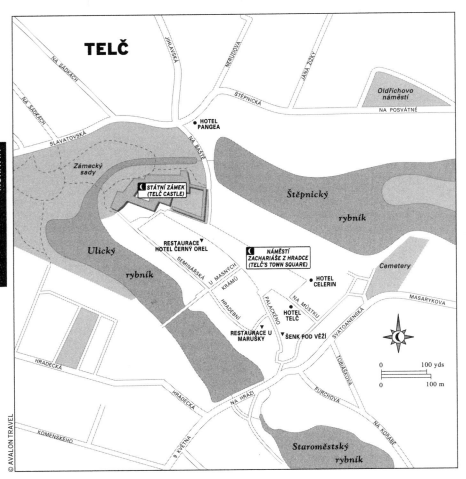

.cz, 1,300–1,600 Kč d) is a romantic, intimate hotel situated right on the main square. The rooms are clean, though simply furnished, and the service is warm and attentive. This hotel is perfect for those fed up with the cold, rather impersonal service that often comes with the bigger chains.

Located in the historic center of town, the **Hotel Telč** (Na Můstku 37, tel. 567 243 109, www.hoteltelc.cz, 1,600 Kč d) is a wonderful option. The staff is professional yet friendly and willing to go out of their way to make you feel at home. There is a distinct family atmosphere to this place and many consider it Telč's best value.

The **Hotel Pangea** (Na Baště 450, tel. 567 213 122, www.pangea.cz, 1,200–1,600 Kč d) is located in a quiet pedestrian zone just two minutes from the town center. The 10 double rooms are clean and comfortable and the desk staff is top-notch. There is a heated swimming pool should you need to get your laps in, and the hotel's location is quite convenient (it's closer to the castle than the Hotel Celerin or Hotel Telč). This is an excellent and affordable three-star hotel that many Czechs opt for when visiting.

FOOD

For an authentic, no-frills Czech culinary sensation, don't miss **Restaurace U Marušky** (Palackého 28, tel. 567 223 866, daily 11 A.M.–11 P.M., mains 70–130 Kč). Popular with the locals, this is the place to come to for fried pork cutlet, goulash, schnitzel, and the like. Wash it all down with tasty, hard-to-find beer like Červeny Drak and grab a heavy dessert like a blueberry dumpling to complete the experience. The delicious daily specials run 60–70 Kč, making this an excellent alternative to the touristy fare served up on the main square.

The **Restaurace Hotel Černý Orel** (Náměstí Zachariáše z Hradce 7, tel. 567 243 220, www.hotelcernyorel.cz, daily 7 A.M.–10 P.M., mains 80–190 Kč) serves up traditional Czech fare to what seems like the entire town's hungry. Extremely popular thanks to its reputation for delicious fresh trout and exceptional pork schnitzel, this is one place where you may have to elbow your way in for a seat.

Arguably the most charming place to eat in town, **Šenk pod věží** (Palackého 116, tel. 567 243 889, daily 11 A.M.–10 P.M., mains 150 Kč) is an excellent choice for tasty Czech fare at reasonable prices. A friendly staff, good selection of domestic wine, and great summer terrace are a few more reasons to stop in no matter what the time of day.

SHOPPING

Not particularly known for its shopping scene, Telč is nevertheless a fine place to pick up a bottle of Moravian wine. If you prefer handicrafts or clothing, try walking through the arcades, which offer all sorts of souvenirs including postcards, books, ceramic miniatures, and marionettes. Be forewarned that the quality of this kind of merchandise isn't particularly high so make sure you're not overpaying.

SPORTS AND RECREATION

Biking around the hills of Telč can be a little trying but the surrounding beauty is so overwhelming that you'll hardly even notice. If you do decide to see the town by bike, contact **Miluše Spázalová** (Náměstí Zachariáše z Hradce 8, tel. 567 243 562). The price is 150 Kč per day.

INFORMATION AND SERVICES

The Information Centre (Náměstí Zachariáše z Hradce 10, tel. 567 112 407, www.telc-etc .cz) is a handy resource for those who would like to learn more about this beautiful town. The kind staff here can help you with information regarding sights, accommodations, restaurants, trips, public transport connections, cultural and sport events, and a whole lot more. Hours are: April Monday–Friday 8 A.M.–noon, 1–5 P.M., Saturday–Sunday 8 A.M.–noon, 1–4 P.M.; May, June, and September Monday–Friday 8 A.M.–5 P.M., Saturday–Sunday 10 A.M.–5 P.M.; July and August Monday–Friday 8 A.M.–6 P.M.,

Saturday–Sunday 10 A.M.–6 P.M.; October Monday–Friday 8 A.M.–5 P.M., Saturday–Sunday 10 A.M.–4 P.M.; November–March Monday and Wednesday 8 A.M.–5 P.M., Tuesday and Thursday 8 A.M.–4 P.M., Friday 8 A.M.–3 P.M.

GETTING THERE
By Bus

Buses leave for Telč a few times a day from Prague's Florenc station, but make sure you get on a direct bus, as the others take twice as long to make the trip. Tickets cost 152 Kč and the ride lasts 2.5 hours.

By Car

Telč is 103 miles from Prague. Leaving Prague, take the D1 highway east in the direction of Brno and exit at Jihlava. After going through Jihlava, take Highway 38 south, then Highway 23 west. The drive should take roughly two hours.

Mikulov

Mikulov, with its enchanting square and dominating 13th-century castle, lies on the Austrian border roughly 155 miles from Prague. The town began to grow economically thanks to its location and climate, which were responsible for the nearly 2,000 acres of vineyards being cultivated here by the 16th century. Mikulov also gained a reputation for being a town of religious tolerance, prompting many Jews to relocate here after being exiled from both Viennese and Czech royal towns. It was home to the Rebbe from the middle of the 16th to the middle of the 19th century, and legendary Rabbi Löw, creator of the Golem, lived here as well, founding a yeshiva during his stay.

Mikulov today continues to be one of Moravia's leading wine centers and is home to Víno Mikulov, the largest producer of still wines in

the town of Mikulov, dominated by its oft-remodeled castle

© TOM DIRLIS

the country, with a total production of approximately 15 million bottles a year. It is home to elegant architecture, numerous nature trails, and the fun-filled Pálava Vintage Wine Festival, which attracts wine enthusiasts from all parts of the Czech Republic and beyond. A short visit here will convince even the most finicky of travelers that few towns are filled with so much history and natural, arresting beauty as this one.

NÁMĚSTÍ (MAIN SQUARE)

Mikulov's main square is a rather irregularly shaped affair that is nonetheless a Renaissance fan's dream come true, lined as it is with gorgeous, well-preserved buildings of the period. One of the square's most prominent features is a **fountain with the statue of Pomona,** who was the Roman goddess of fruit trees, gardens, and orchards. She has sat there with her shield since all the way back in 1680. Another attention-grabbing characteristic of the square is its **Plague Column,** which was designed by Josef Prener and built by Ignác Lengelacher in 1724. It depicts three angels symbolizing faith, hope, and love, as well as the statues of St. Jan Nepomuk, St. Francis Xavier, and St. Karel Boromejský, protector against the black death. The column is ringed with a handful of benches, making it a perfect spot to stop and catch your breath, allowing you to admire the square's remarkable architecture—including the striking, late-16th-century **"U Rytířů"** house decorated with sgraffiti motifs of knights and war. It is the only house of its kind in town and a perfect example of the Late Renaissance style.

ZÁMEK MIKULOV (MIKULOV CASTLE)

Mikulov Castle is a large complex of buildings that was founded by Přemysl Otakar I in 1218. It was acquired by the Liechtensteins in 1249 and went on to change hands and appearances throughout the centuries, being remodeled into Late Romanesque, Gothic, Renaissance, and, after fires in 1719, High Baroque. It was set ablaze by retreating German forces in 1945 and reconstruction began yet again in 1947.

the tower of Mikulov Castle

© TOM DIRLIS

MORAVIA

Since 1959, it has been home to the **Regional Museum of Mikulov** (Zámek 1, tel. 519 510 255, www.rmm.cz), which remains popular due to its interesting exhibition detailing Moravia's long history of wine growing and viticulture. Another object of interest lies in the castle's cellar: Central Europe's second-largest wine barrel, which is 20 feet long, weighs 26 tons, and holds a whopping 26,703 gallons of wine.

PROBOŠTSKÝ KOSTEL SV. VÁCLAVA (CHURCH OF ST. WENCESLAS)

The late Gothic Church of St. Wenceslas (Kostelní náměstí 3) is located just off the main square and stands on the foundations of a former Romanesque church that burned down somewhere around 1426. The relatively modest church sports a five-sided, vaulted presbytery, triple nave, and lavish stucco interiors. It is also home to one of the country's most valuable church organs, which was the work of renowned organ maker Jan Výmola and dates back to 1771.

TOMÁŠ BAT'A: "OUR CUSTOMER IS OUR MASTER"

Born in Zlín on April 3, 1876, Tomáš Baťa became Czechoslovakia's most innovative and important businessman after establishing the Bata Shoe Organization in his hometown on August 24, 1894. To offer some perspective on the matter, Bata has so far managed to sell over 14 billion shoes since its inception – over twice that of the world's population and, indeed, far more than the total amount of people who have ever graced this fair Earth.

Baťa's operation grew significantly in both size and stature during the First World War when the demand for military shoes skyrocketed. When the dust finally settled, economies had been crippled, currencies were rendered practically useless and people had barely enough to spend on food, let alone footwear. Baťa's answer was to slash his prices in half, luring customers back into his stores and forcing the industry to follow suit.

As the company prospered, so did neighboring communities. Baťa began building houses, schools, hospitals, and shops near all his factories, creating an environment that allowed everyone to enjoy his success. Possessing a strong sense of social consciousness and responsibility, he was a pioneer of employment welfare and social advancement programs and once stated, "Let's bear in mind that the chances to multiply wealth are unlimited. All people can become rich." It was this socio-capitalist philosophy that got him elected mayor of Zlín in 1923.

Being a student of Le Corbusier's school of city as machine, Baťa enlisted leading Czech modernist architect František Gahura to design a simple 20-foot-by-20-foot concrete box that could be duplicated quickly and easily. Gahura took the idea and ran with it, adding red brick, glass brick, and steel-framed windows to the mix. The result was that the town's residential buildings now mirrored the factories,

ENTERTAINMENT AND EVENTS

◖ Pálava Vintage Wine Festival

The Pálava Vintage Wine Festival (first half of Sept.) is by far the most important cultural event in Mikulov, drawing thousands of merry-makers from all over the country and beyond. For three days straight, folks celebrate the actions of one Lord John of Lichtenstein, who, in 1403, set free Czech King Wenceslas IV from a Viennese prison. Upon his return, a large feast was held and the same thing has been happening here for the last 50 years. Parades sweep through town, marketplaces spring up, wine is sampled all day and night, and food is consumed with the zeal of hungry noblemen. If you plan on attending this funfest and staying overnight, keep in mind that you'll have to book a room well in advance.

ACCOMMODATIONS

The wonderful ◖ **Eliška Hotel** (Piaristů 4, tel. 519 513 073, www.hoteleliska.cz, 900–1,400 Kč d) offers quality accommodations a mere five-minute walk from the main square. The rooms are clean and comfortable and come equipped with satellite TV, Internet, and the usual amenities. Apartments are available as well and they come with bath and terrace. There's bowling and billiards on the premises, along with indoor golf, tennis, and an Irish pub where the Guinness flows freely. This is easily one of the more stylish and enjoyable hotels in town.

The **Réva Hotel** (Česká 2, tel. 519 512 076, www.hoteleliska.cz, 800–1,200 Kč d) is another excellent and affordable choice. Located right in the historical center, guests have tremendous views of Mikulov Castle, Goat Hill, and St. Wenceslas Church. The rooms are clean and bright with contemporary furnishings and the hotel staff is exceptionally friendly. There is also a restaurant on the premises with a summer terrace for peaceful, romantic dining.

FOOD

The **Hotel Templ Restaurant** (Husova 50, tel. 519 323 095, www.templ.cz, Sun.–Thurs.

stressing Baťa's strong belief of industry being central to one's life.

Baťa continued to modernize the footwear industry by being the first to incorporate factory-style production along with long-distance retailing. He set up factories and companies in a number of countries including Poland, Yugoslavia, India, Holland, Denmark, the UK, and the US. By the time the 1930s rolled around, Baťa and his beloved Czechoslovakia were atop the field of footwear exporters, producing over 80,000 pairs of shoes a day.

Baťa's death came suddenly in 1932 – the result of a fatal plane crash. His half-brother Dr. Jan Antonín Baťa took over the operation until the Nazis invaded in 1939, prompting him to flee to Brazil. When the Communists showed up, they seized all Bata companies and nationalized them – a sign, no doubt, of their distaste for Baťa's egalitarian capitalism, not to mention the fact that Zlín had

already accomplished most of what the Communists were promising, including a level of working conditions unparalleled in Europe at the time.

The company was eventually taken over by Thomas Jan Bata, son of the original, and its headquarters were moved to Toronto, Canada, which is also home to the Bata Shoe Museum. Today, Bata serves roughly one million customers a day, employs over 40,000 people, and is a retail force to be reckoned with in over 50 countries. There is also a Tomáš Baťa University in Zlín, which is currently composed of five faculties: Technology, Management and Economics, Multimedia Communications, Applied Informatics, and Humanity Studies.

Tomáš Baťa may not have lived to see his dream of providing shoes to every man, woman, and child on the planet, but he can rest in peace knowing that he and his devoted family have come pretty darn close.

10 A.M.–11 P.M., Fri.–Sat. 10 A.M.–midnight, mains 135–245 Kč) will catch your eye for no other reason than it's arguably the brightest building in the entire Jewish quarter. Delicious Czech and international dishes are served by a pleasant staff in elegant surroundings that span five successive rooms. The meals are generously portioned and relatively affordable but if you're on a tight budget, make sure to check out their daily specials, which are no less impressive.

❮ Mikulovský Šenk (Videnská 16, tel. 519 510 305, www.mikulovsky-senk.cz, daily 10 A.M.–11 P.M., mains 135–250 Kč) is both a local and tourist favorite that never fails to impress. Mouthwatering Czech dishes are the menu's focus, with meat dishes being grilled on a large open fire. The lovely summer terrace is the scene for lively diners and drinkers enjoying themselves with the occasional live music concert whipping them into more of a fun-loving frenzy. Affordable, friendly, and consistently impressive, a meal here will not only fill your belly but brighten your day as well.

SHOPPING

Pretty much the only thing worth buying here is the local wine that flows like mountain water. There is no shortage of wineries and private wine cellars to choose from, most of which offer visitors samples of their latest creations. Your best bet is to simply walk around, soak up the town's wonderful atmosphere, and, after working up a thirst, experimenting at various shops trying to finds the best deals. Many locals may not know much English but it'll be your taste buds that'll do most of the talking.

SPORTS AND RECREATION

There are plenty of trails to choose from in the region; a visit to the Tourist Information Centre will help you decide which one is best for you.

There is one particularly popular trail of about three miles in length that goes through town, along some natural paths, and then back again. Start at the Chateau Park and continue on to Goat Hill. After you've enjoyed the beautiful view over town, head north to Tur-old Hill. You should come across a blue tourist trail. Follow it through the forest as you climb the northeast side of Holy Hill. Reward yourself with another fabulous view of the town before heading down along the Way of the Cross and back into town.

INFORMATION AND SERVICES

The Tourist Information Centre (Náměstí 30, tel. 519 510 855, www.mikulov.cz) is usually quite busy but very efficient so you won't be waiting long. This is where to come if you have any questions regarding sights or cultural events. The kind people here can also arrange concert tickets and accommodations for you, as well as an evening in one of the town's many wine cellars. If you feel like exploring on your own, you can find helpful maps and brochures that will get you started. The center's hours of operation are: January–March Monday–Friday 8 A.M.–4 P.M.; April–May Monday–Friday 8 A.M.–noon, 1–5 P.M., Saturday–Sunday 9 A.M.–4 P.M.; June Monday–Friday 8 A.M.–6 P.M., Saturday–Sunday 9 A.M.–6 P.M.; July–August Monday–Friday 8 A.M.–7 P.M., Saturday–Sunday 9 A.M.–7 P.M.; September–October Monday–Friday 8 A.M.–noon, 1–5 P.M., Saturday–Sunday 9 A.M.–4 P.M.; November–December Monday–Friday 8 A.M.–4 P.M.

GETTING THERE
By Bus

Buses leave Prague's Florenc station regularly every day; routes, and therefore times and prices, vary widely. A typical trip lasts a little over four hours and costs roughly 35 Kč.

By Car

Mikulov is approximately 155 miles from Prague. Leaving Prague, take the D1 east all the way to Brno, then take Route 52 south to Mikulov.

BUDAPEST

The famed Danube River separates Buda's hilly west bank from Pest's bustling streets, offering travelers the best of both peaceful surroundings and the infectious energy that comes with a modern, cosmopolitan city. Whether it's a stroll through the Belváros or a night spent imbibing the delicious local wine and cuisine, visitors can't help but be affected by the history and romance that blankets this majestic capital.

From the splendor of Buda Castle to the mind-blowing St. Stephen's Basilica, the peaceful paradise of Margaret Island to the other-worldly hills of Buda, there is a delicate mix of nature and architecture that is inspirational. Then there are the glorious spas and grand coffee houses, the broad boulevards and magnificent squares, all serving as reminders of the city's impressive imperial past.

Hungary joined the EU in 2004, and its capital continues to come into its own with countless hotels, shops, and residences going up on a daily basis, as a hungry young generation tries to forge its own unique identity in the new millennium. Budapest is a city clearly on the rise and should be both an artistic and economic force to be reckoned with in the next decade or so. In the meanwhile, come and sip some of the finest wine on the continent, soak those bones in world-class thermal baths, and enjoy a gorgeous city that continues to successfully blend the charm of the old world with the inventiveness of the new.

PLANNING YOUR TIME

Unlike Prague, many of Budapest's major sights are spread throughout the city, resulting

© TOM DIRLIS

HIGHLIGHTS

(Váci utca (Váci Street): The most famous pedestrian street in the country continues to do big business, luring tourists and
residents alike with its memorable mixture
of historical landmarks, sidewalk cafes, and
trendy boutiques (page 200).

(Dunakorzó (Danube Embankment):
A long-time favorite of both locals and tourists, the Danube Embankment exudes an old-
world charm typical of great European capitals
thanks to its pretty outdoor cafes and awe-inspiring views of Buda (page 202).

**(Magyar Állami Operaház (Opera
House):** Put on your finest eveningwear and
head for this neo-Renaissance masterpiece,
where the world's finest musicians dazzle sold-
out crowds night after night (page 212).

(Hősök tere (Heroes' Square): Located
at the end of Andrássy út, this remarkable tribute to Hungary's most important figures will
give you a better understanding of just how seriously the country takes its history (page 218).

**(Széchenyi gyógyfürdő (Széchenyi
Spa Baths):** One of Europe's largest spa
complexes, this majestic, neo-Baroque building boasts an enormous swimming pool that
can be enjoyed year-round, as well as steam
rooms, saunas, and Turkish baths guaran-

teed to leave you feeling as good as new
(page 220).

**(Budavári palota (Royal Palace of
Buda):** Dominating Buda's skyline, the Royal
Palace is one of the country's most revered
architectural achievements and home to the
Hungarian National Gallery, Budapest History
Museum, National Széchenyi Library, and Ludwig
Museum of Contemporary Art (page 227).

(Gellért hegy (Gellért Hill): A trek
up this impressive hill, topped by the battle-
scarred but beautiful Citadella, rewards you
with some of the most spectacular panoramic
views of the city (page 233).

(Aquincum: A short trip on the HÉV will
take you back to the 2nd century, when public
baths and sacrificial altars were de rigueur for
this former Roman capital (page 235).

(Margit sziget (Margaret Island): This
1.6-mile stretch of the sublime offers flower gardens, enchanting ruins, and the incomparable
Palatinus Strand. Its countless paths and near
mystical serenity make this the perfect place to
spend a romantic afternoon (page 236).

(The Railway Circuit: Drink in the scenery as you ride through the vast Buda Hills
on the Cog-Wheel Railway and the Children's
Railway (page 238).

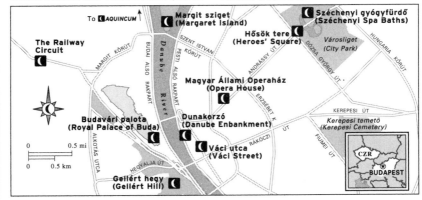

LOOK FOR **(** TO FIND RECOMMENDED SIGHTS, ACTIVITIES, DINING, AND LODGING.

in larger distances to cover and consequently necessitating more time to do so. Many travelers spend a scant three days here, as Budapest is generally just one of many regional capitals they visit while in Europe. Three days will allow you the opportunity to see most of the major sights, though you won't have much time to catch your breath and even less time (if any) to enjoy the city's wonderful museums or spas. The best way to approach planning a trip to Budapest is to think of it in half days: a half day to visit Margaret Island, a half day to visit the Városliget, a half day to visit the Buda Hills, and so forth. Again, should you be interested in visiting any of Budapest's excellent museums or fantastic spas (both of which are highly recommended), simply add however much time you'd like to allot to either. Four days is enough time to give you a decent sense of what Budapest has to offer, though five days to a week would be ideal.

Budapest's public transport system rivals Prague's in convenience and overall service, making the entire city easily accessible via bus or subway. It is also a great city to walk around, with strolls down the Danube Embankment or Andrássy út, as well as over any of its pretty bridges, being wonderful ways to soak up the infectious atmosphere. While the Belváros is clearly tourist central, the city is so big that huge tourist groups are easily avoided in most other districts, thereby allowing you to discover the beauty of Budapest in both comfort and peace.

ORIENTATION
Pest
THE BELVÁROS
(INNER CITY)
Located in Budapest's fifth district, the Belváros, or Inner City, is surrounded by the Kiskörút (Inner Ring), which starts at Szabadság híd (Liberty Bridge) and is comprised of Károly körút, Múzeum körút, Vámház körút, Bajcsy-Zsilinszky út, and József Attila utca before ending at the Chain Bridge. Its main squares are Deák Ferenc tér, which borders Lipótváros; Vörösmarty tér, which is home to the beginning of popular pedestrian shopping

zone Váci utca and neighbors the Danube Embankment; and Ferenciek tere, which is characterized by the Elizabeth Bridge stretching across to Buda's Gellért Hill.

The major subway stops are Deák Ferenc tér, Vörösmarty tér, and Ferenciek tere.

LIPÓTVÁROS
Lipótváros is located in the northern part of the fifth district next to the Belváros and is bordered by Szent István körút, Bajcsy-Zsilinszky út, Deák Ferenc utca, and the Danube. Its main squares are Roosevelt tér, located at the foot of the Chain Bridge; Szabadság tér; and Kossuth Lajos tér, home to the mighty Parliament building.

The major subway stops are Arany János utca, Kossuth Lajos tér, and Nyugati pályaudvar.

TERÉZVÁROS
The city's vibrant sixth district is characterized by the grand boulevard Andrássy út, which stretches all the way to Heroes' Square and marks the border between Terézváros and Lipótváros. Strolling down the boulevard will bring you to Nagymező utca, otherwise known as Budapest's Broadway, as well as vibrant Liszt Ferenc tér and its numerous outdoor cafes and restaurants. Further up still is the bustling, eight-sided square known as the Oktogon, part of the city's Nagykörút (Outer Ring), which begins at Petőfi Bridge and incorporates Ferenc körút, József körút, Erzsébet körút, Teréz körút, and Szent István körút before ending at Margit Bridge.

The major subway stops are Bajcsy-Zsilinszky út, Opera, Oktogon, Vörösmarty utca, Kodály Körönd, and Bajza utca.

ERZSÉBETVÁROS
Situated southeast of Terézváros, Erzsébetváros serves as Budapest's seventh district and is also the location of the capital's colorful Jewish neighborhood. Király utca is a major street full of shops, cafes, and bars, as is Dohány utca, which is home to the magnificent Dohány Synagogue as well. Klauzál tér, deep in the district, is Erzsébetváros' largest square and historic center.

The major subway stop is Astoria.

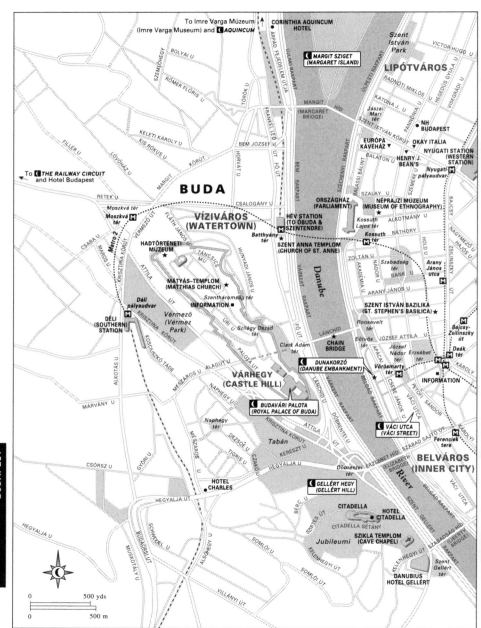

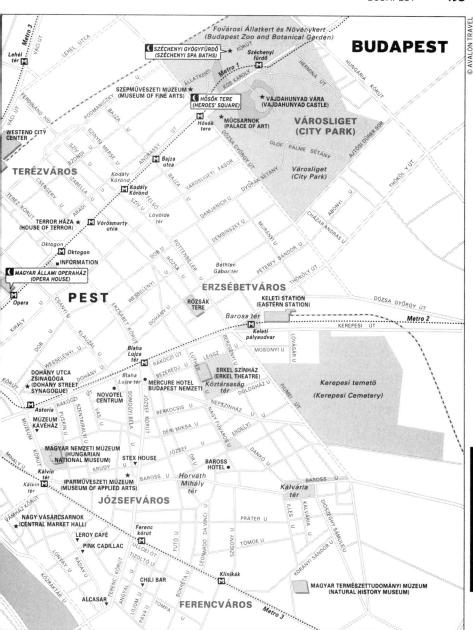

BUDAPEST

Fövárosi Állatkert és Növénykert
(Budapest Zoo and Botanical Garden)

BUDAPEST

© AVALON TRAVEL

Metro 3

Lehel tér

VÁCI ÚT

LEHEL UTCA

☾ SZÉCHENYI GYÓGYFÜRDŐ
(SZÉCHENYI SPA BATHS)

Széchenyi fürdő

KÓS KÁROLY

HERMINA ÚT

HUNGÁRIA KÖRÚT

Metro 1

ÁLLATKERTI KÖRÚT

PODMANICZKY

SZÉPMŰVÉSZETI MÚZEUM ★
(MUSEUM OF FINE ARTS)

HŐSÖK TERE
(HEROES' SQUARE)

★ VAJDAHUNYAD VÁRA
(VAJDAHUNYAD CASTLE)

FERDINÁND HÍD

VÁCI ÚT

BAJZA

WESTEND CITY
CENTER

ANDRÁSSY

ÚT

Hősök tere

Hősök tere

MŰCSARNOK
(PALACE OF ART)

VÁROSLIGET
(CITY PARK)

OLOF   PALME   SÉTÁNY

AJTÓSI DÜRER SOR

TERÉZVÁROS

SZÍV

SZINYEI MERSE U

Bajza utca

VÁROSLIGETI FASOR

DÓZSA GYÖRGY ÚT

Városliget
(City Park)

THÖKÖLY ÚT

SZONDI

IZABELLA

Kodály Körönd

BAJZA

ELSŐ

DVOŘÁK SÉTÁNY

CSENGERY

ARADI

Kodály Körönd

SZÍV U

DAMJANICH U

MURÁNYI U

CHÁZÁR ANDRÁS U

ABONYI U

TERÉZ KÖRÚT

Lövölde tér

DEMBINSZKY U

★ TERROR HÁZA
(HOUSE OF TERROR)

☀ Vörösmarty utca

DOB U

RÓZSA

Bethlen
Gábor tér

PÉTERFY SÁNDOR U

THÖKÖLY ÚT

Oktogon ☀ Oktogon

WESSELÉNYI

■ INFORMATION

☾ MAGYAR ÁLLAMI OPERAHÁZ
(OPERA HOUSE)

ERZSÉBETVÁROS

KELETI STATION
(EASTERN STATION)

DÓZSA   GYÖRGY   ÚT

☀ Opera

CSÁNYI U

ERZSÉBET KÖRÚT

ROTTENBILLER

DOHÁNY U

PEST

RÓZSÁK
TERE

Baross tér

Metro 2

KEREPESI   ÚT

KIRÁLY

DOB

KLAUZÁL U

Keleti
pályaudvar

LOVASÁR U

WESSELÉNYI U

DOHÁNY U

Blaha
Lujza tér

RÁKÓCZI ÚT

LUTHER

LÉGSZ

MOSONYI U

BERZSENYI U

**DOHÁNY UTCA
ZSINAGÓGA**
★ (DOHÁNY STREET
SYNAGOGUE)

KÖRÚT

DOHÁNY U

Blaha
Lujza tér

BEZERÉDJ U

ERKEL SZÍNHÁZ
(ERKEL THEATRE)

FIUMEI ÚT

Kerepesi temetö
(Kerepesi Cemetery)

NOVOTEL
CENTRUM

MERCURE HOTEL
BUDAPEST NEMZETI

Köztársaság
tér

DOLOGHÁZ U

NÉPSZÍNHÁZ

☀ Astoria

RÁKÓCZI

VAS U

JÓZSEF KÖRÚT

BERKOCSIS U

NAGY FUVÁROS U

MÚZEUM
KÁVÉHÁZ

PUSKIN U

SZENTKIRÁLYI U

SOMOGYI BÉLA U

DÉRI MIKSA U

ERDÉLYI U

DANKÓ U

MIHÁLY U

MAGYAR NEMZETI MÚZEUM
(HUNGARIAN
NATIONAL MUSEUM)

STEX HOUSE

JÓZSEF

KRÚDY U

BAROSS
HOTEL ●

Kálvin tér

MÚZEUM KÖRÚT

Kálvin
tér ☀

IPARMŰVÉSZETI MÚZEUM
★ (MUSEUM OF APPLIED ARTS)

BAROSS U

*Horváth
Mihály
tér*

*Kálvária
tér*

BAROSS   U

KÁLVÁRIA U

DIÓSZEGHY SÁMUEL U

VÁMHÁZ KÖRÚT

JÓZSEFVÁROS

LEONARDO DA VINCI U

PRÁTER U

ILLÉS U

NAGY VÁSÁRCSARNOK
★ (CENTRAL MARKET HALL)

Ferenc
körút

FUTÓ U

SZIGONY U

TÖMŐE U

KORÁNYI SÁNDOR U

LŐNYAY U

RÁDAY U

LEROY CAFÉ
▼

PINK CADILLAC
▼

ÜLLŐEI ÚT

TIZOLTÓ U

FERENC KÖRÚT

LILIOM U

PAVA U

BOKRÉTA U

TOMPA

Klinikák
☀

KÖZRAKTÁR U

ANGYAL U

CHILI BAR
▼

ALCASAR
▼

FERENCVÁROS

Metro 3

MAGYAR TERMÉSZETTUDOMÁNYI MÚZEUM
(NATURAL HISTORY MUSEUM)

BUDAPEST

BUDAPEST ADDRESSES AND DISTRICTS

Deciphering an address in Budapest can seem a little daunting at first but it's really rather easy. A Roman numeral or four-digit postal code will precede each address. For example, when looking up the excellent Old Man's Music Pub, you might find its address written as: VII. Akácfa u. 13, or 1072 Budapest, Akácfa u. 13. In the first example, the Roman numeral "VII" tells us that the pub is located in the seventh district (Erzsébetváros). To learn what district the pub is in the second example, simply refer to the middle two digits "07."

There are 22 districts or kerülets in Budapest, with the most common ones listed below.

District I

A small area in central Buda, it includes Gellért hegy, Buda Castle, Matthias Church, Tabán, and Víziváros.

District II

This is the northwest part of Buda, which includes the beautiful and prestigious neighborhood of Rózsadomb as well as hub Moszkva tér.

District III

This district lies on the ancient military camp of Aquincum and includes beautiful Óbuda, the oldest part of Budapest, which has been the site of a commercial revival and is now home to trendy eateries and up-and-coming yuppies.

District V

Representing the Belváros and Lipótváros, it simply doesn't get any more central than this. Sights include Váci Street, the Danube Embankment, Parliament, and St. Stephen's Basilica.

District VI

The cultural center of Budapest, Terézváros is where you'll find the city's famed boulevard Andrássy út, along with the Opera House, Nagymező utca (Budapest's Broadway), and lively Liszt Ferenc tér.

District VII

Otherwise known as Budapest's Jewish district, the Erzsébetváros is surrounded by main roads Károly körút, Király utca, and Rákóczi út. It is also home to the great Dohány Synagogue.

THE VÁROSLIGET (CITY PARK)

The end of Andrássy út leads to the Városliget, Budapest's 14th district. The main square here is the grandiose Hősök tere (Heroes' Square). Its main streets are Dózsa György út, which stretches all the way to Józsefváros, and Állatkerti körút, site of the Circus, Vidám Park, the Zoo, and Széchenyi Spa Baths.

The major subway stops are Hősök tere and Széchenyi fürdő.

JÓZSEFVÁROS

Located southeast of Erzsébetváros, Józsefváros makes up Budapest's eighth district. The Múzeum körút is one of its major routes and is part of the Inner Ring, separating the neighborhood from the Belváros and leading to its main square, Kálvin tér. On the other, less-touristy, and far seedier side of the district, the József körút—part of the Outer Ring—is home to rampant prostitution and organized crime.

The major subway stops are Kálvin tér, Blaha Lujza tér, and Keleti pályaudvar.

FERENCVÁROS

Comprising the city's ninth district, Ferencváros borders Józsefváros to the south and is separated from the Belváros by the Vámház körút. Major road Üllői út stretches through most of the district, while popular pedestrian street Ráday utca offers color in the form of outdoor cafes and restaurants to what is otherwise a primarily working-class district.

District VIII

Józsefváros is a sort of Jekyll and Hyde neighborhood. Sticking to its main roads will reward you with the wonderful National Museum and busy Kálvin tér. Head for the depths, however, and you'll quickly find yourself in a seedy red-light district.

District IX

Ferencváros is a rapidly developing neighborhood that has seen plenty of hip bars, restaurants, and apartment buildings spring up in the last couple of years. Trendy pedestrian street Ráday utca is an excellent place to have a drink and the Central Market Hall just up the street by the Danube is one of the city's most memorable shopping experiences.

District XII

This is home to the beautiful Buda Hills, with winding roads, large houses, and serene hiking trails, not to mention Normafa, which makes for a pleasant summertime getaway or passable ski site in the winter.

District XIII

This is the location of the one and only Margaret Island (Margit sziget).

District XIV

The Városliget is complete with must-see sights such as Heroes' Square, the Museum of Fine Arts, Vajdahunyad Castle, and Széchenyi Baths.

TERMS

Hungarian is obviously a complicated language and its names for various types of roads and streets can cause confusion for the uninitiated. Here are some of the more useful terms that can be learned quickly.

utca (also abbreviated as *u.*) – street
út – road
útja – road of
körút (also abbreviated as *krt*) – boulevard
tér – square
tere – square of
köz – alley or lane
liget – park
sziget – island
híd – bridge
pályaudvar (also abbreviated as *pu.*) – train station
állomás – station

The major subway stops are Ferenc körút and Klinikák.

Buda
VÁRHEGY (CASTLE HILL), THE VÍZIVÁROS (WATERTOWN), AND CENTRAL BUDA

Várhegy, or Castle Hill, is designated as Budapest's first district. On the Buda side of the Chain Bridge is Clark Ádám tér, which is the stepping stone to the funicular leading up the hill and to the Royal Palace. The Castle District's main square is Szentháromság tér, home to Matthias Church and the Fisherman's Bastion.

Running along the Danube below Castle Hill is the Víziváros, also part of Budapest's first district. Its main street is Fő utca, which leads to central Batthyány tér.

The area loosely known as Central Buda is the assortment of small neighborhoods lying below Castle Hill and characterized by bustling Moszkvá tér, located just north of Castle Hill.

The major subway stops are Batthyány tér and Moszkvá tér.

GELLÉRT HEGY (GELLÉRT HILL)

South of Castle Hill is Gellért Hill, part of Budapest's 11th district. The hill is reached via the Elizabeth Bridge and stretches out towards Gellért tér and neighboring Liberty Bridge, home of the world famous Gellért Hotel and Baths.

Gellért Hill is accessed via bus and tram.

ÓBUDA

Located north of Buda along the left bank of the

Danube, Óbuda's centerpiece is its lovely and historic main square Fő tér.

Óbuda is accessed via HÉV train.

THE BUDA HILLS

Beyond central Buda to the east lie the Buda Hills, the majority of which comprise the city's 12th district.

The major subway stop is Moszkvá tér.

Margit sziget (Margaret Island)

Located in the middle of the Danube and representing Budapest's 13th district, Margaret Island is reached via either the Margaret or Árpád Bridge.

Sights

THE BELVÁROS (INNER CITY)

The Belváros is the historic center of Pest and forms the southern half of its fifth district. Abuzz with shops, restaurants, boutique hotels, and bars, it has caught up to the rest of the Western world in terms of consumerism and commerce, though there is still a sense of the old imperial city lurking around corners and down back streets, beckoning those willing to leave the well-worn tourists routes and delve into a glorious past that has yet to fade.

It is home to some of the city's most important sights, like the famed Danube Embankment, whose enchanting views of Buda have inspired romance in the hearts of millions over the centuries. The colorful square Vörösmarty tér is nearby, where street musicians, starving artists, and local peddlers vie for your attention and a few hard-earned forints. Then, of course, there is Váci utca—Budapest's bustling pedestrian avenue lined with countless cafes and shops selling everything from Prada to paprika.

There is always something to do in the Inner City no matter what the time of year. Whether it's sampling the local cuisine and wide variety of wines, taking in a jazz show, or nursing a cup of coffee in glorious, turn-of-the-20th-century surroundings, you'll find it all available here in the lifeblood of the capital.

Deák Ferenc tér (Deák Ferenc Square)

With all three of Budapest's metro lines converging here, Deák Ferenc tér, or simply Deák tér, is quite understandably one of the busiest

squares in town. People on their way to work merge with tourists engrossed in their maps. If you have any questions as to where you are or where you're going, fear not, as the very friendly people at **Tourinform** (V. Sütő utca 2, tel. 1/438-8080, www.budapestinfo.hu, daily 8 A.M.–8 P.M.) will provide you with answers, maps, and all kinds of informative booklets.

Before moving on to Vörösmarty Square and the Inner City proper, take a moment to explore lovely **Erzsébet tér,** whose park across the street merges into Deák Square, forming a sort of border between the Belváros and Lipótváros. In the summertime, the park is constantly full of people young and old chilling out and soaking up the sun. You'll find plenty of beer drinkers here, along with guitar players, in-line skaters, and a bevy of Budapesters cooling their feet in the shallow pool thoughtfully provided in the center of it all. This is a wonderful place to meet locals, read a book, or simply enjoy a beverage and the bustling surroundings.

Vörösmarty tér (Vörösmarty Square)

Vörösmarty Square is undoubtedly the hub of all social activity in the center. Restaurants, cafes, casinos, airline offices, and a myriad of retail establishments are all close by, serving as a busy backdrop for the scores of artists and musicians vying for their livelihood on any given day of the week. This is also the official beginning of Váci utca, Budapest's—make that Hungary's—most famous pedestrian promenade.

Nearby is a statue with lions keeping guard

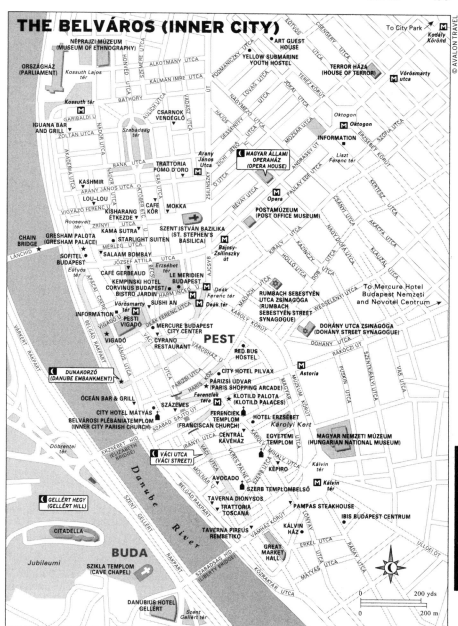

THE BELVÁROS (INNER CITY)

© AVALON TRAVEL

To City Park
Kodály Körönd

NÉPRAJZI MÚZEUM
(MUSEUM OF ETHNOGRAPHY)

ART GUEST HOUSE

YELLOW SUBMARINE YOUTH HOSTEL

TERROR HÁZA (HOUSE OF TERROR)

Vörösmarty utca

ORSZÁGHÁZ (PARLIAMENT)

Kossuth Lajos tér

Kossuth tér

Oktogon

IGUANA BAR AND GRILL

Szabadság tér

CSARNOK VENDÉGLŐ

INFORMATION

Liszt Ferenc tér

Arany János utca

TRATTORIA POMO D'ORO

MAGYAR ÁLLAMI OPERAHÁZ (OPERA HOUSE)

KASHMIR

KISHARANG ÉTKEZDE

LOU-LOU

CAFÉ KÖR

MOKKA

Opera

POSTAMÚZEUM (POST OFFICE MUSEUM)

Roosevelt tér

KAMA SUTRA

STARLIGHT SUITEN

SZENT ISTVÁN BAZILIKA (ST. STEPHEN'S BASILICA)

Bajcsy-Zsilinszky út

CHAIN BRIDGE

GRESHAM PALOTA (GRESHAM PALACE)

SALAAM BOMBAY

SOFITEL BUDAPEST

Eötvös tér

Erzsébet tér

CAFÉ GERBEAUD

KEMPINSKI HOTEL CORVINUS BUDAPEST / BISTRO JARDIN

LE MERIDIEN BUDAPEST

Deák Ferenc tér

To Mercure Hotel Budapest Nemzeti and Novotel Centrum

RUMBACH SEBESTYÉN UTCA ZSINAGÓGA (RUMBACH SEBESTYÉN STREET SYNAGOGUE)

INFORMATION

Vörösmarty tér

SUSHI AN

Deák tér

PESTI VIGADÓ

MERCURE BUDAPEST CITY CENTER

VIGADÓ

CYRANO RESTAURANT

PEST

DOHÁNY UTCA ZSINAGÓGA (DOHÁNY STREET SYNAGOGUE)

DUNAKORZÓ (DANUBE EMBANKMENT)

RED BUS HOSTEL

CITY HOTEL PILVAX

Astoria

ÓCEÁN BAR & GRILL

CITY HOTEL MÁTYÁS

BELVÁROSI PLÉBÁNIATEMPLOM (INNER CITY PARISH CHURCH)

PÁRIZSI UDVAR (PARIS SHOPPING ARCADE)

SZÁZÉVES

Ferenciek tere

KLOTILD PALOTA (KLOTILD PALACES)

FERENCIEK TEMPLOM (FRANCISCAN CHURCH)

HOTEL ERZSÉBET

Károlyi Kert

CENTRÁL KÁVÉHÁZ

EGYETEMI TEMPLOM

MAGYAR NEMZETI MÚZEUM (HUNGARIAN NATIONAL MUSEUM)

Döbrentei tér

VÁCI UTCA (VÁCI STREET)

KÉPIRO

Kálvin tér

AVOCADO

SZERB TEMPLOMBELSŐ

Kálvin tér

GELLÉRT HEGY (GELLÉRT HILL)

TAVERNA DIONYSOS

TRATTORIA TOSCANA

PAMPAS STEAKHOUSE

IBIS BUDAPEST CENTRUM

CITADELLA

KÁLVIN HÁZ

TAVERNA PIREUS REMBETIKO

Jubileumi

BUDA

SZIKLA TEMPLOM (CAVE CHAPEL)

GREAT MARKET HALL

Danube River

DANUBIUS HOTEL GELLÉRT

Szent Gellért tér

ERZSÉBET HÍD (ELIZABETH BRIDGE)

SZABADSÁG HÍD (LIBERTY BRIDGE)

0   200 yds

0   200 m

BUDAPEST

Vörösmarty Square's centerpiece, the statue of Mihály Vörösmarty

© OLIVER HERBST

BUDAPEST

over fountains but it's the **statue of Mihály Vörösmarty,** Hungary's beloved poet and patriot, standing tall in the center of the square that deserves closer scrutiny. Accompanied by a number of eager listeners representing various societal classes (farmer and peasant girl, worker with wife and son, people in traditional Magyar dress), Vörösmarty recites his patriotic *Szózat* (Appeal), the first verse of which is inscribed in the statue's plinth and reads, "To your homeland without fail/Be faithful, O Hungarian!" A popular spot for lounging teenagers and tourists in the summer, the statue is wrapped in plastic sheeting every winter in order to protect the Carrara marble from the unforgiving elements.

At the north side of the square is the one and only **Café Gerbeaud** (Vörösmarty tér, 7-8), a classic Budapest coffee house if there ever was one. Two more nearby sights of historical note are worth mentioning. The first is the **Luxus Department Store** (V. Vörösmarty tér 3). Closed for repair at the time of writing, it is nevertheless housed in pretty Art Nouveau buildings and was *the* place for qual-

ity goods before the beginning of the country's political and economic liberalization in the 1980s. The second sight is the **Entrance to the Underground Railway,** whose original decor was restored in 1996 on its 100th birthday, giving modern commuters a sense of what the public transport side of things used to be like once upon a time.

Vörösmarty Square is in the middle of some serious reconstruction at the time of this writing. Buildings on either side of Cafe Gerbeaud are cordoned off by fences or otherwise covered in plastic sheeting. Many of the buildings that form the square now advertise plenty of office and residential space for rent as well—a sure sign that the times are a-changin', with the lingering question of what exactly comes next.

◖ Váci utca (Váci Street)

Formed in the 18th century and lined with magnificent architecture from the 19th and early 20th centuries, Váci Street is easily the city's most popular street. Starting at Vörösmarty Square and leading all the way to Central Market Hall, Váci Street was originally a shopping district that people of all classes and status could enjoy. That changed during the first decades of the 20th century when it became fashionable for Budapest's elite to stroll down the pedestrian-only avenue and spend freely their hard-earned, or, in most cases, inherited, money. The shops, consequently, became more and more exclusive—and remain so to this day.

Indeed, shoppers today ought to prepare themselves for inflated prices and, while there are many boutiques and popular Western brand outlets to be found, quite a number of shops have adjusted to the healthy jump in tourism and now offer visitors trinkets, t-shirts, and a whole host of kitschy souvenirs. Restaurants, bars, and cafes abound as well, advertising "tourist menus" that typically include meals like goulash, paprika-based meats, and traditional desserts. Some are better than others and you may want to check out the more mom-and-pop-type establishments found on the side streets before making a decision.

A number of colorful characters can be found up and down Váci: musicians young and old busking for a few forints, elderly ladies hawking traditional hand-woven garments, and visual artists publicly plying their trade to the enjoyment of passersby. There are also a handful of "ladies" who like to approach men and lure them into overpriced clubs or offer their company for a fee. All in a day's work on vivid Váci Street.

Quite a few landmarks dot the pleasant avenue. Starting from Vörösmarty Square, your first left is Kristóf tér, where you'll find the pretty **fishergirl statue** amongst shoppers and coffee drinkers. Back onto Váci, make sure to pay special attention to the **Pest Theatre** (Váci utca 9), with an Art Nouveau interior that is worth a moment's look. Still staging popular, classic dramas, it was formerly the Inn of Seven Electors, whose claim to fame is allowing a 12-year-old prodigy by the name of Franz Liszt to take the stage back in 1823. Next door is the **Thonite House** (Váci utca 11), characterized by its Zsolnay tiles and now offering Douglas beauty products and Swarovski jewelry, with traditional Hungarian wine and food at traditional tourist prices being served between the two. A little farther down, at the corner of Váci utca and Regi posta utca, stands a pretty **fountain of Hermes,** messenger of the Greek gods, who points proudly in the direction of the Danube and not (one can assume) at McDonald's. The first, or northern, half of Váci utca ends at busy thoroughfare Szabad sajtó út at the Pest head of the Elizabeth Bridge.

ERZSÉBET HÍD (ELIZABETH BRIDGE)

Originally a decorative chain bridge built between 1897 and 1903, the Elizabeth Bridge was destroyed at the end of World War II by Nazis retreating into Buda. The clean, bright white version of today was finished in 1964, making it Budapest's second-newest bridge which also happens to be situated at the narrowest part of the Danube, spanning a paltry 951 feet. On the Pest side, the bridge passes the Inner City Parish Church while on the Buda side it runs directly

The Inner City Parish Church is the oldest church in Pest.

into Gellért Hill, consequently requiring a complex set of roads to connect to it. Apparently, this design is the result of a wealthy and rather crafty nobleman, who, owning that stretch of riverbank and being a part of the city council at the time, secured himself a fortune by selling off the land for the purposes of construction.

BELVÁROSI PLÉBÁNIATEMPLOM (INNER CITY PARISH CHURCH)

Located next to Elizabeth Bridge, the Inner City Parish Church (V. Március 15 tér 2, Mon.–Sat. 9 a.m.–7 p.m., Sun. 8 a.m.–7:30 p.m.) is the oldest church in Pest, dating all the way back to the 12th century. It is the site of the martyr Saint Gellért's grave, as well as numerous historically poignant events, including Hungarian Royal Princess St. Elizabeth's wedding to the son of the Marquis of Thuringia and the premiere of Liszt's *Missa Choralis* on February 4, 1872, conducted by the composer himself. The church has gone through plenty of transformations over time; it operated as a Gothic hall church in the 15th century, a mosque during the Turkish occupation of the 17th century (a remnant of which includes a prayer niche or *mihrab* found on the right side of the church's main altar), and, after a tremendous fire in 1723, was rebuilt to reflect the Baroque style. As if that weren't enough, it was saved from demolition during the original construction of the Elizabeth Bridge by dint of popular protest and miraculously survived Hitler's bombs in World War II. Something tells me this church will outlive us all, so make sure to pay a visit while *you* still can.

If facing the church, you'll see a small square on the left which is where the foundation of a Roman military fortress, **Contra Aquincum,** is located. An outpost of their settlement at Óbuda at the end of the 3rd century, the first thing you see is a smooth sculpture of faceless Roman soldiers forming a tight circle, shields at the ready. Next to that are the sunken, partial remains of the fort itself—hard rock standing firm against green grass struggling to grow around it, a patch of which now serves as some homeless person's makeshift, though heavily fortified, bed.

To continue on with the southern half of Váci utca, simply backtrack a little (under the Elizabeth Bridge is quickest) and cross the street.

BELVÁROSI SZENT MIHÁLY TEMPLOM (ST. MICHAEL'S CHURCH IN THE CITY)

St. Michael's Church in the City (Váci utca 47/B, tel. 1/337-8116, www.communio.hu/ szentmihaly, Mon.–Sat. 10 A.M.–6 P.M. with Mass at 4 P.M., Sun. 9 A.M.–5 P.M. with Mass at 10 A.M. and 4 P.M.) dates back to 1795, and the church is primarily known for housing one of the city's oldest organs (from 1893). Renovations on its beautiful Baroque style were started in 1999. Walking inside is an eerily quiet affair as most visitors are happy to sit down and get (back) in touch with God, or simply collect their thoughts away from the promenade's tourists and pleasure seekers.

SZERB TEMPLOMBELSŐ (SERBIAN ORTHODOX CHURCH OF ST. GEORGE)

Szerb utca is the appropriate home of the splendid Serbian Orthodox Church of St. George (V. Szerb utca 2-4, tel. 1/337-2970, daily 8 A.M.–6 P.M.), which was built in the Baroque style by the Serbian community in 1698, based on the design of Salzburg architect Andreas Mayerhoffer. It is rather modest sized and far more intimate than you might expect from a church in the center of a capital city. Pews are individual chairs rather than benches and while its interior has seen better days, it is nevertheless charming in its own way. Make sure to note the two icons on the right-hand side above the pews: one of the Apostle Peter and the other of Paul. They are the only two that survived a devastating flood on March 15, 1838, when the water level in the church reached nearly 10 feet high. Outside the church, embedded in the walls on the left, are the headstones of past Serbian residents.

◖ Dunakorzó (Danube Embankment)

In the late 19th and early 20th centuries, the Danube Embankment was the home of elegant hotels such as the Carlton and the Ritz, along with some of the city's finest restaurants and coffee houses. It was a colorful, sophisticated scene, one that included members of the upper classes taking the air to world travelers admiring the view to empty-pocketed Bohemians flirting with ladies of ill repute. The grand promenade was a place where people could come to experience and observe all of society's walks of life—a luxury that was obliterated mercilessly by the savage, relentless destruction of World War II.

While paling in comparison to its former glory, the Dunakorzó nevertheless continues to be one of Budapest's favorite locations for locals and tourists alike, all of whom come to enjoy the romantic atmosphere it has somehow managed to retain. The marvelous, unobstructed view of Buda can be peacefully admired from a chair or park bench at any time of day or night and there are still a healthy number of restaurants and cafes in which to relax and watch the steady flow of human traffic pass by. Also lining the promenade these days are struggling artists, merry musicians, aged vendors selling traditional

Budapest's favorite "place for merriment" – the Vigadó

arts and crafts, as well as a handful of kiosks offering tours down the Danube. It's a pleasant stroll that stretches from the Elizabeth to the Chain Bridge, one that can be savored alone or hand in hand with that special someone.

PETŐFI TÉR
(PETŐFI SQUARE)

Petőfi Square is located at the Elizabeth Bridge end of the Danube Embankment. Its centerpiece is the **statue of Sándor Petőfi,** Hungary's national poet and author of the historically poignant *Talpra Magyar* ("Rise, Hungarian"). It was here on October 23, 1956, that hundreds of students came to protest Matyas Rákosi, the Soviet Union's obedient yes-man.

Opposite Petőfi Square stands the **Greek Orthodox Church** (Petőfi tér 2, tel. 1/266-5988, Services: Sat. 6 P.M., Sun. 10 A.M.). Built between 1791 and 1794 and bankrolled by Greek merchants, it has been a continuous object of dispute between the Patriarchate of Russia, which appropriated it in 1945, and the Orthodox Church of Greece, which maintains

its rightful ownership. Ecclesiastical disagreements aside, visitors are very welcome and a peek inside is recommended, if only to view its beautiful iconostasis.

VIGADÓ

Located at the Danube Embankment's midpoint is Vigadó tér, home to the majestic Vigadó (Vigadó utca 5, www.tabulas.hu), commonly translated as "place for merriment." This is Budapest's second-largest and most beloved concert hall; its 800 seats always sell out any time a concert is announced. Designed originally by Mihály Pollack, it was destroyed in the 1848 War of Independence and was reconstructed in 1865 based on plans drawn up by Frigyes Feszl. One of the most prominent cultural and entertainment venues at the time and throughout the first half of the 20th century, the Vigadó played host to a number of classical music masters, including Brahms, Saint-Saëns, Debussy, and Franz Liszt, who on one occasion in 1875 shared the stage with Richard Wagner. Badly damaged

BUDAPEST

in World War II, it took a full 36 years before opening again in 1980, to the delight of an appreciative crowd who kindly chose to overlook the subpar acoustics. The building also houses its very own gallery, which is considered to be one of the finest contemporary art exhibition centers in the country, though, sadly, both it and the concert hall were closed at the time of writing due to reconstruction.

A few steps from the Vigadó, sitting on a fence opposite the Restaurant Dunacorso, is the **Little Princess Statue,** a tourist favorite, which, judging by the endless stream of smiling and posing going on, has to be the most photographed statue in town.

Ferenciek tere (Franciscan Square)

One of the busier junctions in the Inner City, Ferenciek tere is a mishmash of bustling activity: homeless people asking for change, bus lines from Buda passing through or stopping off, shoppers working their way up and down Váci Street, and tourists unfolding maps trying to figure what to see next. Characterized by the Elizabeth Bridge and looming Klotild Palaces, it is also home to the Franciscan Church and gorgeous Párizsi udvar. No matter which way you're headed, odds are you'll end up passing through here at one point or another.

FERENCIEK TEMPLOM (FRANCISCAN CHURCH)

Dating as far back as the 13th century is the rather inconspicuous yet historically rich Franciscan Church (V. Ferenciek tere, church services Mon.–Sat. 6 A.M., 8 A.M., 10 A.M., 11 A.M., 6:30 P.M., Sun. 6 A.M. then every hour until noon, 5 P.M., 6:30 P.M., 8 P.M.). It was built in 1250 in the Gothic style by Béla IV, a member of the third Franciscan order and widely regarded as Hungary's second founder. Burnt to the ground after the Turkish victory at the Battle of Mohacs in 1526, it was used as a place of Muslim worship until being returned to the Franciscans in 1690 by Emperor Leopold I. Rebuilt in its current Baroque style during the Catholic Reformation, all went well for the

Franciscan brothers until 1950 when the church was outlawed by the Communist regime. Forty years of imposed exile passed before the church and friary were opened once again on September 1, 1990. The church's frescoes are the work of Károly Lotz and Vilmos Tardos Krenner, and its baroque high altar and magnificent statues are worth close inspection. On the Kossuth Lajos Street side of the church, you'll find a touching relief commemorating Miklos Weselenyi's heroic attempts during the tragic Danube flood of 1838, when the river's raging waters claimed the lives of over 400 people.

KLOTILD PALOTA (KLOTILD PALACES)

Framing the Pest end of the Elizabeth Bridge are the Klotild Palaces, named after Grand Duchess Klotild Maria Amalia, who, in 1899, purchased the land and assigned Korb Flóris and Giergl Kálmán the task of building two prestigious palaces there. The architects overcame the challenges the two long and rather narrow plots of land presented them, creating identical neo-Baroque palaces of 157 feet in height, constructed entirely from stone and topped off with two ducal crowns. The palaces became an immediate symbol of the Austro-Hungarian monarchy's cosmopolitan lifestyle. Renovations to the palaces are being done at the time of this writing, with the plan being to open up a multipurpose facility that will include retail outlets on the first three floors, followed by a floor of offices and three floors of swanky residences.

PÁRIZSI UDVAR (PARIS SHOPPING ARCADE)

Another must-see at Ferenciek tere is the Paris Shopping Arcade (V. Ferenciek tere 10-11), located on the north side of the square. Although hardly the bustling shopping center it once was, a walk through it is recommended, if only to see the amazing night and day differences between its two halves. Entering from the square, one feels transported back to 1913, when it was built according to the designs of Henrik Schmahl. Its intricate, ornate features, complete with stained glass cupola, affect the feeling of being in a quiet church rather than a neglected arcade. When you enter the second half, the surprise comes. Following the dull green paint around the corner, you walk into a time warp—one that overwhelms the senses with a lack of architectural imagination (and respect), as well as a full-on functionalism that is a complete come-down from the first (and far better) half. If there's one building in the center that could do with a renovation, it's this one.

EGYETEMI KÖNYVTÁR (UNIVERSITY LIBRARY)

Founded in 1561 by Archbishop of Esztergom Miklós Oláh, the fabulous University Library (V. Ferenciek tere 6, tel. 1/411-6738, www .konyvtar.elte.hu, Mon.–Fri. 10 A.M.–6 P.M.) originally served as the library of the Jesuit College in Nagyszombat (now Trnava, Slovakia). The eclectic design of the palace was drawn up by Antal Szkalnitzky and construction lasted 1873–1876, making it the first library in Hungary to be open to the public. Currently, it boasts a collection of books and periodicals exceeding 1.6 million, the oldest of which is the manuscript of a Beda fragment dating back to the 8th century. While the entire building is something to be admired, it's the main reading room that's truly remarkable, decorated as it is with delicate frescoes by Károly Lotz and a commanding painting of Franz Joseph by Mór Than. Occasionally, the library holds special exhibitions where some of its most prized prints are taken out of storage and made available to the viewing public.

Egyetem tér (University Square)

Dominating Egyetem tér is the **ELTE Law School** (Egyetem tér 1-3) and across the street, on the corner of Király pál utca and Szerb utca, you'll find a **memorial** embedded in the wall in remembrance of the Danube flood of 1838.

EGYETEMI TEMPLOM (THE BUDAPEST UNIVERSITY CHURCH)

The Budapest University (formerly Pau-line) Church (ce—— Papnővelde utca) is est Baroque buildings tween 1715 and 1744, its assumed to be András Maye nobody seems to be able to verify facade bears the coat of arms belong order of St. Paul and between the tw towers you'll find St. Paul the Hermit on left and St. Anthony on the right. This church is distinguished from others by its Baroque organ, considered by many to be the finest in the country, as well as a copy of the black Madonna located above the altar.

PETŐFI IRODALMI MÚZEUM (SÁNDOR PETŐFI LITERATURE MUSEUM)

Named after the country's most important representative of Hungarian letters, the Sándor Petőfi Literature Museum (V. Károlyi Mihály utca 16, tel. 1/317-3611, www.pim.hu, Tues.–Sun. 10 A.M.–6 P.M., 480 Ft) is a fascinating stroll through the country's literary history. Exhibited here are the manuscripts, home movies, and personal effects of various Hungarian writers you've probably never heard of but who nevertheless made vast contributions to the written word. There's also a captivating sculpture of Ady-Altar's death by Miklós Melocco, as well as an ode to ragtime, complete with scratchy, jazzy music streaming through the speakers. The wax figure in blackface, dolls of "negro" musicians, and records on the walls with titles like "Jungle Step" and "My Little Kongo Lady" may seem culturally insensitive by today's standards, but do teach an eye-opening lesson on the history of jazz music in both Hungary and the rest of Europe.

Behind the Sándor Petőfi Literature Museum is **Károlyi Kert** (Henszlmann Imre utca, daily 8 A.M.–dusk), a pretty, well-maintained neighborhood park with swing set and slide, mini soccer field, and fountain with begonias sprouting up around it. A favorite with parents and kids, not to mention the younger set looking to catch up on their reading or gossip, this is a great place to chill out and catch your breath before venturing off elsewhere.

St. Stephen's Basilica

(...)orner of Egyetem tér and (...)arguably one of the fin- (...)in the city. Built be- (...)rchitect is widely (...)hoffer, though (...). The main (...)ng to the (...)o bell (...)he

rös-
iciek
juare
ouple

you'll
Anna
r City
-5536,
30 A.M.,

11:30 A.M., 5:15 P.M.). Built by ... ölbling and János György Paver, its first stone was laid on September 8, 1725—the day of the Blessed Virgin Mary. The facade and bell tower were rebuilt in 1871 and the relief located above the pediment of the portal portrays the founding saints of the Servite Order: St. Peregrin on the left and St. Juliana on the right. Above the pediment stand Servite legislators St. Augustus and St. Phillip of Beniz. The church is still very much functional today, with locals escaping the daily grind of the Belváros and spending a few moments of peace with otherworldly affairs.

Directly in front of the church stands the **Column of the Virgin Mary,** and if when facing the church you take the street on the left named Városház utca (City Hall Street), you'll find two more buildings of note. The first is—you guessed it—**City Hall,** which dominates pretty much the entire street. Designed by Anton Martinelli, this is Budapest's largest Baroque building and was initially used as a hospital in 1711 to care for over 4,000 soldiers that were injured in the Turkish wars. It became the city's main administration building in 1894.

A little farther down you'll find a lime green building, which is **Pest County Hall** (Városház utca 7). Neoclassical in design, this 18th-century building operates as the center of administrations for the entire country. Its three inner courtyards are remarkably beautiful and host the occasional classical concert during the summer.

LIPÓTVÁROS

Lipótváros is located in the northern part of the fifth district, next to the Belváros and bor-dered by Szent István körút, Bajcsy-Zsilinszky út, Deák Ferenc utca, and the Danube. Many of the buildings here were built in the 19th century—an imperial past that is balanced out nicely by modern cafes and restaurants, as well as plenty of financial and administrative buildings. It is a neighborhood that brims with tourists as well, thanks to its being home to some of the capital's most memorable sights, including St. Stephen's Basilica, Gresham Palace, and Parliament.

Szent István Bazilika (St. Stephen's Basilica)

Located in pretty Szent István Square, St. Stephen's Basilica (V. Szent István tér 33, tel. 1/317-2859, www.basilica.hu) is the nation's biggest church and an awe-inspiring sight to behold. Work on the building began in 1851 based on the designs of Jozsef Hild. Unfortunately, Hild died well before the church's completion and Miklós Ybl (architect of the Opera House) was called in to finish the job. Upon close inspection of the structure, Ybl was shocked to find huge cracks in the building's outer walls. The church's vast dome collapsed less than a week later, forcing the entire project to be declared unsound and paving the way for Ybl's neo-Renaissance design. Overcoming tremendous obstacles and great expense, St. Stephen's Basilica was finally opened in 1906.

In the Szent Jobb Chapel lies Catholic Hungary's most revered and rather bizarre relic: the mummified right hand of St. Stephen, Hungary's first monarch. There are plenty of famous and beautiful works of art decorating the interior as well, including mosaics designed by Károly Lotz, Alajos Stróbl's statue of St. Stephen on the main altar, and Gyula Benczúr's depiction of St. Stephen offering the Hungarian crown to the Virgin Mary. Those not afraid of heights should definitely make their way up the tower, which offers visitors an amazing 360-degree view of the capital from a height of 213 feet.

Entrance to the church is free but the treasury costs 300 Ft and the tower 500 Ft. Church hours are: daily 7 A.M.–6 P.M. except during services. The treasury is open daily 9 A.M.–5 P.M. and 10 A.M.–4 P.M. during the winter. Szent Jobb Chapel's hours are Monday–Saturday 9 A.M.–5 P.M. (10 A.M.–4 P.M. in winter) and Sunday 1–5 P.M. The tower is open April–October Monday–Saturday 10 A.M.–6 P.M.

Roosevelt tér (Roosevelt Square)

Positioned at the foot of the Pest side of the Chain Bridge right next to the Dunakorzó, Roosevelt tér is too choked with traffic to be considered a square in any real pedestrian sense. Nevertheless, it's where you'll find some of the city's more upper-class hotels and a couple of noteworthy buildings.

GRESHAM PALOTA (GRESHAM PALACE)

Situated at the very foot of the Lánchid and rightfully considered one of the finest examples of Art Nouveau architecture in Central Europe is Gresham Palace (V. Roosevelt tér 6). Named after Sir Thomas Gresham, it was commissioned by the Gresham Assurance Company of London in 1904 and completed in 1907 based on designs by Zsigmond Quittner, as well as brothers József and Lászlo Vágó. Operating originally as a luxurious palace for British aristocrats, it became the home of Soviet troops during World War II, suffering heavy damage, as it did during the 1956 uprising. The Palace's woes continued as it fell into disrepair and neglect, serving as a private apartment building during the Communist regime. When Hungary once again established itself as a democracy in 1990, ownership of the palace was transferred to the city's fifth district. Purchased years later by the Four Seasons chain, over $85 million was spent in renovations, resulting in sweeping staircases, mosaics, ironwork, and soaring winter gardens all being triumphantly restored, making it one of Budapest's most exclusive luxury hotels.

MAGYAR TUDOMÁNYOS AKADÉMIA (HUNGARIAN ACADEMY OF SCIENCES)

The oldest and undoubtedly most significant building on Roosevelt Square is the Hungarian Academy of Sciences (V. Roosevelt tér 9). The story has it that on November 3, 1825, county delegates criticized magnates for not bothering to make any sacrifices for a Learned Hungarian Society. Not one to be outdone, Count István Széchenyi offered up one year's income from his estate right there and then for just such a purpose. His action was followed by other gentlemen of power and wealth who began moving things along, albeit slowly, in the right direction. The beautiful neo-Renaissance building that eventually came to be was built between 1862 and 1864 based on the designs of Stüler, a prominent architect in Berlin. Lecture and session rooms, along with an invaluable scientific library, lie within; the grand gala hall, which stages the occasional concert, was decorated by the ever-present Károly Lotz. A rather inconspicuous monument to the Count with deep pockets can be found in the small park in the middle of the busy square.

Szabadság tér (Liberty Square)

Strolling through what is arguably one of

Budapest's most picturesque squares, it is hard to believe that the manicured lawns and comfortable park benches were once the site of a large prison or barracks, the sole function of which was to punish "rebellious Hungarians." Punishment came swiftly and mercilessly, particularly in 1848–1849 when scores of Hungarian freedom fighters were executed at this very location. Torn down just before the turn of the 20th century, the gruesome facility was soon replaced with government offices, banks, and residences. Nowadays, kids play pickup games of soccer, dogs frolic, folks read quietly on their own, and couples seal summer love with a kiss, all with the fresh smell of flowers perfuming the light air.

Two breathtaking testaments to capitalism, both built in 1905 and designed by Count Ignác Alpár, stand on opposite ends of the square. To the west, stands the **former Stock Exchange** (Szabadság tér 17), an impressive building influenced by the Secessionist style and full of Greek and Assyrian architectural motifs. It is now home to MTV—not the famed video channel many of us were weaned on but, rather, **Magyar Televizió,** otherwise known as Hungarian Television.

On the opposite side of the square stands the richly decorated **Hungarian National Bank** (Szabadság tér 9, visitors center Mon.–Fri. 9 A.M.–4 P.M.). Take a moment to enjoy sculptor Károly Sennyei's limestone reliefs, a tribute to commerce in the form of rug merchants, Magyar ploughers and herders, as well as Vikings loading their booty onto a longship. Tours through the ornate interiors are possible and worth a peek should you have some extra time on your hands.

Just up the street is the **American Embassy** (Szabadság tér 12), designed by Aladár Kármán and Gyula Ullman and completed in 1900. Originally the home of the Hungarian Hall of Commerce, it has been home to American diplomats since 1935. During World War II, however, it was the Swiss flag that flew out front and the story is that Jewish refugees hid in the building's lower floors. Currently, the building is heavily guarded, as one has unfortunately come to expect from today's political climate.

At the very center of the square you'll find the **Soviet War Memorial,** an obelisk with a Soviet star on top—a thorn in the side of many a proud Hungarian. Although most of Budapest's other Soviet statues and memorials can now be found at Statue Park, this particular one remains standing in remembrance of the sacrifices Soviet troops made during the city's liberation in 1944–1945. This is the result of an agreement Hungary signed in order to continue paying tribute to the Soviet soldiers buried underneath the monument. It has been the object of nationalistic uproars in the past, as a number of Hungarians feel it should be torn down and replaced with, well, a Hungarian memorial. This feeling got so intense during one recent demonstration that nearby cobblestones were uprooted and hurled at police. Now cordoned off by not one but two fences, the memorial's perimeter is also regularly patrolled by a couple of cops to ensure that no more funny business occurs.

Nearby is the interesting **statue of Harry Hill Bandholtz,** a stern-looking general of the U.S. Army who, in 1919, stopped Romanian troops from looting the Hungarian National Museum using the only thing he had at hand—a whip (presumably the one he's holding behind his back). The statue's inscription says it all: "I simply carried out the instructions of my government as I understood them as an officer and gentleman of the United States army."

Around Liberty Square

Leaving the square, head behind the Hungarian National Bank onto Hold Street where you'll find the **former Post Office Savings Bank** (V. Hold utca 4), a magnificent example of Hungarian Art Nouveau. Built in 1901 and designed by famed architect Ödön Lechner, its facade is full of flower and bee motifs, which were meant to symbolize the bank's fervent activity. Both the cornice and majolica roof ornamentation are, quite simply, astounding.

A little farther down, on the opposite side of

the street, is **Bejaras Vásárcsarnok** (V. Hold utca 13, Mon. 6:30 A.M.–5 P.M., Tues.–Fri. 6:30 A.M.–6 P.M., Sat. 6:30 A.M.–2 P.M.), a bustling, wrought-iron market hall full of vendors selling flowers, meat, pastries, clothes, fruit, vegetables, and the like. If visiting on a weekday, try to arrive early, as many of the stalls close up shop at 4 P.M.

Continuing on to the junction where Hold Street meets Bathory Street, an **eternal flame** dedicated to Count Lajos Batthyány stands prominently. It's there to commemorate the man who came to office as prime minister after a republic was declared following the 1848 War of Independence, only to be executed at this very spot by the Habsburgs a year later.

Kossuth Lajos tér (Kossuth Lajos Square)

Kossuth Lajos tér, or simply Kossuth tér, is situated on the bank of the Danube and is easily accessible via the M2 (east–west) line of the subway. Named as such in 1927 after a 19th-century historical figure, the square's previous

name was the more obvious Országház tér (Parliament Square). Before that, between 1853 and 1898, the square was filled with garbage in an effort to raise the level of its low-lying position next to the river and was dubbed the much less romantic Tömő tér (Landfill Square). Its first recorded name dates back to 1820 and comes to us in the form of German: Stadtischer Auswind Platz, which translates into the rather unimaginative-sounding Unloading Square for the Ships.

As you exit Kossuth tér station, cross the #2 Tram tracks and look left to find the melancholy **statue of Attila József.** Looking rather lost and forlorn with his hat in hand and coat discarded carelessly to his left, Attila sports an eternal hundred-yard stare. One of Hungary's most remarkable poets, his work oftentimes focused on poverty, loneliness, and suffering (themes that plagued him throughout his own life) but also expressed his faith in the world's harmony and beauty. He died on December 3, 1937, at the age of 32, when he threw himself under a freight train in Balatonszárszó, an act witnessed by the train's conductor, a sales

BUDAPEST

Patriot Lajos Kossuth points the way to Parliament.

representative, and, perhaps most fittingly, the village lunatic.

Heading straight ahead towards Parliament, the equestrian **statue of Prince Ferenc Rákóczi II** appears on your right. A Transylvanian prince who headed a nearly successful Hungarian uprising against merciless Habsburg rule, he was eventually abandoned by his forces at the Battle of Trenčín (located in present-day Slovakia) on August 3, 1708, when his horse stumbled, throwing him to the ground and knocking him unconscious. Fearing him dead, his forces fled and switched allegiances in the hopes of clemency. It was a slow slide downhill from there when, finally abandoned by his remaining allies in 1711, Rákóczi went into self-imposed exile, drifting to Poland then France, and finally settling in Turkey, where he remained until his death in 1735.

Directly in front of the Rákóczi statue is the **1956 Memorial,** a symbolic grave commemorating the several hundred people who were shot down in cold blood on October 25, 1956, during Hungary's tragic uprising against the Soviet Union. The flag waving just behind it with a large hole in the middle is the result of Hungarian revolutionaries who, a couple of days earlier on October 23, tore out the Soviet star that adorned the center of the flag, thereby cementing it as a symbol of Hungarian independence that remains to this very day.

Standing tall at the northern end of the square, eyes fixed on and pointing directly at Parliament, is the **statue of Lajos Kossuth,** a revolutionary hero of 1848 whom many Hungarians consider the country's purest patriot and greatest orator. After a brief stint as a lawyer, Kossuth moved on to politics, where his liberal-leaning Parliamentary writings landed him in hot water with the Habsburgs, as well as in prison on the grounds of high treason. A national icon by the time of his release, he took over editing duties at *Pesti Hírlap,* a new Liberal party newspaper, and became Hungary's de facto dictator when the Habsburgs invaded in 1848. He escaped to Turkey after the Hungarians surrendered in 1849 but continued fighting for the Hungarian cause, giving highly impassioned speeches in both Britain and America. He died in Turin in 1894 and is buried in Kerepesi Cemetery. His statue continues to be the scene of highly charged national ceremonies and you'll be hard-pressed to find a town in Hungary that doesn't have a street, square, or statue dedicated to him.

Walking past the Kossuth statue and around the right side of Parliament will lead you into a charming little park characterized by Imre Varga's striking **statue of Károly Mihályi.** Hungary's first post–World War I president stands alone, with the help of a cane, under two sloping bars forming a makeshift arch high up above him. Behind the statue lies the Danube, with Castle Hill on the left, Margaret Bridge to the right.

If you're feeling nimble and slightly adventurous, take the stairs on the left leading downward and wait for the right moment to cross the busy two-lane road to the **river embankment.** So close now to the Danube you can smell it, the steps that stretch all the way to Margaret Bridge also lead right down to the water so that you can touch the historic river as well. Heading down the embankment, you get a wonderful view of the back of Parliament and the chance to take a few great photos as well. Be extra careful as you cross the street and back up the stairs at the end of the embankment. You're now basically back to where you started, at the statue of Hungary's beloved but suicidal poet.

Bridging Kossuth tér and Szabadság tér is tiny Vértanuk tér (Martyrs' Square). This is the home of Imre Varga's life-size bronze **statue of Imre Nagy,** the Prime Minister who led the failed uprising in 1956 and was executed two years later. Standing alone on a bridge, hands crossed over one another, he looks pensively towards Parliament, almost as if he knows the end is nigh.

ORSZÁGHÁZ (PARLIAMENT)

Visible from pretty much every riverside point in the city, the Hungarian Parliament (V. Kossuth Lajos tér, ticket reservations tel. 1/441-4904, tours start daily at 10 A.M., noon, 1 P.M., and 2 P.M., 2,300 Ft) is without a doubt one

MIKSA RÓTH

Miksa Róth is easily Hungary's most well-known stained glass and mosaic artist. His colorful work continues to grace numerous sites around the capital, including Gresham Palace, the Music Academy, the Agricultural Museum, St. Stephen's Basilica, and Parliament. Born in 1865, he inherited his father's workshop at the age of 19, back when both he and the craft of glass painting were still in their developmental stages. At 22, Róth was commissioned to decorate the windows of Máriafalva Church (now Mariensdorf, Austria) but his big break came in 1896 when he won a competition that allowed him the privilege of preparing the glass windows for Budapest's House of Parliament. At Budapest's Museum of Fine Arts Christmas Exhibition in 1898, Róth made waves when he unveiled glass windows prepared using a type of Tiffany glass that had never before been seen in the Austro-Hungarian monarchy. As his reputation as an exceptional artists grew, so did the number of awards he received, including the silver medal at the Paris World Exhibition in 1900 and the Grand Prix at the Turin World Exhibition in 1902, as well as at the St. Louis World Exhibition in 1904. Róth continued to represent Hungary's multi-colored turn-of-the-century architecture, creating windows in a number of different styles including Seccessionist, Art Nouveau, and Jugenstil, proving that there was little (if anything) he couldn't do. His work was not limited to Hungary either. He prepared the windows and mosaics for the Royal Palace in Oslo, as well as a magnificent 1,500-square-foot glass cupola for the Teatro Nacional in Mexico City. From the 1920s onward, Róth worked mainly on commissions from the church and state until he decided to close up his workshop once and for all in 1940. He died four years later in 1944.

of the most remarkable achievements in architectural history. Based on Hungarian architect Imre Steindl's design, this monumental structure was supposed to be ready for the 1896 Millennial Celebrations but wasn't completed until 1902. It is Europe's largest parliament building and ranks third in the world, measuring 880 feet long and 404 feet wide at its center. Other statistics are just as staggering, as its central dome measures 315 feet high (the same height as St. Stephen's Basilica) and its interiors boast 691 rooms and over 12.5 miles of corridors. One thousand people worked to bring this building to fruition, using 40 million bricks, 500,000 precious stones, and 88 pounds of gold.

Architecturally speaking, it's an eclectic classic with a Renaissance dome crowning a neo-Gothic facade that stands on a Baroque base. Its white neo-Gothic turrets and arches are complemented by a main cupola decorated with statues of Hungarian kings—just some of the 90 statues and coats of arms that decorate the building's exterior. Tours are offered daily (entrance at Gate X) and are highly recommended. A few of the things you'll see are the Grand Staircase stretching from the main entrance to the Dome Hall, ceiling frescoes by Károly Lotz, fantastic painted glass windows by Miksa Róth, as well as the Holy Crown and the Coronation Insignia, which were worn by Hungarian kings since the Middle Ages. There are not enough superlatives in the world to describe Hungary's Parliament building. It simply must be seen to be believed.

NÉPRAJZI MÚZEUM (MUSEUM OF ETHNOGRAPHY)

With roughly 139,000 Hungarian artifacts, not to mention an additional 53,000 international artifacts, the Museum of Ethnography (V. Kossuth tér 12, tel. 1/473-2400, www.neprajz.hu, Tues.–Sun. 10 A.M.–6 P.M.), located directly opposite Parliament, is one of the largest museums of its kind in Europe. Formerly the Royal Court, this beautiful building combines elements of Renaissance, Baroque, and neoclassical architecture and its huge entrance hall, complete with chandeliers and

BUDAPEST

marble staircases, are reminiscent of a glorious opera house. The fantastic ceiling fresco by Károly Lotz depicts Justitia (the goddess of justice), which reminds visitors of the building's original purpose. The permanent exhibition is no less than fascinating, beginning with the Kováts family's photographic documentation of large, upper-class families, students, and their schooling, as well as various aspects of village life. Following that is the Umling family's tradition of fine-painted furniture from the 18th century, which to this day beats the pants off anything IKEA ever made. The exhibitions continue with wonderful folk costumes, farming tools, musical instruments, and the evolution of village life, churches, towns, and feudal estates. The permanent exhibition is free and an interesting way to spend a couple of hours. Temporary exhibitions come and go but are always affordable (from 1,200 Ft) and well worth any history buff's time.

TERÉZVÁROS

Characterized by Andrássy út, Budapest's grand boulevard, Terézváros is easily one of the busiest, most vibrant parts of the city. You'll find the Opera House here, along with the theater quarter and trendy Liszt Ferenc tér. Shops, museums, cafes, and nightclubs line the streets all the way up to the Oktogon, where the Teréz körút section of the Outer Ring Road cuts through, making it one of the busiest squares in the city and one of the more important intersections for public transportation. Past the Oktogon, the avenue widens, making way for exclusive eateries, neo-Renaissance mansions, and palatial villas, all of which add to the old-world allure of this charming district.

Budapest's finest boulevard, **Andrássy út** is 1.6 miles long, starting from the vicinity of St. Stephen's Basilica and stretching all the way down to Heroes' Square and the Városliget. The traffic, both human and vehicular, is heavy, with cars and motorcycles dueling for position while shoppers and strollers take full advantage of the boutiques, salons, restaurants, and cafes that abound. Continuing past the Oktogon, shops begin to slowly give way to exquisite palaces

and villas, as well as to some of the city's most famous (and expensive) restaurants. Taking in the avenue and its immediate surroundings, it's little wonder that all of it is now a UNESCO-protected World Heritage Site.

Andrássy út from the Basilica to the Oktogon
POSTAMÚZEUM
(POST OFFICE MUSEUM)

Located at the beginning of Andrássy Avenue, the quaint Post Office Museum (VI. Andrássy út 3, Tues.–Sun. 10 A.M.–6 P.M., 200 Ft) is housed in the Saxlehner Mansion, designed by Győző Czigler and built 1884–1886. The lovely frescoes found in the stairwell on the way up to the museum were done by ever-present Károly Lotz, and the stained glass windows are by the one and only Miksa Róth. The museum itself is full of memorabilia from the postal days of yore, including old service desks, wooden telephone booths, and telegram machines. There are also old Communist stamps and swords that postmen carried (as well as guns later on) in order to protect themselves from highway robbers in hot pursuit of the booty they were transporting. The museum is rather small but cute and the pleasant staff is more than happy to explain what you're looking at and answer all your questions.

⬛ MAGYAR ÁLLAMI OPERAHÁZ
(OPERA HOUSE)

The Opera House (VI. Andrássy út 22, www.opera.hu, guided tours daily 3 P.M. and 4 P.M., 2,400 Ft) is one of Budapest's most beautiful structures, adding a historical charm to an already-elegant Andrássy Avenue. This neo-Renaissance masterwork was finished in 1884 and has been attracting classical music fans ever since with the finest of musicians the country has to offer. Couples, families, and friends all don their finest formal attire for an evening out here and it truly is a sight to behold during intermission, when audience members fill the balcony for a breath of fresh air and wondrous views of the boulevard. During the afternoons, a walk around the building often

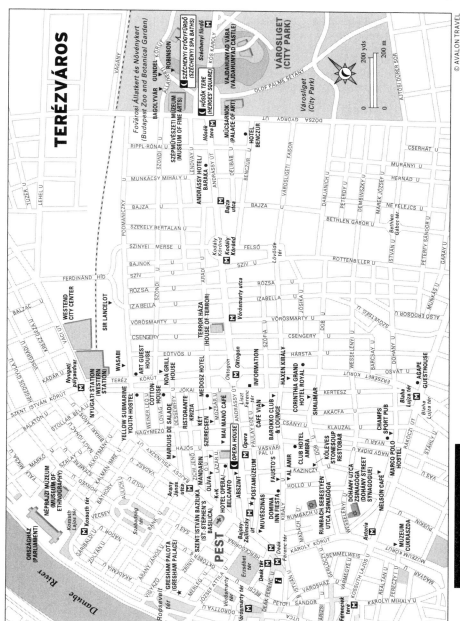

TERÉZVÁROS

© AVALON TRAVEL

rewards visitors with the strains of opera singers warming up for the evening, but if you'd really like an insider's view of this magnificent structure, don't miss out on the informative and entertaining tours offered daily.

NAGYMEZŐ UTCA
(NAGYMEZŐ STREET)

Affectionately referred to as Budapest's Broadway, this picturesque street is full of theaters showcasing original works with provocative titles along with more conventional musicals like *Romeo and Juliet* and *Cabaret*. Plenty of intimate cafes and restaurants can be found here, along with a few casinos and a Moulin Rouge dance club. It even sports its very own miniature walk of fame where the footprints of famous thespians have been immortalized in concrete. This is an excellent place to sit back and drink up the charm before heading back out onto Andrássy.

MAI MANÓ HÁZA
(MAI MANÓ HOUSE OF PHOTOGRAPHY)

If you're a photography fan, postpone that return to Andrássy and venture into the Mai Manó House of Photography (VI. Nagymező utca 20, tel. 1/473-2666, www.maimano.hu, Mon.–Fri. 2–7 P.M., Sat.–Sun. 11 A.M.–7 P.M., 700 Ft). The first floor of the 1894 building served as Mai Manó's residence until the building was bought in 1931 by musical director Sándor Rozsnyai and his wife Mici Rozsnyai, otherwise known as "Miss Arizona." They built a large three-story club in the building's courtyard (aptly named The Arizona), which became an instant success and remained so until 1944, when the couple was senselessly murdered by the Nazis. Following World War II, the building housed a school and presentation hall and operated as a branch of the Hungarian Automobile Club for over 30 years. Today, visitors will find some remarkable exhibitions of contemporary photography within its walls, as well as historical pieces and those chronicling the careers of some of the medium's most important artists.

ERNST MÚZEUM
(ERNST MUSEUM)

The highly respected Ernst Museum (VI. Nagymező utca 8, tel. 1/341-4355, www.ernstmuzeum.hu, Tues.–Sun. 11 A.M.–7 P.M., 700–1,500 Ft) boasts no permanent collection to speak of, instead concentrating its efforts on showcasing a wide variety of constantly evolving modern Hungarian art in interesting new ways. Always one for diversity, the museum also hosts discussions, concerts, and various screenings that continue to grow in popularity.

LISZT FERENC TÉR
(FRANZ LISZT SQUARE)

Home of the diner, drinker, and the super swank, this vibrant square offers opportunities galore to those who want to be seen and heard amongst others of similar style and fashion. Cafes and restaurants line either side of the strip, offering contemporary cuisine and colorful cocktails in an outdoor environment whose ambience has a distinctly trendy yet friendly pulse. This place is always happening, even in the wintertime, when folks simply carry on their fun-loving festivities indoors. At the end of the square is the gorgeous Franz Liszt Academy of Music, a superb Art Nouveau building that doubles as a music university and concert hall.

JÓKAI TÉR
(JÓKAI SQUARE)

If Liszt Ferenc tér is a beloved princess, then Jókai tér is her awkward, unpopular sister. Featuring a tiny playground with abandoned swings and sandbox and peppered with a handful of benches (more often than not occupied by the local homeless populace), this square, located opposite Liszt Ferenc tér, is the ying to its neighbor's zing. Pity poor Mór Jókai, whose literary work was far more romantic than the home his statue was given.

The Oktogon

Continuing along Andrássy, past Liszt Ferenc tér on the way to Heroes' Square, you'll come upon the Oktogon, an eight-sided square/intersection

FRANZ LISZT

Known the world over as a child prodigy and the greatest pianist of his (if not all) time, Franz (Ferenc) Liszt (1811-1886) is easily Hungary's most celebrated composer. Born in Raiding on October 22, 1811, Liszt was the son of a steward who was in the service of the powerful Esterházy family. Pushed hard by his father, who immediately noticed little Franz's genius, Liszt performed publicly for the first time at the age of nine. A scant two years later, Antonio Salieri, an old rival of Mozart, offered the boy free lessons in composition upon hearing a particularly impressive performance at a private home. Liszt studied simultaneously under Carl Czerny, Beethoven's esteemed pupil, and, at the age of 14, wrote his first operetta, *Don Sanche,* which was produced in Paris, where he moved with his family in 1823. Liszt toured extensively and became friends with France's leading artists, including Berlioz and Chopin. In 1833, he began seeing the Comtesse Marie d'Agoult, who eventually left her husband and eloped with Liszt to

Switzerland in 1835. They had three children; the youngest, Cosima, went on to marry another renowned composer and musician, Richard Wagner. Liszt continued touring, solidifying his reputation as virtuoso, performing recitals and composing symphonic poems that both dazzled audiences and changed the direction of music forever. He separated from his mistress in 1844 and went on to live in Vienna, Rome, and finally Budapest where he established the Conservatory of Music and served as its first president. In 1886, Liszt embarked on a final tour that saw him perform in Brussels, Paris, Antwerp, and Windsor Castle for Queen Victoria. Liszt decided to visit a Wagner festival that was being hosted by his daughter Cosima, who was grieving the loss of her dearly departed Richard. Falling gravely ill with pneumonia suddenly, Liszt died under the watchful gaze of his loving daughter on July 31, 1886, leaving behind a legacy that is sure to inspire musicians for centuries to come.

that is as busy at it sounds. Full of shops and fast-food eateries, the buzzing never really stops, especially since the Teréz körút part of the Outer Ring Road runs through here as well. This is also the point where Andrássy widens, allowing for a pleasant walk down the middle of the avenue by way of a pedestrian island.

Andrássy út from the Oktogon to Heroes' Square
TERROR HÁZA
(HOUSE OF TERROR)

During the years 1944–1956, the building on Andrássy út 60 struck fear into the hearts of Hungarians. It was here where first the Hungarian Nazis and then the Communist terror organizations ÁVO and ÁVH tortured and killed hundreds of dissidents. Today, it is home to the House of Terror (VI. Andrássy út 60, tel. 1/374-2600, www.houseofterror.hu, Tues.–Fri. 10 A.M.–6 P.M., Sat.–Sun. 10 A.M.–7:30 P.M., 1,200 Ft), a no-holds-barred memorial dedicated to those who lost their lives on its very

premises. There are quite a few exhibits here, starting with a massive mural of the regimes' victims. Video screens portray the Nazi occupation: Hitler's frenzied speeches, people screaming their support, hundreds of soldiers forming a giant pulsing swastika. Other screens show the Soviet occupation, complete with fires, riots, children left for dead, and adults crying openly over the senselessness of it all. And that's just the first room. A walk through the museum is truly a chilling experience, one that ends in the basement, following an extremely slow elevator ride that features a video explaining in great detail how exactly people were executed. When the elevator finally stops, you find yourself suddenly in the very prison cells that were home to so many unfortunate and innocent people. One cell is so tiny you can barely stand up in it, another is covered in water and yet another is padded. Those thinking of visiting should know that this is not a typical museum; the faint-hearted or extremely sensitive might want to avoid coming here.

BUDAPEST

Those who do visit, however, will be rewarded with a lasting lesson on a treacherous era, as well as one about the dangers of terrorism—no matter what the place or time.

A little farther up the avenue, is the **Kodály körönd,** a circular flowerbed. The grandeur of the square has faded over the years as the massive apartments and mansions that surround it can only be described as majestically decrepit. Nevertheless, it still makes for a nice place to sit and rest for a moment and imagine what must have been.

GYÖRGY RÁTH MÚZEUM
(GYÖRGY RÁTH MUSEUM)
On Városligeti fasor, one block east of Andrássy and running parallel, is the György Ráth Museum (VI. Városligeti fasor 12, tel. 1/342-3916, www.hoppmuzeum.hu, Tues.–Sun. 10 A.M.–6 P.M., free admission), named after the famous art collector and first-ever director of the Museum of Applied Arts. The villa was built in 1870–1871 and was turned into a museum in 1907. In 1955, it began to function as an extension of the Ferenc Hopp Museum and has showcased colorful Eastern Asiatic arts ever since. Among its permanent exhibitions are a large variety of Chinese ceramics and textiles, Japanese ivory, and an Indian collection that covers several major periods, including the Kushana period of Mathura sculpture and the classical style of the Gupta period. There is also a György Ráth Memorial Room, which involves the restoration of the former owner's original dining room.

FERENC HOPP MÚZEUM
(FERENC HOPP MUSEUM)
Those interested in Asian art will do themselves a great service by visiting the fascinating Ferenc Hopp Museum (VI. Andrássy út 103, tel. 1/322-8476, www.hoppmuzeum.hu, Tues.–Sun. 10 A.M.–6 P.M., 400 Ft). Ferenc Hopp visited China during his first trip around the world in 1882–1883, then again during his third and fifth trips, in 1903 and 1913–1914, respectively. The collection available here, in the home he bought specifically to house these treasures, is simply phenomenal. The Chinese collec-

tion alone consists of over 8,000 items, including furniture, paintings, statues, and ceramics, with its earliest piece dating back to the Zhou period (10th–8th centuries B.C.). The Japanese collection is no joke either, boasting over 7,000 pieces, a good number of which can be traced back to the Edo period (1603–1867), as well as the Meiji (1868–1912). The largest part of this particular collection is a stunning group of more than 2,000 works of graphic art.

ERZSÉBETVÁROS
Budapest's seventh district is also the city's Jewish quarter, whose jewel is the remarkable Dohány utca Synagogue. Primarily a blue-collar residential area, the Erzsébetváros oozes character with its crumbling 19th-century buildings, underground bars, and independently run boutiques, mini-markets, and kosher restaurants. It's currently undergoing heavy reconstruction, resulting in a slow but steady increase in brightly colored residences, modern hotels, trendy eateries, and hip cafes. A walk through the district will reveal the neighborhood's strong sense of community, where the streets are filled with warm greetings and a promise of things to come.

The magnificent **Dohány utca Zsinagóga** (Dohány Street Synagogue; VII. Dohány utca 2-8, tel. 1/317-2754) was finished in 1859 and was based on the designs of Ludwig Förster. Built in a neo-Moorish style with additional elements of the Byzantine, Romantic, and Gothic, it is Europe's largest functioning synagogue and the second-largest in the world. It can hold nearly 3,000 people and measures 174 feet long and 87 feet wide, with its two distinct towers reaching over 140 feet in height. In the synagogue's garden is a striking, heart-wrenching Holocaust Memorial, erected in 1989 and designed by Imre Varga. It is in the shape of a weeping willow tree and stands on top of the mass graves of Jews who died during the bitter winter of 1944–1945. Each one of the metallic tree's leaves bears the name of a victim of that terrible time.

Next to the synagogue is the **Nemzeti Zsidó Múzeum** (National Jewish Museum; Dohány utca 2, tel. 1/317-2754), which stands on the site

© TOM DIRLIS

the great Dóhany Street Synagogue, Europe's largest functioning synagogue

of the birthplace of Theodor Herzl, the founder of modern Zionism. Inside is a vast collection of various religious relics and ritual objects of the Sabbath and High Holidays, as well as a Holocaust Room with powerful photographs and anti-Semitic propaganda of the period.

The synagogue and museum share the same hours: November 1–March 1 Monday–Thursday 10 A.M.–2:30 P.M., Friday and Sunday 10 A.M.–1:30 P.M., March 2–October 31 Monday to Thursday 10 A.M.–4:30 P.M., Friday 10 A.M.–2:30 P.M., Sunday 10 A.M.–5:30 P.M. Admission to the synagogue and museum is 1,400 Ft.

Down the road a bit from the Dohány Synagogue on Rumbach Sebestyén Street, you'll come upon the Moorish-looking **Rumbach Sebestyén utca Zsinagóga** (Rumbach Sebestyén Street Synagogue). Easily recognizable by its yellow and red brick facade, the building was restored in recent years but sadly remains closed to the public. A peek through its gates, however, will give you an idea of its beautiful interior. On adjacent Dob Street you'll find the beautiful but rather indescribable **Carl**

Lutz Memorial (Dob #11). It basically features a man lying on his back while another hangs suspended on the wall above him. Lutz was the Swiss vice-consul in Budapest in 1942–1945 and worked relentlessly to save Hungarian Jews from Nazi persecution. His efforts resulted in the saving of roughly 62,000 lives. An inscription from the Talmud pays honor to the man and reads: "Whoever saves a life is considered as if he has saved an entire world."

Continuing along down Dob Street will bring you to the district's largest square and historic center: **Klauzál tér.** It is a friendly neighborhood park complex with a playground for kids, caged surfaces used for impromptu soccer and basketball games, as well as a number of benches where visitors can rest their feet, engross themselves in a book, or enjoy a snack bought from the run-down but atmospheric Vásárcsarnok (District Market Hall, Klauzál tér 11).

THE VÁROSLIGET (CITY PARK)

According to the first available written record circa 1241, the 302-acre-park located behind

BUDAPEST

JOSEPH PULITZER

World-famous journalist and Pulitzer Prize founder Joseph Pulitzer (1847-1911) was born in Budapest during the Austro-Hungarian Empire in April 1847. Pulitzer moved to America in 1864 at the age of 17 and fought in the last year of the Civil War. He was granted U.S. citizenship in 1867 and used his knowledge of the German language to land a job in Saint Louis, Missouri, with a small conservative German language daily named the *Westliche Post*. Working harder than most and showing an exceptional talent for the written word, Pulitzer became part-owner and managing editor of the paper by 1871, but left it in order to pursue far loftier dreams. Working as a correspondent for the *New York Sun*, Pulitzer dabbled in politics, earned a law degree, and made enough money by 1878 to purchase two local St. Louis newspapers, which quickly started to turn a profit under his steady hand. In 1883, already a wealthy man, Pulitzer decided to turn it up a notch

and bought the *New York World*, using it to attack corruption in politics and business and support laborers and their troubled unions. The *New York World* introduced the reading public to investigative reporting, women's fashions, comics, sports, and a whole host of then-innovative light reading. Suffering from debilitating blindness, Pulitzer eventually left the newsroom but continued to run the editorial and business directions of his paper until his death in 1911. In his will, Pulitzer donated $1 million to Columbia University to help build a school of journalism, with the majority of his remaining wealth going towards the funding of the Pulitzer Prize. He wanted to inspire young journalists to seek the truth and report it fearlessly to the public, regardless of established powers and potential consequences. To this day, the Pulitzer Prize remains one of the world's most prestigious awards given to those who have achieved excellence in the field of the written word.

Heroes' Square was originally marshland. The park was formed thanks in large part to tremendous forestation efforts and served as the setting for the all-important Millennial Celebrations that were held in 1896. Nowadays, City Park is a wonderful place to spend the day, be it for a picnic or a stroll around any number of sights, including Vajdahunyad Castle, the Budapest Zoo and Botanical Garden, the Széchenyi Thermal Bath Complex, and, of course, Heroes' Square.

◖ Hősök tere (Heroes' Square)

At the northern end of Andrássy út is the giant, awe-inspiring Heroes' Square, named as such because it is home to the most important figures in Hungarian history. Built in 1896 as part of Hungary's Millennial Celebrations of the Magyar conquest, the striking **Millennial Monument,** dominated by an imposing 118 foot column of the Archangel Gabriel, is the first thing to catch the eye. Gabriel is surrounded by a motley crew on horseback who

represent the seven legendary chieftains responsible for the conquest. A stone tablet rests in front of the column. This is the Monument of National Heroes, also referred to as the **Tomb of the Unknown Soldier,** a solemn tribute to Hungary's nameless heroes of war. Behind the monument is a gorgeous, semi-circular colonnade depicting the most highly regarded men in the country's history, ranging from King Stephen I to Lajos Kossuth. Atop the semi-circles are symbols of War and Peace, Work and Welfare, and Knowledge and Glory. This square has been the site of many historical events, including Socialist holidays during the Communist era, the ceremonial reburial of Imre Nagy (the Hungarian Prime Minister during the Hungarian Revolution who was executed in 1956), a visit by Pope John Paul II, and various heated political demonstrations.

MŰCSARNOK (PALACE OF ART)

On the southern side of Heroes' Square is the

© TOM DIRLIS

majestic Heroes' Square

Palace of Art, also referred to as the Exhibition Hall (XIV. Dózsa György út 37, tel. 1/460-7000, www.mucsarnok.hu, Tues.–Wed. 10 A.M.–6 P.M., Thurs. noon–8 P.M., Fri.–Sun. 10 A.M.–6 P.M., 1,000–2,000 Ft). Designed by Albert Schikedanz and built in 1896 for the Millennial Celebrations, it was renovated in 1995 and now offers the largest exhibition space for contemporary art in the country. It does not have any permanent exhibitions to call its own, but, rather, offers visitors a peek into the development of local and international art with constantly changing programs that receive critical acclaim.

SZÉPMŰVÉSZETI MÚZEUM (MUSEUM OF FINE ARTS)

The grandiose neoclassical building on the northern side of Heroes' Square is the excellent Museum of Fine Arts (XIV. Hősök tere, tel. 1/469-7100, www.szepmuveszeti.hu, Tues.–Wed. 10 A.M.–5:30 P.M., Thurs. 10 A.M.–9:30 P.M., Fri.–Sun. 10 A.M.–5:30 P.M., permanent exhibitions free, special exhibitions 1,000–2,000 Ft), Hungary's premier gallery of non-Hungarian works of art. The gallery began with a donation by Archbishop Pyrker of Eger, but the most significant portion of the collection (now over 100,000 works strong) was purchased by the state in the 1870s from the Esterházy family. Its permanent exhibitions date back to antiquity, including fascinating Egyptian, Greek, and Roman collections totaling over 1,000 artifacts. The upper floors are a treasure trove of art history, including French works from Manet, Pissaro, and Gauguin, a comprehensive collection of 13th–18th-century Italian paintings, and no less than seven masterpieces by El Greco in the Spanish section. Keep an eye out for the museum's special exhibitions, which often bring the world's finest art to Budapest—and for a truly unique experience, visit the museum on a Thursday evening after the crowds have dispersed, leaving you alone with all that genius.

Vajdahunyad vára (Vajdahunyad Castle)

Located behind Heroes' Square is the eclectic Vajdahunyad Castle (XIV. Városliget, daily

BUDAPEST

10 A.M.–5 P.M., free admission to castle complex), which is actually an enclave of buildings rather than a proper castle. It was designed by Ignác Alpár for (what else?) the Millennial Celebrations of 1896 with the intention of displaying the variety of architectural styles found in the Hungarian Kingdom. Indeed, a slow walk around the building will reveal a combination of Gothic, Renaissance, Baroque, and Romanesque elements. Originally constructed out of cardboard as a temporary exhibit for the 1,000-year anniversary, the castle was such a smash that the city decided to turn it into a permanent structure, which is exactly what they did starting in 1904, when reconstruction of the castle began using brick and stone.

Inside the castle you'll find the **Museum of Hungarian Agriculture** (Vajdahunyad Castle, tel. 1/422-0765, www.mmgm.hu, mid-Mar.–mid-Nov. Tues.–Sun. 10 A.M.–5 P.M., mid-Nov.–mid-Mar. Tues.–Fri. 10 A.M.–4 P.M., Sat.–Sun. 10 A.M.–5 P.M., 900 Ft), the largest agricultural museum in Europe and also designed by Ignác Alpár. Visitors are treated to a fascinating lesson on the agrarian evolution in Hungary, complete with tools, pottery, excellent recreations of ancient kitchens and migratory dwellings, as well as informative texts thoughtfully translated into English. Other exhibits include animal skulls and bones, agricultural machines such as the steam engine and tractor, and a light-hearted exhibit on the history of wine-making in Hungary, which includes colorful costumes and jewelry of the period.

In the park, opposite the museum, sits a not-too-friendly-looking hooded figure. Sculpted in 1903 by Miklós Ligeti, this is the famous **Statue of Anonymous,** a monk nobody seems to know much about other than he supposedly lived in the 12th century as the notary to King Béla III. He is also considered to be the author of the *Gesta Hungarorum,* the first-ever book written on the history of the Hungarians. Superstition has it that students who touch his stylus (old-school writing apparatus) will receive help in their studies. It certainly couldn't hurt.

Fővárosi Állatkert és Növénykert (Budapest Zoo and Botanical Garden)

Located just behind the Museum of Fine Arts is the beautiful Budapest Zoo and Botanical Garden (XIV. Állatkerti körút 6-12, tel. 1/273-4900, www.zoobudapest.com, 1,400 Ft). Established in 1886, when the collecting of animals was mostly a luxurious hobby enjoyed by the rich, it is one of the world's oldest and most respected zoos. The zoo showcases over 2,000 animals including elephants, tigers, polar bears, and kangaroos, along with relative newcomer Layla the rhino—the first rhino to be conceived through artificial insemination. You'll find the country's largest tropical garden here, too, boasting roughly 10,000 plant species. Walking past the ornate Art Nouveau entrance is like entering an oasis in the middle of a bustling city. All animal lovers would be wise to make a stop here if time permits. The zoo is open November–February daily 9 A.M.–4 P.M.; March and October Monday–Thursday 9 A.M.–5 P.M., Friday–Sunday 9 A.M.–5:30 P.M.; April and September Monday–Thursday 9 A.M.–5:30 P.M., Friday–Sunday 9 A.M.–6 P.M.; May–August Monday–Thursday 9 A.M.–6:30 P.M., Friday–Sunday 9 A.M.–7 P.M.

◖ Széchenyi gyógyfürdő (Széchenyi Spa Baths)

The large yellow neo-Baroque building opposite the Circus is none other than the Széchenyi Spa Baths (XIV. Állakerti körút 11, tel. 1/363-3210, www.szechenyifurdo.hu, Oct.–Apr. daily 6 A.M.–5 P.M., May–Sept. daily 6 A.M.–10 P.M., 2,000 Ft), one of the largest spa complexes in Europe and certainly one of the most popular in town. Its thermal springs were discovered in 1879 and are the city's deepest, as well as the hottest (165°F). The palatial outdoor swimming pool can be enjoyed year-round, as can the series of steam rooms, saunas, and Turkish baths. Make sure to check out the fantastic whirlpool and if you're a chess fan, bring your own board and join the serious-looking but friendly older men in some competitive fun. If you only have time to visit one bath during your stay, make it this one.

Nagy Cirkusz (Hungarian State Circus)

For thrills, chills, and excitement under the big top, try the Hungarian State Circus (XIV. Állatkerti körút 12/a, tel. 1/343-8300, www.maciva .hu, box office Mon.–Fri. 10 A.M.–6 P.M., Sat. 10 A.M.–7:30 P.M., Sun. 9 A.M.–6 P.M., 1,500 Ft). Putting a smile on the faces of children of all ages since its inception in 1891, this 1850-seat venue is open year-round and continues to draw them in with clowns, trapeze artists, and a wide variety of derring-do. Three different seasons/shows occur every year: January–March, April–August, and October–December.

Vidám Park

Next to the Circus is family favorite Vidám Park (XIV. Állakerti körút 14-16, tel. 1/343-9810, www.vidampark.hu, daily 10 A.M.–8 P.M., admission 300 Ft plus tickets for individual rides). Offering 50 different rides, some of which predate World War II, this delightful fairground has a palpable, old-fashioned charm now lost in the grand, theme-driven amusement parks found elsewhere. Particularly worth your attention is the 100-year-old merry-go-round that comes with authentic Wurlitzer music, the slow-moving (but no less fun) Ferris wheel, and Europe's longest wooden roller coaster. Over one million visitors a year can't be wrong.

Petőfi Csarnok

In the eastern section of the park you'll find Petőfi Csarnok (XIV. Zichy Mihály út 14, tel. 1/363-3730, www.petoficsarnok.hu), a leisure center for the city's youth that has enjoyed immense success since opening in 1985. There is a large hall, as well as an open-air stage that has hosted countless rock, pop, and classical concerts; the center also organizes various community activities run by the local youth. When not rocking the Casbah, or doing its best to keep kids out of trouble, it serves as one of Budapest's most popular flea markets.

Közlekedési Múzeum (Transport Museum)

The Transport Museum (XIV. Városligeti

Széchenyi Spa Baths

körút 11, tel. 1/273-3840, www.km.iif .hu, Tues.–Fri. 10 A.M.–5 P.M., Sat.–Sun. 10 A.M.–6 P.M., 400 Ft) boasts one of the oldest collections in Europe and is full of vintage locomotives, motorcycles, steamboats, and bicycles, not to mention a huge model train set that runs every 15 minutes on the mezzanine level. Well worth a peek if you've bothered to reach this rarely visited section of the park.

JÓZSEFVÁROS

Officially Budapest's eighth district, Józsefváros is seen as having two distinct parts: the grander Kiskörút side (which attracts tourists thanks to its central location near such sights as the National Museum and Ervin Szabó Library) and the darker quarters beyond the Nagykörút (historically associated with prostitutes and various criminal elements). Most visitors stick to the area around Kálvin Square due to its plethora of shops and restaurants, as well as its proximity to Váci Street and the Belváros.

BUDAPEST

© TOM DIRLIS

Múzeum körút
(Museum Boulevard)

Rivaling Andrássy út in terms of shops and majestic buildings, the Múzeum körút separates the Belváros from Józsefváros. As you move along on the way to the National Museum, take a short detour down Bródy Sándor Street until you come upon the historically relevant **Magyar Radio Building** (VIII. Bródy Sándor utca 5-7). On October 23, 1956, this very street was full of angry students and youth demanding access to the airwaves in order to announce their defiant message: "Withdrawal of the Russian troops! An end to Communist dictatorship!" The ÁVO guards on duty weren't about to let that happen so they chose instead to open fire, shooting randomly into the crowd of demonstrators. Things got ugly fast and the masses stormed the building, defending themselves with makeshift weapons they had managed to procure one way or another. The tanks rolled in the following morning and weeks of bloody battle ensued, ending with the revolution's defeat and the start of a 32-year regime of repression.

MAGYAR NEMZETI MÚZEUM
(HUNGARIAN NATIONAL MUSEUM)

Built between 1837 and 1847, the Hungarian National Museum (VIII. Múzeum körút 14-16, tel. 1/338-2122, www.hnm.hu, Tues.–Sun. 10 A.M.–6 P.M., permanent exhibitions free, temporary exhibitions 1,000–2,000 Ft) is easily the largest museum in Hungary. It was on the steps of this inspiring neoclassical structure where beloved poet Sándor Petőfi recited his *National Song*, an inflammatory work meant to provoke revolution against the Habsburgs.

There are a number of permanent exhibitions on display, starting with the Lapidarium in the museum's bottom two floors, which house the Medieval and Early Modern Stone Collection, as well as the Roman Stone Collection, which features tombstones from the 1st and 2nd centuries, sarcophagi, and a gorgeous mosaic pavement from the reception hall of a Roman villa. Another exhibit traces the history of the Carpathian Basin from the Pa-

laeolithic and Mesolithic Eras all the way to the Avar Period in the 8th and 9th centuries. This fascinating section of the museum is full of amazing relics, including stone tools, golden jewelry, weapons, the first minting of coins, and much more.

The final and largest exhibit extends through 20 galleries and is succinctly called "The History of Hungary from the Foundation of the State to 1900." The first group of rooms begins with St. Stephen's reign and it is in this section where you can see a few royal jewels and crowns from the various monarchs who ruled the land. The rise and fall of the Ottoman Empire rounds out the first section and leads into the second, which chronicles Hungarian history through to the Revolution, War of Independence of 1848–1849, and the Millennium anniversary of the country's existence. It is the final leg of the exhibition, however, where things really start heating up, as it's here where you'll find a whole host of period pieces from World War I, World War II, Nazism, and a 40-year legacy of Communism.

The museum is massive and thorough, which means you should be prepared to spend at least two or three hours here in order to get a decent understanding of the region's history. And that's just the permanent exhibitions. There are various temporary exhibitions that come and go regularly, all of which are well worth it.

Kálvin tér
(Kálvin Square)

Under major reconstruction at the time of this writing due to the building of Budapest's fourth subway line, Kálvin Square is typically an incredibly busy intersection with roads heading towards the airport and westwards across the river. Its centerpiece is the neo-Gothic **Inner City Calvinist Church,** whose main entrance is characterized by a four-columned portico that was designed by well-known Hungarian architect József Hild. Miksa Róth, stained-glass artist extraordinaire, is responsible for the church's impressive windows. The treasury has an excellent collection of liturgical objects dating from the 17th and 18th centuries, though, sadly, the church is currently closed due to the aforementioned construction.

Just off Kálvin Square, down busy Baross utca, stands the **Szabo Library** (VIII. Szabó Ervin tér 1, tel. 1/411-5052, www.fszek.hu, Mon.– Fri. 10 A.M.–8 P.M., Sat. 10 A.M.–4 P.M.). Renovated in 1998–2001, this gorgeous neo-Baroque building was once the home of Count Frigyes Wenckheim. Its main entrance is on Revicky utca, which is also the setting for a short stretch of benches and cafes usually busy with students who have had enough education for the day.

Kerepesi temető (Kerepesi Cemetery)
Although it might seem a little odd to describe a cemetery as beautiful, it's apt for Kerepesi (VIII. Fiumei út 16, summer daily 7:30 A.M.–7 P.M., winter daily 7:30 A.M.–5 P.M.). Located just down the street from Keleti Station, it is Budapest's answer to Pere Lachaise, home to everyone who's anyone in Hungarian history. Founded in 1847, its first notable burial was famed poet Mihály Vörösmarty in

Lajos Kossuth's mausoleum in Kerepesi Cemetery

© TOM DIRLIS

1855. Plenty of statesmen, artists, and scientists have followed since then, including Mihály Károlyi, Károly Lotz, Miklós Ybl, Lujza Blaha, and Mór Jókai. There are also three magnificent mausoleums of famous leaders to look for: Lajos Batthyány, Ferenc Deák, and Lajos Kossuth. Along with gorgeous arcades that were built during the years 1908–1911, there is also a striking mausoleum created for the Labor movement during the country's 40-year Socialist period decorated with inspiring images of hard work and all its benefits. Exceptionally well-taken care of and a history lesson in and of itself, the cemetery needs at least two hours of casual strolling to appreciate it fully.

FERENCVÁROS
Development of Budapest's ninth district began in the late 18th century though it was ravaged by floods in 1799 and again in 1838. It is home to FTC—Budapest's most successful soccer team, as well as the Central Market Hall whose massive interior is home to countless stalls offering a wide variety of domestic goods including paprika, sausages, and traditional arts and crafts. Its most fashionable street is the pedestrian-only **Ráday utca,** which is located next to Kálvin tér. Lined on either side with fashionable cafes and restaurants, it is highly popular with people of all ages and walks of life, creating an easy-going, fun-loving atmosphere everybody seems to thrive on. It should be a definite stop during your stay here, whether it's for a delicious meal, cup of coffee, or good old-fashioned stroll through the neighborhood.

Iparművészeti Múzeum (Museum of Applied Arts)
The Museum of Applied Arts (IX. Üllői út 33-37, tel. 1/217-5838, www.imm.hu, Tues.– Sun. 10 A.M.–6 P.M., 700 Ft) was designed by Odön Lechner and completed in 1896, making it the third museum to be built in Europe after its predecessors in London (1857) and Vienna (1864). Its opening had the distinct honor of being the final event of the Millennial Celebrations. This gorgeous Art Nouveau

building, topped off with a dome decorated with colorful Zsolnay ceramics, captures the eye from afar and beckons one and all inside. Its collections are extensive, starting with one dedicated to furniture that consists of roughly 4,000 items from the 14th–20th centuries. Its metalwork collection is vast, totaling over 10,000 pieces, including the astounding Esterházy collection, which gives new meaning to the word "treasures." Art Nouveau jewelry, astronomical clocks, a wide range of textiles, Christian iconography, and one of the world's largest bookplate collections are but a few more of the countless items on display here.

Holokauszt Emlékközpont (Holocaust Memorial Center)

The Holocaust Memorial Center (IX. 39 Páva utca, tel. 1/455-3333, www.hdke.hu, Tues.– Sun. 10 A.M.–6 P.M., 1,000 Ft) is arguably the most architecturally impressive building in the neighborhood, featuring a jagged, asymmetrical exterior and dislocated walls, combining classical elements of form with more modern ones. It's little wonder that architect István Mányi and interior designer István Szenes both won the Ybl prize for their efforts. The center's main motif is "From Deprivation of Rights to Genocide," tracing the persecution and murder of Hungarian Jews and Roma during that most shameful period in history, which began in 1938. Structuring the exhibits to reflect the systematic stages of deprivation, the horror of it all is enhanced by personal accounts that cover the entirety of the exhibition. Opened in 2004, the center continues to grow thanks to private donations of personal relics and memorabilia from survivors of this terrible era.

Magyar Természettudományi Múzeum (Natural History Museum)

Although slightly farther away than where most visitors venture, a trip to the Natural History Museum (IX. Ludovika tér 2-6, tel. 1/210-1085, www.nhmus.hu, Wed.–Mon. 10 A.M.–6 P.M., 1,500 Ft) is nevertheless time well spent, particularly if you have children. Exhibits include over 1,800,000 flora specimens, skeletons of animals throughout the world, a gorgeous underwater room full of aquariums, and dinosaur eggs and huge elephant skulls, not to mention the wide array of human bones ranging from the Neolithic period to the Middle Ages. The excellent permanent exhibition entitled "Man and Nature in Hungary" focuses specifically on how humans have altered the environment over time and what measures can be taken in order to correct some of the bigger mistakes made. If you're looking for a museum that is both educational and interesting, this is it.

VÁRHEGY (CASTLE HILL) AND CENTRAL BUDA

Várhegy is rightfully considered one of the most beautiful districts in all of Europe. Sitting high above its surrounding neighborhoods overlooking the Danube and Pest, its nearly mile-long plateau is Buda's most striking feature.

Dotted with medieval streets, Gothic arches, and Baroque residences, it is where you'll find Buda's majestic palace, the sublime beauty of Matthias Church, and the playful kitsch of Fisherman's Bastion. Filled with tourists in the summer, a shadowy calm falls over the area in the winter, leaving locals in silent contemplation of the palpable history that surrounds them.

Lánchíd (Chain Bridge)

The Chain Bridge is by far Budapest's most famous bridge and a matter of great pride to all Hungarians. Officially opened on November 20, 1849, it was the first bridge to connect Buda and Pest and was responsible for the immediate economic boom that soon followed. As an interesting sidenote, the tunnel located under the hill just opposite the Buda end of the bridge was constructed in a mere seven and a half months just four years later in 1853. It is 32 feet wide, 32 feet tall, and, at 1,146 feet long, exactly the same length as the Chain Bridge, prompting some Hungarians to joke that they can simply push the bridge into the tunnel when it rains so it won't get wet.

Crossing over the Chain Bridge brings

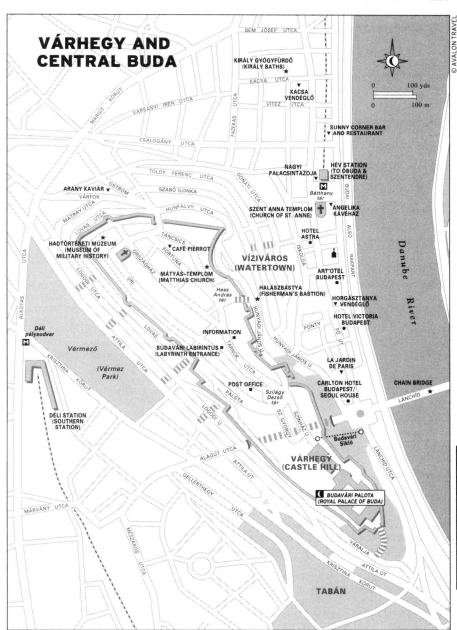

VÁRHEGY AND CENTRAL BUDA

© AVALON TRAVEL

BEM JÓSEF UTCA

KIRÁLY GYÓGYFÜRDŐ (KIRÁLY BATHS) ★

KACSA UTCA

KACSA VENDÉGLŐ ▼

VITEZ UTCA

MARGIT KÖRUT

VARSÁNYI IRÉN UTCA

SUNNY CORNER BAR AND RESTAURANT ▼

CSALOGÁNY UTCA

FAZEKAS UTCA

TOLDY FERENC UTCA

DONÁTI UTCA

NAGYI PALACSINTÁZÓJA ▼

HÉV STATION (TO ÓBUDA & SZENTENDRE)

ARANY KAVIÁR ▼

OSTROM

SZABÓ ILONKA

Bátthany tér

BUDAI

 VÁRFOK

HUNFALVY UTCA

SZENT ANNA TEMPLOM (CHURCH OF ST. ANNE)

ANGELIKA KÁVÉHÁZ

MÁTRAY UTCA

LOVAS UTCA

TÁNCSICS

ISKOLA

ALSÓ

HADTÖRTÉNETI MÚZEUM (MUSEUM OF MILITARY HISTORY) ★

FORTUNA

▼ CAFÉ PIERROT

VÍZIVÁROS (WATERTOWN)

HOTEL ASTRA

RAKPART

ORSZÁGHÁZ

ÚRI

MÁTYÁS-TEMPLOM (MATTHIAS CHURCH) ★

Hess András tér

ART'OTEL BUDAPEST

UTCA

ALKOTAS

LOGODI UTCA

HALÁSZBÁSTYA (FISHERMAN'S BASTION)

HORGÁSZTANYA VENDÉGLŐ ▼

Déli pályaudvar Ⓜ

ATTILA UTCA

LOVAS

HUNYADI JÁNOS U.

HOTEL VICTORIA BUDAPEST

KRISZTINA KÖRUT

Vérmező

(Vérmez Park)

INFORMATION

PONTY

FŐ UT

LOGODI U.

BUDAVÁRI LABIRINTUS (LABYRINTH ENTRANCE) ■

TÁRNOK UTCA

HUNYADI JÁNOS U.

LA JARDIN DE PARIS ▼

POST OFFICE ■

PALOTA

Szilágy Dezső tér

CARLTON HOTEL BUDAPEST/ SEOUL HOUSE

CHAIN BRIDGE ★

DÉLI STATION (SOUTHERN STATION)

SZ GYÖRGY

SZÍNHÁZ U.

LÁNCHÍD

ALAGÚT UTCA

ATTILA UT

Budavári Sikló ○

LÁNCHID UTCA

GELLÉRTHEGY

VÁRHEGY (CASTLE HILL)

MÁRVÁNY UTCA

UTCA

BUDAVÁRI PALOTA (ROYAL PALACE OF BUDA)

MÉSZÁROS UTCA

VARALJA

KRISZTINA KÖRUT

ATTILA UT

TABÁN

Danube River

0   100 yds
0   100 m

BUDAPEST

you to **Clark Ádám tér,** the busy round-about named after the famed Scottish engineer responsible for the Chain Bridge and tunnel. Make sure to look both ways before crossing over to **Budavári Sikló** (daily 7:30 A.M.–10 P.M., closed every second Monday for repairs), the funicular that takes somewhere between 500,000 and one million passengers up the hill every year. Opened in 1870, it was Europe's second funicular and, at the time, the only way to reach the castle grounds. Destroyed in World War II, it was fully restored in 1986 and now uses electricity rather than the steam traction engine that used to power it. The funicular's first carriage offers the least obstructed views; those who are romantically inclined should definitely take a trip up in the evening in order to enjoy the Pest landscape at its floodlit finest.

Coming off the funicular, you can't help but notice a large statue of an eagle. This is the **Turul,** a mythical winged beast that is the symbol of the Hungarian Árpád dynasty kings of Hungary. According to legend, the great bird descended from heaven and impregnated Emeshe, who gave birth to wise leader and brave warrior Álmos. He in turn grew up to marry a prominent family's daughter and through this union a son, Árpád, was born. Marked for greatness, Árpád went on to lead the Magyar conquest of the Carpathian Basin in the 9th century.

Next to the Turul are wrought-iron gates and a set of stairs that lead down to the terrace of the Royal Palace. Here you can enjoy a sweeping view of Pest accentuated by Parliament and St. Stephen's Basilica. A little farther ahead is the **statue of Prince Eugene of Savoy,** considered one of the finer (and there are many) equestrian statues in the city. Prince Eugene was one of the greatest generals to serve the Habsburgs and led successful battles against the Ottoman Turks in the late 17th century. Behind him are the **statues of Csongor and Tünde,** the main characters in Mihály Vörösmarty's time-honored fairy tale *Csongor és Tünde,* which many liken to William Shakespeare's *A Midsummer Night's Dream.*

THE CHAIN BRIDGE

Before the construction of the Chain Bridge, people had been ferried over the Danube in boats. Pontoon bridges were used as well but were highly unreliable as they could be swept away during stormy weather. The story is that during a particularly cold December in 1820, Count István Széchenyi had to wait an entire week to cross as he couldn't find a boatman willing to risk maneuvering between the ice flows. Following this trying experience, he declared the donation of an entire year's income towards the building of a permanent bridge. During a visit to London, he was quite impressed with the work of William Tierney Clark, who had already designed two suspension bridges over the Thames: Hammersmith Bridge and Marlow Bridge. Clark was commissioned immediately and Scottish engineer Adam Clark (no relation) was hired to oversee construction duties. Blown up by retreating Nazis in World War II, the bridge was rebuilt quickly and today remains one of the city's dominant symbols.

© TOM DIRLIS

◖ Budavári palota (Royal Palace of Buda)

Visible from practically any point in the city, the Royal Palace simply dominates the southern skyline of the Castle District. Dating back to the 13th century, its story is a turbulent one full of destruction, resurrection, and, above all, survival.

The palace's first incarnation came after the Mongol Invasion of 1241 and is said to have been built by Béla IV. More of a thick-walled fortress than anything else, it was later developed into a proper palace during the reign of King Lajos the Great. In the 14th century, under Sigismund of Luxembourg, it was expanded once again and reflected the Gothic style of the period. It wasn't until the 15th century, however, that the palace hit its stride when it was remodeled yet again, this time by King Matthias. Considered throughout Europe as one of the continent's most extravagant and important works of Renaissance architecture, it attracted noblemen, scholars, and artists from far and wide, all of whom wished to bask in its majesty.

When the Turks took Buda in 1541, 150 years of rule followed and, while there was some structural damage, it was nothing compared to the complete destruction the palace suffered care of the pan-European Christian army, which liberated Buda in 1686. A new, Baroque building was built by King Charles III of Habsburg during the years of 1714–1723 and was later extended by his daughter, the empress Maria Theresa. A massive fire in 1810, however, not to mention the War of Independence in 1848–1849, caused further damage and reconstruction work began once again. Then came World War II. German occupying forces had been using the building as a command post and, during the final months of the war, the Red Army attacked the palace and gutted it completely. Restored once again, the palace now operates as a cultural center, housing the Hungarian National Gallery and Budapest History Museum, as well as the National Széchenyi Library and Ludwig Museum of Contemporary Art.

MAGYAR NEMZETI GALÉRIA (HUNGARIAN NATIONAL GALLERY)

Opened in 1957, the Hungarian National Gallery (Buda Palace, Buildings B, C, D, tel. 20/439-7325, www.mng.hu, Tues.–Sun. 10 A.M.–6 P.M., permanent exhibitions free, temporary exhibitions 800–1,800 Ft) moved to its present location at Buda Palace in 1975. With roughly 100,000 artifacts on display, it is by far the most comprehensive collection of Hungarian painting and sculpture to be found in the entire country. Beginning with a Medieval and Renaissance stone exhibition that includes a sculpture of King Béla III's head dating back to A.D. 1200, the six permanent exhibitions weave their way through Gothic, Baroque, 19th and 20th century art and include historical masterpieces like Gyula Benczur's *The Recapture of Buda Castle,* Mihály Munkácsy's *The Convict,* and László Hunyadi's *Farewell.* Some remarkable illustrated altars from the Gothic period are not to be missed as well, including triptych *The Altar of the Virgin Mary from the Church of St. Andrew* from 1483. The gallery is enormous and breathtaking in scope and a good four hours or so should be allotted to it should you want to cover the grounds properly. It's one of the more popular sights in the Castle District so getting here early should help you beat the inevitable crowds.

BUDAPESTI TÖRTÉNETI MÚZEUM (BUDAPEST HISTORY MUSEUM)

If you've fallen in love with Budapest and want to learn everything there is to know about its history, as well as that of the Carpathian Basin, make sure to visit the Budapest History Museum (Buda Palace, Building E, tel. 1/224-3700, www.btm.hu, Mar. 1–May 15 Wed.–Mon. 10 A.M.–6 P.M., May 16–Sept. 15 daily 10 A.M.–6 P.M., Sept. 16–Oct. 31 Wed.–Mon. 10 A.M.–6 P.M., Nov. 1–Feb. 28 Wed.–Mon. 10 A.M.–4 P.M., 1,100 Ft). This fascinating collection includes maps and weapons used during the liberation of Buda from the Turks, outstanding statues from the Roman and Medieval eras, as well as "The Medieval

BUDAPEST

Royal Palace and its Gothic Statues" exhibit, which is comprised of rooms and artifacts that were discovered during the excavation and rebuilding of the palace after World War II. A tour through here will give you a fuller understanding and appreciation of what this incredible city has been through over time.

MÁTYÁS KÚT
(KING MATTHIAS FOUNTAIN)
In the Outer Courtyard by the far wall stands the marvelous King Matthias Fountain, whose bronze figures relate the tragic tale of Ilonka, a pretty peasant girl who came upon the King while he was out hunting incognito. When humble Ilonka learned of the hunter's true identity, the impossibility of their ever getting together came crashing down upon her, causing her to die of a broken heart.

SÁNDOR PALOTA
(SÁNDOR PALACE)
Back at the Sikló (funicular) and leading on to the rest of the Castle District is Sándor Palace (I. Szent György tér 1-2) whose full restoration was completed in the spring of 2000 after suffering near total devastation during World War II. Art historians still argue as to whether its architect was Mihály Pollack or Johann Aman but do agree that the building was finished in 1806. The Palace's first residents were the Count Vince Sándor and his wife Countess Anna Szapáry, whose son, Móric Sándor, was a mischievous little fellow known as the Devil's Horseman due to his superb riding skills and habit of entering drawing rooms on horseback. Today, the palace is better known as the official residence of the President of the Republic.

Szentháromság tér
(Szentháromság Square)
Originally a market back in the Middle Ages, Szentháromság tér is not only Castle Hill's highest point, it's also the square all visitors eventually gravitate to as it's here where you'll find two of the area's main attractions: Matthias Church and the Fisherman's Bastion.

Standing smack dab in the center of Szentháromság tér is the **Holy Trinity Column**. Built by Buda's Council and unveiled in 1706, it was meant to serve as a memorial to those who lost their lives during the punishing plague of 1691. When another epidemic broke out in 1709, a bigger, more ornate memorial was built. The column depicts biblical King David praying for an end to the plague while various saints and cherubs are located under the golden Holy Trinity. At the time of this writing, however, the column was being restored. Here's hoping it returns to its rightful place soon.

MÁTYÁS-TEMPLOM
(MATTHIAS CHURCH)
Easily the best-known and most remarkable Catholic Church in Budapest, Matthias Church (I. Szentháromság tér 2, www.matyas-templom.hu, daily 9 A.M.–5 P.M.), officially named the Church of our Lady, was built in the 13th century and has survived countless changes ever since. The church takes its unofficial name from beloved King Matthias, who donated its two towers (his crest is on the south one) and held his two weddings on its premises: the first to Catherine of Podebrad, and, following her death, to Beatrice of Argon.

The church suffered terribly during the 150-year Turkish occupation as most of its invaluable treasures were sent off to Bratislava, and, following the capture of Buda, its role was changed into serving as the city's main mosque. As if that weren't enough, all the magnificent, ornate frescoes that graced the church's interiors were whitewashed and its furnishings were completely stripped. When the Turks were overthrown in 1686, a slew of attempts to reconstruct the building according to the fashionable Baroque style of the time failed miserably. It wasn't until the end of the 19th century when, thanks to the tremendous work of Frigyes Schulek, the church began to regain its former splendor. A number of early Gothic elements were uncovered during the process and Schulek added some of his own spectacular touches, including the diamond-patterned roof tiles and various gargoyles.

The church's interior simply overwhelms the

senses. Colorful geometric patterns cover the walls and ceiling, dazzling frescoes and stained glass windows by Károly Lotz, Mihály Zichy, and Bertalan Székely blend with gilded altars, stone pulpits, coats of arms, and a whole host of ecclesiastical treasures. There are also a large number of sacred relics like chalices and vestments on display at the Ecclesiastical Museum, as are replicas of the Hungarian royal crown and other coronation jewels.

HALÁSZBÁSTYA
(FISHERMEN'S BASTION)

Built in 1905 based on the designs of Frigyes Schulek, the Fishermen's Bastion is a pretty piece of fairy-tale kitsch that comes complete with turrets, parapets, and flowing staircases. Incorporating the styles of both neo-Gothic and neo-Romanesque architecture, its seven round towers are meant to represent the seven Magyar tribes that came to Hungary in 896. The view of Pest is simply breathtaking from here, allowing you to see as far away as Margaret Island and view buildings such as Parliament, St. Stephen's Basilica, the Vigadó, and the Inner City Parish Church. As for its name, a local fish market used to be located behind the church during medieval times and it was the Fishermen's Guild that defended this part of the Castle grounds in the 18th century. The impressive **bronze equestrian statue** standing in front of the Bastion is of St. Stephen. It was unveiled when work on the Bastion was completed.

MAGYAR BOROK HÁZA
(HOUSE OF HUNGARIAN WINES)

Opened to the public on September 2, 1997, the House of Hungarian Wines (I. Szentháromság tér 6, tel. 1/212-1032, www.winehouse.hu, daily noon–8 P.M., wine tasting 4,000 Ft) is an experience wine culture enthusiasts will not want to miss. Guests are given a glass, snacks, and a map of the vast, tasteful cellar, which holds 700 different wines from 22 of Hungary's wine-growing regions. Visitors have the opportunity to taste over 50 wines, either alone or with the help of a friendly guide who can

The **Baroque Erdody Palace** (I. Táncsics Mihály utca 7, tel. 1/214-6770, www.zti.hu) is home to the Musicology Institute of the Hungarian Academy of Sciences, along with the Museum of Music History. Beethoven stayed here in 1800 when the building was a private residence but today visitors can learn about the evolution of musical instruments in Hungarian culture and view such unique and interesting examples like the *tárogató, csákány,* and Schunda pedal-cimbalom. Another permanent exhibition, "In Bartók's workshop," is comprised of the great composer's archives and outlines his compositional methods.

A little farther down, at #26, is the **Medieval Synagogue** (I. Táncsics Mihály utca 26, tel. 1/487-8801, May–Oct. Tues.–Sun. 10 A.M.–5 P.M.), now a small Jewish museum complete with frescoes, inscriptions in their original Hebrew, as well as various artifacts that include maps and prints.

Bécsi Kapu tér
(Bécsi Kapu Square)

At the end of Táncsics Mihály Street is small and unassuming Bécsi Kapu Square. The square's main building is the **National Archives of Hungary** (I. Bécsi Kapu tér 24, closed to the public), a large, neo-Romanesque structure with an eye-catching, multi-colored roof. Around the corner is the **Vienna Gate,** which is actually a replica of the 16th-century original but nevertheless serves as one

s. Heading
ntly lead you to
the opposite cor-
e rather basic-looking,
utheran Church (I. Tánc-
ca 28, tel. 1/356-9736, www
heran.hu/budavar, 9 A.M.–1 P.M.),
ontinues to function by holding the
asional concert in the summer.

Kapisztrán tér
(Kapisztrán Square) and Vicinity

Just west of Bécsi Kapu Square is Kapisztrán tér, named after Friar John Capistranus, whose statue is easily recognizable; he's the one standing on the back of some poor dead Turk.

Opposite the statue stands the neglected and lonely-looking **Mary Magdalene Tower.** The Tower is the only part of this 13th-century Franciscan church that survived World War II and its stone courtyard, crumbling walls, and busted window now produce a slightly melancholic effect. During the Turkish occupation, this was the only church on the Castle's grounds that Christians were allowed to worship in. Catholics were given the choir while Protestants used the nave.

HADTÖRTÉNETI MÚZEUM
(MUSEUM OF MILITARY HISTORY)

The Museum of Military History (I. Tóth Árpád sétány 40, tel. 1/325-1651, Oct.–Mar. Tues.–Sun. 10 A.M.–4 P.M., Apr.–Sept. Tues.–Sun. 10 A.M.–6 P.M., 250 Ft) houses a rather vast collection of weapons dating from before the Turkish wars all the way to the 20th century, as well as uniforms, flags, various military documents, and roughly 28,000 coins. Permanent displays include a commemorative exhibition dedicated to the 150th anniversary of the Hungarian Revolution and War of Independence, and one commemorating the 90 years following the end of World War I.

The entrance to the museum is found around the corner on Tóth Árpád sétány—a pretty **promenade** with a wonderful view of the Buda Hills. Following it past the museum will bring you to a large patriotic flagpole painted in red,

white, and green; still farther along, on your left-hand side, you'll come across the **symbolic grave of Abdurrahmán,** Buda's last Turkish pasha, who died in 1686. The promenade eventually leads back to Bécsi Kapu tér; taking it the other way will bring you to Dísz tér and the Royal Palace.

BUDAVÁRI LABIRINTUS
(LABYRINTH)

Fifty-two feet below Castle Hill is the Labyrinth (I. Úri utca 9, tel. 1/212-0207, www.labyrintus.com, daily 9:30 A.M.–7:30 P.M., 1,500 Ft), a six-mile stretch of caves originally used by the Ottomans. It served as an air-raid shelter during World War II and nearly one mile of the intricate network is now open to the public. There's a waxworks exhibit featuring symbolic figures of Hungarian history, a "Labyrinth of Bravery" wherein you make your way through a section of the caves in total darkness, and a "Nightime Labyrinth" (6–7:30 P.M.) that affords you an oil lamp. A cafe can be found down there as well; it holds jazz and blues concerts throughout the summer. Although very much on the kitschy side of things, the caves are, if nothing else, an excellent way to cool off from the heat aboveground.

THE VÍZIVÁROS (WATERTOWN)
AND SURROUNDINGS

The narrow strip that runs along the Danube from the Castle District to Margaret Bridge is known as the Víziváros. During the Middle Ages, the area was full of fishermen who plied their trade by the river, as well as colorful artisans from all walks of life. Residences here are built into the hillside, and many are reached via narrow alleys and stairs, giving the area an aura of centuries past. The neighborhood's main street is **Fő utca,** which runs the length of the Víziváros in a north–south fashion, one mere block away from the Danube.

The first building worth noticing along Fő utca is the postmodern **French Institute** (I. Fő utca 17, tel. 1/489-4200, www.inst-france.hu, Mon.–Fri. 8 A.M.–9 P.M., Sat. 8:30 A.M.–1:30 P.M.), which was designed by George Marois and has been operating since 1992. The institute stays busy, organizing a large number of classical and jazz concerts, exhibitions, and lectures to a cultured crowd that can't seem to get enough. Aside from a French-language library (Tues.–Fri. 1–7 P.M., Sat. 10 A.M.–1 P.M.), it also houses a bookshop, theater, and rather stylish cafe (Mon.–Fri. 8:30 A.M.–9 P.M., Sat. 9 A.M.–2 P.M.). Farther on down at Corvin tér is the **Budai Vigadó** (I. Corvin tér 8, tel. 1/317-2754, box office daily 10 A.M.–6 P.M.), Buda's answer to a concert hall and home to the critically acclaimed Hungarian State Folk Ensemble.

Szilágyi Dezsó tér (Szilágyi Dezsó Square)

This small but pretty square has a **neo-Gothic Reformed church** at its center. Its interior is rather simple but the church possesses excellent acoustics, making it one of the finer places in town to enjoy classical or choral music concerts.

One block over, at the **Bem Rakpart,** or Danube bank, is where one of Hungary's darkest moments in history occurred. During the brutal winter of 1944–1945, the fascist Arrow Cross (Hungarian Nazis) rounded up thousands of Jews, bound them in small groups then tossed them alive into the freezing river.

Batthyány tér (Batthyány Square)

The main square of the Víziváros, Batthyány tér tends to be busy with shoppers at the **Vásárcsarnok,** a former market hall turned grocery store, or with commuters making full use of the subway/HÉV interchange.

SZENT ANNA TEMPLOM (CHURCH OF ST. ANNE)

On the south side of the square is the Church of St. Anne (I. Batthyány tér 8, only open for services Mon.–Sat. 6:45 A.M.–9 A.M., 4–7 P.M., Sun. 7 A.M.–1 P.M.), one of Budapest's loveliest Baroque buildings. Designed by Kristóf Hamon, construction of the church began in 1740 and was completed by Mátyás Nepauer in 1761. For the next 200 years, the church

withstood the ravages of time, including wars, floods, earthquakes, and a plan to have it demolished due to the construction of the city's subway system. Thankfully, cooler heads prevailed and the church underwent reconstruction between 1970 and 1984. Inside, high altar statues of the Virgin Mary and St. Anne leave an impression, as does the striking ceiling fresco by Pál Molnar. Another interesting thing to note is the church's organ, which was consecrated in 1985 and is known today as being one of the best of its kind in the country.

KIRÁLY GYÓGYFÜRDŐ (KIRÁLY BATHS)

Dating back to the days of the Ottoman Empire, the Király Baths (I. Fő utca 82-84, tel. 1/201-4392, women Mon., Wed., Fri. 7 A.M.–6 P.M., men Tues., Thurs., Sat. 9 A.M.–8 P.M., 1,100 Ft for 90 min.) are truly a step back in time. The steam is so thick you can touch it and visibility is at a minimum since the only light that manages to stream in comes from the star-shaped openings in the cupola that crisscross with a handful of lamps. The maximum time allowed in the bath is an hour and a half on weekdays and two hours on Saturday. Please note that there are no coed days and that the male-only days tend to be popular with the gay community. An open mind and attitude is highly recommended.

Margit híd (Margaret Bridge)

Built in 1872–1876 by a Paris-based firm, the bridge is slightly out of the ordinary due to its V shape; the span twists halfway through to continue along the Nagykörút on one end, while a connecting branch joins the bridge to the southern tip of Margaret Island at the other.

Rózsadomb

Literally meaning "Rose Hill," Rózsadomb was once the neighborhood of choice of the country's past Turkish occupiers but today has the honor of being Budapest's wealthiest and most respectable neighborhood. Many of the city's famous and elite live in the area and it is here

TRAM #2

One of the nicest ways to see most of Budapest's major sights is to hop on the fabled #2 tram and enjoy the ride, all for the price of a regular ticket! The route itself last roughly 20 minutes and should be caught at either of its two ends to be enjoyed to the fullest. Make sure you get on the right tram, however, as there's a #2A out there that doesn't cover the entire route. Highlights include:

Jászai Mari tér
Starting at the Pest end of the Margaret Bridge, you'll see a large conspicuous building between the stop and the river, commonly referred to as "The White House." Formerly serving the Communist Party back in the day, it now houses parliamentary offices.

Szalay utca
To the right is the magnificent Parliament building, and to the left the beautiful Museum of Ethnography, formerly the Palace of Justice.

Kossuth Lajos tér
Named after one of the leaders of both the Uprising and War of Independence of 1948-1949, the square is the common destination for visitors to the Parliament building. Here you'll also find a statue of famed freedom fighter Ferenc Rákóczi II.

Roosevelt tér
The Hungarian Academy of Sciences graces the view on the left while the gorgeous Chain Bridge leading to Buda sits to the right.

Eötvös tér
A handful of modern and luxurious hotels line the river bank on the left as does the historic and still beautiful Dunakorzó, Budapest's romantic promenade, perfect for casual strolls and taking in the breathtaking panoramic view of Buda's skyline.

Vigadó tér
Home to the Vigadó, Budapest's glorious concert hall, the way continues with outdoor restaurants and cafes, as well as the Elizabeth

the historic #2 tram

Bridge, one of the capital's beloved examples of post-World War II architecture.

Március 15. tér
Gellért Hill dominates the skyline here, complete with the statue of Gellért himself and the battle-torn Citadella up top.

Fővám tér
The main sight here is, of course, Central Market Hall, where you'll find a plethora of souvenirs, fruits, and vegetables, as well as clothing, traditional food, and much, much more. There's a reason why hundreds of locals and visitors stop here daily.

Közvágóhíd – Millenniumi Kulturális Központ (Millennium Cultural Centre)
The Közvágóhíd is on the left, while on the right is the National Theatre and Palace of Arts, which is comprised of a concert hall and theatre, as well as the Ludwig Museum of Contemporary Art.

that real estate rates are amongst the highest in the capital. Enjoying easy access to parks, forests, and the hills of Buda, this is a wonderful part of the city to stroll through while admiring both the architectural and natural beauty that surrounds it.

Coming off Margaret Bridge on the Buda side, you'll soon find a street named Mecset (Mosque). A short but rather steep hike up it will lead to a flight of stairs and the **Tomb of Gül Baba** (I. Mecset utca 14, daily 10 A.M.–6 P.M.). It's the final resting place of the Turkish dervish who spread the teachings of Allah with his mighty sword; he died during the first Musulman religious ceremony shortly after the Turks took Buda in 1541. The site itself is a small octagonal building that is surrounded by a splendid colonnaded parapet with a Mediterranean garden that has roses, tropical fruit trees, Turkish fountains, and excellent views of the city.

◀ GELLÉRT HEGY (GELLÉRT HILL)

Rising 450 feet above the Danube, Gellért hegy is as vital to Budapest's landscape as either Parliament or Buda Palace. It is easily identified by the **Gellért Statue,** built right into the hill; the statue is surrounded by a colonnade and overlooks a pretty waterfall. Both the hill and statue are named after the Benedictine abbot Gellért who was an all-important figure during the Magyars' conversion to Christianity under King St. Stephen's reign. Legend has it that shortly following the king's death, Gellért was seized during a pagan rebellion in 1046 and thrown down the hill in a barrel full of nails by those not willing to conform to the Christian faith. A gruesome story to be sure, but not one that should deter you from climbing up and appreciating both the statue and the wonderful view of central Pest down below.

To reach the statue and top of the hill, cross the street upon leaving the Liberty Bridge and follow one of the many footpaths that lead upwards (all paths reach the same point). Even on the hottest of days, the walk up is a pleasant experience as the large number of trees offers plenty of very welcome shade. If you don't feel like making the hike, however, the #27 bus from Móricz Zsigmond körtér will get you there.

The **Liberty Bridge,** or Szabadság híd, connects Fővám tér (home of the Great Market Hall) with Gellért tér at the foot of Gellért Hill. Designed by Hungarian János Feketeházy, the bridge was built between 1894 and 1896 and opened officially in the presence of Emperor Franz Joseph, who hammered home the last silver rivet on the Pest abutment himself. It is 1095 feet long and 66 feet wide and its top four masts are decorated with bronze statues of the Turul, the same mythical winged beast that can be found on Castle Hill. There is currently talk of turning the traffic-plagued bridge into a pedestrian-only crossing upon completion of Budapest's long-awaited fourth subway line.

The Citadella

The top of Gellért Hill is dominated by the Citadella (XI. Citadella sétány, tel. 1/466-5794, www.citadella.hu, 1,200 Ft), built by the Habsburgs between 1850 and 1854 in order to better control the city after their successful suppression of the Hungarian War of Independence. Today, the former barracks operate as budget accommodations and the structure in its entirety serves the busloads of tourists that regularly visit. Numerous stalls sell the usual trinkets, tour books, and t-shirts, and there's a restaurant and a couple of makeshift cafes that make for nice spots to rest and fuel up. The view, of course, is stunning and includes just about every sight you can imagine: Castle Hill, Matthias Church, the Chain Bridge, Margaret Island, Parliament, the Dunakorzó, St. Stephen's Basilica, and the rest of Pest stretching out before you. Make sure you bring your camera or you'll be very sorry.

Felszabadulási emlékmű (Liberation Monument)

Next to the Citadella stands the Liberation Monument, depicting a curiously blank-faced woman holding a leaf up above her head. Erected in 1947, it was built in order to commemorate

© TOM DIRLIS

the Liberation Monument, high atop Gellért Hill

the Soviet soldiers that fought bravely and freed the city from Nazi occupation. Another popular belief, however, is that the statue was originally commissioned by Admiral Horthy, Hungary's wartime leader, who lost his son in a plane crash during World War II. The former version of the story is most likely closest to the truth, which is ironic considering that the statue of the Red Army soldier that used to guard the monument was unceremoniously removed shortly after the collapse of Communism.

Hotel Gellért es Fürdő (Gellért Hotel and Baths)

The Gellért Hotel and Baths (XI. Kelenhegyi út 4, tel. 1/466-6166, summer daily 6 A.M.–7 P.M., winter Mon.–Fri. 6 A.M.–7 P.M., Sat.–Sun. 6 A.M.–5 P.M., 3,000 Ft) is one of Budapest's finest thermal bathing complexes. A huge hit with locals and tourists alike, its decadent Art Nouveau surroundings boast original fittings, mosaics, marble columns, and stained glass windows from 1918, making an afternoon here a most memorable experi-

ence. Luckily, one doesn't have to be a guest at the hotel to take advantage of the lavish indoor swimming pool with gorgeous majolica tiles and stone lion heads spouting water, or the separate thermal baths, steam rooms, and saunas. A modest admission fee includes use of the marvelous outdoor swimming pool during the summer months as well.

In front of the hotel is the **Gellért Fountain,** which stands under a stone dome supported by pillars. A stream of water winds though a complex path that runs in four channels along the ground, representing north, east, south, and west. This is a perfect opportunity to fill up your water bottle, either before or after your trip up the hill, though you'll most likely have to wait your turn alongside manual laborers, businesspeople, tourists, and the elderly.

Szikla templom (Cave Chapel)

Located on Gellért Hill opposite the Gellért Hotel and Baths complex is the interesting Cave Chapel (XI. Gellért Hill, daily 9 A.M.–9 P.M.). Founded by Pauline monks in the 1920s, it was closed down by the Communist police in 1951 and remained sealed until the fall of the regime in 1989. Inside the rather smallish chapel you'll find an intriguing mixture of church elements and natural rock formations that create an extremely calming effect. Services continue to this day, the only time tourists are not allowed in.

ÓBUDA

Having the honorable distinction of being Budapest's oldest district, Óbuda has gone through many significant changes. The Roman Empire founded Aquincum here, a settlement dating back to the 1st and 2nd centuries, the remnants of which can still be seen today. In the Middle Ages, Old Buda was called Buda Castle, as it was here that the royal chancellery made its home. The Turks dominated the area in the 16th century, and the Zichy counts ruled throughout the 17th century, leading to a massive influx of Germans who came to outnumber the Hungarians. In the last hundred years or so, Óbuda has grown from a rural settlement to an industrial area that has increased its population exponentially and brought about a consequent rise in stylish offices and villas erected on its hillside.

Óbuda is a wondrous district whose illustrious past crosses over with a promising and vibrant future. It is also extremely conducive to outdoor activities, given the number of boathouses along the Danube, the bike paths along the riverside, and the numerous hiking paths in the hills. Time spent here will quickly lead you to understand why the area's most famous writer, Gyula Krúdy, referred to his beloved neighborhood as "the grandfather of all cities."

Fő tér
(Main Square)

Linking old Buda and new is Fő tér. The two major roads of ancient Aquincum once crossed each other here and the square still remains an important hub of traffic for passengers using the area's trams, buses, and HÉV. The pretty 18th-century houses that surround the square make a picturesque backdrop for the regular concerts, theater performances, and fairs held here and a walk down its quiet streets will reward you with excellent museums, quaint cafes, and even the occasional Roman ruin.

VASARELY MÚZEUM
(VASARELY MUSEUM)

Located by the hub of buses just outside the Árpád híd stop of the HÉV, the Vasarely Múzeum (III. Szentlélek tér 6, tel. 1/388-7551, www.vasarely.tvn.hu, Tues.–Sun. 10 A.M.–5 P.M., permanent exhibitions free, temporary exhibitions 500–1,800 Ft) is dedicated to Hungarian painter Victor Vasarely, who became renowned throughout the world thanks to his eye-opening op art, which deals primarily with three-dimensional images. The geometrical nature of this extensive collection may indeed induce headaches in those not too interested in modern art but will certainly open the eyes and mind of those who are. Along with various ink, tempera, and collage-oriented works, visitors will also be treated to the artist's vision of utopia and his belief that the world can reach harmony through art. A head trip, to be sure.

ZICHY KÁSTÉLY
(ZICHY CASTLE)

Zichy Castle (Fő tér 1) can be easily missed if you don't have a look into the courtyard on your right as you enter the main square. Completed in 1757, this beautiful baroque building may be crumbling in places but still retains an incontestable elegance. It housed the Zichy counts who ruled Óbuda from 1659 to 1768. Today, it's home to a couple of interesting museums. The **Óbuda Museum** (III. Fő tér 1, tel. 1/388-2534, Tues.–Fri. 2–6 P.M., Sat.–Sun. 10 A.M.–6 P.M., 200 Ft) displays roughly 1,000 historical objects, ranging from pottery, textiles, and carvings to reconstructed living rooms, enlightening visitors on just how differently people lived not that long ago. The **Kassák Museum** (III. Fő tér 1, Wed.–Sun. 10 A.M.–6 P.M., 200 Ft) is dedicated to respected Hungarian artist Lajos Kassák (1887–1967). Permanent exhibits feature a significant collection of his work, including paintings, sculpture, literature, and typography. Firmly devoted to socialism during his youth, his later works conflicted with post-war communism—so much so that public displays of his work were strictly forbidden.

IMRE VARGA MÚZEUM
(IMRE VARGA MUSEUM)

At the end of Laktanya utca rests a slightly shabby-looking yellow building that houses the Imre Varga Museum (III. Laktanya utca 7, tel. 1/250-0274, Tues.–Sun. 10 A.M.–6 P.M., 500 Ft). Quite a few of the famous sculptor's poignant works can be found here, including humorous depictions of military men, as well as sculptures of Hungarian heroes Imre Nagy and Béla Bartók. The courtyard, too, possesses some touching statues accentuated by serene surroundings.

Just off Fő tér and about 100 feet from the museum is Imre Varga's striking set of sculptures entitled *Women with Umbrellas,* which captures both the eye and imagination.

◖ Aquincum

Although nowhere near any other major sights, a 25-minute trip north on the HÉV to Aquincum is well worth the time and effort. A key military post of the Roman province of Pannonia Inferior, Aquincum eventually grew to become its capital, reaching a population of 30,000–40,000 inhabitants and covering a major part of today's Óbuda by the end of the 2nd century. Upon alighting at Aquincum station, you can see a **2nd-century amphitheater** right next door. A little farther down on the other side of the street, however, is where all the action is. The ruins that remain are enough to evoke what life must have been like all the way back then and if you think they were any less civilized, you're wrong. Helpful texts thoughtfully translated into English reveal the layout of the entire complex, which included residential buildings, public baths, shrines, altars for sacrifices, artisans' buildings, and even dwellings that boasted floor heating. A look through a type of viewfinder called a Kronoscope magically recreates what some of the buildings (public bath, market, certain houses) must have looked like in their entirety, illustrating just how developed the Romans were.

If you keep your entrance ticket, you can also visit a tiny but interesting **museum** on the premises that displays various items from the period, including jugs, glass bead necklaces, weaponry, and the slightly chilling mummy of a young woman found in a sarcophagus.

Admission is 700 Ft. The premises are open daily April 15–October 31. Hours for the park are April 15–May 1 9 A.M.–5 P.M., May 2–October 1 9 A.M.–6 P.M., and October 2–31 9 A.M.–5 P.M. The museum is open April 15–May 1 10 A.M.–5 P.M., May 2–October 1 10 A.M.–6 P.M., and October 2–31 10 A.M.–5 P.M.

◖ MARGIT SZIGET (MARGARET ISLAND)

Margaret Island is a little slice of heaven located between the Margaret Bridge to the south and the Árpád Bridge to the north. It is 1.6 miles long and covers 225 acres. Whether you're traveling alone, with friends, a lover, or the whole family, there is no better place to spend the day relaxing, swimming, sunbathing, picnicking, or simply walking around and appreciating natural beauty.

taking a nap on Margaret Island

© TOM DIRLIS

Originally known as Rabbit Island (Nyulak szigete), it was later renamed after Princess Margaret, daughter of King Béla IV, who entered the island's convent and whose burial place is marked to this day amongst its ruins. Favored by monks who appreciated the island's serenity and by kings for its excellent hunting, things changed drastically during the Turkish invasion and the island fell into disuse until the 19th century.

The public opening of a park and entertainment center brought the island back to life, aided by the building of the Margaret Bridge embranchment in 1900, which made it possible for pedestrians to reach the island easily. (Before that, the island could only be approached by boat.) Margaret Island was declared a public park in 1908, right around the time that hot springs were discovered in the area, turning the island into a popular health resort overnight.

Today, the island is a popular destination for tourists and locals in need of escape from the daily rigors of the city. You can spend the entire day strolling up and down the numerous peaceful paths that take you past flower gardens, romantic ruins, a mini zoo, and the Palatinus Strand, Budapest's largest open-air swimming complex. Joggers will love the 3.3-mile rubber-coated track that encircles the island, cyclists will appreciate the opportunity to rent bicycles (fitting one, two, or four people), and there are even electric cars available.

Southern Entrance

Starting at the Margaret Bridge entrance and walking past the Margit Sziget Athletic Center, with its tennis courts and well-kept soccer field, you'll quickly find the **Centenary Monument** directly in front of you. Reminiscent of a futuristic pod or cocoon, it was designed by István Kiss and erected in 1972 to commemorate the 100th anniversary of the union of Buda and Pest. Behind it is the delightful **Musical Fountain,** which pumps water high into the air along to famous classical tunes. This is a favorite with children, who enjoy running around and spraying each another. Should you care to rent a bicycle, electrical car, or take a tour on the "Nostalgia" train, here is where to do so. If you'd rather walk and see how things go, feel free as rental opportunities present themselves throughout the entire course of the island.

A little farther ahead is a pleasant **playground** where children from all over the world make new friends on the slides, swings, and innumerable objects from which to dangle from. Beyond that is the **Hajos Alfred Sportuszoda** (XIII. Margaret Island, tel. 1/340-4946, Mon.–Fri. 6 A.M.–5 P.M., Sat.–Sun. 6 A.M.–7 P.M.), a huge swimming pool complex offering a wide range of aquatic possibilities, from high diving to Olympic-sized facilities. There are a total of six pools, with three of them dedicated exclusively to beginners. This is an excellent place to have either a relaxed or more intensive workout. In fact, odds are you'll probably see a handful of Olympic hopefuls here as plenty of serious athletes come to the center to train.

The first ruins you'll encounter are those of the **Franciscan Priory,** which was established

near the end of the 13th century. Destroyed during Ottoman rule in the 16th century, not much stands today except for a wall and a few crumbling remnants. The flowerbed in front of it is a nice touch, however.

A pleasant stroll through the middle of the island will reward you further with a small **Japanese Garden,** a large **English-style garden,** an **open-air theater,** an octagonal 187-foot-tall Art Nouveau **Water Tower** built in 1911, and a **mini zoo** complete with ponies, baby deer, and horses. At night, popular venues such as Holdudvar and Copacabana Beach host fun-filled dance parties that tend to last until morning.

Palatinus Strand

Originally opened as a beach along the bank of the Danube in 1919, the Palatinus Strand (tel. 1/340-4505, www.palatinusstrand.hu, daily 9 A.M.–7 P.M.) was transformed into an open-air complex upon construction of its immense pool in 1921. Fed by the island's thermal springs, the grounds now boast three thermal pools, an artificial wave pool, a water slide, ping-pong tables, trampolines, and a whole host of snack bars. Very popular and a tremendous amount of fun, this complex is reason to bring your swimsuit if you plan on visiting the island—many have regretted not doing so upon hearing the squeals of laughter and merry-making that emanate from within the grounds.

Dominican Convent

The ruins of the Dominican Convent, dating back to the 13th century, are arguably the most significant site on the island. Founded by King Béla IV following the Mongol invasion, this became the home of his daughter Princess Margaret, famed for curing lepers and performing other selfless deeds. A marble plaque in the nave of the ruins marks the spot where she was buried and is oftentimes adorned with fresh flowers and lit candles by Hungarians who continue to adore her.

The Promenade of Hungarian Artists begins near the convent—a series of busts

BUDAPEST

featuring some of the nation's finest and most important writers, composers, and the like. Among the famous are Béla Bartok, József Attila, and Franz Liszt.

Nearby is the pretty **St. Michael's Provostship Church of the Premonstartensians,** which can be traced back to the 12th century. Completely destroyed during the Turkish wars of 1541, it wasn't until 1923 when its ruins were excavated. It was reconstructed in 1930 and 1931 and possesses Hungary's oldest bell, which was made by Master John Strous in the 15th century.

Northern End

At the far northern end of the island lies a quaint **rock garden** containing twisting little paths and tiny footbridges that wind past pretty ponds, exotic plants, and an artificial waterfall. Turtles and ducklings inhabit the water, something which the kids find entertaining, spending half their time feeding them and the other half frightening them.

THE BUDA HILLS

If you're looking to get away from it all and want to lose yourself in magical, natural surroundings, then the overwhelmingly beautiful Buda Hills are the perfect place to do so. Densely wooded and dotted with the occasional isolated neighborhood, the hills offer peace of mind and fantastic views that simply cannot be beat. Countless trails lead in and around the area, and while relatively busy during the weekends, it's possible to come here on a weekday and stroll for hours without ever being disturbed. It's easy to forget that you're still within the confines of a city while here, falling effortlessly into dream states impossible to experience anywhere down below. When you've had your fill of peace and quiet and want to see what sights draw countless of tourists in year after year, head for the railway circuit and let the trains do the climbing.

◖ The Railway Circuit

One of the most entertaining and breathtaking ways to see the vast Buda Hills is via the railway circuit, which consists of the Cog-Wheel Railway and the Children's Railway. You can spend just a couple of hours if you're in a hurry, or take a more relaxed half-day drinking in the scenery, enjoying the ride more so than any particular destination.

FOGASKEREKŰ VASÚT (COG-WHEEL RAILWAY)

Despite being a rather popular tourist attraction, the Cog-Wheel Railway (Városmajor Station, daily 5 A.M.–11 P.M., standard BKV ticket 170 Ft) is nevertheless an official part of Budapest's tram network. Climbing up 1,066 feet and winding its way through 2.3 miles of track from Városmajor Station (across the street from the Hotel Budapest on Szilágyi Erzsébet fasor in Buda) to Széchenyi Hill, it is a wonderful, picturesque 20-minute trip to the hills that every visitor should experience. Built in 1874 according to the plans of Swiss engineer Ferenc Salesi Cathry, its original purpose was to transport residents of Svábhegy (Swabian Hill) to and from their villas. It was only the third steam-traction carriage in Europe at the time and the line became so popular it was extended in 1890 to its current stop. In 1929, it was converted to electric traction out of respect to the environment. One thing that usually comes as a surprise to first-timers is that the route has very few straight stretches; it mainly runs in curves.

GYERMEKVASÚT (CHILDREN'S RAILWAY)

Located a short walk from the Cog-Wheel Railway's last stop (Széchenyi Hill) is the delightful Children's Railway. Jokingly referred to as the "greatest toy in the world," this 6.8-mile-long stretch through the Buda Hills was completed in 1951; it was formerly called the Pioneer Railway and was run by the Communist Youth Organization. Today, children aged 10–14 operate switches and signals, print tickets, and keep amused passengers informed of upcoming stops—all in full MÁV (Hungarian State Railway) uniforms. For those of you wondering, the driver of the train is indeed an adult. The

SZOBORPARK (STATUE PARK)

When Communism finally ended in Hungary, there was much debate as to what to do with all the statues dedicated to the dreaded political regime that still decorated the streets. Many wanted to throw them out, eager to quickly forget what had brought so much pain and hardship to both themselves and their families. Thankfully, cooler heads prevailed and a collection of 42 statues, memorials, and busts now fill Statue Park – a fascinating outdoor museum that attracts over 40,000 Hungarian and foreign visitors annually, all of whom come to see this remarkable collection reflecting the country's past period of Communist cultural politics. The park includes statues of Lenin, Marx, and Engels, as well as memorials dedicated to the Soviet Soldier, Communist Martyrs, and the Republic of Councils, to name just a few. Designed by Akos Eleőd, Statue Park was opened on June 23, 1993, on the second anniversary of the withdrawal of Russian troops from the country. It is both an eye-opener and history lesson, a living testament to the way things were not that long ago. The park takes approximately 45 minutes to explore and there's a souvenir shop that sells an informative booklet that includes the history of each exhibit, accompanied by interesting photographs depicting their original locations around town. Predictably, the shop also sells a variety of Communist kitsch, including replicas of Lenin statues, Trabant car models, original Soviet medals, postcards, watches, stamps, and, of course, goofy t-shirts. For those wondering why Stalin isn't represented, the answer is easy: The sole Stalin statue in Budapest was destroyed during the revolution of 1956 when an angry mob brought it down and chopped it up into indiscernible little bits.

A direct bus to the park leaves Deák Square daily at 11 A.M. year-round. Tickets can be bought on the bus and cost 3,950 Ft per person. The price includes return and admission to the park. For more information, check out www.mementopark.hu.

railway operates year-round except on Mondays September–April. Trains run roughly every hour 9 A.M.–5 P.M. in the winter and 9 A.M.–7 P.M. in the summer. A one-way trip takes 45 minutes. Round-trip tickets cost 800 Ft.

The railway's first stop is **Normafa.** During the summer, you'll find plenty of locals who have come to escape reality's daily grind down below. In the winter, the place is packed with ski and snowboard enthusiasts who make the best of what little snow stays on the ground.

Another popular stop is **János-hegy.** From here, it's but a few minutes climb up to the top which, at 1,736 feet, is Budapest's highest point. At the summit you'll find the **Erzsébet Lookout Tower,** named after the much-loved Queen during the Austro-Hungarian Empire. The tower is 77 feet tall and offers remarkable panoramic views of the city and hills. Nearby is a **Libegő** (May–Sept. daily 9:30 A.M.–5 P.M., Oct.–Apr. 9:30 A.M.–4 P.M., closed every other Monday, 450 Ft), or chairlift, which, despite the rather lengthy lines during the summer, offers an enjoyable ride down to **Zugliget** from where you can catch a #158 bus back to Moskva tér.

BUDAPEST

Entertainment and Events

Budapest's nightlife is always a vibrant one regardless of the time of year. Whether it's low-key, local wine bars or trendy strips like Liszt Ferenc tér, footloose and fancy-free outdoor summer terraces like Chachacha or legendary live music venues like Old Man's Music Pub, there is always something going on in the big city to satisfy the night owl in everyone.

BARS
The Belváros
If it's tasty pub food you're after, try the ever popular **Irish Cat Pub** (V. Múzeum körút 41, tel. 1/266-4085, www.irishcat.com, daily 11 A.M.–2 A.M.), a traditional Irish pub known for its fast, friendly, and attentive service. A happy-go-lucky mixture of Hungarians, expats, and tourists occupy the bar area, while diners dig into delicious Angus steaks under low, rather romantic, lighting. The burgers here are also delicious and so huge you can barely get your mouth around them. Although slightly pricey by Hungarian standards, it's well within Western traveler budgets and more than fair considering the quality. A fine choice for lunch, dinner, or a couple of drinks when the day's sightseeing is done.

Although no longer the hip, happening place it used to be many years ago, **Fregatt** (V. Molnár utca 26, tel. 1/318-9997, www.club fregatt.hu, Mon.–Fri. 3 P.M.–1 A.M., Sat.–Sun. 5 P.M.–1 A.M.) is nevertheless still a fine place to enjoy a few drinks with friends. Located just off Váci Street, it now tends to mostly attract curious tourists, although locals and students do still frequent this Budapest institution. There's live music every night, as well as a decent menu that delivers very generous portions, making this one of the better offerings in the area.

For a cosy, friendly pub experience, drop into **Janis' Pub** (V. Király Pál utca 8, tel. 1/266-2619, www.janispub.hu, Mon.–Thurs. 4 P.M.–2 A.M., Fri.–Sat. 4 P.M.–3 A.M., Sun. 6 P.M.–2 A.M.) for a pint or two. Frequented mostly by local foreigners and travelers, this is

PÁLINKA

Almost always drunk as a shooter straight up, *pálinka* is an integral part of Hungarian drinking culture. The word's origin comes from the Slavic word *páliť* (distill). Typically made from plums, apples, pears, apricots, and sometimes cherries, it is a type of brandy that was traditionally an essential part of a villager's diet, which also consisted of items such as bread, lard, and fatty bacon. A shot of *pálinka* would help with digestion, not to mention send the imbiber back out to work with a smile on his face. Today, *pálinka* remains an inescapable part of Hungarian culture, finding its way to most tables as the night wears on. Jokingly referred to as "firewater," it typically weighs in at a 40 percent alcohol level but is no match for the more powerful varieties of the drink commonly referred to as *kerítésszaggató* in Hungarian, which literally means "fence-tearer." These merciless homemade concoctions are not available in stores but are nevertheless common. Simply ask a local Hungarian if they have any and they will take great pride in explaining that their home-brewed *pálinka* is not only better than the commercially available kind, but that it will knock your socks off as well. Trust me, they're not kidding.

a laid-back place where you can easily strike up a conversation with strangers or simply enjoy one of the many regularly scheduled concerts. They even have an ongoing karaoke night that tends to liven things up.

Lipótváros
Popular with expats, tourists, foreign businessmen, and beautiful people of all nationalities, **Café Negro** (V. Szent István tér 11, tel. 1/302-0136, Sun.–Thurs. 11 A.M.–2 A.M., Fri.–Sat. 11 A.M.–3 A.M.) is a slick cocktail bar/cafe that

has something going on almost every night of the week. During the summer, its outdoor patio offers stunning, lit-up views of St. Stephen's Basilica, which makes up for the rather pricey drinks.

Advertising itself as Budapest's only authentic Irish pub, **Beckett's Irish Bar** (V. Bajcsy-Zsilinszky út 72, tel. 1/311-1035, www.becketts.hu, Sun.–Thurs. noon–1 A.M., Fri.–Sat. noon–2 A.M.) is a warm, spacious establishment that occupies two vast rooms. Very popular with foreigners, the huge wrap-around bar is the perfect place to knock back a Guinness and the outdoor seating during the summer months is perfect for people-watching. The prices are a little higher than most in the city but the friendly service and extensive drinks menu make it well worth it.

The old adage "time flies when you're having fun" is a fitting description for the addictive **Süss Fel Nap** (V. Szent Istvan körút 11, tel. 1/374-3329, www.sussfelnap.hu, daily 5 P.M.–dawn). An underground, multi-roomed dance spot where you're encouraged to let your hair hang down, it possesses a naturally cheerful atmosphere many other places try yet fail to produce. The music here is eclectic, ranging from raging punk and alternative bands to DJs spinning infectious hip-hop and R&B grooves. It'll be sunrise (a loose translation of the club's name) before you know it.

Terézváros and Erzsébetváros

A mixed crowd of travelers and local revelers can be found drinking and dancing the night away at **Alcatraz** (VII. Nyar utca 1, tel. 1/478-6010, www.alcatraz.hu, Mon.–Wed. 4 P.M.–2 A.M., Thurs.–Sat. 4 P.M.–4 A.M.). As its name suggests, the interior is designed to resemble a prison, though there's certainly nothing here that limits anyone's freedom. The friendly, casual staff can be found enjoying themselves as much as anybody else and the infectious jazz and salsa music will make you beg for an extended sentence.

Warm and friendly **Aloe Kávézó** (VI. Zichy Jenő utca 37, tel. 1/269-4536, daily 5 P.M.–2 A.M.) has built up a reputation as

DAS IST EIN UNIKUM!

Legend has it that when Kaiser Joseph II of Austria was presented with a strong digestive liqueur by his court physician Dr. Zwack, the Habsburg monarch exclaimed, *"Das ist ein Unikum!"* (That is special/unique!). Soon after, a relative of the good doctor standardized the recipe and established the Unicum brand; it went on to become one of Hungary's most requested spirits and has maintained its popularity for over 200 years and counting. Made from 40 different herbs and spices, it is best appreciated at room temperature and is reputed to aid digestion. Tar black in color with a syrupy consistency, it tastes somewhat like Jägermeister but is considerably earthier, has a bitter aftertaste, and packs a punch. Considered a tad too strong for the average Western palate, those not brave enough to try the original might be interested in giving newly launched Unicum Next a try. Thinner, lighter, and cherry-flavored, it has quickly gained both female fans and Western devotees.

having the best (in this case, the cheapest) cocktails in town. Decorated simply with comfortable sofas and armchairs, this is very much a place where one can lounge alongside locals who know how to drink.

You might think that a Wild West theme bar in Budapest would be silly if not downright tacky but **Cactus Juice Pub** (VI. Jókai tér 5, tel. 1/302-2116, Mon.–Thurs. noon–2 A.M., Fri.–Sat. noon–4 A.M., Sun. 4 P.M.–2 A.M.) pulls it off. The secret is that it doesn't take itself seriously, unlike some of the trendier cafes across the street on Liszt Ferenc tér. Very popular with Hungarians, its metal-studded stairs bring you into a typical saloon complete with decorative stains on the walls. There are also 41 different kinds of whiskey on offer, sure to quench the thirst of any High Plains drifter.

BUDAPEST

Located not too far from the Great Synagogue, **Cafe Bobek** (VII, Kazinczy utca 53, tel. 20/774-0103, www.bobek.hu, Mon.–Thurs. 10 A.M.–1 A.M., Fri. 10 A.M.–3 A.M., Sat. 11 A.M.–3 A.M., Sun. 11 A.M.–1 A.M.) is a bright, comfy, local kind of place where you can unwind with a coffee in the afternoon or slosh a few back with friends when the night comes. The very friendly staff and excellent variety of feel-good music makes it difficult to leave, and the free Wi-Fi is a definite plus, as is outdoor seating for the summer months. Should you be heading here on a Thursday, Friday, Saturday, or Sunday, do yourself a favor and reserve yourself a table in advance, as seating is rather limited.

Crazy Café (VI. Jókai utca 30, tel. 1/302-4003, www.crazycafe.hu, Mon.–Sat. 11 A.M.–1 A.M., Sun. 11 A.M.–midnight) is an incredibly popular bar whose long counter and tables in the back are nearly always full. There's plenty of cheer to go around here, as it seems to strike a chord with just about everybody who walks through the door. The vaulted ceiling and walls covered with celebrities give this place its own distinct feel and the reasonable prices, coupled with friendly service, are just the right ingredients to make this a fun, memorable night out.

Cheap beer, street-smart decor, and an overall grungy feel make **Kuplung** (VI. Király utca 46, tel. 30/636-8208, www.kuplung.net, daily 6 P.M.–5 A.M.) a fave with the laid-back, fun-seeking, student crowd. Although about as basic as a bar can get, its lack of pretense and emphasis on simply having a good time make this a must-stop for anyone who appreciates a bar's character more than its fancy cocktails or clientele.

So hip it almost hurts, **SARK** (VII. Klauzál tér 14, tel. 1/328-0752, www.sark.hu, Mon.–Wed. noon–3 A.M., Thurs.–Sat. noon–5 A.M., Sun. 5 P.M.–2 A.M.) generally attracts students, artists, and like-minded Bohemians. A helpful staff, excellent assortment of drinks, and basement disco hosting regular concerts and DJs make this a great choice for anyone looking to rub shoulders with the local cool contingent.

Located just around the corner from the Opera House, **Morrison's Music Pub** (VI. Révay utca 25, tel. 1/269-4060, www.morrisons.hu, Mon.–Sat. 9 P.M.–4 A.M.) packs them in nightly with catchy tunes, karaoke shows, and nightly drinks specials. Popular with the twentysomething expat and traveler crowd, this is one of those places where you can easily strike up a conversation with an utter stranger and end up spending the rest of the night becoming friends. It's ridiculously easy to lose track of the time here as well, but nobody ever seems to complain.

Picasso Point (VI. Hajós utca 31, tel. 1/312-1727, www.picassopoint.hu, Mon.–Wed. noon–midnight, Thurs. noon–3 A.M., Fri. noon–4 A.M., Sat. 6 P.M.–4 A.M., Sun. 4 P.M.–midnight) is a cafe, bar, and restaurant all rolled into one. It was one of the very first Western-style bars to hit the city back in the early 1990s and remains a popular hangout to this very day. Make sure to try the phenomenal pizza, then burn off all those calories by busting a move in the basement disco.

Pótkulcs (VI. Csengery utca 65/b, tel. 1/269-1050, www.potkulcs.hu, Mon.–Sat. 5 P.M.–2:30 A.M., Sun. 5 P.M.–1:30 A.M.) is about as typical a bar as you can find in Budapest. From its laid-back outdoor courtyard in the summer to its friendly, beer-drenched indoor venue during the colder seasons, it's popularity rages on with hipsters who don't seem to need much in the way of ostentatious decoration to enjoy themselves and the people around them. This place is a must for those who want a true taste of the city's bohemian nightlife.

Not far from the Great Synagogue is **Szoda** (VII. Wesselényi utca 18, tel. 1/461-0007, www.szoda.com, Mon.–Fri. 9 A.M.–5 A.M., Sat.–Sun. 2 P.M.–5 A.M.), a comfortable, totally unpretentious, very red bar with old furniture and Japanese anime on the ceiling. It attracts a wide variety of clientele, including students, businessmen, and those who come for the free Wi-Fi. The prices are cheap, the staff friendly, and the music chill. There's a downstairs, too, for those who like their parties on the after-hours side of things.

You can trace the roots of **Fészek** (VII. Kertész utca 36, tel. 1/342-6548, www.feszek -muveszklub.hu, daily noon–1 A.M.) back to the socialist era; formerly it was a Communist artists' club. A huge staircase takes you past large stained glass windows and into a whole lot of fun. There's a beer hall downstairs, a couple of dining areas, a gallery, and TV room. The large pink courtyard is always full in the summertime but that shouldn't stop you from heading here and trying to find a seat.

Located opposite the Great Synagogue, **Katapult** (VII. Dohány utca 1, tel. 1/266-7226, daily 6 P.M.–2 A.M.) is considered one of the better "starter" bars in the area. Loud music and cheap drinks, combined with a hip bar staff and irreverent attitude keep Katapult full till the closing bell. Keep an eye out for the live Latin music shows and guest DJs.

Szimpla kert (VII. Kazinczy utca 14, www .szimpla.hu, daily noon–3 A.M.) is a prime example of Budapest's so-called "ruin bars." Decorated simply (hence the name) with a ragtag mixture of used furniture placed haphazardly throughout its open courtyard, this is one of those places *everybody* in town has been to at least once. Filled with laid-back locals and open-minded visitors looking for a dose of the authentic, its utter lack of pretension and casual atmosphere will most likely have you come back at least once more during your stay.

Józsefváros and Ferencváros

Located behind Corvin Cinema, **West Balkan** (VIII. Futó utca 46, www.west-balkan.com, daily 2 P.M.–late) is a large, lively bar that likes to party till the wee hours. A huge outdoor seating area equipped with two bars fills up quickly during the summer and music aficionados will think they've died and gone to heaven as DJs spin anything from funk to dub to ska. There are smaller rooms upstairs that entertain more intimate events such as poetry readings and film screenings but the large ground-floor hall and packed dance area is typically where the action is.

Those in desperate need of a nightcap ought to seriously consider **Corvintető** (VIII.

Blaha Lujza tér 1-2, tel. 1/461-0007, www .szoda.com, daily 4 P.M.–5 A.M.), a rooftop bar on top of the Corvin Aruház at Blaha Lujza Square. This wide open patio in the center of town offers gorgeous panoramic views of the city and is an excellent place to wind down and watch the sun come up. Entry is possible from Somogyi Béla utca, around the corner from Kaiser's Supermarket.

Following the popular tradition of "ruin bars," the **Tûz Tate** (IX. Tûzoltó utca 54-56, www.tuztate.hu, daily 6 P.M.–2 A.M.) can be found in an abandoned warehouse that looks to be more or less on its last legs. The inner courtyard is the main hub of this laid-back anarchy although people are free to explore the rest of the unlit and unused building. Exhibitions of avant-garde art can be found on the first floor and the roof terrace is an excellent place to chill—at least until you run out of beer and need to head back down to get another.

CLUBS

Bahnhof Music Club (VI. Teréz körút 55, Terézváros, tel. 1/302-4751, www.banhofmusic .hu, Thurs.–Sat. 9 P.M.–4 A.M., 450–900 Ft) is located right behind Nyugati station, making its railway-themed interior all the more appropriate. Spacious, cheap, and open late, its two dance floors fill up quickly with an exuberant crowd that has come to party till they drop.

The **Chachacha Underground Café** (Margaret Island, 300 feet from the Margaret Bridge entrance, tel. 70/554-0670, May–Sept. daily 6 P.M.–5 A.M., no cover charge) came to be after its predecessor (formerly located in Kalvin Square subway underpass) had to close due to construction of the new subway line. Nevertheless, the same bar staff, DJs, and spirit continues on during the summer months at their outdoor terrace on Margaret Island. It's always packed from Thursday to Sunday, with Thursday's Retro Party being the most popular. Lots of dancing, drinking, and romantic escapades are to be expected here, as is a whole lot of fun if you manage to remember whatever it is you did the morning after.

Funk and house are what's usually being

spun at **Club Seven** (VII. Akácfa utca 7, Erzsébetváros, tel. 1/478-9030, daily 10 A.M.–5 A.M., 800–2,000 Ft). The bar area on the left serves as a chilled place to have a drink but the larger room straight ahead is where the dance floor and action is. Very well known for its pick-up potential, this place gets hot, sweaty, and very crowded as the night wears on.

Huge, hedonistic, and pretty much in your face, **E-Klub** (X. Népligeti út 2, Kőbánya, tel. 1/263-1614, www.e-klub.hu, Fri. 9 P.M.–5 A.M., Sat. 10 P.M.–5 A.M., 800–1,000 Ft) is definitely not for the faint-hearted. From scantily clad dancers and strip shows to overtly sexual theme parties, anything goes here and more or less does on the two nights it dares to open. Consider this your fair warning.

Piaf (VI. Nagymező utca 25, Terézváros, tel. 1/312-3823, daily 10 P.M.–6 A.M., 800 Ft) is not only named after the famous crooner, but it evokes the feel of decadent Paris that is impossible not to love. Plush red furnishings, seductive live jazz, and a downstairs disco that gets pretty wild as the night rages on make this a night out on the town you won't soon forget. There's an old woman at the top of the stairs who decides who gets to come in, however, so make sure you're on your best behavior—at least until you get past her.

Located in the basement of the University of Economics, **School Club** (IX. Fővám tér 8, Ferencváros, tel. 1/215-4359, www.schoolclub .hu, Mon.–Sat. 8 P.M.–5 A.M., 500–1,000 Ft) is a student disco/meat market that stays open long enough for everyone to find a friend for the night (or morning). Popular dance music, cheap beer and weekly karaoke keep the place jumping most days of the week.

LIVE MUSIC

Formerly a Ukranian stone-carrier whose seafaring days are now well behind it, **A38** (XI. Petőfi Bridge, Buda side, tel. 1/464-3940, www.a38.hu, daily 11 A.M.–4 A.M., no cover charge) is one of the more unique venues in town to take in a show. Permanently moored on the Buda side of Petőfi Bridge, just south of Gellért hegy, its concert hall is located in the ship's bowels and there is also a restaurant on hand should you get the munchies. During the summer months, the terrace is open and thumps to familiar, dance-friendly beats. A regular host of contemporary musicians representing all genres, A38's former guests include Maceo Parker and Living Color.

Taking its name from colorful New York prohibition agent "Fat Mo" Smith, who, along with his partner Izadore "Izzy" Einstein, made 4,397 arrests and impounded over five million bottles of illegal hooch, **Fat Mo's Music Club** (V. Nyári pál utca 11, The Belváros, tel. 1/267-3199, Mon.–Wed. noon–2 A.M., Thurs.–Fri. noon–4 A.M., Sat. 6 P.M.–4 A.M., Sun. 6 P.M.–2 A.M., live music 700–1,000 Ft) is a must for fans of blues, soul, or jazz. Friendly, English-speaking staff guide you through the extensive menu, which boasts 20 kinds of steak and a cuisine that ranges from Cajun to Mexican fare, not to mention the enviable list of whiskey and wine. Energetic live music whips the crowd into a fun-loving frenzy every night of the week, making this one of the livelier joints off Váci Street. Fat Mo would be proud.

In the heart of Erzsébet tér lies the all-purpose, über-cool **Gödör Club** (V. Erzsébet tér, The Belváros, www.godorklub.hu, daily 4 P.M.–2 A.M., live music 600–2,000 Ft), host to a wide range of exhibits, fairs, music concerts, and just about anything else artistic you can think of. This multi-roomed, versatile space is a favorite during the summer months, when hipsters of all shapes and sizes lounge on the steps with a bottle of beer and soak up the sun's rays. This is a great place to people-watch, chill out with friends, and catch some of the local up-and-coming talent.

If you're a fan of live jazz and blues, make a beeline for the **Old Man's Music Pub** (VII. Akácfa utca 13, Erzsébetváros, tel. 1/322-7645, www.oldmans.hu, daily 3 P.M.–4 A.M., free admission). Attracting some of the finest acts in the country including the phenomenal Cotton Club Singers (jazz circa the 1930s and '40s), it's no wonder this huge club is packed nightly with a friendly, appreciative crowd. Reservations are a must if you feel like sampling their tasty cuisine. Really, there's no excuse not to come here at least once.

THE ARTS

A stroll down Nagymező utca, affectionately dubbed "Budapest's Broadway," is enough to assure fans of the arts that the scene is thriving, but it's not just here that one can indulge themselves. Vörösmarty tér and the underpasses of various subway stations are busy with buskers entertaining passersby with traditional Hungarian folk music and melodies that have soothed the soul for hundreds of years. The Opera House offers its stage to the world's finest musicians, the Merlin International Theatre puts on critically acclaimed English productions, the Madách Theatre hosts performances of the world's most successful musicals, and the Trafó House of Contemporary Arts continues to push the envelope in terms of modern dance. No matter where your tastes lie, Budapest always offers something that it sure to both please and inspire even the most demanding of audiences.

Theater

The **Merlin Nemzetközi Színház** (Merlin International Theatre; V. Gerlóczy utca 4, The Belváros, tel. 1/266-4632, www.merlinszinhaz .hu, box office Mon.–Fri. noon–7 P.M., Sat.– Sun. 2–7 P.M.) is a multi-purpose arts center, cultural institute, and theater all rolled into one. Nearly half of its repertoire is in English and based on famous international works. Fans of the theater, however, should keep their eyes open for the occasional and usually exceptional Hungarian play translated and performed by local English-speaking talent.

Located one block over on the opposite side of the Opera is the often-overlooked **Új Színház** (New Theatre; VI. Paulay Ede utca 35, Terézváros, tel. 1/351-1406, www.ujszinhaz .hu, box office Mon.–Thurs. 10 A.M.–5 P.M., Fri. 10 A.M.–4 P.M.). Built in 1907, its Art Deco facade was designed by Béla Lajta and its grandiose neo-Baroque auditorium comes to us care of László Vágó. Formerly the Ballet

Institute, this theater has gone through plenty of changes over the years but now offers classic and contemporary Hungarian plays, as well as renowned international works. The theater also houses a successful acting school and gallery that offers visual artists the opportunity to introduce their work to a wider audience.

Located in Budapest's vibrant theater district, the **Budapesti Operettszínház** (Budapest Operetta Theatre; VI. Nagymező utca 17, Terézváros, tel. 1/312-4866, www.operettszinhaz .hu, box office Mon.–Fri. 10 A.M.–7 P.M., Sat. 1–7 P.M.) is a wonderful venue. Past shows have included some of the world's most famous musicals, such as *My Fair Lady, Fiddler on the Roof,* and *West Side Story.* Current productions include *Romeo and Juliet* and *Beauty in the Beast,* which have played to sold-out audiences. Fully reconstructed in 2000, the theater now blends the finest in modern stage technology with turn-of-the-20th-century period furnishings to create a warm, inspiring evening at the theater.

The **Madách Színház** (Madách Theatre; VII. Erzsébet körút 29-33, Erzsébetváros, tel. 1/478-2041, www.madachszinhaz.hu, daily 1–6:30 P.M.) was reconstructed in 1999 and possesses three different stages. Its main venue, also known as the Great House, seats just over 800 and regularly plays host to smash musicals like *Cats, Phantom of the Opera,* and *The Producers.* Its second stage is found in the Tolnay Szalon, which typically bases its program on the works of important figures in the world of Hungarian theater. The third stage is found in the Madách Studio, a comfortable theater seating 180 and hosting professional productions of the medium's most famous playwrights, including Shakespeare, Chekhov, and Arthur Miller.

Having survived years of political acrimony, revisions, and cancelled contracts, the **Nemzeti Színház** (Hungarian National Theatre; IX. Bajor Gizi Park 1, Ferencváros, tel. 1/476-6868, www.nemzetiszinhaz.hu, Mon.– Fri. 10 A.M.–6 P.M., Sat.–Sun. 2–6 P.M.) finally managed to open its doors on March 15, 2002. Located along the bank of the Danube, it is part of the ever-expanding Millennium City Center and currently plays host to such classic works as *Master and Margarita, Cinderella,* and *Oedipus.* Despite its spotty and very public history, the theater continues to persevere, believing, as all good theaters do, that the show must go on.

Classical Music and Dance

Designed by Miklós Ybl, Hungary's most important architect in the 19th century, the **Magyar Állami Operaház** (Opera House; VI. Andrássy út 22, Terézváros, www.opera .hu, box office daily 10 A.M.–7 P.M.) is truly a sight to behold. Completed in 1884, this outstanding example of neo-Renaissance elegance is considered one of Hungary's most important buildings and it's easy to see why. Its stunning facade is decorated with 16 statues depicting some of history's greatest classical composers including Mozart, Beethoven, Verdi, and Tchaikovsky. Inside, the massive lobby, grand staircase, and horseshoe-shaped auditorium—in which over seven kilograms (15.4 pounds) of gold were used and whose breathtaking frescoed ceiling was decorated by none other than Károly Lotz—are enough to make you want to return again and again. A tour of the premises is highly recommended, as is a show, where you pay a relatively small amount to be automatically transported back to the 19th century. An absolute must for music fans.

Located at the end of the square is the **Liszt Ferenc Zeneakadémia** (Franz Liszt Academy of Music; VI. Liszt Ferenc tér, Terézváros, www.zeneakademia.hu), an impressive Art Nouveau building that is one of the most recognizable in Budapest. It was founded on November 14, 1875, by none other than the pianist and composer himself, though its current incarnation came in 1907, when it was designed by Flóris Korb and Kálmán Giergl at the behest of then–Minister of Culture Baron Gyula Wlassics. The building's facade includes a statue of Liszt that was sculpted by Alajos Stróbl and its colorful interior is adorned with frescoes, Zsolnay ceramics, and numerous statues of various significant composers. Op-

erating now as both a concert hall and music university, you can often hear students practicing, the strains of their soothing, soaring classical music spilling out onto the street.

Informally referred to as the "Peoples' Opera," the **Erkel Színház** (Erkel Theatre; VIII. Köztársaság tér 30, Józsefváros, tel. 1/333-0540, www.opera.hu, box office Tues.–Sat. 11 A.M.– beginning of performance, Sun. 11 A.M.–1 P.M., 4 P.M.–beginning of performance) is Hungary's largest, seating up to 2,400 people. Built in 1911, it currently serves as the State Opera and Ballet's second home. While some consider it to be subpar to the grand Opera House, it nevertheless fills up nightly with people coming to enjoy the seasonal offerings, which include both classic theatrical works and excellent chamber orchestra concerts.

Built in 1909, the **Trafó Kortárs Művészetek Háza** (Trafó House of Contemporary Arts; IX. Liliom utca 41, Ferencváros, tel. 1/215-1600, www.trafo.hu, box office Mon.–Fri. 2–8 P.M., Sat.–Sun. 5–8 P.M.) is housed in what used to be the electrical transformer station for south Pest. In the early 1990s, a French avant-garde group found the space, which had been left unused for roughly 40 years, and began putting on shows. It was eventually bought by the Budapest City Council and Trafó opened its doors for the first time during the 1998 Budapest Spring Festival. Focusing on a wide variety of modern dance styles and interpretations, it remains on the cutting edge of all things contemporary, including hugely successful dance programs and two annual music festivals focusing on electronic dance music. The building is also home to the **Trafó Gallery** (Tues.–Sun. 4–7 P.M.), presenting eight or nine exhibitions a year in support of young, emerging artists, as well as the hip **Trafó Bar Tango** (tel. 20/319-7061, daily 6 P.M.–4 A.M.), which serves up delicious food and excellent jazz acts in the building's basement. Anyone interested or involved in the arts should definitely make it a point to visit here.

Opened in 2005, the **Művészetek Palotája** (Palace of Arts; IX. Komor Marcell utca 1, Ferencváros, tel. 1/555-3300, www

.muveszetekpalotaja.hu, daily 10 A.M.–10 P.M.) is a remarkable cultural complex that is home to the state-of-the-art National Concert Hall. Awarded the FIABCI Prix d'Excellence in 2006 (which amounts to the same as winning an Oscar for construction and real-estate development), the concert hall seats 1,699 people and hosts the finest acts in classical, jazz, and world music. Top-notch acoustics, a superb audio-visual system, and a remarkable concert organ make an evening here a truly world-class experience.

At Corvin tér you'll find the **Budai Vigadó** (I. Corvin tér 8, The Víziváros, tel. 1/317-2754, box office daily 10 A.M.–6 P.M.), Buda's answer to a concert hall whose "house band" is the superb Hungarian State Folk Ensemble. The group is the oldest of its kind in Hungary and performs folk dances hailing from all four corners of the country. Designed by Arkay Aladár and Kallina Mór, the hall was built between 1898 and 1900, and its Art Nouveau interior with wide marble staircase and richly decorated theater hall make it an excellent venue for fans of traditional music and dance.

Although lacking the distinct charm of older venues around town, the **Budapesti Kogresszusi Központ** (Budapest Congress Center; XII. Jagelló út 1-3, Gellért hegy, tel. 1/372-5400, www.bcc.hu, box office Wed., Fri., and performance days 1:30–6 P.M.), which also functions as a concert hall, is a surprisingly decent place to enjoy a performance. The acoustics are solid, the seats plush, and its main room, the Pátria Hall, seats up to 1,800 and is comfortably spacious. Shows come and go here so make sure to visit the website for upcoming events.

The **Várszínház** (Castle Theatre; I. Színház utca 1-3, Várhegy, tel. 1/201-4407, www.dancetheatre.hu, box office Mon.–Thurs. 10 A.M.–6 P.M., Fri. 10 A.M.–3 P.M., ticket office daily 11 A.M.–6 or 7 P.M. on performance days), originally served as a Carmelite Church in the mid-18th century but was rebuilt into a theater on the order of Emperor Joseph II. Its first Hungarian play was *Igaházi,* written by Kristóf Simai and performed on October 5, 1790. One of the theater's most famous guests was Ludwig van Beethoven, who performed on May 7, 1800. Heavily damaged during World War II, it reopened again in 1978 and is now home to the highly successful National Dance Theatre.

Cinemas

The **Broadway** (VII. Károly krt 3, Erzsébetváros, tel. 1/322-0230) opened in 1938, which would explain its functionalist style architecture. Known for its enormous circular auditorium, it shows its fair share of French art films along with the occasional Hollywood offering. Part of its long, illustrious past is being used as an air raid shelter during World War II, so you know you'll be safe here.

Without a doubt, **Uránia** (VIII. Rákóczi út 21, Józsefváros, tel. 1/486-3400, www.urania -nf.hu) is one of Budapest's most beloved and finest theaters. Designed in a Moorish/ Venetian style by Henrik Schmahl, its gigantic 700-seat auditorium is more often than not the site of lively and enthusiastic crowds, particularly when the latest Hollywood blockbuster hits town.

The **Művész mozi** (VI. Teréz körút 30, Terézváros, tel. 1/332-6726, www.artmozi.hu) is one of the few alternative cinemas to be found in the city, debuting films from all over the world, including Asia, Europe, and America. There are five screens here, which means it shouldn't be too hard to find something interesting, or at least with subtitles you can understand. There's a shop as well in the main hall selling a variety of soundtracks, CDs, and books.

FESTIVALS AND EVENTS

Budapest's events calendar is full of happenings big and small. In the springtime there is the incomparable Budapest Spring Festival, which attracts both musical and visual artists from all over the world. During the summer, the streets and squares are filled with parades, dance festivals, and outdoor concerts on a weekly basis; two of the biggest events are the monumental Sziget Festival and bone-rattling Hungarian Formula 1 Grand Prix. Wine tasting is the name of the game during autumn's Wine Festival and the Christmas Market and Hungarian

Film Week are just two reasons to leave the warmth of your hotel and mingle with winter's merry-makers. No matter when you choose to visit, you can be sure there will be something interesting and entertaining going on.

Spring

The **Budapest Spring Festival** (various venues, www.festivalcity.hu, second half of March) is Hungary's largest cultural event and showcases some of the country's finest musicians, composers, and artists alongside exceptional international talent. First held in 1981, the festival has grown to roughly 200 events put on in 50–60 venues around town and features everything from orchestral and chamber concerts to jazz, contemporary dance, and film screenings. Visitors will do themselves a huge favor by attending at least a handful of the exciting events that keep the city buzzing for two whole weeks.

Summer

The **Sziget Festival** (Óbudai Island, www.sziget.hu, first half of August) is by far the largest musical event to hit Hungary every year and is recognized as one of the world's premier music festivals. Folks from around the globe come to let loose and party hearty on the pretty green island in Óbuda, drinking up the countless shows on multiple stages held in over 60 venues. The island turns into a mini-city that week, offering visitors banking services, restaurants, pubs, and shops, not to mention the opportunity to meet likeminded fans. Day passes, week passes, and camping permits are all available and it's wise to reserve them well in advance as this is one event that is guaranteed to sell out time and time again. Every year has a star-studded list of performers; 2007 alone saw the Chemical Brothers, Nine Inch Nails, Sinéad O'Connor, Tool, and The Killers just to name a few.

The **Budapest Summer Festival** (Margaret Island, tel. 1/340-4196, www.szabadter.hu, June–Sept., box office Wed.–Sun. 4–7 P.M.) delights both cultural tourists and fans of the arts alike. Entertaining performances of the highest degree can be enjoyed at the Margaret Island Open Air Stage, located on the northern tip of the island. A wide variety of Broadway shows, musicals, and children's programs are put on to the enjoyment of thousands, not to mention classical concerts and pop music performances. Tickets can be bought at the island or any number of locations throughout the city, as well as online from the festival's website.

Built in the mid-1980s, the Hungaroring was meant to invite the Formula 1 World Championship behind the then Iron Curtain. Course designers chose Mogyoród, located 11 miles northeast of Budapest, and the **Hungarian Formula 1 Grand Prix** (Mogyoród, www.hungaroinfo.com, early Aug.) was born. Although one of the slowest tracks on the F1 calendar, race fans flock to the weekend event year after year, making it the most popular sporting event of the summer—one that has played host to such race driving greats as Michael Schumacher, Jacques Villeneuve, Ayrton Senna, and Damon Hill. Tickets are typically bought online but can also be purchased at various box offices at the track throughout the three-day affair.

St. Stephen's Day (www.meh.hu, Aug. 20) is a public holiday that falls on August 20 and commemorates Hungary's first king. Stephen's biggest contribution to the Hungarian state was converting the nomadic Magyar people into Christianity and he was canonized on August 20, 1083. One of the day's main events is the procession of St. Stephen's holy right hand around the Basilica before being returned to its home inside. Traditional concerts, food and crafts stalls, children's programs, and a street parade all add to the city's all-round festive mood. At night, follow the crowds to Gellért Hill and cap off the fun-filled day by enjoying the massive fireworks display over the Danube that lasts nearly a half hour.

Few if any events in Hungary are as much fun as the immensely popular **Budapest Parade** (www.budapest.com/BudapestParade, Aug. 26). Celebrated on August 26 and seen as the last official event of the summer, the parade attracts hundreds of thousands of people who fill the city's streets and party the day away. Scantily clad girls, world-renowned DJs, and a convoy of over 50 colorful floats are just some of the things that make their way up Andrássy út all the way to the Városliget. The whole spectacle ends with an elaborate fireworks display and then the real fun begins as most hip bars and clubs hold after-parade parties that rage on till the sun comes up. This is definitely one of those days you want circled on your calendar.

For over 200 years, July 14 has symbolized French independence and national unity and the **Bastille Day Carnival and Market** (I. Fo utca 17, tel. 1/489-4200, www.francia-intezet .hu, July 14 10 A.M.–midnight) is no different. Sponsored by the nearby French Institute, the Bem quay is closed down for the day and turned into a colorful site that includes enthusiastic dancing and heartfelt singing. Countless booths line the street, selling authentic French foods, handicrafts, and sweets, not to mention a large number of delicious wines. Lots of fun for the whole family, this is an excellent opportunity to immerse yourself in a wonderful culture and take part in what amounts to a celebration of an all-encompassing joie de vivre.

One of Budapest's most interesting and cultural events is the hugely successful **Night of Museums** (various venues, www.muzeumoke jszakaja.hu, second half of June). Over 45 cities in Hungary open their museums' doors until the wee hours, allowing visitors access to the usual exhibitions, as well as those that are generally preserved out of the public eye. In Budapest alone, roughly 400 programs are held at over 50 venues and include guided tours, film screenings, talks, concerts, and dance performances. More than 100,000 people took part in 2007, drinking wine and waxing cultural from one end of the city to the other. Entry stickers can be bought at participating museums and allow access to all of them, as well as free transportation on specially marked buses reserved solely for the night's festivities. This is an incredible way to see all the city has to offer for less than a meal at an average restaurant. Highly recommended.

With its first effort coming in 1998, the **Jewish Summer Festival** (Erzsébetváros, tel. 1/413-5531, www.jewishfestival.hu, last week

in August) has gone on to introduce Jewish culture to an ever-growing amount of people. Held on the last week of the summer, visitors get a chance to learn more about a culture that stretches back thousands of years through various artistic forms including film, theater, photography, literature readings, and music. Many local and international artists participate in the festival, making it a truly entertaining and informative week.

Autumn

The **Budapest International Wine and Champagne Festival** (I. Buda Castle, tel. 1/203-8507, www.winefestival.hu, first half of Sept.) takes place during the first half of September and is widely considered to be one of the country's most prestigious events. Visitors get the chance to rub elbows with viniculture's finest and learn all aspects of the industry. Food also plays a large role in the festivities, with a grill corner, fish terrace, and cauldron farm being just a handful of the gastronomical possibilities available to those who don't want to drink on an empty stomach. The festival's most popular event is the Wine Exhibition and Fair, which takes place at beautiful Buda Castle and allows Hungary's finest winemakers, along with top international merchants, to offer their wares to a very thirsty public. No wine lover should miss this.

Established in 1992, the **Budapest Autumn Festival** (various venues, www.festivalcity.hu, mid-Oct.) focuses primarily on the contemporary arts in Hungary and attempts to familiarize the public with new artistic forms, trends, and ideas. The program itself is vast and includes dance, jazz, performance art, music, film, theater, and various exhibitions. Reduced from two weeks to 10 days for financial reasons, the festival nevertheless continues to both educate and entertain art lovers who have been participating annually in ever-increasing numbers.

The **Budapest International Marathon** (throughout the city, tel. 1/273-0939, www .budapestmarathon.com, late Sept.) has been "running" since 1984 and has been growing in size steadily. The marathon's starting point is impressive Heroes' Square, which also hosts a fair full of showmen, concerts, and various booths offering information on both sports and lifestyle. Runners head down Andrássy Avenue then continue on past Gresham Palace, the Chain Bridge, Buda Castle, Margaret Island, and the mighty Parliament building. At the end of it all, competitors are given the opportunity to soak in the superb Széchenyi thermal baths—which almost makes it worth entering.

Winter

The **Christmas Market** (Vörösmarty Square, Dec. 1–24) in Budapest is a time-honored tradition loved and anticipated by both Hungarians and foreigners alike. Considered one of the better Christmas fairs in Europe, the market is an opportunity to buy beautiful hand-made folk art and decorations, as opposed to the kitsch and low-quality goods found in other cities. Roughly 150 programs are scheduled every year with puppet theaters, folk bands, and dance troupes all joining in the Yuletide fun. There's plenty of food available as well, with numerous stalls serving up scrumptious pastries and mulled wine.

Two highlights of the market are a visit by the one and only Santa Claus, who listens to countless kids trying to convince him they've been good, along with Café Gerbeaud becoming a living Advent Calendar as one window is opened daily at 5 P.M. until Christmas Eve.

Established in 1965, **Hungarian Film Week** (various venues, www.szemle.film.hu, first week in Feb.) is the most important film festival in Hungary and is held annually during the first week in February. All the films in competition are made by Hungarian artists looking to receive critical recognition for their work, as well as reach a wider audience. In order to avoid bitter disputes in the past, the festival now has two major awards: Best "Author" Film, which recognizes artistic merit, and Best "Genre" Film, which gives the nod to the film with the most commercial potential. Although nowhere near the stature of the Berlin, Venice, or Cannes film festivals, Hungarian Film Week is nevertheless an excellent opportunity to stay abreast of what's happening in this very exciting and unpredictable medium.

Shopping

When it comes to shopping, the first name on every visitor's lips is Váci utca. This is where locals and tourists with a bit of money to burn come to have a look at what the pricey designer boutiques are offering. You'll find plenty of souvenir and gift shops here as well, peddling everything from traditional costumes to folk art. Many of these shops offer tourist-trap kitsch but a bit of hunting around should reward you with a treasure or two. The Castle District sees its fair share of shoppers as well, with wine shops and art galleries getting the brunt of the business. Shopping malls abound and include Central Europe's largest, WestEnd City Center, and Buda's Mammut, both of which are almost always packed. There's also Andrássy út, which, apart from boasting some of the finer buildings, restaurants, and cafes in town, also has plenty

of gift shops, boutiques, and bookstores to keep upscale shoppers very happy.

THE BELVÁROS
Art

Located in the Párizsi udvar is **Hologram Galéria** (V. Szerb utca 17-19, tel. 1/485-5050, www.hologram.hu, daily 10 A.M.–7 P.M.), a one-of-a-kind gift shop that specializes in holograms. Both two-dimensional and three-dimensional works of art are available, with images ranging from world-famous rock-and-roll bands to dangerous man-eating sharks. The holograms come in all shapes and sizes and make for very unique gifts. There are no shipping services overseas so if you decide on a hefty hologram, be prepared to lug it back with you.

A trip to the **Studio Gallery** (V. Képíró utca

6, tel. 1/411-0235, studio.c3.hu, Tues.–Fri. 4–8 P.M., Sat. noon–4 P.M.) is like a visit to the not-too-distant future. Up-and-coming artists from all over the country and beyond have had their first exhibitions here before going on to critical acclaim. Fans of art who like to be on the cutting edge of the newest trends and movements would be wise to pay this gallery a visit.

Antiques

The state-owned **BÁV** (V. Bécsi utca 1, tel. 1/266-2087, www.bav.hu, Mon.–Fri. 10 A.M.–6 P.M., Sat. 9 A.M.–1 P.M.) has a stronghold on the antiques market in Hungary and has a number of shops throughout the capital. This particular shop is the city's largest and specializes in fine art, chandeliers, porcelain, and carpets. In case you were wondering, most of BÁV's inventory is comprised of goods seized by customs.

Located on a street that's home to more than a few antique shops, **Darius Antiques** (V. Falk Miksa utca 24-26, tel. 1/311-2603, darius@csorge.net, Mon.–Fri. 9 A.M.–6 P.M., Sat. 10 A.M.–1 P.M.) has had no trouble establishing itself over the years. Trying to distance itself and carve out its own niche in the realm of antique hunting, it specializes in Biedermeier furniture, as well as objets d'art and Viennese antiques.

Nagyházi Galéria (V. Balaton utca 8, tel. 1/475-6000, www.nagyhazi.hu, Mon.–Fri. 10 A.M.–6 P.M., Sat. 10 A.M.–1 P.M.) is the largest of its kind in Budapest and mainly stocks furniture, porcelain and paintings from both Hungarian and international artists. Auctions take place monthly and should be taken advantage of by any serious collector of antiques.

The **Polgár Gallery and Auction House** (V. Váci utca 11/B, tel. 1/267-4077, www.polgar-galeria.hu, Mon.–Fri. 10 A.M.–6 P.M.) specializes in valuable works of art, along with jewelry, antique furniture, and various collectibles. Auctions are held regularly and art lovers should definitely have a close look at what's on offer as there are many bargains to be had. Overseas visitors should make sure to confirm whether they'll need an export visa for whatever goods they're interested in before entering the bidding.

Qualitas (V. Kígyó utca 5, tel. 1/318-3246,

Mon.–Fri. 10 A.M.–6 P.M., Sat. 10 A.M.–1 P.M.) is a privately owned company that thus far boasts four locations. This particular one is arguably the most popular and specializes in period furniture, objets d'art, coins, and jewelry, as well as exceptional Herend and Zsolnay porcelain.

Books and Music

Budapest's first English bookshop is the incredibly popular **Bestsellers** (V. Október 6, tel. 1/312-1295, www.bestsellers.hu, Mon.–Fri. 9 A.M.–6:30 P.M., Sat. 10 A.M.–5 P.M., Sun. 10 A.M.–4 P.M.). Opened in 1992, it continues to draw customers from all over the world who are in need of travel books, literary gems, or a good old-fashioned newspaper or magazine. A visit to this bright and well-run shop is a must for any bookworm.

Központi Antikvárium (V. Múzeum körút 13-15, tel. 1/317-3514, Mon.–Fri. 10 A.M.–6:30 P.M., Sat. 10 A.M.–2 P.M.) has the distinct honor of being Budapest's oldest, largest, and some would say best, used bookstore. Located opposite the National Museum, the bookstore is a treasure trove of old prints, maps, and photos, as well as old and rare books covering pretty much any topic you can think of. There is also a small English section that has books ranging from literature to philosophy, travel guides and crime fiction. Always worth a peek inside.

Libri Foreign Language Bookshop (V. Váci utca 22, tel. 1/318-5680, www.libri.hu, Mon.–Fri. 10 A.M.–7 P.M., Sat.–Sun. 10 A.M.–3 P.M.) is Budapest's largest chain of foreign-language bookshops and this particular location couldn't be more convenient. Two floors of books covering all the major categories including new titles, classic literature, nature books, language books, guide books, art, history, film . . . well, you get the picture. Pretty postcards and photo albums can also be bought here and the staff will go out of their way to help you find what you're looking for. English isn't the only language you'll find here either, as books are also available in German, Russian, French, Italian, and Spanish.

A few steps from the Central Market Hall is the excellent music shop **MIND-ZENE**

Zeneáruház (V. Vanhaz krt. 4, tel. 1/318-2390, daily 10 A.M.–8 P.M.). Stocked with some hard-to-find titles of the world's best-known bands, this is also the place to come to if you want to bring home some true blue Hungarian music with you. Not content to concentrate solely on tunes, MIND-ZENE also has a respectable DVD collection of live concerts and movies by some of the mediums more independent-minded filmmakers like Jim Jarmusch, Ingmar Bergman, and John Cassavetes. And if that weren't enough, postcards, trinkets, and action figures of some of the comic world's better and lesser-known superheroes are available as well.

An excellent place to pick up cheap used books is the **Red Bus Bookstore** (V. Semmelweis utca 14, tel. 1/337-7453, www.redbusbudapest.hu, Mon.–Fri. 11 A.M.–6 P.M., Sat. 10 A.M.–2 P.M.). Fiction titles prevail but there are also plenty of non-fiction books, biographies, true crime stories, plays, and even a whole set of crossword puzzles to keep you occupied on those long train rides. With new second-hand titles coming in practically every day, chances are you'll find something that catches your interest no matter when you drop in.

Fashion

Located in the heart of the shopping district, **Matteo and Co.** (V. József Nádor tér 9, tel. 1/266-1813, www.matteoandco.hu, daily 9 A.M.–7 P.M.) is almost always full of shoppers looking for the next great bargain. This is the only shop in town that sells last year's fashions from some of the world's best-known designers (like Versace, Roberto Cavalli, and Dolce & Gabbana) at outlet prices. All serious shoppers should stop in here at least once for a look.

Retrock (V. Ferenczy István utca 28, tel. 30/678-8430, www.retrock.com, Mon.–Fri. 10:30 A.M.–7:30 P.M., Sat. 10:30 A.M.–3:30 P.M.) was established by a group of creative young designers who wanted to buck the mainstream. The result is a chic, colorful boutique where retro meets cutting edge and one-of-a-kind pieces by Hungarian and foreign designers are sold to trendy locals and tourists in the know.

Dresses, jackets, skirts, tops, and accessories can all be found here, as can one or two of the designers themselves on occasion.

Folk Art

Just off Váci Street is the pricey but incomparable **Folkart Kézmúvesház** (V. Régiposta utca 12, tel. 1/318-5143, www.folkartkezmuveshaz.hu, Mon.–Fri. 10 A.M.–7 P.M., Sat. 10 A.M.–4 P.M.). Pretty much any kind of traditional or authentic handcrafted item you can think can be found here including linen, blankets, ceramics, porcelain dolls, wooden toys, and a wide array of knickknacks. The very friendly and knowledgeable staff is more than willing to explain the history of the products and there is never any pressure to buy. This is an excellent place to check out should you want to bring back a piece of the "real" Hungary with you.

Folkart Centrum (V. Váci utca 58, tel. 1/318-5840, www.folkartcentrum.hu, daily 10 A.M.–7 P.M.) is full of authentic, hand-made Hungarian folk art ranging from embroidered goods to ceramics, porcelain, traditional costumes, carpets, and dolls. Far more dependable than the plethora of knock-off shops that line Váci Street, this is one place you can come to and be sure you're getting the real deal.

Food and Drink

The steady business done by **Szamos Marcipán Cukrászda** (V. Párizsi utca 3, tel. 1/317-3643, daily 10 A.M.–7 P.M.) is no accident, for it is here where some of the finest pastries in the capital are to be had. Cakes, sweets, and ice cream so good it should be illegal keep them coming back for more. Don't let the location just off Váci Street fool you; this is no tourist trap. In fact, Hungarians make up the majority of the loyal customers.

Thomas T. Nagy's Cheese Shop (V. Gerlóczy utca 3, tel. 1/317-4268, Mon. 10 A.M.–5 P.M., Tues.–Fri. 9 A.M.–6 P.M., Sat. 8 A.M.–1 P.M.) is one of the few shops in Budapest that focuses solely on cheese and, if you believe the reviews over the last few years, it's also the best. A range of over 300 cheeses are to be found here hailing from the homeland as well as from Italy, Holland, France, and England. Truly a cheese lover's paradise.

Gifts

One of the more beautiful shops on Váci Street is **Philanthia** (V. Váci utca 9, tel. 1/266-1156, www.philanthia.hu, daily 9 A.M.–8 P.M.), a 100-year-old flower shop whose magnificent Art Nouveau interior alone is worth a peek inside. Its flower arrangements are second to none and the beautifully intricate vases, baskets, and various gift items are a throwback to a time Philanthia has chosen to remain in. Should you find something that catches your fancy but is simply too big to carry back with you, the fine folks here will be more than happy to arrange shipping.

Vali Folklor (V. Váci utca 23, tel. 1/337-6301, daily 10 A.M.–8 P.M.) is a refreshing change from the blatant kitsch that pervades Váci Street, offering authentic traditional Hungarian costumes, crafts, ceramics, and a whole host of colorful knick-knacks. The friendly owners are happy to regale you with stories of the past, including the history of much of the Communist-era paraphernalia on the shelves that includes pins, badges, and army headgear. If you're going to buy one souvenir during your stay in Budapest, make sure to drop in here before making that final decision.

If you can't find the right designer gift at **Forma** (V. Ferenciek tere 4, tel. 1/266-5053, www.forma.co.hu, Mon.–Fri. 11 A.M.–7 P.M., Sat. 10 A.M.–1 P.M.), you're just not trying hard enough. Local and greater European talent is represented here in items ranging from furniture to electronics and home accessories to gifts that are just plain fun. There is also an exhibition space on the second floor showcasing the work of young, upcoming talent.

Jewelry

BÁV Jewelry–Rubin Ékszerbolt (V. Párizsi utca 2, tel. 1/318-6217, www.bav.hu, Mon.–Fri. 10 A.M.–6 P.M., Sat. 10 A.M.–1 P.M.) works along the same state-owned lines as all its other shops, including the aforementioned antiques

location. Here, shoppers can delight in savings from the healthy stock of watches and antique gold and silver jewelry available.

TERÉZVÁROS AND ERZSÉBETVÁROS
Books and Music

Four floors of the newest in literature await you at **Alexandra Könyvesház** (VII. Károly körút 3/C, tel. 1/479-7070, www.alexandra.hu, daily 10 A.M.–10 P.M.). There's a decent selection of English books on the second floor, ranging from Penguin classics to Philip Roth and Chuck Palahniuk. A simple yet enticing cafe sits on this level as well, offering an excellent spot to take a load off and dive into a book before venturing back out onto the streets. In case you're interested in Hungarian literature, you'll want to keep an eye out for the various events held here, including popular readings by the country's contemporary authors.

Calling itself "a local bookstore with a global conscience," **Treehugger Dan's Bookstore and Cafe** (VI. Csengery utca 48, tel. 1/322-0774, www.treehugger.hu, Mon.–Fri. 10 A.M.–7 P.M., Sat. 10 A.M.–5 P.M., Sun. 10 A.M.–4 P.M.) is a breath of fresh air (environmental pun intended) in the land of used bookshops. Started in March 2006 by environmental activist Dan Swartz, this tiny space is a favorite meeting spot of locals, travelers, and the green-minded set fully committed to environmental and social justice issues. Poetry readings are held regularly, as are monthly Greenpeace Fridays when films are screened and pressing societal issues are examined. Completely non-smoking and offering Fair Trade coffee and tea, this is one place all lovers of literature and Mother Earth need to check out at least once during their stay.

Hungaroton (VII. Rottenbiller utca 47, tel. 1/322-8839, www.hungaroton.hu, Mon.–Fri. 8 A.M.–3:30 P.M.) is the country's largest publisher of Hungarian classical music, as well as operas, traditional folk music, and contemporary Hungarian music. Fans of these genres should waste no time in making their way down to this factory outlet.

BUDAPEST

WAMP

Founded in July 2006, WAMP is a monthly outdoor Hungarian design market that attracts over 4,500 Hungarians, tourists, and expats to its location in Erzsébet Square. The market houses over 100 local artists and designers, and visitors are often amazed at the wide array of jewelry, textiles, ceramics, glassware, children's toys, and games on display, all of which make for unique gifts and memorable souvenirs. The market's main objective is to create an established forum wherein artists of all disciplines can not only find an outlet to sell their work, but begin a dialogue with conscious consumers as well. WAMP has started to organize its monthly endeavor around themes, the most popular of which thus far have been Earth Day, with recycling as its main design, and Street Art, which included human beat-box performances and urban clothing and merchandise. This is an excellent opportunity to both understand what the country's hottest and most innovative designers are doing, as well as pick up items that far outweigh the usual tourist schlock in both quality and value. For more information, visit www.wamp.hu.

Fashion

Situated next to the Great Synagogue, **Látomás** (VII. Dohány utca 20, tel. 1/266-5052, www .latomas.hu, Mon.–Fri. 11 A.M.–7 P.M., Sat. 11 A.M.–4 P.M.) is where you'll find the country's top contemporary designers all under one roof. Unique, one-piece creations from over 30 designers include bags, jewelry, clothing, and much, much more. This is where all the town's hipsters come to shop.

For the most unique t-shirts in town, check out **Volt Bolt** (VII. Klauzál tér 14, www .voltbolt.hu, Mon.–Fri. 11 A.M.–7 P.M., Sat. 11 A.M.–4 P.M.). Official supplier of major music festivals like Sziget, VOLT, and Balaton Sound, this shop is the ultimate in casual cool. There are also plenty of accessories to sift through including jewelry, watches, bags, and a whole host of souvenirs.

Food and Drink

Not far from the Great Synagogue is **In Vino Veritas** (VII. Dohány utca 58-62, tel. 1/341-0464, www.borkereskedes.hu, Mon.– Fri. 9 A.M.–8 P.M., Sat. 10 A.M.–6 P.M.), a very friendly store filled with an impressive range of domestic wines. Ask the knowledgeable staff for help or enjoy browsing for that perfect bottle. High quality at reasonable prices has made this a popular choice amongst wine lovers for quite some time now.

The **Kosher Store** (VII. Dob utca 12, tel. 1/267-5691, www.rothschild.hu, Mon.– Thurs. 10 A.M.–6 P.M., Fri. 9 A.M.–2 P.M.) is right in the heart of the Jewish district and one of five shops in the Rothschild chain that has been serving customers since 1991. A decent selection of Hungarian wines is to be found here but the real draw is their range of organic and kosher foods. Slightly pricier than other food stores but a whole lot healthier, too.

Open longer than most, **Rana Center ABC** (VII. Ne felejcs utca 27-29, tel. 1/352-2348, Mon.–Sat. 9 A.M.–11 P.M., Sun. 10 A.M.–11 P.M.) is quite a popular choice with the locals. It's home to an excellent selection of Middle Eastern and Mediterranean goods including feta cheese, olives, and a variety of spices; you'll also find a decent selection of fresh meats like lamb and plenty of sweets. Its long hours are a godsend on weekends when most of the city's shops close down.

La Petite Francaise (VII. Rumbach Sebestyén utca 7, tel. 1/321-5711, www.lapetite francaise.com, Mon.–Fri. 10 A.M.–6 P.M., Sat. 10 A.M.–1 P.M.) is a charming little shop specializing in hard-to-find French foods, with offerings that are affordable and of the highest quality. A mouthwatering array of wines, chocolates, cheeses, pates, and sweets are on display in tasteful arrangements that will make you want to devour everything you see before you. Food buffs will do themselves a huge favor by coming here *tout de suite*.

Gifts

Repülő Tehén (VI. Hajós utca 19, tel. 20/204-5574, www.repulotehen.hu, Mon.–Fri. 11 A.M.–7 P.M., Sat. 11 A.M.–4 P.M.), "Flying Cow" in English, is the name of a chain of gift shops that are sure to put a smile on your face. Balancing purity and irony, the artistic and atrociously kitsch, you'll find fun, unusual, and ultimately cool gifts here. From Elvis clocks to Buddha squeeze toys, electronic Sudoku to Michelangelo mugs, this is where you'll find what you're looking for before you even know what that is.

For a truly unique gift, head on over to the Jewish district and check out **Sunship Design Studio** (VII. Király utca 31, tel. 1/352-0229, www.sunship.hu, Mon.–Fri. 11 A.M.–7 P.M., Sat. 11 A.M.–4 P.M.). Colorful and outright gorgeous gift lamps are on sale here from renowned producers Black+Blum and Mathmos, innovators of the hugely successful lava lamp. Also available are the amazing closed ecosystems designed by Globus International—small, living, and breathing spheres that fit right into the palm of your hand.

Shopping Centers

The **WestEnd City Center** (VI. Váci út 1-3, tel. 1/238-7777, www.westend.hu, Mon.–Sat. 10 A.M.–9 P.M., Sun. 10 A.M.–6 P.M.) is located close to Nyugati railway station and is Central Europe's largest shopping mall. Over 400 stores serve eager shoppers, who also have the opportunity to relax in the pretty open-air rooftop garden terrace. Plenty of local shops were hurt by the center's opening in 2000, but that hasn't stopped the steady flow of human traffic through the center's doors.

JÓZSEFVÁROS AND FERENCVÁROS

Fashion

Inspired by American icons that include Hank Williams and Johnny Cash, the **Sunset Star Rock and Roll Shop** (VIII. Bezerédi utca 19, tel. 1/323-1463, Mon.–Fri. 11 A.M.–7 P.M., Sat. noon–2 P.M.) is a remarkable place considering it's nowhere near Highway 61. The shop specializes in rock and roll, rockabilly, psychobilly, and punk fashions and is full of classic and immediately recognizable brands like Lucky 13, King Kat, Liquor Brand, CBGB, and King Kerosin, among others. If you feel the need to shop for the rock star in you, start here.

Food and Drink

Originally founded in 1993 under the name Budapest Wine Society, **Bortársaság** (IX. Ráday utca 7, tel. 1/219-5647, www.bortarsasag.hu, Mon.–Fri. noon–8 P.M., Sat. 10 A.M.–3 P.M.) has grown to become one of the most important wine traders in the country. Turning over roughly 1.5 billion forints a year, it has carved itself a success most wine enthusiasts only dream of. You'll find nearly 500 different kinds of Hungarian or foreign wines, along with spirits, sparkling wines, and champagnes. There are five locations to choose from and you can rest assured that if you can't find what you're looking for, odds are it never made it into the country.

Shopping Centers

Located at the Pest foot of the Liberty Bridge, the **Central Market Hall,** or Nagy Vásárcsarnok (IX. Vámház körút 1-3, tel. 1/366-3300, www.csapi.hu, Mon. 6 A.M.–5 P.M., Tues.–Fri. 6 A.M.–6 P.M., Sat. 6 A.M.–2 P.M.), is Budapest's largest of five market halls and easily its most popular. Opened in 1896, it then included a network of tunnels that allowed incoming barges to unload their merchandise directly under the market floor. Restored in 1994, its two huge floors are packed with bustling stalls selling a remarkable variety of meats, spices, fruits, vegetables, traditional dolls, clothing, and, of course, local wine and liqueurs. Located on the upper floor are a handful of stalls offering Hungarian staples like goulash and *lángos*—a great place to fill up on local food and admire the endless combination of intoxicating colors and smells. If at all possible, visit on a Saturday morning when the market is at its busiest and most vibrant.

Central Market Hall

© TOM DIRLIS

VÁRHEGY AND CENTRAL BUDA

Books

Tucked away in the Fortuna courtyard opposite the Hilton Hotel is **Litea** (I. Hess András tér 4, tel. 1/375-6987, bakobuda@axelro.hu, daily 10 A.M.–6 P.M.), a charming bookshop and tea-house that stands out from the various souvenir peddlers that surround it. Those interested in learning more about Hungary will be happy to find an excellent assortment of books, maps, and CDs dealing with the country's history and culture throughout the centuries. There is also a lovely outdoor courtyard where patrons can sit down with a delicious cup of tea and peruse through their new possessions.

Food and Drink

Located in the Budagyöngye Shopping Center's basement is the infamous **Szega Camembert Cheese Shop** (II. Szilágyi Erzsébet fasor 121, tel. 1/275-0839, www.budagyongye .com, Mon.–Sat. 10 A.M.–7 P.M.), well known throughout Budapest as having one of the city's

finest selections of cheese. Hordes of patrons come here regularly to sample the strange-looking offerings and pick up a chunk of whatever it is they've been craving. Bread, pate, and salads are on sale here, too, along with hard-to-find items such as Canadian maple syrup, rare Greek and Italian olive oils, and more.

Shopping Centers

Not far from the bustling hub of Moszkva tér is **Mammut** (II. Nagyajtai út 4/a, Széna tér, tel. 1/345-8000, www.mammut.hu, Mon.–Fri. 10 A.M.–9 P.M., Sat.–Sun. 10 A.M.–6 P.M.), Budapest's busiest shopping mall. There are loads of shops here including immediately recognizable names like Adidas, Marks & Spencer, and Estée Lauder, as well as smaller outlets geared towards the more discerning shopper. Should you need a break, there are plenty of cafes and restaurants on the upper floors and an outdoor fruit and vegetable market next door. Plenty of variety and regular sales keep Mammut at the top of every local's shopping list.

If you've done the rounds and still crave more Mammut, check out **Mammut II** (II. Lövöház utca 2-6, tel. 1/345-8020, www.mammut.hu, Mon.–Fri. 10 A.M.–9 P.M., Sat.–Sun. 10 A.M.–6 P.M.) located directly across the street. Here you'll find more of what you'd expect with a nice variety of shops that picks up where its counterpart leaves off.

Sports and Recreation

Hungarians like to stay active, if the number of cyclists and in-line skaters are anything to judge by. Traveling around the city by bike is one of the best ways to keep the pounds off, as well as discover neighborhood nooks and crannies you might otherwise never have learned of. For those feeling a little more adventurous, there are caves in the Buda Hills to be explored, and those who simply want to stay fit can head down to Margaret Island and make good use of the rubber track that stretches all around it.

BIKING

If you'd like to see Budapest by bike or simply want to learn more about it, make a beeline for **Yellow Zebra Bikes** (V. Sütő utca 2, The Belváros, tel. 1/266-8777, www.yellowzebra bikes.com, Nov.–Mar. daily 10 A.M.–6 P.M., Apr.–Oct. daily 8:30 A.M.–8 P.M., bike tour 5,000 Ft, bike rental 1,500 Ft for first 5 hours). Here, a friendly and knowledgeable staff will set you up with a bike rental or tour of all of the capital's major sights. Other tours are offered as well, including a walking tour, a wine tour, and a good old-fashioned pub crawl. There's an Internet center on the premises and free handy maps are also available. Being natives or long-term citizens, all of the staff here have an intimate understanding of the city and are more than happy to let you in on its many secrets and off-the-beaten-path sights. If there's anything you need to know about Budapest, this is the place to come to first.

Just down the street from the Great Synagogue opposite the hip Szoda bar are the very friendly and helpful folks at **Budapest Bike** (VII. Wesselényi utca 18, Erzsébetváros, tel. 30/944-5533, www.budapestbike.hu, daily 9 A.M.–10 P.M., bike tour 5,000 Ft, bike rental 2,000 Ft first 6 hours). Started up in 2005, they quickly carved out a place for themselves on the market thanks to entertaining and informative tours that continue to grow in popularity. Various trips through the city include the general Budapest tour, the Budapest lifestyle tour, Budapest by bridge, and the enchanting Sunset tour. There is also a fun-filled pub crawl led by natives who are determined to show visitors a good time. This is an excellent, affordable option for the budget traveler.

Bringóhintó (XIII. Margaret Island, Alfréd sétány 1, tel. 1/329-2746, www.bringohinto .hu, daily 8 A.M.–dusk, 1,000–4,000 Ft/hour) started up in 1991 and has been renting out odd-looking but fun vehicles ever since. Normal mountain and city bikes are available, as are two-seater tandem bicycles and four-person bike-car contraptions. This is a healthy, fun, and relatively easy way to cover all of Margaret Island, especially if you're traveling in a group or with family.

Another fun way to explore Margaret Island is to first visit **Sétacikli** (XIII. Margaret Island, Palatinus Strand, tel. 30/966-6453, www.setacikli.hu, daily 10 A.M.–6 P.M., 1,800 Ft/hour). Their pedal-operated cars are a big hit with kids but plenty of adults get into the spirit as well. Open year-round but only on weekends during the winter.

CAVING

Páivölgyi Cave (II. Szépvölgyi út 162, tel. 1/325-9505, Tues.–Sun. 10 A.M.–4 P.M., 700 Ft) is the prettiest and longest cave in the Buda Hills, stretching a whopping 11 miles under the city. Unfortunately, less than half a mile of it is open to the public, but visitors can still enjoy doing something a little more adventurous than the usual sightseeing while viewing hundreds of remarkable stalactites firsthand. Tours leave every hour and last roughly 50 minutes. The temperature in the caves dips down to about 46°F so wearing something warm is a good idea. Although there are ladders and stairs to help with your progress, the tour is not recommended for children, the elderly, or those with physical disabilities. To get to Pálvölgyi Cave, take the #65 bus from Kolosy tér in Óbuda.

Located not far away from Pálvölgyi Cave is the smaller but no less interesting **Szemlőhegyi Cave** (II. Pusztaszeri út 35, tel. 1/325-6001, Wed.–Fri. 9 A.M.–3 P.M., Sat.–Sun. 9 A.M.–4 P.M., 600 Ft), covered in unique mineral formations that alternately look like cauliflower or bunches of grapes. Visitors can also enjoy an informative exhibition regarding the caves of Budapest at the entrance hall. Tours run hourly and last approximately 45 minutes. Warm clothing is necessary. To get to Szemlőhegyi Cave, take the #29 bus from Kolosy tér in Óbuda.

FITNESS CLUBS

Considered by many to be the finest and most comprehensive fitness center in town, the excellent **Danubius Premier** (XIII. Margaret Island, tel. 1/889-4914, www.premier fitness.hu, daily 6:30 A.M.–9:30 P.M., day rate 5,700–7,200 Ft) does not disappoint. Located on peaceful Margaret Island, visitors will find pretty much any service or treatment they can think of. Yoga, tai-chi, aqua aerobics, and Pilates are a few of the more popular choices, and those interested in simple, straight-up weight and cardiovascular training will be very satisfied as well. The Danubius has plenty of top-of-the-line equipment available, along with more luxurious options like thermal baths, a whirlpool tub, and indoor and outdoor swimming pools. A full range of massages and medical services are on offer too, making it clear that when it comes time to take care of both mind and body, the Danubius should be at the top of your list.

Located within the Hotel Marriott is the **World Class Fitness Center Budapest** (V. Apáczai Csere János út 4-6, The Belváros, tel. 1/266-4290, www.worldclassfitness.net). Famous around the globe for having state-of-the-art equipment and a friendly, invigorating atmosphere, this Budapest chapter is certainly no different. Luxurious settings, a wide variety of programs and services (including aerobics, spinning, dance, yoga, Pilates, and top-of-the-line cardiovascular and weight training equipment), and a helpful English-speaking staff make it a treat to work out here.

ICE SKATING

City Park Ice Rink (XIV. Olof Pálme sétány 5, Városliget, tel. 1/364-0013) is Europe's largest and oldest open-air ice-skating rink. Built way back in the middle of the 19th century, the rink has brought plenty of smiles on children's faces and been the spark of many a romance as well. This is a wonderful place to mingle with locals and stay in shape, all with awe-inspiring Heroes' Square right next door. Skate rental is available and complete beginners can look to any number of teachers and helpers that are always available.

SKIING

With a panoramic view 1,565 feet above the city, it's little wonder that the gorgeous piece of green otherwise known as **Normafa** (XII. Buda Hills, www.normafa.hu) is one of the most popular destinations for Budapesters to escape to during the summer. Located high up in the Buda Hills, it's often overrun by hikers, families, and young lovers enjoying the more-than-idyllic surroundings. In the winter, the area is flooded with skiers, snowboarders, and sledders hoping that the snow will stay on the ground long enough for them to enjoy it. Those who decide to join in the fun should keep in mind that there is no ski lift or anything resembling it to bring you back up the hill for a second run. Should the time come for you to warm your bones or fill your belly, try a cup of mulled wine or a delicious snack at the pleasant **Normafa Ski House** (XII. Eötvös út 59, tel. 1/395-6508, daily 9 A.M.–5 P.M.).

SPECTATOR SPORTS

Soccer is by far the country's most popular sport and if you're a fan as well, you'll have no shortage of opportunities to root for the home team, be it league-dominating Ferencvarós FC, wildly popular Ujpest Football Club, or perennial underdogs MTK Budapest. Tickets are very cheap in relation to Western standards and the enthusiastic crowds more than infectious. A lazy day at the track is also possible March–November at aging, but nevertheless enjoyable, Kincsem Park.

Soccer

Hungary's most successful football club, Ferencvarós FC plays at **Ülloi út Stadium** (IX. Üllői út 129, Ferencvarós, tel. 1/215-6025, www.ftc.hu). Known affectionately as either Fradi or FTC, they have won the Hungarian football league 28 times and the cup 20 times. Aside from their successes, the team is also known for having the most vocal and violent fans, many of whom are skinheads and those linked to the extreme political right. Currently, the club is suffering from major financial problems and speculation has it they will either be sold to or co-owned with British investors.

Hidegkuti Nándor Stadium (XIII. Salgótarjáni út 12-14, Józsefváros, tel. 1/333-8368, www.mtkhungaria.hu, tickets 500–1,800 Ft) is a relatively small stadium that officially opened in 1912. Home to MTK Budapest, its 12,700 seats are rarely filled to capacity, but those who do drop by to support the team create more of a family atmosphere than the violent, hooliganesque environment commonly associated with bigger clubs. If a laid-back day watching soccer with old fans is your thing, then order up your very affordable tickets now.

Szusza Ferenc Stadium (IV. Megyeri út 13, Újpest, tel. 1/231-0088, www.ujpestfc .hu) is home to Ujpest Football Club, one of the more popular soccer teams in the country. Originally opened in 1922, the stadium went through extensive renovations in 2000–2001 and now stands as one of the more modern sports facilities in the region. Bathed in purple and white (the team's colors), this has

BUDAPEST WOLVES

When one thinks of Hungary, football isn't exactly the first thing that springs to mind, but the Budapest Wolves, founded in 2004, would like to change all that. Sponsored by Sport 1 television and run by Zsolt Damosy, who is also the promoter of world boxing champion Zsolt Erdei, the Wolves' rough-and-tumble style and never-say-die on-field attitude has done plenty to introduce the sport to Hungarians and win over a few fans in the process. Currently a force to be reckoned with in the Southeastern European League of American Football (SELAF), they pull in anywhere from 2,000-4,000 fans per game – not bad considering last year's Eurobowl final drew just over 4,000 spectators. The Wolves have high hopes and are constantly on the lookout for ways to improve their organization. Qualified and experienced coaches and players for any of their three teams (Wolves, Wolves 2 Rookies, and under 17 Wolves Juniors) are always a necessity, so if you think you have what it takes, perhaps you can become a star athlete this side of the pond. For more information on the Budapest Wolves and European football in general, have a look at www.wolves.hu, www.selaf .com, and www.eurobowl.com.

been the setting of many a lively game; fans of the sport may very well want to make the trek out here to join in the fervor. Note that green is the color of bitter rivals Ferencváros and wearing it will most likely land you in unwanted hot water.

Horse Racing

Originally founded as a gallop track back in 1925, **Kincsem Park** (X. Albertirsai út 2-4, Kőbánya, tel. 1/433-0520, www.kincsempark .com) was then known as one of the more beautiful courses in Europe. Named after a Hungarian wonder horse who won all 54 of her races, the track was redone in 2005 and now allows for trotting races as well. The grandstand was expanded to seat 3,500 visitors and there is also a restaurant with a panoramic view of the proceedings on the top floor. Trotting races are held year-round and are usually run on Wednesdays and Saturdays. Gallop races run March–November every Sunday.

Accommodations

The hotel scene in Budapest is a wide and varied one, ranging from grand, historical landmarks like the Hotel Gellért to more unsophisticated, functionalist buildings found in the outer districts. You'll find pricey, internationally recognized four- and five-star chain hotels in the Belváros and affordable, cozy pensions (guesthouses) farther away in the Buda Hills. Budapest's public transportation system is excellent, making it easy to reach the center and all major sights no matter where you choose to stay. If coming in the summer, reserving well in advance is very much recommended and you'll save a bundle if you do it online. Also, those wanting a double bed should make sure to clearly specify as a double room here usually means twin beds.

THE BELVÁROS
Under 10,000 Ft
Red Bus Hostel (V. Semmelweis utca 14, tel. 1/266-0136, www.redbusbudapest.hu, 9,500 Ft d) is a centrally located, reputable hostel that stands a cut above most others in Budapest. Single, double, and triple bedrooms are offered as are four-, six-, and eight-bed dormitories, all of which are kept tidy on a regular basis. The usual services are available, including laundry, Internet access, and full kitchen facilities. The strict policy against stag parties and loud, drunken behavior ensures guests the restful sleep they need during their stay.

20,000–30,000 Ft
If it's location you're looking for, you cannot do better than the **City Hotel Pilvax** (V. Pilvax köz 1-3, tel. 1/266-7660, www.taverna.hu, 25,500 Ft d). Tucked away on a side street mere minutes from the Danube and busy Váci Street,

its accessibility to all the major sights and shops ensure you never have to step foot onto public transportation. The 32 simply furnished rooms are neat and functional and, while they admittedly lack the charm of other hotels, are good enough for those uninterested in frills and inflated rates. This is an excellent choice for budget travelers who care more about location than they do bells and whistles.

Originally opened in 1873, the **Hotel Erzsébet** (V. Károlyi Mihály utca 11-15, tel. 1/889-3700, www.danubiushotels.com/erzsebet, 26,500 Ft d) took its name from Queen Elizabeth, wife of Emperor Francis Joseph who ruled the Austro-Hungarian Empire at the time. Located a few minutes stroll away from Váci Street, the Danube embankment, and as many shops, sights, restaurants, and bars you can handle, guests will most likely never have to see the inside of a bus or subway. Rooms were refurbished in 2002 and fitted with air-conditioning, satellite and pay TV, telephone, Internet access, and sound-proof windows. If you're looking for something simple and central that won't break the bank, you just found it.

Located in bustling downtown Pest, the **City Hotel Mátyás** (V. Március 15 tér 7-8, tel. 20/460-2134, www.ohb.hu/matyas, 28,000 Ft d) is close to all the sights, restaurants, shops, and bars you could hope for. A bar, brasserie, 24-hour reception, and helpful tour desk are available to guests, as are decent service, clean, affordable rooms, and the hotel's famous Matthias Cellar Restaurant. This is an excellent choice for those who only have a handful of days in the capital and want to maximize their time without paying an arm and a leg for location.

30,000-40,000 Ft

Formerly the Hotel Taverna, the **Mercure Budapest City Center** (V. Váci utca 20, tel. 1/485-3100, www.mercure.com, 40,000 Ft d) continues on in the same tradition, offering high-class service and comfort to all its guests. Located on bustling Váci Street near the Gerbeaud Cafe and Danube Embankment, its 227 rooms and four exclusive suites are well-sized, tastefully designed, and fully equipped. Its widely acclaimed Gambrinus restaurant serves excellent international and Hungarian cuisine and its Zsolnay cafe offers over 100 varieties of cake. With a top-notch buffet breakfast and a location that can't be beat, it's little wonder guests always seem to leave the premises with a huge smile.

◖ **Starlight Suiten** (V. Mérleg utca 6, tel. 1/484-3700, www.starlighthotels.com, 40,000 Ft d) may be overshadowed by the large, internationally renowned hotel chains that surround it, but location is location and this place has got it at a fraction of the price. All the rooms are suites and come with living room, bedroom, bathroom, and living and working areas, as well as two phones, two TVs, a mini bar, and microwave. In addition, the hotel also has a sauna, fitness center, and Turkish bath. A location mere minutes from Váci Street, the Chain Bridge, a mini-market, and the subway makes this hotel an excellent choice for travelers of all budgets.

Over 50,000 Ft

Kempinski Hotel Corvinus Budapest (V. Erzsébet tér 7-8, tel. 1/429-3777, www .kempinski-budapest.com, 65,000–113,000 Ft d) is quite often the hotel of choice for celebrities and international businessmen. Overlooking Elizabeth Park, its 335 rooms, 29 suites, and two presidential suites all come with floor heating in the bathroom, built-in safes, and high-tech infotainment systems. Ten meeting rooms, as well as a fully equipped business center satisfy every workaholic's needs, while the ballroom is usually the scene of quite a few lavish parties. The Kempinski Spa is also a favorite among guests who take full advantage of the sauna, solarium, steam bath, pool, gym, and massage treatments.

Sofitel Budapest (V. Roosevelt tér 2, tel. 1/266-1234, www.sofitel-budapest.com, 69,000–78,000 Ft d) went through extensive renovations in 2005 with a modern French flair in mind. It boasts 351 rooms, the majority of which offer fantastic views of both the Chain Bridge and Buda Palace. There are also 52 luxury and two presidential suites that radiate the ultimate in contemporary comfort. Facilities include a well-equipped fitness center, a ballroom, 16 state-of-the-art multi-functional rooms, and an impressive high-tech boardroom for the plethora of conferences that find their way here. Its new restaurant, the Paris-Budapest Café, has won raves for its French, Mediterranean, and Hungarian cuisines.

In the heart of the city lies **Le Meridien Budapest** (V. Erzsébet tér 9-10, tel. 1/429-5500, www.lemeridien.com, 100,000 Ft d), proud member of the Leading Hotels of the World and the sole hotel in Hungary accredited with the Five Star Diamond Award. Its 218 rooms and 26 suites are fully equipped with Wi-Fi, high-speed Internet access, flat-screen TVs, and, of course, top-notch service. There's a health club, ballroom, and eight boardrooms as well, making this a favorite with businesspeople, diplomats, and high rollers. Its excellent French restaurant, Le Bourbon, has won several awards and remains one of the finer dining experiences in the capital.

LIPÓTVÁROS
Under 10,000 Ft

The **Art Guest House** (V. Podmaniczky utca 19, tel. 1/302-3739, artguests@citromail.hu, 7,100 Ft d) is a mere two-minute walk from Nyugati train station, making it a popular choice with weary backpackers. Close to restaurants, shops, bars, and cafes, it's also within walking distance of all the major sites. Private rooms are available as are four- and seven-bed dorms and most find the absence of bunk beds a major plus. There's a kitchen available for those interested in cooking up their own grub and the free Internet terminal allows you

BUDAPEST

to keep up on your emails. Many of you will also be happy to know that this is a smoke-free hostel.

30,000-40,000 Ft

The **NH Budapest** (XIII. Vígszínház utca 3, tel. 1/814-0000, www.nh-hotels.com, 33,000 Ft d) is situated behind the Vígszínházis, Budapest's oldest theater. This elegant hotel is home to 160 air-conditioned and soundproofed rooms, all of which are equipped with a workspace that features Wi-Fi, ISDN, and LAN, as well as the usual amenities. Guests are invited to use the fitness room and sauna free of charge and unwind in the chilled out Afterwork Bar with a vintage wine and the chef's special tapas. The WestEnd City Center, Nyugati train station, and the Danube River are all close by, as are countless means of public transportation, making it easy to get to wherever you need to be.

TERÉZVÁROS AND ERZSÉBETVÁROS
Under 10,000 Ft

Marco Polo Hostel (VII. Nyár utca 6, tel. 1/413-2555, www.marcopolohostel.hu, 8,700 Ft d) is a popular choice amongst both individual travelers and larger groups who appreciate the clean rooms and beds, as well as there being no curfew or lockout. There are double and quad rooms with telephone and TV, along with 12-bed dormitories with adjoining bathrooms and showers. Its proximity to sights and numerous dining, shopping, and nightlife options make choosing the Marco Polo a no-brainer.

The **Yellow Submarine Youth Hostel** (VI. Podmaniczky utca 27, tel. 1/331-9896, www .yellowsubmarinehostel.com, 9,600 Ft d) seems to be very much a hit-or-miss kind of place. While some appreciate the extremely laid-back, almost aloof way things are run, others find it not only inconvenient, but unacceptable as well. Most reports agree that the place could be cleaner and that the owner could be nicer. The location is a couple minutes' walk from Nyugati train station and a few minutes more from just about everything else worth seeing. Tours

are organized through the hostel, laundry services are available, and the common room has cable TV, Internet, and a swapping library. If you're in a pinch or feel kind of lucky, give the Yellow Submarine a try.

10,000-20,000 Ft

Located in busy Blaha Lujza tér, the ☾ **Agape Guesthouse** (VII. Erzsébet körút 2, doorbell 11, tel. 1/317-4833, www.agapeguesthouse .hu, 12,600 Ft d) is a simple subway stop from Keleti Station and a 15–20 minute walk to Váci Street, the Basilica, and Liszt Ferenc tér. The tiny guesthouse offers clean rooms equipped with TV and fridge and furnished with old-school Communist furniture. There are also two apartments available with small kitchens should you want a home away from home. Excellent value for the location.

Located in the heart of Budapest's theater district, the **Medosz Hotel** (VI. Jókai tér 9, tel. 1/374-3000, www.medoszhotel.hu, 17,600 Ft d) is an excellent choice for no-frills travelers looking to remain close to the action without paying an arm and a leg. All the rooms are furnished cheaply with small simple beds, old yet clean bathrooms, and the occasional phone. There is no air-conditioning and you shouldn't expect anything but an inexpensive place to lay your head at the end of the day. Close to the Opera, Liszt Ferenc tér, and pretty much anything worth seeing, this is an obvious choice for those who don't mind roughing it a little.

20,000-30,000 Ft

Hotel Benczúr (VI. Benczúr utca 35, tel. 1/479-5650, www.hotelbenczur.hu, 20,220–27,800 Ft d) is located in the heart of the city's diplomatic region and a scant two minutes' walk from Heroes' Square. Its 153 simple but clean and comfortable rooms are fitted out with all the usual amenities and the hotel's restaurant and cafe are fine places to relax and enjoy some contemporary local cuisine. There's also a souvenir shop and a garden for those who like their peace and quiet outdoors.

Baross Hotel (VII. Baross tér 15, tel. 1/461-3010, www.barosshotel.hu, 24,200 Ft

d) is a three-star hotel known for being of decent value for the money. With its location near Keleti Station and plenty of public transportation, guests have no problem reaching any and all of Budapest's sights. All 40 rooms and five suites are well maintained and offer air-conditioning, telephone, satellite TV, and private safe. An excellent all-you-can-eat buffet is included in the price and the helpful staff will do its best to make your stay a memorable one. Simple and unpretentious, this is a good choice for those who like to keep costs down without having to sacrifice basic comforts.

Just off Andrássy Avenue is the **C Club Hotel Ambra** (VII. Kisdiófa utca 13, tel. 1/321-1533, www.hotelambra.hu, 28,000 Ft d), a casual yet professional apartment-hotel. Its 21 rooms are all decked out with striking decor done by local artists, as well as the usual amenities (such as kitchen, satellite TV, minibar, and safe). Close to the Opera House, Basilica, and Liszt Ferenc tér, this hotel is an excellent choice for those wanting to stay close to the action.

The **Cotton House** (VI. Jókai utca 26, tel. 1/354-0886, www.cotton-house-hotel -budapest.com, 28,000 Ft d) is a charming hotel with a Jazz Age theme. Each of its 23 rooms is named after a famous celebrity, such as Louis Armstrong, Frank Sinatra, Ginger Rogers, and Marilyn Monroe. The hotel is spotlessly clean and presided over by extremely helpful staff. Guests can take advantage of an excellent restaurant in the basement that features an after-dinner live show complete with cigars and cabaret-style entertainment. Fun, affordable, and within 10–15 minutes' walking distance of the main sights, this hotel is a smart choice for those who like a little distance between themselves and the center of town.

30,000–40,000 Ft

The **Domina Inn Fiesta** (VI. Király Utca 20, tel. 1/328-3000, www.dominahotels.com, 38,000 Ft d) boasts an amazing downtown location as well as a reputation for being one of Budapest's best value three-star hotels. All

112 tastefully decorated rooms have air-conditioning and en-suite facilities, as well as TV, minibar, telephone, and modem jack. Guests have access to the hotel's excellent fitness center and sauna. Being well within walking distance of major sights like Parliament, Váci utca, the Chain Bridge, and the Opera House makes this hotel a sound choice for all travelers.

Over 50,000 Ft

Andrássy Hotel (VI. Andrássy út 111, tel. 1/462-2100, www.andrassyhotel.com, 51,000–68,000 Ft d) is a five-star boutique hotel located within walking distance of the Széchenyi Thermal Baths, Museum of Fine Arts, the Zoo, and Gundel Restaurant, to name but a few. Built in a Bauhaus style in 1937, its 62 guest rooms and seven suites were completely renovated in 2001 and now offer the highest in quality and comfort, including all the modern amenities you can imagine. As an added bonus, fans of gourmet dining will be pleased to know that the award-winning Baraka restaurant is now part of the hotel.

Voted the best five-star hotel in Hungary in 2003 and 2004, the **C Corinthia Grand Hotel Royal** (VII. Erzsébet körút 43-49, tel. 1/479-4000, www.corinthia.hu, 55,000–85,000 Ft d) is a hard act to beat. Opulently designed and offering guests an unparalleled level of luxury, its 414 rooms plus fully equipped one two-, and three-bedroom apartments have been home to politicians, artists, and upper-stratosphere businessmen alike. Boasting the country's largest state-of-the art Conference and Exhibition Center, as well as the incredibly beautiful Royal Spa, the hotel has firmly established itself as one of Hungary's finest accommodations.

K+K Hotel Opera (VI. Révay utca 24, tel. 1/269-0222, www.kkhotels.com, 56,000–60,000 Ft) is one of a distinguished group of privately owned boutique hotels found all over Europe. Its location next to the Opera House is hard to beat and the hotel's bright, stylish interiors make guests feel immediately at home. Known throughout the continent for its excellent service, the hotel offers 206 tastefully furnished rooms fitted out with state-of-the-art amenities that include air-conditioning, high-speed Internet, and international TV.

FERENCVÁROS AND JÓZSEFVÁROS
20,000-30,000 Ft

Centrally located, the **Mercure Hotel Budapest Nemzeti** (VIII. József körút 4, tel. 1/477-2000, www.mercure.com, 21,500–28,000 Ft d) happens to sit smack dab in the center of Blaha Lujza tér, one of the city's busiest and noisiest squares. Out of the 76 air-conditioned rooms available, ask for one that faces the courtyard or else you will be doomed to desperately trying to ignore the non-stop traffic passing below your window. Spacious, tasteful, and sporting a helpful staff, the hotel is a sound choice for the discriminating traveler and its convenient proximity to the city's most important sights, shops, and nightlife cannot be overlooked.

Right in the thick of hip and happening Ráday Street, **Ibis Budapest Centrum** (IX. Ráday utca 6, tel. 1/456-4100, www.ibishotel .com, 24,000 Ft d) is both a dependable and affordable option in the center of town. Its 126 rooms are comfortable and well maintained, as is the hotel in general, including its bar and garden with terrace. Within walking distance of all the major sights and close to major hubs of public transportation, this is one hotel all visitors to Budapest should consider.

Located on a quiet street close to Kálvin Square, **Kálvin Ház** (IX. Gönczy pál utca 6, tel. 1/216-4365, www.kalvinhouse.hu, 24,000 Ft d) is an exceptionally friendly, warm, and professionally run hotel. Thirty large rooms decorated with tasteful turn-of-the-20th-century furniture are available, all of which have been equipped with newly renovated bathrooms, telephone, and satellite TV. Within easy walking distance of the Liberty Bridge, Váci Street, the National Museum, and Central Market Hall, the Kalvin House is a great, affordable choice for travelers seeking service and comfort with a personal touch.

30,000-40,000 Ft

First opened in 1911, the Art Nouveau building that now houses the 🌙 **Novotel Centrum** (VIII. Rákóczi út 43-45, tel. 1/477-5300, www .novotel-bud-centrum.hu, 40,000 Ft d) has been recently renovated in order to make the surroundings more comfortable and pleasant for guests. Spacious, colorful, and air-conditioned rooms come with personal safe, telephone, satellite TV, and Internet access. The helpful staff is more than willing to help you arrange trips and tours around town and those guests who prefer to stay close to home can enjoy various services including sauna, whirlpool tub, fitness room, and massage. Simply put, this is a four-star hotel that lives up to its rating.

VÁRHEGY AND CENTRAL BUDA
20,000-30,000 Ft

The **Hotel Charles** (I. Hegyalja út 23, tel. 1/212-9169, www.charleshotel.hu, 20,000–22,500 Ft d) may not be the prettiest hotel you've ever seen, but it definitely gets the job done. Offering fully furnished apartments that can fit 1–4 people, guests have the option of choosing the Standard or Executive Studio, or the bigger Standard and Executive Apartments. The bus stop directly in front of the hotel allows guests to reach all parts of the city with relative ease and the 24-hour multilingual reception office can help you plan day trips or simply answer whatever questions you might have. Low on frills but high on service, this hotel is a sensible choice for bargain hunters.

The 🌙 **Hotel Astra** (I. Vám utca 6, tel. 1/214-1906, www.hotelastra.hu, 25,000 Ft d) is a well-kept secret in Buda's picturesque Watertown neighborhood. Housed in a completely reconstructed 300-year-old building, the hotel oozes history and charm, helped in no small part by the tasteful and elegant decorations found throughout the premises. Clean, spacious, well-furnished rooms await with satellite TV, telephone, and minibar, and the ever-friendly staff goes out of its way to ensure your stay is a comfortable one. Travelers looking for a homey environment while being a mere five minutes away from the center of town should start thinking of booking a room now.

The **Carlton Hotel Budapest** (I. Apor Péter utca 3, tel. 1/224-0999, www.carltonhotel.hu, 28,000 Ft d) is conveniently located at the foot of Fisherman's Bastion and the Castle District, making sightseeing on both the Buda and Pest sides as easy as pie. The hotel offers guests 95 rooms complete with air-conditioning, cable TV, ISDN, minibar, and a whole bunch more. Helpful staff and spotlessly clean surroundings are two more reasons to enjoy your stay at a hotel that is widely agreed to be great value for the money.

30,000-40,000 Ft

The **Hotel Victoria Budapest** (I. Bem rakpart 11, tel. 1/457-8080, www.victoria.hu, 31,000 Ft d) is situated on the Buda embankment allowing all of its 27 air-conditioned rooms to enjoy spectacular panoramic views of the city, including two that have their own balcony. Decked out with the usual amenities like satellite TV, high-speed Internet, telephone, and personal safe, the rooms and hotel in general are known for being well maintained and spotlessly clean. Buffet-style breakfast, laundry services, free sauna, and professional service are just a few more reasons to consider a stay in this wonderful hotel.

Over 50,000 Ft

On the Danube embankment sitting opposite the magnificent Parliament building is the trendy and colorful **(Art'otel Budapest** (I. Bem rakpart 16-19, tel. 1/487-9487, www.artotel.de, 55,000 Ft d). Comprised of a modern seven-story building and four 18th-century Baroque Buda townhouses, guests can choose from being enveloped in a modern or turn-of-the-20th-century atmosphere. Its 164 rooms contain state-of-the-art amenities, including IDD telephones, ISDN lines, satellite TV, and air-conditioning. Renowned American artist Donald Sultan created over 600 works of art for the hotel, which are displayed in all guest rooms as well as common areas. The hotel also boasts an art gallery, art

shop, sauna, fitness room, hair stylist, beauty parlor, and valet parking. Its balancing of art and modernity, along with its proximity to the Castle District and the Chain Bridge leading to Pest, make this a very popular choice among travelers who enjoy and can afford the finer things in life.

GELLÉRT HEGY AND THE TABÁN 10,000-20,000 Ft

Built in 1854 by the Habsburgs following the suppression of both the 1848–1849 Hungarian revolution and War of Independence, the **(Hotel Citadella** (XI. Citadella sétány, tel. 1/466-5794, www.citadella.hu, 16,500 Ft d) is steeped in history, to say the least. Battle-scarred and bullet-ridden, it continues to stand tall on Gellért Hill, offering guests the finest views of the entire city bar none. Its five large dormitories are basic but passable, as are the 15 quad bedrooms and handful of single and double rooms. Location-wise, guests are a short walk away from the statue of St. Gellért and the Liberation Monument, not to mention all the major sights of the Castle District. While certainly not fancy, the Citadella is easily one of the city's better budget accommodations.

The cylindrical, B-movie-looking **Hotel Budapest** (II. Szilágyi Erzsébet fasor 47, tel. 1/889-4200, www.danubiushotels.com/budapest, 15,500–21,500 Ft d) might be considered by many to be a blight on the landscape, but it also offers travelers an excellent choice in relatively cheap accommodations. All 289 clean, no-frills rooms come with a full wall of windows offering great views of either the Danube or Buda Hills, as well as the usual amenities like satellite TV, private bath, and telephone. The Restaurant Budapest serves international and Hungarian dishes, while the souvenir shop, newsstand, and business center take care of most travelers' immediate needs. Its proximity to Moskva tér and the Cog Wheel Railway means easy access to Pest and the Buda Hills. A smart choice for those needing to keep costs down.

BUDAPEST

30,000-40,000 Ft

Built just after World War I, the **[** **Danubius Hotel Gellért** (XI. Szent Gellért tér 1, tel. 1/889-5500, www.danubiushotels.com/gellert, 33,000–53,000 Ft d) remains one of Budapest's most well-known and charming hotels. Undergoing steady renovations since 2000, its 234 rooms vary greatly in size and quality depending on whether they've been redone or not. For those wanting to play it safe, make sure to ask for a refurbished room. The hotel also offers a wide range of health treatments and services including indoor and outdoor swimming pools, whirlpool tub, wave bath, steam room, manicure, pedicure, and even Thai massage. Then, of course, there are the world-famous Gellért baths, which are free to hotel guests. The service and food here remain as good as ever and the hotel's decaying Art Nouveau elegance continues to draw them in.

ÓBUDA AND MARGIT SZIGET
Over 50,000 Ft

Situated on the Danube bank, the **Corinthia Aquincum Hotel** (III. Árpád fejedelem útja 94, tel. 1/436-4100, www.corinthia.hu, 58,000 Ft) is a highly reputable hotel whose focus is on balancing business with pleasure. The exclusive Executive Club offers those in town on business the most modern of facilities for meetings, functions, and presentations, while the natural thermal spa encourages guests to indulge in the large number of wellness and beauty treatments available. Keeping with the wellness theme, the hotel's Apicius restaurant maintains a delicious menu that revolves around health-conscious cuisine.

THE BUDA HILLS
10,000-20,000 Ft

High up in the Buda Hills is the **Budai** (XII. Rácz Aladár utca 45-47, tel. 1/249-0208, www.hotelbudai.hu, 13,900 Ft d). Clean, affordable, and a mere 10–15-minute bus ride from the center, this hotel is perfect for those on a tight budget who prefer calm surroundings to bustling city squares. Rooms are basic but well maintained and come with minibar, satellite TV, and telephone. For the best view of the hills, ask for a room on the top floor and make sure to enjoy a meal or coffee on the hotel restaurant's terrace.

[**Hotel Molnár** (XII. Fodor utca 143, tel. 1/395-1872, www.hotel-molnar.hu, 13,800–19,000 Ft d) is a pleasant, family-owned and -run hotel in the lush greenbelt of Buda. All rooms are spacious and furnished with satellite TV, minibar, and telephone, and offer attractive views over either the city or the Buda Hills. Occasional goulash and grill parties are held in the hotel's garden, the after-effects of which can be burned off in the Scandinavian sauna and fitness room. Its location three miles outside the city center makes this a perfect choice for travelers who appreciate the warm, personal atmosphere of an intimate, out-of-the-way hotel, as opposed to the rash of formulaic chain hotels occupying the city center.

20,000-30,000 Ft

Gizella Panzió (XII. Arató utca 42/b, tel. 1/249-2281, www.gizellapanzio.hu, 20,000 Ft d) is a friendly, charming guesthouse built into the side of a hill. It has several terraced gardens that lead to a swimming pool and its quaint, artfully decorated rooms add to the overall cozy atmosphere. The heart of the city is a brief 10 minutes away via public transportation or taxi and a sightseeing car and driver can be arranged on request. The Gizella Panzió also rents apartments in the center of Pest.

Helios Hotel & Pension (XII. Lidérc utca 5/a, tel. 1/246-4658, www.heliospanzio.hu, 22,000–28,700 Ft d) is a warm and friendly family-run guesthouse located in the Buda Hills. All rooms are comfortably furnished and most come with a balcony overlooking the city. A direct bus whisks guests to the city center in 15 minutes and the 24-hour reception is more than happy to answer questions and arrange any number of sightseeing trips or cultural activities. Charming, affordable, and the perfect solution to those who like a little peace and quiet with their holiday.

Food

Hungarians love to eat, which might explain the huge number of restaurants found throughout the city. Magyar cuisine continues to dominate the landscape, with establishments ranging from the gourmet to the greasy spoon. Traditional dishes like goulash, fish soup, or wild game should be tried at least once and snacks like *lángos*—a deep-fried flatbread made from potato-based dough—will keep you going during your long walks about town. Ethnic restaurants continue to crop up everywhere, making it easy to find anything from Indian to Greek, Asian to South American, regardless of what district you're in. Prices are reasonable by Western standards and the service, while spotty, continues to improve with most wait-staff being able to speak at least some English, particularly in the downtown core.

THE BELVÁROS
Asian
Just off Vörösmarty tér, next door to the British Embassy, is **Sushi An** (V. Harmincad utca 4, tel. 1/317-4239, daily noon–10 P.M., mains 800–3,400 Ft). Simple and traditional, it offers moderately priced sushi and sashimi prepared right before your very eyes. It's rather small and odds are you may not find a seat so if you're in a rush or just don't feel like waiting around, you'll be happy to know that you can order to go.

Cafes
At the north side of Vörösmartytér is the one and only 🅒 **Café Gerbeaud** (Vörösmarty tér, 7-8, tel. 1/429-9000, www.gerbeaud.hu, daily noon–11 P.M., 3,500–6,900 Ft), a classic Budapest coffee house if there ever was one. Established in 1858, it was bought in 1884 by Swiss confectioner Emile Gerbeaud, whose homemade desserts quickly became the talk of the town and remain unbeatable to this very day. Its elegant, ornately designed salons are furnished with chandeliers, marble tables, and gilded ceilings, making it the perfect place

to read a newspaper, have a coffee, or simply imagine you're reliving the 19th century. While plenty of outdoor seating is made available during the summer months, it's almost always a challenge to find a vacant table. Do yourself a favor, however, and don't give up as this is one of those places where you should definitely believe the hype.

Laid-back, filled with ambience, and just plain gorgeous, **Centrál Kávéház** (V. Károlyi Mihály utca 9, tel. 1/266-2110, www .centralkavehaz.hu, daily 7 A.M.–midnight, mains 2,200–3,500 Ft) was founded back when Budapest was still an imperial city and it shows. A perfect example of a "Grande Café," its attentive, bow-tied waiters serve you with a smile and are very happy to help with the menu. Choice selections include the Wiener schnitzel, mixed grill plate, and the marinated fillet of salmon in cream sauce. Wash it all down with one of the better espressos to be found in the area or with a fine Hungarian wine.

Continental
Bistro Jardin (Kempinski Hotel Corvinus Budapest, V. Erzsébet tér 7-8, tel. 1/429-3990, www.kempinksy-budapest.com, daily noon–11:30 P.M., buffet 6,950–7,950 Ft) may be a little pricey, but it's worth every forint. Whether you go for the business buffet offered on weekdays, the seafood buffet on Friday nights, or the award-winning brunch they lay out every Sunday, you are guaranteed a memorable culinary experience. If buffet isn't your thing, wait till the evening and try some of the Hungarian specialties à la carte or ask for the Taste of Hungary menu. Over 100 local wines are available as well, some of them dating all the way back to the 1950s.

Képiro (V. Képiro utca 3, tel. 1/266-0430, www.kepirorestaurant.com, daily noon–3 P.M., 6–11 P.M., mains 2,200–4,500 Ft) is a slick, understated, and elegant restaurant that has built up a solid reputation for offering the finest in contemporary Hungarian and Continental

GIMME THE GOULASH

Popular among herdsmen in the 18th century, Hungary's most popular dish became a staple of Hungarian cuisine in the late 19th century when the country deemed it necessary to establish its national identity and independence from the ruling Habsburgs. For those wondering if the term *gulyás* actually means anything, it does: herdsman.

Every grandmother in the country has her own "authentic" recipe, but *gulyás* is typically a beef dish cooked with onions, paprika, tomatoes, and green pepper. It is neither soup nor stew, lurking, rather, somewhere in between. Below is a typical recipe.

Hungarian Goulash (for four people)

600 g (1.3 lb.) beef sheen or shoulder, or any tender part of the beef cut into 2x2 cm (0.8 in. per side) cubes
2 tbsp. oil or lard
2 medium onions, chopped
2 cloves of garlic
1-2 carrots, diced
1 parsnip, diced
1-2 celery leaves
2 medium tomatoes, peeled and chopped, or 1 tbsp. tomato paste
2 green peppers
2-3 medium potatoes, sliced
1 tbsp. Hungarian paprika powder
1 tsp. ground caraway seed
1 bay leaf
Ground black pepper and salt according to taste
Water

Heat oil or lard in a pot and stir in chopped onions until they turn golden brown.

Sprinkle onions with paprika powder; continue stirring to prevent paprika from burning.

Add beef cubes and sauté until they turn white and get a bit of brownish color as well.

Let beef cubes simmer. Add garlic, ground caraway seed, salt, ground black pepper, and the bay leaf. Then pour enough water to fill the pot and let it simmer on low heat for a while.

When the meat is half-cooked (approximately 1.5 hours), add the diced carrots, parsnip, potatoes, celery leaf, and more salt if necessary. You'll probably have to add some more (2-3 cups) water, too.

When the vegetables and meat are almost done, add the tomato cubes and sliced green peppers. Cook on low heat for a few more minutes and keep pot uncovered if you'd like a thicker consistency.

Enjoy!

cuisine at affordable prices. Standout choices include the phenomenal goose liver and exceptional seafood soufflé. The rabbit and trout are also highly recommended, along with excellent French cheeses and snails. Special business lunches are available from noon–3 P.M., allowing those with tightened belts to relax them a little and join in the culinary fun.

Hungarian

Cyrano Restaurant (V. Kristóf tér 7-8, tel. 1/226-3096, daily 11 A.M.–5 P.M., 6:30 P.M.–midnight, mains 2,500–5,600 Ft) is a slick establishment just off Váci Street that focuses on contemporary Hungarian cuisine. Standards such as goose liver and wild duck breast

are expertly prepared and the wide array of pasta dishes delights diners from all over the world. The cocktails here are fantastic, as is the lively atmosphere and friendly staff. Definitely pricey, but well worth it.

If being made to feel like a king is something you enjoy, head for well-known **Kárpátia** (V. Ferenciek tere 7-8, tel. 1/317-3596, www .karpatia.hu, daily 11 A.M.–11 P.M., mains 3,900–6,900 Ft). Its rich interior reminds diners of the majesty that once enveloped the city, and traditional Hungarian dishes like Lake Balaton pike perch and saddle of venison are perennial winners. All the desserts are homemade—the Emperor's strudel in particular stands out. If too pricey for your budget, check out the less formal Brasserie, which is a favorite amongst locals.

Tiny and inexpensive, **Kisharang Étkezde** (V. Október 6 utca 17, tel. 1/269-3861, Mon.–Fri. 11 A.M.–8 P.M., Sat.–Sun. 11:30 A.M.–4:30 P.M., mains 690–950 Ft) is a family-run bistro that serves up hearty Hungarian staples like fish soup, stuffed cabbage, and *rakott,* a dish made from layers of potato and meat. Dishes change daily and can be ordered to go and in half-sized amounts should you not want to go overboard. An excellent choice for those in a hurry or on a budget.

Százéves (V. Pesti Barnabás utca 2, tel. 1/318-3608, www.taverna.hu/szazeves, daily 11 A.M.–midnight, mains 2,500–5,000 Ft) is the oldest restaurant in Budapest and its rustic yet elegant interior makes one feel like they've traveled back in time. Hungarian and international cuisine dominate the menu, with the grilled fillet of pike perch and sirloin steak roasted on stone being two of its highlights. At night, light gypsy music fills the air and the bottles of excellent Hungarian wine start to flow. This is a great place to enjoy your meal and leave the pressures of the modern world behind.

Indian

Kashmir (V. Arany János utca 13, tel. 1/354-1806, www.kashmiretterem.hu, daily noon–4 P.M., 6–11 P.M., mains 890–2,690 Ft) is a warm, unpretentious restaurant with an extensive menu of both classic and creative Indian cuisine. Beef, fish, and tandoori dishes make up the majority of the menu, with the lamb chops and tandoori mixed platter being particularly impressive. Vegetarians will be happy to know that there are plenty of tasty options for them, including the mushroom-based Shabnam curry and spicy vegetable vindaloo. For dessert, the mango mousse and unique chocolate samosa are a must. Those on a strict budget need not worry as there is a reasonably priced buffet-style business lunch available until 6 P.M.

Classic Indian food adapted to the modern palate is what awaits at **Kama Sutra** (V. Október 6 utca 19, tel. 1/373-0093, www.kamasutrarestaurant.hu, daily noon–11 P.M., mains 1,050–3,200 Ft). Its relaxed decor, inspired by traditional Indian motifs, makes for a perfect environment to sample such delicacies as shrimp in curry sauce, chicken tikka, and exquisite kadhi lamb. For those on the go, a takeout service is available, as is home delivery.

Focusing on contemporary Indian cuisine, **Salaam Bombay** (V. Mérleg utca 6, tel. 1/411-1252, www.salaambombay.hu, daily noon–3 P.M., 6–11 P.M., mains 1,500–3,200 Ft) has established itself firmly in Budapest's restaurant scene. Unusual dishes like the chicken momo or more common choices like vegetarian curries and tandoori shrimp are excellent, as is the service and atmosphere. Many argue that this is the city's finest Indian restaurant.

International

Located near the Basilica, **Mokka** (V. Sas utca 4, tel. 1/328-0081, www.mokkarestaurant.hu, daily noon–midnight, mains 2,480–5,680 Ft) remains at the cutting edge of international fusion cuisine with an irresistible menu that changes seasonally. There are plenty of tapas to choose from and house specialties such as Brazilian beefsteak, wild duck breast, and swordfish in passionfruit sauce should not be overlooked. There's an exceptional dessert menu as well, so make sure to leave some room.

Avocado Restaurant and Music Café (V. Nyáry Pál utca 9, tel. 1/266-3277, www.avocadomusiccafe.hu, daily 10:30 A.M.–midnight, cafe midnight–5 A.M., mains 1,300–5,790 Ft) couldn't have a more central spot, located as it is just off Váci utca. Hip, funky, and usually full, you'll oftentimes find diners preferring to gorge on their delicious meals rather than talk to those around them. The menu offers a wide selection of Hungarian, French, Italian, and Asian dishes, as well as plenty of Hungarian and international wines, drinks, and cocktails. The staff is attentive but not intrusive and there is an excellent music bar downstairs should you want to burn off all that rich food afterwards. While admittedly a little pricey by typical Hungarian standards, the quality of the food and experience far outweigh the bill.

Latin American

If you love steak, you most certainly cannot overlook **Pampas Steakhouse** (V. Vámház körút 6, tel. 1/411-1750, www.steak.hu, daily noon–2 A.M., mains 2,100–4,000 Ft). At this tastefully designed and reasonably priced Argentinean restaurant, you'll simply devour house specialties like the New Zealand lamb chops and grilled crayfish. There are plenty of Angus steaks to choose from as well, along with various grilled chicken and salmon dishes. Do leave room for the chocolate mousse though or you'll be very sorry.

Mediterranean

Trattoria Toscana (V. Belgrád rakpart 13, tel. 1/327-0045, www.toscana.hu, noon–midnight daily, mains 1,450–3,950 Ft) is a wonderful Italian restaurant that focuses on Tuscan cuisine. The tomato soup makes a particularly tasty starter and mains like the linguine with lobster, duck breast, or gigantic house fish mix are popular choices. There are plenty of pastas and pizzas to choose from and the traditional tiramisu and variety of ice creams are exceptional. If you're a coffee drinker, make sure to try the traditional espresso.

Entering **Taverna Dionysos** (V. Belgrád rakpart 16, tel. 1/318-1222, www.dionysos .hu, daily noon–midnight, mains 2,000–8,000 Ft) is a bit like entering Greece itself. Bathed in the traditional colors of blue and white, the taverna offers diners delicious, authentic cuisine including fish, seafood, lamb, and salads. Try the heavenly homemade noodles with chunks of lobster or the excellent grilled lamb, both of which will have you begging for more. The atmosphere is infectious here so don't be surprised if people start dancing suddenly. Odds are you'll soon join them. Reservations recommended.

Taverna Pireus Rembetiko (V. Fővám tér 2-3, tel. 1/266-0292, www.pireus.hu, Mon.–Fri. noon–midnight, Sat.–Sun. noon–1 A.M., mains 1,890–4,290 Ft) is located opposite the Great Market Hall, making it a popular choice amongst tourists and daytime shoppers. The Greek mixed platter with stuffed vine leaves, cheese balls, tzatziki, and meatballs is an excellent starter, as is the calamari and spinach pie. Can't-miss mains include the wide variety of grilled dishes available, as well as Jorgos steak and the beef stew in red wine sauce known as *stifado*. A fine place for lunch before hitting Váci Street.

Seafood

Seafood fans will want to waste no time visiting **Óceán Bar & Grill** (V. Petőfi tér 3, tel. 1/266-1826, www.oceanbargrill.hu, daily noon–midnight, mains 2,390–7,000 Ft). Tuscan chef Giuseppe Mosti's emphasis on the freshest of ingredients makes starters like the king crab and shiitake mushrooms, along with the Cote D'Azur bouillabaisse, outstanding options. A wide range of mains will satisfy even the most finicky of palates with the sea bass roulade being of particular note. There's also an adjacent delicatessen that sells and delivers plenty of fresh fish, seafood, lobster, and specialty foods from around the world.

LIPÓTVÁROS
American

Henry J. Bean's Bar & Grill (V. Szent István körút 13, tel. 1/302-3112, www.hjb .hu, Mon.–Wed. noon–midnight, Thurs.–Sat. noon–1 A.M., Sun. noon–10 P.M., mains 1,600–3,000 Ft) may not be the most original idea in the world, but it's done well. American classics are offered here: classic grilled chicken and turkey sandwiches, BBQ ribs, hot dogs, steaks, and an excellent chili cheeseburger. Reasonably priced and also offering a decent range of cocktails, HJB's livens up in the evenings when the live music begins. If you're feeling a little homesick, a trip to Hank's should cure it.

Cafes

Located between Nyugati train station and Margaret Bridge, **Európa Kávéház** (V. Szent István körút 7-9, tel. 1/312-2362, www.europakavehaz.hu, Nov.–Apr. daily 9 A.M.–10 P.M., May–Oct. daily 9 A.M.–11 P.M.) is usually busy with shoppers and strollers in need of a break. A large selection of cakes, as well as homemade sandwiches await, as does a very pleasant atmosphere and rather friendly service. A simple yet filling breakfast is available as well.

French

⟨ Lou-Lou (V. Vigyázó Ferenc utca 4, tel. 1/312-4505, www.loulourestaurant.com, Mon.–Sat. noon–3 P.M., 7–11 P.M., mains 2,340–5,400 Ft) may not be known to most tourists, but it is treasured by local gourmands. Its gorgeous interior balances Louis XVI–style chairs with modern elements of design to create an intimate and romantic dining experience. The salmon bisque is an excellent starter and the duck parmentier and baby Bretagne veal chop are hearty and delicious mains. Both the international cheese selection and wine list are impressive to say the least and desserts like the exquisite chocolate parfait will leave you in a state of divine fulfillment. Reservations most definitely recommended.

Hungarian

Popular with both Hungarians and expats, **⟨ Cafe Kör** (V. Sas utca 17, tel. 1/311-0053, Mon.–Sat. 10 A.M.–10 P.M., mains 1,600–3,580 Ft) remains as popular as ever due to the simple fact that it continually serves high-quality food at remarkably reasonable prices. Boasting a rather creative Hungarian menu, which is far lighter than other traditional restaurants, you can't go wrong with the grilled duck medallions or beef tenderloin. Make sure to save room for dessert as both the *aranygaluska* (a traditional Hungarian coffee cake) with vanilla sauce and sour cherry biscuit are prepared with the love and attention only a grandmother could give. Highly recommended.

Csarnok Vendéglő (V. Hold utca 11, tel. 1/269-4906, Mon.–Sat. 9 A.M.–midnight, Sun. 9 A.M.–10 P.M., mains 600–1,500 Ft) is a cheap local restaurant located near the U.S. Embassy that remains mostly unknown to visitors. Steeped in tradition, the menu is heavy on meats and sweets and light on pomp and circumstance. If you want a hearty meal and need

to keep the costs down, you won't find many places offering more bang for your buck.

Mediterranean

Okay Italia (V. Nyugatí tér 6, tel. 1/332-6960, www.okayitalia.com, Mon.–Fri. 11 A.M.–midnight, Sat.–Sun. noon–midnight, mains 1,890–3,650 Ft) is the kind of restaurant that gains loyal, returning customers day after day. Known for its friendly service, generous portions, and affordable prices, the menu ranges from fresh pasta made on the premises to over 20 types of pizza, as well as a large variety of salads, meats, and fish courses. The minestrone makes for an excellent starter and mains like homemade pasta with salmon and broccoli and penne with traditional Italian sausage and grilled peppers are first-rate. For dessert, do yourself a big favor and order the outstanding tiramisu.

Trattoria Pomo D'oro (V. Arany János utca 9, tel. 1/302-6473, www.pomodorobudapest .com, Mon.–Fri. 11 A.M.–midnight, Sat.–Sun. noon–midnight, 1,890–4,290 Ft) is a warm, intimate restaurant that offers a wide variety of excellent Italian dishes. The fresh branzino is quite good and the Italian Fiorentina, a Florentine T-bone steak grilled on charcoal, will satisfy even the most finicky of carnivores. For dessert, you have to try Chef Viti's Tenerina—a delicious dark chocolate brownie served with vanilla custard. You might also want to consider the flambéed strawberries with ice cream, which is as decadent as it sounds. All of this scrumptious fare can be washed down with one of the 200 award-winning Italian and Hungarian wines available.

Mexican

For delicious and authentic Mexican-American eats, you can't go wrong with **⟨ Iguana Bar and Grill** (V. Zóltán utca 16, tel. 1/331-4352, www.iguana.hu, Sun.–Thurs. 11:30 A.M.–12:30 A.M., Fri.–Sat. 11:30 A.M.–1:30 A.M., mains 1,800–3,300 Ft). Located around the corner from Szabadság tér, this expat staple is colorfully decorated with comical if kitschy retro pictures of old Mexican films, cigarette advertisements, license plates, and mariachi players. The menu has everything you'd want in a restaurant like this, offering generous portions of tacos, burritos, quesadillas, fajitas, chilies, and vegetarian options to boot. "Jenő's Quesadilla" and the aptly named "Whoop Ass Chilli" are popular choices but pretty much anything you order is bound to please the palate. Highly recommended, as are reservations in advance.

TERÉZVÁROS AND ERZSÉBETVÁROS
Asian
Wasabi (VI. Podmaniczky utca 21, tel. 1/374-0008, www.wasabi.hu, daily 11:30 A.M.–11:30 P.M., all you can eat: lunch 3,790 Ft, dinner 4,790 Ft) caught the public's attention by being the first restaurant to serve its fare via a slowly moving conveyor belt. Of course, it's the food that keeps people coming back. Asian staples such as miso soup, sashimi, and kimchi are excellent, and the all-you-can-eat sushi is a must for those who can handle it. If you're traveling with kids, you'll be happy to know that children under three eat for free, while those aged 3–12 receive a 40 percent discount.

Cafes
Mai Manó Café (VI. Nagymező utca 20, tel. 1/269-5642, daily 10 A.M.–1 A.M., mains 600–1,500 Ft) is housed in the elegant Mai Manó House on Budapest's Broadway. An excellent and ever-evolving selection of coffees, wines, desserts, salads, and sandwiches, combined with its central location, makes this an excellent choice for unwinding and people-watching. Perfect for those lazy afternoons.

Café Vian (VI. Liszt Ferenc tér 9, tel. 1/268-1154, www.cafevian.com, daily 9 A.M.–1 A.M., mains 1,500–4,000 Ft) is located on trendy Liszt Ferenc tér and tends to fill up rather quickly in the evenings. There's lots to choose from here, including a large variety of international breakfasts, salads, pastas, and sandwiches. The grilled honey orange duck breast and Norwegian salmon are superb, as is

the decent selection of desserts and coffees. An extensive drinks menu is one more reason to visit and soak up the strip's atmosphere.

Just down the street from the Great Synagogue, the **Nelson Café** (VII. Dohány utca 12, tel. 1/411-1804, www.nelsoncafe.hu, Mon.–Fri. 7 A.M.–midnight, Sat.–Sun. 8 A.M.–midnight, 590–1,390 Ft) is a laid-back, friendly place with an affordable menu. Nachos and sausages are two scrumptious snacks available and their hot and cold sandwiches aren't too shabby either. The jewel of this place, however, is the breakfast menu, a rarity in Budapest. Choose from a wide range of breakfasts including U.S.-style and Continental. Worth the trip no matter how bleary-eyed you might be in the morning.

Múzeum Cukrászda (VII. Múzeum körút 10, tel. 1/338-4415, 24 hours, mains 600–1,700 Ft) is located between the museum district's university and the National Museum, attracting an eclectic mix of patrons who can oftentimes be found gorging on the scrumptious desserts on offer, as well as light salads and sandwiches. An excellent place to start the day or to end the evening, it's open 24 hours a day—a fact many night owls take full advantage of.

Continental
Now located in the Hotel Andrássy, **Baraka** (VI. Andrássy út 111, tel. 1/483-1355, www.barakarestaurant.hu, daily noon–3:30 P.M., 6–11 P.M., mains 4,800–6,900 Ft) continues to serve some of the most imaginative and tasty dishes in the city. Enjoy the sophisticated Art Deco interior while savoring such delicacies as the seared wild duck breast and New Zealand lamb chops. If interested in sampling a wide variety of the restaurant's fare, opt for the nine-course *menu de gustacion,* and, if there's room for dessert, give the mouth-watering molten chocolate volcano with homemade ice cream a try. The menu changes often so make sure to check the website for current menu recommendations.

Located in the heart of Budapest's Broadway, **Két Szerecsen** (VI. Nagymező utca 14, tel.

1/343-1984, www.ketszerecsen.hu, Mon.–Fri. 8 A.M.–1 A.M., Sat.–Sun. 9 A.M.–1 A.M., 1,480–2,860 Ft) is a popular choice with Hungarian celebrities and savvy locals. A very laid-back, warm, and friendly atmosphere pervades, making it an excellent place to have a drink or grab a bite with a handful of close friends. The arugula salad is excellent, as is the deer goulash and unique homemade ravioli filled with ricotta and pumpkin. This is the kind of place that can easily make a regular out of you.

If you're on the lookout for mouth-watering, traditional Hungarian food, you cannot overlook **Haxen Király** (VI. Király utca 100, tel. 1/351-6793, www.haxen.hu, daily noon–midnight, mains 1,470–2,990 Ft). Huge portions served with a smile in a rustic, comfortable setting keep this place busy more often than not so reservations may not be a bad idea. Devoted carnivores have got to try the crispy spit-roasted pork knuckle, while those looking for a rich, tasty alternative should opt for the duck casserole. There's a reasonably priced all-you-can-eat buffet lunch on Sundays, too. You really can't go wrong here.

Köleves Stonesoup Restobar (VII. Kazinczy utca 35, tel. 1/322-1011, www.koleves.com, daily 11 A.M.–2 A.M., mains 980–2,580 Ft) is a comfortable, laid-back spot in the heart of the Jewish district. The menu reflects Hungarian, Mediterranean, and Jewish (not kosher) delights, with an emphasis on beef, chicken, and lamb. You can also find staples such as duck breast and smoked turkey leg, both of which are scrumptious. There are a handful of options for vegetarians and a small number of desserts, including crepe suzette and sponge cake. This local favorite also has free Wi-Fi and the occasional live music event on the weekends.

Champs Sport Pub (VII. Dohány utca 20, tel. 1/413-1655, www.champs.hu, daily noon–2 A.M., mains 950–2,800 Ft) is owned by a group of five Olympic medalists who decided to join forces and open up a restaurant where diners could enjoy delicious food while watching a vast array of sports. The menu is extensive, with plenty of varieties of salads, fish, pasta, and chicken and the service, while spotty, is generally helpful. This is very much a guy's hangout and is also popular with stag party groups so things can get rather rowdy. If you're looking for a quiet or romantic place to enjoy your meal, you may want to try somewhere else.

French

Located on bustling Andrássy út, **Abszint** (VI. Andrássy út 34, tel. 1/332-4993, www.abszint.hu, daily 10 A.M.–midnight, mains 1,600–4,000 Ft) has built a solid reputation around town thanks to its imaginative dishes reflecting the southern region of France. Sporting both a seasonal and daily menu, solid picks include the basil goat cheese mousse as a starter, along with the rosé duck breast and saddle of lamb. Chocolate truffles seem to be the dessert of choice here, as well as the cheese board, which includes Stilton Vieux, Emental Suisse, Brie De Maux, and Tomme De Savoie. The drinks menu is quite good and even includes cocktails made with the magical beverage from which the restaurant took its name.

Hungarian

One of the more elegant restaurants in town, **Muvészinas** (VI. Bajcsy-Zsilinszky út 9, tel. 1/268-1439, daily noon–midnight, mains 1,700–4,800 Ft) is a trip back to the turn of the 20th century. Decorated with faded books, old photos, and candlelit tables, it is the perfect place to enjoy a romantic dinner with that special someone. The menu includes fish, game dishes, and the odd vegetarian dish, with the broccoli soup, shashlik, and salmon with lemon sauce being pretty near unbeatable. Reservations are essential.

Located across the street from the Opera, **Belcanto** (VI. Dalszínház utca 8, tel. 1/269-2786, www.belcanto.hu, daily noon–3 P.M., 6 P.M.–2 A.M., mains 2,200–6,200 Ft) is a hit with local artists, as well as the city's sophisticated crowd. Starters like the goose liver pate and mushroom soup with pasta are perfectly prepared while standard mains such as the sirloin strips or pork medallions never

PAPRIKA POWER

If you weren't aware of paprika's popularity before landing in Hungary, you most certainly will be when you get there. Strung up and sold everywhere, Hungarian paprika is the national ingredient, spicing up soups, poultry, and countless meat-based dishes. Below are a few facts that will help you to better understand Hungary's association and love of the fabled red powder.

FACTS ABOUT PAPRIKA

- Paprika powder is produced by grinding the dried deep red paprika pods of the pepper plant.

- Although *the* symbol of Hungarian cuisine, the plant was originally introduced by the Turks during their rule in the 16th and 17th centuries.

- Red paprika isn't the hottest you can find. It's the orange-colored one that will really make you sweat.

- Paprika's heat is caused by capsaicin, a chemical that is extracted from paprika plants and used in pharmaceutical production due to its pain-killing properties.

- Paprika is rich in vitamin C (150mg/100g paprika), a fact that was discovered by Hungarian scientist Albert Szent-Györgyi, who was consequently awarded the Nobel Prize in 1937.

- Kalocsa and Szeged in the south are the heart and soul of Hungary's paprika production.

TYPES OF HUNGARIAN PAPRIKA

There are eight different brands of paprika generally available in the shops, all of which vary in potency and color.

1. Special quality (Különleges) – the mildest of all paprikas; sports the most vibrant red color
2. Delicate (csípősmentes csemege) – mild paprika full of rich flavor
3. Exquisite delicate (csemege paprika) – slightly more potent than the Delicate
4. Pungent exquisite delicate (csípős csemege) – getting warmer
5. Noble sweet (édesnemes) – the most common type, slightly potent with a bright red color
6. Half-sweet (félédes) – a medium-potent paprika
7. Rose (rózsa) – light red color and mild
8. Hot (erős) – the papa bear of paprikas; sporting a light brown-orange color, it'll make you blow smoke out your ears

---

fail to satisfy. For dessert, opt for the chestnut puree and wash it down with a smooth glass of Hungarian wine. If on a tight budget, try the inexpensive lunch buffet served on weekdays, which is quite popular with opera singers and musicians filling up before the big show.

Indian

◖ **Shalimar** (VII. Dob utca 50, tel. 1/352-0305, daily noon–4 P.M., 6–11 P.M., mains 1,700–3,000 Ft) has consistently placed in the top three as Best Indian Restaurant of the Year in the local papers for a decade now and the first bite into anything on the menu will quickly show you why. Whether it's the

chicken makhani, or various beef, lamb, and vegetarian dishes, you simply will not be disappointed. The service is excellent, the atmosphere relaxed, and the naan, poppadums, and parathas unbeatable. Highly recommended.

International

Barokko Club & Lounge (VI. Liszt Ferenc tér 5, tel. 1/322-0700, www.barokko.hu, Sun.–Tues. noon–2 A.M., Wed.–Sat. noon–3 A.M., mains 1,990–3,750 Ft) is a hip restaurant, bar, and weekend dance club all rolled into one. Located on fashionable Liszt Ferenc tér, it serves up trendy, international fare like tasty tapas platters, excellent spicy king prawns, and melt-in-your-mouth veal fillet steak. Their chocolate mousse is a big hit, as is their international "greatest hits" wine list. Fun and lively, this place is almost always packed, so get there early or phone ahead to reserve a table.

Mandarin Bar & Restaurant (VI. Ó utca 22, tel. 1/688-1696, www.mandarin bar.hu, Mon.–Sat. 11 A.M.–midnight, mains 1,460–2,680 Ft) has quickly become the local restaurant of choice for plenty of foreigners due in large part to its friendly service, unpretentious attitude, and amazing dishes. The prawn salad in avocado is an interesting starter and mains like the salmon steak in lemon sauce, butterfish, and the chili-honey chicken are cooked to perfection. For dessert, try the chocolate fondante and wash it all down with Mandarin's special non-alcoholic beverages. Reservations, as well as wasting no time to get here, are both very much recommended.

C **Marquis de Salade** (VI. Hajós utca 43, tel. 1/302-4086, daily 11 A.M.–1 A.M., mains 2,500–4,000 Ft) offers a remarkably wide selection of dishes from all over the world including Russia, Azerbaijan, Georgia, Bengal, Greece, and China to name but a few. Vegetarians will be happy as there are numerous veggie options; carnivores should not ignore the lamb, which is prepared especially well. Highlights include *pyty,* which is a traditional Georgian lamb and vegetable soup, the chickpea curry, coq au vin, and diced chicken breast in a piquant sauce. Pretty much everything on offer is excellent, which would explain why it's constantly filled with all walks of life. Make sure to stop by here at least once.

Noa Grill House (VI. Teréz körút 54, tel. 1/354-1670, daily 10 A.M.–11:30 P.M., www .noarestaurant.com, mains 1,400–4,600 Ft) was voted Best New Restaurant in 2006 and it's easy to see why. Generous portions are served by smiling staff, who are very happy to help with the large and varied menu. International dishes ranging from Indonesian honey-chili chicken to lamb ribs with green curry satisfy all tastes, and sports fans will be happy to know that widescreen TVs broadcast the day's games from all over the world. Try the tricolor chocolate mousse or three-chocolate-and-walnut brownie for dessert then head upstairs to the lounge and chill till the wee hours. If in a hurry, the gyros buffet has the finest falafel in town.

Medieval

Those who feel cutlery is bourgeois nonsense will be happy to know that the people at **Sir Lancelot** (VI. Podmaniczky utca 14, tel. 1/302-4456, www.sirlancelot.hu, daily noon–midnight, mains 1,990–4,290 Ft) couldn't agree more. Grab a table in the long medieval dining hall and order from the set, meat-heavy menus or opt for some of the more colorful, à la carte titles, like "Calf of Mrs. Baker" or "We tortured and broke it with onion." Be warned that the portions here are enormous, so either starve yourself beforehand or be prepared to stay a while. Diners will be happy to know that entertainment also plays a great role and includes sword fighting, belly dancing, and a whole host of surprises.

Mediterranean

Not far from the Oktogon is **Ristorante Krizia** (VI. Mozsár utca 12, tel. 1/331-8711, www .ristorantekrizia.hu, Mon.–Sat. noon–3 P.M., 6:30 P.M.–midnight, mains 1,400–6,200 Ft). By mixing the creative and traditional sides of Italian cuisine, owner/chef Graziano Cattaneo has managed to create one of the better Italian restaurants in Budapest. Start off with the excellent porcini mushroom soup and follow up with any number of homemade dishes, including the goose liver stuffed tortelloni, veal ossobuco, or truffled Italian risotto with asiago cheese. Definitely leave room for dessert as you'll want to try the bitter chocolate mousse and caramelized fruit pancakes. Reservations are recommended if planning on visiting in the evening.

Fans of fine Italian dining will be more than pleased with **Fausto's** (VI. Székely Mihály utca 2, tel. 1/877-6210, www.fausto.hu, Mon.–Fri. noon–3 P.M., 7–11 P.M., Sat. 6–11 P.M., mains 2,300–5,500 Ft), a consistent favorite on the restaurant scene. Its new minimalist setting sets the stage for authentic Italian dishes served with a contemporary twist. Try the spinach ravioli filled with minced monkfish or branzino served with avocado cream and top it all off with a very chocolaty chocolate pine nut cake. Although on the pricey side, rest assured this is money well spent.

Olíva (VI. Lázár utca 1, tel. 1/312-0080, www.oliva.hu, daily noon–midnight, mains 1,190–2,450 Ft) is a warm, friendly restaurant perfect for family dinners or more intimate tête-à-têtes. A complimentary bowl of olives is placed on your table as you peruse the menu, which offers an excellent selection of starters, soups, salads, meat dishes, pizza, and pasta. There is a distinct Italian bent to the cuisine but there are also a few Hungarian dishes available should you wish to "go local." The portions are huge, the staff animated, and the atmosphere casual, making this place one to seek out should you find yourself anywhere near Andrássy Street.

Middle Eastern

Al Amir (VII. Király utca 17, tel. 1/352-1422, Mon.–Sat. noon–11 P.M., Sun. 1–11 P.M., mains 1,000–2,500 Ft) is an exceptional Syrian restaurant beloved by all Budapesters. The usual Middle Eastern starters like eggplant dip and lentil soup are available here, as is the best hummus you'll find in town. Grilled meat is another specialty and the minced lamb, kebabs, and shawarma are all first rate. Those with a sweet tooth have to top off the experience with the famous baklava, which is simply unbeatable. Mouth-watering meals and excellent value for the money make this an impossible restaurant to ignore.

THE VÁROSLIGET
Continental

Close to Heroes' Square and located on its own island in City Park Lake, **Robinson** (XIV. Városligeti tó Sziget, tel. 1/422-0222, www .robinsonrestaurant.hu, daily noon–4 P.M., 6 P.M.–midnight, mains 2,850–5,250 Ft) is an ideal restaurant to enjoy a romantic dinner for two. Its summer terrace affords peaceful views of the surrounding landscape, while a fireplace keeps things nice and cozy during the winter. The Thai soup with coconut and chili king prawn makes for an excellent starter, while main courses like the Norwegian salmon steak with pineapple and New Zealand lamb cutlets continue to be among diners' favorites. The friendly, family atmosphere, complemented by wonderful live Latin guitar in the evening, add to a memorable dining experience.

Hungarian

Gundel (XIV. Állatkertí út 2, tel. 1/468-4040, www.gundel.hu, daily noon–4 P.M., 6:30 P.M.–midnight, Sunday brunch 11:30 A.M.–3 P.M., mains 4,870–10,620 Ft) is one of Budapest's best-known restaurants and is equated with the finest in Hungarian cuisine. An impressive art collection covers the walls of its main dining room, giving it an immediate old-world charm lacking in other upscale restaurants. Dishes like the smoked fillet of beef and classic crepe à la Gundel are impressive to say the least and can be washed down with over 100 wines available, including those from Gundel's own wineries. Those on a budget will want to check out the affordable lunch menus, and if you're one of those people who lives for brunch, look no further.

Located next to Gundel, **Bagolyvár** (XIV. Állatkerti út 2, tel. 1/468-3110, www .bagolyvar.hu, daily noon–11 P.M., mains 1,300–3,700 Ft) is a far less expensive choice that doesn't sacrifice any of the quality. Simple, homemade Hungarian dishes are cooked by an all-female kitchen staff and served by waitresses who are consistently warm and friendly. The permanent menu is comprised of about half a dozen choices including the tasty but heavy garlic-roasted barbecue pork and veal with egg dumplings. Daily specials are something to keep an eye out for and desserts like the walnut pancake with chocolate sauce are superb. This is an excellent choice for the budget traveler who'd like to sample well-cooked, authentic Hungarian cuisine.

JÓZSEFVÁROS AND FERENCVÁROS
Cafes

So hip it has outdoor seating on both sides of the Raday strip, the **Leroy Café** (IX. Ráday utca 11-13, tel. 30/207-9220, www.leroyraday.hu, daily noon–midnight, mains 1,550–2,950 Ft) is sleek, stylish, and here to stay. Boasting a truly international menu, diners will have a hard time deciding between sushi, salmon steaks, nouveau soups and salads, Mexican, Italian, Hungarian cuisine, and steaks made from free-range organic beef imported from South America. This is a great place to come on a date or with somebody who likes current, creative cuisine.

The award-winning **⟨ Múzeum Kávéház** (VIII. Muzeum körút 12, tel. 1/338-4221, www.muzeumkavehaz.hu, Mon.–Sat. noon–midnight, mains 2,800–5,500 Ft) is a time-honored establishment that serves some of Hungary's finest domestic cuisine. Its gorgeous dining rooms are decorated with antique Zsolnay tiles and possess a stunning ceiling fresco by none other than famed artist Károly Lotz. Pretty much anything on the menu is a hit, particularly the salmon carpaccio and unbelievable venison fillet "Lucullus." For dessert, try the chocolate soufflé or house favorite pancake "Muzeum" with Unicum sauce. A class act all the way.

For a tasty lunch or light dinner, try **Chili Bar** (IX. Tompa utca 7, tel. 1/216-1637, www.chilibar.hu, Mon.–Fri. 10 A.M.–midnight, Sat.–Sun. noon–midnight, mains 780–1,280 Ft). Small and unpretentious, with a warm and friendly atmosphere, it's the perfect place to enjoy fresh, homemade fare. Big hits are the bruschetta, Caesar salad, and steak sandwich, as well as mouthwatering desserts like tiramisu and cognac chocolate cream. Definitely worth dropping by if you happen to be in the neighborhood.

Continental

Stex House (VIII. József körút 55-57, tel. 1/318-5716, www.stexhaz.hu, Mon.–Tues. 8 A.M.–2 A.M., Wed.–Sat. 8 A.M.–6 A.M., Sun. 9 A.M.–2 A.M., mains 1,000–3,000 Ft) is a larger-than-life venue offering pool, darts, gambling, a huge sports screen, and, oh yeah, food! Continental cuisine ranging from pizzas to traditional Hungarian dishes comes in generous portions and the kitchen stays open until 4 A.M. more often than not. Very popular with locals and expats alike, there's also terrace seating during the summer months. Friendly and always busy, this is one of those places that has to be experienced to be understood.

French

Although a little off the beaten tourist path, **Alcasar** (IX. Ferenc tér 2-3, tel. 1/216-0483, www.alcasar.hu, daily noon–midnight, mains 1,390–3,990 Ft) is nevertheless worth the trek. There are so many fantastic dishes offered here that it's nearly impossible to pick just one. Highlights include the interesting spiced deer carpaccio as starter, as well as the roasted mahi-mahi and assortment of French cheeses. The crème brûlée is a must and reservations in advance might be a good idea as well.

Mediterranean

Pink Cadillac (IX. Ráday utca 22, tel. 1/216-1412, www.pinkcadillac.hu, daily 11 A.M.–1 A.M., mains 750–2,490 Ft) is an affordable pizza and pasta restaurant whose reputation is far greater than the rather small space made available to its patrons. Countless top-notch dishes are offered, and the quality is so good that many restaurants along the Ráday strip offer them up as their own. Always an excellent choice.

VÁRHEGY, THE VÍZIVÁROS, AND CENTRAL BUDA
Asian

Located near the Chain Bridge on the Buda side is **Seoul House** (I. Fő utca 8, tel. 1/201-7452, Mon.–Sat. noon–3 P.M., 6–11 P.M., mains 2,000–5,000 Ft). Although rather pricey, it is said to have some of the best Korean food around, thanks in no small part to its location next to the South Korean Embassy. There are plenty of mains and side dishes available; the kimchi and pulgogi are standouts. An excellent option for those not too worried about spending a little more than usual while on holiday.

Cafes

Angelika Kávéház (I. Batthyány tér 7, tel. 1/201-0668, www.angelikakavehaz.hu, daily 10 A.M.–10 P.M., mains 1,500–3,000 Ft) is wonderful place to take a break from the day's activities and enjoy a light meal or snack in elegant, turn-of-the-20th-century surroundings. If you get there early, you can choose from a number of breakfast options like three-egg omelettes or toasted sandwiches. There are plenty of soups and salads to choose from, and the entree highlights include grilled salmon and Caribbean chicken wings. The cakes, pastries, and teas are all in a class of their own and coffee drinkers will be happy to know that there are plenty of iced and piping hot possibilities.

An institution of sophistication for over 25 years now, **Café Pierrot** (I. Fortuna utca 14, tel. 1/375-6971, www.pierrot.hu, daily 11 A.M.–midnight, mains 2,500–4,500 Ft) combines a stylish setting and unrivalled level of service to create an atmosphere no diner will soon forget. The Hungarian goose liver trilogy is absolutely divine; heartier appetites will appreciate the perfectly prepared venison steak. A comprehensive selection of Hungarian wines is ready for the tasting and the crème brûlée may very well be the best in town. Softly played live piano music in the background completes the effect.

◖ **Nagyi Palacsintazoja** (I. Batthyányi tér 5, tel. 1/212-4866, www.nagyipali.hu, open 24 hours, mains 200–1,000 Ft) has many locations but it's generally agreed that the one in Batthyányi tér is the best. Soak up the amazing view of both the Castle and Parliament while diving into scrumptious, gut-busting pancakes that vary from salty to sweet. The ham and mushroom and Hungarian stew pancakes are solid choices, and those with a sweet tooth cannot miss the opportunity to try the famous chestnut pancake. This is a very affordable choice for those who like quality without extravagance.

Continental

Horgásztanya Vendéglő (I. Fő utca 27, tel. 1/212-3780, daily noon–11 P.M., mains 1,300–2,500 Ft) has been around for as long as anyone can remember and is still considered one of the finest fish restaurants in town. The fish soup is hard to beat and the trout makes for a memorable main. There are also meat-based Hungarian specialties but it would be a shame to ignore the variety of fishy delights. If you care for dessert, try the Somloi Galuska and wash it all down with a light Hungarian wine. Few, if any, leave here disappointed.

French

Le Jardin de Paris (I. Fő utca 20, tel. 1/201-0047, www.lejardindeparis.hu, daily noon–midnight, mains 1,650–4,650 Ft) was the first authentic French restaurant to open in Budapest and automatically raised the bar in the possibilities of fine dining. Tastefully decorated and sporting one of the more romantic courtyards to be found during the summer months, diners can be found enjoying house specialties such as goose breast with green pepper sauce and goose liver pâté. Of course, there is also a fine selection of French cheeses available, as well as a top-notch selection of wines, champagnes, and Godet cognacs.

Hungarian

Kacsa Vendéglo (I. Fő utca 75, tel. 1/201-9992, www.kacsavendeglo.hu, daily 6 P.M.–1 A.M., mains 3,800–5,600 Ft) is an elegant, comfortable, upscale restaurant specializing in duck. While various beef and wild game dishes can be had, it's the duck in all its forms that most are drawn to. Try the crispy duck with sour cherry, pineapple, or orange sauce, or the wild duck stuffed with plums—or any other interesting combination that strikes your fancy. With live music in the evening, this is a perfect place to celebrate an anniversary or enjoy a romantic dinner for two.

International

Brightly lit and incredibly funky, **Sunny Corner Bar and Restaurant** (II. Bem

Rakpart 30, tel. 1/488-0115, www.sunny corner.hu, Sun.–Thurs. 11 A.M.–midnight, Fri.–Sat. 11 A.M.–2 A.M., mains 1,190–3,290 Ft) is located on the Buda side of the river, opposite Parliament. Its large terrace affords wonderfully peaceful views and its diverse offerings include steaks, seafood, pizza, pastas, Thai, vegetarian, and even a classic American diner menu that includes old-fashioned hot dogs and hamburgers. At night, things heat up with DJs and dancing.

Russian

Arany Kaviár (I. Ostrom utca 19, tel. 1/201-6737, www.aranykaviar.hu, daily noon–midnight, mains 1,850–3,950 Ft) is an upscale Buda restaurant with an elegant, finely lit interior: the perfect place to have a romantic dinner with that special someone. The French-influenced Russian menu is carefully selected every month and offers delicious choices such as home-smoked kamchata salmon bundles and Boyar-style roast veal on a sword. If undecided, consider the "Gourmet Menu" option, which is comprised of the finest assortment of food available at the restaurant, selected from the most popular courses on offer.

ÓBUDA AND MARGIT SZIGET
Hungarian

One of the more popular choices on the Buda side is **Kisbuda Gyöngye** (III. Kenyeres utca 34, tel. 1/368-6402, www.remiz.hu, Mon.–Sat. noon–midnight, mains 1,400–2,600 Ft). Its antique furniture and frescoed ceiling provide a very intimate environment for savoring international gourmet dishes, as well as Hungarian favorites. The pike perch fillet and veal fillet with pasta come highly recommended, as does the strudel with sour cherries, a sinfully delicious variation on the traditional dessert.

International

Humphrey's Restaurant (III. Bécsi út 136, tel. 1/439-2444, www.bowlingonline.hu, daily 10 A.M.–midnight, mains 700–3,000 Ft) is a funky, friendly establishment located in the north part of old Buda. The menu consists of authentic international cuisine with a strong focus on Mexican and Hungarian dishes. There are also buffet-type menus available that are large enough to feed a small army. An extensive wine list and fantastic cocktails are two reasons to stay awhile after your meal, not to mention the third and most important reason: the bowling alley waiting for you upstairs.

Information and Services

TOURIST INFORMATION OFFICES

There is no shortage of tourist information possibilities in Budapest but the main company that handles most visitors is Tourinform (Main office, VI. Liszt Ferenc tér 9-11, tel. 1/322-4098, www.budapestinfo.hu). A helpful, efficient, and English-speaking staff is more than happy to provide you with information regarding sights, tours, day trips outside the capital, and much more. You can also pick up plenty of free leaflets, booklets, and maps which are quite comprehensive and invaluable to the first-time visitor. Hours are November–April Monday–Friday 10 A.M.–6 P.M., Saturday 10 A.M.–4 P.M.; May Monday–Friday 10 A.M.–6 P.M., Saturday 10 A.M.–4 P.M.; June–September daily 10 A.M.–7 P.M.; October Monday–Friday 10 A.M.–6 P.M., Saturday 10 A.M.–4 P.M.

Another centrally located office is Tourinform Deák (V. Sötő utca 2, tel. 1/316-9800, www.budapestinfo.hu, daily 8 A.M.–8 P.M.), which provides the same useful information and is mere minutes away from many of the more popular sights, including Váci Street, Vörösmarty tér, and the Danube Embankment. Those flying to Budapest should make sure to check out the Tourinform Ferihegy (Terminal 1, tel. 1/438-8080, www.budapestinfo.hu,

BUDAPEST

daily 9 A.M.–10 P.M.) branch for all pertinent information before heading into the heart of the city. If you think you might need instant information at any given hour of the day, be sure to note the tourist information 24-hour hotline (tel. 1/438-8080).

EMERGENCY SERVICES

The Budapest Police Command (V. Sütő utca 2) is available to tourists 24/7 at its Deák Square location. If your passport is lost or stolen, report it immediately to the Budapest and Pest County Directorate of the Office for Immigration and Citizenship (XI. Budafoki út 60, tel. 1/463-9165, open 24 hours) or your respective embassy.

Should an emergency occur, contact the appropriate number immediately:

- Ambulance: 104
- Police: 107
- Fire: 105
- General emergency: 112

MEDICAL SERVICES

There are many hospitals in Budapest, including MÁV Kórház (VI. Rippl-Rónai utca 37, emergency room entrance, tel. 1/269-5656) and Országos Traumatológiai Intézet (VIII. Fiumeti út 17, tel. 1/333-7599), which serve both adults and children. For adults only, there is the BM Kórház (VII. Városligeti fasor 9-11, tel. 1/322-7620), while the Heim Pál Gyermekkórház (VIII. Ülloi út 86, tel. 1/210-0720) deals exclusively with children.

FirstMed Centers (I. Hattyú utca 14, Hattyúház, 5th floor, tel. 1/224-9090, www .firstmedcenters.com, open 24 hours) is an English-speaking clinic that offers emergency care around the clock. Medicover Health Centre (XIII. Váci út 22-24, ground floor, tel. 1/465-3100, www.medicover.com/hu, Mon.– Fri. 7 A.M.–7 P.M.) is the leading private health care provider in the region that charges either a flat fee or fee for specific services.

For immediate 24-hour dental care try SOS Dental Service (VI. Király utca 14, tel. 1/322-

0602, open 24 hours) or Profident (VII. Karoly körút 1, tel. 1/342-6972, open 24 hours).

The word for pharmacy in Hungarian is *gyógyszertár*. All pharmacies will be able to provide you with the proper medicine you need to control or cure most common ailments. Should you need a pharmacy after regular business hours, the location of the nearest 24-hour one is displayed on all pharmacy doors. Don't panic if the pharmacy looks closed when you get there. Ring the bell and wait patiently. A small fee is added for nighttime service. Some all-night pharmacies around town are Déli Pharmacy (XII. Alkotás út 1/b, tel. 1/355-4691), Óbuda Pharmacy (III. Vörösvári út 86, tel. 1/368-6430), Örs VezérPharmacy (XIV. Örs vezér tere, tel. 1/211-3861), Szent Margit Pharmacy (II. Frankel Leó út 22, tel. 1/212-4311), and Teréz Pharmacy (VI. Teréz körút 41, tel. 1/311-4439).

BANKS AND CURRENCY EXCHANGE

Banks tend to offer the best rates in Budapest but keep relatively short hours. They are generally open Monday–Thursday 8 A.M.–4 P.M. and Friday 8 A.M.–3 P.M. The most reputable banks around town are CIB Bank (II. Medve utca 4-14, tel. 1/212-1420, www.cib .hu), Erste Bank (V. Párisi utca 3, www.erste bank.hu, Mon. 8 A.M.–6 P.M., Tues.–Thurs. 8 A.M.–4 P.M., Fri. 8 A.M.–3 P.M.), and OTP Bank (V. Nádor utca 6, tel. 1/483-2300, www .otpbank.hu, Mon. 7:45 A.M.–5 P.M., Tues.–Fri. 7:45 A.M.–4 P.M.).

Currency exchange offices are all over the city. Should you want to forgo the banks or you need to change money after they've closed, hunt around for the best deal as rates vary widely.

POSTAL SERVICES

Budapest has plenty of postal outlets throughout the city so there really is no excuse for not sending that postcard to Mom. All post offices are open Monday–Friday 8 A.M.–6 P.M., with the exception of the two head post offices near the city's main railway stations.

The first is near Nyugati Railway Station (VI. Teréz körút 51, Mon.–Sat. 7 A.M.–9 P.M.) and the second by Keleti Station (VIII. Baross tér 11, Mon.–Sat. 7 A.M.–9 P.M., Sun. 8 A.M.–8 P.M.). Most post offices offer both the sending and receiving of faxes, as well as encashment possibilities for VISA, VISA Electron, Eurocard/Mastercard, Maestro cards, Eurocheques, and American Express travelers checks.

INTERNET

There are countless Internet cafes throughout the city; prices vary wildly, typically depending on their proximity to the city center. A few of the more reputable ones are LamiNet Internet (II. Lövőház utca 32, tel. 1/212-9878, www.lamin.axelro.net, daily 9 A.M.–11 P.M., 20 terminals, 200 Ft/hr), Electric Café (VII. Dohány utca 37, tel. 1/413-1803, www.electric cafe.hu, daily 9 A.M.–midnight, 27 terminals, 200 Ft/hr), OLIVNet (V. Váci utca 8, tel. 1/266-1085, www.music-animation -product.t-online.hu, daily 9 A.M.–10 P.M., 14 terminals, 400 Ft/hr), and Private Link Hungary (VIII. József körút 52, tel. 1/334-2057, www.private-link.hu, open 24 hours, 96 terminals, 700 Ft/hr). Those traveling with a laptop will be happy to know that many cafes, bars, and restaurants offer free Wi-Fi to their patrons. These establishments advertise this service on their doors or windows, making it incredibly easy for you to choose whichever one strikes your fancy.

LAUNDRY

There are very few coin-op laundrettes to be found in Budapest, as most Hungarians have their own washing machine. The Liliom Textilcare Salon (IX. Liliom utca 7-9, tel. 1/215-6782, www.liliomszalon.hu, Mon.–Fri. 7 A.M.–7:30 P.M., Sat. 8 A.M.–2 P.M.), however, is just such a place, with modern facilities and English-speaking staff. For full-service washing and dry cleaning, try the highly rated Tiszta Kék (VI. Teréz körút 62, Mon.–Fri. 7 A.M.–8 P.M., Sat. 8 A.M.–2 P.M.) or Oláhné Horváth Krisztina (VIII. Népszínház utca 53, tel. 1/313-4508, www.kelmefesto.hu, Mon.–Thurs. 7:30 A.M.–5 P.M., Fri. 7:30 A.M.–4 P.M.). Any of these places will have you clean as a whistle again in no time.

Getting There

BY AIR

Ferihegy Airport (tel. 1/296-7000, www.bud .hu) is located in southeast Pest approximately 15 miles from the center of town. The airport is served by two main terminals.

Taking a cab downtown can cost anywhere from 3,500–4,500 Ft and while it's the most convenient option, there is a cheaper alternative. The airport's regularly running minibus service (tel. 1/296-8555, daily 6 A.M.–10 P.M.) offers trips to the center for 2,500 Ft per person, with each vehicle seating anywhere from 8 to 11 passengers. Tickets can be purchased from the company's service desks located in both the airport's terminals. While certainly cheaper, it does, however, have one slight disadvantage: Depending on the number of people in the vehicle, as well as the distances between destinations, it might be a while before you finally make it to your hotel.

BY TRAIN

A large number of trains from across Europe roll into Keleti Station (VIII. Kerepesi út 2/6, tel. 1/313-6835), which is located in Pest's sketchy Baross tér. The station is conveniently located on the red subway line, making it easy to reach and a snap to get to any part of the city.

Other major railway stations include Nyugati Station and Déli Station. The occasional international train arrives at Nyugati Station (VI. Teréz krt. 55, tel. 1/349-8503), but it mainly serves the Danube Bend and Great Plain. It is located on the Outer Ring and borders the fifth, sixth and thirteenth districts. It can be reached

BUDAPEST

via the M3 Budapest subway line (Nyugati pá-lyaudvar). Déli Station (I. Krisztina krt. 37/A, tel. 1/355-8657) is located in central Buda at the terminus of the M2 Budapest subway line. Few international trains arrive here; most routes serve Lake Balaton and Transdanubia.

Trains from Prague to Budapest leave around the clock and number up to 10 a day, with the trip lasting 7–9 hours.

The national train website, www.elvira.hu, is very useful, offering complete, up-to-date information regarding Hungary's railway system and schedules.

BY BUS

Just about all international buses hailing from the UK and the rest of the continent make Népliget Station (Népliget autóbusz-állomás, Ferencváros, IX. Üllői út 131, tel. 1/219-8063) their final destination.

Volánbusz (www.volanbusz.hu) is the country's main international bus line and serves the three weekly routes coming from Prague. The trip generally lasts 7.5–8 hours, and prices start at 770 Kč; passengers are asked to check in one hour beforehand (or 15 minutes prior to leaving at the very latest). Fares and schedules change often so make sure to check the Volánbusz website for the most up-to-date information.

BY CAR

An International Driver's License is no longer necessary in order to drive legally in Hungary, but a valid UK, U.S., or Canadian license most certainly is. A handful of highways connect Hungary to the rest of Europe; the most important are the E60 (or M1), which connects Budapest with Vienna and the west, and the E65, which connects Budapest with Prague and points north. The roads are generally hassle-free, as are the Austrian and Slovakian borders, though you may be required to present your driver's license and registration.

In regards to distances, Prague is 347 miles, Vienna is 154 miles, Warsaw is 339 miles, and Berlin is 428 miles.

Getting Around

Budapest is a rather large city, which means you'll most likely have to jump on a bus, tram, or subway at some point during your stay. The system is efficient and rather simple to get the hang of, so don't worry and just jump right in. If in need of a taxi, use caution and stick to the companies recommended below. If traveling around by car, know that Hungarians are rather aggressive drivers and don't always follow the common rules of the road; keep your eyes open at all times.

BY PUBLIC TRANSPORT

Budapest's highly efficient network of public transportation services includes roughly 200 bus lines, 34 tram lines, three subway lines, and four above-ground suburban train lines (HÉV). The majority of services run 4:30 A.M.–11:30 P.M. When the trams and subways close, night buses run along the major routes. The two most useful buses are the 78É, which follows the Red subway line route, and the 14É, which follows the Blue subway line route. All three subway lines connect at Deák tér station, with trains running every two minutes during peak times and up to every 15 minutes late in the evening. The HÉV's lines run to and from various points of the city's outskirts but only the one running to Szentendre in the north (located at Buda's Batthyány tér station) is of any real concern to visitors.

BKV (Budapest Transport Company) runs Budapest's public transport system including all buses, trams, subways, suburban railways, and trolleys, as well as the Cog-Wheel Railway and funicular leading to Buda Palace. For more

© OLIVER HERBST

the funicular leading to Buda Palace

information regarding all things public transport, have a look at www.bkv.hu.

Tickets

Tickets are available at subway kiosks, newsstands, and machines located at bus and tram stops throughout the city. Typical tickets are good for one entire journey of any length without transfer. This includes the Cog-Wheel Railway but not the HÉV stops that lie outside the city's borders. (Special tickets can be bought to allow for a change of route and travel beyond Budapest.) A single ticket costs 230 Ft and 300 Ft if bought from the driver.

There is a large range of books of tickets and day/week/month passes that are available as well. A one-day pass costs 1,350 Ft, a three-day pass 3,100 Ft, and a seven-day pass 3,600 Ft. It's a good idea to buy a book of 10 tickets at a discounted price of 2,050 Ft, though this depends on how much you plan on using the public transport system.

Tickets must be validated at the start of each trip by inserting them into the orange boxes found near the doors of all buses, trolleybuses, trams, and HÉV trains, and in front of the escalators at subway stations. Make sure to validate your ticket, as there are plenty of inspectors patrolling the routes. Some wear uniforms while others travel undercover, but all sport a blue armband and carry badges with photo ID. The old "I'm a foreigner, how could I be so stupid?" routine has worn thin and inspectors no longer allow their lack of English language skills to get in the way of their job. If you haven't validated your ticket, be sure that you will be penalized.

BY TAXI

There are two kinds of taxis in Budapest: the ones that belong to large, organized fleets and the ones that are run privately. Whatever you do, avoid the latter as they are legally allowed to determine their own rates and are oftentimes on the hunt for tourists who just don't know any better. Hailing a cab on the street or choosing one from a taxi stand guarantees the base rate you will be charged before getting in will

BUDAPEST

be significantly higher than if you had called ahead. The most reputable taxi company to contact when in need of a driver is City Taxi (tel. 1/211-1111, www.citytaxi.hu). Other dependable companies include Fő Taxi (tel. 1/222-2222, www.fotaxi.hu), Buda Taxi (tel. 1/233-3333, www.budataxi.hu), and Rádió Taxi (tel. 1/777-7777, www.radiotaxi.hu).

There is a basic charge of 300 Ft during the day and 420 Ft at night upon entering the taxi. Rates are then calculated by kilometers traveled; a maximum of 240 Ft per kilometer is charged during the day and a maximum of 336 Ft at night. Larger, more well-known taxi companies occasionally offer lower rates, depending on time of day and distance traveled. If you are happy with the driver and service, rounding the bill up or tipping 10 percent is common practice.

BY CAR

Driving in and around Budapest is not an enviable task, as traffic is a common problem thanks to pedestrian zones and neverending construction. Reckless drivers who change lanes at the last possible second or speed up suddenly in order to beat out a red light add to the maddening equation, making Budapest's excellent public transport system a logical and less stressful alternative.

Despite the capital's unpredictable roads, Hungary has an excellent highway system that makes it easy to get around the country, as well as to connect to neighboring ones. There are three main types of roads. The first is Motorways (preceded by an M), which link Budapest with Lake Balaton and Vienna via Győr and run to Miskolc via Debrecen and Szegred via Kecsemét. The second type is National Highways, which are characterized by a single number and spread out from the capital. The third type is the secondary or tertiary roads, which are identified by two or three digits. Traveling the open road is not free and your car must have an appropriate highway sticker that can be bought at gas stations and some kiosks. For further information regarding prices, routes, and maps, check out www.motorway.hu.

Parking

Parking is very difficult to find in the center of both Pest and Buda but relatively easy elsewhere. Tickets can be purchased from machines located on the respective street and must be left on the dashboard, clearly visible through the windshield. Fees change often and vary depending on location.

Car Rental

Renting a car can be an expensive affair, but a bit of hunting ought to reward you with a decent deal. Make sure to have your passport and credit card handy, and if reserving a car before arriving in Hungary, double-check to ensure you've got the reservation confirmation with you.

Hertz (VIII. Marriott Hotel, Apáczai Csere János utca 4, tel. 1/266-4361, www .hertz.com, daily 7 A.M.–7 P.M., from 18,000 Ft/day) is a reliable though pricey option, with offices at the airport as well. Fox Autorent (XXII. Nagytétényi út 48-50, tel. 1/382-9000, www.fox-autorent.com, from 9,900 Ft/day) has gained plenty of repeat business and is highly recommended. Don't let their address in the boondocks scare you away; they provide free delivery and pickup anywhere within Budapest. Avis (V. Szervita tér, tel. 1/318-4240, www.avis.com, Mon.– Sat. 7 A.M.–6 P.M., from 8,900 Ft/day) is another solid option and it, too, has offices at the airport for your convenience.

BEYOND BUDAPEST

Flowing for 1,775 miles through nine different countries, the Danube is Europe's second-longest river, behind the Volga. As the Danube enters the Carpathian Basin, it is forced by surrounding hills and mountains through a narrow, twisting valley before continuing on its merry way to the capital. The shape of the river at this point is commonly referred to as the Danube Bend or Dunakanyar. It is a remarkably scenic part of the country, with green valleys and forested hills rising up from the river. There are also a handful of pretty little towns along the bend that are easily reached from Budapest and make for delightful day trips.

The most popular town in the region is undoubtedly the charming artist colony Szentendre. Characterized by a romantic embankment, lively cafes, and winding cobblestone streets, it is a picturesque part of Hungarian history that simply cannot be missed. Esztergom, too, is well worth a trip out of the big city as it is the birthplace of the one and only St. Stephen, as well as the site of the great Basilica, Hungary's largest church. And who can overlook lovely Lake Balaton? Central Europe's largest lake fills up quickly and not so quietly over the summer months, as visitors from all around the world come to satisfy their Dionysian desires in Siófok, sip from the springs of Balatonfüred, imbibe the mouthwatering wines of Badacsony, and bask in the beauty of Keszthely.

While life might be a little slower outside the capital, it's certainly no less exciting. The wine flows as freely as the waters of the Danube, colorful festivals appear out of nowhere throughout the summer months, and locals

© TOM DIRLIS

HIGHLIGHTS

LOOK FOR ◖ TO FIND RECOMMENDED SIGHTS, ACTIVITIES, DINING, AND LODGING.

◖ **Szabadtéri Néprajzi Múzeum (Skanzen Open Air Ethnographical Museum):** Just two miles southwest of Szentendre, this ambitious museum has recreated villages from the 18th and 19th centuries that house over 300 buildings, including a fire station, tavern, and shepherd's hut. Spend the afternoon immersing yourself in Hungary's colorful past and grab yourself some authentic souvenirs or traditional grub while you're at it (page 292).

◖ **Bazilika (The Basilica):** Esztergom's main attraction is the largest church in the country. Check out the world's largest oil painting inside, as well as the creepy crypt before heading up to the cupola for stunning panoramic views of St. Stephen's birthplace (page 293).

◖ **Siófoki Nagystrand (Siófok Beach):** Suntan central by day, hedonistic heaven by night, Hungary's most visited beach entertains approximately 13,000 people a day during the high season. Whether it's a fun game of beach volleyball, rockin' outdoor concert, or Dionysian disco you're looking for, you'll find it all here and then some (page 299).

◖ **Tihanyi Apátság (Tihany Benedictine Abbey):** This gorgeous abbey was established in 1055 and contains the world's oldest existing document featuring the Hungarian language. Reconstructed in the Baroque style after being destroyed during the Turkish occupation, its carved pulpit is arguably the finest in the country; the adjoining Tihany Museum will teach you everything you ever wanted to know about the region's turbulent past (page 306).

◖ **Balaton Festival:** Held annually during the second half of May, the Balaton Festival officially kicks off the summer season with a multitude of street performers, outdoor concerts, and theater productions before winding down with the highly anticipated Balaton Ballroom Dance Competition. This is by far Keszthely's biggest cultural event of the year and is not to be missed (page 313).

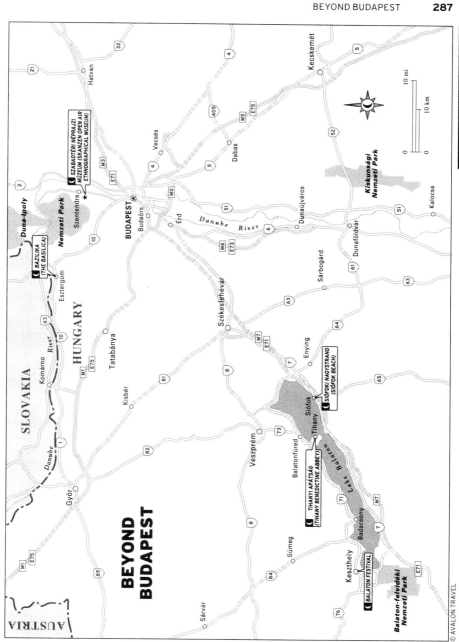

BEYOND BUDAPEST

© AVALON TRAVEL

mix with foreigners to create an international air of fun and adventure that is as uplifting as it is memorable.

PLANNING YOUR TIME

How much time one spends beyond Budapest really is up to the traveler and what they're hoping to get from their trip. To be sure, the traditional way of seeing Szentendre and Esztergom is to leave the capital in the morning and return in time for dinner and a nightcap. This is definitely the best way to appreciate each town and, unless you fall particularly in love with either destination, an overnight stay will not be necessary.

Lake Balaton, on the other hand, is a whole other kettle of goulash. While most places are easily accessible, there really is no point in heading there unless you plan on spending at least two or three days there. Keep in mind, however, that this is the absolute minimum you should schedule for and it will most likely restrict your trip to a quick tour of the nearest towns or a couple of hangovers care of Siófok shenanigans. If you plan on touring a substantial part of the lake and want to soak up its endless beauty, three to four days will give you a good start; five days to a week will feel like you've died and gone to Hungarian heaven. Siófok, Balatonfüred, and Keszthely are all well worth an overnight stay if not more, while Tihany and Badacsony can be enjoyed in half a day apiece if time is short.

Travel outside of Budapest is easier than you think. The HÉV from Batthyány tér in Buda serves those headed for Szentendre, and numerous buses, trains and boats leave for Esztergom on a daily basis. Lake Balaton is also easily reached by bus, train, or boat, and travel in and around the Balaton region is likewise easily managed via the same modes of transport.

Szentendre

Despite being choked with tourists during the summer months, Szentendre nevertheless remains an atmospheric, picturesque town whose location a mere 13 miles north of Budapest makes it an easy and logical choice for either a half- or full-day trip. Serbian settlers established themselves here in the Middle Ages, which accounts for the handful of Serbian Orthodox churches located around town, as well as the nearly palpable Mediterranean feel of Szentendre's own Dunakorzó—a romantic embankment lined with lively outdoor cafes and restaurants. The town's inherent beauty inspired an artist colony to develop here in the early 20th century and continues to serve as home and muse to roughly 100 artists. Most visitors stick close to Fő tér and its environs, preferring the shopping opportunities to almost anything else, but if you're feeling slightly adventurous, try losing yourself down one of the town's many winding, cobblestone streets. Odds are you'll end up losing the masses and come upon a more residential area of town which you'll be happily surprised to note is just as pretty and romantic as Szentendre's well-worn main drag.

FŐ TÉR (MAIN SQUARE) AND VICINITY

Szentendre's main square is chock full of pretty Baroque and Rococo architecture, as well as tons of tourists who fill the surrounding cafes, shops, and restaurants all day and night throughout the summer months. Busy Bogdányi utca, with its long strip of shopping opportunities begins here, while the remaining streets twist and turn in different directions, leading to various churches, museums, and (eventually) quieter locales. Here on the square, there are two immediate buildings that add to the square's illustrious history and romantic atmosphere: Blagovestenska Church and Ferenczy Museum.

© AVALON TRAVEL

Blagovesztenszka szerb ortodox templom (Blagovestenska Church)

Blagovestenska Church (Fő tér 4, Tues.–Sun. 10 A.M.–5 P.M., 200 Ft) is one of the finer examples of Baroque architecture found on the main square. It is a Serbian Orthodox church that was built in 1752 based on the designs of Andreas Mayerhoffer. The main entrance windows and bell tower sport Rococo flourishes, as does the iconostasis found inside. Many of the furnishings located under the vaulted nave are all authentic pieces dating back to the 18th century. For those wondering, "Blagovestenska" means the feast of the Annunciation of the Blessed Virgin Mary, to whom the church is dedicated.

Ferenczy Múzeum (Ferenczy Museum)

Named after Károly Ferenczy, the Ferenczy Museum (Fő tér 6, tel. 26/310-244, Tues.–Sun.

ETYEKWOOD

Located roughly 15 miles from Budapest, Etyek is home to a nearly 5,000-acre wine-growing region known for producing dry, acidic, light wines. More recently, however, Etyek has become synonymous with production of a much different sort — movies. Nicknamed "Etyekwood" by the press, the tiny town is now home to Korda Studios, which came to be thanks to Hungarian-born American producer Andrew G. Vajna and businessman Sándor Demján, who is responsible for the very successful WestEnd City Center. This major film production studio boasts a state-of-the-art post-production suite, 65,000-square-foot soundstage, and the largest indoor water tank in Europe. There are big plans for the studio with both founders banking on American productions being lured to Hungary in an effort to save costs, as well as domestic filmmakers looking to capitalize on the government's pledge to reimburse 20 percent of productions costs for each film made at Korda. The hope is that Hungary will once again be thrust into the limelight of international film production, and, judging by the growing number of films that have been bypassing Prague due to its absurdly unfair tax laws, it looks like that this is one dream that just might come true.

10 A.M.–5 P.M., 500 Ft) pays homage to one of the country's finest Impressionist painters, who made Szentendre his home between 1889 and 1892. There are nearly 8,000 works on display chronicling the work of local artists from the 19th century to the present day. Included is the work of Ferenczy's children, twins Noémi (a tapestry artist) and Béni (a sculptor).

Kovács Margit Múzeum (Margit Kovács Museum)

Dedicated to Hungary's most famous ceramics artist, the Margit Kovács Museum (Vastagh György utca 1, tel. 26/310-244, Apr.–Oct. Tues.–Sun. 10 A.M.–6 P.M., Nov.–Mar. Tues.–Sun. 10 A.M.–4 P.M., 600 Ft) was for years the country's most visited collection of art. Visitors will be amazed by the range and imagination of this remarkable artist, whose works here include an extensive selection of friezes, folk art, and heartbreakingly realistic statuettes of dear old ladies.

ENTERTAINMENT AND EVENTS

Szentendre's cultural calendar is full throughout the year. A good idea is to check listings while in Budapest and then make the short trip into town should something strike your fancy.

The **Szentendre Summer Festival and Theatre** (Duna-parti Művelődési Ház, Duna korzó 11/A, tel. 26/301-701, www.szentendre .hu, late June–late Aug.) is a highly anticipated event that involves a wide range of theater, concerts, exhibitions, and children's programs that take place all over town. Very entertaining children's shows are performed every Sunday morning and popular jazz and folk evenings are held in the Barcsay Museum garden every Saturday night.

The **Spring Days of Szentendre** (second half of March) coincides with Budapest's Spring Festival, whose tremendous popularity has inspired a chain of similarly spirited events throughout the country. The aim of the festival is to promote the outstanding work of local artists and musicians. Chamber orchestras, choirs, folk dance ensembles, and amateur theater are a few of the things visitors can expect from this fun and animated festival.

ACCOMMODATIONS

There are plenty of options for those who would like to stay in Szentendre overnight. Most come in the form of *panziós* (guesthouses), which vary greatly in price. To properly enjoy everything the island has to offer, try staying somewhere that isn't directly in the thick of all the tourist action. This will ensure peaceful surroundings and a better understanding of what the people here are really like.

   The Bükkös Hotel (Bükkös part 16, tel. 26/312-021, www.bukkoshotel.hu, 13,000 Ft d) is a popular choice for many travelers thanks to its affordable rates and proximity to the town center. There are 16 clean, simply furnished rooms in all and a restaurant that serves authentic Hungarian and wild game specialties. This is a good choice for the budget traveler who likes comfort but doesn't need anything fancy.

   ◖ **Horváth Fogadó Panzió** (Darupiac 2, tel. 26/313-950, www.everyoneweb.com/ horvath.fogado, 12,000 Ft d) is a charming, family-run guesthouse located a 5–10 minute walk away from the hustle and bustle of the tourist-driven center. Peaceful surroundings complement a warm, friendly environment that features seven comfortable rooms with wood paneling and an overall cabin-type feel. In the summertime, guests are allowed to use the barbecue in the garden, the scene of many an impromptu party. This place gets plenty of return business.

   The three-star **Hotel Róz** (Pannónia utca 6/b, tel. 26/311-737, www.hotelrozszentendre .hu, 13,000 Ft d) offers guests 10 clean and comfortable air-conditioned rooms that are furnished simply and boast pretty views of the Danube. Its fine restaurant serves up filling breakfasts and old-fashioned Hungarian dishes, which can be enjoyed in the elegant dining room or lovely outdoor terrace.

FOOD

Restaurants operating in heavily visited tourist destinations are bound to be pricier than the norm and Szentendre is no different, particularly the dining establishments located at Fő tér. There are, however, renowned restaurants serving authentic Hungarian fare at reasonable prices, a few of which are listed here.

   Housed in a former 18th-century smithery, **Rab Ráby** (Kucsera Ferenc utca 1/a, tel. 26/310-819, www.dunakanyar.net, daily noon–10 P.M.) is a very popular restaurant that serves delicious traditional Hungarian fare, including the finest goulash in town. Its lovely summer patio makes for pleasant, relaxed dining and its rather chaotic interior, filled with handcuffs, chains, full suits of armor, and a wide array of metallic doohickeys, make this a memorable time for both the visual and tactile senses.

   Almost always busy with both Hungarians and the tourist trade, ◖ **Aranysárkány Vendéglö** (Alkotmány utca 1/a, tel. 26/301-479, www.aranysarkany.hu, daily noon–10 P.M., mains 1,900–2,600 Ft) is an excellent traditional Hungarian eatery that offers up tasty meat dishes like lamb and steak, as well as standard Eastern European fare that includes stuffed cabbage and dumplings. The long wooden tables and friendly service provide a warm, hospitable atmosphere that has become legendary in these parts.

   A lovely, intimate interior and romantic (albeit tiny) outdoor seating are just two reasons to not miss **Nosztalgia Kávéház** (Bogdányi utca 2, tel. 26/311-660, daily 10 A.M.–8 P.M., desserts 250–800 Ft). Then there's the wide array of mouthwatering desserts that includes house favorite *Dobos torta,* a divine layer cake named after József Dobos, the Habsburg emperor's baker. A tiny museum honoring the man is located upstairs. Those who want to take a little piece of the coffeehouse home with them are able to choose from a nice selection of sauces and jams for sale, along with other more conventional souvenirs, like CDs and coffee mugs.

SHOPPING

There is no shortage of shopping opportunities in Szentendre. Indeed, it can feel sometimes like the whole town is one big marketplace. The main square, Fő tér, has a number of shops selling various handicrafts and souvenirs. Just off the square is Bogdányi utca, a street filled with shops selling crystal, folk costumes, antiques, fabrics, shirts, and, of course, local artwork from resident painters. There is also a collection of kiosks by the Dunakorzó selling more of the same.

INFORMATION AND SERVICES

Tourinform Szentendre (Dumtsa Jenő utca 22, tel. 26/317-965, www.tourinform.hu, Apr.–Oct. Mon.–Fri. 9 A.M.–7 P.M., Sat.–Sun. 9 A.M.–2 P.M., Nov.–Mar. Mon.–Fri. 9 A.M.–5 P.M.) is staffed with very helpful people who can provide you with maps of the area, as well as help regarding concert and exhibition schedules, accommodations, and common side trips outside of Szentendre.

GETTING THERE
By HÉV

Take the HÉV from Batthyány tér in Buda. Trains leave roughly every 20 minutes from 4:30 A.M.–11:30 P.M. The trip lasts approximately 45 minutes.

By Car

Szentendre is 13 miles from Budapest. Take Lajos utca across from Margaret Island north until it becomes Szentendrei út in north Budapest. This then becomes Rákóczi utca, Batthyány utca, and finally Dózsa György út, which will lead you directly to Szentendre.

By Boat

You can catch a boat from Vigadó tér on the Danube Embankment each morning at 10:30 A.M. It returns from Szentendre at 5 P.M. The trip is roughly 1.5 hours and costs 1,490 Ft. Various kiosks line the embankment representing companies who may offer different departure and arrival times. Boats tend to run from May until the end of September to middle of October.

VICINITY OF SZENTENDRE

If you're looking for something outside of town that's both educational and fascinating, try the Skanzen Open Air Ethnographical Museum. The huge outdoor museum is located two miles southwest of Szentendre. A bus leaving platform 8 of Szentendre's bus station (located adjacent to the HÉV) will get you there quickly and easily. If driving, follow Route 10 north and turn left on Sztaravodai út.

◖ Szabadtéri Néprajzi Múzeum (Skanzen Open Air Ethnographical Museum)

Founded in 1967, the Skanzen Open Air Ethnographical Museum (Sztaravodai út, tel. 26/502-500, www.skanzen.hu, Apr.–Oct. daily 9 A.M.–5 P.M., 1,000 Ft) is an ambitious collection of over 300 buildings representing the past architecture, life, and traditions of Hungary's different regions. Situated in Duna-Ipoly National Park, the museum is comprised of several recreated villages from the 18th and 19th centuries that include buildings like a fire station, tavern, and shepherd's hut. Arguably the most fascinating part of the immense collection is the furniture, textiles, and household equipment that give visitors a clear and fascinating picture of what life was really like back then. Shops selling traditional crafts, souvenirs, and food are also on the premises.

Esztergom

Located approximately 31 miles northeast of Budapest a mere stone's throw from the Slovakian border, Esztergom served as both the capital of Hungary between the 10th century and mid-13th century, as well as the Royal Seat up to the end of King Béla IV's reign. Esztergom is also famous for being the birthplace of Vajk, otherwise known as St. Stephen, Hungary's beloved king who was crowned here in the year 1000. The town went on to flourish, particularly during the 14th and 15th centuries when it rivaled Buda in cultural significance. Its importance and stature disappeared altogether, however, during the unforgiving 150-year Turkish rule of the 16th and 17th centuries. Today, Esztergom's winding streets, church towers, narrow stairs, and alleys continue to evoke an atmosphere of historical importance

© MEG RICHARDS

Esztergom Basilica, Hungary's largest church

and artistic beauty, particularly when it comes to the magnificent Basilica, Hungary's largest and grandest church.

◖ BAZILIKA (THE BASILICA)

The mighty masterpiece known simply as the Basilica (Szent István tér 2, tel. 33/411-895, www.bazilika-esztergom.hu, daily 6 A.M.–6 P.M.) is the largest church in the country, measuring an impressive 328 feet tall and 351 feet long. From 1543 to 1683, the Basilica suffered both negligence and damage under Ottoman rule, except for the beautiful **Bakócz Chapel,** which somehow survived relatively intact. Built by Tamás Bakócz (archbishop from 1497 to 1521), it is one of Hungary's finest examples of Renaissance architecture and boasts elaborately carved red marble. Following the expulsion of the Turks, the Hungarian Catholic Church re-established itself in Esztergom in 1819 and it was a few years later in 1822 that Primate-Archbishop Sándor Rudnay laid the foundation stone of a new cathedral. Two architects, Pál Kühnel and then,

following his death, János Packh, were responsible for the masterpiece we enjoy today which had its ceremonial consecration on August 31, 1856. Franz Liszt composed his *Esztergom Mass* for the occasion and conducted its first performance from the organ loft.

The centerpiece of the great Basilica's interior is the vast altarpiece depicting the Assumption of the Blessed Virgin Mary. Painted by Michelangelo Grigoletti, it measures 44 feet by 21.7 feet, making it the world's largest oil painting done on a single piece of canvas. Upstairs, an interesting collection of liturgical objects in the **treasury** includes some very pretty chalices, jewels, and vestments from the Baroque period, as well as the coronation cross dating all the way back to the Árpád era—the same one Hungarian kings swore on. A creepy **crypt** where the remains of archbishops, assistant bishops, canons, and exiled anti-Communist Cardinal Mindszenty's rest is also open to visitors, as is a **cupola** whose steep climb pays off with a wonderful view of the entire town. The treasury is open daily 9:30 A.M.–4:30 P.M.

and costs 450 Ft. The cupola is open daily 9 A.M.–4:30 P.M. and costs 200 Ft, while the crypt is open daily 9 A.M.–4:30 P.M. and costs 100 Ft.

KERESZTÉNY MUZEUM (CHRISTIAN MUSEUM)

The Christian Museum (Mindszenty tér 2, tel. 33/413-880, www.christianmuseum.hu, Mar. 13–Oct. 28 Tues.–Sun. 10 A.M.–6 P.M., Oct. 30–Jan. 1 Tues.–Sun. 11 A.M.–3 P.M., 600 Ft) is located on the second floor of the Primate's Palace and boasts the country's largest collection of ecclesiastical artwork, ranking just behind the National Gallery and Museum of Fine Arts in scope and significance. The museum was founded in 1875 by Archbishop János Simor and contains remarkable Hungarian work from the late Gothic period, along with Austrian, German, Italian, and Flemish paintings ranging from the 13th to 18th centuries. There are also a large number of tapestries and icons on display, rounding out a fascinating set of exhibitions outlining religion's vital role in Hungarian history.

ENTERTAINMENT AND EVENTS

Esztergom isn't exactly known for its nightlife and many restaurants pull double duty, offering diners tasty grub and well-made drinks. One or two trendy or all-night bars do crop up now again and simply asking the locals will put you in the right direction. The cultural calendar is filled with various art exhibitions and classical music concerts, though the two biggest events are clearly the St. Stephen's celebrations and summer theater performances at the Basilica.

Nightlife

Múzeumkert Restaurant és Cocktail Bár (Batthyány Lajos utca 1, tel. 33/404-440, muzeumkert@tvn.hu, Sun.–Thurs. noon–midnight, Fri.–Sat. noon–3 A.M.) is a spacious establishment bathed in black and red with animal skins decorating the booths and walls. Not much happens during the weekdays but a few stick around after their meals on the weekend, taking their time perusing the impressive list of cocktails available.

Festivals and Events

The Basilica offers up a gorgeous backdrop during the **Esztergom Castle Theatre Festival** (June–Aug.) as a wide variety of plays ranging from historical epics, operas, comedies, and musicals are performed during warm summer nights. Performances are in Hungarian but nonetheless enchanting with such fantastic scenery.

August 20 is St. Stephen's Day in Hungary, one of the biggest holidays of the year as the entire country celebrates the King and founding of the Hungarian state. Imagine then, the popularity of **St. Stephen's Days** (Aug. 18–20) in Esztergom, which is where he was crowned on Christmas 1000. The party starts early and ends late with a whole host of outdoor concerts, theater, food, fun, and frolicking in between. This is one of the more highly anticipated events on the town's cultural calendar and not to be missed.

ACCOMMODATIONS

Most people come to Esztergom for the day and leave well before the need for sleep and shelter arises. Should you get smitten with the place, however, and want to stay overnight, you'll find no shortage of guesthouses and small hotels in and around the city center.

Alabárdos Panzió (Bajcsy Zsilinszky utca 49, tel. 33/312-640, ww.alabardospanzio.hu, 10,500 Ft d) is a charming little bed-and-breakfast located right in the heart of Esztergom. Its cheerful atmosphere is infectious and while their rooms are a little on the small side, they are nevertheless clean, comfortable, and quiet.

Ria Panzió (Batthany utca 11-13, tel. 33/313-115, www.riapanzio.com, from 13,000 Ft d) is a quiet and charming guesthouse located within short walking distance of both the Basilica and Danube. Rooms are a little on the small side, though clean and comfortable, and blend in nicely with the overall friendly, family-run atmosphere. Breakfast is generous

FUN FACTS

- Susan Polgar, daughter of internationally renowned chess coach Polgar Laszlo, made chess history by breaking the game's gender barrier when she became the first woman ever to both qualify for the men's World Chess Championship and earn a Grandmaster title.

- Those old enough to remember television in the 1980s will undoubtedly recall the acerbic yet lovable prime-time alien, ALF. Sporting a huge snout and orange fur, he was played by three-foot tall Hungarian actor Michu Meszaros, who got into the hairy suit every time full body shots were required.

- On June 9, 2007, a whopping 6,637 Hungarian couples entered the *Guinness Book of World Records* for the largest gathering of simultaneous kissing. The record was previously held by the Philippines, which only got to enjoy its place at the top for a handful of months before the Hungarians smooched their way into history.

- World-famous philanthropist George Soros was born in Hungary and grew up during the Holocaust. He left to study at the London School of Economics and has had a hand in shaking up the world's finances ever since, including predicting the fall of the British pound back in the early 1990s.

- Ex-Lax, the chocolate-flavored laxative that has provided relief the world over, is the brainchild of Hungarian inventor Max Kiss. Tired of the unpleasant bitter taste that was synonymous with laxatives at the turn of the 20th century, Kiss sweetened the taste of active ingredient phenolphthalein to produce the second-best selling laxative in the world.

- Edward Teller, father of the hydrogen bomb, was born in Budapest in 1908. He moved to the United States in the 1930s where he eventually became a member of the Manhattan Project. Teller was also an important figure in the development of thermonuclear energy.

- Beloved actor Tony Curtis is the child of Hungarian natives who left for America in search of a better life. Though born in the Bronx, Curtis never forgot his roots and returned to Hungary in 2003 to shoot two 30-second spots for Hungarian tourism.

- During the Middle Ages, the Carpathian Basin was home to Europe's most developed mining system and was responsible for the production of 80 percent of the continent's gold.

---

and tasty and the excellent restaurant Csülök Csárda is located right next door as well.

The **Ⓒ Gran Camping Pension and Youth Hostel** (Nagy-Duna sétány 3, tel. 30/948-9563, www.grancamping-fortanex.hu, from 4,500 Ft d) is a great choice for budget travelers and those who would like to meet like-minded wanderers. Situated on Prímás Island, it offers guests spacious, brightly lit bungalows, simple but clean guest rooms, as well as a well-maintained hostel boasting 160 beds. Recreational possibilities are endless, with tennis courts, soccer field, playground, and swimming pool on the premises, along with a restaurant and shop. The town center is an easy 10-minute walk from the grounds

and Slovakia is a hop, skip, and a jump from neighboring Maria-Valeria Bridge.

FOOD

Esztergom has plenty of restaurants, with most offering traditional Hungarian dishes at relatively reasonable prices. The following are some of the better dining experiences to be had about town.

Located underneath the Basilica is the very well-known **Prímás Pince** (Szent István tér 4, tel. 33/313-495, Jan.–Mar. daily 10 A.M.–4 P.M., Apr.–Oct. daily 10 A.M.–6 P.M., Nov.–Dec. 10 A.M.–4 P.M., mains 1,600–2,800 Ft). Enjoy traditional Hungarian dishes like goulash, wild game soup, and pike-perch in its cavernous cellars, which ooze a mysterious medieval atmosphere that somehow seems to make the already great food better.

Not just another cellar restaurant, **Csülök Csárda** (Batthyány utca 9, tel. 33/412-420, www.csulokcsarda.hu, daily noon–10 P.M., mains 1,690–2,690 Ft) offers plenty of Csülök (trotter) specialties, as well as a delicious paprika chicken and wide array of pork, turkey, and steak dishes. Generous portions, friendly service, and a rustic looking but well-lit environment make this an excellent choice for either lunch or dinner any day of the week.

◖ Anonim Vendéglő (Berényi utca 4, tel. 33/411-880, daily noon–10 P.M., mains 1,500–2,800 Ft) is located inside a historic townhouse decorated in a traditional Hungarian style and offering some of the most mouthwatering dishes in town. Top Hungarian specialties like Cserhat saddle of lamb with *tocsin, racponty* (fillets of carp), and venison ragout Pilis-style are all made to perfection and can be washed down with one of the many Hungarian and international wines on offer. Highly recommended.

SHOPPING

While certainly not a shopping Mecca by any stretch of the imagination, Rákóczi tér does offer supermarkets, banks, and bustle. There is also a daily outdoor market on Simor János Street with stalls selling fruits and vegetables, as well as clothes, souvenirs, wine, and a whole bunch of reasonably priced bric-a-brac.

INFORMATION AND SERVICES

Centrally located Gran Tours (Széchenyi tér 25, tel. 33/502-001, grantours@freemail.hu, summer Mon.–Fri. 8 A.M.–4 P.M., Sat. 9 A.M.– noon, winter Mon.–Fri. 8 A.M.–4 P.M.) is where you should head to if you need any information about Esztergom. Apart from providing visitors with city maps, brochures, and general information, the staff here are also happy to help you exchange money, book accommodations, reserve concert tickets, and arrange for a guided tour of the area.

GETTING THERE
By Bus

Numerous buses depart frequently from Árpád híd bus terminal, which is located at the subway station of the same name in Budapest's 13th district. The faster ride (via Dorog) takes roughly 75 minutes but can vary depending on traffic. Tickets cost approximately 700 Ft.

By Train

Trains to Esztergom leave Budapest's Nyugati station every half-hour. Tickets cost 900 Ft, and the trip lasts roughly 1.5 hours. Note that the Esztergom train station is about a 15–20-minute walk from the center and all major sights.

By Car

Leave Budapest by taking Route #11 north (Szentendre-Visegrad-Esztergom, 40 miles) or Route #10 (Budapest–Dorog–Esztergom, 28 miles).

By Boat

If you have the time and extra cash, traveling by boat can be a pleasurable experience. The popular river tour provider MAHART (V. Belgrád rakpart, tel. 1/484-4000, www .mahartpassnave.hu) has a boat leaving every morning at 8 A.M. from Vigadó tér on the Danube Embankment. The trip lasts 5.5 hours and costs 2,535 Ft.

Lake Balaton

Affectionately nicknamed the "Hungarian Sea," Lake Balaton is both Central Europe's largest lake and Hungary's premier holiday destination. Its 124 miles of shoreline offers visitors a multitude of activities, from enjoying a swim in silky waters to sailing, windsurfing, fishing, and a whole lot more. The rolling hills and historic vineyards of the north will please hikers and wine enthusiasts alike, while the lively southern shore will prove to be more than enough fun for even the most energetic of party-goers. Waterfront towns, spa resorts, natural wonders, and picture-perfect historical landmarks all come with the territory, making Lake Balaton an excellent choice for families, couples, and lone travelers looking for fun, relaxation, adventure, and the quintessential Hungarian summer experience.

The lake's **south shore** is easily reached from Budapest, which is one reason why it attracts thousands of tourists year after year. Another is its famed nightlife that knows no end

and has few, if any, limits. Filled to near capacity with countless resorts, high-rises, shops, bars, restaurants, and discos, it is *the* place in Hungary to spend long days at the beach and even longer nights out on the town. Siófok, the south's largest and busiest resort, remains the lake's HQ of hedonism, luring hordes of fun-loving students and twentysomethings looking to work on their tan before drinking and dancing till they drop. If it's a nonstop party you're after, you'll most definitely find it here.

Lake Balaton's **north shore** is the ying to the south's yang—a destination for travelers more interested in a journey through the country's history and culture, where teeming resorts and drunken revelers are replaced with picturesque towns and centuries-old vineyards. At the far west of the shore is Keszthely, one of the region's largest towns and home to the gorgeous Festetics Palace. Nearby are the fine wines and basalt hills of Badacsony, whose natural environs are some of the finest in the entire region.

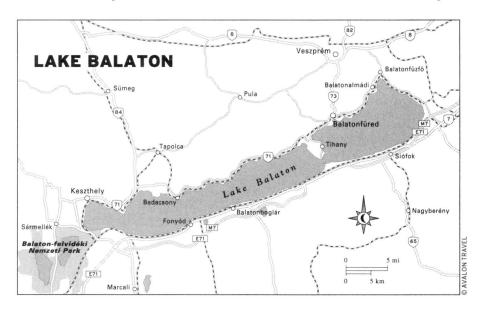

© AVALON TRAVEL

There is also the beautiful, 18th-century Baroque Benedictine Abbey of Tihany, as well as the popular Balatonfüred, Hungary's oldest spa resort. No matter where you go in the north, you'll find peaceful surroundings, old-world hospitality, and a relaxation of spirit that is as rare as it is invigorating.

SIÓFOK

Located on the southeastern end of the lake, Siófok began to come into its own during the 1860s when it was first connected to Budapest by rail. Easily accessible from the capital, it quickly grew into the largest resort town on the lake and continues to be the country's prime location for hedonists the world over. Lined with bars, restaurants, hotels, and clubs,

Siófok attracts a young, student crowd that comes to soak up rays during the day and get their freak on at night. Despite the countless hotels, burger joints, strip bars, and nightclubs, however, the town has somehow managed to preserve some of its old-world charm. Tree-lined promenades take visitors past majestic villas while both the Gold Coast (Aranypart) to the east and the Silver Coast (Ezüstpart) beckon bathers into their soothing shallow waters. Buildings such as the Water Tower in central Szabadság Square, as well as the Evangelical Lutheran Church are worth noting as well, as is peaceful Millennium Park. For the most part, however, people come to Siófok to eat, drink, and be merry, though not necessarily in that order.

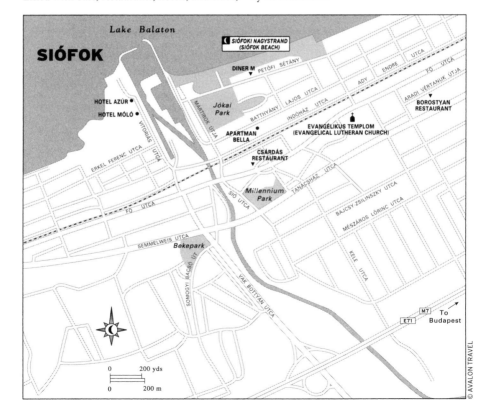

© AVALON TRAVEL

◀ Siófoki Nagystrand (Siófok Beach)

The most visited beach in the country, let alone the lake, Siófok Beach covers an area of over 20 acres and holds roughly 13,000 people. During the day, sun-lovers young and old take a dip, catch some rays, or engage in one of the many water sports on offer. By night, the beach turns into a hedonist's heaven with numerous bars, discos, concerts, and casinos. The beach is also the site of the world famous Coca-Cola Beach House, which attracts thousands of tourists every year thanks to its non-stop nightlife and excellent outdoor concerts.

Millennium Park

Built in 1994, Millennium Park is a peaceful oasis in the center of town spanning well over 170,000 square feet. Well-manicured lawns are home to gorgeous flowers and statues, along with a picturesque musical pavilion and water fountain. At night, the small lake is a wonderfully romantic spot for lovers bathed in the park's lights. Always open, it is the perfect place for those who need to get away from the frantic activity that tends to envelop the rest of the town during the summer months.

Evangélikus templom (Evangelical Lutheran Church)

Siófok's Evangelical Lutheran Church (Fő utca 220, tel. 84/310-549, May–Sept. Mon., Wed., Sat. 10 A.M.–noon, 4–6 P.M., Tues. 10 A.M.–noon) was designed by Ybl-prize-winning architect Imre Makovecz and stands as one of the town's most original and architecturally thought-provoking buildings. Combining traditional elements with modern touches, the church is 80 percent wooden and was mainly financed by Siófok's Finnish sister town Oulu, which is also the name of the park the church resides in. Massive angel wings stretch above either side of the main entrance, protecting all those who enter. Inside, the church seats 120 people and is home to László Péterffy's noteworthy *Statue of the Resurrected,* located above the eastern altar.

Entertainment and Events

Siófok is without a doubt the nightlife capital of Lake Balaton and finding somewhere to quench your thirst or put your dancing shoes to good use will not be a problem. There are countless bars, clubs, cafes, and the like vying for your attention, time, and money, and they are all full of likeminded fun-lovers and thrill seekers. Most people come here to party and you can hear them doing so well into the night.

NIGHTLIFE

The **Palace Dance Club** (Deák Ferenc sétány 2, tel. 84/351-295, www.palace.hu, daily 10 P.M.–5 A.M., entrance depends on theme night/party) is Siófok's most well-known club, attracting over 300,000 visitors a year. Inside are two stories full of house, techno, and trance fans partying on the dance floor and tables, as well as in the massive outdoor garden, which is perfect during warm summer nights. Plenty of weekend programs and theme nights are scheduled, including the very popular Foam and Free Beer Parties. Free Palace buses leave from the water tower in the center of town every hour starting at 9 P.M., and if you see one cruising around town, simply wave and the kind bus driver will stop and let you on. This place is a must for any serious clubber.

Bacardi Music Café (Petofi sétány 5, www.bacardi-music-cafe.hu, daily 9 P.M.–5 A.M., entrance depends on party or theme night) is another institution in Siófok that packs in both students and tourists on a regular basis. Inside you'll find a spacious seating area done up in comfortable bamboo, as well as a dance floor that heats up as the hours fly by. There is also an outdoor patio where people can chill from the block rockin' beats and catch up with friends or attempt to make new ones.

Flört Dance Club (Sió utca, tel. 20/333-3303, www.flort.hu, daily 9 P.M.–5 A.M., cover charge depends on party/theme night) was established in 1989 and has not looked back since. Done up in faux beach decor complete with palm trees and suspended surf boards, this twin-level club is almost always packed with the lake's most beautiful men and women. Trance, house, and techno are spun by international DJs on a nightly basis and the club's various theme nights and parties are almost always sellouts.

FESTIVALS AND EVENTS

During the **Golden Shell Folklore Festival** (first week of July), Siófok changes from a hedonistic party town into a slightly more cultured, international folklore center. Dance troupes from all over the world perform traditional dances to adoring audiences that are invited to take part in the demonstrations and learn a few moves themselves. There are plenty of parades, performances, and concerts throughout the week offering a nice break from the usual club fare that typically overruns the town.

An annual three-day event, the **Balaton International Egg Festival** (mid-October) honors and attempts to further promote the consumption of eggs. Plenty of outdoor concerts take place during the festival, as well as a number of egg-based contests, including a children's egg-drawing event and an adult egg-based recipe contest. One of the most entertaining events is the Egg Ball, which offers dancers the opportunity to party until the sun comes up. Although an egg festival may sound a little strange to some travelers, the event brings in thousands of visitors every year.

Accommodations

There are plenty of accommodation options for visitors to choose from, ranging from upscale wellness centers to guesthouses and hostels. Many affordable guest rooms are available in private homes with remarkably low prices and a family atmosphere to boot. A trip to the Tourinform office will arm you with plenty of phone numbers and addresses but bear in mind that Siófok is a ridiculously popular tourist destination and that you take your chances by not reserving a room ahead of time.

The four-star **C Hotel Azúr** (Vitorlás utca 11, tel. 84/501-413, www.hotelazur.hu, 39,000 Ft d) is situated directly on the shore and has the distinction of being the largest wellness and conference hotel in Balaton. Its brightly colored

and tasteful Mediterranean decor provides a warm, welcoming environment that is home to 222 clean, comfortable, and spacious rooms and luxury suites. The rooms are all fashioned with balconies and equipped with movie channels, Wi-Fi, safe, mini-bar, and air conditioning. The hotel also boasts its own beach, as well as a number of saunas and steam rooms, a thermal bath, and one of the finest indoor pools you'll ever see. As far as the region goes, this is quite simply as good as it gets.

Located next to the railway and bus station, the **Hotel Vértes** (Batthyány utca 24, tel. 84/312-422, www.hotelvertes.hu, 29,000 Ft d) was transformed a few years back from a two-star hotel into a four-star wellness hotel offering guests everything from a thermal bath and sauna to solarium and massage therapy. Its 58 rooms all come with satellite TV and air-conditioning, and, though spartanly furnished, are nevertheless comfortable. A mere five minutes away from all the action, it remains a convenient, if somewhat pricey, choice.

The **Hotel Móló** (Vitorlás utca 16, tel. 84/310-047, www.balatonihajozas.hu, 16,700 Ft d) is a pleasant, affordable hotel located next to the marina. All 37 of the simply furnished but cozy double rooms come with TV, fridge, and balcony and the friendly staff is always on call to make your stay as comfortable as possible. The hotel has its own lido, as well as a children's pool, bar, and hall for various social and business functions.

Apartman Bella (Batthyány Lajos utca 14, tel. 84/510-078, www.siofokbella.hu, 11,500–13,000 Ft d) is a reasonably priced, popular option. The 12 apartments vary in size, with 1–3 bedrooms holding 2–6 people. All apartments have their own terrace, as well as kitchen or kitchenette, fridge, satellite TV, and minibar. Located a couple minutes' walk from the beach, port, and center, it is an excellent choice for travelers of all tastes and budgets.

Food

Most of the food in town is of the traditional Hungarian variety, but there are plenty of kiosks and smallish eateries serving up a variety of snacks and foods like hamburgers and pizza. Prices vary greatly, so have a look around before settling on a place that suits both your tastes and budget.

Csárdás Restaurant (Fő utca 105, tel. 84/310-642, www.csardasetterem.hu, daily noon–9 P.M., 1,350–2,690 Ft) is a highly reputable establishment located in the center of town that serves up tasty Hungarian fish and meat dishes. Its three halls are decorated with light traditional touches and its outdoor seating is nearly always full during the holiday season. Also on offer are over 20 kinds of Hungarian wine, which go down splendidly during the live gypsy music concerts in the summertime.

Near the railway is **Hintaló Vendéglő** (Vécsey út 6, tel. 84/350-494, May 15–Sept. 20 daily noon–midnight, 1,200–3,000 Ft), an excellent traditional Hungarian restaurant that should not be missed. It's decorated in a charming rustic style, and the friendly staff delivers mouth-watering meat, fish, and wild game delights that are sure to please all palates. Dinnertime is the right time here as dishes are prepared in a *bogrács* (cauldron), as well as grilled on an open fire outdoors.

Diner M (Petofi stny. 3, tel. 84/510-074, www.dinerm.hu, late May–June and Sept. daily 10 A.M.–2 A.M., July–Aug. 24 hours, mains 1,290–1,490 Ft) is not only a step back in time, but an American one at that. Playing off the classic diners of the 1950s, Diner M incorporates booths, stools, jukeboxes, and muscle cars to recreate a piece of Americana known and loved the world over. Diners can choose from club sandwiches and chili dogs, burgers and milkshakes, while listening to old Elvis and rockabilly records. Some say it's kitsch, others say it doesn't belong. Whatever it is, it certainly distances itself from the usual fare found around town.

Borostyan Restaurant (Aradi vértanúk utca 57, tel. 84/311-707, www.borostyan etterem.hu, daily 11 A.M.–10 P.M., mains 1,050–2,050 Ft) is another traditional Hungarian restaurant worth paying a visit. Spacious and tastefully decorated, diners are able to comfortably enjoy a number of Hun-garian specialties, including grilled meat, trout, and wild game. The friendly service, excellent wines, and family atmosphere are three more reasons to stop in for a memorable lunch or dinner.

Shopping
Sometimes it feels like Siófok is one big souvenir stand pulsing with tourists in dire need of souvenirs and beach accessories. The center of town, particularly Kálmán Promenade, is jam-packed with shops and stalls managed by smiling shopkeepers eager to make a sale. Postcards, beach towels, leather goods, embroidery, and a whole host of arts and crafts are available, all of which make for a memorable gift item or souvenir. Prices can be rather inflated at times so don't be embarrassed to haggle should you feel it necessary.

Information and Services
Tourinform Siófok (Water Tower, tel. 84/315-355, www.tourinform.hu, summer daily 8 A.M.–8 P.M., winter daily 8 A.M.–5 P.M.) is located right under the town's massive water tower and provides visitors with maps and information regarding Siófok, its sights, and Lake Balaton in general. Help is available if you need to find accommodations and tickets for various events can be arranged here as well.

Getting There
BY TRAIN
Trains leave regularly from Budapest's Keleti and Déli train stations. The journey typically lasts 2–3 hours depending on route taken and costs 2,200–2,600 Ft.

BY CAR
Siófok is 70 miles from Budapest. Driving from Budapest to Siófok couldn't be easier. Simply take Highway M7 south all the way to town, then follow the "Siófok Centrum" sign into the center of town.

BALATONFÜRED
Located at the northeastern end of the lake, Balatonfüred is a picturesque town surrounded

by gently sloping hills that grew in popularity as a result of its curative springs and warm, invigorating climate. First mentioned in the estate registration of Tihany Abbey in 1211, it was home to spa houses as early as the 18th century and quickly became a favorite destination of liberal-minded politicians and artists. A lively and sophisticated social and cultural scene followed, leading to a boom of development in the 19th century. Today, it is home to remarkable villas, residential districts, and

BALATONFÜRED

churches, as well as modern hotels and pulsating clubs, managing somehow to strike a balance between the old world and the new. Among the town's highlights are the Lajos Kossuth Spring and Reformed Church, not to mention a romantic stroll along the pier.

Kossuth Lajos-forrás (Lajos Kossuth Spring)

Situated in the center of town in Gyógy Square is the Lajos Kossuth Spring, also referred to as the "Drinking Hall." Built in 1800 in a neoclassical style, it was originally named after Emperor Joseph Francis I, who visited Balatonfüred in 1852, but was renamed to honor Hungary's beloved radical after the end of World War II. Originally used to treat stomach and kidney conditions, its several springs are used today primarily to relieve cardiovascular ailments.

Lóczy-barlang (Lóczy Cave)

Though not particularly impressive in size, Lóczy Cave (Öreghegyi utca, tel. 87/555-291, May–Sept. daily 10 A.M.–6 P.M.), with a 394-foot-long, 63-foot-deep subterranean setting, is a must for cave enthusiasts. Discovered in 1882, its pretty calcium carbonate formations coupled with layers of limestone dating back millions of years ago leave an indelible impression, as do the bubbling hot waters below. The site is named after the famed Lajos Loczy, who spearheaded countless forays into Hungary's caves. The 20-minute guided tour offered here is an excellent lesson in the region's evolution over the centuries.

Református templom (Christian Reformed Church)

Commonly referred to as the "white church," the Christian Reformed Church (Óvoda utca 1, tel. 87/342-795, Mass Sun. 8 A.M.) is a single-towered classicist beauty whose foundation stone was laid in 1828. Inside, the whitewashed walls and alluring plainness of its huge hall provoke silent fascination, while its large choir on the northern side is reminiscent of the grandeur of Tihany Abbey. Behind the church is a relatively new multistory rectory that is home to offices and a congregation hall, adding to what is already one of the town's most valuable and recognizable landmarks.

Entertainment and Events

Balatonfüred's nightlife heats up during the summer with plenty of Hungarians and visitors from all over the world shedding their bathing suits and suiting up in their sexiest outfits. Clubs tend to open around 9 or 10 P.M. and close whenever the party seems to finally be over. Many go club hopping while others pick a place and settle in for the long night ahead. Whatever your strategy, you're bound to have a ball.

NIGHTLIFE

Columbus Dance Club (Honvéd utca 3, tel. 30/268-3399, www.columbusclub.hu, daily 6 P.M.–4 A.M., cover charge ranges free–800 Ft) is a spacious club with plenty of booze and neon lights to get the party started. The sunken dance floor is often packed to capacity on weekends, as well as during the multitude of theme nights and alcohol-promotion parties.

Named after the notorious party island in Greece, **Club Santorini** (Fürdő utca 35, tel. 30/956-2536, www.santorini.hu, daily 6 P.M.–5 A.M., no cover charge) has adopted a distinctly Mediterranean feel what with the light-blue paint job, exposed brick, and fun-loving atmosphere. It seems like there's a theme party here every night of the week showcasing various musical genres and offering huge discounts on the chosen cocktail of the night. Things heat up here quickly on the weekends, encouraging the party to rave on till the sun comes up.

FESTIVALS AND EVENTS

In 2007, Hungary entered the *Guinness Book of Records* by holding a 192-hour mega concert during the **International Guitar Festival** (end of June). The event, like years past, was a huge success. When not breaking records, the festival hosts leading guitarists from all over the world whose styles range from classical to rock

to flamenco. This is one festival that no lover of the six-string should miss.

The **Blue Ribbon Regatta** (middle of July) was first held on Lake Balaton in 1934 and has been going strong ever since. The route runs Balatonfüred–Balatonkenese–Siófok–Keszthely–Balatonfüred and, at 124 miles, is Europe's longest round-the-lake race. Held every odd-numbered year, this is arguably the Hungarian sailing season's most popular race.

Held annually since 1825, the **Anna Ball** (end of July) is undoubtedly Balatonfüred's most eagerly anticipated social event of the year and is celebrated on whatever weekend falls closest to July 26—the day the name Anna is celebrated. The entire town gets dressed up for the occasion and takes part in a street ball held in Vitorlás Square. The highlight of the event is the choosing of the Belle of the Ball, who, along with her runners-up, rides across town in carriages before taking a trip around the lake on *Nemere II*, one of the town's most impressive sailing boats. Other events during this fun and romantic weekend are dance performances, brass band concerts, and theater productions.

Accommodations

The **Flamingó Wellness Hotel** (Széchenyi utca 16, tel. 87/581-060, www.flamingohotel.hu, 30,250–35,200 Ft d) is a modern four-star hotel situated right on the shores of Lake Balaton. Its 181 rooms, apartments, and family suites are both spacious and spotlessly clean, offering gorgeous views of Tihany and its abbey. There are plenty of shops and restaurants nearby and the hotel's wellness and spa services include an indoor pool, whirlpool tub, steam bath, sauna, massage, beauty salon, and solarium. Those looking for a bit of pampering while on holiday will definitely want to consider the Flamingó.

The very affordable three-star **Blaha Lujza Hotel** (Blaha Lujza utca 4, tel. 87/581-210, www.hotelblaha.hu, 13,350–14,600 Ft d) is a pretty period piece of a hotel that used to serve as home to the famous Hungarian singer of the same name. Its 22 rooms are simply

© OLIVER HERBST

peace and quiet along Balatonfüred's pier

furnished yet comfortable, but there is no air conditioning available. Nevertheless, its traditional decor, friendly staff, and proximity to the lake all add up to a sensible choice for those who appreciate intimate surroundings without paying exorbitant rates.

Less than half a mile from the lake you'll find the reasonably priced **Green Guest House** (Nádor str. 47, tel. 87/481-505, www.green guesthouse.hu, 11,000 Ft d). Its nine rooms are all outfitted with TV, fridge, and a balcony that's perfect for morning coffees. Though certainly not luxurious, it is clean and well run by helpful, friendly staff who are able to arrange sailing and fishing trips, as well as cultural events and goulash parties. There is also a modest-sized swimming pool and sun deck to help guests relax before and after they hit the town. Perfect for those on a tight budget.

Füred Camping (Széchenyi utca 24, tel. 87/580-241, fured@balatontourist.hu, 6,800–8,600 Ft, open Apr. 15–Oct. 15) is a huge campsite with plenty of room for all to enjoy the sun and lake. A large water slide is

its main attraction and there is also a small beach nearby for kids. The premises also boast a modern swimming pool, supermarket, sauna, playground, and comfortable toilet facilities. There are plenty of options in the food and drink department, as well as a number of sports activities including tennis, volleyball, and mini golf.

Food

The ⟨ **Cimbora Grill Garden** (Széchenyi utca 23, tel. 87/482-512, www.cimboragrillkert.hu, daily noon–11 P.M., mains 1,300–2,400 Ft) is an outdoor affair that seats up to 150 people who have come with an appetite. A wide variety of grilled meat dishes including ribs, pork chops, chicken, goose, and turkey is available, along with a salad bar offering 10 types of salad. Be prepared to eat plenty and get your hands a little dirty in the process.

Located next to the pier, **Stefánia Vitorlás Restaurant** (Tagore Promenade 1, tel. 87/343-407, www.vitorlasetterem.hu, daily 10 A.M.–midnight, mains 1,450–2,600 Ft) is home to a huge sunny terrace that seats up to 600 people. Diners will be impressed with both the quality of the food—which includes delicious Hungarian specialties like veal in smoked cheese and Balaton fish soup—and professional service. There are also over 40 desserts to tempt you, including a mouthwatering strawberry yogurt cake. Aside from the tasty fare, guests can't discount the remarkable view where you can dine and daydream at the same time.

Hordó Csárda (Széchenyi utca 33, tel. 87/482-017, www.hordocsarda.click.hu, daily noon–11 P.M., mains 1,300–2,600 Ft) is a family-run inn and restaurant boasting a number of Hungarian specialties like fish soup and paprika chicken. There are also Transylvanian specialties available like the Gypsy pork chops, as well as a hearty selection of poultry, fish, and wild game dishes. Hungarian music and folk programs are often performed in the evenings, but keep in mind that the restaurant only operates during the tourist season (Apr.–Oct.).

Shopping

There are plenty of shopping opportunities in town, with local establishments selling everything from wine to wooden toys and souvenirs. The most controversial shopping experience, however, can be had at Annagora Park (www.annagorapark.com), a mock Greek village that was completed just a few short years ago. Brightly colored shops and kiosks hawk everything from handmade crafts, paintings, and clothing, as well as a myriad of cheap and not-so-cheap gift items. There are also restaurants, casinos, and pubs for those needing a break. The reason it's controversial is because many find it to be remarkably kitschy and an enormous eyesore. Establishments with names like the Akropolis Café only strengthen their argument. Nevertheless, the park continues to be packed with visitors looking for a decent deal, which can be had if you look hard enough.

Information and Services

The accommodating folks at Tourinform (Kisfaludy utca 1, tel. 87/580-480, www.tourinform.hu) are happy to arm visitors with a number of brochures and publications regarding the region and country in general. Information about cultural events, restaurants, hotels, and sights is readily available, as are plenty of books, maps, postcards, and CDs. Office hours are May, June, September Monday–Friday 9 A.M.–5 P.M., Saturday 9 A.M.–1 P.M.; July–August Monday–Friday 9 A.M.–7 P.M., Saturday 9 A.M.–6 P.M., Sunday 9 A.M.–1 P.M.; October Monday–Friday 9 A.M.–4 P.M.

Getting There
BY TRAIN
Trains leave Budapest regularly from both Keleti and Déli stations. The trip takes 3–4 hours depending on routes taken and costs 2,000–2,500 Ft.

BY CAR
Balatonfüred is located roughly 87 miles from Budapest along main road #71. If coming via Veszprém, take main road #73 and change to #71 in Csopak.

BY BOAT
The town's port is very active during the summer season and can be reached from a number of spots, including Tihany and Siófok.

TIHANY
The Tihany Peninsula became Hungary's first nationally protected area in 1952 and has managed to maintain its charming traditional fishing village quality despite the surge of development elsewhere in Balaton. Its unique landscape is characterized by the Inner and Outer Lake (both formed in volcanic craters), as well as Csúcs, Nyereg, and Apáti Hills, which were once the setting for very active volcanoes. Due to the peninsula's thermal activity, approximately 50 geyser cones cover the area, not to mention the Geyser Field, which was formed over three million years ago. Tihany village, the area's main historical attraction, dates back to 1055, when it was founded by King Andrew I; its beautiful, 18th-century Baroque Benedictine Abbey is undoubtedly its most well-known and impressive monument.

◖ Tihanyi Apátság (Tihany Benedictine Abbey)

Established by King Andrew I in 1055, the Benedictine Abbey (András tér 1, tel. 87/538-200, daily 9 A.M.–5:30 P.M.) was erected in honor of St. Anianus. It is home to its founder's sarcophagus, as well as a copy of the abbey's deed, which is the oldest existing document containing the Hungarian language. During the Turkish occupation of the 16th and 17th centuries, the medieval monastery was transformed into a fortress and eventually destroyed. Reconstruction began in 1716 and finished in 1752, giving the two-steeple church its present Baroque form. Its interior is filled with remarkable wood carvings, as well as banisters decorated with angels and arguably the most beautiful carved Baroque pulpit in the country, all of which came care of gifted artist Sebestyen Stuhlhof. Next door is the **Tihany Museum** (tel. 87/448-650), which is likewise housed in a pretty Baroque building and

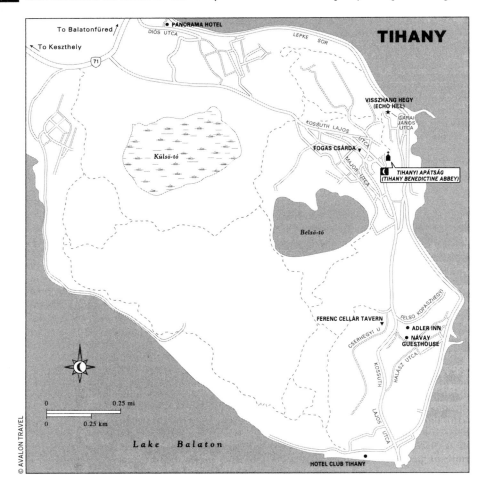

features a wealth of information about the region's tumultuous past and enduring culture. Both the abbey and museum can be visited by paying a single entrance fee of 500 Ft.

Visszhang hegy (Echo Hill)

A path on the left side of the church leads up to Echo Hill, which affords splendid views of the lake. Words shouted from the top of the hill reverberate back from the walls of the church and produce an echo. Sadly, the effect has begun to wane in the last few years due to increased noise and building but can nevertheless still be heard—at least for now.

Entertainment and Events

The **Lavender Festival** (late June–early July) in Tihany is a unique opportunity to visit an enormous lavender plantation and take part in the lavender harvest. Visitors are taken on organized trips by professionals who are happy to inform them on the flora and fauna of the area, as well as help them pick the fragrant flowers.

Every year, Tihany's **Summer Theatre Festival** (early July–late August) hosts a wide array of popular cultural programs in an open-air theater. Locals and visitors from all over the world have enjoyed spectacular performances, which have included productions of both Hungarian and internationally known plays, as well as concerts, dance performances, and children's theater. Tickets can be secured at the Tourinform office in town.

Accommodations

Located at the top of the Tihany Peninsula is the four-star **Hotel Club Tihany** (Tihany-Rév Pf. 31, tel. 87/538-500, www.clubtihany.hu, 14,000 Ft d). Its 330 rooms and bungalows are always filled to capacity in the summer. The rooms themselves are brightly decorated and come with TV and Internet access, though odds are you won't be using them much. A swimming pool and Cure Center offering everything from physiotherapy to total health packages are also available. Those traveling with children will be hard-pressed to find better accommodations, but those who'd rather stay away from the hoots and hollers of young ones might want to look elsewhere.

The **Panorama Hotel** (Lepke sor 9-11, tel. 87/538-220, www.panoramaht.com, 18,000 Ft d) is situated in beautiful Tihany Bay and surrounded by peace and quiet. Town is just a short walk from the hotel, while Balatonfüred's active nightlife is a scant 1.2 miles away. Offering 39 basically furnished but comfortable rooms equipped with TV, phone, minibar, and safe, the hotel also has a popular sauna and solarium available for guests. This is an excellent choice for those who like to be relatively near the action but look forward to going home to a peaceful night's sleep when the fun's over. Reservations in advance are highly recommended, as is asking for a room with a view of the bay.

The **Adler Inn** (Felsőkopaszhegyi utca 1a, tel. 87/538-000, www.adler-tihany.hu, 11,280 Ft d) is an elegant hotel situated amongst Tihany's vineyards less than a mile from the center. Open from the middle of March to the end of October, its 11 rooms and apartments are spacious and stylishly furnished, adding to the overall beauty of the natural surroundings. A peaceful swimming pool and terrace, along with top-notch sauna, complete the perfect getaway.

The **Návay Guesthouse** (Alsókopaszhegyi utca 1, tel. 70/382-2369, www.navaypanzio.hu, room 9,000 Ft d, apartment 11,000 Ft d) is a charming and affordable option located high up above on Felsőkopasz Hill. While the center of town is a 15-minute walk away, guests here are nevertheless awed by the wonderful views and pleased with the friendly service and family atmosphere. A swimming pool, terrace, and garden are on the premises; non-smokers will be relieved to know that the guesthouse is completely smoke free.

Food

The **Fogas Csárda** (Kossuth Lajos 9, tel. 87/448-658, www.fogascsarda.hu, Mar. 1–Nov. 15 daily 11 A.M.–11 P.M., Nov. 16–Feb. 28 Fri.–Sun. 11 A.M.–11 P.M., mains 1,500–2,700 Ft) is the oldest traditional restaurant in Tihany and very well known to both tourists and Hungarians. Located near the Abbey, it offers fish, wild

© OLIVER HERBST

Tihany Benedictine Abbey

game, and traditional dishes in a rustic setting decorated with handcrafted furniture and local art and crafts. This is an excellent choice for those wanting a taste of the authentic, though it can get overrun by tour groups now and again.

Amongst the vineyards on Mount Cser you'll find the exemplary **Ferenc Cellar Tavern** (Cser utca, Mt. Cser, tel. 87/448-575, www.ferencpince.hu, mains 1,550–2,800 Ft), which serves up delicious Hungarian fare like red hot goulash, garlic pork chops, and fresh pike-perch and zander. Diners enjoy both the grub and the extraordinary view, washing it all down with any number of locally produced wines.

Shopping

Part of the fun in Tihany is to stroll around and have a look at all the wares being sold along the cobblestone streets. There is certainly no shortage of local handicrafts, embroidery, wine, and earthenware pots to choose from, as well as a wide variety of wooden trinkets ranging from bracelets to chess sets. Take your time and try striking up a conversation or two. And remem-ber: Never accept the first price given. Don't be afraid to haggle until you get to a price you're comfortable with.

Information and Services

Brochures, books, and a whole range of information can be found at the Tourinform Office (Kossuth utca 20, tel. 87/448-804, www.tourinform.hu). The friendly staff there will happy to answer your questions and also sell postcards, stamps, maps, and various books offering more detailed information about the region. The office's hours are January 2–April 15 Monday–Friday 10 A.M.–4 P.M.; April 16–May 31 Monday–Friday 9 A.M.–5 P.M., Saturday 10 A.M.–4 P.M.; June 1–June 15 Monday–Friday 9 A.M.–5 P.M., Saturday–Sunday 10 A.M.–4 P.M.; June 16–September 15 Monday–Friday 9 A.M.–7 P.M., Saturday–Sunday 10 A.M.–6 P.M.; September 16–30 Monday–Friday 9 A.M.–5 P.M., Saturday 10 A.M.–4 P.M.; October 1–31 Monday–Friday 9 A.M.–4 P.M.; November 1–December 31 Monday–Friday 10 A.M.–4 P.M.

Getting There

BY BUS

A local bus to Tihany can be taken from Aszófő, which is a mere three miles away. Balatonfüred also has a bus serving Tihany, which can be caught just outside its railway station. Buses run hourly; the trip lasts about a half-hour and the fare is 132 Ft.

BY CAR

Tihany is roughly 89 miles from Budapest. From Budapest, take Highway M7 south then main road #71 from Balatonaliga.

BY BOAT

You can opt to travel via ferry (340 Ft) from Szántód. The trip lasts 10 minutes, with ferries leaving every 40 minutes.

BADACSONY

Hungary's finest poets and painters have for hundreds of years described Badacsony and its surroundings, located at the western end of the lake, as the most beautiful landscape in the country. It is characterized by enormous basalt hills, the most famous of which are the Badacsony (1,227 feet), the Gulács (1,289 feet), the Csobánc (1,234 feet), and Szent György-hegy (1,362 feet). A winding, 500-foot path makes its way up Badacsony Hill and is lined with charming old wine cellars selling the local produce—which just happens to be some of the country's most famous and delicious wines. Calm, quiet, and surrounded by awe-inspiring natural beauty, Badacsony makes for a wonderful day or two away from the rigors of reality.

Basalt Hills

These wondrous geological relics resemble coffins from a distance, adding another poetic layer of beauty and mystique to the area. The various formations of solidified basalt are legendary, with some of the more popular examples being the Stone Gate of Badacsony and the "organs" of Szent György. The hills' numerous shapes and geological souvenirs of the past outline the development of volcanic activity in the area, and it is interesting to note that one reason given for the region's superiority in wine is the volcanic ash found in the soil. Badacsony's famous vineyards, meanwhile, are located on the southern slopes between Badacsony Hill and the lake.

Entertainment and Events

What else can one expect from a town revered far and wide for its tasty wine than a festival honoring the godly grape? All of the region's traditions come to life during the carefree days of the **Badacsony Wine Festival** (late July–early August), which includes demonstrations on winemaking then and now, as well as a number of outdoor concerts and theatrical performances guaranteed to keep one and all happily in their cups.

Accommodations

The **Badacsony Hotel** (Balatoni út 14, tel. 87/471-040, www.badacsonyhotel.hu, 21,000 Ft d) is situated right on Lake Balaton's shore, making a stay here a near heavenly experience. Its 70 comfortable, brightly decorated rooms complement a gorgeous summer terrace and swimming pool, which you will be loathe to leave when your holiday time is up. Friendly staff and a warm English pub are two more reasons to start thinking about reservations today.

Borbarátok Panzió (Római út 78, tel. 87/471-000, www.borbaratok.hu, 8,500 Ft d, breakfast 900 Ft) is a friendly, family-run restaurant and guesthouse located near the beach and village center. Its small number of rooms and traditional Hungarian restaurant lend an air of authenticity that differs greatly from the larger, more commercial type of hotels populating the region. Live entertainment is often scheduled in the evenings and guests can also arrange a number of leisure activities, such as wine tasting and fishing. This is a fine choice for budget travelers who like to dive deep into the native culture.

Food

The **Szent Orban Wine-House and Restaurant** (Str. Kisfaludy 5, tel. 87/431-382, daily 10 A.M.–10 P.M., mains 1,500–3,650 Ft) is a gourmet restaurant that adds an element

taking a break in beautiful Badacsony

of traditional elegance to Badacsony's limited dining options. Serving regional dishes that include pike-perch and wild game, it is also an excellent place to imbibe some of the country's finest wines while absorbed in the lovely panoramic view from the summer terrace.

Shopping

Pretty much the only thing worth buying in Badacsony is some of its delicious wine; the **Sipos Wine House** (Szőlő utca 13, tel. 87/471-153, www.siposborhaz.hu, daily 10 A.M.–6 P.M.) is an excellent place to start. The vineyard is located at the foot of Badacsony Mountain, ensuring this decades-old family business the finest of harvests season after season. Apart from offering excellent vintages at remarkably affordable prices, they are also happy to arrange wine tastings at similarly reasonable fees (800–1,800 Ft per person).

Information and Services

Maps, guides, and a whole host of information on the region can be acquired at Tourin- form Iroda (Park utca 6, tel. 87/531-013, www .badacsonytomaj.hu). Guided tours can be arranged here and various souvenirs, postcards, and the like are on sale as well. The office's hours are May 1–June 14 Monday–Friday 9 A.M.–5 P.M., Saturday 9 A.M.–1 P.M.; June 15–August 31 Monday–Friday 9 A.M.–7 P.M., Saturday–Sunday 9 A.M.–6 P.M.; September 1–15 Monday–Friday 9 A.M.–6 P.M., Saturday–Sunday 9 A.M.–5 P.M.; September 16–30 Monday–Friday 9 A.M.–5 P.M., Saturday 9 A.M.–2 P.M.; October 1–30 Monday– Friday 9 A.M.–5 P.M.; November 1–April 30 Monday–Friday 9 A.M.–3:30 P.M.

Those who spend at least one night in Badacsony qualify for the Badacsony Card, which can be obtained from local lodgings. The card allows holders to use all beaches for free and entitles them to 10 percent off at participating restaurants and wine cellars.

Getting There
BY TRAIN

The easiest way to get to Badacsony is by train. If coming from Budapest, trains leave frequently from both Keleti and Déli stations. Trips last 3.5–4.5 hours and cost 2,800–4,200 Ft. If coming from anywhere else in the region, simply alight at Badacsony train stop.

KESZTHELY

Situated at the far western tip of the lake, Keszthely is not only one of the region's largest towns, but one of its most beautiful as well, attracting thousands of tourists during the warm summer months. The town began to develop rapidly in the 14th century when crossing trade routes brought unprecedented wealth and commerce. Destroyed during the Turkish Wars, it was brought back to life in the 18th century by the powerful Festetics family, who became the area's sole landowner and was responsible for the building of a city hospital, grammar school, and Europe's first agricultural college, the Georgikon. By the end of the 19th century, Keszthely had firmly established itself as a premier bathing resort that boasted soothing waters and an architecturally eclectic town center. Today, much of the era's architecture remains and the town's numerous museums, monuments, and landmarks, particularly the elegant Festetics Palace, help make it one of the lake's finest holiday destinations.

Festetics Palota (Festetics Palace)

Festetics Palace (Kastély utca 1, tel. 83/312-190, Tues.–Sun. 10 A.M.–5 P.M., free admission) is the fourth-largest palace in Hungary, boasting 101 rooms, a protected park, and museum tracing the history of the town's most influential family. Commissioned by Kristóf Festetics, construction of the U-shaped, twin-story Baroque palace began in 1745 and was extended and altered over the years by sons Pál and György. Visitors to the palace will be treated to an amazing collection of exhibitions found in the Helikon Palace Museum (Kastély utca 1, tel. 83/312-190, May 31–Sept. 1 Tues.–Sun. 9 A.M.–5 P.M., July 1–Aug. 31 daily 9 A.M.–6 P.M., 1,300 Ft). Highlights include the outstanding Helikon Library, whose floor-to-ceiling oak bookcases were built by a local

carpenter and have managed to remain intact over the years, as well as various trophies, weapons, and residential rooms furnished with invaluable pieces from the period. To the west of the palace are the immaculately kept Festetics Palace Grounds, which are decorated with pretty statues and fountains, reminding visitors of an elegance and style long since gone.

Balatoni Múzeum (Balaton Museum)

Founded in 1898, Balaton Museum (Múzeum utca 2, tel. 83/312-351, May–Oct. Tues.–Sun. 10 A.M.–6 P.M., Nov.–Apr. Tues.–Sat. 9 A.M.–5 P.M., 350 Ft) has the distinct honor of being the oldest museum in the country. Inside, visitors will find numerous educational exhibits covering everything there is to know about the region. An impressive diorama outlines the lake's enormous variety of flora and fauna, while other rooms detail the region's local dress, jewelry, and pottery, as well as its rich history of fishing, boating, and bathing. This is a must for those interested in familiarizing themselves intimately with the area's rich archeological, geological, and natural evolution.

Georgikon Majormúzeum (Georgikon Manor Museum)

Detailing the area's agricultural history, the Georgikon Manor Museum (Bercsényi utca 67, tel. 83/311-563, Apr. and Oct. Mon.–Fri. 10 A.M.–5 P.M., May–Sept. Tues.–Sun. 10 A.M.–5 P.M., 300 Ft) is located on the site of Europe's first ever agricultural college. A wide variety of exhibitions concerning the college's history, the traditions of viticulture and viniculture, and the hard life of farmers and servants help visitors understand the unforgiving challenges of agriculture throughout the centuries. Tools, carts, coaches, and farming machinery complete the effect.

Entertainment and Events

Most of the bars and clubs are sadly of the neon-lit or strip variety, but there are a number of loose and friendly establishments that are second homes to students and night owls alike.

A stroll through town will quickly enlighten you as to which ones are up your alley.

NIGHTLIFE

John's Pub (Kossuth Lajos út 46, 309931140, www.johnspub.hu, Mon.–Fri. noon–midnight, Sat.–Sun. 6 P.M.–midnight, no cover charge) is a pretty straightforward type of pub, with plenty of wood furnishings and tons of drink-happy youngsters. This place gets pretty busy on weekends and even busier during theme nights and special parties. It's loads of fun if you can keep up.

For a walk on the wild side, try **512 Club** (Georgikon utca 1, tel. 70/250-2950, www.512club.hu, Sun.–Thurs. 4 P.M.–1 A.M., Fri.–Sat. 4 P.M.–3 A.M., no cover charge), a long, dark alternative bar that can get pretty rowdy, especially when it hosts live concerts. Music ranges from ska and punk to rock, providing a refreshing change from the countless techno beats that typically fill the night air.

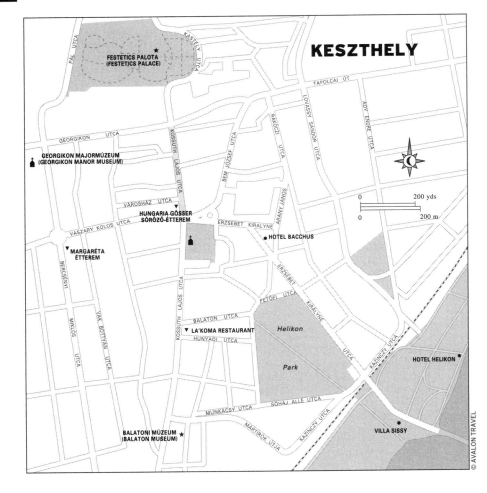

KESZTHELY

© AVALON TRAVEL

Club Inside (Szalasztó utca 18, tel. 30/325-5699, www.clubin.hu, Sun.–Thurs. 2 p.m.–midnight, Fri.–Sat. 2 p.m.–4 a.m., cover charge ranges free–2,500 Ft) is a dance club very much like every other dance club you've been to. Strobe lights, DJs, the young and ecstatic all pull together to have as much debauched fun as possible. Clubbers will appreciate the loose vibe, while those interested in quieter settings and getting to know the person they're with will definitely want to seek shelter elsewhere.

◖ BALATON FESTIVAL

The Balaton Festival (second half of May) is easily Keszthely's biggest and most important cultural event. It is held to symbolically usher in the lake's summer season and is an eclectic mix of what some might call "high" and "low" art. It traditionally opens with a classical concert at Balaton Theatre, which paves the way for a variety of similar concerts held at various upscale venues. The streets, on the other hand, are filled with jugglers, clowns, and various other street performers, all getting in on the act and entertaining the swelling crowds. Outdoor pop and rock shows fill the night air and there are plenty of other dance and theater productions to enjoy as well. The festival closes with the hugely popular Balaton Ballroom Dance Competition, capping off two weeks of not-to-be-missed fun.

Accommodations

There are plenty of places to choose from, ranging from huge hotels to pretty pensions. As always, the best deals are to be found at guesthouses and private rooms, the addresses and contacts of which can be made readily available to you with a simple visit to the town's Tourinform office.

Open from early spring to late fall, the **Hotel Helikon** (Balatonpart 5, tel. 83/889-636, www .danubiushotels.com/helikon, 29,300 Ft d) is a pricey, three-star affair situated right on the shore. Its 232 rooms and suites are comfortable, well kept, and equipped with satellite TV, minibar, and balcony offering nice views of the lake.

A wide variety of sports facilities and health services are available, including indoor and outdoor tennis courts, swimming pool, sauna, solarium, bowling, hairdresser, manicure and pedicure. This is a reliable option for those who prefer big hotels and a certain level of luxury.

The **Hotel Kakadu** (Pázmány Péter utca 14, tel. 20/460-2134, www.ohb.hu/kakadu, 16,400 Ft d) is a calm, quiet, and picturesque three-star hotel located 20 minutes' walking distance from the center. Guests will be impressed by the friendly and helpful staff, as well as the tastefully decorated rooms that come with all modern amenities (except for air-conditioning) and a balcony to boot. There's also a gorgeous indoor swimming pool, peaceful garden, and large terrace on the roof that's perfect for sunbathing. This is an excellent choice for those who like to be treated as honored guests, as opposed to just one of the masses at any given chain hotel.

The **Hotel Bacchus** (Erzsébet királyné st 18, tel. 83/510-450, www.bacchushotel.hu, 14,600 Ft d) is hard to beat when it comes to location, situated as it is right in the heart of town. The friendly staff does their best to make your stay a pleasant one and the basically furnished but relatively comfortable rooms should be suitable for most easy-going travelers. The onsite restaurant serves excellent Hungarian fare, including fish and wild game specialties, and the hotel's wine cellar/museum allows guests to both learn about and purchase some of the country's finest wines. Overall, this is a solid choice but a few have observed that the value for money is somewhat on the lower end of the scale.

The **Villa Sissy** (Erzsébet királyné utca 70, tel. 83/321-673, www.villasissy.hu, 9,000–13,000 Ft d) is a quiet, romantic getaway located a mere two-minute walk from the lakefront. Clean, spacious, tastefully decorated rooms and apartments accommodate a maximum of 13 people, which helps maintain an intimate, family-type atmosphere. This is a great and affordable option for budget travelers who will be staying a night or two and want to stay close to the action.

Food

Margaréta Étterem (Bercsényi M. utca 60, tel. 83/314-882, www.margaretaetterem.hu, daily 11 A.M.–11 P.M., mains 750–1,800 Ft) is a very affordable, very traditional Hungarian eatery that serves up all the classics: goulash, paprika chicken, fish soup, and a load of wild game dishes. Basic furnishings with no frills lend an air of the authentic, as does the delicious homemade grub.

Hungaria Gösser Söröző-Étterem (Kossuth Lajos utca 35, tel. 83/312-265, daily 9 A.M.–11 P.M., mains 1,200–2,700 Ft) is a spacious, traditionally decorated Hungarian restaurant with outdoor seating that is always packed in the summertime. Mouthwatering meat dishes and spicy soups are the most popular choices here, and there's an excellent selection of local wines. In the evenings, music and entertainment are provided, which tends to get the guests excited and, not surprisingly, a lot more thirsty.

La'Koma Restaurant (Balaton utca 9, tel. 83/313-129, www.lakomaetterem.hu, May 1–Sept. 30 daily 11 A.M.–11 P.M., rest of the year daily noon–10 P.M., mains 990–1,890 Ft) is a peaceful, lightly decorated restaurant offering a staggering amount of dishes that include soups, fish, poultry, grilled meat, Hungarian favorites, house specialties, and a rather impressive drinks list. Just about everything on the menu is good here, particularly the wild game and rib eye steaks. Just about everybody leaves here full and satisfied.

Shopping

There are plenty of shops and street vendors catering to the tourist trade by selling handmade arts and crafts, embroidery, wine, and various gift items. The best shopping in town, however, is located just down the hill from the main square. There you'll find Keszthely's open-air market, which buzzes with activity from dawn to mid-afternoon. Plenty of good buys are to be found, with vendors selling everything from fruit and vegetables, spices, trinkets, clothing, and lots more. One word of advice: If you feel the price is a little high, it probably is. Don't be afraid to haggle!

Information and Services

Tourinform Keszthely (Kossuth utca 28, tel. 83/314-144, www.tourinform.hu, Mon.–Fri. 9 A.M.–6 P.M., Sat. 9 A.M.–2 P.M.) will be able to address any questions or concerns you may have. They provide plenty of information about the town and its surroundings, as well as help finding accommodation, dining tips, and tickets for any cultural event that may tickle your fancy.

Getting There

BY TRAIN

Trains leave Budapest's Keleti and Déli stations more or less hourly on a daily basis. The trip last approximately 4–5 hours and costs 3,400–3,800 Ft.

BY CAR

Keszthely is 117 miles from Budapest. If coming from Budapest, take the M7 motorway south towards Balaton. When you get to Balatonszentgyörgy, keep your eyes open for Route #76, which will take you to Keszthely.

BACKGROUND

The Land

GEOGRAPHY
The Czech Republic

Covering an area of approximately 30,450 square miles, the Czech Republic is geographically considered to be a mid-sized European country on par with Austria or Ireland, representing a scant 2 percent of the European Union and sporting a relatively low population that hovers somewhere around 10.2 million.

Located smack dab in the heart of Europe, it shares borders with Germany to the west, Poland to the north, Austria to the south, and former family member Slovakia to the east. The country is comprised of Bohemia and Moravia, as well as the tiny southern tip of Silesia; these three lands are further broken down into 14 regions, the largest being Central Bohemia, which is home to the nation's capital.

The Czech Republic lies in between two mountain ranges, characterized by the Czech Highlands, along with the Šumava, Český les, Krušné hory, Krkonoše, Orlické hory, and Jeseníky Mountains, which form the hilly central and western parts of Bohemia, and the West Carpathian Mountains (Beskydy), which are located in Moravia along the Slovakian border. Krkonoše, which creates a natural border with neighboring Poland, is the country's highest mountain range and is

© OLIVER HERBST

also home to Sněžka, the Czech Republic's tallest mountain, which stretches to a height of 5,256 feet.

Being a landlocked country, the Czech Republic does not have access to the sea. The nation's famed river, the Vltava, runs 269 miles long and is navigable from Prague to Mělník, where it empties into the Elbe. The Elbe, meanwhile, runs southwest across Bohemia, receiving the Vltava, Jizera, and Ohre Rivers before continuing on its way to Germany. The Morava River flows south towards the Danube River, draining most of Moravia in the east, while the Oder River rises in the northeastern part of the country, flowing northward towards Poland.

Hungary

Hungary is approximately 35,919 square miles in size (roughly that of the state of Indiana). Measuring about 155 miles from north to south and 326 miles from east to west, it shares borders with Slovakia to the north, the Ukraine to the northeast, Romania to the east, Serbia and Croatia to the south, Slovenia to the southwest, and Austria to the west.

Hungary is comprised of three regions: the Great Plain, the Transdanube, and the Northern Hills. The Great Plain is situated east of the Danube River and makes up over half of the country's overall territory. Surrounded by mountains, it is characterized by its wastelands, swamps, sandy areas, and fertile soil. The Transdanube, meanwhile, lies in the west, bounded by the Danube and Drava Rivers, and consists for the most part of rolling hills leading to the Austrian Alps. It is home as well to the Bakony Mountains, which feature dolomite and limestone plateaus and reach heights of anywhere between 1,300 and 2,300 feet. Finally, the Northern Hills lie north of Budapest, running in a northeastern direction towards the border with Slovakia. Forested ridges, rich coal and iron deposits, as well as the production of world-famous Tokaj wine personify the region.

When it comes to bodies of water, the mighty Danube leads the way, with a third of it located in Hungary; the rest flows through Germany, Austria, the former Yugoslavia, and Romania. The Drava River runs along the Serbian–Croatian border, while the Rába, Azamos, Sio, and Ipoly Rivers make their way along the Slovak line. Lake Balaton is, of course, the country's largest and best-known lake. It overshadows Lake Velence, which is located southeast of Budapest, and Lake Ferto on the Austrian border.

CLIMATE
Prague

Prague's **winter** temperatures range 22–37°F, with the season literally being the night to summer's day, averaging a mere 2–3 hours of sunshine daily. Long, cold, and grey winters in the capital are best battled with a piping hot cup of *svařák* (hot mulled wine) and a firm belief that the sun will indeed rise again one day. On the upside, there are few tourists choking the streets so a walk down the cobblestones is a far more pleasant experience, and Christmas time is a colorful, enchanting affair with carp peddlers and brightly lit outdoor markets filling the center's squares. Occasionally, virgin white snow blankets the city for a magical day or two, adding a wintry layer of almost unbearable beauty to all of Prague's marvelous monuments.

Temperatures naturally start to rise come **spring** time, averaging 30–65°F. The city slowly starts to awaken from its deep slumber, smiles begin to appear on people's faces, and gardens and castles once again open their doors to the public.

Things are in full swing by the time **summer** rolls into town with tourists descending on the capital in full force. The streets are crowded; the bars, beer gardens, and cafes are packed; and business booms all around. Temperatures remain at a reasonable 75–80°F and the sun doesn't set till 9:30 P.M. or so, making up, it would seem, for all its time off in the winter.

The most colorful time of year and arguably the prettiest, the **fall** season sees its temperatures begin to decrease steadily from the comfortable mid-60s in September to low 30s in November. Days begin to perceptibly shorten with the sun starting to set around dinner time, letting us all know that the party's over and winter's darkness is just around the corner.

Budapest

January and February are **winter**'s coldest months in Budapest, with temperatures ranging 30–35°F, though they can (and do) quickly fall well below that. Damp, snowy, and devoid of tourists, the city is best experienced with friends and loved ones over a glass of wine at your favorite local restaurant or bar.

Things start to pick up around the capital in the **spring** time, its warmer temperatures (38–62°F) and promises of sunshine adding a discernible bounce to everybody's step. It can get rather wet, however, particularly during May, when showers seem to appear out of nowhere.

Summer temperatures in Budapest average around 68–72°F but often reach Mediterranean proportions of more than 80°F. Tourist season reaches its zenith, Hungarians head for Lake Balaton, and a wide range of outdoor concerts and festivals pop up on a regular basis. While easily the busiest time in the capital, it is also the most lively and exciting.

The **fall** brings with it milder temperatures that make September and October best, most comfortable months for sightseeing. Starting at around the mid-60s, the mercury starts dropping to the low 40s by the time November rolls around.

FLORA AND FAUNA
The Czech Republic

Despite the fact that large areas of original Czech forests have been cleared due to expanding development and the need for timber, woodlands remain a distinct and beloved characteristic of the country's landscape. The average forest is comprised of a healthy mixture of oaks, fir, and spruce, but the country's symbolic tree is the linden. The country's oldest tree, dating back almost 1,000 years, is called the Klokočovská linden; it can be found in the Železné Mountains. Various regions in the country have established nature reserves to protect what have been designated particularly important landscapes, the most notable of which are the Šumava Forest, Moravian karst, and the Jizera Mountains.

Considering its small size, the Czech Republic has a relatively diverse wildlife. In its forests and wetlands, the most common types of species you are bound to come across include hares, otters, martens, minks, and marmots. The woods and fields are home to pheasants and partridges, as well as plenty of wild boars, ducks, red deer, and geese. Occasionally, you might catch a lucky break and get to see an eagle, vulture, or heron, and if you happen to find yourself in the northeastern part of Moravia, you may even see a wolf or brown bear. The country's rarer species are protected by various organizations sponsored by the state and include storks, ospreys, bustards, and eagle owls.

Hungary

Just over 12 percent of Hungarian land is covered by meadows and pastures, while roughly a further 19 percent is made up of forests (mainly deciduous). The forests are covered with oak, lime, and beech, with oak being by far the predominant type of tree.

There are some 2,200 species of plant to be found in the country, most of which are indigenous to Central Europe. Quite a few rare and endangered flowers are protected, the most important of which are the fragrant hellebore (*Helleborus odorus*) in the Mecsek Mountains, the wild peony (*Paeonia officinalis var. banatica*), the pheasant's eye (*Adonis vernalis L.*), sage (*Salvia nutans*) on the Great Plain, and the meadow anemone (*Pulsatilla pratensis ssp. hungarica*) in the Nyírség.

Somewhere in the neighborhood of 45,000 animal species live in Hungary. The forests abound in roe-deer, wild boar, and foxes, while lower-lying regions and cultivated areas are home to rabbits, partridges, quails, and pheasants.

The country's rivers and lakes are full of a wide variety of fish including carp, catfish, pike, eel, trout, and Lake Balaton's world-famous (and delicious) pike perch.

The Great Plain is a huge migration center for a large range of birds, the most common of which are storks and swallows, as well as laughing geese, wild geese, and herons. During the spring and autumn, huge flocks of migratory birds make their way from north to south and then back again, while some head to Africa for the winter.

Hungary's bird reserves protect many endangered species like the peregrine falcon, striped-headed reed-warbler, spoonbill, ibis, aigrette, bittern and red heron, while protected waterbirds include the bustard, avocet, and aigrette.

History

THE CZECH REPUBLIC
In the Beginning . . .
The oldest settlers of Czech lands are believed to be a Celtic tribe called the Boii, who inhabited the area somewhere around the 4th century B.C. They gave Bohemia its name and defended the region successfully for nearly 1,000 years before being ousted by Germanic tribes who were in turn destroyed by Attila the Hun in A.D. 451.

The Great Moravian Empire
It wasn't until the 6th century A.D. that Slavs entered the picture and began to settle the territory. Slavic leader Mojmir established the Great Moravian Empire along the Morava River in 830, which grew to encompass modern-day Bohemia, Slovakia, southern Poland, and western Hungary. The empire found itself between the powerful Frankish Kingdom to the west and the Byzantium to the east. Not wanting to be overcome by the influence of the Frankish Kingdom, Mojmir's successor Prince Rostislav sent word to the Byzantine Empire to send aid in the form of priests. Two missionaries named Cyril and Methodius arrived and began spreading Eastern Christianity. Most famously, they created a Slavonic script, known better as the Cyrillic alphabet, which continues to be used to this day in countries such as Russia and Bulgaria.

The Přemyslid Dynasty
The short-lived empire was replaced by the 400-year-long rule of the Přemyslid Dynasty, the first prince of which, Bořivoj, founded the Prague Castle in 880. His grandson, "Good

King" Wenceslas, went on to become of the most famous rulers in the Přemyslid line and is today the patron saint of the Czech people. He was murdered by his jealous younger brother Boleslav, who vied for political power of his own and got it—only to lose it to Saxon King Otto I, who conquered Bohemia in 950 and made it a part of the Holy Roman Empire. Prague became a bishopric in 976, a Slav alliance was formed with Přemysl princes ruling the land on the German's behalf, and Bohemia began to boom. Prague grew rapidly as a result of its advantageous geographic position at the crossroads of several trade routes. Construction of the Judith Bridge (now the Charles Bridge) began in 1172, Old Town was founded in 1234, Lesser Town in 1257, and Přemysl Otakar II saw his Czech kingdom expand all the way to the Mediterranean Sea. Nothing lasts forever, however, and things started to go quickly downhill when Otakar II was killed in 1278 at the Battle of Moravske Pole by the invading Roman King Rudolph Habsburg. The final nail in the coffin came in 1306 when the last Přemysl, Wenceslas III, was assassinated in Olomouc.

John of Luxembourg and Charles IV
John of Luxembourg ascended to the Czech throne in 1310 and stayed there until his death in 1346. During this time, both Prague and the Czech territory continued to grow, seeing the foundation of the Hradčany district in 1320, as well as Old Town Hall in 1338. In 1346, despite being blind, he entered the Battle of Crécy and was killed. His son fought, too,

but managed to survive and go on to bring Bohemia into a golden age, establishing Prague as a cultural capital and turning it into one of the most prosperous cities in the region. His name was Charles IV.

In 1344, he elevated the Prague bishopric to an archbishopric. On April 7, 1348, he established what is now called Charles University, the oldest university in Central Europe. Charles IV didn't stop there, however. He began construction of New Town and Charles Bridge, as well as the reconstruction of St. Vitus Cathedral and the building of Karlštejn, the Czech Republic's most famous and popular castle. All of his historic accomplishments led to him being crowned Holy Roman Emperor in 1355—one more reason why he is still lovingly referred to today as the Father of the Czech Nation.

The Hussite Era

Charles IV's son, Wenceslas IV, was having a heck of a time. Private wars, highwaymen, plague—not to mention the fact that the Church had started focusing far more on wealth and power than the good word of God. Critics began to demand that the Church renounce its power and property, something that wasn't going to happen any time soon. Consequently, a reform movement began; it was led by Jan Hus, who, in 1403, started preaching and fighting against the outright corruption of the church. The number of his enemies within the church grew and he was eventually arrested and burned at the stake on July 6, 1415.

The murder of Hus sparked a massive protest by his followers, the Hussites. In 1419, the first Defenestration of Prague occurred, which culminated in seven councillors being thrown out the window of Prague's New Town Hall. Religious battles swept the country in 1420–1434, and in 1436 an agreement was finally reached. The Catholic Church, for the first time in its history, would allow more than one religion to be practiced on the territory it controlled; this was a foreshadowing of the European Reformation to come and a huge step forward for religious freedom. In 1458, George of Poděbrady, a moderate Hussite, became the country's new king and based his rule on peace, tolerance, and diplomacy, despite being largely ignored by many European rulers and the Pope himself.

The Habsburg Dynasty to Joseph II

In 1526, Ferdinand I of Habsburg took over the Czech throne and immediately moved the seat of power to Vienna, reducing Prague Castle to little more than a Habsburg vacation home. He was succeeded by Rudolf II, who was crowned in 1576 and moved the court back to Prague in 1583. Obsessed with art and science, it was under his reign that the nickname "Magic Prague" came to be, attracting the likes of Tycho de Brahe and Johannes Kepler and creating an environment where legends like The Golem were born.

Rudolf II's brother, Matthias, took over and took little time in stripping Protestants of the rights they had been granted in the past. This, of course, sparked Prague's Second Defenestration and, in 1618, out the window (Prague Castle this time) went more oppressive councillors, starting what was to become the hugely destructive Thirty Years' War. The Protestants were routed in 1620 at the Battle of White Mountain and, less than a year later, 27 Protestant leaders were rounded up and executed in Old Town Square. What followed was the banning of all religions save Catholicism, the suppression of the Czech language, the overtaking of Protestant properties, and the killing of anyone who dared get in the way. Little wonder this period is often referred to as The Dark Age.

Things finally began to improve under Marie Therese's rule of the Austrian Empire between 1740 and 1780. She and her son (and successor) Joseph II mercifully reduced the power of the Catholic Church, kicked the pushy Jesuits out in 1773, and issued the Edict of Tolerance in 1781, which allowed for religious minorities to have political and religious rights.

The National Revival

As the 18th century came to an end, a National Revival attempting to resurrect the Czech language, culture, and identity began. Josef

Dobrovský and Josef Jungmann were two figures who successfully introduced the study of the Czech language in schools, while historian František Palacký authored a much-needed *History of the Czech People*. Czech literature saw the light of day again with novelist Božena Němcová and poet Karel Hynek Mácha, the first Czech dictionary was published between 1834 and 1839, and Czech cultural institutions began to appear in the form of the National Theatre and National Museum.

Fighting for more and more political rights, a group called the Young Czechs attacked the establishment and older, passive Czechs who remained unsuccessful in their negotiations with the Habsburgs. Their efforts were finally rewarded in 1891 when they swept the elections to the Diet with the help and support of Realist Party leader Tomáš Garrigue Masaryk.

The 19th century was also characterized by the Industrial Revolution, which saw the introduction of factories, the building of a railway between Prague and Vienna, and a massive influx of people moving to the city from the countryside in search of new and exciting work. A nation was slowly being formed.

The First Republic and World War II

Following the collapse of the Austro-Hungarian Empire at the conclusion of World War I, an independent Czechoslovakia was born on October 28, 1918. Two years later, a Czechoslovak Constitution was drafted and the nation's first elected president, Tomáš Garrigue Masaryk, set up shop at Prague Castle.

Czechoslovakia enjoyed a parliamentary democracy, absorbed 70 percent of the industry from the former Austro-Hungarian Empire, and ranked among the strongest of the world's economies. In the mid-1930s, however, German inhabitants of the border areas began calling for autonomy. When diplomacy between the Czech and German governments failed, the Czechoslovak armed forces seized the disputed areas. In 1938, Britain and France, no friends of the Germans but admittedly unprepared for war, signed the Munich Pact along with Germany and Italy, allowing Adolf Hitler the right to invade and claim Czechoslovakia's border areas. The utter selling out of the land and its people still stings some of the older Czechs, who recall a bitter phrase repeated over and over again at the time: *O nás, bez nás* ("About us, without us").

Hitler invaded Czechoslovakia on March 15, 1939 and occupied the country until the end of World War II in 1945. May 5, 1945, marks the day of the Prague Uprising when citizens took matters into their own hands. Their cause was helped by the Soviet Red Army on May 9, which helped ensure the liberation of Prague. In the western part of the country, meanwhile, it was the American army that liberated town after town (like Plzeň, which still commemorates the day with a parade) under the leadership of General Patton.

The Communist Era

Following the end of World War II, the Communist Party won the national election in 1946, with further elections to come in the following two years. Interested in gaining complete power, however, the party staged a coup on February 25, 1948, marking the beginning of a totalitarian regime that would last the next 40 years. Approximately 95 percent of all privately owned companies became properties of the state and political trials and executions were handed down to anyone who opposed the new law of the land.

In the 1960s, a wave of political and cultural freedom was briefly enjoyed when Alexander Dubček, secretary of the Communist Party, attempted to create a brand of "socialism with a human face," guaranteeing people's basic rights and decreasing the number of political persecutions that had plagued the country for so long. The famed "Prague Spring," an outward and effusive display of the people's growing freedoms and happiness, began to disturb the Soviet Union, which saw these changes as potential threats to the system. So, on August 21, 1968, five Warsaw Pact member countries invaded Czechoslovakia and the nation's representatives, including

Dubček, were dragged to Mother Russia for a "chat." There, they signed the Moscow Protocol, which allowed Soviet forces to "temporarily" stay on in Czechoslovakia, just to make sure everything ran smoothly.

The period that followed (1968–mid-1980s) is known as the "normalization" period, where the party tried to right the wrongs of the last couple of years and bring things back to the way they were before the attempted reforms. This sparked the Charter 77 movement, whose members spoke out as proponents of freedom and human rights. One of those members was a young Václav Havel, who grew more and more vocal against the Communists' blatant lack of respect for the people and the truth.

Finally, in 1985, Mikhail Gorbachev found his way to the top of the Soviet Union and, realizing that the entire Soviet bloc was starting to crumble under the weight of severe economic problems, things slowly began to change.

The Velvet Revolution and Beyond

Gorbachev's *perestroika* and the fall of the Berlin Wall in the autumn of 1989 were signs that fundamental changes were on their way. On November 17, 1989, police in Prague violently broke up a demonstration commemorating the 50th anniversary of the closing down of Czech universities under Nazi rule. The papers circulated the story widely and three days later, the streets were filled with roughly 200,000 people demanding the government's immediate resignation.

Things moved quickly and in January 1990, former dissident and political prisoner Václav Havel was elected to power following the country's first democratic elections in over 40 years.

Unable to find a mutually beneficial bilateral model for the co-existence of the Czech and Slovak nations, Czechoslovakia split in two on January 1, 1993, becoming the Czech Republic and Slovakia respectively.

The Czech Republic has gone on to blossom into one of the more successful post-Communist countries since then, joining NATO in 1999 and the EU in May 1, 2004. With a robust tourist industry and the Communist hangover just about cured, the future looks bright indeed.

HUNGARY
The History of the Carpathian Basin

Celts settled Gellért Hill in the mid-1st century B.C. and were eventually conquered by the Romans, who extended their rule to the region lying west of the Danube. Their settlement of Aquincum grew into the capital of Pannonia province, which was inhabited by an impressive 30,000 people. After four centuries of rule, the Romans created a sophisticated civilization that was responsible for the founding of many of western Hungary's present-day towns.

Mass migrations brought the Visigoths, Ostrogoths, and Lombards, as well as the Huns and Avars, whose empires eventually collapsed, leaving western and southern Slavs to settle the Basin.

King Stephen

In 896, the Carpathian Basin was conquered by Magyar tribes who made the mighty Danube the heart of their homeland. They made the flatlands their first home, including what is today's downtown Pest, which was then a large island. On Christmas Day, 1000, King Stephen was crowned with the blessing of the Pope and became Hungary's first king. Believing firmly in the importance of bringing Christianity to the pagan practices of the Magyars, King Stephen invited Bishop Gellért to come help, who was in turn rewarded by being thrown into a barrel and pitched off the hill by pagans who had little interest in being converted. King Stephen nevertheless succeeded, introducing measure after measure until he eventually Christianized the land.

The Mongol Invasion

The Mongols invaded and destroyed Pest in 1241, besieging the Magyar army and effectively ending Hungary after a mere 300 years of existence. All looked lost but internal conflicts within the Mongol Empire resulted in their leaving the country the following summer. King Béla IV began reconstruction of the country, building castles and fortifying towns, inviting in the meanwhile German and Italian settlers whom he encouraged to participate in the urban development of the land. Known as "the second founder of the state," King Béla IV went on to plan the construction of Buda Castle, raise Buda and Pest to the rank of towns (after which they began to flourish), and found the Dominican convent on Margaret Island.

King Matthias

The rule of King Matthias (1458–1490) is widely considered to be the golden age of Medieval Hungary. Through sheer will and political savvy, he built a centralized monarchy, created a highly respected mercenary army, and laid down the foundations for the development of commerce and industry.

The first printing press was established in 1473, the study of science flourished, and, by the time of his unexpected death in 1490, Matthias left behind a rapidly growing economy that ranked alongside the most developed of European countries.

The Turkish Occupation

In 1541, Buda was occupied by the Turks, kicking off 150 years of rule that saw the entire Great Plain become part of the Ottoman Empire, which already stretched across three continents. The law of Islam prevailed over Christianity and the Ottoman tax system hit Hungarian serfs hard. The law restricted their freedom of movement, stone houses were not allowed to be built, and damaged ones could not be repaired without permission. Battles broke out intermittently but the Turks beat the insurgents back again and again, destroying and plundering the country along the way.

The Habsburgs

Under Habsburg rule in the 18th century, Hungary began undergoing reconstruction, including Buda Palace which had been gut-

ted and left for naught. In 1848, however, the country joined the rest of Europe in widespread revolution, culminating on March 15 with Sándor Petőfi's passionate reading of his "National Song" from the steps of Pest's National Museum. The revolution was quelled the following year, but a corner had been turned and Hungarians began to have more of a say concerning matters that directly affected them. The result was the Compromise of 1867, which brought with it both stability and prosperity. It also reorganized the Habsburg Empire on a dualist basis where both the Austrian Empire and Hungarian kingdom became independent states with separate legislative bodies and governments.

Budapest developed at an astonishing speed and in 1873 Buda and Pest were joined with Óbuda, creating a new and thriving capital. New bridges were built, as were streetlights, the first underground railway in continental Europe, and Andrássy Avenue. The compromise's high point came in 1896 when massive Magyar Millennium celebrations took place to commemorate 1,000 years of the Magyars settling the land. A new Parliament building was constructed, as was monumental Heroes' Square. By the time the turn of the century rolled around, Budapest rivaled Vienna as a capital of culture and had truly come into its own as a political, administrative, and commercial force.

The World Wars

The assassination of heir to the Austro-Hungarian throne Archduke Ferdinand in Sarajevo on June 28, 1914, aligned Hungary with the Central Powers. This alliance forced the country into World War I, resulting in the loss of one million Hungarian lives. By the summer of 1918, a Hungarian National Council had come into existence. Headed by Count Mihály Károlyi, it demanded a separate peace and Hungarian independence. Bending under immense pressure, Archduke Joseph appointed Károlyi Prime Minister and on November 16, 1918, Hungary was proclaimed a republic.

The Treaty of Trianon was signed following the end of the Great War, the provisions of which were remarkably severe. Hungary's territory was reduced to a third of its former size, resulting in the sudden estrangement of roughly three million Hungarians. Then there was the enormous indemnity it was forced to pay, immediately destroying an economic region that had thrived for centuries.

In the hopes of recovering at least some of the land lost due to the treaty, Hungary began to slowly align herself with the Axis Powers who brought about the Vienna Verdicts in 1938 and 1940, returning some of the land previously annexed to Slovakia and Romania. Hungary's alliance with the Axis Powers however, meant participating in what was shaping up to be another world war, and in 1941, Hungary found herself entering World War II. Casualties that numbered in the hundreds of thousands, plus damages to towns inflicted by the Allies, inspired country-wide resistance to the war. Sensing this and not wanting to lose support, Hitler occupied Hungary in March 1944, setting up a puppet government that was more than happy to follow orders. More troops were sent to the front and Hungarian Jews were sent to the German death camps. By the time the Soviet army drove out the last of the Germans in April 1945, roughly half a million Hungarian lives had been lost and over 40 percent of the country's national resources destroyed. The Treaty of Trianon raised its ugly head once again and Hungary was for a second time made to pay crippling reparations.

1956

A much-needed period of reconstruction took place after the war while democratically held elections brought about the formation of a coalition government. This did not go down well with the Hungarian Communist Party, however, who, with the support of the occupying Soviet army, began a series of unlawful arrests and deportations to dreaded Siberia, managing in a short time to assume power and introduce the country to a relentless reign of terror.

Resistance began to grow over time and on October 23, 1956, a revolution erupted in the streets, toppling Mátyás Rákosi's regime and introducing the government of Imre Nagy, who announced the beginning of a new Hungary and her withdrawal from the Warsaw Pact. As Soviet troops withdrew, the people celebrated and began to feel that things would finally return to normal. On November 4, however, Soviet tanks rolled in and crushed the uprising within days, arresting, deporting, or simply executing anyone who stood in their way. Imre Nagy was deported to Romania, only to be brought back to Hungary for a circus of a trial that ended with his execution in 1958.

Goulash Communism

The 1960s saw the introduction of what was commonly referred to as "goulash communism." By improving the overall living standard (albeit slightly) and allowing a modicum of flexibility in regards to travel to the west, the regime of János Kádár tried to appease a wary public. He also incorporated the slogan "Who is not against us is with us" into the daily vocabulary in the hopes of building solidarity.

The economy began to suffer under this system of "socialist planning," however, and massive debts began to be amassed. This led to inflation, a lower standard of living, and an overall feeling of hopelessness that was now felt by those within the Communist Party as well. In the end, János Kádár was forced to resign and Miklós Németh's reform-Communist government took over.

1989 and the New Millennium

In the summer of 1989, representatives of the government met with budding opposition parties to discuss the possibilities and potential of a multi-party democracy. Simultaneously, Hungary opened its borders to citizens of Soviet-occupied East Germany who were looking to flee westward. The result was the beginning of a domino effect that led to the eventual fall of Communism and a democratically elected government that took power in May 1990.

A new and revitalized economy led to a flurry of construction and renovation that saw the restoration of such architectural gems as Gresham Palace and the conversion of Váci Street into a pedestrian zone. The political, economic, and cultural changes continued to evolve, and, in 2004, Hungary joined the EU, solidifying its opportunity to once again become a key player in Central Europe.

Government and Economy

THE CZECH REPUBLIC
Government
On December 16, 1992, a new constitution was adopted, establishing the Czech Republic as a parliamentary democracy. Having adopted many of the Western world's liberal governmental principles, the constitution calls for a bicameral Parliament comprised of a Chamber of Deputies that is elected every four years, as well as a Senate that is elected on a district basis every six years. Both the President and Prime Minister share executive power; the former selects the latter, who runs the government and keeps the President abreast of all appointments to it.

There are a number of political parties representing the country's various interests, including the Civic Democratic Party, the Civic Democratic Alliance, the Freedom Union, the Christian and Democratic Union-Czech People's Party, the Czech Social Democratic Party, and the Communist Party, which surprised (and worried) a number of people when it won nearly 20 percent of the popular vote a few years ago. Interesting to note is the Green Party, which entered Parliament for the first time in its history during the last elections. A relative newcomer on the scene, it enjoyed modest success with its youth-oriented campaigns, making it a party to keep an eye on in the coming years.

Economy
When Communism fell in 1989, the Czech government introduced a new economic program that included price liberalization, the opening of markets to foreign trade and investment, internal convertibility of the country's currency, privatization of state-owned enterprises, and tax reform. Led by President Havel and Prime Minister Klaus, the country's well-educated and skilled labor force, proximity to Western Europe, and low level of foreign debt resulted in its becoming one of the great post-Communist success stories of the East. The tourism and service industries began to flourish, too, as reports of the capital's astonishing beauty and liberal atmosphere began to surface. The fairy-tale ended within a few years, however, as it became painfully clear that the government was not restructuring key sectors of the economy, nor was it creating transparent financial market regulations. In 1996, out and out corruption in the banking sector resulted in the collapse of eight state-controlled banks. Necessarily severe economic measures followed, leading to a major depreciation of the Czech crown and a recession in the late 1990s. The economy rebounded at the turn of the century and grew quickly once again when the Czech Republic entered the European Union in 2004. Today, Czechs enjoy a higher standard of living than most former Communist states, particularly those who live in Prague where business continues to grow steadily and the unemployment rate is a microscopic 1 percent.

HUNGARY
Government
Throughout the 19th and 20th centuries, Hungary's political system was mostly autocratic in nature, though the period between 1867 and 1948 did see a functioning parliament, multi-party system, and independent judiciary. Then came the Communist takeover

in 1948 and a Soviet-style system was incorporated, wherein all legislative and executive branches of the government fell under the control of the Communist Party. Opposing political parties were abolished and the Hungarian Social Democratic Party was forcefully merged with the Communist Party to form the Hungarian Workers' Party.

After the fall of Communism in 1989, dramatic political reforms began to take place, beginning with an all-encompassing revision of the 1949 constitution, which included approximately 100 changes and re-introduced a multi-party parliamentary system of democracy that included free elections. The legislative and executive branches were once again separated, and an independent judicial system was established, as was a constitutional court elected by parliament.

Today, the National Assembly holds ultimate legislative power, electing the president of the republic, the Council of Ministers, the president of the Supreme Court, and the chief prosecutor. The Council of Ministers is led by the Prime Minister and is responsible for the administration of the state. The President, meanwhile, commands the armed forces but otherwise has limited authority.

Economy

Up to World War II, Hungary was primarily an agrarian country but in 1948, the Soviet Union introduced an industrialization policy and a centrally planned economy that created millions of new jobs. As time passed, the number of those employed in the agriculture sector began to decline significantly, representing a mere eighth of the population by the end of the 1980s. Meanwhile, the industrial workforce grew to roughly one-third of the employed population, with iron, steel, and engineering being given the highest priority. New technologies and high-tech industries were ignored however, and by 1989, Hungary's new market and parliamentary system inherited an economy plagued with debt and underdeveloped export sectors. The sudden opening of the country and abolition of state subsidies led to the eventual collapse of its iron, steel, and engineering industries, as well as a GDP that decreased by 25 percent, leading to a 14 percent unemployment rate in the early 1990s. Things started to look up by the new millennium, however, thanks in large part to Hungary's very welcoming foreign investment policies, along with the modernization of telecommunications and establishment of new industries like automobile manufacturing. Today, roughly one million SMEs operate in the country, state ownership of businesses has fallen to approximately 20 percent, and an increasingly profitable tourist industry indicate that Hungary has finally begun to right itself.

People and Culture

THE CZECH REPUBLIC

The Czech Republic's population weighs in at just over 10 million people, with roughly 1.2 million people living in Prague. The capital remains rather homogenous, as the vast majority of people are of Czech origin. Slovak and Roma minorities comprise the second and third largest ethnic groups, just ahead of the significantly sized expatriate community, which numbers in the tens of thousands and is mostly comprised of Americans, Brits, Germans, and the French. Minority groups from South Asia, as well as Africa and Russia, have continued to grow in size, adding a cosmopolitan flavor and appeal to Prague that was obviously lacking before Communism fell and the floodgates opened.

Culture

While just as friendly, considerate, and warm as anybody else, Czech people can seem rather distant and at times downright rude to first-time visitors, particularly when it comes to the service industry. This is in large part due to a still lingering Communist hangover, where many don't feel the necessity to over-exert themselves at their jobs or are simply tired of the nonstop flow of foreigners that come and go. Nevertheless, Czechs will open up to you quickly if you attempt a word or two of their language or somehow demonstrate that you're a respectful visitor and not just one of the masses who have come for the booze and bordellos. Typically mild-mannered, understated, and sporting a wicked, dark sense of humor, Czechs are also often very tolerant people, sexually open-minded, proud of their absurdly delicious beer, and fiercely loyal to their national soccer and hockey teams. Many Czechs love the outdoors and often leave the rigors of the city on the weekend, heading to their cottages for rest, relaxation, and outdoor recreation.

Religion

If there's a heaven for atheists, then the Czech Republic is most certainly it. Thanks to 40 years of Communist rule that taught atheism as part of the curriculum and systematically stripped the church of all its power, Czechs are the most atheistic people in Europe and admit as much with a certain sense of pride. Catholicism is the country's traditional religion, but only 30 percent of people claim to loosely believe in "something," while less than 10 percent of the population claims to attend church services more than once a month. When asked about their distaste and disinterest in all things ecclesiastical, most Czechs will tell you they have a hard time distinguishing between Communism and religion; after all, both limit one's freedom and demand that people comply with their ideals. Not exactly Bohemian, now is it?

Language

As you might expect, the Czech language is the predominant tongue spoken in the Czech Republic, though some of the older Czechs can speak German and Russian, which was mandatory in schools before the Velvet Revolution. Prague is no different, of course, but many do speak at least a modicum of English, primarily in the shops, restaurants, and bars located in the downtown core. As you leave the center, however, your chances of finding someone to communicate with in English begin to diminish.

Food and Drink

Typical Czech meals focus primarily on bread, meat, and potatoes, with fresh fruit and vegetables being an afterthought at best. A standard breakfast usually involves a bread roll smothered in jam and/or butter, a touch of yogurt, or eggs and sausage. Bakeries serving croissants and pastries are also popular stops for those on their way to work. Lunch is the average Czech's main meal of the day and is generally had between noon and 2 P.M. This is the time when the nation's most common meal—dumplings, sauerkraut, and roast pork—is typically enjoyed. Dinner, served anywhere from 5 to 7 P.M., is oftentimes a much smaller and simpler affair consisting of rye bread and an assortment of sausage and deli meats. Vegetarians will most likely be limited to soups and salads when patronizing a Czech establishment; restaurants specializing in various foreign cuisines (Asian and Indian, for example) may offer more of a variety. Beer is the standard alcoholic drink throughout the country, followed by wine and any number of spirits. Coffee and a wide assortment of teas top the nonalcoholic category.

HUNGARY

Historically speaking, Hungary was a multicultural country since its beginnings in the 10th century; but the geographical changes that came after the end of World War I left it with a predominantly homogeneous population of ethnic Hungarians—a fact that remains to this day. Over 90 percent, in fact, of Budapest's two million people are Hungarian, with the Roma being the largest of ethnic minority groups, followed by the Slovaks. Plenty more minority groups make Hungary their home, however, including Germans, Russians, Greeks, and Poles. There is also a small expatriate community comprised mostly of North

Americans and Brits who have either opened up small businesses or work for any number of multinationals.

Culture

Hungarians are a hospitable people who generally will go out of their way to make a guest feel welcome. They are typically very friendly to foreigners and will do what they can to help if able to communicate in English. Lively, active, and fun-loving, Hungarians also often enjoy having dinner and drinks with friends, following the latest soccer game, and unwinding at any one of the country's many baths. They are generally fiercely proud of their culture and will talk to you at length about their glorious history, as well as their admittedly uncertain future, if prodded.

Religion

Despite having been exposed to a wide variety of religions as a result of being ruled by everyone from the Austrian Habsburgs to the Ottomans, Hungary nevertheless remains a relatively secular country, with roughly one-third of the population claiming no religious affiliation whatsoever. About 50 percent of Hungarians are Roman Catholic, most of whom live in the northern and western sections of the country. Protestants account for just over 20 percent of the populace, while the Jewish community, which spans a centuries-long tie to the country, was estimated to be around 400,000 strong before 1939. Today, following the decimation of World War II, that number is closer to 80,000.

Language

Hungarian is the main language spoken widely throughout the country, posing quite a few difficulties for visitors who find it nigh impossible to make heads or tails of the bizarre sounding Finn-Ugric language. Most Hungarians who can't speak English will throw in a German word or two in hopes of making themselves clearer, rarely realizing that this doesn't help most tourists. English is generally spoken by most under the age of 30, though, particularly in the service industry and at most museums and city sights. The odds of finding someone who speaks English do start to work against you, however, the farther you stray from the capital.

Food and Drink

Typical Hungarian meals are generally known to be meat-heavy and generously spiced with paprika, though there are plenty of other options such as goose liver, wild game, and pike-perch. Breakfast can be a typical eggs-and-sausage affair or a lighter meal consisting of yogurt, fresh fruit, pastry, or fruit-filled pancake. Lunch is mainly served at noon and is the day's most important meal. It usually begins with a seasonal or fish soup and is followed by a meat dish like paprika chicken or traditional favorite *gulyás* (goulash). Dinner is typically served between 6 and 7 P.M. and can range from an assortment of fantastic Hungarian salamis to a fish or meat dish. If you're looking for something other than meat, you'll usually have a handful of fish-based meals to choose from, as well as the occasional salad, but that's about it. There are countless dessert options, as the country abounds in mouthwatering pastries, ice creams, and cakes, all of which are guaranteed to satisfy your sweet tooth. Wine is by far the alcoholic drink of choice as Hungarians have no shortage of domestic product to choose from. On the nonalcoholic side of things, coffee tops the list, with tiny cups of espresso being the most popular.

The Arts

THE CZECH REPUBLIC
Cinema

For such a small country, it really is amazing just how many quality films are made in the Czech Republic. While only 15 or so films are produced each year, a handful have managed over the years to win the prestigious Academy Award for Best Foreign Picture: *Obchod na korze (The Shop on Main Street,* by Jan Kadar and Elmar Klos), *Ostře sledované vlaky (Closely Observed Trains,* directed by Jiří Menzel), and, most recently, *Kolja* (by Jan Svěrák). Recent nominations for the coveted prize include 2000's *Musíme si pomáhat (Divided We Fall,* by Jan Hřebejk), as well as 2003's offering, *Želary* (directed by Ondřej Trojan). The country's most successful filmmaker, however, is undoubtedly the incomparable Miloš Forman, responsible for such classics as *One Flew over the Cuckoo's Nest, Amadeus,* and *Man on the Moon.*

Czech films are typically offbeat in nature, wielding a dark sense of humor and unconventional narratives that make for unique cinematic experiences. Lately, however, it seems that the originality films here are known for has begun to suffer thanks in large part due to having to compete with international (primarily American) releases. The result is a tendency to rely on formulaic storytelling or a nostalgic revisiting of the nation's past, usually in the form of World War II mini-epics or Communist-era dramedies.

Aside from its domestic endeavors, Prague also hosts a large number of foreign productions that come here to capitalize on professional crews and exceptional locations at relatively low costs. Past productions include *Mission Impossible, The Brothers Grimm, Hart's War, From Hell,* and *Oliver Twist.*

Literature

With a roster of literary giants that includes Bohumil Hrabal, Milan Kundera, Franz Kafka, and Nobel Prize–winner Jaroslav Seifert, the Czech Republic is clearly well represented in the field of *belles lettres.* Dating back to the 12th century in the form of folk poetry and liturgical texts, Czech literature hit its stride during the national revival of the mid-19th century with the outlandish and oftentimes nightmarish works of Karel Jaromír Erben *(Kytice),* Božena Němcová *(Babicka),* and the country's greatest Romantic poet, Karel Hynek Mácha, known primarily for his exceptional lyrical work, *Maj.*

The start of the 20th century, particularly the years 1918–1939, represents a high point in Czech literature, with an incredible body of work coming from masters of the narrative form like Franz Kafka *(The Metamorphosis),* Karel Čapek *(RUR),* and Jaroslav Hašek *(The Good Soldier Svejk).*

Following the Communist takeover, it wasn't until the 1960s that things started to look up again, as writers such as Vaclav Havel *(The Garden Party),* Josef Škvorecký *(Cowards),* Milan Kundera *(The Unbearable Lightness of Being),* Bohumil Hrabal *(Closely Observed Trains),* and Ivan Klíma *(A Ship Named Hope)* came into form, fighting the powers that be with their pens on home turf or producing some of their finest work while in exile abroad. This rebellious streak continued on into the 1970s when samizdat, the practice of reproducing banned works on personal typewriters and distributing copies secretly both inside and outside the country, took off, lending much needed exposure to the powerfully subversive material.

The fall of Communism has seen a sharp decline in the number of celebrated Czech writers, with the possible exception being Jachym Topol, whose down-and-dirty vision of post-Communist Prague made for excellent reading when it first came out in 1994, but now seems already out of date due to Prague's rapidly changing nature.

Music

The Czech Republic has a rich and diverse musical history that notably starts in the 18th century with influential composer Johann Stamitz, who founded the Mannheim school of symphonists and had a significant effect on the great Mozart himself. Also influential was Josef Mysliveček, who wrote operas and symphonies that were highly respected in Italy, where he came to be known as "il divino Boemo"—the divine Bohemian.

Classical music began to blossom during the 19th century with renowned composers such as Bedrich Smetana, who was the first to incorporate Czech nationalism into his work, like in his famed opera *Prodaná nevesta (The Bartered Bride)* and his powerful cycle of symphonic poems *Má vlast (My Country)*. Then, of course, there was Antonín Dvořák, as well as Leoš Janáček and Bohuslav Martinů, each of whom left his mark on international stages and who continue to be immortalized today with concerts performed regularly by orchestras around the world.

Today, the Czech Republic's most famous (and oldest) recording artist is still Karel Gott—dubbed "the Czech Elvis" by his fans, who remain loyal to the cheesy pop singer who started soon after the King himself. On the alternative, indie side of things, there is no shortage of bands gracing Prague's stages. Monkey Business is a hugely successful funk band led by the vocal stylings of American Tonya Graves; Support Lesbiens, Tatabojs, and MiG21 continue to churn out light, radio-friendly rock and pop tunes; Kabat reigns supreme in the heavy metal department (still a popular genre here); and Cechomor blends traditional folk and rock to create a catchy and unique rootsy Czech sound.

HUNGARY
Cinema

In 1948, the provisional Soviet-led government established the Hungarian Film Industry, which was to promote the land and its people through a nationalistic context. In essence a sophisticated propaganda machine, young filmmakers coming up in the system began after the 1956 uprising to make films filled with symbolic and allegorical inside jokes that bit the hand greasing the machine. A Hungarian New Wave was born and by the early 1970s, Hungarian cinema was widely considered to be one of the most exciting, daring, and original in Eastern Europe. Ironically, it was the collapse of Communism that led to the particularly troubling state domestic cinema finds itself in today. Now that the gates to the world are open, audience members are far more inclined to spend their money watching a genre film rather than one dealing with intricate social conflict. In other words, Hungarian art films have taken a backseat to American blockbusters, reaching maybe a few thousand viewers and are unable, therefore, to make much of their money back, let alone earn a profit.

There have been a few success stories, however, particularly with famed director Istvan Szabo's Oscar for Best Foreign Film for his hugely popular *Mephisto*. Hungarian expatriates have made quite a name for themselves abroad as well, starting with Michael Curtis *(Casablanca),* the Korda Borthers, and Adolph Zukor (the founder of Paramount Studios) in the 1920s–1940s. Hungarians who fled after the 1956 uprising have continued the tradition in the form of producer Andrew Vajna *(Nixon, Lethal Weapon),* Peter Medak *(The Ruling Class, Let Him Have It)* and screenwriter Joe Eszterhas *(Flashdance, Basic Instinct).*

Literature

The earliest and most significant examples of the written Hungarian language can be found in the *Halotti Beszéd és Könyörgés (Death Speech and Prayer),* as well as *Ómagyar Máriasiralom (Old-Hungarian Mary-Lamentation),* the first Hungarian poem, which dates all the way back to 1300.

The 16th century saw the rise of Gáspár Heltai and his moralistic fairy tales; Sebestyén Tinódi Lantos, whose verse recounted famous battles against the dreaded Turks; and the religious, heroic, and romantic elements of Bálint Balassi, widely agreed to be one of the country's finest poets.

The next major movement came in the 19th century when some of the country's most revered writers began expressing themselves in the Romantic style. There was Ferenc Kölcsey, who composed the Hungarian national anthem; Mihály Vörösmarty, who became poet laureate after penning his epic poem *Zalán futása (Zalan's Run)*; Sándor Petőfi, who stirred the country's heart with his patriotic and revolutionary poems; and János Arany, credited with single-handedly introducing Hungary to the ballad form.

Attila József reworked popular poetry and took it in the direction of the avant-garde during the first half of the 20th century, while the second half saw Dezső Tandori and Ottó Orbán delve deeply into post-modernist narrative. Péter Esterházy's *Termelési regény (Production Novel)*, Péter Nádas' *Emlékiratok könyve (Book of Memoirs)* and György Konrád's *A cinkos (The Accomplice)* all enjoyed significant success in the 1980s, while Imre Kertész received the Nobel Prize for Literature in the new millennium (2002) for his heartbreakingly beautiful novel *Sorstalanság (Fateless)*, which dealt with the Holocaust as seen through the eyes of a young boy.

Music

Hungary has enjoyed a rich musical culture for centuries, mixing classical elements with folk music and gypsy rhythms to create a sound unique to its land and people. *Verbunkos,* a traditional Hungarian dance music that was coupled with Western harmonies and forms, was made popular by Ferenc Erkel (1810–1893), who was also the first to use the Hungarian language in opera with *László Hunyadi* and *Bánk bán.* Representing a high point in Hungarian classical music was, of course, the incomparable Franz Liszt (1811–1886), whose blend of European romanticism and Hungarian traditions catapulted him to the top of the

classical music scene in the second half of the 19th century. Operettas enjoyed a respectable degree of success at the turn of the 20th century with composers Ferenc Lehár (1870–1948), Imre Kálmán (1882–1953), and Jenő Huszka (1875–1960) representing their country on the international stage. Then came Béla Bartók (1881–1945), another seminal Hungarian composer of international repute who turned to the traditions of Hungarian folk music and made them into his own unique works, including the opera *Bluebeard's Castle,* ballets *Wooden Prince* and *Miraculous Mandarin,* and numerous string quartets and piano concertos. During the oppressive 1960s, rock music was the rebellious melody of choice with bands like Illés, Omega, Lokomotiv GT, along with singers Klári Katona, Zsuzsa Koncz, and Kati Kovács expressing their distaste and disillusionment in the form of political protest. Things loosened up and by the mid-1980s, all sorts of musical genres were coming into their own including, of all things, the rock opera whose popularity can be attributed to its national and religious themes more so than the music itself. Hits of the time included *István the King* and *The Excommunicated.*

Today, Hungary's contemporary music scene continues on in vibrant style spanning any number of genres. Electronic dance music started gaining popularity after the changes in 1989 and continues on today, with Anima Sound System, Yonderboi, and Neo being some of the more popular acts. Ganxsta Zolee pioneered gangsta rap in Hungary, while Dopeman and LL Junior provide mainstream hip-hop to the masses. Ektomorf sits atop the heavy metal scene and bands like Aurora, PICSA, and Prosecura continue to prove that punk's not dead.

Architecture

Both Prague and Budapest boast some of the most breathtaking architecture to be found in the world, let alone Europe. From palaces to churches, museums to hotels, visitors are treated to a wide range of styles that span centuries and inspire awe in all who lay eyes on them.

Perhaps the biggest difference between the two cities is the fact that a number of Budapest's buildings and monuments were destroyed over and over again throughout the years due to bloody wars, whereas Prague's were for the most part (and rather miraculously) spared from any significant damage. As a result, some of Budapest's finest architecture is actually an amalgamation of styles. For example, take its magnificent Parliament building, which incorporates Renaissance, neo-Gothic, and Baroque elements, or the Royal Palace of Buda, which was originally designed in the Gothic style, later rebuilt to gel with the Renaissance tastes of the time, and finally reconstructed as a Baroque building.

Painstaking care is taken in both countries to restore historical landmarks to their original designs. Even the most casual passerby will be hard pressed not to be amazed at the overwhelming aesthetic beauty found in both cities. Below is a small sampling of some of the architectural gems to be found.

GOTHIC

The Gothic style of architecture flourished in this part of the world from the 13th to the 16th century and was particularly embraced in Prague. Its main characteristic features are pointed arches, ribbed vaults, and flying buttresses, with an emphasis on verticality meant to signify a sort of "reaching up to God." There are plenty of well-preserved examples of Gothic architecture in Prague today, with the Church of our Lady Before Týn in Old Town Square and the mind-blowing Charles Bridge being its most famous examples. Other notable sights are the Powder Tower, Old-New Synagogue in Josefov, and the eastern side of St. Vitus Cathedral at Prague Castle.

RENAISSANCE AND NEO-RENAISSANCE

The Renaissance movement began in the 16th century and its style emphasized symmetry, proportion, and an overall influence by the architecture of Classical antiquity. In Prague, the Royal Summer Palace (otherwise referred to as "The Belvedere") and Schwarzenberg Palace are two shining examples. St. Stephen's Basilica, the Hungarian Academy of Sciences, and Budapest's majestic Opera House are the Hungarian capital's m ost significant contributions to the neo-Renaissance movement.

BAROQUE AND NEO-BAROQUE

The Baroque movement swept through Europe during the 17th and 18th centuries, focusing primarily on broader forms, adding colonnades, domes, and large ceiling frescoes to works, as well as dramatic contrasts in the usage of light and shade. Neither Prague nor Budapest lack for wonderful demonstrations of the style. Prague's most exquisite example is undoubtedly the magnificent St. Nicholas Church in Malá Strana, which never ceases to wow visitors. Not to be outdone, the Church of St. Nicholas in Staré Město as well as the Clementinum, Wallenstein Palace, and the Loreto also serve as fine examples of the period. In Budapest, the enormous City Hall, Franciscan Church, and Church of St. Anne are just a handful of buildings displaying an undeniable mastery of the form. The Klotild Palaces and Széchenyi Spa Baths are must-sees for those interested in neo-Baroque.

ART NOUVEAU

The highly stylized and dynamic curvilinear designs that characterize Art Nouveau began cropping up at the end of the 19th century and peaked in popularity at the turn of the

20th century. Oftentimes incorporating floral motifs and basking in opulence, the buildings are a symphony for the eyes. In Prague, the most well-known examples of the flamboyant style are the gorgeous Municipal House and the well-preserved exterior of the Grand Hotel Evropa. In Budapest, the Art Nouveau movement was influenced by Middle Eastern design and incorporated more traditional Hungarian elements as well, creating a unique synthesis of styles that are noticeable in the Museum of Applied Arts, Gresham Palace, and the incomparably lavish Gellért Hotel and Baths.

CUBIST

Prague was a hotbed of Cubist activity in Central Europe, primarily during the years 1910–1920. The style is easily recognizable, thanks to its emphasis on striking triangular and pyramidal forms, as well as its focus on diagonal lines instead of horizontal or vertical ones. The most celebrated architectural examples of the movement are undoubtedly Adria Palace and the House of the Black Madonna, which is also home to the thoroughly interesting and informative Museum of Czech Cubism.

Cubism did not have an impact on the architecture of Budapest.

MODERNIST

The modernist movement began shortly after the establishment of an independent Czechoslovakia in 1918 and flourished during the years leading up to World War II. Linking design with function (hence the term "functionalism"), as well as uncommon beauty with purpose, its use of brick, stone, prefab materials, and glass swept the city and left behind many exemplary uses of the form, including the incomparable Church of the Most Sacred Heart of our Lord, Veletržní palác (Trade Fair Palace, home to the National Gallery Collection of 19th-, 20th-, and 21st-Century Art), Mánes Gallery, and the residential Baba Settlement.

In Budapest, the influence of modernism can be found primarily in residential architecture.

ESSENTIALS

Getting There

BY AIR
Prague

Ruzyně Airport (tel. 220 113 314, www.csl .cz) is located in Dejvice, roughly 12.5 miles northwest of the downtown core. The Czech Airline CSA (tel. 220 113 417, www.csa.cz) provides direct flights from North America. Other major airlines regularly stopping in Prague are Lufthansa (tel. 234 008 234, www.lufthansa.com), Air France (tel. 220 113 737, www.airfrance.com), Austrian Airlines (tel. 220 114 324, www.aua.com), and British Airways (tel. 220 113 477, www.british airways.com).

Budapest

Ferihegy Airport (tel. 1/296-7000, www.bud .hu) is located in southeast Pest approximately 15 miles from the center of town. The airport is served by two main terminals. Recently renovated Terminal 1 generally handles airlines offering budget travel, including EasyJet (www .easyjet.com), Germanwings (www.german wings.com), Norwegian Air Shuttle (www .norwegian.no), and Sky Europe (tel. 1/296-9035, www2.skyeurope.com). Terminal 2 is home to Hungarian airline Malév (tel. 1/235-3888, www.malev.hu), which offers direct flights from North America to Budapest, as well

as leading carriers British Airways (tel. 1/777-4747, www.britishairways.com), Delta Airlines (tel. 1/301-6680, www.delta.com), and Lufthansa (tel. 1/292-1970, www.lufthansa.com).

BY TRAIN

A multitude of regional and continental rail passes are available, and they're a very good idea for anyone who would like to travel extensively throughout the continent. If you're coming from North America, you'll want to book ahead online. The two most important sites are www.eurorailways.com and www.raileurope.com, both of which offer scores of deals depending on age, length of stay, and distances traveled.

Prague

All international trains make their final stop at either Nádraží Holešovice (Holešovice Station; Vrbenského 1, Holešovice, tel. 220 806 790) or Hlavní nádraží (Main Station; Wilsonova 2, Nové Město, tel. 972 241 883).

Trains from Budapest to Prague leave 5–6 times a day, and the trip takes 7–9 hours.

Visit www.idos.cz for schedules and fares of all trains, buses, and planes both leaving and crisscrossing the country.

Budapest

A large number of trains from across Europe roll into Keleti Station (VIII. Kerepesi út 2/6, tel. 1/313-6835), which is located in Pest's sketchy Baross tér.

Trains from Prague to Budapest leave around the clock and number up to 10 a day, with the trip lasting 7–9 hours.

The national train website, www.elvira.hu, is very useful, offering complete, up-to-date information regarding Hungary's railway system and schedules.

BY BUS
Prague

Florenc bus station (Křižíkova 4, Žižkov, tel. 900 144 444, www.csad.cz) is where all domestic and international coaches come and go. On the premises is a Eurolines office

(Křižíkova 6, tel. 224 218 680, www.eurolines.cz, daily 5:45 A.M.–10:15 P.M.), which can help you reserve a seat on any one of their numerous buses connecting Prague with the rest of the continent.

Buses leave Budapest for Prague three times a week. The trip lasts 7.5 hours, and a round-trip ticket costs 15,900 Ft.

Visit www.idos.cz for schedules and fares of all trains, buses, and planes both leaving and crisscrossing the country.

Budapest

Just about all international buses hailing from the UK and the rest of the continent make Népliget Station (Népliget autóbusz-állomás, Ferencváros, IX. Üllői út 131, tel. 1/219-8063) their final destination.

Volánbusz (www.volanbusz.hu) is the country's main international bus line and serves the three weekly routes coming from Prague. The trip generally lasts 7.5–8 hours, and prices start at 770 Kč; passengers are asked to check in one hour beforehand (or 15 minutes prior to leaving at the very latest). Fares and schedules change often so make sure to check the Volánbusz website for the most up-to-date information.

BY CAR
Prague

A valid UK, U.S., or Canadian license is required for you to lawfully drive in the Czech Republic. The country's highways are continually being upgraded, which means that traffic jams and various delays are not out of the ordinary. For travel on the highways, a sticker needs to be bought at a border crossing, gas station, or post office and affixed to your windshield. The validity of coupons is as follows: "R" is valid for one year, "M" for one month, and "D" for one week.

If you're approaching Prague from the east, you'll cross through Zilina, Slovakia; those from the south will pass through Linz, Austria. If coming from the west, Waldhaus/Rozvadov will serve as your border and Reitzenhain/Pohraničí will greet those coming from the northwest.

© TOM DIRLIS

getting ready to leave Keleti Station in Budapest

While Prague boasts highway connections from five major directions, the country's highway network leaves plenty to be desired, as it is incomplete and suffers from poor upkeep. Nevertheless, two major highways lead to the Czech border: the D5 (or international E50) stretches southwest past Plzeň and on to Germany, while the D1 (or international E65) heads to Brno and continues on to Slovakia.

With regard to distances, Budapest is 347 miles, Vienna is 194 miles, Warsaw is 320 miles, and Berlin is 220 miles.

RULES OF THE ROAD

People drive on the right side of the road in the Czech Republic. Wearing your seatbelt is mandatory and child seats for young children are required on all roads. There is absolutely zero tolerance when it comes to drinking and driving. That means you cannot have had anything alcoholic to drink before getting behind the wheel, no matter how tiny or insignificant the amount. Use of a cell phone while driving is against the law (though hands free is okay).

Headlights must be on no matter what time of day you're driving. Always stop behind trams when passengers are getting on and off at a stop where there is no pedestrian island, and avoid driving on tram tracks unless there is no other choice. Speed traps are a common thing in the Czech Republic so it's always best to observe the speed limits: 130 kph (81 mph) on the motorways, 90 kph (56 mph) on roads, and 50 kph (31 mph) in towns and villages.

Budapest

An International Driver's License is no longer necessary in order to drive legally in Hungary, but a valid UK, U.S., or Canadian license most certainly is. A handful of highways connect Hungary to the rest of Europe; the most important are the E60 (or M1), which connects Budapest with Vienna and the west, and the E65, which connects Budapest with Prague and points north. The roads are generally hassle-free, as are the Austrian and Slovakian borders, though you may be required to present your driver's license and registration.

In regards to distances, Prague is 347 miles, Vienna is 154 miles, Warsaw is 339 miles, and Berlin is 428 miles.

RULES OF THE ROAD

People drive on the right side of the road in Hungary. Those sitting in the front seat are required to wear seat belts at all times. Children under the age of six cannot sit up front and must always have their seat belts on. There is a zero tolerance rule in effect regarding alcohol consumption before getting behind the wheel. Headlights must be on at all times. All cars in Hungary must be equipped with a first-aid kit, reflective warning triangle, and spare bulbs (any officer who stops you and finds you without one or more of these items will most likely write you up). The car should also have a clearly visible sticker indicating the country it's been registered in. The speed limits are 130 kph (81 mph) on the motorways, 90 kph (56 mph) on roads, and 50 kph (31 mph) in towns and villages.

Visas and Officialdom

PRAGUE
Visa Requirements

Those wishing to visit the Czech Republic will be wise to consult their local Czech embassy or consulate before traveling, as requirements change often. Currently, citizens of the EU, U.S., and Canada do not need a visa for visits under 90 days. Keep in mind that visas cannot be obtained at the border; they must be applied for in advance at a Czech embassy outside of the Czech Republic (but not necessarily the one in your country). The entire process can be quite frustrating and time consuming so it's best to start this process well in advance. For further information, check out the Ministry of Foreign Affair's website at www.mzv.cz.

Customs

EU nationals visiting the Czech Republic are not required to make a formal customs declaration, provided the quantities of such personal products as alcohol and tobacco fall within the limits set. Visitors bringing in goods bought in other EU countries where tax and duty has already been paid will not be required to pay tax and duty in the Czech Republic. Non-EU citizens who have bought products in the EU and have already paid tax and duty on them will be required to produce a receipt in order not to pay a second time. Personal effects including laptops, cameras, clothing, and gifts totaling no more than 6,000 Kč are not subject to duties. Prohibited goods include narcotics, pornographic or offensive material, firearms, ammunition, and animal/plant products. Customs allowances for non-EU nationals include 200 cigarettes, 100 cigarillos, 50 cigars or 250 grams of tobacco, 1 liter of spirits over 22 percent volume or 2 liters of fortified wine, sparkling wine or other liqueurs, 2 liters of still table wine. For goods bought in the EU, the allowances are considerably more generous: 800 cigarettes, 400 cigarillos, 200 cigars, or 1,000 grams smoking tobacco, 110 liters of beer, 20 liters of fortified wine, 90 liters of wine, 10 liters of spirits. For more information, visit the official website of the Czech Customs Administration at www.cs.mfcr.cz.

Embassies and Consulates

Most major embassies and consulates can be found in the center of Prague. The U.S. Embassy (Tržiště 15, tel. 257 022 000, prague. usembassy.gov) is located in Malá Strana, not far from the square. The British Embassy (Thunovská 14, tel. 257 402 111, www.britain .cz) is also in Malá Strana, along with the French Embassy (Velkopřevorské Náměstí 2, tel. 251 171 711, www.france.cz), which is situated opposite the John Lennon Wall. The Canadian Embassy (Muchová 6, tel. 272 101 800, www.canada.cz), meanwhile, can be found near the Hradčanská subway stop in Prague 6.

BUDAPEST
Visa Requirements

Visitors to Hungary will need a valid passport to gain entry, except for citizens of Austria, Belgium, Croatia, France, Germany, Italy, Liechtenstein, Luxembourg, Slovenia, Spain, and Switzerland, who need only produce a national identity card. Citizens of the EU, U.S., Canada, Australia, and New Zealand do not need a visa. U.S. and Canadian citizens are allowed to stay in Hungary for a maximum of 90 days. Those citizens who enter the country with the intention of becoming employed or staying longer than 90 days, however, do need a travel visa. Hungarian visa requirements tend to change often so it's best to consult with your local Hungarian embassy or consulate before traveling.

Customs

EU nationals visiting Hungary are not required to make a formal customs declaration provided the quantities of such personal products as alcohol and tobacco fall within the limits set. Visitors bringing in goods bought in other EU countries where tax and duty has already been paid will not be required to pay tax and duty in Hungary. Non-EU citizens who have bought products in the EU and have already paid tax and duty on them will be required to produce a receipt in order not to pay a second time. Personal effects including laptops, cameras, clothing, and gifts totaling no more than 29,500 Ft are not subject to duties. Prohibited goods include narcotics, pornographic or offensive material, firearms, ammunition, and animal/plant products. Customs allowances for non-EU nationals include 200 cigarettes, 100 cigarillos, 50 cigars or 250 grams of tobacco, 1 liter of spirits over 22 percent volume or 2 liters of fortified wine, sparkling wine or other liqueurs, 2 liters of still table wine. For goods bought in the EU, the allowances are considerably more generous: 800 cigarettes, 400 cigarillos, 200 cigars, or 1,000 grams smoking tobacco, 110 liters of beer, 20 liters of fortified wine, 90 liters of wine, 10 liters of spirits. For more information, visit the official website of the Hungarian Customs and Finance Guard at www.vam.hu.

Embassies and Consulates

Every major country has an embassy or consulate in Budapest. The heavily fortified U.S. Embassy (V. Szabadság tér, tel. 1/475-4400, www.usembassy.hu) is located close to Parliament in pretty Szabadság Square. The Canadian Embassy (II. Ganz utca 12-14, tel. 1/392-3360, www.dfait-maeci.gc.ca/canadaeuropa/hungary) is located on the Buda side in an area currently going through heavy development. The British Embassy (V. Harmincad utca 6, tel. 1/266-2888, www.britishembassy.hu) is located very near the main pedestrian shopping street Váci utca, and the French Embassy (VI. Lendvay utca 27, tel. 1/374-1100, www.ambafrance-hu.org) is just a short walk from Heroes' Square.

Tips for Travelers

TRAVELERS WITH DISABILITIES

Odds are that travelers with disabilities will encounter a bit of difficulty in Prague, as quite a number of buildings (not to mention subway stations, hotels, and the like) do not provide proper wheelchair access. The Prague Wheelchair Association (Benediktská 6, tel. 224 827 210) publishes a free brochure outlining barrier-free sightseeing routes, galleries, restaurants, and shops that can be picked up at its office. You can also contact Accessible Prague (Moravanu 51, tel. 608 531 753, www.accessibleprague.com), whose services include help arranging transportation, accommodations, and personal assistance.

Budapest is another European capital that sadly lacks in wheelchair access. While an increasing number of hotels are slowly starting to catch on, there are still plenty of barriers around town. An excellent resource, however, is MEOSZ (III. San Marco utca 76, tel. 1/388-5529, www.meosz.hu), which is the National Association of People with Mobility Impairments. Scroll down a little on their website until you find the icon of the British flag on the left. It will lead you to a list of sights, restaurants, hotels, museums, and the like that have caught on and offer comfort and accessibility to all their visitors.

GAY AND LESBIAN TRAVELERS

While definitely not as loud and proud as in other major cities, the gay community in Prague is nevertheless a thriving one. There are a small number of bars and clubs that cater specifically to both homosexual men and lesbians, many of which are friendlier than their straight counterparts. For up-to-date listings regarding the scene, check out the very helpful and informative http://prague.gayguide.net.

The gay community in Budapest is a healthy, albeit low-key, one. Plenty of bars and clubs spring up only to close moments later, leaving everyone to wonder what comes next. In order to find out and stay on top of an ever-changing scene, make sure to visit www.budapestgaycity.net or http://budapest.gayguide.net.

WOMEN TRAVELERS

Some women may be initially surprised or put off by the blatant sexuality found on billboards and reflected in the rather provocative styles of dress in both countries, but they are simply reflections of a generally liberal attitude towards sex. Both cities abound in strip clubs and "gentlemen's clubs" (i.e., brothels), and women, while strong-willed and independent, have little, if any, motivation not to flaunt what they've got. Despite the overt exhibitions of flesh and open displays of interest and affection, women here are generally far safer than in most large American cities, with attacks being very low in number. Of course, caution and common sense are always a good thing to practice, which means dark alleys, train stations, parks, underpasses, and

the outer districts should generally be avoided if traveling alone at night.

CONDUCT AND CUSTOMS
Prague
GENERAL ETIQUETTE

It's rare to hear Czech people raise their voice in public, with the exception of the occasional drinker barking at the moon after the bars let out (and that's usually a tourist). North Americans and southwestern Europeans tend to be a whole lot louder when entering shops or having a conversation over coffee or dinner—a habit that Czechs and those having lived here long enough oftentimes find hard to take. Try to keep your voice at whatever level the establishment is operating at. Of course, all this goes right out the window when entering a bar or club. Other shining examples of good behavior are helping mothers with baby carriages up/down stairs or getting on/off trams. Always offer your seat to an elder when on public transport and try to remember to say "Dobry den" (good day) when entering a shop. Finally, if invited to a Czech home, make sure to take your shoes off as most wear slippers indoors. Some of the more thoughtful hosts provide guests with slippers of their own.

TERMS OF ADDRESS

Although generally polite and pleasant, Czechs as a whole tend to be rather reserved when meeting new people; much more so than North Americans and Western Europeans who think nothing of hugging, kissing, and exchanging jokes from the get go. A smile and firm handshake will suffice during initial introductions. Always address elders and those you are meeting for the first time in the plural form, which is a clear sign of societal courtesy and respect. Typically, both you and the person being addressed will switch to more informal speech before you know it. Although Czech is a very complex and difficult language, learning a few pleasantries will go a long way in ingratiating yourself, as all Czechs appreciate foreigners making an effort to speak their language.

Budapest
GENERAL ETIQUETTE

Having a good time is paramount to Hungarians so as long as your behavior is on par with everybody else's, you'll be okay. If invited to a Hungarian's home for dinner, be on time (or at least no more than five minutes late) and always bring a gift. Preferred items are chocolates, flowers, or Western liquor. Do not bring wine, as Hungarians pride themselves on their own ability to choose something suitably tasty. On the streets, helping the elderly and mothers with children is commonplace and expected.

TERMS OF ADDRESS

While close friends kiss each other on both cheeks, a friendly handshake is just fine when being introduced for the first time. If a man is greeting a woman, he should wait for the woman to extend her hand first. When addressing elders or people in a business context, use titles, surnames, and the plural (more polite) form.

Hungarian tradition dictates that all names appear surname first, followed by the person's given name. This practice can be found everywhere, from the addressing of a postcard to the names of streets.

HEALTH AND SAFETY
Common Afflictions

The most common complaints from travelers to these destinations are minor in nature and usually revolve around sunburn and insect bites. In Prague, however, you may want to steer clear from traditional mayonnaise-heavy salads sold in supermarkets; they often sit out for hours and have been the cause of quite a few cases of salmonella. Tap water in both Prague and Budapest is perfectly safe.

Medical Services

Medical care is decent in both countries, and payment by cash will automatically get you the quick and proper attention most locals on insurance only dream of. Rates rival those of Western countries; you'll be wise to double-check your health plan and see what kind of coverage (if any) it provides you in Central and Eastern Europe. If on medication, make sure to bring enough to last you the entire trip; bringing copies of prescriptions may not be a bad idea either.

Insurance

It's a good idea to confirm beforehand whether your insurance policy covers treatment in the Czech Republic and Hungary. If it does, verify whether any incurred costs will be covered by the policy up-front or whether you will be reimbursed upon your return home. Should your particular policy not provide coverage in this part of the world, find a travel medical insurance company that does, either online or through a trusted travel agent.

Safety

Prague is remarkably safe both during the day and at night. The biggest problem continues to be petty theft, be it a scarf or pair of gloves that goes missing at a bar or restaurant, the occasional shortchange at a kiosk or by a particularly clever waiter, and pickpocketing, which usually occurs wherever there are large groups of tourists or on the trams heading for Prague Castle. Your best bet is to keep your valuables in your hotel safe and just enough money on you to get through the day.

Budapest is a relatively safe city with little violent crime, but a number of pickpockets work the public transportation system. Always keep your valuables in the hotel safe and your money in an inside or front pocket. Watch for the numerous underpasses used to cross some of the major streets. If it's late at night and you're having second thoughts, feel free to bend the law and jaywalk.

Information and Services

MONEY
Prague
CURRENCY

The currency used in the Czech Republic is the crown or *koruna,* as well as hellers, with one crown equaling 100 hellers. The crown's two most common abbreviations are Kč and CZK. Bills come in denominations of 50, 100, 200, 500, 1,000, 2,000, and 5,000 Kč. Most shops will happily provide change for up to 1,000 Kč but if you have a 2,000 or 5,000 Kč bill, you're best off using it at a boutique, bar, restaurant, or supermarket. Coins come in denominations of 1, 2, 5, 10, 20, and 50. There are also 50 heller coins, which are made from a lighter material. At the time of writing, the crown was roughly 20 Kč to both the American and Canadian dollar, 40 Kč to the British pound, and 28 Kč to the euro. For the most up-to-date rates, be sure to check out www.xe.com.

CHANGING MONEY

Exchange rates vary slightly across town and it's a good idea to do a bit of comparison shopping before making a transaction. Banks generally charge less commission but you are confined to their business hours (Mon.–Fri. 8 A.M.–5 P.M.). Be wary of those offering "No Commission," as their rates are usually the worst and oftentimes result in creative calculations. Exchanging money on the street is strongly discouraged, no matter what rates you are offered. It's a common-enough occurrence for visitors to walk away from a transaction thinking they've made the deal of a lifetime only to realize soon afterward that the money they received in return for theirs was not Czech currency (usually it's Bulgarian).

CREDIT CARDS AND ATMS

Although certainly not as commonplace as in North America or Western Europe, credit cards are becoming more and more common as an alternative method of payment. Most restaurants and shops in the city center will accept the world's better-known plastic, as well as euros, but it never hurts to ask if you're not sure. Plenty of ATMs are to be found around town, with most paying out on major credit and charge networks like Visa, MasterCard, Cirrus, and Delta. Just be certain that the symbol on your card matches one of those advertised on a given machine.

TAXES

A 19 percent value added tax (VAT) is added beforehand to all goods, so there is no pesky arithmetic for visitors to get bogged down in. In other words, the price you see is the one you pay. Non-residents are eligible for VAT reimbursement if they purchase products at shops advertising "Tax Free Shopping" and obtain the appropriate VAT Refund Form from staff. Refunds can be obtained at the border or from Ruzyně Airport at the customs desk in the Departure hall. You must be prepared to present your sales receipt, passport, and refund form. Eligible purchases are those totaling over 1,000 CZK that are taken out of the country within 30 days of sale.

COSTS

The cost of living in Prague is nowhere near as low and alluring as it once was, but it is still relatively affordable for Western visitors. Meals in the city center generally run 150–250 Kč a plate but can easily reach 800–1,000 Kč at some of the fancier places. A glass of domestic wine should cost roughly 35–50 Kč, while a beer hovers somewhere around 25–50 Kč. These, of course, are average prices and can easily grow exponentially depending on location and establishment.

TIPPING

Czechs aren't necessarily the best tippers, which may account for some of the surly service you're bound to encounter. Foreigners are expected to tip the standard 10–15 percent but feel free to

PRAGUE TOURIST CARD

The Prague Tourist Card is a four-day pass to more than 50 museums and monuments about town, including the Prague Castle, the Powder Tower, Old Town Hall, and the National Museum. It can be purchased at tourist information centers all over town, as well as travel agencies, hotels, and the airport. The cost is 740 Kč, which is a considerable amount, though quite practical if you're planning on soaking up as much culture as possible. If you're only interested in visiting a handful of museums and sights, however, individual tickets to the respective places is definitely the way to go.

tip nothing if the service was particularly unprofessional. One common form of payment is for the waiter to come to your table and tell you the total cost of your meal. The diner then hands over the money and tells the waiter how much tip to keep. For example, if your bill comes out to 225 Kč and you'd like to leave a 25 Kč tip, simply hand over your money and say "250." The waiter will then give you back the appropriate change. When taking a cab, keep your eye on the meter. If you feel like your driver was honest, then an appropriate tip would be to round up to the next 10 or 20 Kč.

Budapest
CURRENCY
Hungary's unit of currency is the forint, typically abbreviated as Ft or HUF. Bills come in denominations of 200, 500, 1,000, 5,000, 10,000, and 20,000, while coins come in denominations of 1, 2, 5, 10, 20, 50, and 100 Ft. Should you get either a 10,000 or 20,000 Ft bill from the ATM, save it for purchases totaling over 1,000 or 2,000 Ft, as it's generally too large an amount to use when buying something small like a cup of coffee. At the time of writing, the forint was roughly 178 Ft to the Canadian and American dollar, 358 Ft to the

British pound, and 250 Ft to the euro. For current rates, head to www.xe.com.

CHANGING MONEY
Although you'll have no problem finding plenty of independent currency exchange booths throughout the city center, it is widely understood that they generally charge higher rates than most, despite their large signs advertising 0 percent commission. Changing money on the street, no matter how sweet the offer may sound, is even worse, not to mention illegal. Individual banks and travel agencies are far more reliable and recommended. Keep in mind that they are free to set their own rates so a bit of comparison shopping won't hurt. You will also see signs throughout the downtown core, as well as at train stations and the airport, that read *Bureau de Change*. They typically have the fairest rates so make sure to have a look at what they're offering as well.

CREDIT CARDS AND ATMS
Withdrawing forints shouldn't be a problem as plenty of banks have 24-hour ATMs that accept most, if not all, popular credit, debit, and charge cards including AMEX, Diners Club, Cirrus, EnRoute, Euro/Mastercard, JCB, and VISA. These cards can also be used in hotels, restaurants, and shops. Many establishments have signs at the front entrance advertising which cards they accept.

TAXES
A 20 percent tax called ÁFA (VAT) is included in the sales price of goods in Hungary. Foreigners are entitled to a refund if: items bought in stores advertising "Tax Free Shopping" total a minimum of 50,000 Ft, less than 90 days pass between the time of purchase and time of export, and items leaving the country remain in new condition (cannot have been used in Hungary). Make sure to ask the sales staff for a Fiscal Receipt and VAT Reclaim Form (as it is your export and tax refund document), as well as a Tax Free envelope. Put the credit card receipt into the envelope, or, if paying by cash, include the

sales receipt and your receipts from changing money into forints. You can be refunded in cash at the airport IBUSZ office or be reimbursed via bank check or transfer by mailing all original documents (VAT invoice, VAT refund form, exchange or credit card receipt) in the Tax Free envelope within six months of the date of purchase. Make sure you have all relevant documents stamped by Hungary Customs before leaving or else a refund will not be possible.

COSTS

Hungary remains a very affordable place for travelers, who have the luxury of choosing from a wide variety of hotels, restaurants, and shops. An average meal will cost 1,300–2,200 Ft, while a glass of beer goes for roughly 400–800 Ft, depending on the brand. Clearly, prices in general are slightly more expensive in the downtown core but still a bargain when compared to Hungary's Western neighbors. One big advantage is that Budapest has stocked its collective commercial shelves with many of the same products found elsewhere but at a noticeably lower price.

TIPPING

Tipping is a big deal in Hungary, with everyone from the hairdresser, waiter, taxi driver, or thermal spa attendant getting a piece of the action. This is not to suggest, however, that tipping is mandatory. If the service was particularly bad, feel free to tip nothing as an expression of your dissatisfaction. When in restaurants, always ask if a service charge has been added to your bill, as it's a relatively commonplace procedure. If it has been added, a tip is not necessary. If it hasn't, then 10–15 percent is standard. Do not leave your tip on the table. If your bill was brought in a booklet, leave the tip inside. If not, give the tip to the waiter.

BUSINESS HOURS
Prague

Most shops in Prague open at 8:30 or 9 A.M. on weekdays and close at either 5 or 6 P.M. Sat-

---

BUDAPEST CARD

Those planning on packing in as much sightseeing as possible during their stay might want to opt for the Budapest Card. Available at tourist information offices, hotels, travel agencies, subway ticket offices, and the airport, it offers a number of discounts about town including: unlimited travel on public transport, free or discounted entry to 60 museums, and discounts on selected restaurants like Gerbeaud, spas like Széchenyi and Palatinus Strand, and services like Budget Rent-A-Car. Valid for either 48 or 72 hours, the card's rather hefty price tag comes in at 6,450 or 7,950 Ft respectively. While certainly offering a wide array of potential savings, keep in mind that many of the major museums offer free admission, so check out the card's specifics at www .tourinform.hu, or simply ask one of the tourist information assistants if already in town before deciding whether the card is for you or not.

---

urdays begin at the same time but end earlier, usually around 1 or 2 P.M. Specialty shops, department stores, and supermarkets, particularly those close to the city center, may stay open as late as 9 or 10 P.M. Banks, on the other hand, tend to share the same operating hours of Monday–Friday from 8 or 9 A.M. to 4:30 or 5 P.M.

Budapest

The majority of shops are open Monday–Friday 10 A.M.–6 P.M. and Saturday 10 A.M.–1 or 2 P.M. Most shops close on Sunday, though those in central shopping areas usually stay open, following Saturday's schedule. Food shops tend to open earlier, at either 6 or 7 A.M. and close at 6 or 7 P.M. on weekdays, while weekends have them opening at 7 or 8 A.M. and closing at 1 or 2 P.M. Certain ones (designated as "nonstops") operate 24/7. Most banks, meanwhile, are open Monday–Thursday 8 A.M.–3 P.M. and Friday 8 A.M.–2 P.M.

MAPS AND TOURIST INFORMATION
Prague

The Prague Information Service (tel. 221 714 444, www.pis.cz, Mon.–Fri. 8 A.M.–7 P.M.) is the first and foremost tourist authority on all things Praha. Whether it's basic information regarding the country, culture, transportation, accommodations, cultural events, day trips, or organized tours, you'll find everything you need right here. Plenty of maps and brochures can be picked up at their four branches: Rytířská 31 (Apr.–Oct. daily 9 A.M.–7 P.M., Nov.–Mar. daily 9 A.M.–6 P.M.); Staroměstské náměstí 1 (Apr.–Oct. Mon.–Fri. 9 A.M.–7 P.M., Sat.–Sun. 9 A.M.–6 P.M., Nov.–Mar. Mon.–Fri. 9 A.M.–6 P.M., Sat.–Sun. 9 A.M.–5 P.M.); Wilsonova 8 (Apr.–Oct. Mon.–Fri. 9 A.M.–7 P.M., Sat.–Sun. 9 A.M.–6 P.M., Nov.–Mar. Mon.–Fri. 9 A.M.–6 P.M., Sat.–Sun. 9 A.M.–5 P.M.); Lesser Town Bridge Tower, Malá Strana (Apr.–Oct. daily 10 A.M.–6 P.M.).

For general country information, three websites will help you get the ball rolling. The first is www.czechtourism.com, which is the Czech Republic's official tourism site, run as it is by the Czech Tourist Authority. The second is www.czech.cz, which is overseen by the Czech Republic's Ministry of Foreign Affairs. Last, but not least, there's www.czecot.com, a highly informative Czech tourist server.

Maps of Prague can be bought at pretty much any bookshop, newsstand, or hotel, and can be had for free at various tourist information offices. Most consider the series of maps published by Kartographie Praha called *Plán města Prahy* to be the best. They vary in terms of size and detail so you should be able to find the one that's perfect for your particular trip.

Budapest

There is no shortage of tourist information possibilities in Budapest but the main company that handles most visitors is Tourinform (Main office, VI. Liszt Ferenc tér 9-11, tel. 1/322-4098, www.budapestinfo.hu, Nov.–Apr. Mon.–Fri. 10 A.M.–6 P.M., Sat. 10 A.M.–4 P.M., May Mon.–Fri. 10 A.M.–6 P.M., Sat. 10 A.M.–4 P.M., June–Sept. daily 10 A.M.–7 P.M., Oct. Mon.–Fri. 10 A.M.–6 P.M., Sat. 10 A.M.–4 P.M.). A helpful, efficient, and English-speaking staff is more than happy to provide you with information regarding sights, tours, day trips outside the capital, and much more. You can also pick up plenty of free leaflets, booklets, and maps that are quite comprehensive and invaluable to the first-time visitor.

Another centrally located office is Tourinform Deák (V. Sötő utca 2, tel. 1/316-9800, www.budapestinfo.hu, daily 8 A.M.–8 P.M.), which provides the same useful information and is mere minutes away from many of the more popular sights, including Váci Street, Vörösmarty tér, and the Danube Embankment. Those flying to Budapest should make sure to check out the Tourinform Ferihegy (Terminal 1, tel. 1/438-8080, www.budapestinfo.hu, daily 9 A.M.–10 P.M.) branch for all pertinent information before heading into the heart of the city. If you think you might need instant information at any given hour of the day, be sure to note the tourist information 24-hour hotline (tel. 1/438-8080).

For general information regarding the entire country, contact the Hungarian National Tourist Office, 350 Fifth Avenue, Suite 7107, New York, NY 10118, 212/695-1221, or visit their helpful website www.gotohungary.com. Other informative sights include www.hungarystartshere.com and www.budapest.com.

Free maps can be obtained from all tourist centers and can also be found at the back of local publication *Budapest Funzine*. Mr. Gordonsky's colorful City Spy maps (www.cityspy.info) are also quite useful but if you want a bona fide, detailed map outlining the entire city and its environs, a trip to any bookstore in the center will have a number of them to choose from.

COMMUNICATIONS
Prague
POSTAL SERVICES

When sending mail, be patient as odds are there will be a lengthy line to wait in. Make sure whatever it is you're sending is properly and clearly addressed and, in the case of packages, wrapped in plain paper where all pertinent information can be easily found and read. Postcards and letters can be dropped into any of the orange mailboxes located outside all post offices and around the city.

Both postcards and letters weighing up to 20 grams cost 11 Kč if sent within Europe. Sending either outside of Europe will run you 20 Kč.

TELEPHONE
Prague's telephone lines underwent a major digital overhaul in 2002 and now all numbers have nine digits; regional and mobile prefixes are integrated into the nine-digit number. The Czech Republic's international dialing code is 420. If you'd like to make a long distance call from here to your loved ones abroad, simply dial 00 followed by the country and city codes. The prefix for Canada and the U.S. is 1, while the UK's is 44.

There are a few public pay phones that take coins, but they are few and far between, not to mention perpetually broken. Most nowadays take prepaid calling cards, which can be bought at kiosks and newsstands. They come in denominations of 50 and 150 units and can be used at pay phones to make local and long-distance calls. However, your best (and far cheaper) bet for international calls is to purchase a Trick card. These can be bought at kiosks and newsstands as well and go for 200 and 300 Kč each. Rates are highest 7 A.M.–7 P.M. on weekdays and lowest after hours, as well as on weekends and public holidays.

NEWSPAPERS AND MAGAZINES
There are plenty of international newspapers and magazines available in Prague, including *The Guardian, International Herald Tribune,* and *Atlantic Monthly.* Most can be found at centralized kiosks or English-language bookshops, as can plenty of locally produced news and coverage. The most established English newspaper in town is the weekly *Prague Post* (www.praguepost.com), which has as many critics as it does readers. Nevertheless, it delivers the country's news and has an excellent arts and entertainment section detailing all of the city's most important cultural happenings. For financial news, the *Czech Business Weekly* (www.cbw.cz) covers markets, trends, and all things moving and shaking in a region that continues to develop rapidly. Independently produced local mags dealing with life in the expat lane, as well as literary 'zines showcasing some of the local talent, come and go overnight and are hard to pin down. Whatever is being printed at the time of your visit, however, will surely be available at all English-language bookshops.

RADIO AND TV
Czech television centers around four main stations. ČT1 and ČT2 are both state-funded channels and offer viewers anything from domestically produced dramas to the latest episode of *Lost.* ČT2 does have some programs of interest, including a weekly film club that often plays English movies, as well as jazz and classical concerts. The country's two private stations, Prima and Nova, serve up the usual sitcom and dramatic fare imported from the United States, Canada, Germany, and France. Keep in mind that everything is dubbed here so even if you do manage to find something you like, odds are you won't understand it. Most residents opt for a cable package of some kind, which usually includes channels like CNN or SKY.

Radio stations in Prague tend to play the same old pop and top 40 formats that we're all accustomed to. There is, however, the excellent Radio 1 (91.9 FM), which spins everything from hip-hop to indigenous music. This, of course, is both its strength and its weakness, as it's very eclectic but rather unpredictable as well. To stay abreast of what's happening in the world, tune in to the BBC World Service on 101.1 FM.

Budapest
POSTAL SERVICES
When sending mail, be patient as odds are there will be a lengthy line to wait in. Make

sure whatever it is you're sending is properly and clearly addressed and, in the case of packages, wrapped in plain paper where all pertinent information can be easily found and read. Postcards and letters can be dropped into any of the red boxes found outside all post offices and on numerous streets around the city.

Stamps for postcards sent within Europe cost 120 Ft, while those for letters weighing up to 20 grams cost 170 Ft. Sending mail to North America is slightly pricier, with stamps costing 140 Ft for postcards and 190 Ft for letters up to 20 grams. For a full list of rates, check out www.posta.hu.

TELEPHONE

Phone numbers in Budapest have seven digits, plus the area code 1. Phone numbers outside Budapest have six digits, plus a two-digit area code. If you want to reach somebody staying in another part of the country, dial 06, wait for the tone, then dial the area code and phone number. Mobile phones begin with 06-20, 06-30, or 06-70 and are then followed by seven digits. You must dial all the numbers (06 prefix included) if you are calling from a land line or pay phone, as well as if you are calling from another mobile phone provider. If calling someone who uses the same provider, dialing the first four numbers (e.g., 06-30) is not necessary. Hungary's international access code is 36, while the outgoing code is 00 plus the relevant country and city codes.

Public pay phones operate on 20, 50, and 100 Ft coins or prepaid phone cards, which can be bought at post offices, newsstands, and most kiosks. They come in denominations of 50 and 120 units and can be used for both local and long distance calls. As always, international calls are cheapest when made after hours or on weekends and public holidays.

NEWSPAPERS AND MAGAZINES

Aside from the plethora of foreign newspapers available at most English-language bookshops, there are a handful of domestically produced English publications that have significant circulations. The first is the fluffy, tabloid-leaning *Budapest Sun* (www.budapestsun.com), which reports the country's news on a daily basis. Many buy the paper simply for its entertainment and events listings. Those interested in matters political or business-oriented will want to grab a copy of the more respectable *Budapest Business Journal* (www.bbj.hu), which keeps readers informed of the massive changes the country and region are currently going through. People who would like to know what's going on about town should definitely pick up *Budapest Funzine* (www.funzine.hu). This is a free publication geared towards both tourists and expats with plenty of tips and inside information on shopping, restaurants, nightlife, and a whole lot more. It's very informative, and not a bad read either.

RADIO AND TV

Hungarian television is led by national channel MTV, a barren landscape of dreary variety shows, game shows, and soap operas. Commercial channels such as Duna TV, TV2, and RTL Klub are not much better. Many spring for a satellite package of some sort but most of the channels end up being in German, with the occasional Russian, Polish, or Italian one thrown in just to spice things up. If staying at one of the pricier hotels, you may get CNN, which may not sound like much but it will make you appreciate the boob tube all the more when you finally return home.

On the radio, you can catch the excellent BBC on 92.1 FM, which is more or less the only thing in English on a regular basis. Some stations have the occasional hour or two of an English-speaking DJ or interview but those are few and far in between.

WEIGHTS AND MEASURES

Electricity in the Czech Republic and Hungary is 220V and 50 Hz. Most outlets have the typical European two-pin socket (also referred to as "Europlugs"), while some also have a protruding third (earth) pin. If planning on using any North American appliances or electronic equipment while in the country, make sure to bring an adaptor as they are not easy to find and overpriced when available.

Both the Czech Republic and Hungary are on Central European Time (CET). This puts Prague and Budapest one hour ahead of London, six ahead of New York, and nine ahead of Los Angeles. The 24-hour clock is used officially and oftentimes in conversation as well.

Czechs and Hungarians use the metric system. Road signs display distances/speeds in kilometers and you fill up your car with liters of gas. A large glass of beer is half a liter, while smaller items are measured using decagrams or *deka* (10 gram units) and deciliters or *deci* (10 centiliter units). For example, enough lunchmeat for a couple of sandwiches would be 10 deka (100 grams) and a typical glass of wine would be 2 deci.

RESOURCES
Glossary

CZECH
antikvariát second-hand bookshop
cukrárna sweet shop
divadlo theater
dům house or building
hospoda pub
hrad castle
jízdenka ticket for public transport
kavárna cafe or coffee shop
Kč Czech crown (also abbreviated CZK)
kino cinema
knihkupectví bookshop
kostel church
lékárna pharmacy
město town
most bridge
nádraží train station
náměstí town/public square
obchod shop
ostrov island
pěší zóna pedestrian zone
pivo beer
potraviny food shop or mini-market
sleva discount
trh market
ulice street
vinárna wine bar
vlak train
zahrada garden, park
zastávka bus, tram, or train stop

HUNGARIAN
antikvárium second-hand bookshop
bolt shop
borozó wine bar
édességbolt sweet shop
egyház church
élelmiszerbolt grocery shop or mini-market
Ft Hungarian forint (also abbreviated HUF)
gyógyszertár pharmacy
ház house or building
híd bridge
jegy ticket
kávéház cafe or coffee shop
könyvesbolt bookshop
leszámítolás discount
megálló bus, tram, or train stop
mozi cinema
pályaudvar train station
park garden, park
piac market
sétálóutca pedestrian zone
sör beer
söröző pub
sziget island
színház theater
tér town/public square
utca street
vár castle
város town
vonat train

Czech Phrasebook

PRONUNCIATION GUIDE

Czech is a relatively difficult language to learn. Just ask the multitude of foreigners who have lived here for years and still trip over their tongues. Nevertheless, it's the effort that counts and many Czechs will be both pleased and flattered that you tried. When reading signs, menus, etc., keep in mind that the language is written phonetically, so there are no tricky silent letters. Also helpful to know is that most words are stressed on the first syllable.

a as in "lap"
á as in "father"
c "ts" as in "gets"
č "ch" as in "choose"
ch like an "h" but throatier
e as in "bet"
é as in "fair"
i, y as in "knit"
í, ý as in "knee"
j like "y" in "yellow"
ň like "ny" as in "canyon"
o as in "cot"
ó as in "boring"
ř no English equivalent; a combination of a rolled "r" and soft "g"
š "sh" as in "shore"
u as in "look"
ú, ů as in "doom"
ž like "s" in "measure"

BASIC AND COURTEOUS EXPRESSIONS

Hello/Good day *Dobrý den*
Hi *Ahoj*
Good morning *Dobré ráno*
Good evening *Dobrý večer*
Good night *Dobrou noc*
How are you? *Jak se mate?*
I'm fine *Mám se dobře*
Please/You're welcome *Prosím*
Thank you *Děkuji*
Yes *ano*

No *ne*
And/or *a, nebo*
Excuse me *Promiňte*
Sorry *Pardon*
Goodbye *Nashledanou*
Cheers *Na zdraví*
Bon appetit *Dobrou chuť*
I don't speak Czech *Nemluvím Česky*
Do you speak English? *Mluvíte Anglicky?*
My name is . . . *Jmenuji se . . .*
I understand *Rozumím*
I don't understand *Nerozumím*
I don't know *Nevím*

TERMS OF ADDRESS

I *já*
you *vy* (formal), *ty* (informal)
he *on*
she *ona*
we *my*
they *oni*
Mr./sir *pan*
Mrs./madam *paní*
Miss *slečna*
friend *přítel*

TRANSPORTATION AND DIRECTIONS

Where is . . . ? *Kde je . . . ?*
from/to *od/do*
here *tady*
far *daleko*
near *blízko*
map *plán*
downtown *centrum*
highway *silnice*
straight *rovně*
go right *doprava*
go left *doleva*
address *adresa*
north *sever*
south *jih*
east *východ*
west *západ*

ACCOMMODATIONS
hotel *hotel*
guesthouse/family hotel *penzion*
key *klíč*
bathroom *toaleta*
shower *sprcha*
bath *koupel*
manager *ředitel*
towel *ručník*
soap *mýdlo*
toilet paper *toaletní papír*

FOOD
breakfast *snídaně*
lunch *oběd*
dinner *večeře*
menu *jídelní lístek*
water *voda*
juice *džus*
coffee *káva*
tea *čaj*
milk *mléko*
eggs *vejce*
fruit *ovoce*
vegetables *zelenina*
bread *chléb*
meat *maso*
chicken *kuře*
beef *hovězí*
pork *vepřové*
fish *ryba*
soup *polévka*
french fries *hranolky*
salt *sůl*
pepper *pepř*
the bill *účet*

SHOPPING
I need . . . *Potřebuji . . .*
I want . . . *Já chci . . .*
I would like . . . *Rád bych (teď) . . .*
How much does it cost? *Kolik to stojí?*
money *peníze*

SIGNS
Out of Service *Mimo Provoz*
Open *Otevřeno*
Closed *Zavřeno*

Toilets *Toalety*
Men *Páni/Muži*
Women *Dámy/Ženy*
Entrance *Vchod*
Exit *Východ*

NUMBERS
0 *nula*
1 *jeden*
2 *dva*
3 *tři*
4 *čtyři*
5 *pět*
6 *šest*
7 *sedm*
8 *osm*
9 *devět*
10 *deset*
11 *jedenáct*
12 *dvanáct*
13 *třináct*
14 *čtrnáct*
15 *patnáct*
16 *šestnáct*
17 *sedmnáct*
18 *osmnáct*
19 *devtenáct*
20 *dvacet*
21 *dvacet jedna*
22 *dvacet dva*
23 *dvacet tři*
30 *třicet*
40 *čtyřicet*
50 *padesát*
60 *šedesát*
70 *sedmdesát*
80 *osmdesát*
90 *devadesát*
100 *sto*
1,000 *tisíc*

TIME AND DATES
What time is it? *Kolik je hodin?*
today *dnes*
tomorrow *zítra*
yesterday *včera*
now *teď*
next week *příští týden*

day *den*
week *týden*
month *měsíc*
year *rok*
century *století*

Days
Monday *pondělí*
Tuesday *úterý*
Wednesday *středa*
Thursday *čtvrtek*
Friday *pátek*
Saturday *sobota*
Sunday *neděle*

Months
January *leden*
February *únor*
March *březen*
April *duben*
May *květen*
June *červen*
July *červenec*
August *srpen*
September *září*
October *říjen*
November *listopad*
December *prosinec*

Seasons
spring *jaro*
summer *léto*
fall *podzím*
winter *zima*

Hungarian Phrasebook

PRONUNCIATION GUIDE
The Hungarian language is hands down one of the most difficult and complex languages on the continent, if not the world, so learning even the basics will take some work. Understanding pronunciation is key, as is a lot of practice. Like anywhere else, an honest attempt at using the language will put you in the good graces of any native speaker. Like the Czech language, stress almost always falls on the first syllable. Long vowels have either a single or double acute accent while short vowels have no accent or the two-dot umlaut. In most cases, the sound of long vowels is slightly elongated.

a "o" as in "not"
á as in "father"
c "ts" as in "lets"
cs "ch" as in "church"
e as in "let"
é as in "say"
gy like "di" in "medium"
i like "ee" in "feet" (short)
í like "ee" in "feet" (long)
j like "y" in "yes"
ly like "y" in "yes"
ny like "ny" in "canyon"
o like "a" in "fall"
ó as in "law"
ö like "u" in "fur" (short)
ő like "u" in "fur" (long)
r rolled "r"
s "sh" as in "shop"
sz "s" as in "sofa"
u as in "full"
ú as in "root"
ü as in German *über* (short)
ű as in German *über* (long)
w "v" as in "very"
zs like the "s" in "pleasure"

BASIC AND COURTEOUS EXPRESSIONS
Hello/Good day *Jó napot*
Hi *Szia!*
Good morning *Jó reggelt*
Good evening *Jó estét*
Good night *Jó éjszakát*
How are you? *Hogy van?*
I'm fine *Jól*
Please *Kérek/Kérem*
Thank you *Köszönöm*

Yes *Igen*
No *Nem*
And/Or *És/Vagy*
Excuse me *Elnézést*
Sorry *Bocsánat*
Goodbye *Viszlát!/Viszontlátásra!*
Cheers *Egészégedre*
Bon appetit *Jó étvágyat*
I can't speak Hungarian *Nem beszélek magyarul*
Do you speak English? *Beszél angolul?*
My name is . . . *A nevem . . .*
I understand *Értem*
I don't understand *Nem értem*
I don't know *Nem tudom*

TERMS OF ADDRESS
I *én*
you *ön* (formal), *te* (informal)
he/she *ő*
we *mi*
they *ők*
Mr./sir *úr*
Mrs./madam *hölgy*
friend *barát*

TRANSPORTATION AND DIRECTIONS
Where is . . . ? *Hol van . . . ?*
from/to *honnan/hova*
here *itt*
far *messze*
near *közel*
map *térkép*
downtown *belváros*
highway *autópálya*
straight *egyenesen*
right *jobb*
left *bal*
address *cím*
north *észak*
south *dél*
east *kelet*
west *nyugat*

ACCOMMODATIONS
hotel *szálloda*
bathroom *fürdőszoba*

shower *zuhany*
bath *kád*
towel *törülköző*
toilet paper *vécépapír*

FOOD
breakfast *reggeli*
lunch *ebéd*
dinner *vacsora*
menu *étlap*
water *víz*
juice *gyümölcslé*
coffee *kávé*
tea *tea*
milk *tej*
eggs *tojás*
fruit *gyümölcs*
vegetable *zöldség*
bread *kenyér*
meat *hús*
chicken *csirke*
beef *marhahús*
pork *sertéshús*
fish *hal*
soup *leves*
french fries *hasábburgonya*
salt *só*
pepper *bors*
the bill *fizetek*

SHOPPING
I need . . . *. . . van szükségem*
I want . . . *Kérek . . .*
I would like . . . *Szeretnék . . .*
How much does it cost? *Mennyibe kerül?*
money *pénz*

SIGNS
Out of Service *Nem működik/Üzemen kívül*
Open *Nyitva*
Closed *Zárva*
Toilets *Toalettek*
Men *Férfi*
Women *Női*
Entrance *Bejárat*
Exit *Kijárat*

NUMBERS

0 *nulla*
1 *egy*
2 *kettő (két)*
3 *három*
4 *négy*
5 *öt*
6 *hat*
7 *hét*
8 *nyolc*
9 *kilenc*
10 *tíz*
11 *tizenegy*
12 *tizenkettó*
13 *tizenhárom*
14 *tizennégy*
15 *tizenöt*
16 *tizenhat*
17 *tizenhét*
18 *tizennyolc*
19 *tizenkilenc*
20 *húsz*
21 *huszonegy*
22 *huszonkettó*
23 *huszonhárom*
30 *harminc*
40 *negyven*
50 *ötven*
60 *hatvan*
70 *hetven*
80 *nyolcvan*
90 *kilencven*
100 *száz*
1000 *ezer*

TIME AND DATES

What time is it? *Mennyi az idő?*

today *ma*
tomorrow *holnap*
yesterday *tegnap*
now *most*
day *nap*
week *hét*
month *hónap*
year *év*
century *évszázad*

Days

Monday *hétfő*
Tuesday *kedd*
Wednesday *szerda*
Thursday *csütörtök*
Friday *péntek*
Saturday *szombat*
Sunday *vasárnap*

Months

January *január*
February *február*
March *március*
April *április*
May *május*
June *június*
July *július*
August *augusztus*
September *szeptember*
October *október*
November *november*
December *december*

Seasons

spring *tavasz*
summer *nyár*
fall *ösz*
winter *tél*

Suggested Reading

All of the books listed below can be found online at most of the web's major book sites (such as www.amazon.com), as well as at the local English-language bookshops listed in the *Shopping* sections of both cities.

PRAGUE
Literature

Hašek, Jaroslav. *The Good Soldier Švejk.* Czech literary icon Jaroslav Hašek's most famous and celebrated work, this is a subversive satire illustrating the futility of war through the eyes of a solider far more interested in drinking and card playing than the bureaucratic machine he's caught up in.

Havel, Václav. *The Memorandum; Three Vaněk Plays; Temptation.* Impressive body of work from the Czech Republic's former president, whose roles as intellectual, politician, and public figure never diminished his literary ability, though they certainly overshadowed it. Much of his work deals with language's power to persuade, as well as interfere with rational thought.

Hrabal, Bohumil. *I Served the King of England.* The story of Ditie, an ambitious waiter focused on accumulating $1 million and as many sensuous experiences as he can, is a classic of Czech comedic literature. Depicting the absurdities of the nation's history during the middle of the 20th century, it is a work full of memorable characters and situations ranging from the hilarious to the downright tragic.

Kafka, Franz. *The Castle, The Metamorphosis,* and *The Trial.* The masterworks from Prague's most famous writer blend perfectly with the city's cobblestone streets and Gothic atmosphere. Perfect during the cold, dark, and mysterious winter months.

Klíma, Ivan. *Love and Garbage.* Poetic novel focusing on a banned Czech writer who now cleans Prague's streets alongside a motley crew that is likewise outcast from society. A moving meditation on love, freedom, and death from one of the country's premier writers.

Kundera, Milan. *The Joke, The Book of Laughter and Forgetting,* and *The Unbearable Lightness of Being.* The Czech Republic's most successful literary export is a must-read for anyone interested in familiarizing themselves with the absurdity and romance of the land and its people.

Meyrink, Gustav. *The Golem.* This is the classic telling of Rabbi Loew's fabled monster. Phantasmagorical, surreal, and wonderfully weird, Meyrink paints a picture of Prague that is much different from Kafka's, or anyone else's for that matter.

Neruda, Jan. *Prague Tales.* Famous collection of bittersweet vignettes depicting life back in 19th-century Malá Strana. Half the fun is reading the stories, while the other half is walking down the streets immortalized in them.

History, Politics, and Culture

Banville, John. *Prague Pictures: A Portrait of the City.* A wonderfully written collection of anecdotes dealing with Banville's pre- and post-Communist visits to Prague mixed in with interesting and enlightening tidbits of historical fact.

Farley, David and Sholl, Jesse. *Travelers' Tales Prague and the Czech Republic: True Stories.* Politics, history, and sociology all find their way into this excellent mix of entertaining personal experiences and memorable adventures. From well-known Czechs to foreigners who live and love in the country, these stories range from the poetically poignant to the laugh out loud funny.

Havel, Václav. *Disturbing the Peace, Living in Truth,* and *Letters to Olga.* These works offer remarkable insight to one of the country's most important and influential leaders. In these three volumes we find his thoughts, letters written to his wife while imprisoned, and his most significant contributions to political writing.

Ripellino, Angelo Maria. *Magic Prague.* A wild and wonderful blend of art, literature, history, and fantasy that celebrates the magical capital's haunted heart.

Sayer, Derek. *The Coasts of Bohemia: A Czech History.* A thoroughly researched book detailing the Czech peoples centuries-long search for their national identity, offering a treasure trove of information regarding Czech art, theater, architecture, language, music, and literature.

BUDAPEST
Literature

Esterházy, Péter. *Celestial Harmonies.* This ambitious literary work attempts to outline the lives of the writer's aristocratic family, who played no small role in Hungarian history. Split into two parts-the first, an exercise in post-modern vignettes and the second a more traditional form of narrative-the book takes a bit of effort to get through but nevertheless rewards readers with a deeper understanding of the land, its politics, and its people.

Fischer, Tibor. *Under the Frog.* This satirical novel follows the exploits of two basketball players representing the Hungarian national team from the end of World War II to the Hungarian uprising in 1956. Although a remarkably funny read, the book also manages to intelligently examine the repression leading up to the uprising, as well as the brutality of its bloody end.

Kertész, Imre. *Fateless.* This haunting novel by Nobel prize winner Imre Kertész is an absolute must for visitors to the country, as well as literature fans in general. Written from the

perspective of a 14-year-old Hungarian Jew imprisoned in Auschwitz and Buchenwald, it is guaranteed to stay with readers long after they've finished.

Kosztolányi, Dezső. *Skylark.* Widely regarded as a masterpiece of 20th-century Hungarian literature, Kosztolányi's beautiful book portrays provincial life during the Austro-Hungarian monarchy. Centering around an elderly Hungarian couple and their unattractive spinster daughter (Skylark), the author turns family sentiment upside down in this short, very enjoyable read.

Nádas, Péter. *A Book of Memories.* Jumping back and forth between the Stalinist era and post-Communist Eastern Europe, this exceptional though demanding work portrays a society full of secrets, tension, and fear, where the personal and political often become the same thing.

History, Politics and Culture

Frigyesi, Judit. *Béla Bartók and Turn-of-the-Century Budapest.* An interesting perspective on one of Hungary's most acclaimed composers. Frigyesi delves deep into the country's intellectual society at the time-a remarkably talented and diverse group of individuals who collectively attempted to find wholeness and identity in a rapidly developing world.

Kontler, Laszlo. *A History of Hungary.* This comprehensive review of Hungarian history begins with the pre-historic age and takes the reader all the way to the present day. Kontler examines the country's economics, revolutions, geographical setting, and social structure in an attempt to understand the country's current challenges in a new Europe.

Lessing, Erich. *Revolution in Hungary: The 1956 Budapest Uprising.* Lessing was the one of the first photographers to document the uprising and its aftermath. The remarkable photos he took during the period are found in this eye-opening volume. Interspersed with easy-to-read essays highlighting this painful, bloody chapter in Hungarian history, the book relies heavily on the photographs to tell the time's stories, which range from hope and jubilation to the bitterness of broken dreams.

Schopflin, George. *Politics in Eastern Europe, 1945-1992.* An impressive analysis of Communism and its aspirations, as well as how it was able to stabilize its grip on the people and the reasons that led to its collapse.

Internet Resources

PRAGUE
Travel
www.pis.cz

One of Prague's official tourist information websites, this site offers plenty of help regarding historical sites, accommodations, and city events. You can also learn more about reserving tickets for various cultural events going on around town, as well as arrange day or overnight trips out of the city.

www.discoverczech.com

Another informative site that has all kinds of pages dedicated to the Czech Republic, including detailed information regarding apartments, hotels, car rental agencies, and a whole lot more.

www.myczechrepublic.com

This is an excellent resource for learning all kinds of interesting things regarding Czech culture, history, cuisine, and language. The site also features a blog, chat function, and message boards that offer plenty of opportunities to interact with past visitors and current residents.

Culture
www.expats.cz
www.prague.tv

Both of these sites are treasure troves of invaluable information, providing visitors to and residents of Prague with a remarkable amount of up-to-date travel, cultural, and relocation material, as well as classifieds, message boards, job opportunities, and lots more to keep you occupied for hours. If you want to keep your finger on the pulse of Prague, bookmark both sites.

News and Information
www.prague-tribune.cz

The business lifestyle set will enjoy this site, which keeps readers informed of all the moneyed movers and shakers in this volatile region.

www.praguemonitor.com

Those wanting to stay abreast of politics and culture will do themselves a favor by visiting this highly informative and typically well-written site.

www.radio.cz

Radio Praha's site serves up-to-the-minute articles covering every major news event in the country and region. Visitors to the site also have the option of listening on demand or connecting to live broadcasts.

BUDAPEST
Travel
www.budapestinfo.hu

Sponsored by the Budapest Tourist Office, this is a highly informative site that also assists in booking hotels and securing tickets for a wide range of events.

www.gotohungary.com

The Hungarian National Tourist Office in New York has an exceptional site that includes historical information, as well as a cultural calendar, suggested itineraries, tour packages, and a whole lot more.

www.hungary.com

If you're still looking for more information

after researching those two sites, try the aptly named www.hungary.com.

Culture
www.pestiside.hu

For a light-hearted and typically zany look at life in Hungary, make sure to visit this highly entertaining and informative site.

www.caboodle.hu

At www.pestiside.hu, you'll find a link to this site, also an excellent and fun portal that is loaded with information regarding all the important happenings around town.

www.winesofhungary.com

For wine enthusiasts, a visit to this site will get you started on better understanding the country's history of wine, as well as its relevant wineries and regions.

News and Information
www.insidehungary.com

Current news and information can be found here.

www.budapestweek.com

In addition to current news and information, this site also boasts an excellent arts and entertainment section, cultural listings, and classified ads.

www.met.hu

Up-to-the-minute weather reports from around the country.

Index

www.moon.com

For helpful advice on planning a trip, visit www.moon.com for the **TRAVEL PLANNER** and get access to useful travel strategies and valuable information about great places to visit. When you travel with Moon, expect an experience that is uncommon and truly unique.

HANDBOOKS | METRO | OUTDOORS | LIVING ABROAD

MAP SYMBOLS

	Expressway	**ᑕ**	Highlight	✈	Airfield	⚓	Golf Course
	Primary Road	○	City/Town	✈	Airport	**P**	Parking Area
	Secondary Road	◉	State Capital	▲	Mountain	⏚	Archaeological Site
	Unpaved Road	✸	National Capital	✛	Unique Natural Feature	⬛	Church
	Trail	★	Point of Interest			🅶	Gas Station
	Ferry	•	Accommodation	⋐	Waterfall		Glacier
	Railroad	▼	Restaurant/Bar	▲	Park		Mangrove
	Pedestrian Walkway	■	Other Location	⬛	Trailhead		Reef
	Stairs	⋀	Campground	⬥	Skiing Area		Swamp

CONVERSION TABLES

°C = (°F - 32) / 1.8
°F = (°C x 1.8) + 32
1 inch = 2.54 centimeters (cm)
1 foot = 0.304 meters (m)
1 yard = 0.914 meters
1 mile = 1.6093 kilometers (km)
1 km = 0.6214 miles
1 fathom = 1.8288 m
1 chain = 20.1168 m
1 furlong = 201.168 m
1 acre = 0.4047 hectares
1 sq km = 100 hectares
1 sq mile = 2.59 square km
1 ounce = 28.35 grams
1 pound = 0.4536 kilograms
1 short ton = 0.90718 metric ton
1 short ton = 2,000 pounds
1 long ton = 1.016 metric tons
1 long ton = 2,240 pounds
1 metric ton = 1,000 kilograms
1 quart = 0.94635 liters
1 US gallon = 3.7854 liters
1 Imperial gallon = 4.5459 liters
1 nautical mile = 1.852 km

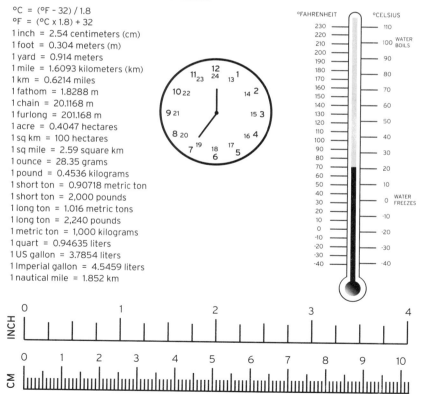

MOON PRAGUE & BUDAPEST

Avalon Travel
a member of the Perseus Books Group
1700 Fourth Street
Berkeley, CA 94710, USA
www.moon.com

Editor and Series Manager: Kathryn Ettinger
Copy Editor: Ellie Behrstock
Graphics Coordinator: Tabitha Lahr
Production Coordinators: Domini Dragoone,
  Nicole Schultz
Cover Designer: Domini Dragoone
Map Editor: Kevin Anglin
Cartographers: Kat Bennett, Chris Markiewicz,
  Brice Ticen
Indexer: Valerie Sellers Blanton

ISBN-10: 1-59880-133-3
ISBN-13: 978-1-59880-133-0
ISSN: 1941-4773

Printing History
1st Edition – May 2008
5 4 3 2 1

Some photos and illustrations are used by permission and are the property of the original copyright owners.

Front cover photo:
© Maurizio Borgese/Hemis.fr/Aurora Photos.
  Astronomical Clock, Old Town Square, Prague
Title Page:
© Frits Meyst/Adventure4ever.com/digitalrailroad
  .net. Old Town Square
Interior Photos:
Page 6 © Bill Bachmann/digitalrailroad.net; Page 7
  © Robert Adler Peckerar; Page 8 © Tom Dirlis; Page
  9 © Oliver Herbst; Page 10 © Tom Dirlis; Page 11:
  first photo © Tom Dirlis, second photo © Oliver
  Herbst, third photo © Tom Dirlis; Page 19 © Tom
  Dirlis; Page 20 © Oliver Herbst; Page 22 © Tom
  Dirlis; Page 23 © Tom Dirlis; Page 25 © Tom Dirlis;
  Page 26 © Corine Tachtiris; Page 28: all three photos
  © Corine Tachtiris; Page 30 © Tom Dirlis

Printed in the United States by RR Donnelley

KEEPING CURRENT

If you have a favorite gem you'd like to see included in the next edition, or see anything that needs updating, clarification, or correction, please drop us a line. Send your comments via email to feedback@moon.com, or use the address above.